kunstmuseum basel

MUSEUM BARBERINI

POTSDAM

Under the patronage of Her Excellency Hedda Samson,
Ambassador of the Kingdom of the Netherlands in Switzerland,
and His Excellency Wepke Kingma,
Ambassador of the Kingdom of the Netherlands in Germany

Kingdom of the Netherlands

Rembrandt's Orient

West Meets East in Dutch Art of the Seventeenth Century

Exhibition:
Gary Schwartz

Catalog:
Bodo Brinkmann, Gabriel Dette,
Michael Philipp, Gary Schwartz

Edited by
Bodo Brinkmann, Gabriel Dette,
Michael Philipp, Ortrud Westheider

With contributions by
Bodo Brinkmann
Jan de Hond
Gabriel Dette
Corinna Forberg
Susanne Henriette Karau
Michael Philipp
Gary Schwartz
Erik Spaans
Jolanta Talbierska
Roelof van Gelder
Arnoud Vrolijk

PRESTEL Munich · London · New York

Lenders

Stedelijk Museum Alkmaar
Allard Pierson, University of Amsterdam
Amsterdam Museum
Rijksmuseum, Amsterdam
Stadsarchief Amsterdam
Tropenmuseum, Amsterdam
Universitätsbibliothek Basel
The Barber Institute of Fine Arts, Birmingham
Herzog Anton Ulrich-Museum, Braunschweig, Kunstmuseum des Landes Niedersachsen
Szépművészeti Múzeum, Budapest
Statens Museum for Kunst—National Gallery of Denmark, Copenhagen
Dordrechts Museum
Gemäldegalerie Alte Meister, Staatliche Kunstsammlungen Dresden
Trustees of the Chester Beatty Library, Dublin
Kunstpalast, Düsseldorf
Musée de Grenoble
Frans Hals Museum, Haarlem
Leiden University Libraries, Special Collections
The British Museum, London, Department of Prints and Drawings
The National Gallery, London
Victoria and Albert Museum, London
The J. Paul Getty Museum, Los Angeles
Musée des Beaux-Arts, Lyon
Museo Nacional del Prado, Madrid
Museo Nacional Thyssen-Bornemisza, Madrid
Milwaukee Art Museum
Musée Fabre, Montpellier
Bayerische Staatsgemäldesammlungen, Alte Pinakothek, Munich
Ashmolean Museum of Art and Archaeology, University of Oxford
Bodleian Library, University of Oxford
Bibliothèque de l'Arsenal, Bibliothèque nationale de France, Paris
Fondation Custodia/Collection Frits Lugt, Paris
North Carolina Museum of Art, Raleigh
Residenzgalerie Salzburg
The State Hermitage Museum, St. Petersburg
Mauritshuis, The Hague
Centraal Museum Utrecht
Albertina, Vienna
Gemäldegalerie der Akademie der bildenden Künste, Vienna
Kunsthistorisches Museum Wien, Gemäldegalerie, Vienna
Schönbrunn Palace, Vienna
Stichting Duivenvoorde, Voorschoten
University of Warsaw Library
National Gallery of Art, Washington, DC
Kunst Museum Winterthur
York Museums Trust (York Art Gallery)
Emil Bührle Collection, Zurich
The Earl of Derby
The Kremer Collection
Natan Saban Collection, Israel
The National Trust
as well as other lenders who wish to remain anonymous

The exhibition in Basel received generous support from:

Pierrette Schlettwein
Anonymous
Sulger-Stiftung
Novartis International AG
L. & Th. La Roche Stiftung
Annetta Grisard-Schrafl (catalog)
BLKB
HEIVISCH
Karl und Luise Nicolai-Stiftung
Stiftung zur Förderung niederländischer Kunst in Basel
Isaac Dreyfus-Bernheim Stiftung
Stiftung für das Kunstmuseum Basel

Contents

Foreword

Turbans and carpets, sabers and silk robes—Rembrandt and his contemporaries repeatedly painted objects from distant lands. The resulting works of art provide evidence of the first wave of globalization and reflect the influence of foreign cultures on the Netherlands of the seventeenth century. This significant art-historical period was shaped by a thirst for knowledge, a passion for collecting, and a pride in possession; it also inspired painters to create novel history scenes, portraits, and still lifes. However, what is especially striking today in this kind of cultural appropriation is the failure to represent its negative side: the power gap between cultures that was also evident in slavery, violence, exploitation, and trade wars.

This exhibition addresses images of foreign subjects from this period with full awareness of these issues. In antiquity, the terms *Orient* and *Occident* were used to describe regions of the world. In Rembrandt's time, the East was known as "the Orient." In the nineteenth and twentieth centuries, a Eurocentric attitude emerged with the notion of "Orientalism," which asserted a claim to authority over the countries of the Middle East and the Arab world. Although the term *Orient* remains burdened by this history today, in the exhibition's title, *Rembrandt's Orient: West Meets East in Dutch Art of the Seventeenth Century*, the possessive case indicates that it is concerned with the ideas *then* associated with the term.

The exhibition examines how the painters of the Dutch Golden Age reacted to the regions of the Middle and Far East of which they had become increasingly aware through trade, travel, and publications. Rembrandt is the starting point for all this. His fascination for "the East" is reflected in his biblical histories featuring Orientalizing garments, in the *tronies* of "Orientals," and in his collection of exotic objects. Many of Rembrandt's students, like their teacher, also used fanciful turbans in their biblical scenes. In *portraits historiés* they even provided the sitters with "Oriental" costumes. The self-staging in such clothing, often in front of "Oriental" carpets, indicates the role of these items as status symbols for well-to-do citizens.

The show also explores the global trade in exotic objects, such as porcelain and nautilus cups, presented in still lifes as evidence of a passion for collecting and cultural appropriation. Only a few works of art, however, document concrete encounters between West and East, and the problematic aspects of international trade were seldom given artistic expression: the wealth of the Dutch upper class was the result, moreover, of violence and oppression in the Far East and came at high human cost, even among the country's own sailors.

Guest curator Gary Schwartz has been involved with Rembrandt for decades and has also produced major monographs on Pieter Saenredam (1989), Hieronymus Bosch (2016), and Johannes Vermeer (2017). His book *Rembrandt, His Life, His Paintings: A New Biography* was published in 1985. In it, he situated the artist in his world, examined the intellectual climate of his time, and emphasized the role of his patrons. The inclusion of this social and intellectual context certainly represented a progressive approach. The historical background of Rembrandt's artistic endeavor is also the basis of the exhibition *Rembrandt's Orient*. We consider ourselves fortunate to have succeeded in persuading Gary Schwartz to work on our exhibition. Without the weight of his reputation, this ambitious project could not have been realized.

The exhibition is a collaboration between the Kunstmuseum Basel and the Museum Barberini. Its genesis dates back to 2010, when one of our catalog authors, Erik Spaans, raised the idea in conversation with Michael Philipp, who is now chief curator at the Museum Barberini, and shortly afterwards established the connection to Gary Schwartz. Bodo Brinkmann, curator of Old Masters at the Kunstmuseum Basel, brought the project to his institution, where, in addition to Rembrandt's painting *David with the Head of Goliath before Saul* (cat. 60), the Rembrandt prints preserved in its own collection provided a compelling connection to the subject. In recent years, these holdings have been significantly expanded thanks to the donation of 150 important prints by the collector Dr. h.c. Eberhard W. Kornfeld of Bern, Switzerland.

The scholarly collaboration on the catalog was overseen by Michael Philipp, who has distinguished himself in the field of Dutch and Flemish art history with such exhibitions as *Rubens*, *Van Dyck*, *Jordaens: Baroque from Antwerp* (2010) as well as *The World Upside Down: Hieronymus Bosch's Century* (2016). Gabriel Dette, assistant curator of Old Masters at the Kunstmuseum Basel, joined the team of catalog editors. The essays in this catalog originated in a symposium in Potsdam in June 2019, to which Gary Schwartz invited a number of renowned researchers. We would like to thank all the authors for their investigation of specific aspects of a highly complex subject.

The "Orient" was present in seventeenth-century Dutch townhouses in the form of exotic objects and clothing, and numerous accounts of journeys to the East were published, but hardly any artists of this period actually explored these distant countries themselves. Thus, the "Orient" and the "Oriental" remained constructs of set pieces, stereotypes, and imagination in Netherlandish visual culture of the time. Foreign things were appreciated and incorporated into Dutch lifestyle. But this was for the most part no more than a pose, since there was less real interest in other cultures than in their material manifestations and products, coveted for their preciousness and the associated prestige. The encounter of West and East was not a meeting on the same level; there was no sense of an equal exchange. Foreignness represented an appealing contrast to the familiar, but it hardly aroused a more profound level of sympathy. This was no different in Rembrandt's case than for his contemporaries, and this attitude—which this exhibition invites us to reflect upon—has not changed in large parts of the Western world. The show thus offers us the opportunity to more closely question this persistent Eurocentrism.

Josef Helfenstein
Director of the Kunstmuseum Basel

Ortrud Westheider
Director of the Museum Barberini

Distant Inspiration
An Introduction to the Exhibition

Gary Schwartz

In 1479 the Great Council, the *Signoria*, of Venice, received a request from the Ottoman sultan Mehmed II to send a painter and a sculptor in bronze to the sultan's court, the Sublime Porte in Constantinople. As the painter for this high-level artistic-diplomatic mission the *Signoria* chose Gentile Bellini, who at that time was virtually the official painter of the Republic.[1] During his eighteen months in Constantinople he made paintings for the court and drawings for himself. The main relic of his production there is his 1480 portrait of Mehmed II (The National Gallery, London). Before Gentile left for home, the sultan honored him with the titles *eques auratus* (golden knight) and *comes palatinus* (palace companion). The images Gentile brought back, together with those by other artists who had visited Turkey, became standard features of the Venetian visual vocabulary. Venetian state processions found form in what has been called the "Oriental mode," and entire suites of portraits of Ottoman sultans were executed in paint and in medals.

The Dutch reaction was different when, in 1656, a provincial governor of the Mughal Empire of India submitted a request from his master, Grand Mughal Shah Jahan, to the leading functionary of the Dutch East India Company (Vereenigde Oostindische Compagnie, or VOC) in Western Asia, Hendrik van Wijck. Having heard that there was a painter in the service of the VOC, Shah Jahan requested the Company to send the artist to him at his court in Agra. Van Wijck was annoyed. Where did an Indian chieftain come off deciding how an individual in his employ was going to spend his working hours? Moreover, this was not the first time he had obliged the *padishah* in this way, and he had had a devil of a time getting his personnel back again. But in view of the possible nasty consequences for the Company of an outright refusal, Van Wijck decided to honor the request.[2]

This was not a unique case. Between 1602 and 1656, six Dutch painters served three successive rulers of Persia, Abbas I, Safi I, and Abbas II, as "painters to the shah." None of them was supported gladly by the VOC, let alone the Dutch government, which farmed out its foreign policy to the Company. They were not artists of recognized stature, and all of them came to a bad end. Not a single work any of them made in Persia has survived or was documented after their time.

The contrast between the early Italian and later Dutch situations typifies East-West artistic relations in the cultures concerned. Whereas rulers in India and Persia were eager to patronize

Dutch artists—Abbas II even took drawing lessons from Philips Angel (see cat. 44–45) and Hendrick Boudewijn van Lockhorst—no Dutch political organ ever played into this interest. The Dutch East India Company obliged only when its hand was forced, with the kind of ill will displayed by Hendrik van Wijck. This attitude was incomprehensible to other foreign bodies in Isfahan. As the Carmelite fathers in the city noted in their chronicle, "Nothing could be more useful to the Mission than if we had here a good painter, the Shah taking great pleasure in painting; and in these countries good artists are rare. There is a Dutchman who works for the Company, who has done very little, and yet has received very good rewards, and the Shah has conferred great favours on him."[3] Even though the VOC had actually been introduced into the Safavid court by the painter Jan Lucasz. van Hasselt, a familiar of the shah, the Company could not care less.

Not only were the diplomatic and commercial opportunities opened by Oriental interest in Western art neglected by the Dutch. So were the artistic ones. Of the hundreds of Dutch painters active in the seventeenth century, none is known to have traveled to the East in search of artistic possibilities or patronage. No portraits after life of an Oriental ruler by a Dutch artist are recorded. Wallerant Vaillant's mezzotint (cat. 90) is captioned "Soliman III. Empereur des Turcs." Actually, Süleyman II (there was never a third) did not become sultan until 1687, ten years after the death of the artist. This is typical of the quality of information on the subject.[4] The only complete Dutch series of portraits from the East depicts the VOC governors-general in Batavia (Rijksmuseum, Amsterdam). We can only dream of what might have been had the States General sent Rembrandt to Agra in 1656 to paint a portrait of Shah Jahan. However, nothing like that happened.

In the century intervening between Gentile Bellini and Rembrandt, firsthand images of Oriental countries were made by no more than two Dutch artists. Jan van Scorel went on a pilgrimage to Jerusalem in 1520 and incorporated drawings he brought back (themselves lost) into his *Entry of Christ in Jerusalem* (Centraal Museum, Utrecht); the only portraits that emerged from the trip were of fellow pilgrims whose visit to the Holy Sepulchre entitled them to membership in a prestigious Utrecht or Haarlem brotherhood.

It was left to Scorel's pupil Jan Cornelisz. Vermeyen to create the greatest ensemble of pictures of non-European subject matter made by a Dutch artist of the sixteenth century. In 1535 Vermeyen accompanied Emperor Charles V to Tunis as a war artist. Ten of a set of twelve monumental tapestries, woven in Antwerp in the 1550s after his cartoons, are preserved in the royal collections in Madrid. That Vermeyen was a Dutchman is incidental to the work as a whole.

In the seventeenth century only one Dutch artistic campaign can be compared in scope and daring to *The Conquest of Tunis*. That is the group of drawings and paintings made by Albert Eckhout and Frans Post for the governor of Dutch Brazil, Johan Maurits of Nassau-Siegen. They form a unique documentation of the flora, fauna, inhabitants, and landscape of the country. In this case as well the initiative lay with the patron, whose agenda determined the shape of events and the nature of the artistic production required. Once again, the nationality of the artists was incidental. No governor of the Dutch East India Company ever commissioned that kind of record of the natural history and culture of the localities under his control. The object that comes closest is the modest sketchbook of drawings of Sri Lanka by Esaias Boursse (cat. 88), but no paintings were ever made of the motifs Boursse sketched with such obvious curiosity and humaneness.

The dearth of firsthand images of Oriental people and places in Dutch art of the seventeenth century stands in obverse relation to the prominence of Orientalism in that school. Two kinds of painting in particular were produced in great abundance. One type was the *tronie*. This Dutch word, meaning "face," refers to an image of a man or woman that is seen not as the portrait of an individual but as a type of humanity (cat. 3, 99–104, 106, 119). Even more common are the paintings of biblical subjects in which the figures are given "Oriental" garb (cat. 54–79, 81–82). Some of them are *portraits historiés*—portraits, usually of a couple or family, in which the living sitters take on the guise of biblical or historical personages, as in Ferdinand Bol's *Couple in a Landscape* (cat. 6).

The mode of Orientalism we encounter in Dutch art of Rembrandt's time is not a serious attempt to penetrate the meanings and customs of the East on their own terms. For the most part, what we see is an appropriation of exotic appearances to fit Dutch circumstances. Dutchmen who gained a measure of repute from service in the East will not neglect to have the painter build that into their portraits (cat. 14–15, 25–26). Collectors showed off weapons and jewelry from abroad as attributes of their own sophistication. The owner of a *japonse rok* (Japanese robe) will put it on for the painter (cat. 11–13, 15, 34). A specialty within still-life painting made an emphatic point of including precious vessels or *naturalia* from the Orient, as well as from the Americas (see cat. 20–53 and the essays by Erik Spaans, pp. 12–23, and Michael Philipp, pp. 24–39).

In attempting to find general meaning in these images and practices, it is well to be aware of something we do *not* encounter. That is, knee-jerk xenophobia, aversion, or derogation. There are no images ridiculing or satirizing Orientals as such, despite the real threat presented to Dutch maritime shipping by Barbary pirates of the North African territories that were also labeled "Oriental" (see the essay by Roelof van Gelder, pp. 74–85). What we do find, unavoidably, is principled antagonism to Islam. The painted *Parody of Religious Tolerance* of 1659 (cat. 46), which brings together representatives of various religious denominations, gives undiluted expression to this prejudice. To reduce Islam to the most intolerant attitude is unfortunately a running theme through Christian history from the early Middle Ages to our time.[5]

This distorted view was so deeply embedded in Christian belief and culture, independent of the exploration of the Orient, for example, through collecting manuscripts at the University of Leiden (see the essay by Arnoud Vrolijk, pp. 86–101), that even honest attempts to instruct Dutch readers about the nature of Islam fall into that groove. Of the six etchings in an illustrated Quran translation of 1696 (cat. 49), the first four show Muslims sunk in prayer or approaching a mosque. The last two plates refer to anti-Islamic stories about the prophet Muhammad, as they were proffered in medieval Christian sources. According to them the divine revelations received by Muhammad were delusions sprouting from epileptic attacks or had been staged by him on his own. *The Arabic Quran, by the Saracen and Turkish Prophet Muhammed, Divided into Three Discreet Sections . . .* (cat. 48), which had been published in Dutch in 1641, had been less polemical.

On the whole, the image of the Oriental in Dutch art of Rembrandt's time is respectful. Studio models for *tronies* were often dressed up as Orientals. By contrast, very rare were those with Catholic attributes, and rarer still—despite the common labeling of male *tronies* as Jewish rabbis or merchants—with items of Jewish dress. The weakness for Oriental *tronies* has been related, convincingly, to a defiant catchword of the Dutch revolt against Spanish Spain: "Liever Turks dan Paaps" (I'd rather be a Turk than a Papist). For Dutch individuals to take on, in portraiture, the identity of an Oriental, as in a *portrait historié*, goes further than that. But just where it goes is not very clear.[6]

The Easternness of the image may not always have been apparent. The description of such paintings in notarial records of the time most often call them "op sijn antijcks" (in the ancient mode). This highlights a certain peculiarity we encounter in the dressing of biblical figures. That is, that contemporaneous writers on the subject seem to have thought that the dress and customs current in the Middle East of their time were the same as in the age of the Bible. Philips Angel praises Rembrandt, in his *Samson Proposing the Riddle at the Wedding Feast* (cat. 73), for rendering the guests reclining at the table according to the Ottoman fashion of the day. He saw observation of Turkish or Levantine manners as research into the ways of Old Testament personages (cat. 44).

Whereas Persian, Indian, and later Japanese artists studied and imitated models in European art closely—mainly in the form of prints from the Netherlands—nothing of the sort took place in Europe in the seventeenth century. A handful of collectors took pride in ownership of Indian miniatures (Arabic and Persian manuscripts were collected only for their texts), but almost no artists repaid the compliment that their colleagues in Asia were paying them by incorporating artistic inventions or conventions into their own work. No artist, that is, except for two. In mid-century two Dutch painters turned their gaze in admiration to the creations of artists from the Mughal court of India.

One was Rembrandt, who copied a lost set of Mughal miniatures (see my essay, pp. 56–73). But he was not the only Amsterdam artist to have been given access to those rare collectors' items. Adaptations of one of the motifs recur in two paintings by a younger contemporary of Rembrandt's, Willem Schellinks. While Rembrandt made literal copies of the miniatures, Schellinks did the opposite. He made them more exotic than the originals (fig. 5, p. 45; cat. 94).

The paintings of Indian phantasmagoria were not the only tribute Schellinks paid to Indian art. His fantasies are dated to the 1660s, but in 1657 he came out with an extraordinary poem in hyperbolic praise of that school, entitled *On Benjan [Indian] Painting* (cat. 92). The fact that the author plays off Indian painting, of which he cannot have known more than a few examples, against all other art, only makes his message all the more striking: ultimate quality in art has now been achieved by Indian artists (see the essay by Jan de Hond, pp. 40–55).

The proximity in time and place between Rembrandt's and Schellinks's response to one and the same Mughal motif shows that they were in contact with each other and with the owner of the miniatures. I see them pondering, discussing, and copying the strange drawings together, in the company of the owner, the only artists of their time to incorporate art from the Oriental world into their own. That this exceptionality took place in the Netherlands is not coincidence. If Italy in the fifteenth and sixteenth centuries took the lead in incorporating Oriental imagery into its art, that role was taken over in the seventeenth century, in less authentic but more widely diffuse fashion, by artists in the Netherlands.

1 Istanbul 2000, no. 1.
2 Cf. Schwartz 2014, 37, with source.
3 Cited from Floor 1979, 154.
4 Cf. Wuestman/Webb 2006, 65.
5 Cf. Daniel 2000.
6 Cf. Van Leeuwen 2018, 73.

The Fascination of the East
Trade and Art in the Netherlands in the Seventeenth Century

Erik Spaans

In 1681 the Amsterdam poet and jurist Andries Pels (1631–1681) published a treatise entitled *Gebruik én Misbruik des Tooneels* (Use and Misuse of the Theater). It includes a direct attack on the popular dramatist Jan Vos, but also on Rembrandt, who had died twelve years earlier.[1] Pels had nothing good to say about Rembrandt's realistic style of painting with its "sagging breasts and twisted hands." At the same time he reported that Rembrandt had searched eagerly "for armor, morions, Japanese daggers, furs, and ruffs at the Nieuwe and Noordermarkt, all of which he found very picturesque."[2]

Despite his partiality, there is little reason to doubt Pels's words. Contemporary sources confirm Rembrandt's preference for exotic and picturesque bric-a-brac. The inventory of his possessions taken in July 1656 on the occasion of his bankruptcy shows that his art chamber must have been an impressive cabinet of curiosities.[3] The painter owned, among other things, the busts of Greek philosophers and Roman emperors, globes, branches of coral, musical instruments, a death mask of Prince Maurits, a "pissing child," dozens of animals that had been stuffed ("from the sea as well as land"), armor, arrows, bows, guns, and even a small canon.

The large number of Asian objects is noteworthy: "Twee Oost-Indische backiens" (two East Indian saucers), a "dito nap met een Sineessien" (ditto saucer with a small Chinese person), two "porceleyne cazuwarisen" (porcelain cassowaries),[4] an "Oost-Indische naeydoos" (East Indian sewing box), a "Japanse hellemet" (a Japanese helmet, perhaps a samurai's), a "carbaetse helmet" (Carpathian helmet), an "Oost-Indische poeverdoos" (East Indian powder box), "60 stucks soo indiaens hantgeweer, pijlen, schichten, asegayen en bogen" (sixty items including Indian handguns, arrows, spears, assegais,[5] and bows), and an "Indies koppie" (little Indian head).[6] "Indiaense" (Indian) fans in two other rooms were also mentioned.[7]

Rembrandt repeatedly used objects from his collection of rarities in his work, in particular to depict exotic clothing or weapons. Presumably he also designed the stabbing weapon in *The Blinding of Samson* (fig. 1), which the armor-clad soldier uses to put out the eye of the biblical hero as he lies on the ground, after a piece from his own collection. Its blade has the same shape as an Indonesian *kris*.[8]

Thus, Rembrandt here painted a story from the Old Testament ornamented with weaponry that came from a part of the world thousands of kilometers distant from the Holy Land. A viewer in Rembrandt's time would not have been aware of the fact that such an Indonesian weapon in this setting was a truly odd detail. This was true, however, of many depictions from the Bible in the seventeenth century. Artists were accustomed to taking necessary liberties since the opportunity to obtain information about the real appearance of the cities, houses, palaces, streets, headwear, garments, everyday objects, and animals mentioned in the Bible was limited. Exotic objects, even if they came from a different part of the world, were a welcome addition to the available props needed to furnish biblical scenes. Like the meals that seventeenth-century households seasoned with spices from India such as pepper, cloves, mace, cinnamon, and nutmeg, artists of the Dutch Republic "seasoned" their historical pictures with exotic objects from East Asia.

Player in World Trade

The Dutch interest in products from "foreign" lands increased significantly at the end of the sixteenth century due to turbulent new activities in trade. Until this time, the radius of action of Dutch merchants had been limited for the most part to harbors on the North and Baltic Seas. Ships traveled to England, Norway, Spain, France, and Portugal as well, but sailors did not dare go farther. The first attempts to expand their horizon date from the 1590s.

One reason among others for this expansion were the embargos imposed because of the war that made trade with Spanish and Portuguese ports difficult. In addition, in previous years Portugal had succeeded in establishing a monopoly on the extremely lucrative spice trade. Thus it became—for military as well as commercial interests—more and more tempting for the Dutch to sail directly to Asia and obtain spices themselves, and thereby to eliminate the Portuguese.

Because they had no experience in this area, the Dutch first engaged in a kind of industrial espionage. In 1592 Amsterdam merchants sent the brothers Cornelis and Frederik de Houtman to Lisbon with orders to collect information about trade with India.[9] Three years later the time was ripe for the first expedition. In April 1595 a fleet of four ships under the command of Cornelis de Houtman set out by sea for East India. Two years and four months passed before three of the four ships returned to the Dutch Republic. The sailors had endured many hardships, and more than a third of them did not survive the voyage. Furthermore, the money earned from the spices that De Houtman obtained in India was barely enough to cover the cost of the expedition.[10] Nonetheless this first India voyage was the start of a series of further voyages in which the yields gradually increased, and soon they were making substantial profits.

The Dutch expansion was facilitated by the failure of the strategy of Philip III, the king of Spain. In 1598, two months after his accession to the throne, he had demanded stricter observance of the ban on trade with the northern Netherlands. The new orders denied Dutch merchants access to Spain and Portugal, and commercial agents working in Spanish ports were imprisoned. These measures proved counterproductive since Dutch merchants were compelled to intensify their colonial efforts.[11] As a result, new companies that sent ships to India were founded in Amsterdam, Middelburg, Veere, and Rotterdam.

The unbridled spread of colonial trading organizations around 1600 also led to competition among them. Grand Pensionary Johan van Oldenbarnevelt used a strong hand to put a stop to the imminent fragmentation by forcing merchants in various cities to work together. This peaked in 1602 with the founding of the Dutch East India Company (Vereenigde Oostindische Compagnie, known as VOC), a multinational enterprise avant la lettre, which was able to get off to an excellent start thanks to initial capital amounting to just over 6.5 million guilders. The States General gave the new company a free hand in the development of policy in Asia, the naming of directors, the construction of forts, the resolution of conflicts, and the conclusion of treaties.

In the years that followed, the Dutch East India Company would strengthen its position of power in southeast Asia to such a degree that competing traders from Portugal and England were practically excluded from the market.[12] Not only did the company's success have economic consequences; it also influenced the self-image of the young Dutch Republic, which after 1581 had grown rapidly from a modest region under the dominion of the Habsburgs to an independent nation, and was considered an up-and-coming colonial superpower and a player in the world economy that had to be taken seriously.

Transported to the Homeland from all Directions

A painting made by Pieter Isaacsz. and Karel van Mander in 1606 for a commission from the Amsterdam town government portrays the city as a powerful trading center from which ships set out to every corner of the world (fig. 2).[13] The exotic figures betoken distant regions and, in particular, the trade with India, which had experienced an enormous upturn in a very short time. In this painting Amsterdam is portrayed as a dynamic city overflowing with a passion for trade and a colonial spirit of enterprise.

The East India Company not only gave a powerful boost to shipbuilding, but also to a long list of associated trades, from making rope and sails to baking bread and brewing beer. In Dutch ports, warehouses, shipyards, storage facilities, and offices were built at a rapid pace. A hall was constructed in Amsterdam specifically for the storage of cowrie shells, the currency used in Africa and Asia.

The rise of the Dutch Republic to a colonial power did not have only economic and political effects, however. It was also apparent in science and culture. Books and prints relating to areas overseas were in great demand. The report about the catastrophe-plagued voyage of Captain Willem Ysbrantz. Bontekoe to India (1646) even became a bestseller.[14] Distant continents were mapped for the first time. Their flora and fauna became an object of research and scientific publications. Tropical plants and crops were cultivated and studied in the botanical gardens of Leiden and (later) Amsterdam.[15] Foreign animal species reached the Republic by ship, and they could be seen at fairs and in menageries. And any animal that did not survive the long sea journey, which unfortunately happened quite often, could always be stuffed.[16]

New products from the East (and also from the West) made their way into Dutch households. Works of art and arts and craft products that had been virtually unknown until that time found their way into Dutch interior decoration or were acquired by collectors (see the essay by Michael Philipp, pp. 24–39). The influence of the exotic new products was even noticeable in the personal appearance of well-to-do burghers. Indian, Chinese, and Japanese clothing and luxury accessories played an increasingly ostentatious role in fashion.

That Asian cuisine also enjoyed a certain prestige is shown by the visit in 1638 of the queen mother of France, Maria de' Medici, to the East India House in Amsterdam (see cat. 18), where an *Indische rijsttafel*, a collection of Asian dishes, was served. According to the scholar Caspar Barleus, the queen was very impressed "and seeing and tasting the foreign and unusual banquet, she imagined that she was the guest of Indians, Moluccans, Persians, Arabs, Japanese, and Chinese."[17]

Stimulants such as tea and coffee from Asia and tobacco from America reached the Republic and became increasingly popular.[18] The clearest change for the common citizen was in the wider availability of spices, whose use in earlier centuries, because of their high prices, had been limited to the wealthy. That now changed since they were being imported on a large scale directly from India.

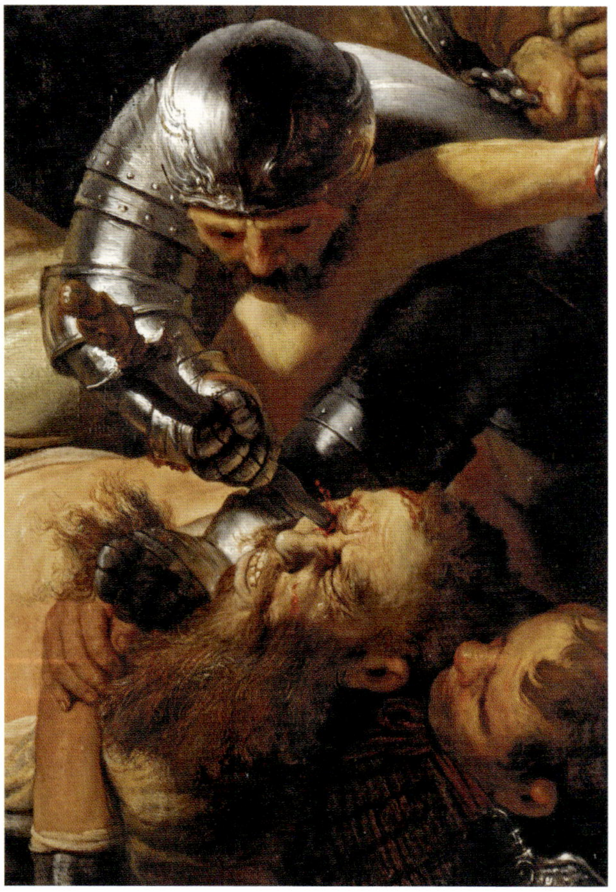

1 Rembrandt,
The Blinding of Samson (detail), 1636,
Städel Museum, Frankfurt am Main

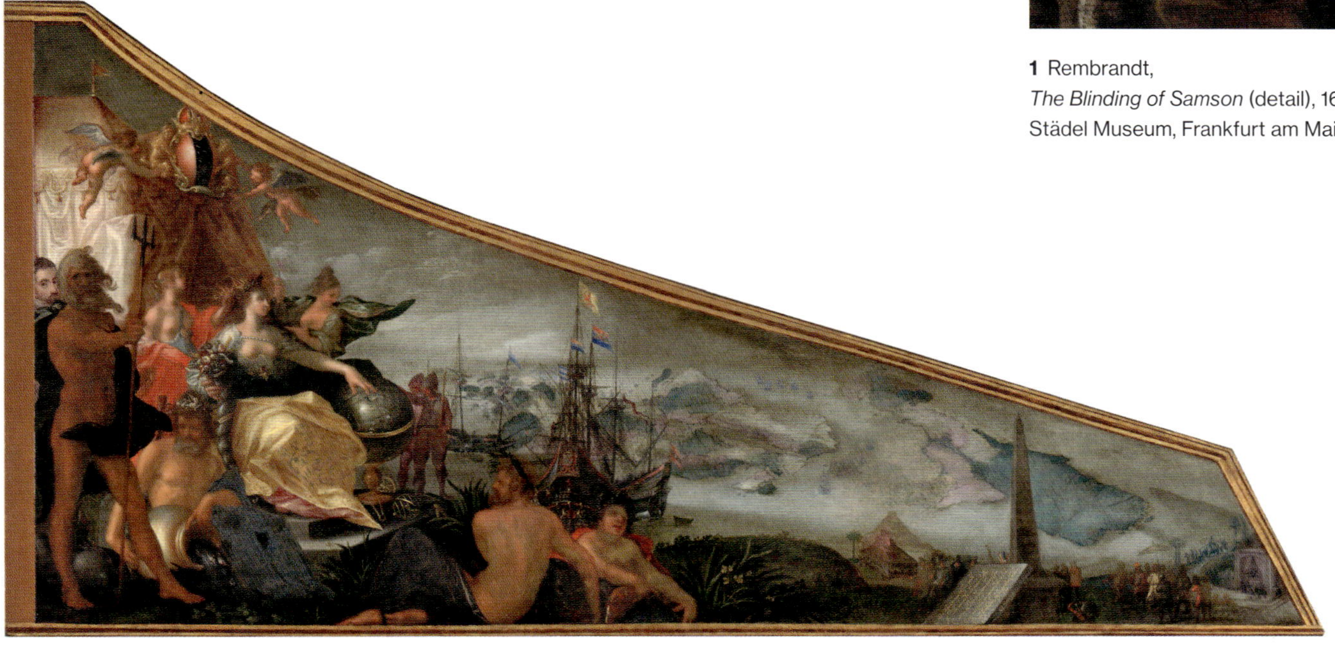

2 Pieter Isaacsz. and Karel van Mander,
Allegorical Representation of Amsterdam as the Center of World Trade, 1606,
Rijksmuseum, Amsterdam

The storehouses were full of pepper, mace, nutmeg, and cloves, and the enormous increase in the supply meant lower prices. All these spices and herbs were said to have a medical effect that was effusively praised in contemporary publications.[19] In the popular songbook *De Vermakelijcke Buys-Man, ofte Koddige Boots-Geselletje* (The Entertaining Herring Fisherman, or The Droll Sailor) it is put so: "The Dutch pharmacy / gets its strength through them [the herbs] / The Medicine: because the drugs / Which are from all sides / transported to the Fatherland / With many large and small ships."[20]

Imports and Imitations

The wealth in spices made its way into still-life painting as well, particularly well-illustrated by the *banketjes* (banquet pictures) by the Haarlem painters Pieter Claesz. and Willem Claesz. Heda. Among the food on display in their pictures, there are often pages from old almanacs rolled up into small cones and filled with peppercorns (fig. p. 32), which were known as *peperhuysjes* (little pepper houses). Shiny hams that are studded with hundreds of cloves can also be seen.

Porcelain had a special function in still-life painting (cat. 50–51). The Portuguese had started importing Chinese porcelain to Europe in the second half of the sixteenth century. The exact moment at which the Dutch Republic fell completely under its spell can be pinpointed in relation to two major auctions. The public sale of the cargo of two Portuguese ships captured by the East India Company, one in Middelburg in 1602 and the other in Amsterdam in 1604, was the prelude to a genuine mania. The captured property consisted of tens of thousands of porcelain items, the proceeds of which came to millions of guilders. The Portuguese ships that were looted were of the type known as *carraca*, or *kraak* in Dutch, which explains why *kraakporselein* became common in popular parlance after the auction. The company could hardly meet the demand afterwards. In the first half of the seventeenth century alone, an estimated three million porcelain objects were shipped to the Netherlands.[21] As early as 1614 one chronicler noted that the use of porcelain had become a habit among the common people.[22]

However, with the fall of the Ming Dynasty and the accession to power of new leaders, the export of porcelain from China abruptly stopped in 1644. Imports dropped significantly, although Japanese manufacturers who made Kakiemon porcelain enabled the East India Company to get around the problem. At the same time the manufacture of ceramic increased in the Netherlands. Domestic manufacturers managed to improve quality and to expand their range of products. Delft Blue, a tin-glazed ceramic, was an economical alternative to Chinese porcelain. In the second half of the seventeenth century, the manufacturers in Delft developed into a thriving, independent industry that produced a high-quality characteristic type of faience.

Japanese and Chinese lacquerware shipped to the Netherlands by the East India Company was also popular. The demand was so great that the officials of the company traded on a large scale to their own advantage.[23] In 1654 Amalia von Solms, the widow of Stadtholder Frederik Hendrik, had one of her rooms decorated completely with Japanese lacquer panels. Such lacquer cabinets were later emulated by other European courts.[24] Because lacquerware was extremely expensive, Dutch craftsmen tried to duplicate it. The problem there was that an essential ingredient, the sap of the lacquer tree, was only found in East Asia. Nevertheless, specialists, such as the Amsterdam lacquerer Willem Kick, were able to produce imitations of high quality "in the Chinese manner."[25] The production of artificial lacquer imitations became known as *verlakken*, a Dutch term that to this day is a synonym for fraud.

Willem Kick owned a shop in which various treasures of the East were sold, and he was by no means the only one. In his 1664 book *Beschreibung der Stadt Amsterdam* (Description of the City Amsterdam), the writer Philipp von Zesen wrote of a store for East Indian goods on the Prinsengracht and gave an enthusiastic description of the many "köstligkeiten" (delicacies) that could be purchased there: valuable porcelain, little boxes with mother-of-pearl inlays, wondrous articles of clothing, strangely painted jars, walking sticks decorated with tortoiseshell, all sorts of lacquer work, "and other similarly strange things, sent to us from the other world."[26]

Fashion and Accessories in Portraiture

Other dealers specialized in fashion, selling fans, Japanese garments, silk fabrics, hand-painted Indian chintz, ostrich feathers, and rattan walking sticks. A document from 1664 cites the dizzying number of 1,700 such *rottings* (rattan sticks) in the inventory of one shop in Amsterdam. This fashionable accessory must have made its first appearance shortly before 1640, when a group of dealers purchased all of the rattan sticks in the East India Company's stock.[27] Regents, merchants, and respected citizens liked being painted holding a rattan stick—including Frans Banninck Cocq, the central figure in Rembrandt's *Night Watch* (fig. 3). His gloved right hand, which holds his second glove, is resting on a one-and-a-half-meter-long *rotting*.

In the case of some objects in seventeenth-century paintings, the present-day observer probably does not realize that they came from overseas. This is true, for example, of the large, graceful feathers that adorn headwear in portraits. These ostrich feathers were imported from Africa (see cat. 1, 57, 72).[28] Other accessories that flaunted lavishness were fans and parasols. In Indonesia *pajongs* (parasols) played an important role in ceremonial life. Dignitaries used them to show their status, and this was copied—although in a different context—in the West (cat. 25, 27–28, 62, 66–67, 75, 86, 94). Such parasols also appear in depictions of biblical scenes such as Rembrandt's *The Baptism of the Eunuch* (cat. 62), where they function as picturesque props and at the same time as a sign of the special status of the person being baptized.

The most popular article of clothing from Asia was the *japonse rok*, a lined, silk dressing gown very similar to the traditional kimono but without the long, wide sleeves (cat. 11–13, 15, 34). The garment was worn inside the house, but occasionally on the street as well. Originally worn only by men, it became increasingly popular among women and children as well toward the end of the seventeenth century.[29] The 1673 inventory of Bartelt Jansz. Bruijnvis, a dealer in goods from the East on Warmoesstraat, lists no fewer than forty-four *japonse rokken* imported from Asia, seven of which were for children.[30] Because the supply from Japan was much too small to meet the steadily growing demand, part of the production was outsourced to India. However, successful imitations were made in the Netherlands too.[31] The best-known examples of *japonse rokken* in seventeenth-century paintings are *The Geographer* (fig. 4) and *The Astronomer* (1668, Musée du Louvre, Paris) by Johannes Vermeer.[32]

Camels with Long Necks

Exotic animals such as camels, lions, and elephants were considered special attractions at fairs and festivals. Certain species, in particular tropical birds, could be seen in menageries, the precursors to zoos. Just one of the marvels of the menagerie of Prince Maurits in Rijswijk was a cassowary that an East India Company official had presented to the governor in 1614.[33]

When portraying exotic animals, artists frequently based their work on prints by colleagues or predecessors. Albrecht Dürer's 1515 engraving of a rhinoceros was for nearly two hundred years the only image artists could use as reference due to the lack of exact information about what the animal looked like.[34] Dürer, however, had mistakenly given the animal a second horn between its shoulder blades. As a result that mistake was often repeated by others.[35]

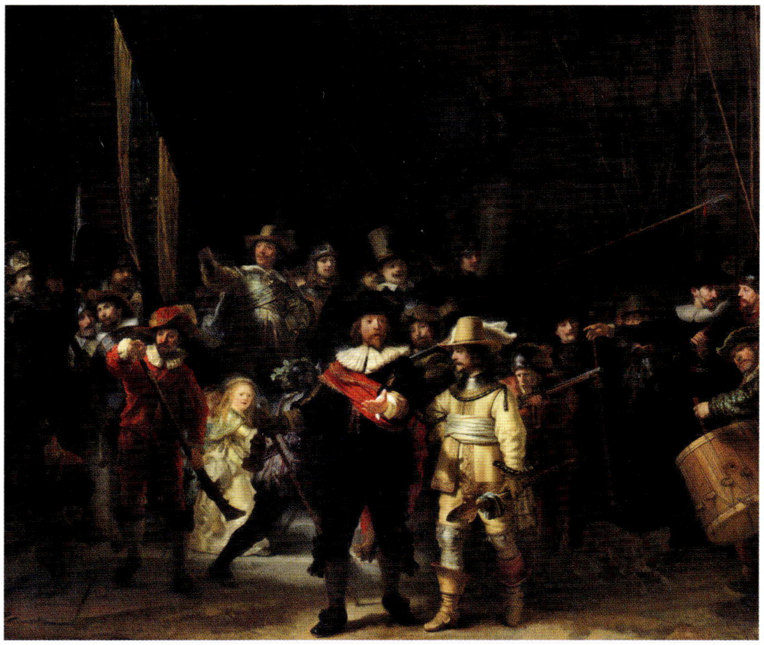

3 Rembrandt,
The Militia Company of District II under the Command of Captain Frans Banninck Cocq (The Night Watch), 1642,
Rijksmuseum, Amsterdam

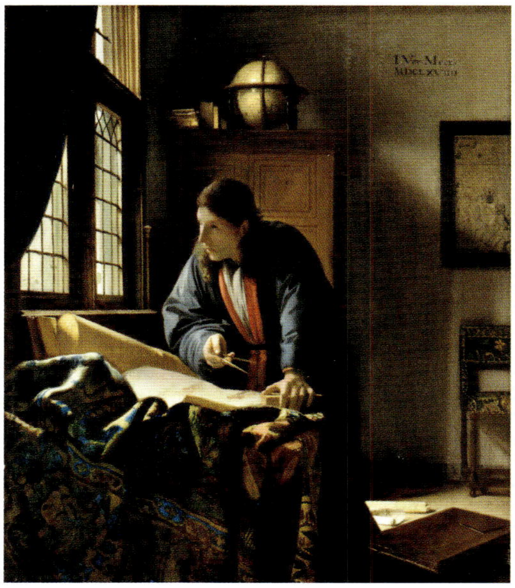

4 Johannes Vermeer,
The Geographer, 1669,
Städel Museum, Frankfurt am Main

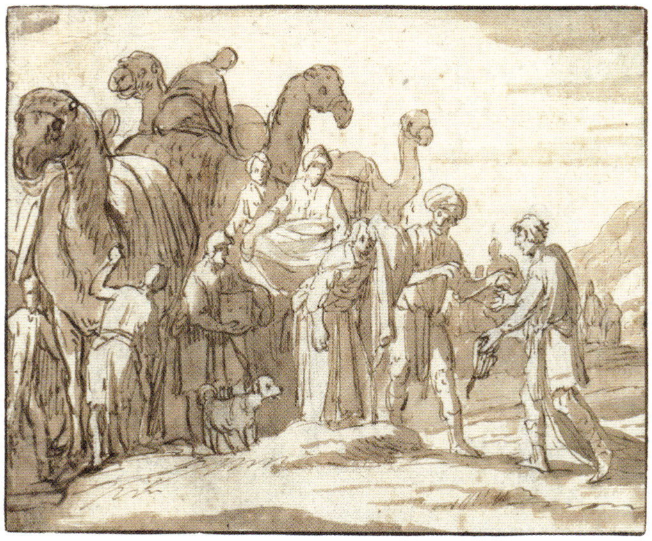

5 Nicolaes Moeyaert (1591–1669),
The Meeting of Rebecca and Eliezer,
Fondation Custodia, Collection Frits Lugt, Paris

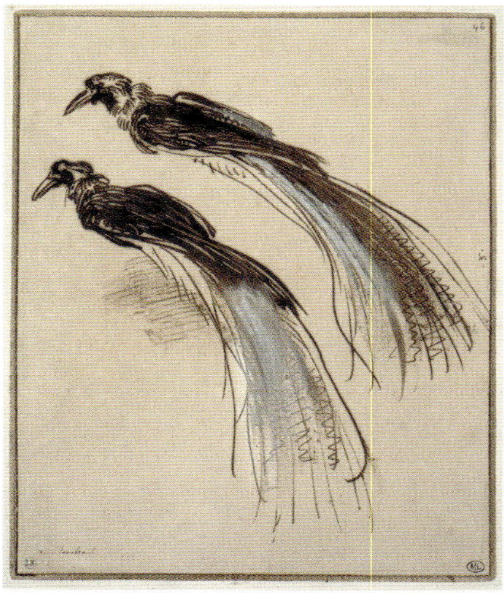

6 Rembrandt,
Two Studies of a Bird of Paradise, ca. 1639,
Musée du Louvre, Paris

Certain animals were required for the depiction of scenes from the Bible. Camels, for example, played an essential role in the Old Testament story of Rebecca and Eliezer.[36] An artist who had never seen a camel had no other choice but to find another print that showed this animal and hope that the proportions were more or less correct. In Nicolaes Moeyaert's drawing *The Meeting of Rebecca and Eliezer* (fig. 5), the camels have unrealistically long necks and the proportions of elephants. The artist was obviously not familiar with the real appearance of these animals.

Sketches by Rembrandt of lions, elephants, and camels survive which were most probably made at fairs.[37] In an early etching of *Saint Jerome Reading* by Rembrandt of 1634, the lion resembles an awkward variation on a housecat; in later works the artist depicts the lion correctly (fig. p. 83). When necessary, Rembrandt could fall back on his own collection, which included dead and stuffed animals or individual parts. The inventory of his possessions prepared in 1656 lists "Skins of a lion and a lioness" as well as "A drawer with a bird of paradise."[38] He also made drawings of this colorful bird (fig. 6). That he depicted it without legs or feet corresponds to the object because the animals were prepared thusly before they were shipped.[39]

The "Oriental" in Dutch Painting

There is a long tradition of the depiction of Oriental characters in the context of biblical scenes. Since all the stories in the Old and New Testaments take place in the Middle East, artists had to give them, somehow, an "Oriental" decor. That was particularly true of the story of the Adoration of the Magi, since the three princes who brought the Infant Jesus gifts were "wise men" from the East, one of whom had dark skin.[40] Consequently, they were shown in sumptuous garments that not only emphasized their kingly status but also gave them an exotic appearance. Thus arose a pictorial tradition in which the three Magi were portrayed with large turbans provided with small crowns.

The general idea of the "Oriental" arose from the pictorial tradition of the three wise men. This character type, which in seventeenth-century painting appeared in history pictures, cityscapes, harbor views, portraits and *tronies*, and occasionally even as a minor figure in still lifes, could never be pinned to a particular place of geographical origin or ethnic group. Although the Dutch in Asia—in an area that stretched from Japan to Iran—were confronted with numerous peoples (Javanese, Chinese, Singhalese, Tamil, Japanese, Moluccan), their specific facial features almost never appear in the artwork of the time. The "Orientals" that we see in the paintings are more a synthesis of different inhabitants of the distant lands and regions that inspired so much fantasy. They were Arabs just as much as they were Moors, Persians, Indians, and Turks. Since Polish and Hungarian articles of clothing were sometimes also used, they are sometimes even a bit Eastern European.

In the depiction of Mediterranean harbors and genrelike scenes with markets and ships by painters like Jan Baptist Weenix, Johannes Lingelbach, and Thomas Wijck (fig. 7, cat. 26–27), Oriental characters were eye-catching extras.[41] Against a backdrop of merchant ships and galleys one sees on the bustling docks, where the most varied of goods are piled, merchants with distinctive headwear in long coats and colorful caftans. Similar Oriental merchants are found in city scenes like those by the brothers Gerrit and Job Berckheyde. They show individuals in Oriental garb chatting with their Dutch colleagues in Amsterdam on the Dam (fig. 8, cat. 21) or in the Exchange. Pieter Jansz. Saenredam even painted a man in Oriental clothing and turban who was looking with interest at the interior of a church in Utrecht (fig. 9). Even if such figures did occasionally walk around the large cities of the Dutch Republic, it does not mean that these are realistic depictions of foreign visitors. In these pictures, too, the "Orientals" are colorful extras, the product of fantasy, who are intended primarily to emphasize the cosmopolitan character of Dutch trading cities.

Visits of diplomatic delegations offered Dutch citizens and artists the chance to admire men in exotic regalia in real life. Around 1610 the Moroccan ambassador and his entourage stayed for a time in Amsterdam, where they attracted much attention. A delegation from Persia visited The Hague in 1625, at which time the Dutch painter Jan Lucasz. van Hasselt, who was a member of the shah's court, was one of the principals of the mission.

Eccentric Headwear and Sparkling Jewelry

Oriental clothing also played a role in Dutch portrait painting. In some cases men and women were portrayed in historical scenes in which a biblical setting provided an excuse for an elaborate exotic garment. A double portrait that refers to the Old Testament and at the same time testifies to fashionable elegance is the picture of an unknown *Couple in a Landscape* painted by Ferdinand Bol (cat. 6). Quite often, however, there does not seem to be any concrete reason for the fancy dress, so that the motivation of the individuals portrayed can only be sought in their luxurious, almost glamorous appearance. There could also be a practical explanation for the choice of Oriental garments in portraits. Artists might have taken pains to avoid contemporary fashion, which might have soon looked outdated.[42]

Aelbert Cuyp created a painting in which the costumes display striking contradictions. In a large family portrait (cat. 7) half of the figures are wearing a type of simple black-and-white clothing normally associated with strict Calvinism. The other half, in contrast, is sumptuously dressed. These family members are wearing colorful garments with Turkish and Hungarian elements. One of the young men is decked out in a gigantic turban. In addition, there are various attributes of the hunt present. Exactly what this remarkable contrast in clothing could mean remains a secret for now.

Most depictions of "Orientals" in seventeenth-century Dutch art are *tronies*, striking heads with powerful facial features where the identity of the portrayed person is not relevant. Rembrandt and his numerous successors worked a great deal in this genre (cat. 99–104, 106, 119). It enabled them to leave sober reality behind and paint a more imaginative world, with figures wearing costly garments, eccentric headwear, and jewelry that sparkles in the twilight.

In Rembrandt's portrait of a *Man in Oriental Clothing* (cat. 101) the first thing one notices is the enormous turban made from an unbelievable amount of white fabric wound together and the narrow, gem-studded ribbon that is wrapped around it. The turban is much larger than the man's head; his face has no specifically "Oriental" or even foreign characteristics. He could be a neighbor of Rembrandt's. This particular kind of turban is not very realistic, but that did not matter at all to Rembrandt and his pupils. They were not interested in what an "Oriental" person really looked like. They painted them how they *should* have looked. Thus, they continued the pictorial tradition of the three Magi, which requires a huge turban, decorated with an impressive number of gems, and, occasionally, with a little crown.

Two opposite developments are evident in the depiction of Oriental themes and figures in the first half of the seventeenth century. There is enormous growth in knowledge about the Orient and a growing interest in Oriental items that ranged from food and luxury products to ink and rubber and articles of clothing. These products made their way into everyday life in many ways, and by extension also into painting as well. At the same time, this interest did not lead to a more precise or realistic image of the "Oriental" and its way of life. The "Oriental," for Rembrandt and his contemporaries, is an abstract, exotic ideal. Samuel van Hoogstraten says it explicitly at the end of his thorough description of all kinds of foreign peoples: "And from this the painter's spirit can conclude that he has far-reaching freedom in the depiction of armed peoples; and need not be sparing or conscientious when he considers his own discoveries."[43]

Translated from Dutch to German by Susanne Henriette Karau and from German to English by Gerald E. Brennan

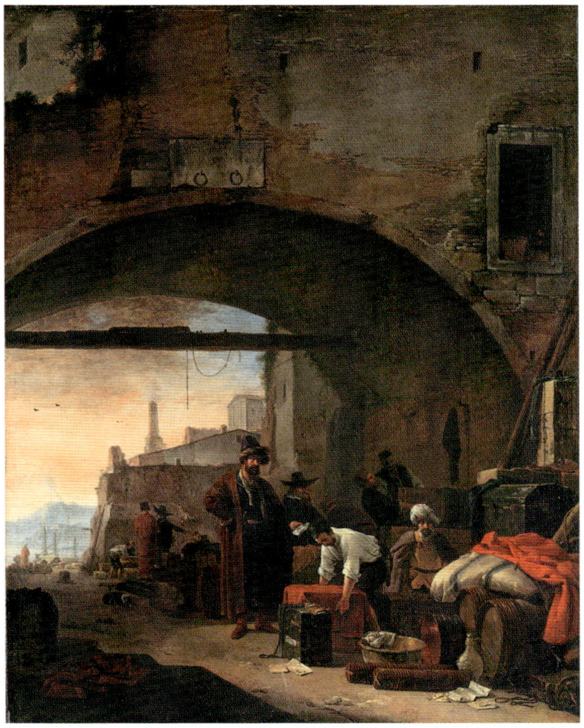

7 Thomas Wijck,
View of a Levantine Port, ca. 1640–77,
Rijksmuseum, Amsterdam

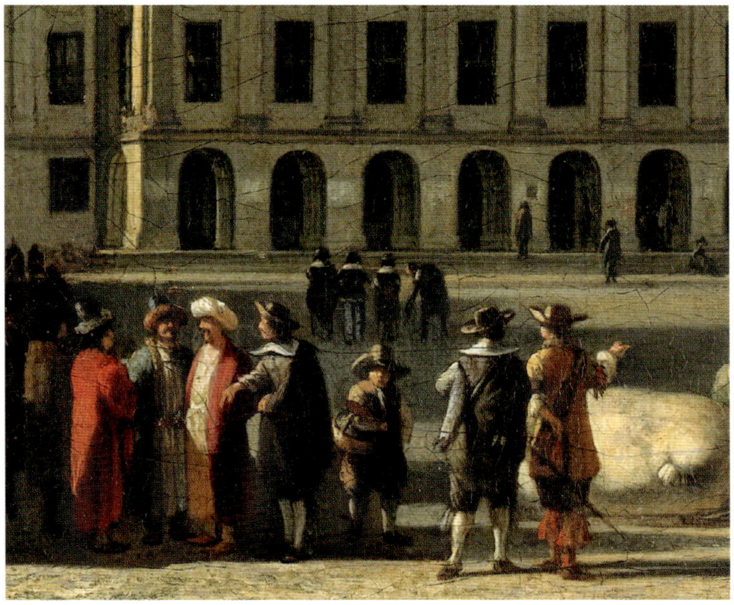

8 Gerrit Adriaensz. Berckheyde,
The Town Hall on Dam Square in Amsterdam (detail), 1672,
Rijksmuseum, Amsterdam (cat. 21)

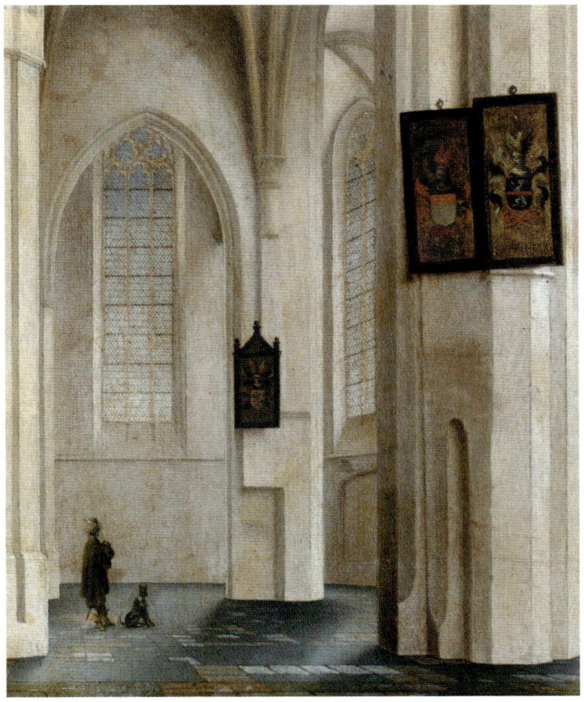

9 Pieter Jansz. Saenredam,
The Interior of the Sint Jacobskerk in Utrecht (detail), 1642,
Bayerische Staatsgemäldesammlungen,
Alte Pinakothek, Munich

[1] Cf. Andries Pels, *Gebruik én Misbruik des Tooneels*, ed. Maria A. Schenkeveld-van der Dussen, Culemborg 1978, 78: "In Pels's treatise, Rembrandt serves as an example of *pictor vulgaris* who demonstrates the dangers of unrestrained art." All Dutch quotations were translated by Susanne Henriette Karau.

[2] Andries Pels, *Gebruik én Misbruik des Tooneels*, Amsterdam 1681, 36: "Op Nieuwe en Noordermarkt zeer yv'rig op ging zoeken / Harnassen, Moriljons, Japansche Ponjerts, bont / En rafelkragen die hy schilderachtig vond." A morion is a type of helmet without a visor that developed from the Spanish *cabasset* (kettle helmet) in the sixteenth century.

[3] The inventory has been published in Amsterdam 1999a, 147–52, Appendix 2: "Rembrandts boedelinventaris" (1656).

[4] The cassowary is a large flightless bird that lives in New Guinea and Indonesia.

[5] An assegai is an African spear.

[6] Contrary to the common interpretation of "Indies koppie" as cup, I believe that it refers to a "little head," that is, a fragment of a sculpture.

[7] Cf. Amsterdam 1999a, Appendix 2, nos. 143–44, 146, 148, 150, 153, 158–59, 313.

[8] A *kris* or *keris* is an Indonesian dagger with a wavy blade. Mystical powers are ascribed to the weapon.

[9] Information about the most important trade routes to the East also came from seaman and author Jan Huygen van Linschoten (1562–1611), who during his expeditions in the Portuguese service collected information about Asian lands. After his return to Enkhuizen in the year 1592, he wrote of his experiences in a much-read account of his voyage; cf. Jan Huyghen van Linschoten, *Itinerario: Voyage ofte schipvaert . . . naer Oost ofte Portugaels Indien . . .*, Amsterdam 1596.

[10] For the early colonial history of the Dutch Republic, cf. George Masselman, *The Cradle of Colonialism*, London 1963.

[11] Maarten Prak, *Gouden Eeuw: Het raadsel van de Republiek*, Amsterdam 2002, 110–11.

[12] A description of the competition between the Dutch and English in the years 1616–20 can be found in Giles Milton, *Nathaniel's Nutmeg, or, The True and Incredible Adventures of the Spice Trader Who Changed the Course of History*, New York 1999.

[13] The picture by Isaacsz. is painted on the lid of a harpsichord that had a representative purpose in Amsterdam. The instrument was played by the renowned composer Jan Pietersz. Sweelinck, who was the City Organist there.

[14] The full title is *Journael ofte Gedenckwaerdige Beschrijvinghe van de Oost-Indische Reyse van Willem Ysbrantsz. Bonte-koe van Hoorn.* The book was reprinted more than sixty times between 1646 and 1810.

[15] The Hortus Botanicus in Leiden was established in 1594. The Hortus in Amsterdam, also known as the "medicinal herb garden," was laid out in 1638.

[16] Ria Winters, *Exotische dieren in historisch Amsterdam*, Amsterdam 2017.

[17] Joost van den Vondel, "Blyde Inkomst der allerdoorluchtighste Koninginne, Maria de Medicis, t'Amsterdam, vertaeld uit het Latijn des hooghgeleerden heeren Kasper van Baerle," Amsterdam 1639, in *De werken van Vondel*, vol. 3: *1627–1640*, ed. J. F. M. Sterck et al., Amsterdam 1929, 617–38, here 630: "en zy beelde zich in, ziende en aentastende 'tuitheemsche en ongewoone bancket, datze by den Indiaenen, Molucken, Persianen, Arabiers, Japonesen, en Chinesen te gast was," https://www.dbnl.org/tekst/vond001dewe03_01/rond001dewe03_01_0137.php (accessed February 26, 2020).

[18] The first tea was imported to the Netherlands in 1610 from Japan. After 1660 the interest in tea and coffee increased so significantly that imports rose and prices started to drop; cf. Roelofs 2015, 238. Cf. also F. M. G. de Feyfer, "Cornelis Bontekoe Tractatus de herba Thee," in *Opuscula Selecta Neerlandicorum de arte medica* 14 (1937), 52–99.

[19] For the (supposed) medicinal efficacy of herbs, cf. Wim Wennekes, *Gouden handel: De eerste Nederlanders overzee, en wat zij daar haalden*, Amsterdam 1996, 73–80.

[20] Anonymous, "Het Lof van Oost-Indiën," in *De Vermakelijcke Buys-Man, ofte Koddige Boots-Geselletje*, Amsterdam 1694, 66–72, here 68: "De Nederlands Aptheeckery, / Krijght door u haer Heer-schappy, / Der Genees-konst: want de Medecijn, / Die wort van alle kant / Gevoert na 't Vaderlant, / Met veel schepen groot en kleyn." Cf. also Bert Paasman, "Lof van Oost-Indiën: Liedjes uit de VOC-tijd," in *Indische Letteren* 6,1 (1991), 1–17, here 4.

[21] Cf. Charles Ralph Boxer, *The Dutch Seaborne Empire 1600–1800*, London 1965, 174.

[22] Karina H. Corrigan, "Asia on the Herengracht: Furnishing Amsterdam with Asian Imports," in Amsterdam 2015, 123–33, here 132, note 16: "tot het ghebruyck des ghemeenen volcks ghemeyn gheworden is."

[23] The German Engelbert Kaempfer (1651–1716), who worked from 1690 until 1692 at the East India Company trading post Deshima (Japan), indicated that much money could be earned with this trade. Cf. Amsterdam 2011b, 23–26, here 26.

[24] Ibid., 23–26.

[25] Reinier Baarsen, "Lacquer from the Far East and Dutch Japanning," in *Furniture in Holland's Golden Age*, Amsterdam 2007, 200–05, here 201: "in the Chinese manner."

[26] Philipp von Zesen, *Beschreibung der Stadt Amsterdam,* Amsterdam 1664, 463. Philipp von Zesen (1619–1689) was a German writer, poet, translator, and diplomat who lived in Amsterdam for a large part of his life.

[27] Jaap van der Veen, "East Indies Shops in Amsterdam," in Amsterdam 2015, 134–228, here 139–40.

[28] A portrait of a woman by Rembrandt from around 1656–58 (National Gallery of Art, Washington, DC) shows a large ostrich feather that is used as a fan.

[29] Mariëlle Hageman, *Amsterdam in de wereld: Sporen van Nederlands gedeelde verleden*, Amsterdam 2016, 227.

[30] Van der Veen 2015 (see note 27), 195.

[31] Copies were produced in Amsterdam from imported Chinese silk. In India the East India Company ordered house coats in the Japanese style from hand-painted chintz.

[32] It was assumed that the young man depicted in these two pictures might be the natural scientist Antoni van Leeuwenhoek, who was the curator of Vermeer's estate. Cf. Laura J. Snyder, *Eye of the Beholder: Johannes Vermeer, Antoni van Leeuwenhoek, and the Reinvention of Seeing*, New York 2015.

[33] It concerned a gift from Captain Willem Jacobsz. The librarian Ernst Brinck from Harderwijk described this cassowary. He reported that the animal was extremely aggressive and that it had inflicted a wound on Hellebardier's thigh with its claws. Cf. Winters 2017 (see note 16), 119.

[34] Dürer's woodcut shows an Indian rhinoceros that had arrived at the harbor of Lisbon in 1515 as a gift for Manuel I, the king of Portugal. Dürer did not see the rhinoceros with his own eyes; he based his depiction on a quick sketch made by an anonymous artist and a detailed description of the animal. Cf. Tim H. Clarke, *The Rhinoceros from Dürer to Stubbs, 1515–1799*, London 1986.

[35] See also Erik Spaans, "Een dodo in de Lage Landen," in *Origine: Het tijdschrift voor kunst, antiek en design* 6 (August 2015), 110–11.

[36] In Genesis 24:19 Abraham instructed Eliezer to find a wife for his son Isaac. When he reached a well with his followers he met Rebecca. She gave Eliezer and his companions water to drink and also cared for his ten camels. This convinced Eliezer that he had found a suitable bride for Isaac.

[37] Michiel Roscam Abbing, *Rembrandts olifant: In het spoor van Hansken*, Amstelveen 2016.

[38] Cf. Amsterdam 1999a, Appendix 2, nos. 346 and 280: "Een leeue- en een leeuwinnenhuyt," "Een laede daerin een paradijsvogel en ses wayers."

[39] Marrigje Rikken, *Dieren verbeeld: Diervoorstellingen in tekeningen, prenten en schilderijen door kunstenaars uit de Zuidelijke Nederlanden tussen 1550 en 1630*, PhD diss. Leiden 2016, 196, note 22.

[40] The wise men are mentioned in Matthew 2:1–12, and their description is general. Neither their number nor their names are mentioned anywhere in the New Testament. Since the Middle Ages it has been assumed that there were three persons with the names Balthasar, Melchior, and Caspar.

[41] Cf. Skeeles Schloss 1982, 7–17.

[42] Cf. Emilie Gordenker, "Cuyp's Horsemen: What Do Costumes Tell Us?," in *Aelbert Cuyp*, exh. cat., National Gallery of Art, Washington, DC, 2001, 53–63.

[43] Samuel van Hoogstraten, *Inleyding tot de hooge schoole der schilderkonst: Anders de zichtbaere werelt*, Rotterdam 1678, 154: "En hier uit kan de Schildergeest gewaer worden, dat hy in't uitbeelden van gewapende volken, een wijtuitgestrekte vryheyt heeft; en niet kaerich noch naeuw gezet in eyge vonden behoeft te zijn."

"The Exquisiteness of the Goods the Indian Gives Us" Non-European Objects in Seventeenth-Century Dutch Still Lifes and Interiors

Michael Philipp

On July 27, 1599, the bells tolled in Amsterdam as a fleet of four ships arrived "uyt Indie" after having embarked for Asia fifteen months earlier under Admiral Jacob Cornelisz. van Neck.[1] They were "received happily and with great astonishment"—never before had ships with such large amounts of exotic goods reached the northern Netherlands. As Pieter Christiaensz. Bor, an early seventeenth-century chronicler, noted, they bore "four hundred loads of pepper, one hundred loads of cloves, as well as mace, nuts, nutmeg and cinnamon, porcelain, silk and silk cloth, and other valuables."[2]

This event, documented in images by Hendrik Cornelisz. Vroom (fig. 1), was the start of a commercial boom in the city of Amsterdam, which within a few years' time became the center of world trade. That was connected with a previously unknown availability of all kinds of goods never seen before. The variety and abundance of exotic goods amazed contemporaries. René Descartes, who had been in the Netherlands since 1629, wrote to a friend in May 1631 about how much he enjoyed watching the arrival of ships in Amsterdam that brought everything in abundance that was produced in the two Indies[3] and was rare in Europe: "What other place in the world could you choose where all the goods and all the curiosities that you could want are so easy to find as in this city?"[4]

This essay will investigate the cultural appropriation of non-European goods and curiosities in the genres of still life and interiors in seventeenth-century painting in the northern Netherlands.[5] The former are examined not only because still lifes are a leading genre in seventeenth-century Dutch painting;[6] they also document the appropriation of exotic objects and the significance attributed to them. The latter are included due to their realistic or fictitious depiction of living spaces, since interiors show the actual or idealized pictorial integration of exotic objects into everyday surroundings.[7] While paintings remain an important source of information about the Dutch seventeenth century in critical art history, over the past few years the deficits of a viewpoint focused on aesthetic idealization has been increasingly criticized.[8]

The appeal of these exotic objects derived from their unfamiliarity, their rarity, their resulting costliness, and frequently also their beauty. From the Western point of view, the term *exotic* refers to a place of origin outside Europe,[9] which in the Netherlands of the seventeenth century was often generalized as the East, India, or the "Orient"[10]—thus tobacco from America was considered "Oriental," as a *cartellino* in a painting by Hubert van Ravesteyn from 1670 shows (fig. 2). The goods that reached Amsterdam from foreign trade had the status of luxury goods until late in the seventeenth century.[11] They did not serve to satisfy the essential needs of everyday life, but rather sensuous enjoyment. Due to their price and rarity, they were not available to just anyone; as status symbols they brought their owners social prestige. The material culture of the Netherlands in the seventeenth century was not only a part—and a motor—of early globalization;[12] it also stood at the beginning of the formation of modern consumer culture.[13]

The preconditions for this phenomenon were complex. They were based on long-term social and intellectual developments in the sixteenth century: the decline of the orientation on the hereafter, a turn toward the world of things, the *zichtbaere werelt*[14] as expressed in still lifes, the increasing discovery of the world by means of encyclopedically applied science, and finally the formation of a civil society with an interest in status and the mechanisms of social distinction. In addition there were other short-term economic and social developments, such as the influx of immigrants from the southern Netherlands after the fall of Antwerp in 1585, which led to both an enormous growth in Amsterdam's population[15] and its rapidly expanding economy, and a rational economy based on efficiency and increasing profit, as illustrated, for example, by the founding of the Dutch East India Company (Vereenigde Oostindische Compagnie, or VOC), a monopoly, in 1602.[16] Finally, technological advances in shipbuilding and navigation, which led to exponential increases in maritime transport capacity and speed, contributed to commercial successes.[17]

This essay investigates the contemporary view of the city of Amsterdam and Dutch foreign trade as depicted in seventeenth-century allegories.

The True Cornucopia

The frontispiece in a new edition of seaman Joris van Spilbergen's report about his first trip to the Indies, published posthumously in 1664, announced the book's contents in a few lines. In the words of Spilbergen, it described "veel vreemdigeyt, en d'kost'lijckheyt der Waren / Die d'Indiaen ons geeft" (many strange things and the exquisiteness of the goods the Indian gives us).[18] *Strangeness* and *exquisiteness* are two key terms that describe aspects of the European fascination with exotic goods. This reference is illustrated by an engraving of the allegorical figure of Fama hovering above a globe and proclaiming the fame of Spilbergen the circumnavigator.[19]

The depiction shows neither the rich goods nor "the Indian" from whom these goods came—although these two motifs were part of the most common topoi of Dutch descriptions of travel to Asia as well as of allegorical depictions of the city of Amsterdam in the seventeenth century. The 1672 ethnographic study of some regions in Asia by Philippus Baldaeus,[20] for example, features a frontispiece (fig. 3) in which several scantily clad figures, who are meant to be local natives, are hauling fruit, ivory, fabrics, jewelry, and other goods in baskets and crates in front of a large elephant. The close-up view and the crowdedness indicate an abundance that seems to invite the viewer to partake in it.

Although such depictions portray in a fantastic manner the purportedly idyllic conditions and the simple and lavish availability of goods in distant lands, the depiction of trade and the amount of trade could only take the form of allegories in the Dutch homeland. In this context, a type of picture developed in which the personification of Amsterdam, the *stedenmaagd*, usually sits in an elevated position, as if on a throne, and allegories of the four continents, rendering homage, present goods at her feet. This composition can be found, for example, on the frontispiece of the 1663 history of the city of Amsterdam by Olfert Dapper[21] and on the tympanum of the west façade of the massive

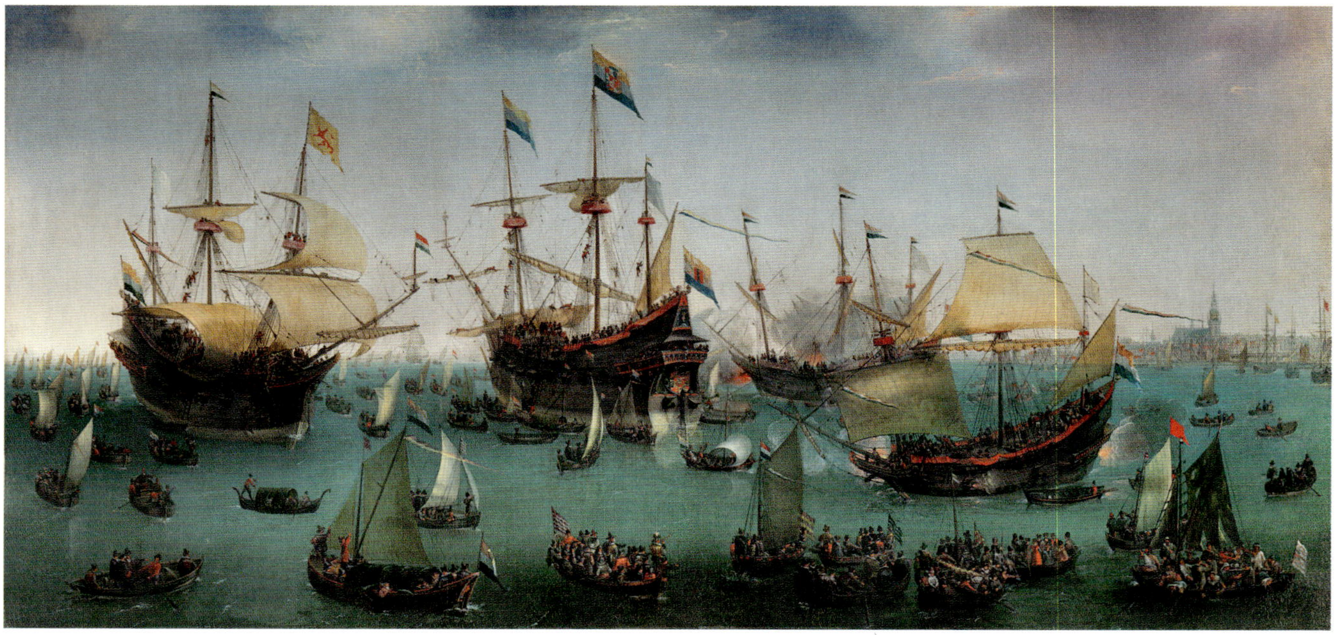

1 Hendrik Cornelisz. Vroom,
The Return of the Second East Indian Expedition to Amsterdam, 1599,
Rijksmuseum, Amsterdam

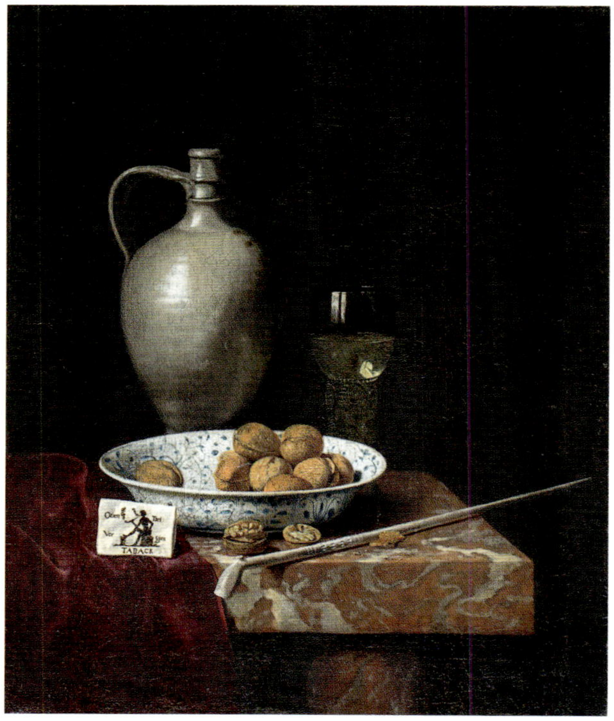

2 Hubert van Ravesteyn,
Still Life with Pipe, Nuts, Jug, and Tobacco Pouch, 1670,
Museum voor Schone Kunsten, Ghent

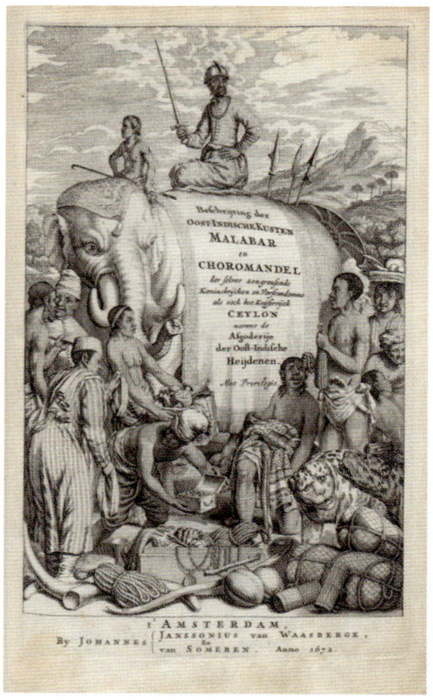

3 Anonymous,
frontispiece, in Philippus Baldaeus,
Naauwkeurige Beschriyvinge van Malabar en Choromandel, der zelver aangrenzende Ryken, en het machtige Eyland Ceylon,
Amsterdam 1672

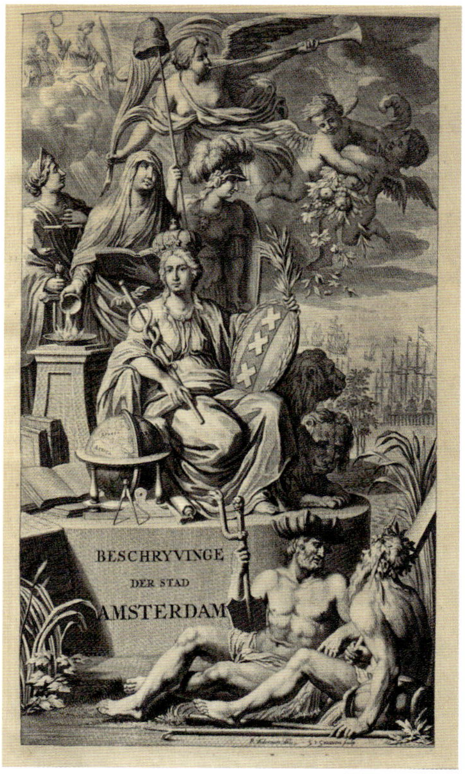

4 Anonymous,
frontispiece, in Olfert Dapper,
Beschryvinge van Amsterdam,
Amsterdam 1663 (1693 edition)

Amsterdam town hall, which had been inaugurated only a few years earlier (see cat. 21).[22] Maritime symbols such as the figure of Neptune or a ship and the globe are frequently part of the multifigural depictions, and the tympanum is crowned by a monumental bronze figure of Atlas bearing the earth.

The most characteristic motif of such scenes is a cornucopia, which has been a symbol of opulence and fertility and an attribute of the goddess Fortuna since ancient times. This motif is also found in depictions of Antwerp, Amsterdam's predecessor as the metropolis of world trade.[23] The cornucopia is often presented to the *stedenmaagd* by another figure, as in the above-mentioned frontispiece in Dapper's city history from 1663. It might be emptied on her, as in the frontispiece of the 1693 edition (fig. 4).[24] Or she holds it in her hands, as she does in the allegory *Amsterdam as the Center of World Trade* by Pieter Isaacsz. and Karel van Mander (fig. p. 15). In all cases, it signals that wealth has come to Amsterdam without effort and as if of its own accord.[25]

Most depictions from the seventeenth century reproduce this idea without reflection as self-evident, although in some works astonishment can be felt at the suddenness of the abundance. The detailed inscription on the 1611 etching *View of Amsterdam, Seen from the IJ* by Claes Jansz. Visscher II and Pieter Bast (fig. 5, cat. 17)—just a dozen years after the arrival of the first cargos from Asia—repeatedly refers to the scarcely imaginable amount of goods. It states that the abundance of goods was so large that it could hardly be described or its value expressed. After a long list of all the goods possible, which like the pictorial allegories is intended to overwhelm, it strikes a balance: "Everything that is of service for the care of the body or the stimulation of the mind is here in such abundance that one recognizes that God's merciful blessing, the true *keras Amaltheias*, or cornucopia, has clearly been poured out upon us." In less than ten years since its founding in 1602, the East India Company brought a total cargo of 22,580 tons to the Netherlands in forty-nine ships, an inconceivable amount at the time.[26]

For part of the population—a small part—the immense trade set loose large amounts of money that was used not only for accumulation of capital but was also available for conspicuous consumption.[27] Thus, the town houses of Amsterdam in the seventeenth century were characterized by plenitude and wealth. In his description of the city, which came out in 1662 during a new expansion of the ring of canals, Melchior Fokkens wrote that the magnificent new buildings on the Keizersgracht resembled the palaces of kings more than the houses of merchants.

Fokkens admired the extraordinary furnishings with their works of art and luxury goods, paying particular attention to Asian objects. He wrote that these houses—perhaps similar to the buildings in the architectural fantasies painted by Bartholomeus van Bassen and Esaias van de Velde in the 1620s (fig. 6)—were furnished so sumptuously with paintings and Asian decorations that their value was incalculable. Nonetheless, Fokkens did make a calculation of the amounts invested, and he wrote that the expensive furnishings of some houses were worth fifty thousand guilders, while for others they were valued at one hundred thousand or even twice as much.[28] In any case, he noted that some houses had more foreign rarities than others and that the difference could easily amount to fifty or eighty thousand guilders.[29]

While the passage indicates competition among the homeowners over the prestige of their property, it also shows the degeneration of aesthetic luxury goods to their quantifiable material value.[30] Toward the end Fokkens refers to the "uytheemsche rariteyten" (foreign rarities) that were kept visibly in the state rooms open to visitors. He equated the significance of these works with that of the paintings in the state rooms, which suggests that they were visibly—or ostentatiously—presented. The exotic objects, which were not described in any greater detail, were just as omnipresent as they were special. The specialness, the rareness, and the preciousness of *exotica* made them desirable objects to collect and that was also the attraction for frequently depicting them in seventeenth-century still lifes.

The Collected Beauty of Creation

Collecting valuable and rare objects in a chamber of curiosities was the privilege of princes during the Renaissance, but in the seventeenth century it was widespread among well-to-do citizens in the Netherlands. More than 150 collections have been documented, 90 of them in Amsterdam alone.[31] Along with traditional areas of collecting, such as coins or paintings, they frequently included exotic objects: *artificialia, naturalia,* and *ethnographica.* Rembrandt was also a collector of *exotica,* among other things.[32] Due to the inventory of the auction taken in connection with his bankruptcy in 1656, the makeup of his collection is known. It included two East Indian boxes, an East Indian powder compact, a Japanese helmet, a bird of paradise, six fans, a large selection of sea snails and sea plants, non-European weapons and clothing, and two lion skins.[33]

In spite of the popularity of collecting and the amount of capital that was expended on it, hardly any paintings from the seventeenth century exist that document this passion. One of the few collectors who had his portrait painted as a collector was Jan Govertsz. of Haarlem, who displayed a few choice items from his shell collection for Hendrick Goltzius in 1603 (Museum Boijmans Van Beuningen, Rotterdam). In his hand he holds a magnificent specimen of *Turbo marmoratus Linnaeus*, with its surface polished down to the silvery-shiny layer of mother-of-pearl. However, there are no paintings in the northern Netherlands that depict entire collections or chambers of art.[34]

In Flanders, on the other hand, painters such as Frans Francken the Younger or Willem van Haecht developed the genre of gallery paintings, which illustrated the abundance and diversity of collections at the time (fig. 7).[35] Other painters in Antwerp such as Jan Brueghel the Elder and Peter Paul Rubens celebrated the products of nature and arts in rich splendor in a series of allegories of *The Five Senses* (1617–18, Museo Nacional del Prado, Madrid). The Calvinist North shied away from such material-saturated exuberance. These painters integrated exotic objects into the composition of their still lifes.

In almost all varieties of still lifes—including vanitas, flower, banquet, fish, or trompe l'oeil—*exotica* appear as elements of more or less plausible arrangements. That is true for *artificialia*—handcrafted objects such as porcelain—as well as for *naturalia*—for example, shells or coral—and *ethnographica,* such as cult objects or weapons. These exotic elements had several functions in still lifes. Thus, because of their rarity, they created an atmosphere of preciousness and exceptionality. They also stood for affluence, like intricately worked tableware made of precious metal. Such still lifes identified their customers or owners as collectors and therefore as connoisseurs. For Dutch artists, who strove to capture the different materials and their surfaces with the utmost exactness in their still lifes, reproducing the properties of something like porcelain or shells was a technical challenge.

The most-frequently-depicted exoticum was Chinese porcelain,[36] called *kraakporselein* after a type of ship, the carrack, that was known as *kraak* in Dutch.[37] The material, produced in Ming Dynasty China (until 1644) in particular for export and previously unknown in Europe, was fascinating because of its material properties—a high degree of hardness with a low degree of thickness—and its aesthetic qualities—the blue decor on a milky white ground. Porcelain appears in countless still lifes in the form of a bowl with fruit, for example, or a large vessel such as the ginger pot seen in a painting by Willem Kalf (fig. 8). The harmonic effect of the forms and surfaces of the vessels are shown to great advantage in front of a dark background. Besides such aesthetic moments, a still life can also use porcelain to communicate a symbolic message. Often-used motifs such as birds or plants could be seen as a link between nature and culture. Its fragility could also refer to the fragility of human existence.

Shells have many material characteristics similar to porcelain and because of their wealth of shapes they were considered miracles of God. In 1614 the poet Philibert van Borsselen published a didactic ode to shells, "tot lof vanden schepper aller dinghen" (In Praise of the Creator of All Things).[38] Although popular as precious collector's objects from foreign waters, they were only rarely appreciated as individual objects. Their physical presence was more impressive than their representativeness in pictures.

Rembrandt's etching of a *Conus marmoreus* from 1650 is an exception. In this work the black-and-white pattern was perhaps more important to him than a correct rendering: corresponding to the reversal of the printing process, his seashell has a right-handed twist instead of a left-handed one. Few still-life painters have depicted shells. Balthasar van der Ast painted them most frequently and often combined them with flowers. In such paintings, the shells invoke a comparison of hardness and softness, of transience and endurance. Jan Davidsz. de Heem used a *Turbo marmoratus* next to a bouquet of flowers and a skull as a vanitas symbol in his *Memento Mori* (fig. 9).

Everything Is Vanity

The nautilus has a special role among seashells.[39] Since the Renaissance, the housing of this cephalopod from the Pacific and Indian Oceans has been sanded down to its mother-of-pearl layer, embellished with gold or silver fittings, and made into magnificent drinking vessels. Modified in this way, it became a hybrid of nature and art. Even though the trading colony of the East India Company founded in the Moluccas in 1609 discovered nautilus shells in great quantities on the coast of Ambon,[40] they remained a precious, coveted good and a striking element in still lifes (fig. 10).

That is also true for some of the plants shown in flower still lifes, including tulips. The tulip, whose name stems from the Persian word for "turban," *tulband*, which was adapted in Dutch, had been cultivated for centuries in Persia and the Ottoman Empire before they were planted for the first time in the botanical garden in Leiden in 1593. Soon cultivated widely in the Netherlands, the flowers remained precious and had the aura of something valuable. They were usually integrated into flower still lifes but also appreciated as individual objects. In 1636–37 the crazed speculation of tulip mania started in the Netherlands with horrendous sums being paid for single tulip bulbs.[41] Even after the bubble burst, tulips continued to be cultivated, gathered with other flowers in vases, displayed in living rooms,[42] and reproduced in still lifes (fig. 11) in the Netherlands.[43]

Exotica are usually presented with other precious materials, such as gold or silverwork, or domestic products, and they are frequently shown as a distinctive but not dominant element. Nonetheless, there are also still lifes in which exotic objects play a dominant role—for example, in Cornelis de Man's *Still Life with Servant and Parrot* (fig. 12), in which the sheer dimensions of the porcelain vessel and the large macaw emphasize the exoticness.

In De Man's painting, the characteristic format of the still life, which includes the surface of a table, is expanded by the presence of a person. This is also the case in Jan van der Heyden's *Room Corner with Curiosities* (cat. 53), which shows various *exotica* such as a Chinese carpet, a Turkish carpet, a stuffed armadillo, a Japanese Kakiemon cup, and a *naginata* weapon. The rolled-up map leaning against the wall and the open copy of cartographer Joan Blaeu's *Atlas Maior* indicate the far-flung origins of the objects.

Still lifes create a connection with the objects depicted that extends into the personal space of the observer. These objects are presented like practically tangible consumer goods. However, it is left to the individual to establish this relationship. Although in still lifes each object is shown to its best advantage, also as objects of admiration, *exotica* in interiors are presented in a domestic context—even if they are usually idealized—and thus as part of an overall structure that expresses prestige.

The Strange Becomes Familiar

Although wealth and abundance are often invoked in the allegories of the city of Amsterdam and of its trade as well as in the topographical description of the city, it is rare that depictions of this opulence of goods are found in the northern Netherlands outside of this context. *Exotica* in the townhouses of the Keizersgracht, which Melchior Fokkens praised as conspicuous and defining features, were portrayed by painters in a discreet manner, often in the background of depictions of domestic settings. This is also true of popular genre pictures, for example, by Johannes Vermeer, Frans van Mieris, and Pieter de Hooch, which show courtly or merry scenes with standardized figures as well as of portraits of real people.

The settings could have corresponded to real circumstances in either case, but they did not have to by any means.[44] That is also true of furniture and decor: the particular furnishings make it possible to read what the ideal of a middle-class reception room was. Still, an aristocratic attitude was by no means obligatory in interiors—Rembrandt, for example, did not depict an interior in his *Old Man Sleeping* (ca. 1629, Galleria Sabauda, Turin), and Caspar Netscher did without furnishings in his family portrait of 1649–84 (Rijksmuseum, Amsterdam). This grim family is shown in a room with a magnificent fireplace; some paintings are hinted at in the background, but there is no trace of any *exotica*.

The most common—and most noticeable—non-European object in seventeenth-century pictures of interiors is a carpet spread on a table.[45] The occasional Anatolian carpet must have been present in the Netherlands by the fifteenth century,[46] but it was only after the founding of the East India Company that carpets from Persia and India—and in large quantities—reached the northern Netherlands. It is not possible to say how many of the Oriental carpets shown in approximately one thousand seventeenth-century paintings[47] could also be found on the tables of citizens. It is obvious, though, that their frequent depiction was a reflection of current fashion. The carpet motif was also attractive to painters because its powerful color palette, in pictures of regents, for example, could provide color accents in settings that were not exactly colorful with gentlemen in dark clothing in front of brown-toned walls. An Oriental carpet frequently lay on the table in monumental group portraits, such as in *The Headmen of the Arquebus Civic Guard House* by Bartholomeus van der Helst (cat. 10). The rendering of its pattern with the distortion of perspective due to the folds was an artistic challenge, particularly when the carpet had been pushed to one side, as Gabriel Metsu often does, for example, in *A Young Woman Composing a Piece of Music* (fig. 13).

While Oriental carpets, due to their high price, were items not available to just anyone, porcelain was an Asian product that was soon found in all households.[48] In the course of the seventeenth century the Dutch East India Company imported hundreds of thousands of plates, cups, bowls, and vases from China and at times from Japan as well. The aesthetic qualities of porcelain also played a role in interiors—painters often depicted individual vases and plates with the typical blue-white design on mantelpieces and cabinets. Their placement so high that they were difficult to reach indicates their role as pure decoration.

A portrait of a family from Dordrecht by Nicolaes Maes painted in 1656 (Norton Simon Museum, Pasadena) includes as the room's only prominent decoration two Chinese plates and a porcelain bowl on a ledge along the wall. The way they are presented leads to the conclusion that they were not used as dining utensils. That is also true of the porcelain in the *Family Group in an Interior* attributed to Quiringh Gerritsz. van Brekelenkam (fig. 14). Five porcelain items are symmetrically arranged on the cabinet—in front of a painting of a ship that refers to the origin of the objects. The family gathered in the foreground has just finished their meal. Bread and cheese have not yet been cleared from the table. Traditional tin was used as tableware, not the expensive porcelain, as the plate still on the table shows.

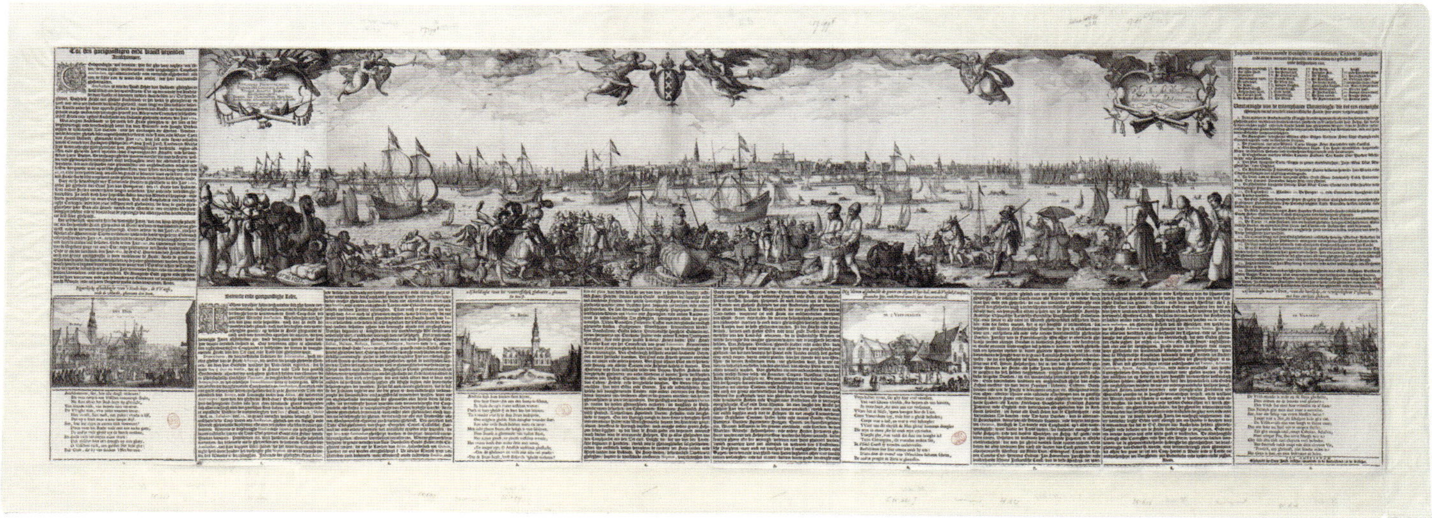

5 Claes Jansz. Visscher II and Pieter Bast,
View of Amsterdam, Seen from the IJ, 1611 (cat. 17)

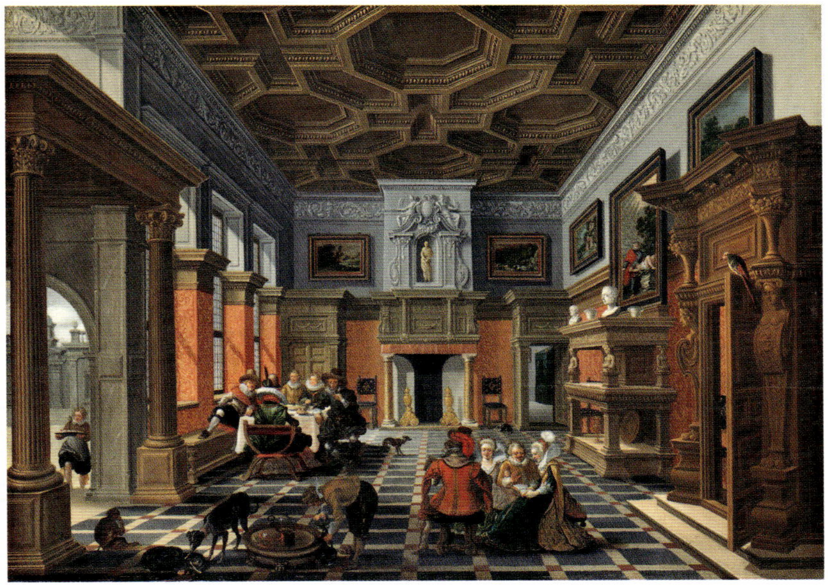

6 Bartholomeus van Bassen and Esaias van de Velde,
Interior with a Company, 1622–24,
Rijksmuseum, Amsterdam

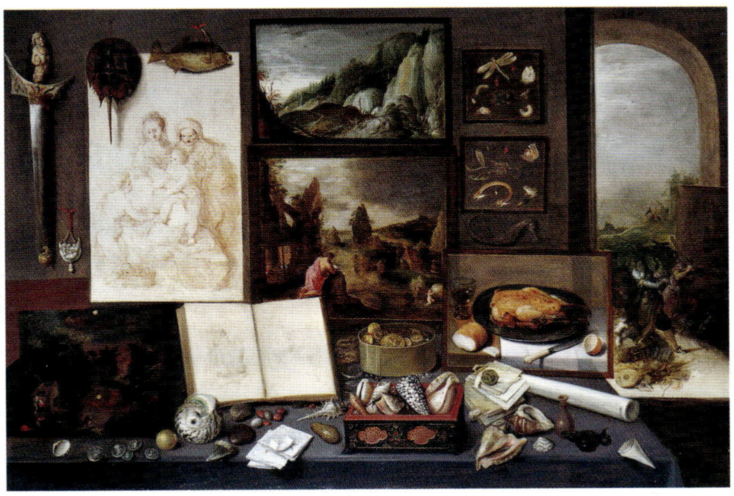

7 Frans Francken the Younger,
The Cabinet of a Collector, 1617,
The Royal Collection Trust, London

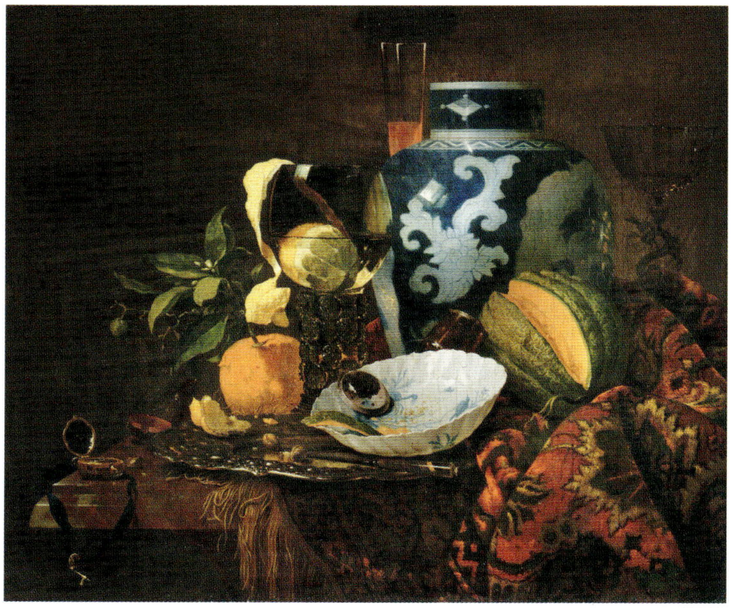

8 Willem Kalf,
Still Life with Ginger Pot and Porcelain Cup, ca. 1660,
Musée du Louvre, Paris

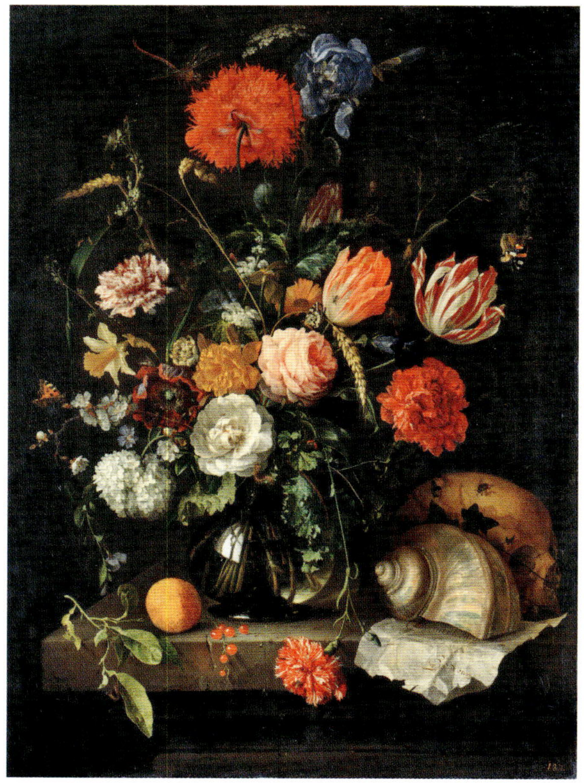

9 Jan Davidsz. de Heem,
Memento Mori, ca. 1655–60,
Gemäldegalerie Alte Meister,
Staatliche Kunstsammlungen Dresden

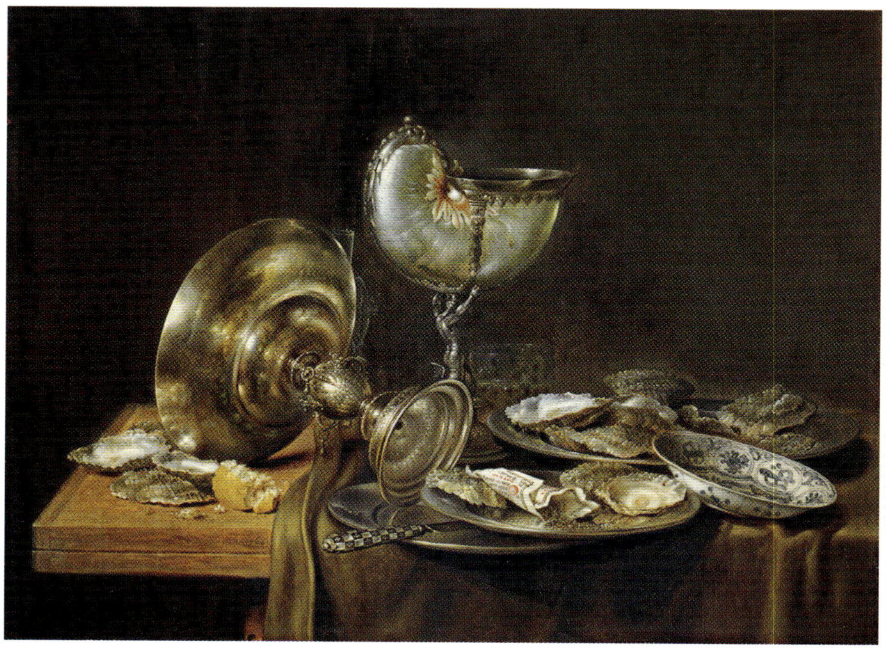

10 Willem Claesz. Heda,
Still Life with Nautilus Cup, 1649,
Staatliches Museum Schwerin

Exotica brought to the Netherlands from non-European countries also included live animals such as parrots and primates. Kept as pets, they found their way into depictions of interiors. Two long-tailed monkeys from southern Africa were painted by Pieter Bruegel the Elder in 1562 (Gemäldegalerie, Staatliche Museen zu Berlin). Such an animal is sitting in the left foreground of the above-mentioned *Interior with a Company* by Bartholomeus van Bassen and Esaias van de Velde (fig. 6). While the guenon monkey here stands for the upper class or courtly lifestyle, in the domestic scene of Jan Miense Molenaer's *Woman Playing the Virginal* (fig. 15) it has a moral function. One of the many meanings that have been attributed to apes in art since the Middle Ages was sexual passion. The animal on the harpsichord is sitting above a painting that depicts a pair of lovers in a landscape. The cavalier is already coming through the door while the young woman at the virginal looks out from the picture with a provocative gaze.

Parrots appear more frequently than monkeys in interiors.[49] They were often imported and could be seen in public in Amsterdam, for example, in the aviary in the garden of the inn Blaauw Jan at the Kloveniersburgwal that was established around 1675.[50] Their use in parodistic genre pictures, such as Jan Steen's *As the Old Sing, So Pipe the Young* from around 1668–70 (Mauritshuis, The Hague), substantiates their general familiarity in a domestic context. The *Ara macao* from Central and South America has a two-fold symbolic meaning in this picture: while its screeching is contrasted ironically with the singing of the merry group, the parrot, with its ability to imitate speech, also represents the figure of speech in the title.

While scenes like these are bits of fantasy, in the case of a 1657 portrait by Rembrandt, the actual existence of the bird pictured, possibly a parrotlet, is documented: Catrina Hooghsaet, the sitter in the portrait (fig. 16), mentioned the bird in her will.[51] That Rembrandt placed his signature in the immediate area of the bird might also be a reference to its ability to imitate. Although the question of whether the bird in the Hooghsaet house actually sat on a ring over the table must remain open, the painting is evidence of the intimacy of the person portrayed with her exotic housemate.

Cultural Appropriation

Although exotic objects are often depicted in seventeenth-century Dutch still lifes and interiors, it is not always the case. When they are included, they are shown discreetly but clearly. Their integration into paintings testifies to their presence in Dutch life and to the high regard they enjoyed, but it does not necessarily indicate how they were actually used in everyday life or in what numbers.

The paintings do not reflect the abundance of goods invoked by the contemporary allegories and descriptions of the city of Amsterdam, an abundance that flowed as if from a cornucopia. This did not necessarily correspond to the actual conditions at the time; it is evidence only of a certain restraint in the depiction that expressed the self-conception and/or wishful thinking of the owners of such paintings. This restraint was due to the impact of Calvinism, which emphasized sobriety. According to Calvinists, wealth was in no way bad; on the contrary, it was a sign of God's blessing. However, an excessive display of accumulated wealth and an overly demonstrative attachment to earthly goods was considered indecent.[52] In this respect too, the symbolic message that often accompanies these pictures, for example, a vanitas allegory, should be understood as one of several layers of meaning.

Exotica played an important role in these paintings. They were signifiers of an affluent lifestyle, enhancing prestige, and presenting their owners as worldly and up-to-date, as a participant in the latest trends in bourgeois society. As citations from other parts of the world with which the Netherlands traded, they referred to distant regions where the wealth had its origin. The exotic objects were fashionable and prestigious elements of the domestic setting. Separated from the circumstances of their origin, which were for the most part undocumented, there was no connection to their original cultural function or their place of geographical origin. No interest in any of these objects beyond an appreciation of the aesthetic or material can be seen in these paintings. From this point of view, it is more the case of a material than a cultural transfer from East to West.[53] Even if there was an acculturation process with porcelain and tulips, as these were produced or raised in the Netherlands over the course of the seventeenth century, the transcultural aspect was not a theme in painting.

The focus of the paintings on the aspects of aesthetics and the documentation of status also excludes any consideration of the specific circumstances of this transfer. That the overflowing wealth of goods in seventeenth-century Amsterdam also claimed human lives—including travelers to Asia, many of whom died in transit,[54] but above all the Asians and Africans themselves who were repeatedly subjected to violence[55] or enslaved[56]—is never referred to in still lifes or interior scenes of Dutch painters. It cannot be assumed that these circumstances would have been of particular interest to contemporaries of the seventeenth century. A remark in Joris van Spilbergen's travel journal reflects the self-righteous perception of the origin of the goods. At the end of August 1603, after the ships in Bantam were laden with "5,500 sacks of pepper, as well as precious stones, ambergris, cinnamon, silk, porcelain, mace, indigo, and 200 sacks of nuts," the commander noted, "dit alles heeft God de Heere ons toegevoecht" (all this God the Lord has given to us).[57]

Seventeenth-century still-life painting reflects the transition of the Dutch economy from sheer subsistence to widespread consumerism. Among the changes in society accompanying this major shift we find the cultural appropriation of non-European goods. These would be appropriated and integrated into local life in two ways: materially, through purchase, and behaviorally, by being taken up in the practices of everyday life. This extended to everyday use—for example, luxury foods such as tea, tobacco, or spices and articles of daily use such as clothing or porcelain—or to the aestheticization as artifacts, as was the case with nautilus cups. Still lifes and interiors documented this process in the seventeenth century while supporting it in two ways: by defining the standards of social prestige and by anchoring exotic objects in the current collective visual memory.

Translated from German by Gerald E. Brennan

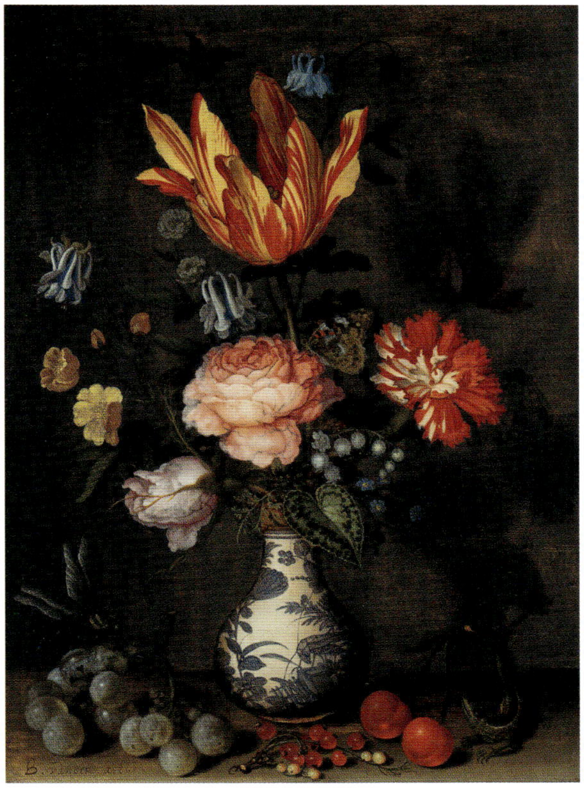

11 Balthasar van der Ast,
Flowers in a Wanli Vase, 1620s,
Suermondt-Ludwig-Museum, Aachen

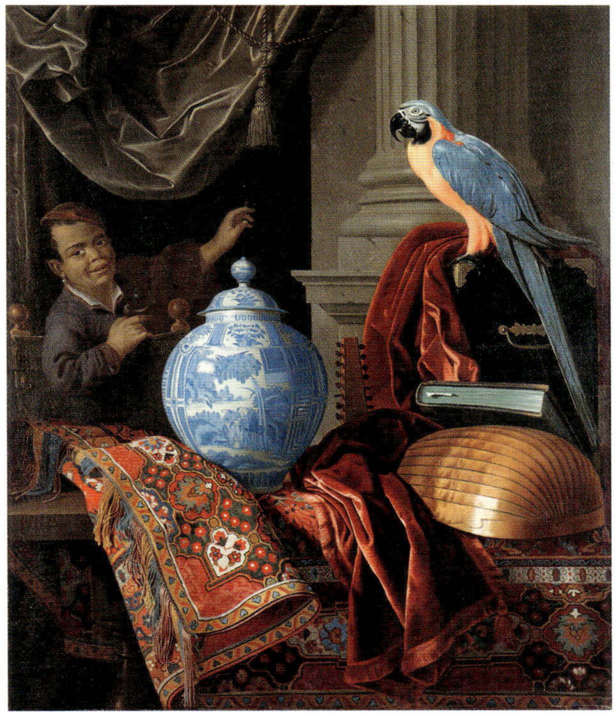

12 Cornelis de Man,
Still Life with Servant and Parrot, 1667 or later,
Historisches Museum Frankfurt

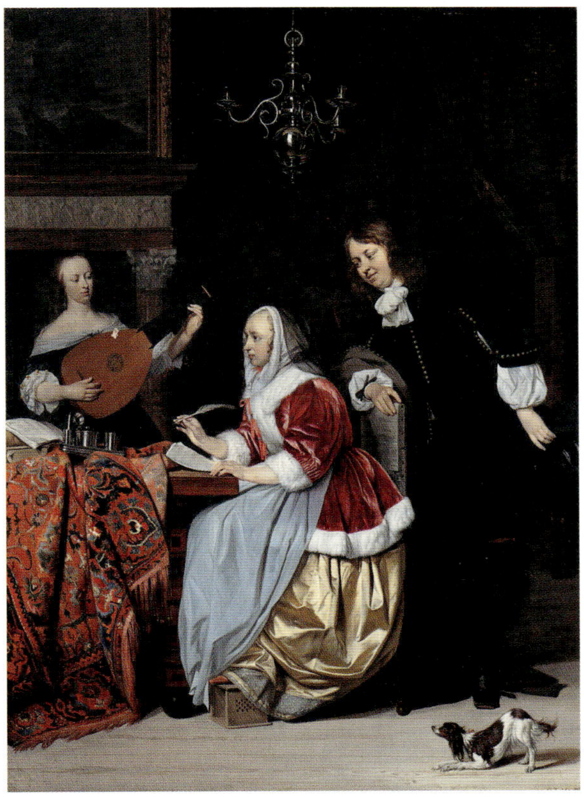

13 Gabriel Metsu,
A Young Woman Composing a Piece of Music, ca. 1664,
Mauritshuis, The Hague

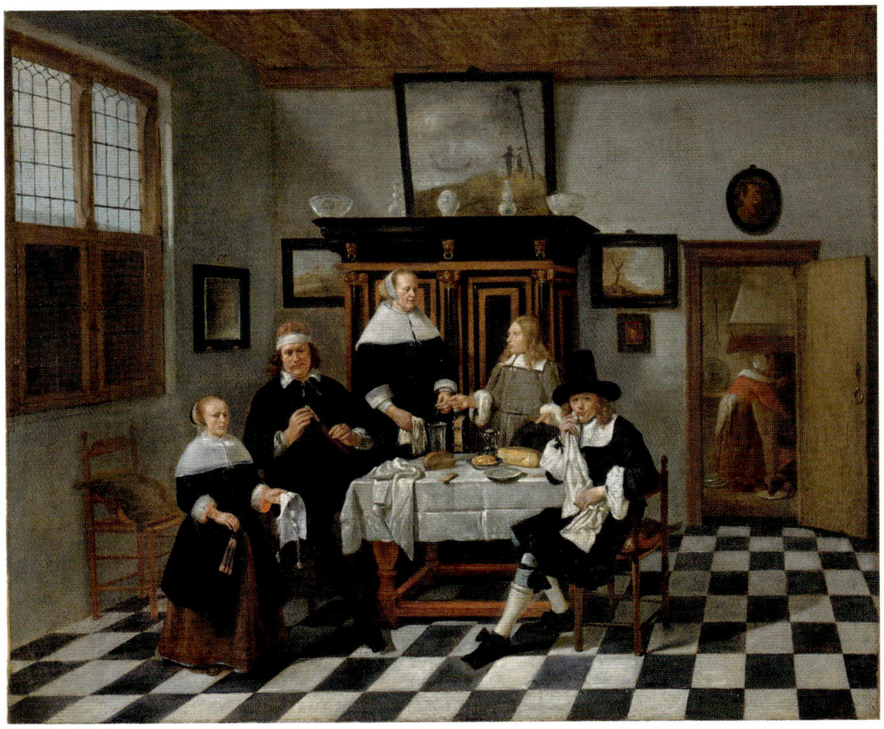

14 Attributed to Quiringh Gerritsz. van Brekelenkam,
Family Group in an Interior, ca. 1658–60,
The J. Paul Getty Museum, Los Angeles

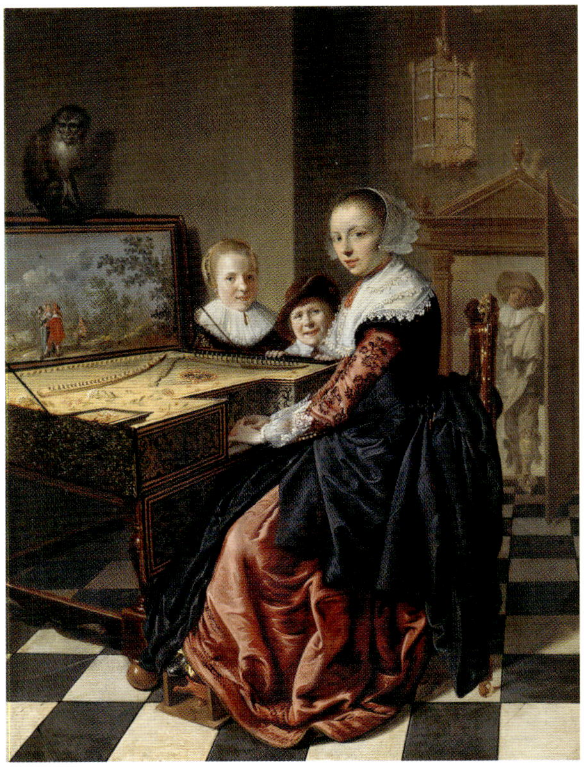

15 Jan Miense Molenaer,
Woman Playing the Virginal, 1630–40,
Rijksmuseum, Amsterdam

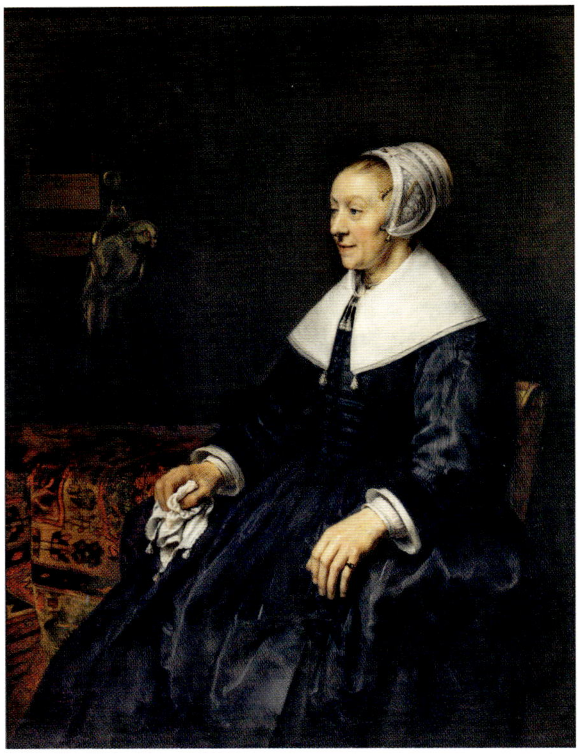

16 Rembrandt,
Catrina Hooghsaet, 1657,
National Museum Cardiff

1 On this journey, cf. Van Neck's report, "Reisverhaal van Jacob van Neck (1598–1599): Medegedeeld door Dr. H. T. Colenbrander," in *Bijdragen en Mededeelingen van het Historisch Genootschap* 21 (1900), 194–329, https://www.dbnl.org/tekst/_bij005190001_01/_bij005190001_01_0007.php (accessed May 21, 2019).

2 Pieter Christiaensz. Bor, *Oorsprongk, begin, en vervolgh der Nederlandsche oorlogen, beroerten, en borgerlyke oneenigheden*, part 4, Amsterdam 1679, 561, https://archive.org/details/oorsprongkbegine04borp_0/page/n9 (accessed April 29, 2019); all citations from Dutch were translated by Michael Philipp. The unit of measurement "shipload" designates a weight of approximately two thousand kilograms. Spices played a central role in Dutch foreign trade but were rarely shown in paintings. Cf. Julie Berger Hochstrasser, "The Conquest of Spice and the Dutch Colonial Imaginary: Seen and Unseen in the Visual Culture of Trade," in Schiebinger/Swan 2005, 169–86.

3 "The two Indies" refers to the then-used terms *West Indies* for America and *East Indies* for Asia, which was also reflected in the names of the seventeenth-century Dutch trade organizations the United East India Company, better known as the Dutch East India Company (Vereenigde Oostindische Compagnie, or VOC), and the West India Company (West-Indische Compagnie, or WIC).

4 Letter from René Descartes to Jean Louis Guez de Balzac (May 5, 1631), http://ckcc.huygens.knaw.nl/epistolarium/letter.html?id=desc004/1041 (accessed March 24, 2019); translated from French by Michael Philipp.

5 For a basic introduction to spices, shells, tea, porcelain, lacquerware, weapons, fabric, and *naturalia,* as well as an extensive bibliography, see Roelofs 2015.

6 This refers not only to the quantity of Dutch still lifes and the differentiation of the genre in the seventeenth century, but also to their historical explanatory power in terms of the orientation to the world of things, the development of optical perception, and moral discourse; cf. Claus Grimm, *Stilleben: Die niederländischen und deutschen Meister*, 2nd ed., Stuttgart and Zurich 1993, 7–16.

7 On the interior, with numerous pictorial examples, cf. Thornton 1979; on the question of the reference to reality in seventeenth-century Dutch interior paintings, see C. Willemijn Fock, "Semblance or Reality? The Domestic Interior in Seventeenth-Century Dutch Genre Painting," in Newark 2001, 83–101; cf. also The Hague 2001; Fock 2006.

8 Material and historical aspects of economy, globalization, and colonialism are given much weight, for example, in Hochstrasser 2007, Rittersma 2010, Hahn/Weiss 2013, Weststeijn 2016, and De Zwart 2016.

9 On the concept of the exotic, cf. Swan 2013; Schmidt 2015, 1–23; the essays in Stuttgart 1987 provide an overview that extends into the twentieth century; cf. also Bandmann 1962.

10 Although the term *Orient* indicates the direction of the rising sun, since Said 1978 the term *Orientalism* has usually been understood as a particular Eurocentric view of Arabic countries of the West that includes a claim of superiority; for a history of the concept and an analysis of Edward W. Said, cf. Schwarz 2003, 19–71; De Hond 2008, 12–18. A naive use of the term *Orient* is seen, for example, in Berlin 1989 and Lemaire 2000.

11 For the idea of luxury in the Netherlands since the early modern period, cf. the essays in Rittersma 2010, esp. Rengenier C. Rittersma, "Putting Social Status and Social Aspirations on Display: A Panoramic Study on Manifestations of Luxury in the Low Countries, 1500 to the Present," 9–24.

12 For the concept of globalization in connection with the Netherlands in the seventeenth century, cf. among others De Zwart 2016, esp. 31–77.

13 Aspects of consumer culture in the Netherlands since the early modern period are discussed in Schama 1988, 289–371; Batchelor 2006; Rittersma 2010; and Amsterdam 2015.

14 The term *zichtbaere werelt* refers not only to the object of painting, but also to an important textbook of the seventeenth century, Samuel van Hoogstraten, *Inleyding tot de hooge schoole der schilderkonst: Anders de zichtbaere werelt*, Rotterdam 1678, cf. *De Zichtbaere Werelt: Schilderkunst uit de Gouden Eeuw in Hollands oudste stad*, exh. cat. Dordrechts Museum, Dordrecht 1992, 10.

15 In 1570 Amsterdam had a population of 30,000; the number had doubled to 60,000 by 1600. In 1620 the city had 105,000 inhabitants; in 1670 there were 200,000; cf. Elmer Kolfin, "Amsterdam, stad van prenten: Amsterdamse prentuitgevers in de 17de eeuw," in Amsterdam 2011a, 11–57, here 12.

16 On the history of the East India Company, cf. Bamberg 1988, Gaastra/Bruijn 1993, and Kuipers 2014.

17 The books of Lucas Jansz. Waghenaer (1533/34–1605/06) were pioneering, with navigational charts and instructions for navigation: *Spieghel der Zeevaerdt*, Leiden 1584, and *Thresoor der zeevaert*, Amsterdam 1596. On the development of Dutch seafaring in the seventeenth century, cf. Beekman 1996, 17–38.

18 Joris van Spilbergen, *Journael van de voyagie gedaen met drie schepen, uyt Zeelandt, naer Oost-Indien, onder het beleydt van den commandeur Joris van Spilbergen, zijn eerste reyse, uytghevaren in den jare 1601, 1602, 1603 en 1604*, Amsterdam [ca. 1664], frontispiece. The frontispiece and verse are not included in the first edition, Delft 1605.

19 From 1614 to 1617 Spilbergen undertook circumnavigation of the world on behalf of the East India Company; cf. Joris van Spilbergen, *Oost ende West-Indische Spieghel waer in beschreven werden de twee laetste navigatien . . .*, Zutphen 1621; new edition retitled *De reis om de wereld van Joris van Spilbergen 1614–1617*, ed. J. C. M. Warnsinck, The Hague 1943.

20 Philippus Baldaeus, *Naauwkeurige Beschryvinge van Malabar en Choromandel, der zelver aangrenzende Ryken, en het machtige Eyland Ceylon*, Amsterdam 1672. The book describes Indonesia, Coromandel (the south-eastern coastal region of the Indian subcontinent), and what was then Ceylon.

21 Anonymous, *Amsterdam and the Four Continents*, etching, in Olfert Dapper, *Historische Beschryving der Stadt Amsterdam*, Amsterdam 1663. For the iconography of Amsterdam in the seventeenth century, cf. Kolfin 2011; for a contemporary description of the city, cf. Haitsma Mulier 1997.

22 Artus Quellinus after a draft by Jacob van Campen, *The Continents of the World Bring Their Goods to Amsterdam*, 1648–50, Amsterdam city hall, tympanum on the west pediment.

23 See, for example, Abraham Janssens's paintings *Scaldis and Antverpia*, 1609, and *Harmony, Love, Sincerity*, 1622 (both Koninklijk Museum voor Schone Kunsten, Antwerp), or the relief of the Antwerp Waterpoort: *The River God Scaldis with Cornucopia*, 1624 (originally located on Vlasmarkt, currently on Gillisplaats). For exotic objects in Antwerp in the seventeenth century, cf. Göttler 2013.

24 Olfert Dapper, *Beschryvinge van Amsterdam*, Amsterdam 1693.

25 A curious allegory can be found in Boëtius Adamsz. Bolswert's etching *The Stock Exchange of Amsterdam*, 1609 (Rijksmuseum, Amsterdam), in which putti with symbols of welfare and trade fly over the stock exchange. Some of the merchants depicted in the interior courtyard are wearing turbans and are thus shown to be foreign.

26 Until the end of the seventeenth century, it is supposed to have been a total of 680,000 tons. The largest transport volume was reached in the eighteenth century. In the decade between 1720 and 1730 alone, the volume imported amounted to more than 250,000 tons; cf. Gaastra/Bruijn 1993, 179.

27 In this regard, cf. Thorstein Veblen, *Theorie der feinen Leute: Eine ökonomische Untersuchung der Institutionen* (1899), Munich 1981.

28 Around the middle of the seventeenth century, the weekly wages of a craftsman was 2.80 guilders and the annual salary of a teacher 200 guilders; cf. Schama 1988, 617.

29 Melchior Fokkens, *Beschrijvinge der wijdt-vermaarde koop-stadt Amstelredam . . .*, Amsterdam 1662, 69.

30 Fokkens also mentions an owner of one painting, whose value the author estimated to be between three and four thousand guilders, who said that he would not have sold it for ten times that amount. Ibid., 69–70.

31 Cf. Amsterdam 1992, 313–37. For Dutch chambers of art, cf. Jorink 2010, 257–345; for *naturalia,* Claudia Swan, "Collecting *Naturalia* in the Shadow of Early Modern Dutch Trade," in Schiebinger/Swan 2005, 223–36; Florike Egmond, "Precious Nature: Rare *Naturalia* as Collectors' Items and Gifts in Early Modern Europe," in Rittersma 2010, 47–65. Cf. also Monika Kopplin, "'Was frembd und seltsam ist': Exotica in Kunst- und Wunderkammern," in Stuttgart 1987, 296–303; Marr 2006; Daniela Bleichmar, "Seeing the World in a Room: Looking at Exotica in Early Modern Collections," in Bleichmar/Mancall 2011, 15–30.

[32] Cf. Scheller 1969 and Amsterdam 1999a.

[33] The inventory with 363 individual positions, in Amsterdam 1999a, 147–52.

[34] A painting with a depiction of an Amsterdam art collection was not made until the end of the eighteenth century, Adriaan de Lelie, *The Art Gallery of Jan Gildemeester in his House on Herengracht*, ca. 1794–97 (Rijksmuseum, Amsterdam).

[35] Cf. in this regard Ganz 2006, 195–227; *Kamers vol kunst in zeventiende-eeuws Antwerpen*, exh. cat. Rubenshuis, Antwerp 2009; Dupré 2010; Rijks 2015.

[36] For porcelain, cf. Batchelor 2006, with a focus on consumer society and international exchange.

[37] The term *kraakporselein* came into being after two hundred thousand pieces of Chinese porcelain, originally from the cargo of the captured Portuguese *kraak* (Spanish: *carraca*) *Santa Caterina,* were sold at auction in Amsterdam in 1603 (see the essay by Erik Spaans, pp. 12–23).

[38] Philibert van Borsselen, *Strande oft Ghedichte van de Schelpen, Kinckhornen, ende andere wonderlicke Zee-schepselen*, Amsterdam 1614. For shell collecting in the seventeenth century cf. Leonhard 2007.

[39] On the use of nautilus shells as drinking vessels and in still lifes, cf. Mette 1995; Kassel 1996; Schwerin 2013, 146–71.

[40] Kassel 1996, 19.

[41] At the high point of the speculation in 1637, the going rate for three Semper Augustus bulbs, the most expansive sort, was thirty thousand guilders; this was three times the value of an Amsterdam canal house; cf. Dresden 2004, 150. On tulip mania, cf. also Dash 1999; Anne Goldgar, "The Use and Misuse of Flowers: Tulipmania and the Concept of Luxury," in Rittersma 2010, 67–84. On flowers as status symbols, cf. Segal 1987.

[42] Cf. Thornton 1979, 265–67.

[43] Cf. Pieter Biesboer, "Tulpomanie: Tulpenzucht und Tulpenhandel in den Niederlanden," in Dresden 2004, 47–53; Anne Goldgar, "Nature as Art: The Case of the Tulip," in Smith/Findlen 2002, 324–47; Anne Goldgar, "Kunst und Natur: Sammellust und Tulpenhandel in den Niederlanden," in Dresden 2004, 55–61.

[44] On the problem of realism in paintings of Dutch interiors of the seventeenth century, cf. Fock 2006.

[45] The most thorough study of Oriental carpets is Ydema 1991; cf. also Thornton 1979, 109–11; Schwarz 1990.

[46] Cf., for example, Jan van Eyck, *Virgin and Child with Saints and Donor*, 1437 (Gemäldegalerie Alte Meister, Staatliche Kunstsammlungen Dresden).

[47] Ydema 1991 lists 960 seventeenth-century Dutch paintings by a number of artists.

[48] For porcelain in the Netherlands in the seventeenth century, cf., among others, Spriggs 1964–66; Batchelor 2006; Van Campen/Eliens 2014; Roelofs 2015, 235–36. For the presentation of porcelain in living spaces, cf. Thornton 1979, 247–52.

[49] On the depiction of parrots in Dutch art, cf. Van de Velde 2014.

[50] Cf. Roelof van Gelder, "De wereld binnen handbereik: Nederlandse kunst- en rarieteitenverzamelingen, 1585–1735," in Amsterdam 1992, 15–38, here 20.

[51] Cf. http://resources.huygens.knaw.nl/vrouwenlexicon/lemmata/data/Hoogsaet (accessed May 3, 2019).

[52] On the display of property as a cultural practice in the Netherlands of the seventeenth and eighteenth centuries and the related church attitudes, cf. Hester Dibbits, "Pronken as Practice: Material Culture in the Netherlands, 1650–1800," in Rittersma 2010, 135–58, here 144–45.

[53] Cf. among others, Weststeijn 2016, esp. 15.

[54] In the period 1602–1795, only about one third of those who traveled to Asia returned to Europe; many died of malnourishment or disease during the journey or while abroad, or as a result of maritime disasters or acts of war, cf. Gaastra/Bruijn 1993, 198–203.

[55] Governor General Jan Pietersz. Coen (1587–1629), considered the founder of Batavia, for example, emerged as an advocate of brutal military force against European competitors and the populations of Asia; there is a brief portrayal in Hochstrasser 2005 (see note 2), 174–76.

[56] On the Dutch slave trade, cf. among others Johannes Postma, *The Dutch in the Atlantic Slave Trade, 1600–1815*, Cambridge 1990; the inclusion of these aspects in art historiography in Hochstrasser 2007.

[57] Joris van Spilbergen, *'t Historiael journael van tghene ghepasseert is van weghen drie schepen, ghenaemt den Ram, Schaep ende t' Lam . . .*, Delft 1605, 65. Though Spilbergen, ibid., also noted that this was accomplished, after a long journey, poverty, and danger, by the grace of God. The reference to God's support is not found in the edition of 1664. The ambergris mentioned (*ambra grisea*) is a material produced in the digestive tract of sperm whales that is used in the production of perfume.

"Utterly Artless" or "Exceedingly Noble" Ottoman, Mughal, and Safavid Art in the Dutch Republic in the Seventeenth and Eighteenth Centuries

Jan de Hond

Rembrandt's Amsterdam was a global city. Goods from all over the world were traded, from wood and grain from the Baltic region and spices from the Indonesian archipelago to cinnamon from Sri Lanka and sugar from the Americas. Luxury items from Asia were also part of this steady stream of exotic wares[1]—including Japanese screens, Chinese porcelain, and Indian chintz, which were admired for their high level of craftsmanship.

The Dutch collected far fewer works of visual art than valuable handicrafts from Islamic countries. There are many reasons for this. First of all, the supply was limited. In the Ottoman Empire, the Mughal Empire, and the Safavid Empire, monumental painting played a less dominant role than it did in Christian Europe, where imposing altarpieces decorated churches and paintings covered the walls of palaces and houses.[2] While in Europe painting was at the top of the artistic hierarchy, this privileged position was held by calligraphy in most Islamic cultures. The tradition of miniature painting blossomed, but it was a typical art of the court, which only a private circle of connoisseurs enjoyed. The best miniatures were almost always done on commission and not for the open market, which made access to Oriental paintings complicated for European merchants and travelers. That would only change over the course of the seventeenth century.

There was no great demand for Eastern paintings in Europe because they were unappreciated in the West. In the opinion of Europeans, Western painting, which since the Renaissance had strived for a realistic depiction of the world, was superior to any tradition that did not use one-point perspective and shadow effects. The description given by the painter and traveler Cornelis de Bruijn of a Persian painter of miniatures whom de Bruijn met while he was traveling in Persia in 1703–04 is characteristic: "Indeed I cannot say he knew anything of lights and shades, and in this all the country are ignorant, whence it is that their paintings are very imperfect." For the Dutchman, therefore, the work of the Persian artist was "poor, flat, stiff, and utterly artless."[3]

Despite the frequent lack of aesthetic appreciation, Islamic miniatures were collected in the Netherlands to a limited degree. The focus of this essay is the painting of the great Islamic cultures with which the Dutch Republic maintained commercial and diplomatic relations: the Ottoman Empire, the Mughal Empire, and the empire of the Safavids. Although Mughal miniatures are found rather often in inventories and auction catalogs, Ottoman paintings are never mentioned. Until recently, it was assumed that Safavid miniatures were rarely—or never at all—collected in the Netherlands. This essay will attempt a more nuanced view. Instead of merely inventorying Eastern miniatures in Dutch collections, the following will also look at a few artists who were touched by their beauty and who used them as a source of inspiration for their own work.

Painted Memories from Constantinople

Europe's oldest connections to the Islamic world were the lands around the Mediterranean. Despite military confrontations, there had been intensive commercial, diplomatic, and cultural contacts since the Middle Ages. In 1612 the young Dutch Republic signed a treaty with the Ottoman sultan that gave the Netherlands the right to pursue a trade concession and to establish trading posts.

As early as the sixteenth century, Western artists traveled with diplomatic and trade missions to the Ottoman Empire to record in pictures its landscapes, cities, and inhabitants. Among them were painters from the Netherlands, such as Lambert de Vos from Mechelen, who was part of the entourage of Karel Rym, the ambassador of the Holy Roman Empire in Constantinople. A costume book from his hand made in 1574 has been preserved (fig. 1), with 104 drawings, most of which can be traced back to earlier costume books.[4] These kinds of books with pictures of various peoples and of the clothing that indicated various ranks and social levels in the Ottoman Empire were so popular in the sixteenth and seventeenth centuries that some also appeared in print editions. Costume books such as those by the Frenchman Nicolas de Nicolay or the Fleming Abraham de Bruyn remained a source of inspiration for Western artists who wanted to depict Eastern subjects until well into the seventeenth century.[5]

As a result of the increasing demand from Western travelers for visual information about the Ottoman Empire, in the last decades of the sixteenth century local artists began producing costume and memorial albums.[6] These were initially Western artists who had settled in Constantinople. At the beginning of the seventeenth century, however, they were joined in this work by Ottoman artists.[7] In this regard, Western painters did not rely only on their own perceptions but probably also on pictures by Ottoman makers of costume books. These, in turn, used Western models. Although patrons could also order drawings that depicted their own travel experiences, the design of most costume books was quite uniform. Many of the compositions appear again and again, sometimes with minor variations, which suggests that they were made in specialized studios from which they circulated.

Owners of costume albums prized them as sources of information and as souvenirs. The English traveler Peter Mundy, for example, mentions that his album, which was created in 1618, had been painted "by the Turcks themselves." Regarding the importance of the collection he wrote "although no great art therein, yet enough to satisfie concerning that Matter."[8] He was interested in content and authenticity and not in aesthetic pleasure. In a letter of 1614, the Italian Pietro della Valle wrote in a similar vein about a costume album he had ordered in Constantinople. He wrote that the pictures would undoubtedly be considered very special in Italy although the Turks couldn't paint figures well because they were "being simply painters of pots."[9] Such albums, which were generally of lesser artistic value, were sold in abundance in the bazaar in Constantinople, where they were extremely popular with European visitors.[10] When Peter Paul Rubens drew several Ottoman women in a sketchbook with costume studies around 1610, he relied on these local products as well as costume books printed in the West (fig. 2).[11]

In the seventeenth and eighteenth centuries, these locally produced costume books showed almost no stylistic development. They were far removed from the sophisticated artistry of miniatures from the workshops in the court of Constantinople, and no evidence has yet been produced that such miniatures were present in European collections of the sixteenth or seventeenth centuries. Apparently, Western travelers had no access to these studios, where the best Ottoman and Persian artists worked for the sultan and his entourage.

The Most Secret Particularities of India

The situation was different in India, where it was much easier for Western travelers to acquire original miniatures. The Dutch East India Company (Vereenigde Oostindische Compagnie, known as VOC) imported large amounts of miniatures, of which a part was specially painted for the Western market.[12] In the seventeenth and eighteenth centuries the Netherlands became *the* European trading hub for Indian miniatures.[13] The earliest mention of an Indian miniature in a Dutch collection is dated 1655, but the real flood did not set in until a few decades later.[14] Nonetheless, a few Indian miniatures must have made their way into the country in the first half of the seventeenth century, such as the portrait of Jahangir, the Mughal emperor, which was the source of the title page of *De Imperio Magni Mogolis sive India Vera Commentarius*, a description of the Mughal Empire by Johannes de Laet published in 1631 (fig. 3). These works were collected primarily by the owners of the popular cabinets of curiosities in the Republic. Some miniatures found their way to other European collections via the Netherlands. Maria Theresia, the empress of Austria, for example, sent her agents to the Dutch Republic in the middle of the eighteenth century, where they obtained several hundred Indian miniatures for the decoration of Schönbrunn Palace in Vienna.

Estate inventories and auction catalogs often describe these works very vaguely as "Oostindise" (East Indian), "Indiaense" (Indian), "Moorse" (Moorish), "Mogolse" (Mughal), or "Suratse" (from the Surat region on the western coast of India), but also as "Chinese," "Japanse" (Japanese), or "Persiaense" (Persian).[15] The general public could probably not tell the difference between these categories, and it is doubtful whether the owners themselves even knew the difference. Those works that have been identified all seem to have originated in India. Old Dutch inscriptions have been found on the front or back of a significant number of these works, which suggests that they were in the possession of a Dutch collector in the seventeenth or eighteenth century (fig. 4).[16]

Like Ottoman costume books, Indian miniatures were appreciated in Europe for the historical, ethnographic, or religious information they provided. The French physician and numismatist Charles Patin, who visited the Netherlands in 1672 and saw Indian and Chinese miniatures there, wrote for example: "We discover in these the most secret particularities of the history, the way of life & the religion of the countries."[17] This was the reason authors like Philippus Baldaeus, Olfert Dapper, and Athanasius Kircher included prints based on Indian miniatures as illustrations in their travel literature and publications on world religions.[18]

As has already been mentioned, the artistic abilities of the Eastern painters were not highly valued by Europeans. Nevertheless, two Dutch artists seem to belie this view. Rembrandt and Willem Schellinks were very interested in the aesthetic aspects of the works of their Indian colleagues. About twenty-five drawings by Rembrandt after Mughal miniatures are known (see the essay by Gary Schwartz, pp. 56–73).[19] Schellinks's occupation with Indian painting was much more intensive and varied. He was not only a painter; he was also a poet. He is the only Dutchman—and probably the only European—to dedicate an entire poem to the subject of Indian miniatures in the seventeenth century. His ode *Op de schilder-konst der Benjanen* (On Benjan [Indian] Painting) was part of *Klioos Kraam* (The Confinement of the Muse Clio), a collection of poetry published in 1657 (cat. 92).[20]

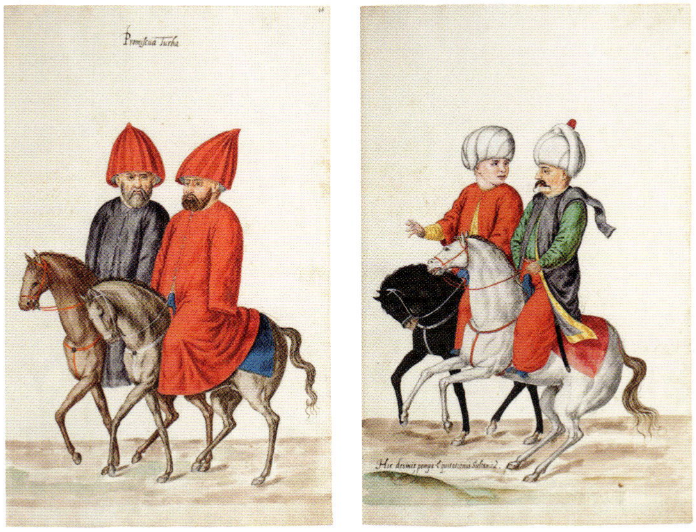

1 Lambert de Vos,
Turkish Costume Book, 1574, fols. 48r and 49r,
Staats- und Universitätsbibliothek Bremen

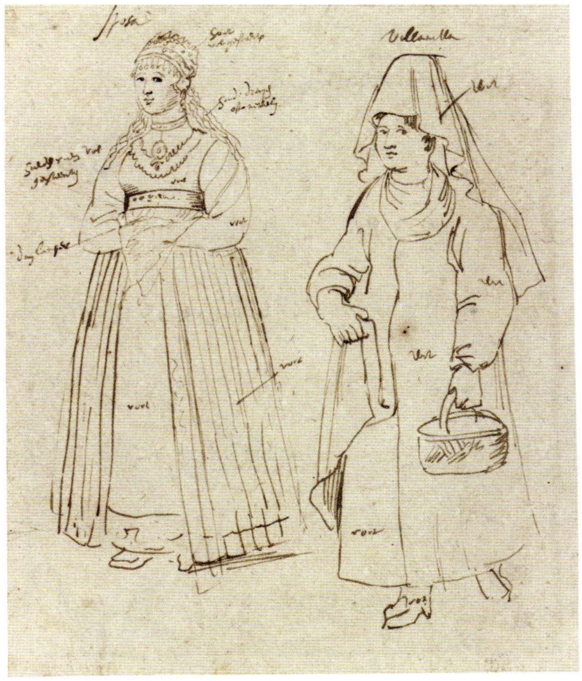

2 Peter Paul Rubens,
Two Women from Turkey,
from his *Costume Book,* 1609–12, fol. 33,
The British Museum, London

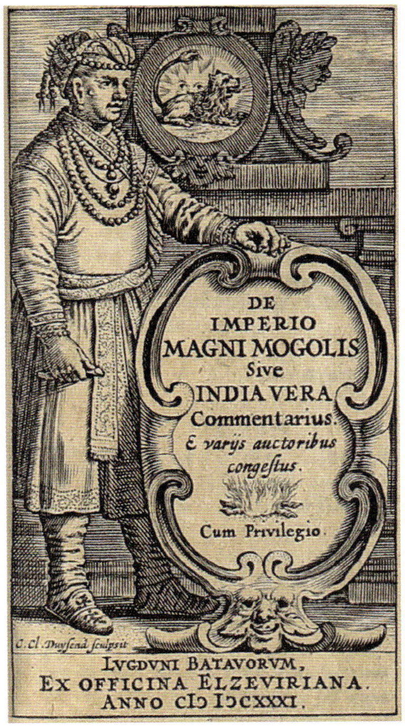

3 Cornelis Claesz. Duysend,
title etching, in Johannes de Laet,
De Imperio Magni Mogolis sive India Vera Commentarius, Leiden 1631

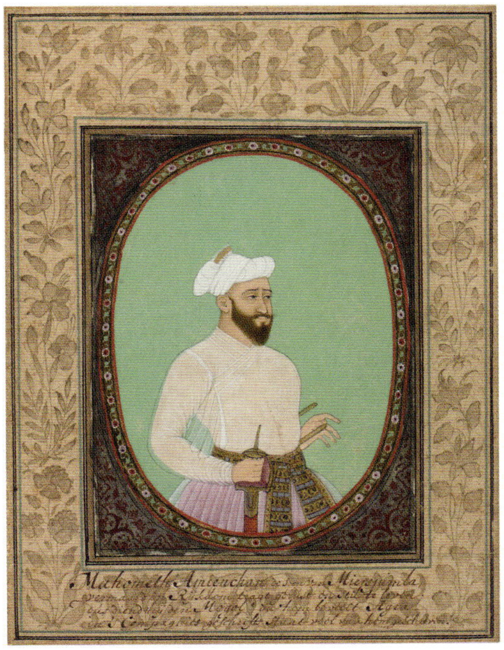

4 Anonymous,
Portrait of Muhammad Amin Khan,
with Dutch inscription, 1670s,
Rijksmuseum, Amsterdam

In this poem Schellinks says painting had its origin in biblical times with the Chaldeans. They gave their "konst-kroon" (artistic crown) to the Greeks and Romans, who later passed it on to the Germans, Dutch, and French. However, then this crown went to India, completely unexpectedly, where the Mughal artists had created painting of unparalleled beauty: "His painting as exeedingly noble / As an artist's brush ever made."[21]

Schellinks's central idea—painting arose in the biblical East and was exported from there to Europe—is not new. Giorgio Vasari in 1568 and later Karel van Mander in 1604 traced the origins of fine art back to the biblical East, from which it spread to Greece and Rome, and finally came to full flower in Italy (Vasari) and the Netherlands (Van Mander).[22] Schellinks goes further, however. He does not stop with Italian and Dutch art but returns the painterly crown to the India of his own day. And thus the circle closes—painting is back in the East where it arose.

Schellinks does not go deeper into the question of what makes these miniatures so special. He praises Mughal painting only in general terms: "zeer heerlyk" (absolutely splendid) and "wonder eel" (exceedingly noble).[23] But his judgment that Indian painting is of equal value, if not superior, to the European tradition, is unusual. Presumably it is the earliest evidence of European artists admiring the aesthetic qualities of Indian painting.

The Futility of War

Schellinks's appreciation of Mughal miniatures is also evident in an unusual series of "Indian" paintings that he made, presumably between 1660 and 1675. All five works were concerned with the history of Emperor Shah Jahan.[24] The two most striking works show Shah Jahan in front of a theater set while he watches a parade of his four sons, who are sitting in a litter or on a horse, elephant, or camel—all composites made up of female figures (fig. 5, cat. 94). Shah Jahan's forebears, his grandfather, Akbar, and his father, Jahangir, appear high in the clouds. Another painting shows the shah and his sons on horses, hunting with falcons, before the backdrop of a broad landscape (fig. 6).

Schellinks must have based these pictures on the original Indian miniatures of which he had sung with such inspiration in his ode. The composite animals on which Shah Jahan's sons are riding are also found in the tradition of Mughal painting.[25] Instead of simply adopting his models, Schellinks transformed them according to Western traditions, modeling them three-dimensionally with shadow effects and set in an architectural or natural setting rendered with Western perspective. The result is a combination of protagonists based on original miniatures depicted in detail, secondary figures with a fanciful, vaguely Oriental appearance, and a background that looks Western with some exotic details added, such as palm trees or elephants.

How Schellinks, who was never in Asia, came to his visual sources is not known.[26] Perhaps he obtained his originals from his brother Laurens, who worked for the VOC, or from the owner of a cabinet of curiosities, such as the Amsterdam lawyer Laurens van der Hem, who owned a comprehensive topographical atlas that also contained material about India. Schellinks knew Van der Hem because he had worked for the attorney. However, there is a direct connection with the miniatures that Rembrandt copied. Schellinks and Rembrandt—who moved in the same circles, lived in the same quarter of the city, and likely knew each other—probably studied the same series of Mughal miniatures. Thus, Rembrandt drew a picture of Akbar and Jahangir in apotheosis, which is similar to the same group in Schellinks's painting. There are several known Mughal miniatures with this composition as well (figs. 7, 8).[27]

Much has been written about the iconography of Schellinks's Indian paintings, but the meaning of the works remains a mystery.[28] The pictures take as their main subject Shah Jahan

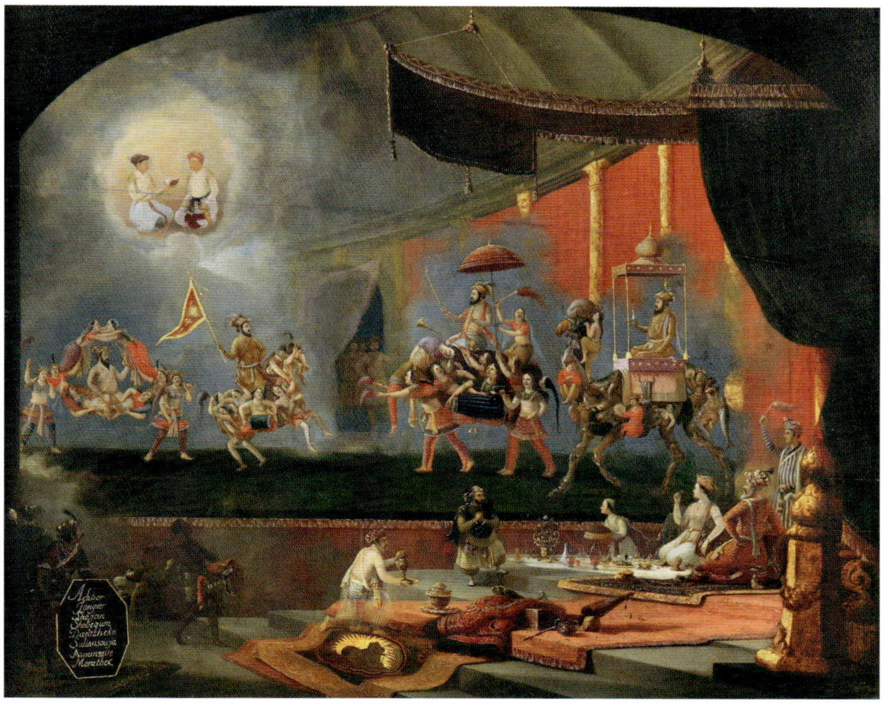

5 Willem Schellinks,
Shah Jahan and His Four Sons, 1660–75,
Musée Guimet—Musée national des arts asiatiques, Paris

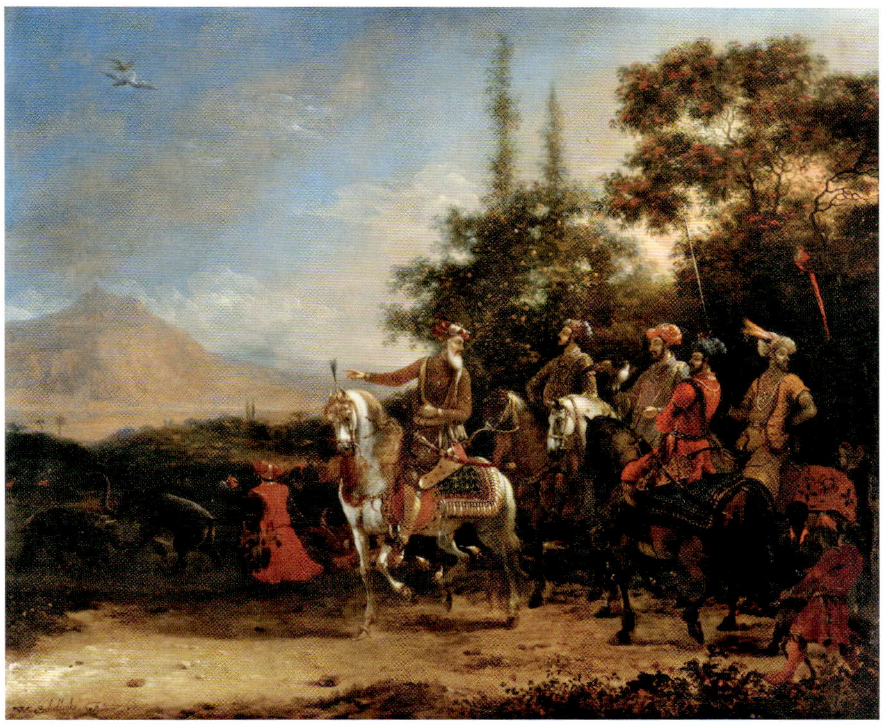

6 Willem Schellinks,
Shah Jahan and His Sons Hawking, 1660–75,
Orientalist Museum, Doha

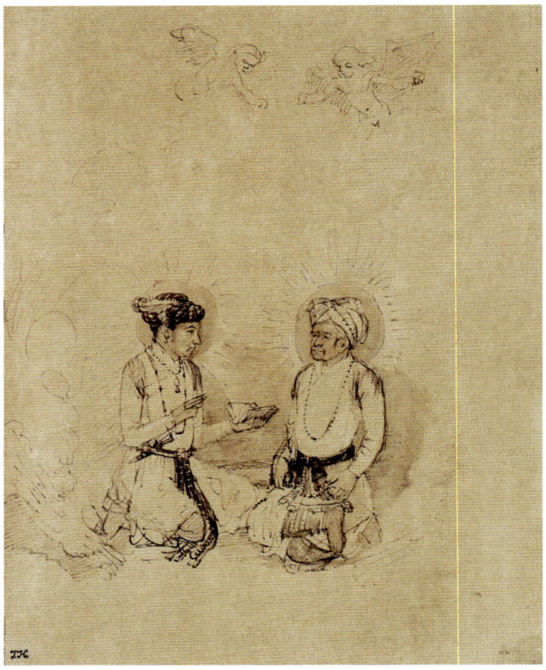

7 Rembrandt,
The Emperors Akbar and Jahangir in Apotheosis,
after a Mughal miniature, 1656–61,
Museum Boijmans Van Beuningen, Rotterdam

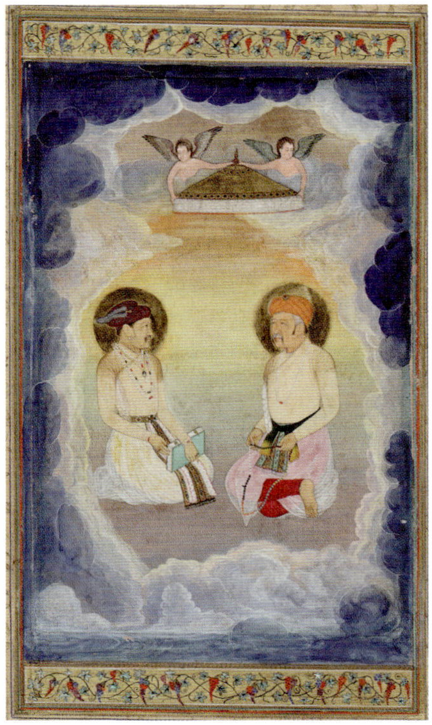

8 Indian,
The Emperors Akbar and Jahangir in Apotheosis, in an album of Mughal paintings and calligraphy, Shah Jahan period, ca. 1650, fol. 19a, Bodleian Library, University of Oxford

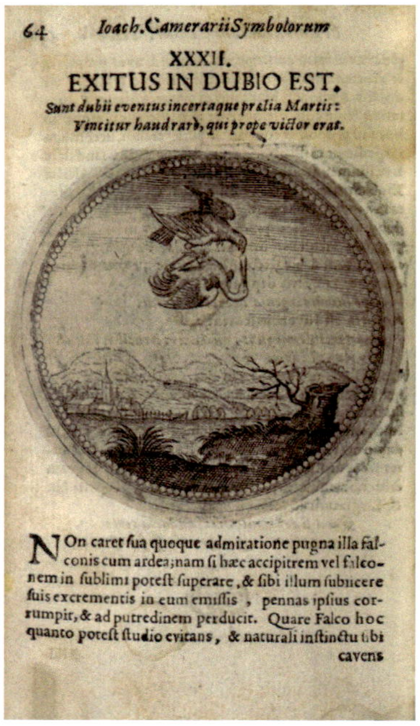

64 Ioach. Camerarii Symbolorum

XXXII.
EXITUS IN DUBIO EST.

Sunt dubii eventus incertaque prælia Martis:
Vincitur haud rarò, qui prope victor erat.

Non caret sua quoque admiratione pugna illa falconis cum ardea; nam si hæc accipitrem vel falconem in sublimi potest superare, & sibi illum subiicere suis excrementis in eum emissis, pennas ipsius corrumpit, & ad putredinem perducit. Quare Falco hoc quanto potest studio evitans, & naturali instinctu sibi cavens

9 *Falcon and Heron*,
in Joachim Camerarius,
Symbolorum et Emblematum . . .,
Mainz 1677, III, 32

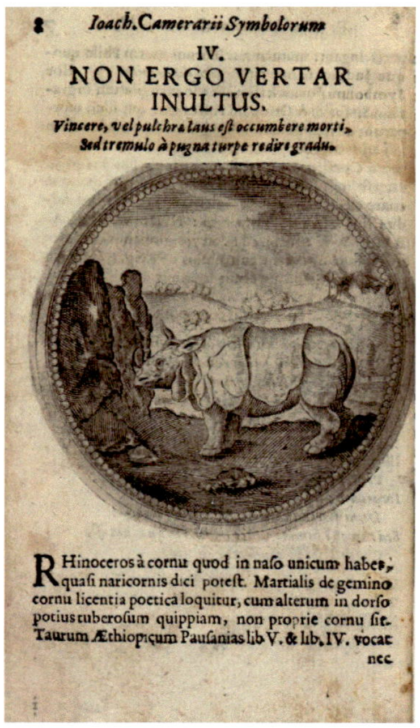

8 Ioach. Camerarii Symbolorum

IV.
NON ERGO VERTAR INULTUS.

Vincere, vel pulchra laus est occumbere morti,
Sed tremulo à pugna turpe redire gradu.

Rhinoceros à cornu quod in naso unicum habet, quasi naricornis dici potest. Martialis de gemino cornu licentia poetica loquitur, cum alterum in dorso potius tuberosum quippiam, non proprie cornu sit. Taurum Æthiopicum Pausanias lib V. & lib. IV. vocat nec

10 *Rhinoceros,*
in Joachim Camerarius,
Symbolorum et Emblematum . . .,
Mainz 1677, II, 4

and his four sons. It is clear that they are related to the bloody civil war that shook the Mughal Empire from 1658 until 1661. The sudden illness of Shah Jahan in 1657 had led to a bitter war of succession among his four sons, one of whom, Aurangzeb, won in the end. He killed his three brothers and imprisoned his father until the latter's death in 1666.

Why, however, would this war of succession on the other side of the world have been relevant for a European audience? Perhaps the falconry picture, which shows a popular pastime of both the European and Indian nobility, offers a clue (fig. 6). On the right we see Shah Jahan and his four sons on horseback. On the left an elephant is fighting with a rhinoceros, and the rhino is ramming his horn into the elephant's stomach. A similar drama is being played out in the air. A falcon is diving at a heron or crane, which pierces the attacker with its long beak.

Both scenes are also included in the emblem book *Symbola et Emblemata* (1595–1604) by Joachim Camerarius. Above the picture with the falcon battling the heron (fig. 9) is the motto "Exitus in dubio est" (The outcome [of a war] is always uncertain).[29] In another passage there is a reference to the fight between the rhinoceros and the elephant. However, it is not the battle itself that is depicted, but the preparation for it—the rhino is sharpening its horn on a boulder (fig. 10).[30] The motto on this emblem reads "Non ergo [re]vertar inultus" (I will not return unavenged). The text praises the tenacity of the attacking rhino. It knows that if it is not immediately successful, it will be killed by its opponent. Consequently, the rhinoceros either leaves the battle as victor or loses its life on the battlefield.

In both battles, the participants die. The falcon and the crane or heron crash to earth together, and the rhinoceros will be buried under the elephant as it falls to the ground. There are no victors: war knows only losers. This message concerning the uncertain outcome and the uselessness of war is very appropriate for the Indian war of succession between Shah Jahan's sons. It was also recognizable and relevant for the population of Europe, which in the seventeenth century was torn apart by countless wars.

Schellinks was perhaps thinking of a particular war. The English poet Richard Lovelace (1617–1657) had used the same emblems from Camerarius's *Symbola et Emblemata* in his verse about the English Civil War.[31] Lovelace was a cavalier poet who fought on the side of the English king. The code of the cavalier sung the praises of courage and loyalty to his friends and king, ideals that Lovelace sang in his animal poems. An example is *The Falcon*, a poem written in the early 1650s but first published posthumously in 1659, in which this noble bird stands for loyalty to the king and the royal cause. It has typical kingly virtues like unconditional faithfulness and courage and fights bravely in battle, even when it can mean his own death. The confrontation with the heron might end in the death of both adversaries; however, the falcon is at least the moral victor and an example of self-sacrifice for the good cause.[32] His defeat can serve as a source of inspiration for future generations. In another animal poem, Lovelace refers to the rhinoceros as a deadly assailant who is successful in bringing down the elephant, but in the end is crushed under its weight and dies.

There may be a connection between Lovelace's poems and Schellinks's pictures. The Dutchman spent almost two years between 1661 and 1663 in England and was familiar with the chaotic period of the English Civil War from personal experience. Was Schellinks's *Shah Jahan and His Sons Hawking* perhaps painted for an English client? And was the Indian war of succession a subtle reference to the English Civil War? In that case, Schellinks was not only the first to use Indian miniatures for his paintings; he also introduced Indian history into Western history painting and made it meaningful for a European audience.

Models from Persia

While Indian miniatures were found in Dutch collections, that seems not to be the case for Persian miniatures. Auction catalogs show that the collections of Roeter Ernst (1663), Johannes Swammerdam (1679), Constant Sennepart (1704), and Nicolaas Witsen (1717) included Persian miniatures or at least miniatures with Persian subjects. However, this does not mean that they were made by Persian artists.[33] Persian dignitaries were often integrated into series of ruler portraits made in India.

The only Persian miniatures that can be directly connected to the Netherlands are two architectural views: *Palace Garden of Hazar Jarib in Aliabad* and *Private Audience Hall of Shah Safi I in Isfahan* (figs. 11, 12).[34] Both have a short handwritten description in Dutch next to an annotation in Persian on the back, from which it can be concluded that they were already in the Netherlands in the seventeenth or early eighteenth century.[35] How they got there is not known.

A small, seventeenth-century publication on Persia also suggests that an important series of Persian miniatures of extraordinary quality had arrived in the Netherlands around 1625. The book, *Persia seu Regni Persici Status* (cat. 91), which was published in 1633, was written by the prolific Johannes de Laet (1581–1649), who was also responsible for the abovementioned book *De Imperio Magni Mogolis sive India Vera Commentarius* (1631) with the portrait of Jahangir on its title page.[36] De Laet himself never visited Persia. His book on Persia is a compilation of the best-known, primarily foreign, travel reports. The book's title page as well as eight woodcuts were made by Cornelis Claesz. Duysend. The illustrations show men and women in local garb, rendered according to Western conventions, that is, three-dimensionally, with shadowing and European facial features. The quality of these illustrations is not very sophisticated, and they are very small. That is probably why they have thus far been widely ignored.[37]

Nonetheless, these woodcuts are important. The originals on which they were modeled were Safavid miniatures from the first quarter of the seventeenth century. Persian miniatures were traditionally an integral part of precious manuscripts, on which several artists had worked. They thus usually dealt with literary themes. They were created in the court studios, where calligraphers and painters working in close cooperation produced manuscripts that were frequently quite extensive. That changed, however, in the course of the sixteenth and seventeenth centuries.[38] Persian painters no longer worked exclusively for monarchs and princes but for the free market as well. This had an effect on the form and content of the works. Instead of very expensive illuminated manuscripts, the artists now more and more often created individual miniatures that could later be put in albums. These sheets were not only less expensive and thus available to a larger circle of customers; their subjects were new and appealed more to the tastes of the rising urban elite of merchants and administrative officials: scenes of city life, depictions of European visitors,[39] itinerant dervishes, and elegant young men and women enjoying music, wine, or each other's company. One of the best-known painters who specialized in such pictures of attractive young people in graceful style was Reza Abbasi (1565–1635), who was the favorite artist of Shah Abbas (1557–1628). This painter was associated with the royal studio, but he also worked for a clientele outside the walls of the palace.[40] He and his successors made depictions of the Persian jeunesse dorée popular.

The woodcuts in De Laet's *Persia seu Regni Persici Status* also showed elegantly dressed young men with striking headwear and frequently holding a bottle of wine, a bowl, or a cup. Although it is not known which originals were used as models, all indications are that they were by Reza Abbasi or a painter close to him from the school of Isfahan.[41] The woodcut with the depiction of a man with a fur hat, jacket, and trousers (fig. 13) bears resemblance to Abbasi's *Standing Youth with Cup and Bottle*, signed and dated in 1624 (fig. 14). The clothing, the dagger through the knot of the

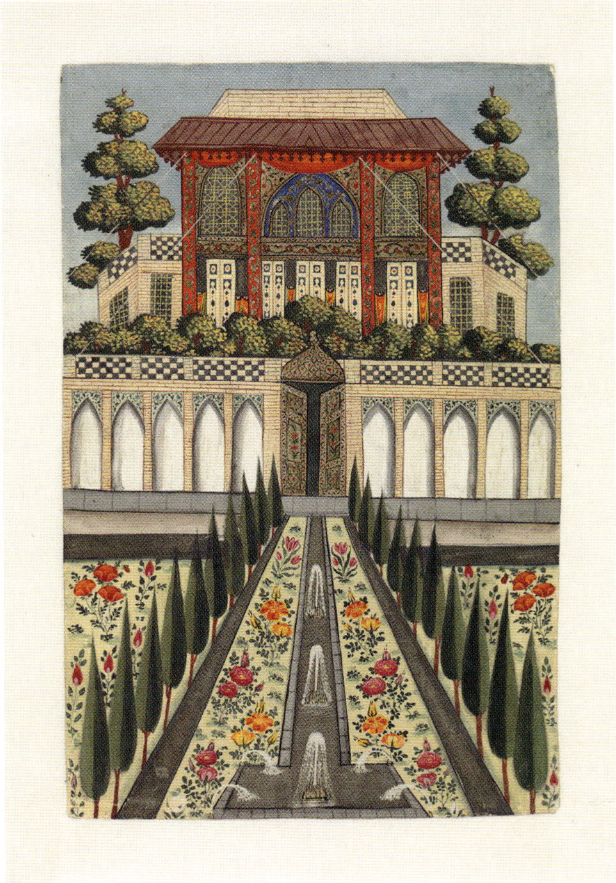

11 Persian,
Palace Garden of Hazar Jarib in Aliabad, ca. 1700,
Rijksmuseum, Amsterdam

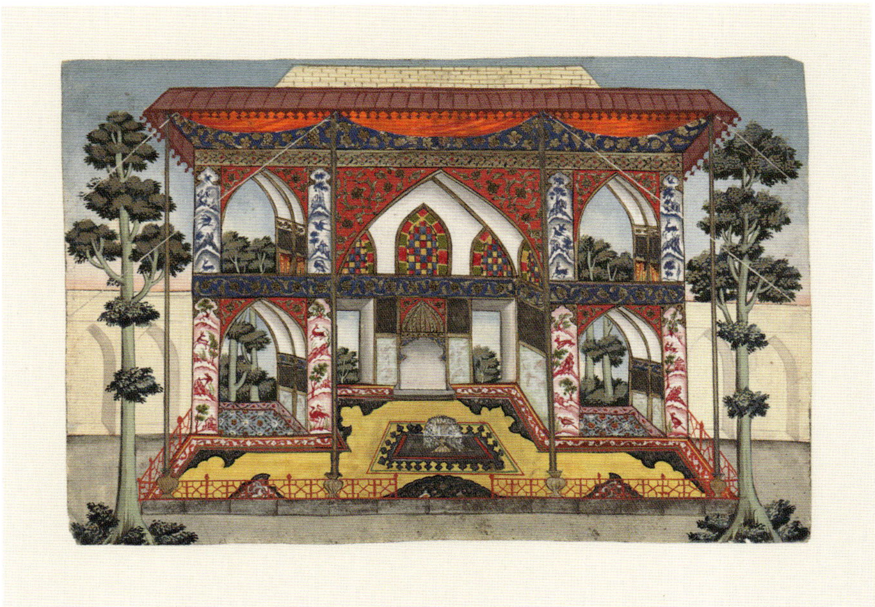

12 Persian,
Private Audience Hall of Shah Safi I in Isfahan, ca. 1700,
Rijksmuseum, Amsterdam

scarf, and the pose are identical, although there are also differences. The man in the miniature is holding a cup; in the woodcut he has two small branches or flowers. The most obvious difference is the headwear. Nonetheless, the type of fur hat of the man in the woodcut corresponds to the hat of another of Abbasi's cupbearers from the same time (Chester Beatty Library, Dublin).[42]

De Laet mentions the source of the woodcut in his publication. His models came from a certain Nicolaus Hemmius, who spent time in Isfahan in 1623–24.[43] Nicolaus Hemmius is the Latin form of the name Niclaes Hem, a merchant of the VOC who accompanied ambassador Hubert Visnich in 1623 on a journey to Isfahan. Working on behalf of the company, the purpose of the trip was the conclusion of a trade agreement with Shah Abbas the Great.[44] In Isfahan Visnich became acquainted with his countryman the painter Jan Lucasz. van Hasselt (see cat. 5), who had been working in Isfahan for several years.[45] He had arrived in the city in 1617 and became court painter of Shah Abbas.

Niclaes Hem, who was part of the Dutch negotiating team, must have known Van Hasselt well. If Hem, as we read in De Laet, obtained a series of Persian miniatures during his stay in Isfahan, it is reasonable to conclude that Van Hasselt was involved in the transaction. As court painter he had access to his Persian colleagues, with whom he worked in the royal workshops on a daily basis. One of these colleagues was Reza Abbasi, whose composition seems to be the basis for the woodcut in De Laet's *Persia seu Regni Persici Status.* With help from Van Hasselt, Hem was probably able to get a series of drawings by or after Reza Abbasi.

A Reworked Persian Miniature

An album from the late seventeenth century has been preserved in the collections of the Rijksmuseum since 1890, in which a portrait of a *Persian Youth* can be found (fig. 15, cat. 98).[46] It is the family album of the painter Gesina ter Borch (1631–1691), who was a member of the famous Ter Borch family of artists in the provincial town of Zwolle.[47] She began this impressive work in 1660. At first, her plan was to fill the empty pages with her own watercolor miniatures of scenes from everyday life in her hometown of Zwolle, a genre in which she had specialized. Gradually, however, she added the work of others, which she glued in the remaining empty pages. In addition to drawings by her father and brothers, this also included the work of other artists, copies of other masters, or cut-out pictures and children's drawings by her nephews.[48]

Some details of the miniature of the youth, which has remained largely unknown, seem to have been modified or added later. The uniform black background, a feature that is never found in original Persian miniatures, is particularly striking. Under close examination, it is evident that the drawing originally had a rounded upper and lower edge, and that a piece is missing on the lower right. It was probably Ter Borch who—for aesthetic reasons—rendered the background black and provided the entire drawing with a rectangular frame. She painted similar borders elsewhere in the album.

In addition to the black background, the scarves tied around the waist of the youth, the feather in the turban, and the white collar also catch the eye. These details are more loosely painted, with clearly visible brushwork and distinctive white highlights. Their three-dimensional effects are in contrast to the flatter rendering of other parts of the figure. Ter Borch presumably followed the contours of the body and clothing when she blackened the background, with the result that she covered the feather and part of the wafting cloth with black paint, on which she then painted a new feather and white scarf. At the same time, she modified the rest of the scarves, the collar, the turban, and the sword, and provided everything with highlights. Such later additions can also be found on other drawings in her album. She had no qualms about "enlivening" the work of other

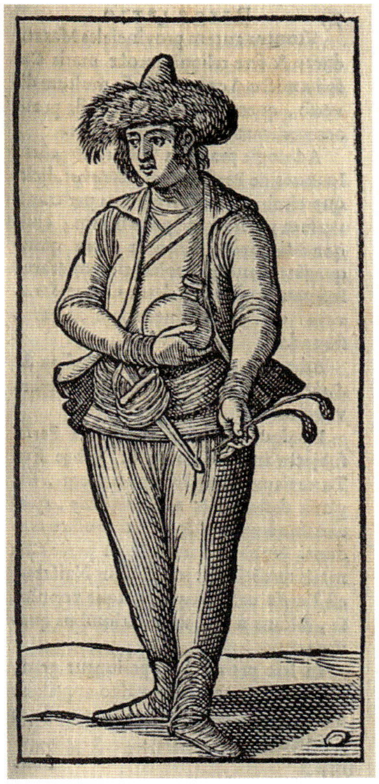

13 Cornelis Claesz. Duysend, title woodcut, in Johannes de Laet, *Persia seu Regni Persici Status,* Leiden 1633

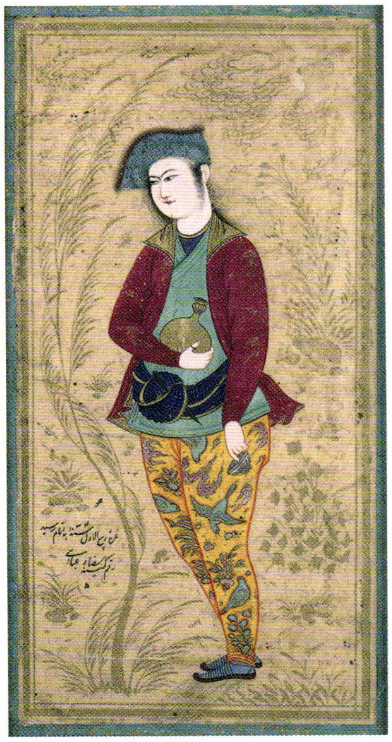

14 Reza Abbasi, *Standing Youth with Cup and Bottle,* 1624. From the Collection of Prince and Princess Sadruddin Aga Khan

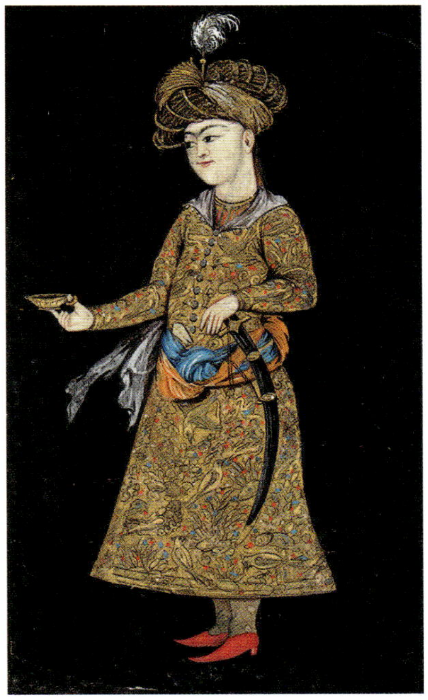

15 School of Isfahan, *Persian Youth,* ca. 1650–80, in the family album of Gesina ter Borch (detail), fol. 40r, Rijksmuseum, Amsterdam (cat. 98)

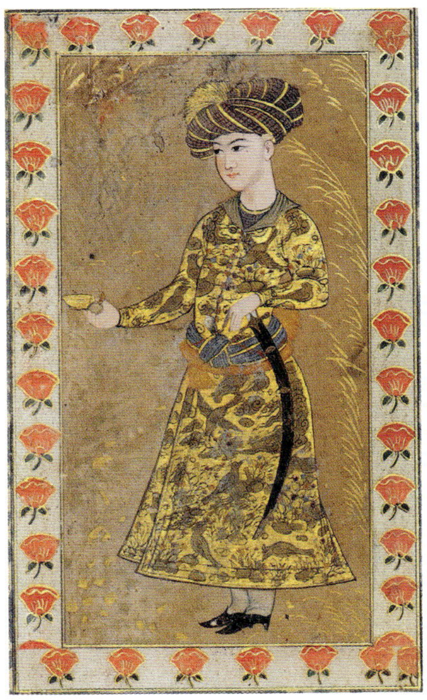

16 School of Isfahan, *A Young Man Holding a Wine Cup* (detail), 1650–70, private collection (see fig. p. 282)

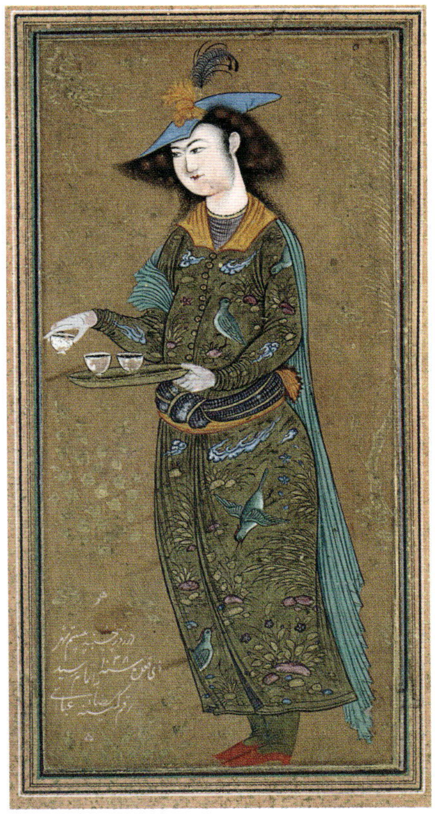

17 Reza Abbasi, *Young Man with Three Wine Cups* (detail), 1629. From the Collection of Prince and Princess Sadruddin Aga Khan

masters at her own discretion. As in the case of the *Persian Youth*, she added most bright colors and white highlights.[49]

The overpainting that is visible to the naked eye was the occasion for a thorough technical analysis in the Rijksmuseum.[50] It revealed that under the scarves that can be seen today a different cloth had been painted that corresponds to the style of the other clothing. The original background showed plants and trees. This kind of stylized landscape in gold or sepia can be found in Persian miniatures from this time. Furthermore, much less of the original material seems to have been retained. Large parts of the coat and the face showed serious damage and were later painted over. The white lead used was not from the Netherlands but presumably originated in Persia.

The Persian source of the drawing in Gesina ter Borch's album remained unknown until late 2019, when a Persian miniature very similar to her copy was auctioned at Christie's in London (fig. 16). Although the page was dated to the end of the sixteenth century by the auction house, stylistic features indicate that it more likely originated in the 1650s or 1660s.[51] This miniature was probably made by a painter from the Isfahan school. The original condition of the copy in Ter Borch's album—that is, without her additions and modifications—differs from the miniature at Christie's only in minor details, including the bird pattern on the right sleeve of the garment and the vegetation in the stylized landscape, which was later painted over in black.

The similarities are much more noticeable, however. The side whiskers are missing from both works, which is unusual for Safavid art of this time. The motif of the elegant youth serving wine is already seen in the woodcuts after Reza Abbasi or someone from his immediate circle in De Laet's *Persia seu Regni Persici Status*. The miniature at Christie's does not have the refinement and elegance of Abbasi's works, and the depiction of the face is also different. However, the painter, who is presumably from the school of Isfahan, oriented himself closely on Abbasi and, like many other artists, worked in this tradition. The robe's pattern indicates a direct connection with Abbasi's work. It consists of birds looking at one another in a stylized landscape with vegetation, cliffs, and clouds. Instead of imitating any existing material, it was probably an invention of the master, who used it in the trousers and robes of his elegant youths (fig. 17).[52]

In seventeenth-century Safavid painting, compositions were frequently used over and over, and Abbasi too made several variations on the same composition, which were then used frequently by his followers. Thus, it is very possible that the miniature at Christie's also refers back to an older prototype, perhaps to a miniature by Reza Abbasi from the 1620s, when he was using this bird pattern frequently.

The question remains as to who made the copy in Gesina ter Borch's album? Her changes make it difficult to evaluate the quality of the original Persian painting. However, the composition recalls miniatures that were painted in or around a studio of the court. The original details seem to confirm this: the original portions of the pattern on the clothing are painted very freely. Technical analyses have revealed that the birds, plants and a part of the clouds were originally executed in silver, which formed a striking contrast to the gold background, and which must have given the clothing—as in the miniature at Christie's—a more precious appearance. The neck too with its very fine hatching, which clearly differs from the coarser treatment of the eyes that was later painted over, shows that the original drawing must have been of very high quality—the work of an artist of the school of Isfahan from the circle of the painter of the miniature at Christie's, if not from his own hand.

If that is the case, Niclaes Hem would not only have brought a few Persian miniatures to the Netherlands around 1624; such a painting must also have reached the Republic around 1650–60. Hem's series was by Reza Abbasi or someone in his immediate circle, while the single drawing in Gesina ter Borch's album was by an artist from the school of Isfahan who, a generation later, was presumably inspired by an earlier composition by Abbasi. How the drawing got to Ter Borch's album in Zwolle remains a mystery for the time being.

Conclusion

Although the aesthetic quality of paintings from the Ottoman, Mughal, and Safavid Empires was generally disdained in the Dutch Republic, a few artists were inspired by miniatures from the East. Rembrandt copied a series of Mughal miniatures in the 1650s. The influence of Indian painting on the work of Rembrandt's contemporary Willem Schellinks is undisputed. In addition to a series of oil paintings with motifs from Indian history, Schellinks also fashioned his main figures on models from original Indian miniatures that he had studied carefully. Schellinks drew parallels between the dramatic events in Mughal India—the subjects of his paintings—and contemporary developments in Europe. Gesina ter Borch seems to have nurtured a similar admiration of the beauty of Eastern miniatures. The painter from Zwolle put a drawing of a Persian youth—despite damage—into her album and took care in her reworking to retain the original style.

Rembrandt's drawings, Schellinks's paintings, and the copy in Ter Borch's album are certainly exceptions that nonetheless indicate the global range of Dutch painting in the seventeenth century.

Translated from Dutch to German by Susanne Henriette Karau and from German to English by Gerald E. Brennan

I would like to thank Amélie Couvrat Desvergnes and Leila Sauvage at the restoration workshop of the Rijksmuseum, Amsterdam, for preparing and interpreting the infrared and XRF images. Additional thanks to Sheila Canby, Massumeh Farhad, Willem Floor, Paolo d'Imporzano, Axel Langer, Petria Nobel, Forough Sajadi, and Arnoud Vrolijk.

1 Cf. Amsterdam 2015. See also the essays by Erik Spaans, pp. 12–23, and Michael Philipp, pp. 24–39.

2 There is no tradition of decorating interiors with paintings in most Islamic countries. One exception is seventeenth-century Persia, where a few large paintings are known.

3 Cited in De Hond 1994, 67 (translation modified). On the appreciation of Persian art by the Dutch and vice versa, see Schwartz 2014.

4 Lambert de Vos, *Turkish Costume Book, 1574* (see fig. p. 43), Staats- und Universitätsbibliothek Bremen, msor 009; https://brema.suub.uni-bremen.de/ms/content/thumbview/1616750 (accessed February 17, 2020). Cf. Brussels 2015, 145.

5 Robert Born, "Kostuumprenten en herinneringsalbums: Overdracht van beelden en informatie tussen Oost en West," in Brussels 2015, 65–66.

6 Several examples of costume books from the sixteenth and early seventeenth centuries that were produced in Constantinople by native artists for the Western market or by traveling artists from the West, in Brussels 2015, 145, 148, 152.

7 William Kynan-Wilson, "The Origins of Orientalism: A Plurality of Orients and Occidents (c. 1500–1800)," in London 2019, 30–41, here 34.

8 Cited in Kynan-Wilson, "'Painted by the Turcks Themselves': Reading Peter Mundy's Ottoman Costume Album in Context," in *The Mercantile Effect: Art and Exchange in the Islamicate World during the 17th and 18th Centuries*, ed. Sussan Babaie and Melanie Gibson, London 2017, 38–50, here 41–43.

9 Cited in ibid., 43.

10 In the seventeenth century costume books were also purchased by Ottoman customers. Kynan-Wilson 2019 (see note 7), 34.

11 For the pages with Ottoman and Persian figures in Rubens's *Costume Book* see Ingrams 1974.

12 For examples of Indian miniatures produced for the Western market, see Lunsingh Scheurleer 1996 and Lunsingh Scheurleer 2016.

13 For Indian miniatures in Dutch collections, see Lightbown 1969; Lunsingh Scheurleer 1996; Forberg 2014; Forberg 2015, 46–65; Schrader 2018.

14 Lunsingh Scheurleer 1996, 211–30.

15 Ibid.

16 Ibid., 229–30.

17 Cited in ibid., 214.

18 Forberg 2015, 67–185.

19 For Rembrandt's Indian drawings, see Lunsingh Scheurleer 1980; Lunsingh Scheurleer 1991, 96; Courtright 1996; Filipczak 2007–08; Forberg 2014; Forberg 2015, 46–65; Los Angeles 2018.

20 Willem Schellinks, "Op de schilder-konst der Benjanen," in *Klioos Kraam, vol verscheiden gedichten: De tweede opening*, Leeuwarden 1657, 351–53. Concerning this poem cf. Gommans/De Hond 2015.

21 Schellinks 1657 (see note 20), 352: "Zyn Schildery zo wonder eel / Als oit kon maalen 't konst-penceel."

22 Gommans/De Hond 2015, 81.

23 Schellinks 1657, 352.

24 Auboyer 1955; Loewenstein 1958; Forberg 2015, 46–62; Gommans/De Hond 2015.

25 Cf., for example, Indian, *Rider on a Horse Composed of Female Figures*, seventeenth century, NORDICO Stadtmuseum Linz.

26 Gommans/De Hond 2015, 75, 76.

27 Lunsingh Scheurleer 1980; Forberg 2015, 46–48; Glynn 2018, 34–35. Forberg 2015, 49–62, also presents other examples of Indian sources Schellinks could have used.

28 Gommans/De Hond 2015; Forberg 2015, 46–62.

29 Cf. Joachim Camerarius, *Symbolorum et Emblematum . . .*, Mainz 1677, III, 32.

30 Ibid., II, 4.

31 An interpretation of Lovelace's animal poems against the background of the English Civil Wars and the use of Camerarius's emblems can be found in Raymond A. Anselment, "'Griefe Triumphant' and 'Victorious Sorrow': A Reading of Richard Lovelace's 'The Falcon,'" in *The Journal of English and Germanic Philology* 70,3 (1971), 404–17; Erna Kelly, "'Small Types of Great Ones': Richard Lovelace's Separate Peace," in *The English Civil Wars in the Literary Imagination*, ed. Claude J. Summers and Ted-Larry Pebworth, Columbia, MO, 1999, 81–101; Susan A. Clarke, "'Bright Heir t' th' Bird Imperial': Richard Lovelace's 'The Falcon' in Context," in *The Review of English Studies* 56,224 (April 2005), 263–75.

32 Anselment 1971 (see note 31), 415.

33 Lunsingh Scheurleer 1996, 211–30, appendix I.

34 Axel Langer, “European Influences on Seventeenth-Century Persian Painting: Of Handsome Europeans, Naked Ladies, and Parisian Timepieces,” in Zurich 2013, 170–237, here 197.

35 The Dutch and Persian texts for the miniature with the inv. RP-T-1895-A-3069 (fig. 11) read: “’t poort vand tuijn Desarjerib” and عالياباد (āli ābād), and for the miniature with inv. RP-T-1895-A-3070 (fig. 12): “Chal wat Choene van sjah Sefie in Haram” and عمارت خلوت خانه باغ سعاداتاباد (Emārat Khalvat Khān-e Bāgh-e Sa‘ādat ābād, or “Building with privy chamber in Sa’adat Abad”).

36 Cf. Bremmer/Hoftijzer 1998.

37 Schwartz 2014, 29: “The original drawings, simple depictions of individual figures in typical dress, have never surfaced.”

38 For the changes in Persian miniature art in the second half of the sixteenth and the first half of the seventeenth century, cf. Sheila Canby, *The Rebellious Reformer: The Drawings and Paintings of Riza-yi ‘Abbasi of Isfahan*, London 1996, 9–18; *Splendeurs persanes: Manuscrits du XIIe au XVIIe siècle*, exh. cat. Bibliothèque nationale de France, Paris 1997, 165–223; *Hunt for Paradise: Court Arts of Safavid Iran, 1501–1576*, exh. cat. Asia Society Museum, New York 2003, 122–23.

39 Langer 2013 (see note 34).

40 Canby 1996 (see note 38).

41 The school of Isfahan refers to artists who worked for the court of the shah after it was moved to Isfahan starting in 1598, including Reza Abbasi, Muhammad Qasim, and Muin Musavvir.

42 The other woodcut in De Laet with the depiction of a young man with a wine bottle and cup also bears a strong resemblance to a miniature that was at one time ascribed to Reza Abbasi but is now considered the work of one of his successors (thanks to Sheila Canby). Once again differences can be discovered, like the neck of the wine bottle, the cup, and the shape of the headwear. On the other hand, the pose and the clothing are almost identical. That is also true of the long hair that almost touches the floor, something that would hardly stand out in the Persian drawing but in the woodcut is much more clearly worked out, presumably because the Dutch block-cutter was particularly fascinated by that detail.

43 Johannes de Laet, *Persia seu Regni Persici Status*, Leiden 1633, 119: “Accepimus a Nicolao Hemmio nostrate icones duas, quarum prima exprimitur habitus Tartari Uzbequii. Altera habitus & cultus filiae Uzbequii Tartari.” Thus, De Laet wrote only that he acquired the two pictures of an Uzbek man and an Uzbek woman of Tatar descent through Hemmius, but since it is obvious that the other six woodcuts are based on models from the same series, they must also be from Hemmius.

44 Heert Terpstra, *De Opkomst der Westerkwartieren van de Oost-Indische Compagnie (Suratte, Arabië, Perzië)*, The Hague 1918, 149, 292, 293. Niclaes Hem is also mentioned in VOC bookkeeping in Persia in 1623–24. See Hendrik Dunlop, *Bronnen tot de Geschiedenis der Oostindische Compagnie in Perzië*, The Hague 1930, 55, 73, 76–80, 82, 86.

45 For Jan van Hasselt, see Vermeulen 1975–78, Floor 1979, Vermeulen 1979, Schwartz 2009, and Schwartz 2013.

46 The following is the abridged version of an essay by Jan de Hond, Amélie Couvrat Desvergnes, Leila Sauvage, Paolo d’Imporzano, and Forough Sajadi that appeared in *Bulletin of the Rijksmuseum* 68,3 (2020); see De Hond et al. 2020.

47 The artistic estate of the Ter Borch family has been held by the Rijksmuseum since 1890. See Kettering 1988.

48 Every page of the family album is described and reproduced in ibid., vol. 2, 615–760. A discussion of the drawing with the Persian youth, fol. 40r, 632.

49 A discussion of other drawings later modified by Gesina ter Borch can be found in ibid., 632–33 (fols. 42, 44, 45).

50 The findings of the technical examination (infrared imaging, pigment analysis, Macro-XRF scans, and isotope analysis) are described in De Hond et al. 2020. The historical and art-historical aspects of this drawing are dealt with in greater detail there.

51 My thanks to Massumeh Farhad for the corrected dating and identification.

52 Canby 1996 (see note 38), 151–58. See also Scarce 2013, 62.

Convention and Uniqueness
Rembrandt's Response to the East

Gary Schwartz

When Rembrandt's artistic career began in the 1620s, a hazy form of Orientalism had already established itself among Dutch artists. Nonetheless, the suggestive play of light and shadow with which he depicted his Oriental heads and biblical costume scenes make this subgenre seem like his own invention. His self-portraits as an "Oriental" in prints (cat. 107) and paintings also contributed to this impression, so that by 1642—the year of his creative crisis following the death of his wife, Saskia—Rembrandt had made a name for himself based on his understanding of Eastern customs. Later, numerous successors continued to work on his themes, to which they added the Oriental *portrait historié* in a Rembrandtesque style that he had never utilized—the beginnings of the so-called Rembrandt school. In this way the image of the Orient became conflated with the Rembrandt look and assumed a life of its own.

At a given moment in his later life Rembrandt van Rijn performed the most unconventional artistic deed of his career. He took the time to draw some twenty-five copies of miniature paintings by artists from half way around the globe, artists whose names he did not know and who had been studied by no other European master. He carried this out conscientiously and respectfully on expensive Asian paper that he never used before or after for drawings. This campaign was not only out of the ordinary for Rembrandt. It remained unique in European artistic practice throughout the seventeenth century. The better to understand the significance of this group of works, which stand outside the pictorial tradition in which Rembrandt was trained and worked, let us first inspect Oriental motifs in the tradition he did inherit, and his way with it.

Domestic Objects and Collectors' Items

If there ever was a time in Rembrandt's life as an artist before there was the Orient, it would have been in the studio of his first master, Jacob Isaacsz. van Swanenburg (1571–1638). This rather eccentric artist had spent twenty-five years in Italy. His preferred subject matter was the inferno, whether in classical mythology or Christian belief. For decors, he preferred references to Roman architecture, and for armor and costumes nonspecific European fashions of past decades. What the young Rembrandt would have acquired from his master was a license to fantasize.

This will have made Rembrandt's confrontation with the East in the studio of his next master all the more striking. Pieter Lastman (1583–1633) was incapable of painting a scene from the Old Testament and certain scenes from the New Testament without dressing his figures in Eastern fashion and dropping hints that the action was taking place in the lands of the Bible (cat. 54–55). Other Amsterdam painters that Rembrandt came to know were also attached to this habit. The compositions they created were never attempts to recreate a historically or ethnographically correct image of the East. The landscapes in which they placed the scenes were imaginary mountains that were never presented in any detail. If there is architecture in the background, it tends to be Roman ruins (cat. 56). The model of Jan van Scorel (1495–1562), who in 1520 visited Jerusalem and drew its skyline and its architecture in order to later integrate them into his biblical paintings, had long faded by the seventeenth century.

The main manufactured objects encountered in Amsterdam painting in the 1620s that were actually imported from the East are carpets, which came from Turkey, Persia, and Egypt. Several paintings by Lastman display Anatolian carpets (fig. 1) of the type named Lotto, after the Venetian painter Lorenzo Lotto (ca. 1480–1556; fig. 2). He was, however, not the first artist to depict them in his pictures. Flemish and Italian painters of the fifteenth and even the fourteenth century included accurate renditions of Oriental carpets, especially in paintings of the Madonna, where their geometrics fed into numerological symbolism. Later in Venice Paolo Veronese (1528–1588) used colorful Oriental textiles and tapestries in his paintings, but mainly decoratively rather than iconographically, which is also true of the extremely sparse numbers of Oriental carpets in Dutch painting of the sixteenth century.

Around the year 1600 a reversal took place. In the seventeenth century the overwhelming preponderance of Oriental carpets is found in Netherlandish rather than Italian painting.[1] A key role in this development was played by Pieter Lastman. It is in his paintings, starting in 1608 after his return from Italy, that we find deliberate placing of Oriental attributes not only in biblical but also in historical subjects. These include carpets, but also weapons and turbans. It has been suggested that he acquired this taste from Veronese when he visited Venice about 1603.[2]

In paintings by Lastman we find various patterns that can only have been drawn from existing textiles, such as cartouche borders and the cloud band motif derived from Chinese models. These could have been painted from entire carpets or, as was mainly the case with articles of clothing, fragments that were cheap and easy to keep in the studio.[3] The latter makes it understandable that the forms of Lastman's Oriental carpets and textiles do not add up to complete recognizable wholes. The same is true of the textile designs in Rembrandt's paintings. Neither artist was out for ethnographical accuracy.[4] What they did achieve, aside from giving the viewer a small thrill, was placing markers of difference.

A natural product that can only have come from the East is the nautilus shell, which Dutch goldsmiths would put into precious mounts (cat. 50–51; see the essay by Michael Philipp, pp. 24–39). Lastman's brother, Zeeger Pietersz., was a goldsmith, and the painter used whatever chances he had to show products of that craft to good advantage. Birds such as the parrot and the peacock and animals such as the camel found their way into Lastman paintings of the Bible lands. The inventory taken after Lastman's death in March 1633 includes these intriguing items: "een cocodril" (a crocodile) and "een gaytge" (a parrot).[5] These may well have been stuffed animals brought back by employees of the Dutch East India Company. In this way he could also have come into possession of the Asian ceramics and chest in his will. They look more like household items than collectors' objects, but they may have been the first objects from the East

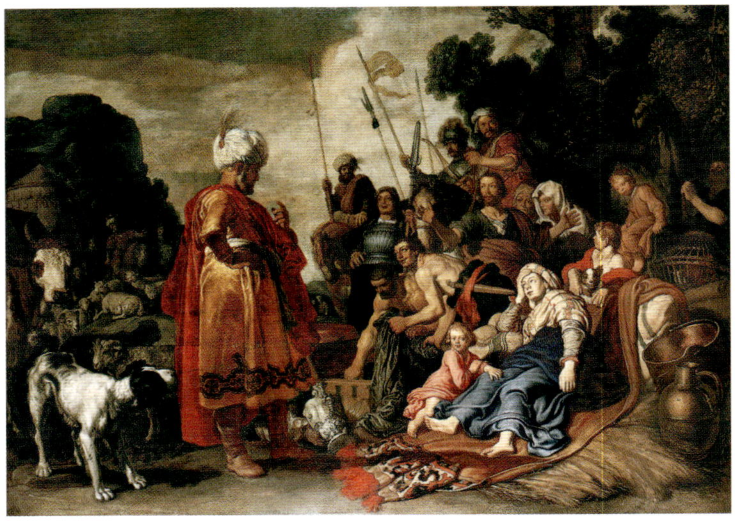

1 Pieter Lastman,
Laban Searching for the Lost Idols, 1622,
Musée Boulogne-sur-Mer

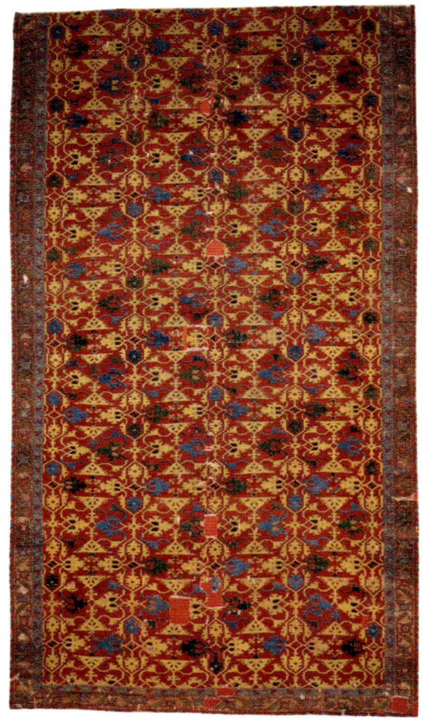

2 Anatolian carpet,
known as Lotto carpet, 16th century,
Museum für Islamische Kunst,
Staatliche Museen zu Berlin

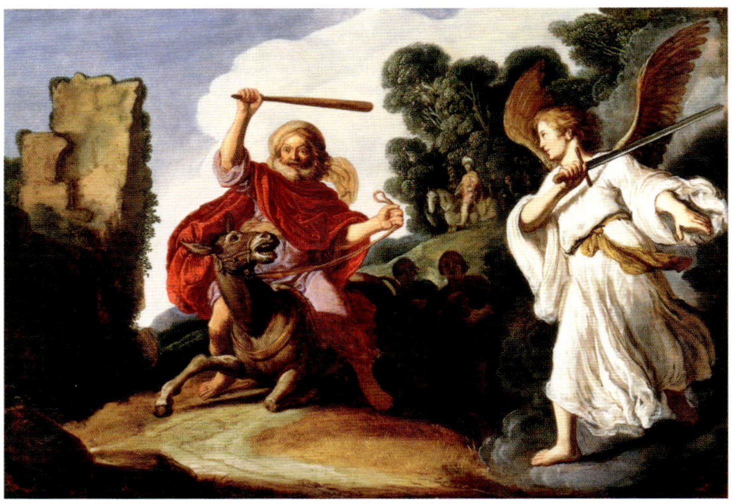

3 Pieter Lastman,
Balaam and his Ass, 1622,
The Israel Museum, Jerusalem

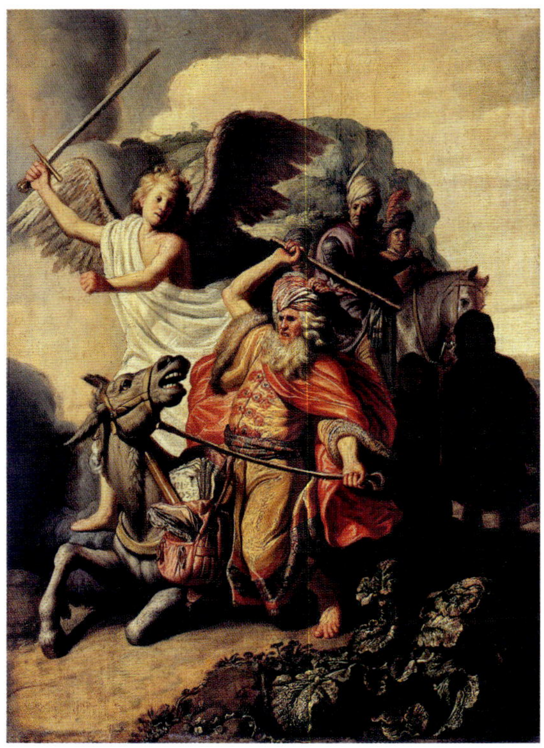

4 Rembrandt,
The Ass of the Prophet Balaam, 1626,
Musée Cognacq-Jay, Paris

the young Rembrandt saw with his own eyes. Not on a large scale, we see in the work of both artists an occasional weapon made in Asia or a parasol of a kind associated with too sunny countries far from the Netherlands (cat. 75).

The way Lastman dresses his biblical figures is clearly intended to evoke the Orient. They wear long, loosely fitting robes, often brightly colored and patterned, and sashes around the waist. Women might have headscarves. Some of the fabrics are imported Indian cottons. Royal persons are given capes set off in ermine and joined at the front with ornate golden clasps. Few of these garments were typically Oriental in origin or use.

Lastman and his Amsterdam colleagues were perfectly able to dress mythological and historical figures in the same way. However, one fixed rule is that the turban is never put on the head of a Christian. Although the apostles were just as Levantine as the kings from the East or Jews like Abraham, Joseph, King David, and Mordecai, who are turbaned by Lastman, the Twelve are not marked this way. A borderline case is Nicodemus, who paid Christ the honor of arranging for his burial. Lastman painted him in 1612 in *The Entombment of Christ* (Palais des Beaux-Arts, Lille) with a turban, identifying him, in accord with the gospel of Saint John, as a Pharisee and member of the Jewish high court. The turban was a sign of heathendom or Jewishness, not of disrespect.

Ambivalent Turban Wearers

There are few biblical subjects in Rembrandt's art that had not been depicted earlier by Pieter Lastman.[6] Much the same can be said of his Orientalizing tactics, with three main exceptions that we will come to below one by one. A striking early example is Rembrandt's adaption from 1626 of Lastman's painting of Balaam's ass (figs. 3–4). One by one, Rembrandt adapts motifs from his master's composition: most literally the ass, but also the figure and dress of the barefoot Balaam, the accompanying servants on horseback, the angel, and the setting. Rembrandt enhances the Oriental features by giving real turbans to Balaam and his servants. Balaam is Rembrandt's first biblical "Oriental." Lastman's Balaam however wears only a long headscarf that flutters in the breeze.

The story of Balaam (Numbers 22–24) is more complex than you would know from its iconography. Known as a prophet whose blessings and curses were particularly effective, Balaam was called upon by King Balak of Moab to curse the Jews, with the promise of a "fee for divination." Balaam consulted God, who first told him not to go, but in the second instance commanded him to go after all, with the proviso that he say only what God told him to. Although Balaam seems to have been following divine instruction, God grew angry with him and sent an angel to block his way. The angel was visible only to Balaam's ass, who balked and was thereupon whipped by the prophet. When Balaam struck the ass the third time, God opened the mouth of the ass, who protested his beatings to Balaam, and unblocked the eyes of Balaam, who was now allowed to see the angel. Both Lastman and Rembrandt depict the moment when the ass was struck the first time. When he reached Balak, Balaam told him that he could only say what God told him to say, no matter how much money he was offered, and he then proceeded to enunciate blessings on Israel in seven messages. Balaam's contradictory relationship to God and his angel, to Balak, to the Jews, and to his mount makes him an ambiguous figure.

It is known to whom Rembrandt sold his painting of Balaam's ass, and the identity of this man seems to be relevant to the subject of the picture. Fifteen years after its creation in 1626, in November 1641, the French artist Claude Vignon wrote this in a letter to the publisher and art dealer François Langlois: "In Amsterdam give my greetings to Mr. Rembrandt and bring back something by him. Tell him also that yesterday I appraised his painting *The Prophet Balaam* which Mr. Lopez bought from him."[7]

Alfonso Lopez was a Portuguese Jew converted to Catholicism, but the sincerity of whose conversion was widely doubted. He was a jeweler by trade, with something like a monopoly on diamond cutting in Paris. He also worked as an agent for Cardinal Richelieu of France, who valued his services so highly that Lopez's position was unassailable to Jew-hating detractors. Lopez was sent by Cardinal Richelieu on diplomatic and military supply missions at the highest level, especially to the Netherlands. In addition, however, to buying ships, cannon, gunpowder, saltpeter, and miscellaneous matériel for the French navy, he also bought collectors' items, diamonds, tapestries, Dutch textiles, laces, and pictures. A mid-seventeenth-century account about Lopez stated: "In Holland he bought a thousand curios from the East; [his display of them in Paris] looked like an abridged version of the Saint Germain fair."[8]

That this man bought from Rembrandt himself that particular painting is highly suggestive. He may well have seen himself as a latter-day Balaam, a mistrusted outsider who served the interests of the powers that be and brought blessing to the Jewish people. In the 1610s Lopez played a key role in assuring safe passage to France for Jews expelled from Portugal.

That Rembrandt framed Balaam as a turbaned "Oriental" tells us no more than that the wearer is from the countries of the East, that he is not a Christian and not without means. A figure marked in this way takes on an air of otherness that is not necessarily antagonistic but may be. The ambivalent Balaam, with his reception by an ambivalent "converted" Jew, is exemplary for the image of the Orient in Rembrandt's biblical creations.

Oriental Decor

Pieter Lastman has been called "the Dutch Rubens." The two artists must have met when they were both in Rome and kept in touch thereafter.[9] Rembrandt knew about the famous Fleming from engravings that Jacob van Swanenburg's brother Willem made of Rubens's paintings, but working with Lastman raised his awareness and interest to a new level.

An early borrowing from Rubens is the figure of King Saul in Rembrandt's *David with the Head of Goliath before Saul* of 1627 (fig. 6, cat. 60). The little boy pages holding the king's cape and Saul himself are adapted from one of the wise men from the East in a print of 1621 after a Rubens *Adoration of the Magi*. Perhaps the nicest little touch is Saul's extended left hand, the thumb lowered, like that of the Magus (fig. 5, cat. 61). The Jewish king is given a robe and turban on the model of an Oriental heathen.

For Rembrandt, this was more a matter of decor than principle. That was not always true of Rubens. Starting at the time he worked for the Gonzaga court in Mantua in the early years of the seventeenth century, he was acutely aware of the strained relations between Europe—mainly Habsburg Europe—and the Ottoman Empire. Current developments as well as history played into his imagery of the Oriental.

Was Rembrandt, like Rubens, thinking of politics? It would be fitting if he were. In 1621 the Twelve-Year Truce in what was to become an Eighty-Year War between the Seven United Provinces of the Netherlands and Spain was to expire, and the Dutch too were looking for military cooperation with Muslim forces. In fact, the Dutch and the Ottomans, both at war with the Habsburgs, saw each other as natural allies. This thought was as old as the revolt itself, since 1568, and it went further than just shared antagonism to a common foe. The Dutch rebels against Catholic Spain praised the Ottomans for the religious tolerance in their realm, a compliment that was returned by the Turks, giving rise to the denigrating expression "Calvino-Turcisme" for Dutch geo-religious policy.[10] And it went even further: the rebels took the Ottoman crescent moon as an emblem of their own struggle and propagated the war cry "Liever Turks dan Paaps" (I'd rather be a Turk than a Papist). Although

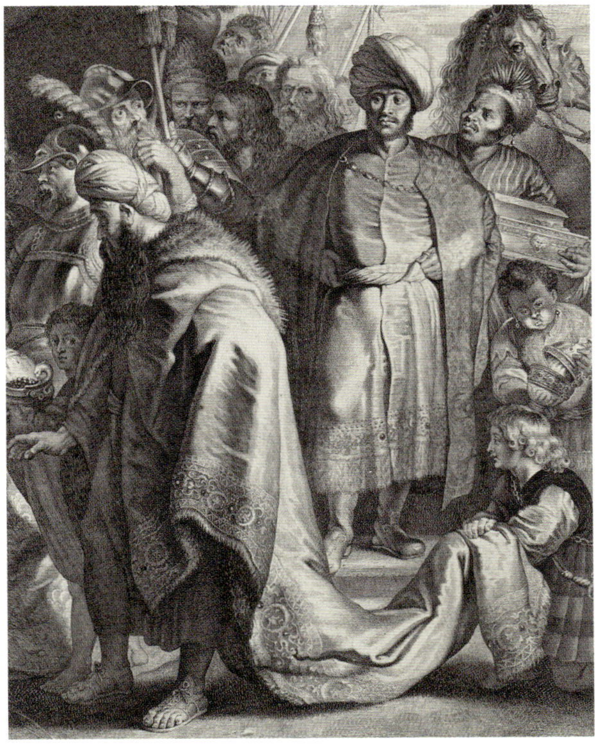

5 Lucas Vorsterman after Peter Paul Rubens,
The Adoration of the Magi (detail), 1621 (cat. 61)

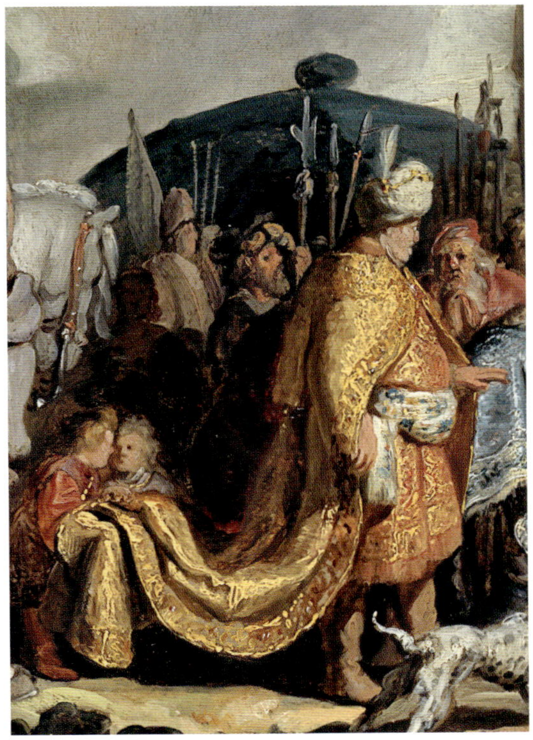

6 Rembrandt,
David with the Head of Goliath before Saul (detail), 1627 (cat. 60)

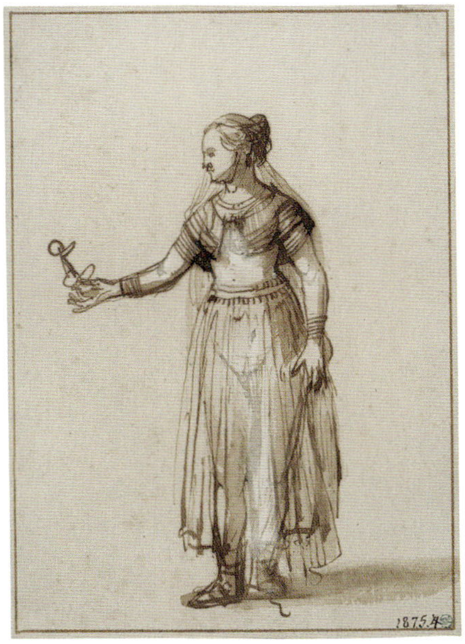

7 Rembrandt,
A Young Indian Woman,
after an Indian Miniature, ca. 1638–40,
Nationalmuseum, Stockholm

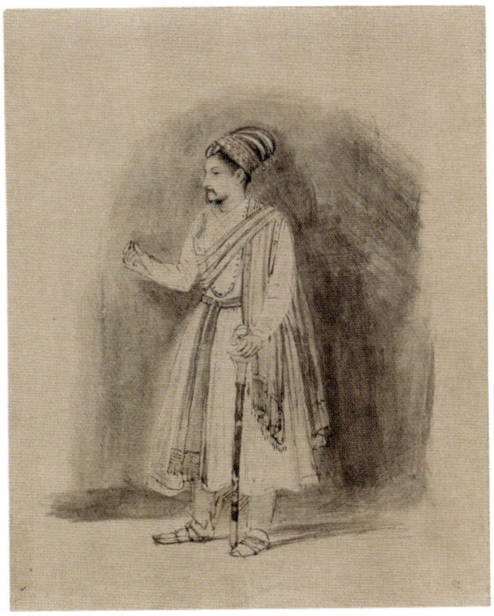

8 Rembrandt,
A Deccan Nobleman Standing
(Muhammad 'Adil Shah of Bijapur), 1656–61,
The British Museum, London

it never came to an actual two-front war against the Holy Roman Empire, and although these expressions of mutual admiration went only so far, they were part of Dutch culture and helped define the stance of the Republic in world affairs.

This was however a fairly abstract part of the background against which Rembrandt's Orientalism played off. More concrete were the ongoing depredations against European shipping by Barbary pirates. They operated from ports in the Maghreb and captured Christians to be sold as slaves or held for ransom (see the essay by Roelof van Gelder, pp. 74–85). This engendered in the West an enemy image of a barbarous people, marked by the barbarity that gave the Maghreb its name.

Rembrandt was not the only Lastman pupil to go Oriental. His Leiden friend Jan Lievens (1607–1674) had been to Lastman's studio first and had already worked with the theme (fig. 9). Constantijn Huygens, secretary to Stadtholder Frederik Hendrik, remarked in his memoirs: "There is, in my Prince's house, a portrait [by Jan Lievens] of a so-called Turkish potentate, done from the head of some Dutchman or other."[11] Although this is how all but the most credulous contemporaries would have seen that painting, it was nonetheless listed in later inventories of the collections of the House of Orange as "the Great Turk" and "Sultan Soliman by Rembrandt."[12] To my knowledge, not a single portrait of a known personality from the Orient was ever made by a Dutch artist in the seventeenth century.[13]

Rembrandt too played this game. The engraver Jan Gillisz. van Vliet immortalized a lost Rembrandt "head of some Dutchman or other" in a turban that closely resembles Rembrandt's earliest known painted *tronie* of an "Oriental" (fig. 11). Early paintings by or after him are listed in the inventory of the Leeuwarden painter Lambert Jacobsz. as "A fine young Turkish prince" and "A small *tronie* of an Oriental woman, the likeness of H. Uylenburgh's wife."[14] The inventory of Lambert Jacobsz. also lists a painting that it gives to Rembrandt: "A *tronie* of an old man with a long, full beard by Master Rembrandt van Rijn himself." There is a good chance that the work referred to—among others—is the *tronie* from the Earl of Derby's collection (cat. 106).

The Noble Easterner

The climax of Rembrandt's faux-Oriental figures is the so-called *Noble Slav*, more properly *Man in Oriental Costume* (fig. 10). It is unusually large for what it is—a three-quarter-length *tronie* of a studio model posing as an "Oriental." At life size, it is the largest non-portrait figure painting Rembrandt ever made. He painted it in 1632, the year he presented his calling card to the city of Amsterdam, beginning with the *Anatomy Lesson of Dr. Nicolaas Tulp* (Mauritshuis, The Hague). The man emanates regality, dressed as richly as can be imagined. He wears a glowing golden robe, embroidered and lined with precious fur, which in front reveals a more closely fitting tunic bound by a sash. His turban, with its voluminous tassels, is wrapped four or five times around his head and is painted with immense delicacy and finesse, the light picking up the smallest strands and shadows. Around the man's neck hangs a chain with a golden pendant, suggestive of a sign of distinction. The fall of light on the right embraces the figure, nearly like an aureole. It seems unlikely that Rembrandt disposed over garments and accessories of a kind that would have been worn by any particular person. His *Man in Oriental Costume* is therefore a hybrid product—a paid Dutch model (the man occurs in paintings by other Amsterdam artists of the time) dressed in an assortment of clothing intended to convey an Oriental look.

At that time such a picture would have appealed to just about anyone. Owners of Oriental *tronies* from these years we have already met are Stadtholder Frederik Hendrik in The Hague, and the painter Lambert Jacobsz. in Leeuwarden, covering the full price range of Dutch paintings, from high to low. Rembrandt's *Man in Oriental Costume* is obviously aimed at the high end of the market.

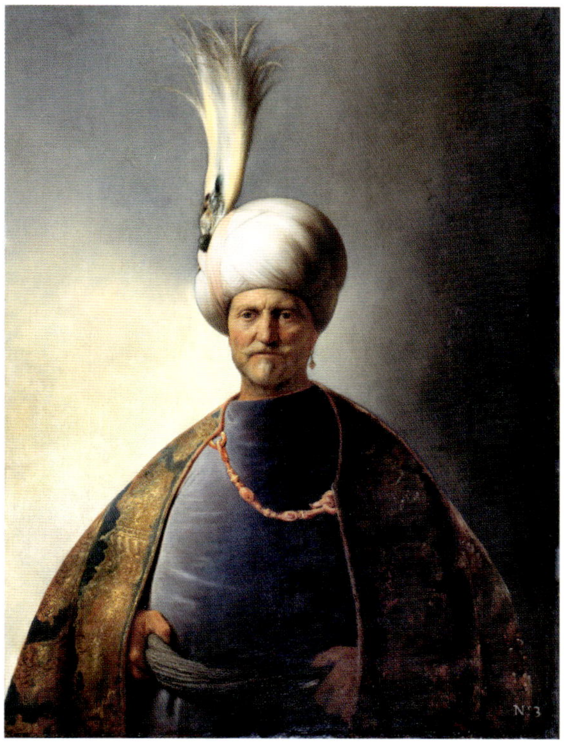

9 Jan Lievens,
Man in Oriental Costume, ca. 1629,
Stiftung Preussische Schlösser und Gärten
Berlin-Brandenburg, Potsdam

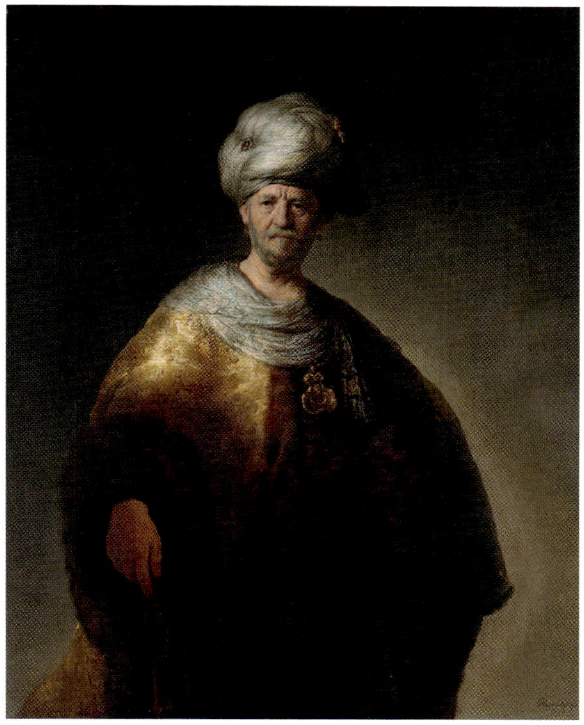

10 Rembrandt,
Man in Oriental Costume (The Noble Slav), 1632,
The Metropolitan Museum of Art, New York

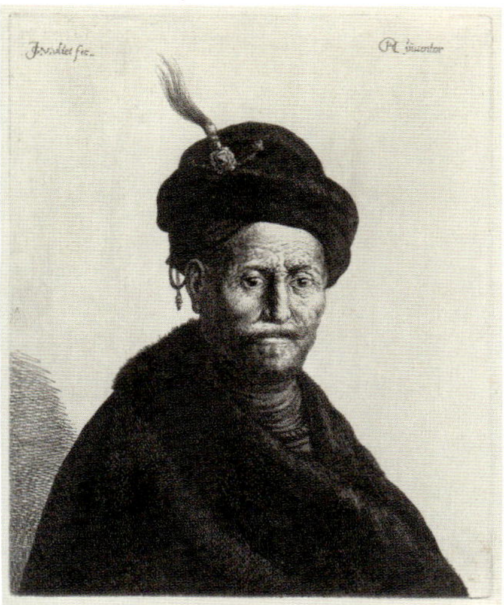

11 Jan Gillisz. van Vliet after Rembrandt,
Bust of an Oriental, ca. 1634,
etching on paper

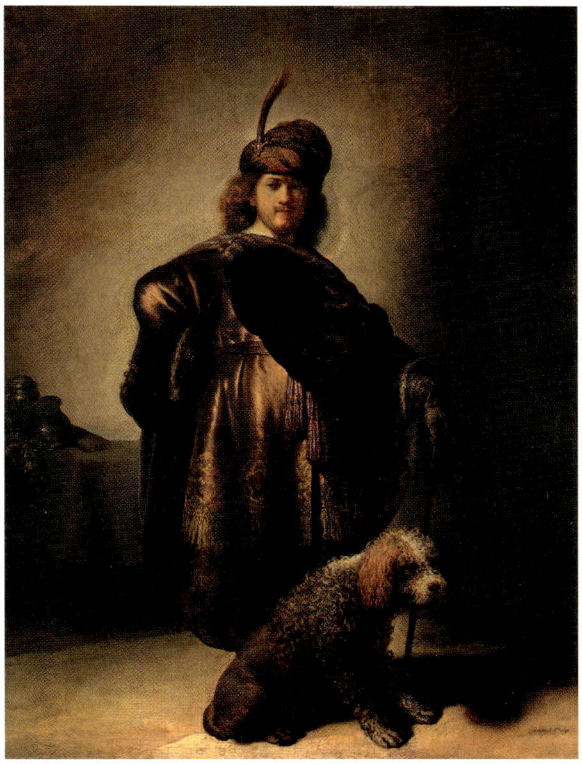

12 Rembrandt,
Self-Portrait in Oriental Attire with Poodle, 1631–33,
Petit Palais—Musée des Beaux-Arts de la Ville de Paris

There were enough Amsterdam merchants in his new location who could afford it. Another possible function for the painting was to serve as an ad for Rembrandt's skill as a portraitist. In the year of *Man in Oriental Costume*, he painted one other portrait of similar pose and format in The Hague and two in Amsterdam, of men in their own clothing. One of those sitters, Marten Looten, may well have been the first owner of *Man in Oriental Costume.* The estate of a grandson of Marten Looten's, Govert Looten, sold on March 31, 1729, in Amsterdam, included "A Turkish ruler or Grand Vizier, painted skillfully and powerfully by Rembrandt."[15]

That Rembrandt followed the lead of Jan Lievens in the creation of Oriental visages cannot be denied or ignored. In 1635 Rembrandt produced four copies of etchings made by Lievens a few years before, with big, eye-catching inscriptions on each saying they were "retouched" by him (cat. 103–04). The four so-called *Oriental Heads* were the last Orientalizing *tronies* Rembrandt ever made. It is as if he had to satisfy himself that he could defeat Lievens at his own game before he could let the genre rest.

Rembrandt as "Oriental"

The most interested sitter for a portrait in Oriental garb was Rembrandt himself. In 1631 he stood up in front of the mirror and painted what was to be his only full-length self-portrait, in garments of the same kind as the *Man in Oriental Costume*, though in smaller size (fig. 12). He adopts a commanding pose in the picture. He is wearing a gold-hued tunic and a colored sash around his waist that resembles the scarf of *Man in Oriental Costume*. Three gold buttons hold the heavy cloak together on his right shoulder. A feather attached by a small cruciform ornamental pin adorns the dark turban. Behind Rembrandt, on a table, lies a helmet and a silver vessel, neither of them particularly suggestive of the East. Nor is the large poodle at his feet, a dog that originated in Germany or France. In depicting himself as an "Oriental," Rembrandt forges links to artists who were the sources of his inspiration.

One likely source for the figure is the same print of *The Adoration of the Magi* by Lucas Vorsterman after a painting by Rubens from which Rembrandt had already borrowed one of the kings from the East for his King Saul (fig. 15, cat. 60). Another of the kings stands in pretty much the same pose, although dressed differently. Rembrandt will not have been aware of it, but Rubens drew on Italian pictorial sources going back to a drawing made in Constantinople by Gentile Bellini during his stay there around 1480 (figs. 13–14, 16). For 150 years, one can say, an observation from life enjoyed an afterlife that no longer had any direct connection to Eastern reality.

Rembrandt was playing with the identities not only of a wise man from the East and a knight of the Holy Sepulchre but also that of an Oriental prince who rules by the sword. In a self-portrait etching of 1634 he wears an ermine collar with a gold chain and holds a *kris* (cat. 107).

Thorough Reflection

None of Rembrandt's *tronies* with an Eastern look are overtly xenophobic. This is all the more true of the other main genre in Rembrandt's art that invokes the Orient. That is, as we saw above, the way he depicts biblical figures in Oriental style. In 1642, in an address to the painters of Leiden, Philips Angel praised Rembrandt's practice (cat. 44), saying: "I once saw a depiction by Rembrandt of the Wedding of Samson, of which we read in Judges, chapter 14, verse 10. You can see in it how that keen intelligence, by thinking hard about the actual way the guests sit (or in this case recline) at table—since the ancients used small beds on which to lie, not sitting at table the way we do today, but lying on their elbows the way the Turks still do in that part of the world—showed it very nicely."[16]

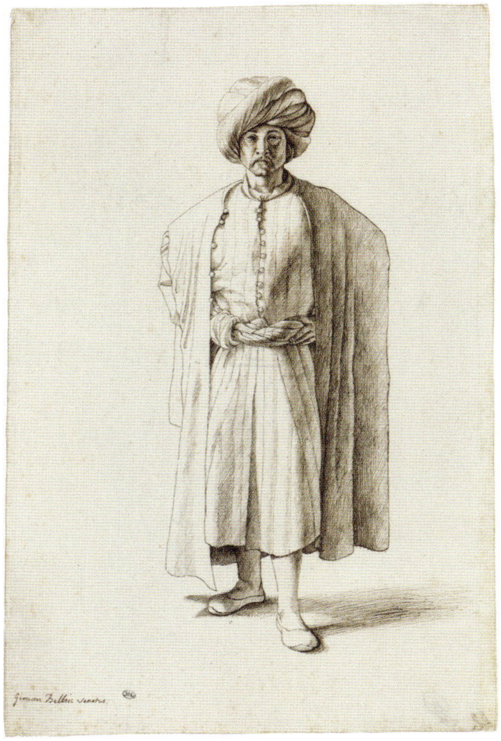

13 Costanzo da Ferrara after Gentile Bellini,
Turkish Man Standing, ca. 1495,
Musée du Louvre, Paris

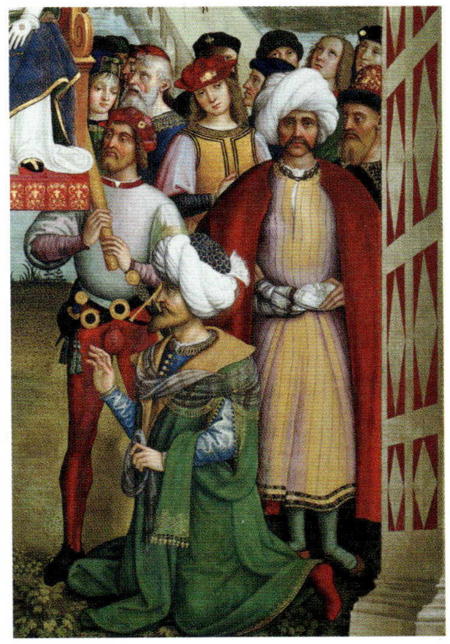

14 Bernardo Pinturicchio,
Pope Pius II Arriving in Ancona (detail),
ca. 1502–07, Siena, Cathedral,
Biblioteca Piccolomini

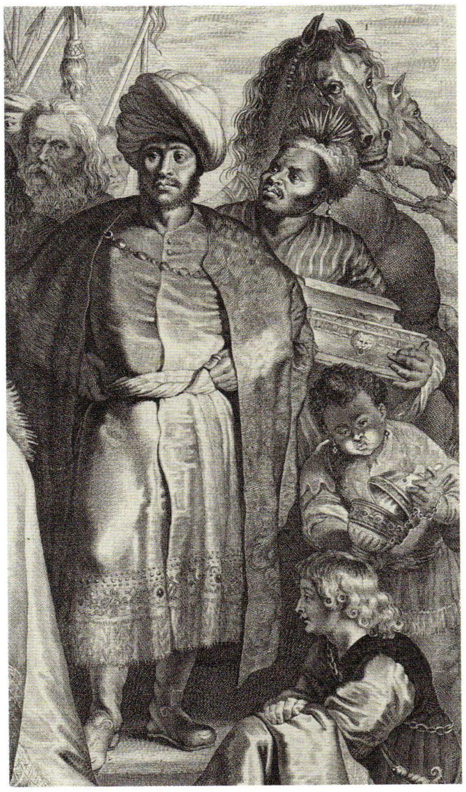

15 Lucas Vorsterman after Peter Paul Rubens,
The Adoration of the Magi (detail), 1621 (cat. 61)

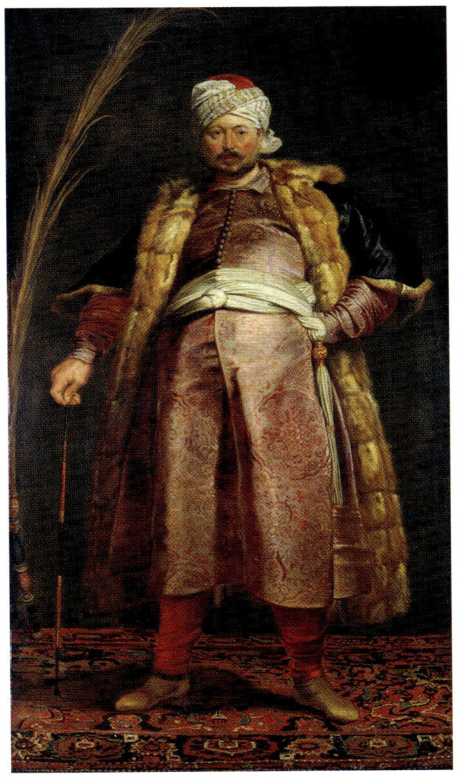

16 Peter Paul Rubens,
Nicolas de Respaigne, 1620 or earlier,
Gemäldegalerie Alte Meister, Kassel

Angel's talk ended with the words: "These fruits of natural representation, true to the subject, come into being by reading the story well and analyzing it in lofty and wide reflections."[17]

Angel uses Rembrandt's painting to illustrate a point about artistic license in relation to the literal depiction of a story. Artists who think that artistic license allows them to give free rein to their imaginations abuse that privilege. Their first allegiance must be to the meaning of the story and the specificity of the actions and objects displayed. In this, Angel writes, the "highly renowned Rembrandt" sets a standard with his painting of Samson's wedding. In saying that, he implies that the behavior of contemporaneous denizens of "that [Eastern] part of the world" had changed so little since biblical times that it can still provide authentic particularities for the painter. Other details in *Samson Proposing the Riddle at the Wedding Feast* (cat. 73) that can be seen in this light are the feathered hat of a man at the left and costume features, including the attire of Samson and his bride.

What Angel does not say is that Rembrandt was looking not only at Turkish custom (if he was) but also at a Dutch group portrait made a few years before his of another Oriental wedding (cat. 4). Here too a similarly composed company is seated at a table covered with a white tablecloth, with a baldachin behind the central figure. The groom wears the same kind of crown Rembrandt gives to Samson's Philistine bride. The carpet in the portrait, with small lobes connecting larger lozenges, suggests an origin in the Persian center of Shiraz. Rembrandt's carpets, on the other hand, are not identifiably Oriental.

The bride in the painting is known to be Grietje Hermans van Hasselt, who married Jochum Berntsen van Haecken in Utrecht on May 15, 1636; the canvas is signed "J. Hasselt fe 1636." Of the various painters with that name, the one who stands out in this connection is Jan Lucasz. van Hasselt (see cat. 5).[18] He had traveled in the East, in the cortege of the Italian adventurer Pietro della Valle, before leaving his service in 1617 for that of Shah Abbas in Isfahan. Van Hasselt was a painter to the shah until 1631, when he overplayed his hand in a mission to the Netherlands and found himself stranded back where he started. However, there is no further documentation that would identify the painter of this bridal *portrait historié* as Jan Lucasz. van Hasselt.

Jan Lucasz. van Hasselt participated as a familiar of the shah of Persia in the extensive culture of conviviality at Abbas's court.[19] He is even reported to have been responsible for the decoration of the Safavid royal palace on the Caspian Sea. An English envoy, Thomas Herbert, wrote of the reception hall there that "the seeling was garnished with gold, and pencill'd with Story in lively colours; all which seem'd to strive whether Art or Nature to a judicious eye would be more acceptable. One John a Dutch-man (who had long served the King) celebrated his skill here to the admiration of the Persians and his own advantage."[20] From an artist with that kind of access to one of the greatest Muslim courts in the world of its time, one could have expected more. If the wedding portrait in Utrecht was painted by him, we can only conclude that Jan Lucasz. van Hasselt was no more interested than Pieter Lastman or Rembrandt in truth to Oriental life.

There is a further indirect connection between Rembrandt's *Samson Proposing the Riddle at the Wedding Feast* and the Persian court. Ten years after writing his commendation of Rembrandt's attention to the customs of the East, Philips Angel, like Van Hasselt before him, became a painter to the shah of Persia, Abbas II. And he too created palace decorations for his imperial patron. Several frescoes in the Chehel Sotoun pavilion in Isfahan are very likely based on his designs, if not executed by him.

Neither these works nor any other possible creations of Angel in Persia had an impact on the image in the Netherlands of Eastern art, but another of his works did, in arcane form. In 1658, for the director-general of Netherlands East India, Carel Hartsinck, Angel produced an illustrated translation of a book on the avatars of Vishnu (fig. p. 260). The manuscript reached Europe in 1664 and provided (without credit to the artist) part of the contents of Athanasius Kircher's *China*

Illustrata, published in Amsterdam in 1667. The man who lauded Rembrandt for his familiarity with Eastern customs became the author of the single most significant contribution by a European artist to knowledge of an Eastern religion.[21]

Unusual Copies

Until the mid-1650s the extent and nature of the Oriental touches in Rembrandt's work was limited to adaptations of work or motifs from Pieter Lastman, Jan Lievens, Peter Paul Rubens, Jan Lucasz. van Hasselt, and miscellaneous sources: weapons from Japan and the East Indies, and snatches of Oriental patterning from nowhere in particular. His copies of Mughal portrait miniatures[22]—twenty-five are known to have been made—were made under different circumstances. Although they were called "copies," they are no more than sketchy impressions of the main motif of the originals, lacking color and context. Twenty-three of these works are still extant.

This set of works is unique. While Rembrandt emulated Albrecht Dürer and made incidental copies of compositions by Andrea Mantegna, Leonardo da Vinci, and others, we know of no other even remotely similar suite of copies. This being so uncharacteristic of Rembrandt, an uncharacteristic explanation of how they came into being might be in order.

The paintings of the highest artistic quality that served as models had been produced just a few decades earlier in royal Mughal ateliers under the imperial patronage of Emperor Jahangir (r. 1605–27) and his son, Shah Jahan (r. 1627–58).[23] For each of the drawings a corresponding composition has been identified in surviving Mughal portraits, but never an exact model. Only in two cases, the famous drawing of *Four Mullahs Seated under a Tree* (fig. 18) and one of *Emperor Jahangir Receiving an Officer* (The British Museum, London), is it at all possible that the models are known. The candidate miniatures were cut up and incorporated into decorative cartouches in Schönbrunn Palace in Vienna (fig. 17, cat. 95).[24]

The lack of comparative material makes it difficult to date the drawings. By the year 1656, when Rembrandt adapted the composition of the miniature of four mullahs under a tree for an etching, *Abraham Entertaining the Angels* (figs. 18–19, cat. 118), he knew at least one and probably all of the Mughal models. Regardless of when these copies were made the question arises whether his exposure to Indian art impacted his own practice and concept of art and why he made copies of the miniatures.

One clue is that Rembrandt copies are focused on certain details in the sheets he copied—faces, clothing, and accessories such as weapons, turbans, sashes, jewelry, and shoes.[25] This led the Berlin archeologist and Orientalist Friedrich Sarre to speculate that Rembrandt made these copies to serve as models for figures in his own biblical histories.[26] However, since he never quoted directly from them, and since the costume of his biblical figures shows no change after 1656, this is unpersuasive. Equally unconvincing, to my mind are the various attempts to seek in Rembrandt's late work reflections of the style or iconography he encountered in the Mughal miniatures.[27] He is said to have found in them new insights into the style of ancient art;[28] or to have endeavored to merge the cultures of East and West.[29] These opinions take for granted that the impulse to make the copies was an autonomous artistic choice on Rembrandt's part. But what if it wasn't? What if it was a commission? There is an argument to be made that it was.[30]

Commission or Artistic Adaptation?

Among the drawings and paintings from India documented in the Netherlands in the seventeenth and early eighteenth centuries, the Mughal miniatures copied by Rembrandt are the second oldest.[31] The 1655 inventory of the estate of Aletheia Talbot, Lady Arundel, lists a "a small book with several

East Indian drawings."[32] This book came into the possession of the tax collector Joannes Wtenbogaert, a collector of prints and drawings in Amsterdam.[33] He could have known Rembrandt since his studies in Leiden, where from 1626 on he lodged with a relative of Rembrandt's. In 1639 Rembrandt made a portrait etching of him (cat. 36). In 1650 Rembrandt was still in artistic contact with Wtenbogaert, when he etched two landscape fantasies with Wtenbogaert's country house and made a stunning drawing of the estate.[34]

According to a contemporary account, Wtenbogaert owned a book of Mughal miniatures. On Thursday, January 5, 1668, he paid a visit to Cosimo III de' Medici, the future grand duke of Tuscany, who was making a study trip to the Netherlands. Wtenbogaert presented the crown prince with "a quite valuable book of Mughal portraits" along with two coins and a dagger from that part of the world.[35] This description matches the lost album of Mughal portraits of which Rembrandt made copies.

The question now arises: given the existence of a "small book with East Indian drawings" (1655) and a "quite valuable book of Mughal portraits" (1668) in Rembrandt's close environment, with a strong presumption of a tie between the two through Joannes Wtenbogaert, why should we think they were not one and the same object? That would help explain why we know of nearly no direct models for Rembrandt's copies. Cosimo would have taken the original miniatures to Florence, where they were lost to sight. The two miniatures that seem to have been Rembrandt's actual models will have been removed from the album by Wtenbogaert before he gave it to Cosimo.

Wtenbogaert's audience with Cosimo III was a return visit. A few days earlier on Wednesday, December 28, 1667, Cosimo had visited the house of Wtenbogaert, about which the chronicle states: "Following his inclination, for forty years he has found pleasure in collecting, type by type, shells and minerals that come in on all the ships from Italy and other parts of the world. He has formed a most intriguing cabinet, adorned with paintings of some quality."[36] That evening Cosimo met with a merchant experienced in the Indian trade, presumably to acquire information for his own ambitions in that direction, and the next day he visited Rembrandt.[37]

Cosimo might have told Wtenbogaert about his interest in India. Wtenbogaert thereupon could have decided to present the prince three Indian items from his collection, including an album of Mughal portraits. In order to preserve the memory of this proud possession he commissioned Rembrandt to draw copies of its contents. The copies will therefore have been made during the week between December 28, 1667, and January 5, 1668.

Rembrandt in fact had earlier, in 1638, copied an Indian miniature, in a form that seems to have served as a model for this speed job. That drawing after an Asian costume study is the same size as his Mughal copies (figs. 7–8).[38] Because Mughal miniatures were exceedingly rare in Europe, the question arises where Rembrandt could have seen one. Of all his known patrons, customers, and connections of the 1630s, there is however one who is a documented possibility as owner of such an object. That was Alfonso Lopez, who—as already cited—"in Holland bought a thousand curiosities from the Indies." The impulse to create such copies probably originated with collectors—who were used to having copies made of items they owned—rather than with artists.[39]

The theory presented here is rooted in documented events and objects, and puts a different cast on the entire subject. If the creation of the miniatures was the result of a one-off commission, toward the end of Rembrandt's life, the assumption that the copying was artistically significant for him falls away. His drawings came into being not as a deliberate transcultural choice, but in the interest of a collector friend. Rembrandt was not acting as a visionary with a transcultural aesthetic but as a simple hired hand.

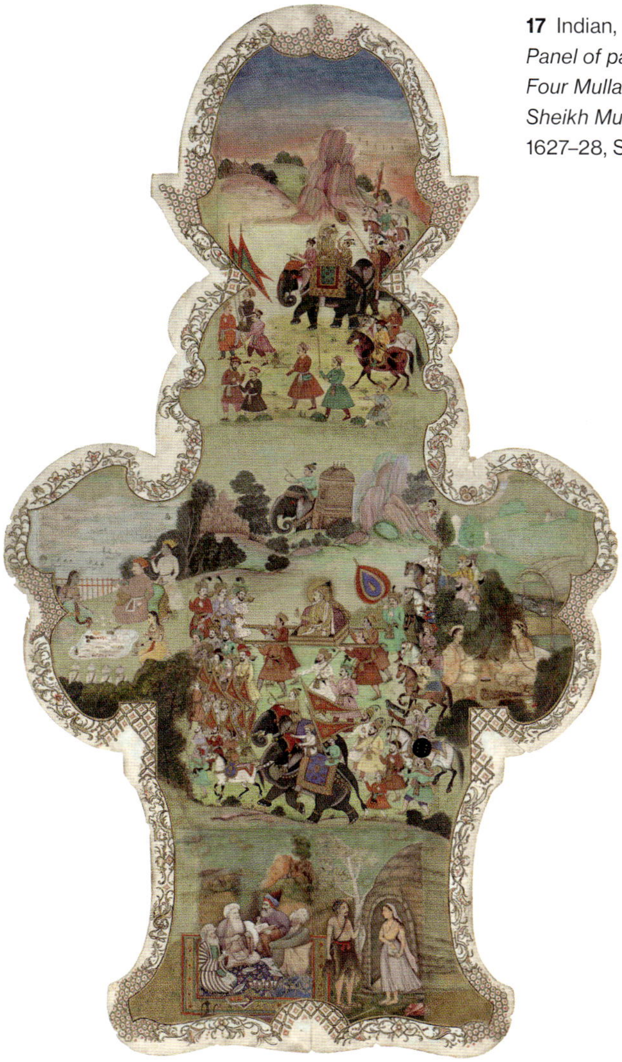

17 Indian, mounted in the eighteenth century in Vienna, *Panel of paintings from the Millionenzimmer*, including *Four Mullahs (Sheikh Husain Jami, Sheikh Husain Ajmeri, Sheikh Muhammad Mazandarani, and Sheikh Miyan Mir),* 1627–28, Schönbrunn Palace, Vienna

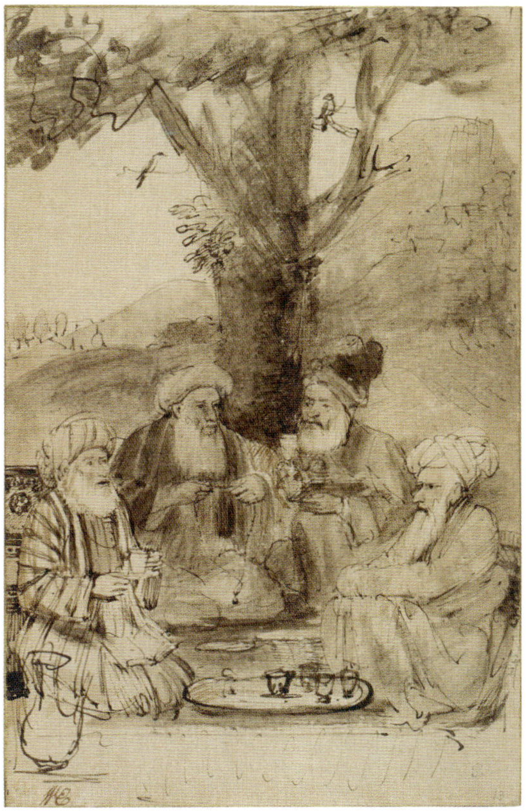

18 Rembrandt,
Four Mullahs Seated under a Tree,
copied after a Mughal miniature, 1656–61,
The British Museum, London

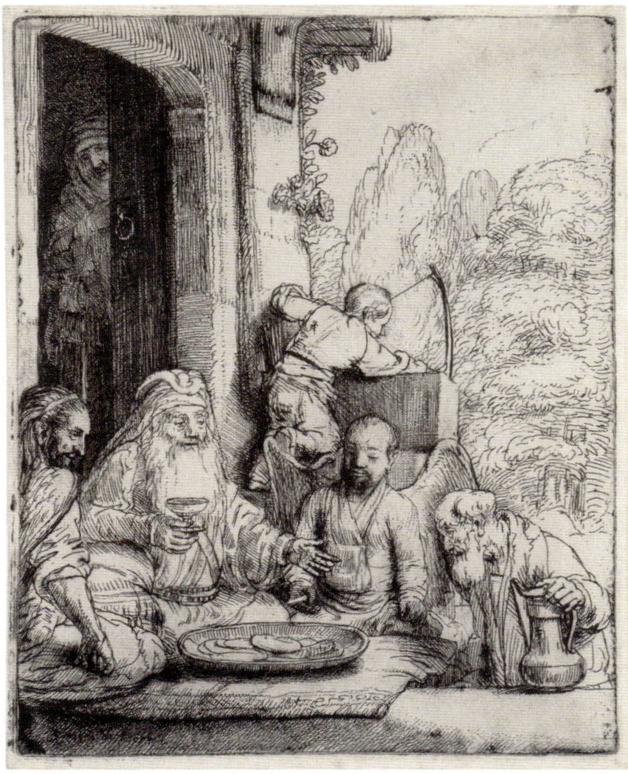

19 Rembrandt,
Abraham Entertaining the Angels, 1656 (cat. 118)

Rembrandt let himself be inspired by his master Pieter Lastman, his buddy Jan Lievens, and the hero of them all, Peter Paul Rubens, to employ an assorted mix of Eastern-leaning elements in *tronies* and biblical paintings. Some of the elements derive from older art, in sixteenth-century prints of the kind he collected. Nowhere do we encounter direct knowledge of an Eastern source (as sometimes in the work of Rubens).

Although Rembrandt was following contemporary convention in his Eastern motifs, his twenty-five free copies of Mughal miniatures were one of a kind. One could say that this is the opposite constellation to the above. Rembrandt's appropriation of Oriental motifs had almost nothing to do with the authentic imagery of the East but had an aura in his home surroundings. However, the moment in Rembrandt's art with uniquely authentic input had no impact at all. Had this moment been primarily artistic, one would expect it to have had consequences and to have yielded responses. That this did not happen, is the result of the artist's role as a contract worker. Rembrandt was not out to inject a dose of the Orient into Western art or into his own art. He was serving the purposes of private and princely collectors who preceded European artists in cultivating a taste for the art of foreign cultures.

This view puts Rembrandt into a global context far greater than even the expansionistic Dutch world of art, with its emanations into all the countries of Europe. Rembrandt's first-degree network in his meetings with the East extended from the Arundel exile in Italy and the Netherlands to a French royal agent from Paris to a voracious Amsterdam collector. In second degree they reached to the courts of the Bourbons in Paris, the Medici in Florence, the Safavids in Isfahan, and the Mughals in Agra, connected by the Dutch East India Company and intermediate agents. If Rembrandt's contribution to this nexus was less autonomous than has been supposed, that does not diminish its importance. It takes his achievement outside the studio and the privacy of his own mind to the great chain of interdependent realms where West truly met East.

See the more detailed version including the research on Rembrandt's copies after Mughal miniatures published online: http://www.garyschwartzarthistorian.nl/convention-and-uniqueness-in-rembrandts-response-to-the-east/.

1. Ydema 1991, 10.
2. Seifert 2011, 32.
3. De Winkel 2006, 169–70.
4. Therefore it would be a mistake to accuse them of imprecision. This point was made by Claudia Swan in criticism of remarks by myself and Marieke de Winkel, cf. Swan 2013, 113–14.
5. Seifert 2011, 312–20.
6. Josua Bruyn, *Rembrandt's keuze van Bijbelse onderwerpen*, Utrecht 1959.
7. Cited in Strauss/Van der Meulen 1979, 212.
8. Gédéon Tallement de Réaux, *Les historiettes: Mémoires pour servir à l'histoire du XVII*^e^ *siècle*, vol. 2, Paris 1834, 40; translated from French by Gary Schwartz. Cf. also Henri Baraude, *Lopez, agent financier et confident de Richelieu*, Paris 1933, 147.
9. Seifert 2011, 236–39.
10. Nicolette Mout, "Calvinoturcisme in de zeventiende eeuw: Comenius, Leidse oriëntalisten en de Turkse bijbel," in *Tijdschrift voor Geschiedenis* 91 (1978), 576–607.
11. Cited in J. Worp, "Constantyn Huygens over de schilders van zijn tijd," in *Oud Holland* 9 (1891), 106–36, here 128; translated from Dutch by Gary Schwartz.
12. CRP, vol. 2, 156.
13. For portrait prints of Persian emissaries to the court of Rudolf II by Flemish artists, see Schwartz 2014. Portrait prints by Flemish and Italian artists of a Persian dignitary who accompanied Robert Sherley on a mission to European courts are discussed by Gary Schwartz in "The Sherleys and the Shah: Persia as the Stakes in a Rogue's Gambit," in Zurich 2013, 78–99, 294–97, 300–20.
14. Cf. Strauss/Van der Meulen 1979, 144, document of October 2, 1637. The British Royal Collection contains a painting that could be the same as the prince mentioned.
15. Gerard Hoet, *Catalogus of naamlyst van schilderyen*, vol. 1, The Hague 1752, 333. Cited in CRP, vol. 2, 157.
16. Philips Angel, *Lof der schilder-konst*, Leiden 1642, 47, https://www.dbnl.org/tekst/ange001lofd01_01 (accessed April 7, 2020); translated from Dutch by Gary Schwartz.
17. Ibid., 48.
18. In this I follow the conviction of Slatkes 1983b. Cf. the discussion of this painting in Van Leeuwen 2018, 672. Van Leeuwen calls the painting a biblical *portrait historié,* depicting either the marriage of Esther and Ahasuerus or Samson's wedding.
19. For the centrality of this side of life, see Sussan Babaie, *Isfahan and its Palaces: Statecraft, Shi'ism and the Architecture of Conviviality in Early Modern Iran*, Edinburgh 2008.
20. [Thomas Herbert], *A Relation of Some Yeares Travaile, Begunne Anno 1626 . . .*, London 1634, 175.

[21] See Stolte 2012.

[22] Martin Royalton-Kisch ascribes the copies after the Mughal miniatures to Arent de Gelder; cf. Martin Royalton-Kisch, *Catalogue of Drawings by Rembrandt and His School in the British Museum,* https://projets.britishmuseum.org/research/publications/online_research_catalogues/rembrandt_drawings/drawings_by_rembrandt.aspx, no. 56 (accessed February 12, 2020).

[23] Cf. Glynn, 2018.

[24] Los Angeles 2018, pl. nos. 20, 21, 29, 30. The fundamental study of Rembrandt's drawings in relation to their models is by Lunsingh Scheurleer 1980; cf. also Forberg 2015, 22–23.

[25] Cf. for this and the following: William W. Robinson, "A Book of Indian Drawings by Rembrandt, 25 in Number," in Los Angeles 2018, 43–62, here 54.

[26] Cf. Friedrich Sarre, "Rembrandts Zeichnungen nach indisch-islamischen Miniaturen," in *Jahrbuch der Königlich Preussischen Kunstsammlungen* 25,3 (1904), 143–58.

[27] Cf. Filipczak 2007–08, 177, 179; Stephanie Schrader: "Rembrandt and the Mughal Line: Artistic Inspiration in the Global City of Amsterdam," in Los Angeles 2018, 5–27, here 21.

[28] Cf. Nicola Courtright, "Origins and Meanings of Rembrandt's Late Drawing Style," in *The Art Bulletin* 78,1 (1996), 485–510.

[29] Forberg 2015, 30, 33–39.

[30] The question of whether Rembrandt made these drawings of his own accord or on commission was raised by Marian Bisanz-Prakken: "[cat. 146] Indischer Fürst, vermutlich Kaiser Jahangir," in Vienna 2004, 304.

[31] Lunsingh Scheurleer 1996, with the appendix "Aanwijzingen voor de aanwezigheid van Indiase miniaturen in de Republiek in de zeventiende en achttiende eeuw," 211–22. It is frequently said that Rembrandt owned the miniatures he copied and that they were part of a lot described in the inventory of 1656 "vol curieuse minyateur teeckeninge nevens verscheyde hout en kopere printen van alderhande dragt" (Amsterdam 1999a, Appendix 2, no. 203). This assumption is doubtful because the originals were far too precious and special to be described so casually.

[32] "Noch een boexken met eenige Oostindise tekeningen," S. A. C. Dudok van Heel, "Een Holbein uit de collectie Six," in *Maandblad Amstelodamum* 79 (1992), 51–55, here 55; cf. also M. Roscam Abbing, ed., *Rembrandt 2006: New Rembrandt Documents*, Leiden 2006, 73–76, esp. note 6.

[33] Dudok van Heel 1978; Pierre Tuynman, "Manuscript Caption to the 1639 Portrait of Joannes Wtenbogaert, Receiver of Inland Revenue in the Service of the States of Holland in Amsterdam and District," in Roscam Abbing 2006 (see note 32), 155–68.

[34] The etchings *Canal with a Fisherman and Two Swans* and *Canal with a Large Boat and a Bridge* (B 235, 236) place Wtenbogaert's country house Kommerrust in distant landscapes. Rembrandt's drawing of Kommerrust is in the J. Paul Getty Museum, Los Angeles (inv. 83.GA.363).

[35] G. J. Hoogewerff, *De twee reizen van Cosimo de' Medici prins van Toscane door de Nederlanden (1667–1669): journalen en documenten,* Amsterdam 1919, 83 (with great thanks to Pauline Lunsingh Scheurleer for bringing this passage to my attention). See also Lodewijk Wagenaar and Bertie Eringa, *Een toscaanse prins bezoekt Nederland: de twee reizen van Cosimo de' Medici 1667–1669*, Amsterdam 2014, 85. Eringa's translation into Dutch calls the book "een fraai boek met afbeeldingen van de Mogol" (a beautiful book with illustrations of the Moguls), which Wagenaar interprets as a printed book on East India, doubting that Wtenbogaert would have given the prince a costly gift.

[36] Hoogewerff 1919 (see note 35), 64.

[37] Ibid., 65. For the artistic traffic between Florence and India, see *A Mirror of Princes: The Mughals and the Medici,* ed. Dalu Jones, Mumbai 1987.

[38] Benesch 450, cf. http://rembrandtcatalogue.net/benesch-427/4594602024 (accessed February 12, 2020), and Benesch 1200, cf. Royalton-Kisch n.d. (see note 22), no. 59; cf. also Robinson 2018 (see note 25), esp. note 60.

[39] Thomas Howard is reported to have commissioned Joachim von Sandrart to make copies of portraits from his collection. See Jean-Baptiste Descamps, *La Vie des peintres flamands, allemands et hollandois*, vol. 2, Paris 1754, 102, http://digi.ub.uni-heidelberg.de/diglit/descamps1754bd2/0112/image (accessed June 17, 2018). A few incidences of Dutch collectors having drawn or engraved copies of their possessions are to be found in Marion Peters, *De wijze koopman: het wereldwjde onderzoek van Nicolaes Witsen (1641–1717), burgemeester en VOC-bewindhebber van Amsterdam*, Amsterdam 2010. In correspondence, Pauline Lunsingh Scheurleer takes distance from the hypothesis I here present. She does not dismiss the idea that Rembrandt was the owner of the originals, "bought when he was wealthy." While she posits alternative possibilities for all the factors involved, her arguments do not dispute the facts behind the theory presented here.

The Fear of Barbary Pirates
Privateers and Christian Slaves in the Seventeenth Century

Roelof van Gelder

The year 1642 was an emotional one for Rembrandt. His wife, Saskia van Uylenburgh, who was only twenty-nine, died on June 14, and not long after that he completed his masterwork, *The Militia Company of District II under the Command of Captain Frans Banninck Cocq*, better known as *The Night Watch* (Rijksmuseum, Amsterdam, fig. p. 18). Less dramatic but nonetheless relevant for what follows is a notarized file dated November 1, 1642, in Edam, a small city fifteen kilometers north of Amsterdam. Rembrandt's name appears in the file.[1] According to the file's contents, Rembrandt, who is listed not as a painter but as a merchant, vouched for an amount of twelve hundred guilders, which was needed to purchase the freedom of Cornelis Jansz., a ship carpenter from Edam. The ship on which the twenty-six-year-old Edammer sailed had been captured in the Mediterranean by Barbary pirates. The expression "Barbary pirates," which strongly suggests the term "barbarian" (which has its origin in the Greek work *barbaroi* for "foreigner"), refers to the regions resembling states in North Africa at the time of the Ottoman Empire. The area was named the Barbary Coast for its largest ethnic group, the Berbers.

Together with the entire crew and cargo, Cornelis Jansz. was taken to Algiers where he was sold. His was the fate of tens of thousands of unfortunates who were reduced to slavery. At that time few had twelve hundred guilders in cash. Anyone who promised to pay such an amount and who could not put the cash readily on the table needed a well-to-do, reliable guarantor. In the case of Cornelis Jansz. that was Rembrandt, who in those years was well-off and apparently in a position to do it. The document referred to earlier in which Rembrandt plays an important role gives rise to the question who this Cornelis Jansz. was and what his relationship to Rembrandt was. It is also an indication that the events in the Mediterranean affected those who remained in the Netherlands. The aggressive behavior of the pirates during a capture was the subject in the work of a number of painters at the time and shall be briefly described here.

Opponents and Trading Partners

In Rembrandt's lifetime the Ottoman Empire was a world power on which Europeans, for political, religious, economic, and cultural reasons, kept a constant watch. By the sixteenth century it had grown to an immense size, extending from its heartland in Anatolia to Iraq, the Levant, and North Africa as well as to eastern and central Europe. In 1453 the Ottomans had subjugated the city of Constantinople, which was to be their springboard to Europe. They conquered Greece, the Balkans, large parts of Hungary, and in spring 1529 they were standing at the gates of Vienna.

The Ottomans posed a threat, a true danger for the Europeans because wherever they went, they subjected the population to their laws and to Islam. Above all, the Catholic princes of Europe, in Spain, France, and the Holy Roman Empire, for example, felt just as threatened as the Pope. They were constantly occupied with preventing, on land and sea, further incursions of the Ottomans into the West. Now and then they were successful, such as in the Battle of Lepanto in 1571, in which the fleet of the Holy League (an alliance of western Catholic states) crushed the Ottoman fleet and thus brought about a turning point.

By the fifteenth century, as the result of intense Catholic propaganda in both words and pictures, a negative image of "Turks" was created as cruel and godless. But there were other voices as well. Protestant nations, for example, saw the Ottoman Empire as an ally in their struggle against Catholic monarchs. Trade relations with the Turks also proved to be very good, which led to an increasing interest in Turkish culture.

The Netherlands were involved with the Ottoman Empire in various ways. During the uprising against Spain that began in 1568, for example, the Turks eased some of the Spanish pressure on the Dutch. From about 1590 on Dutch traders sailed more and more frequently in the Mediterranean. On their trips through the Strait of Gibraltar, they transported grain from the Baltic region as well as textiles, dairy products, fish, and spices. On their return voyages, they purchased wine, tropical fruits, oil, silk, wool, cotton, and marble at the Mediterranean harbors of Marseille, Genoa, Livorno, and Venice. In 1612 the first ambassador of the Netherlands was appointed in Constantinople, the capital of the Ottoman Empire, in which the Dutch could travel freely from that time on. They were permitted to engage in trade and to settle there. Smyrna, present-day İzmir, became an important Dutch trading post. Dutch trading communities were also established in Aleppo, Tripoli, Sidon, Acre, Jaffa, Alexandria, and Cairo.

Privateers and Pirates

These trade contacts were by no means without problems. From their home in northwestern Africa, the Barbary pirates cruised the Mediterranean and the Atlantic coast as far as France, Ireland, and even Iceland. It was there that the Barbary states were located—Tripoli (present-day Libya), Tunis, Algeria, and Morocco. The first three were formally part of the Ottoman Empire. They were, however, so far distant from the capital of Constantinople that the long arm of the sultan did not reach them. As vassal states, they were able to achieve an almost autonomous status. In contrast, Morocco was an independent state whose most important city, Salé, because of Morocco's extremely weak central government, effectively became an independent city-state in the 1640s and 1650s. The privateer ships sailed out into the Mediterranean from Salé, Tripoli, Tunis, and Algiers, the largest and most dangerous of the ports.

According to the views of the time, privateering was a legal activity. Seafarers were termed privateers when, with the written authorization of their government—the letter of marque and reprisal—they attacked enemy ships in times of war, looted them, and then brought them to the privateers' home harbors, where the ships and their cargo were auctioned. The crew and passengers were imprisoned or also auctioned and enslaved in North Africa. In times of peace there was no privateering. Sailors who attacked other ships without a letter of marque—and that is the essential difference—were termed pirates, buccaneers, or freebooters. They were outlaws, and if they were captured could expect no mercy. Although the Barbary pirates were called Turks because they were subjects of the Ottoman Empire, ethnically they were Arabs and Berbers. Their home countries, the Barbary states, were able to wage wars independently of Constantinople.

A tragic fate awaited the sailors, traders, and passengers captured by the Barbary pirates. They were sold as slaves at markets and forced to work, for example, as stonemasons for fortifications, as bearers or road workers, as farm help, or as rowers on the galleys (fig. 1). Only a few led a more humane life as house slaves. Europeans who were captured frequently converted to Islam and entered the service of an Arab; a few were even able to become advisors to the bey, the local ruler. If they were gunners, carpenters, or other specialists, their special knowledge was in great demand. A few Dutchmen became infamous privateers themselves. They were given dazzling names like Simon de Danser (Simon the Dancer), Thomas de Gauwdief (Thomas the Sneak-Thief), and Jacob de Hoerenwaard (Jacob the Pimp). The Barbary pirates were a great danger to European cargo ships from between around 1600 and 1800. Their ships were primarily galleys—long, flat ships propelled forward by oars (fig. 2).

The number of European ships captured during these two centuries and of men enslaved cannot be precisely ascertained—it involves thousands of ships and as many as 1.25 million slaves. In Algiers alone seven thousand Dutchmen may have been captured.[2] It is not surprising that those who traveled on ships along the Atlantic coast or in the Mediterranean were in constant fear of the privateers. There is hardly a log book from a ship that sailed the Mediterranean or along Africa's northwest coast that does not contain reports of Barbary pirates. Between the lines, one reads the fear of being attacked by these corsairs.

Slaves as Merchandise

Privateering by the Barbary pirates wreaked untold damage on the European and thus on the Dutch merchant fleet. It brought the slaves almost hopeless suffering and their loved ones enormous grief. As a result, initiatives arose in all European nations to end it—by means of either violence or diplomacy. The States General of the Netherlands, for instance, ordered ships to be armed, which naturally led to an increase in shipping costs. Ships sailed together or in convoys. Several retaliatory expeditions were mounted; heavily armed warships sailed into the Mediterranean to put a stop to piracy and privateering (fig. 3).

However, regular efforts were also made by the Dutch to win the favor of the Algerians and Moroccans by diplomatic means. Now and then the States General sent a legation to Tripoli, Algiers, or Morocco on a mission to purchase the freedom of captives. This involved enormous sums, which made up a significant portion of the income of the Barbary princes. The size of the ransom stood in direct proportion to the rank of the prisoner. A captain brought three to four thousand guilders, a helmsman or a surgeon about two thousand guilders, a carpenter or a sailmaker fifteen hundred to two thousand guilders, and a simple sailor one thousand guilders. Thus the twelve hundred guilders that Rembrandt put up would not have been enough to ransom the ship's carpenter Cornelis Jansz. It can, therefore, be assumed that several individuals must have provided backing in this case.

Monastic orders specializing in the ransoming of prisoners were active in the Catholic countries around the Mediterranean. However, such orders did not exist in the Protestant Netherlands; collections were taken up and lotteries organized there—sometimes by the government, more

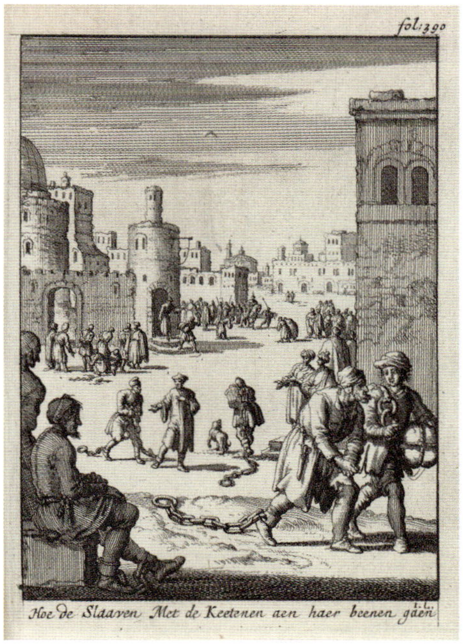

1 Jan Luyken,
Slaves Walk with Chains on Their Ankles (detail),
in Simon de Vries et al., *Historie van Barbaryen,
en des zelfs zeeroovers . . . ,*
Amsterdam 1684, between pp. 390 and 391

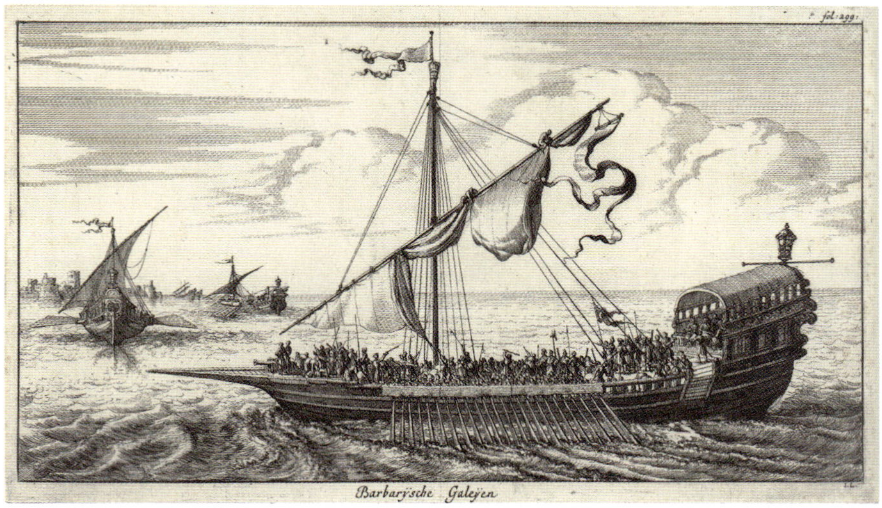

2 Jan Luyken,
Galleys of the Barbary Pirates, in Simon de Vries et al.,
Historie van Barbaryen, en des zelfs zeeroovers . . . ,
Amsterdam 1684, between pp. 298 and 299

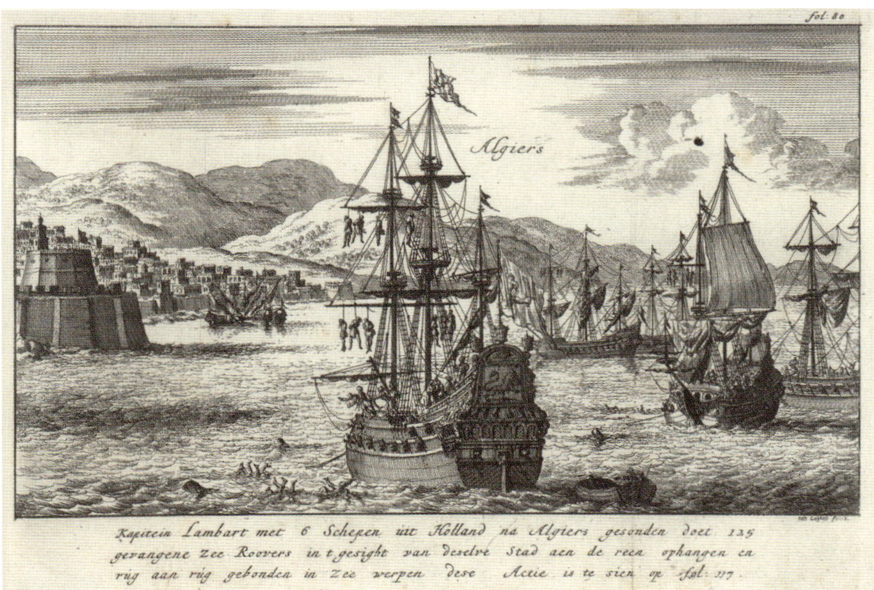

3 Jan Luyken,
Captain Lambert Hendrikszoon Hangs 125 Pirates, ca. 1619,
in Simon de Vries et al., *Historie van Barbaryen,
en des zelfs zee-roovers . . . ,*
Amsterdam 1684, between pp. 80 and 81

commonly by fellow citizens, friends, and family. In a few harbor towns there were even special "slave funds," in which monies specifically for ransoms were kept. While a poor person might donate only one stuiver, others deposited hundreds of guilders, as the case of Rembrandt and Cornelis Jansz. from Edam shows. Great efforts were made to raise the necessary funds, and a few went deeply into debt in order to be able to ransom imprisoned family members. An additional method of freeing prisoners was an exchange for North African prisoners.

The attitude of the Barbary princes was ambivalent. On the one hand, they needed the lucrative income that privateering brought; however, from time to time it seemed more advantageous, in view of the balance of power, to make peace. Moreover, they received valuable gifts as part of diplomatic settlements and could demand cannons, gunpowder, and ammunition. But these times of peace were few and rarely lasted long. Christian slaves were essentially merchandise that could bring in sizable sums. For this reason, slaves were also forced to write home and insist on a speedy release.

Imposition of Hard Labor

What did people at home actually know about the situation in the Mediterranean? Were they able to form a picture of the Barbary pirates and of the life of a slave on the galleys or on the coast of North Africa? Thanks to various media this was actually entirely possible. All in all, it can be assumed that all Dutch—particularly in coastal areas—were informed about the practices of the Barbary pirates. Even if they did not have a family member or acquaintance who was imprisoned, they nonetheless heard stories about men who had returned and the horrible things they had undergone. A few put down their experiences in writing.

News from the Ottoman Empire filled a great deal of space in Dutch newspapers in the seventeenth century. The most important was the *Oprechte Haerlemse Courant*, in which in 1667 nearly every edition included reports about Turkish affairs, that is, about acts of war, uprisings in the Ottoman Empire, court intrigues, and captured ships.[3] In addition, a flood of pamphlets appeared in the seventeenth century with reports about the Barbary pirates. The general tendency of the articles was that they were cruel, unreliable, reckless, and tyrannical.

The few books about the Barbary Coast that were published in the Netherlands presented extremely negative reports about this part of the Ottoman Empire. In 1657, for example, the *Historie van de Turckse slavernie* was published in The Hague, a Dutch translation of a book written in French a year earlier by Emmanuel de Aranda from Bruges. The ship on which De Aranda had left San Sebastián for Flanders in 1640 was captured off the Breton coast by Barbary pirates. De Aranda was sold at the market of Algiers. Two years later he regained his freedom and was able to return to Bruges, where in 1656 he published his book about his experiences.

Another book that devoted a great deal of attention to the Barbary Coast and Morocco was the compilation *Naukeurige Beschrijvinge der Afrikaensche Gewesten* (Amsterdam, 1668) by the Amsterdam physician and prolific writer Olfert Dapper (see cat. 43). As his basis he used the book *Pertinente Beschryvinge van Africa* (Amsterdam, 1665), a work by Leo Africanus, a Muslim who converted to Christianity. Originally written in Arabic and published in Italian in 1550, it contained a great deal of information about Morocco. In his book, Dapper described terrible punishments. "Most slaves there lead a wretched and pitiable life and are treated disgracefully, with blows and the obligation to perform the heaviest of labor; a few, however, who are fortunate enough to end up with good patrons or lords, are treated with more consideration."[4] He goes on to describe life on the galleys, where the slaves had to row under blows of the bullwhip, their best food consisting only of ship's biscuit and water. When they returned to land, they were set in heavy chains and taken to underground cellars where they slept on the bare ground.

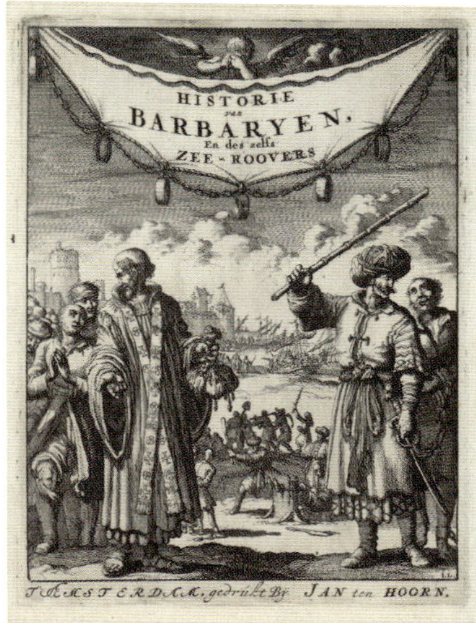

4 Jan Luyken,
title engraving,
in Simon de Vries et al.,
Historie van Barbaryen,
en des zelfs zeeroovers . . . ,
Amsterdam 1684

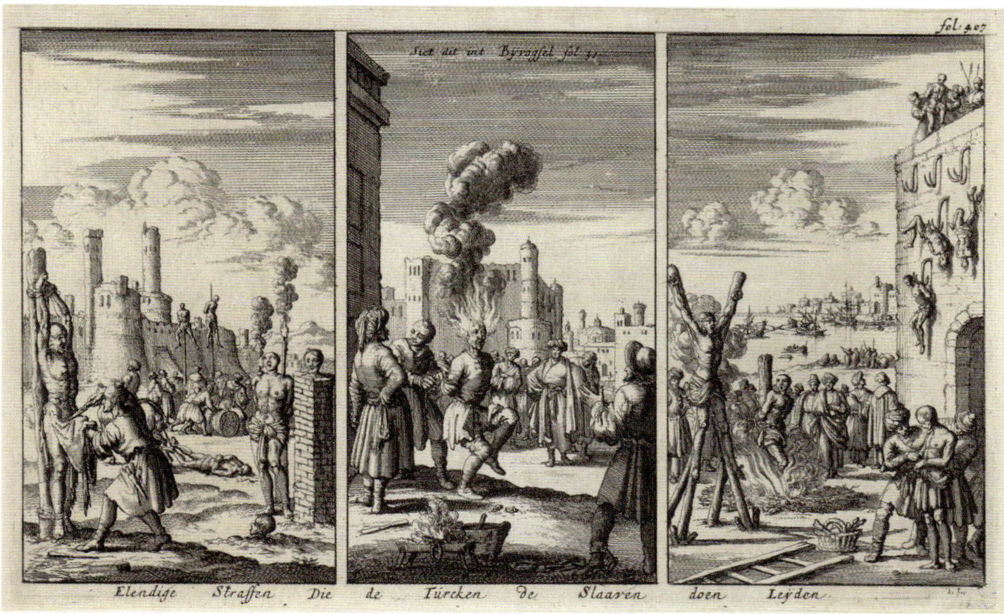

5 Jan Luyken,
Abject Punishments the Turks Inflict on Slaves,
in Simon de Vries et al., *Historie van Barbaryen,*
en des zelfs zeeroovers . . . ,
Amsterdam 1684, between pp. 406 and 407

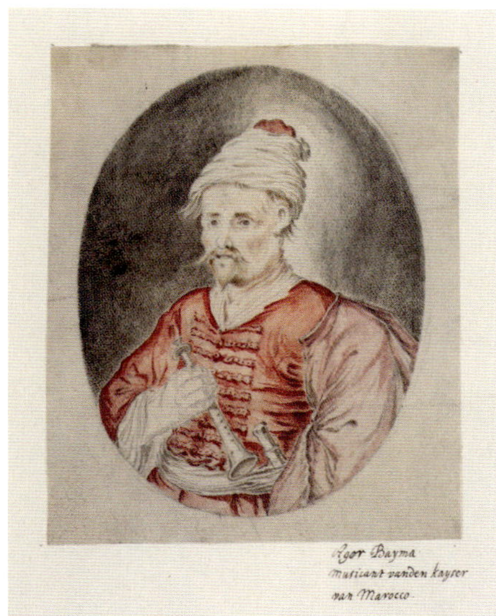

6 Adriaen Matham,
Musician at the Court of the Sultan of
Morocco, 1640, in *Atlas Blaeu–Van der Hem,*
Amsterdam 1662–78, vol. 37:24b, fol. 49,
Austrian National Library, Vienna

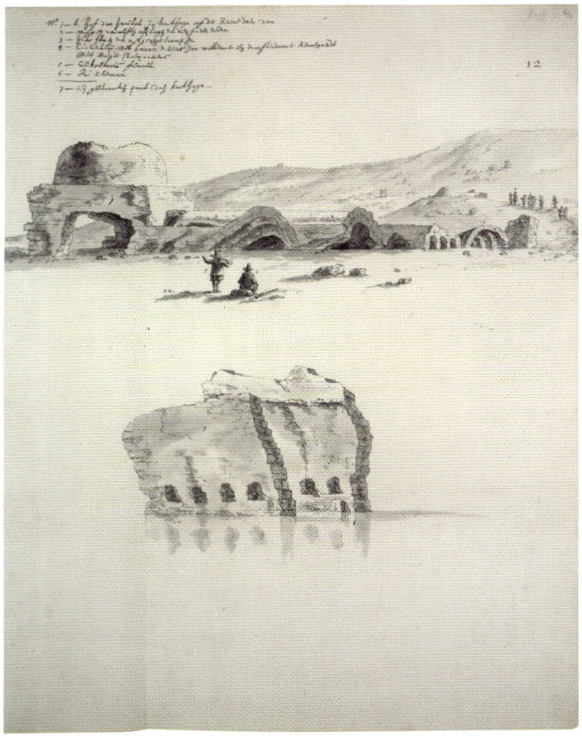

7 Reinier Nooms,
The Ruins of Carthage, 1663,
in *Atlas Blaeu-Van der Hem,*
Amsterdam 1662–78, vol. 35:17, fols. 43–44,
Austrian National Library, Vienna

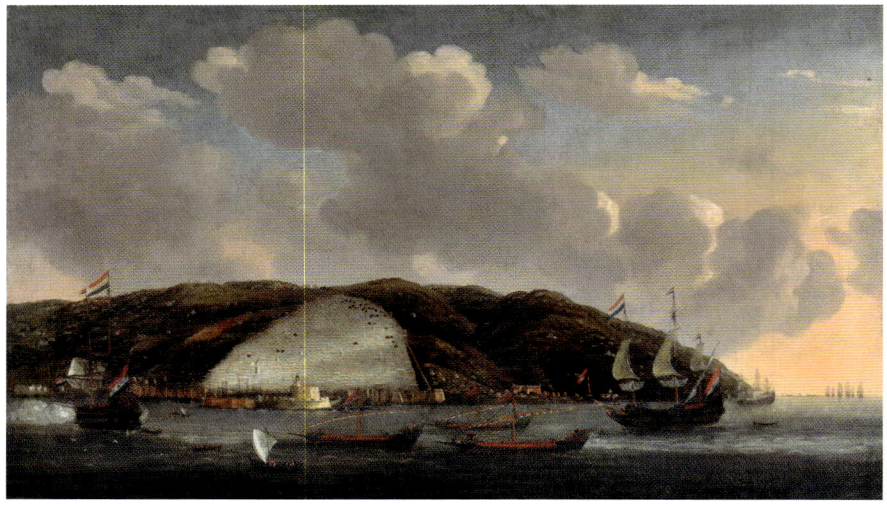

8 Reinier Nooms,
View of Algiers, 1662–68,
Rijksmuseum, Amsterdam

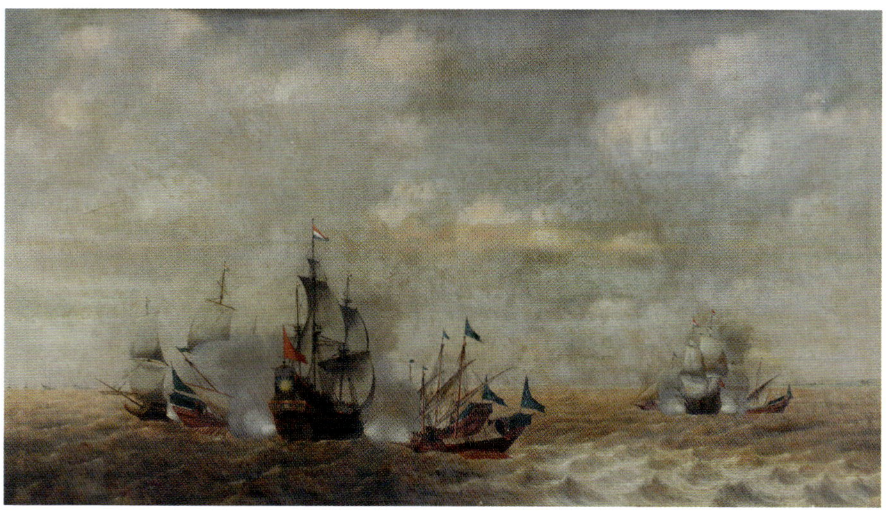

9 Aert Anthonisz.,
Three Dutch Ships Attacked by Galleys of the Barbary Pirates, 1600,
MAS/Museum aan de Stroom, Antwerp

An important source for Dapper's book was the *Histoire de Barbarie et de ses corsaires* written by the French priest Pierre Dan and published in 1637. This summary of all the atrocities of the Barbary pirates was reprinted and translated many times. A Dutch translation of Dan's shocking book came out in 1684 under the title *Historie van Barbaryen, en des zelfs zeerovers*. The illustrations were made by the productive Amsterdam poet and graphic artist Jan Luyken, who had a fondness for the depiction of cruelties like torture, executions, and war scenes, which his etchings showed in all their detail.[5] The text and images in these publications tended to be frightening, as can be seen in the fearsome heads of the "kings" of Tunis and Algiers on the title page (figs. 4–5).[6]

Cruelties and Vedutas

Jan Luyken never visited Turkey, but there is an entire series of prints based on drawings by Dutch eyewitnesses. Two contemporary diplomatic missions to Algiers and Morocco even had a professional artist among the travelers. One of these journeys took Anthonis van Liedekerke, envoy of the States General, to the sultan of Morocco in 1640–41. On the ship was Adriaen Matham, who called himself a "Constrijck Schilder" (artful painter) and reported on this mission in words and images.[7] Especially remarkable are his drawings of individuals—members of the diplomatic mission, but also a gardener and one of the Moroccan sultan's musicians (fig. 6)—as well as various street figures and a large view of Marrakesh.

In contrast to Morocco, relations with the Algerians were more problematic. Algiers practiced privateering much more intensively than Morocco. Wars broke out regularly between the Dutch and Algerians, some of which were allayed by vague promises of the bey, but which also resulted in naval operations and forced peace treaties. Sometimes it was possible to purchase the freedom of Dutch slaves.

Michiel de Ruyter, the most significant Dutch admiral, was sent repeatedly to North Africa. Although treaties were signed and the bey of Algiers promised peaceful dealings with Dutch ships, the privateers continued to carry out their terrible business until into the nineteenth century. In 1661 the States General sent De Ruyter with a fleet to Algiers with an order to sink as many Barbary galleys as possible and to pacify the troublesome pirate-cities Algiers, Tunis, and Tripoli. He had been provided with money to purchase the freedom of Christian slaves.

Also on the expedition was painter and draftsman Reinier Nooms, who made views of the coast and harbors of Algiers, Tangier, Tunis, and Tripoli. They show Dutch ships and North African galleys as well as scenes of Algiers with its harbor fortress and city gate. Nooms recorded, for example, the body of an executed man that had been hung from a hook at the city gate as a deterrent. According to an accompanying text, he portrayed himself as a draftsman at the gate of Carthage (fig. 7).

It is known that Jan Linsen, a painter from Hoorn, was actually taken prisoner by North African privateers and was a slave in Tunis around 1625. Another painter, Justus Stuyling from Delft, served against his will as court painter in Marrakesh from 1620 on. There is no known work by either of these artists concerning their captivity.

Prints like those of Jan Luyken were distributed in great numbers; drawings, in contrast, were one of a kind and meant for a limited audience. A few colleagues of Rembrandt selected the Barbary Coast and its pirates as pictorial motifs, which can be divided into two types: on the one hand peaceful views of the coast and the ports of the Barbary pirates, Tripoli, Tunis, Algiers, and Salé, and on the other hand violent sea battles between the Barbary pirates and European cargo ships.

Of the views of the coast, the most impressive are the pictures by Reinier Nooms. After his return to Amsterdam he worked out his sketches. He created four large paintings with views of Algiers, Tunis, Tripoli, and Salé for the Admiralty and possibly also for the States General (fig. 8).[8] The vistas of the Barbary Coast offer a tranquil view of the countryside; the drawings from the diplomatic journeys also have a peaceful quality. The situation is different in the depictions of the confrontations of European freighters and warships with the Barbary galleys, part of the genre of seascapes in which some painters specialized during the seventeenth century. These pictures show dramatic scenes, a confusion of ships' hulls, powder fumes, masts, rigging, and people drowning. The flags indicate whether the ships are Dutch, English, French, or Spanish. The galleys of the Barbary pirates fly green flags with three silver half-moons. Such paintings were frequently titled "Battle of Lepanto (1571)" or "Sea Battle between Christians and Turks." The first is incorrect because the type of ship pictured was not built until the seventeenth century; the second title is too general. The title might better read "Battle between a European Trading Ship (or Warship) and Barbary Pirates." One painter who produced a series of such pictures was Johannes Lingelbach (cat. 33).[9]

Two examples from the early seventeenth century were by Aert Anthonisz. (fig. 9). In 1615 a painting by Hendrik Cornelisz. Vroom was made in which a Spanish warship can be seen in battle with Barbary pirates (fig. 10). This extremely dramatic scene shows the sinking of a galley, which recalls that the oarsmen of the ship were chained slaves who, in such a situation, faced certain death by drowning. Vroom was able to reproduce this drama so realistically because he had himself been shipwrecked off the coast of Portugal. The famous naval painter Willem van de Velde the Younger tried his hand at this subgenre too. From 1672 on he lived in London, where he painted battle scenes between English ships and Barbary pirates (fig. 11).[10]

A Mixed Picture

For whom were these terrifying paintings made? Maybe for the open market, or perhaps they were commissioned by someone who had survived such a sea battle. Perhaps Cornelis Jansz., the ship's carpenter from Edam for whose ransom Rembrandt acted as guarantor, had seen or even commissioned such a painting. He eventually returned to his hometown, according to a court document drawn up there on September 13, 1643, which included the testimony of Cornelis Jansz. In it he explains that in Algiers he had witnessed the ransom of Cornelis Dircksz. from IJsselstein.[11] Cornelis Dircksz., Cornelis Jansz., and another man were prisoners of a certain Hamet. The man who purchased the freedom of Cornelis Dircksz. was a Jewish merchant who, after many entreaties, paid 175 pieces of eight.[12]

Cornelis Jansz.'s relation to Rembrandt remains unclear. Jansz. could have been a relative of Geertje Dircx, who was the wet nurse or nanny of Rembrandt's son, Titus,[13] and came from the region of Edam. Her father was Dirck Pietersz., and her mother Jannetje Jansdr. Cornelis might have been the brother of her mother and thus Geertje's uncle.[14]

Rembrandt never used the Barbary pirates as a motif for a painting, print, or drawing; he was simply not interested in naval pictures. Nonetheless, in addition to the notary's file in Edam, there is another connection between Rembrandt and the Barbary Coast. In 1656 Michiel de Ruyter brought a young lion from North Africa to Amsterdam. It attracted a great deal of attention and was also seen by Rembrandt, who made a series of drawings of the animal (fig. 12). Besides the lion, Rembrandt's drawings of the animal were also admired, as the number of copies suggests.

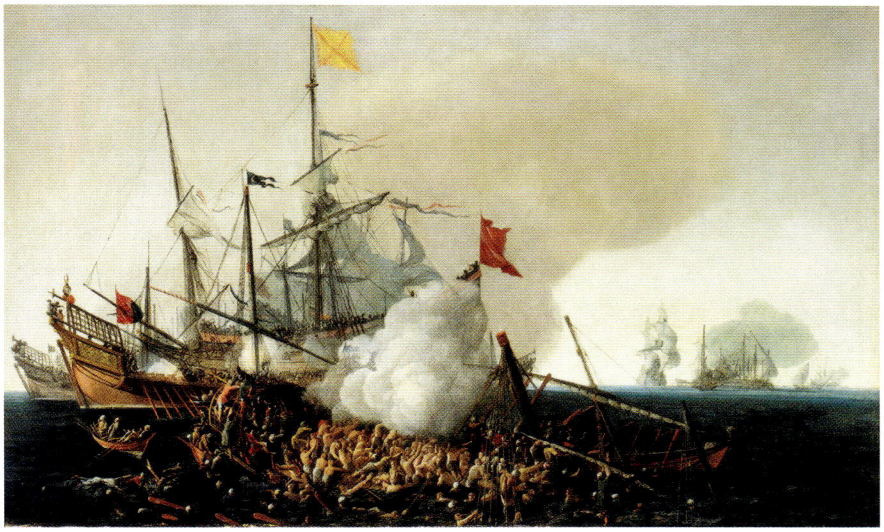

10 Hendrik Cornelisz. Vroom,
Spanish Men-of-War Engaging Barbary Corsairs, 1615,
National Maritime Museum, Greenwich, London, Caird Collection

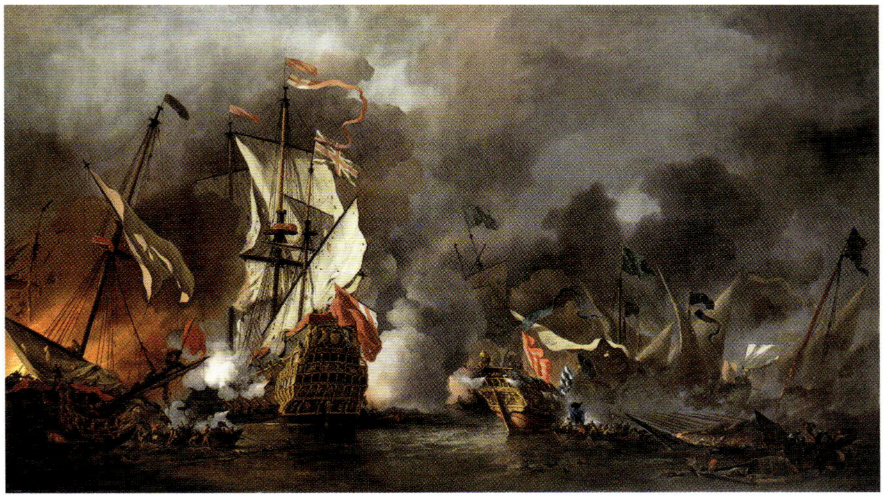

11 Willem van de Velde the Younger,
An English Ship in Action with Barbary Vessels, 1678,
National Maritime Museum, Greenwich, London, Caird Collection

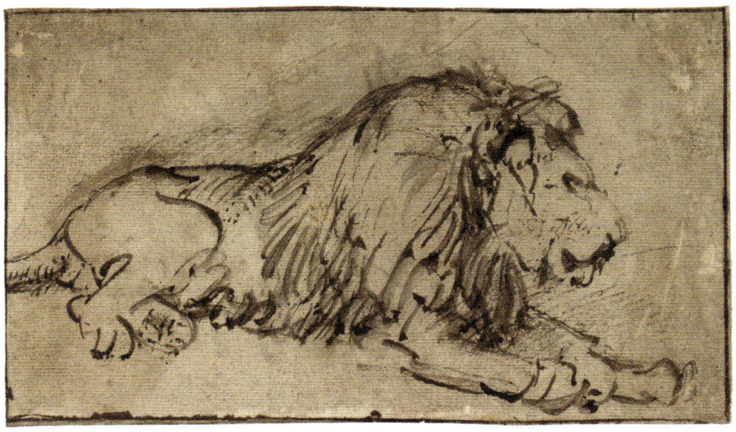

12 Rembrandt,
Recumbent Lion Facing Right, ca. 1660,
Rijksmuseum, Amsterdam

The image the Dutch had of the Ottoman Empire was mixed. They were political and commercial allies. The Dutch admired the pomp, the splendor, and the magnificence of the sultan's court in Constantinople. They were familiar with the tulips, the coffee, İznik ceramic, and tea pavilions *à la turque*, and they paid high prices for Turkish carpets. Plays and poems also stimulated the fascination with the fairy-tale "Orient." However, this did not apply to the North African part of the Empire—Tripoli, Algiers, Tunis, and Morocco—where the sultan had less influence. This region had an extremely negative reputation among the Dutch. The image was determined by the Barbary pirates. It was a nightmare, the picture of cruelty, ruthlessness, and greed. A single lion could not change that; it probably strengthened the fear of the Barbary pirates.

Translated from Dutch to German by Susanne Henriette Karau and from German to English by Gerald E. Brennan

1 Notary Lambert Adriaensz. Schorel, November 1, 1642 (Waterlands Archief, Purmerend, Oud-Notarieel Archief Edam, inv. 486).

2 Cf. *Christenslaven: De slavernij-ervaringen van Cornelis Stout in Algiers (1678–1680) en Maria ter Meetelen in Marokko (1731–1743)*, ed. Laura van den Broek and Maaike Jacobs, Zutphen 2006, 12; cf. also “Lyst der schepen,” in Jacques Philippe Laugier de Tassy, *Beschryving van het Koningryk en de stadt Algiers*, Amsterdam 1725, 277–96; Cornelis Pynacker, “Historysch verhael van den steden Thunes, Algiers ende andere steden in Barbarien gelegen,” ed. Gerard S. van Grieken, The Hague 1975, 5; Robert C. Davis, *Christian Slaves, Muslim Masters: White Slavery in the Mediterranean, the Barbary Coast, and Italy, 1500–1800*, Basingstoke and New York 2003, XIV–XVI.

3 Cf. Frans R. E. Blom, “Het venster op het Ottomaanse Rijk: De import van theater en nieuws over de Turk in de Republiek,” in *De zeventiende eeuw* 29,1 (2013), 20–31; seventy-six issues were examined.

4 Olfert Dapper, *Naukeurige Beschrijvinge der Afrikaensche Gewesten*, Amsterdam 1668, 177: “Al de meeste slaven leiden aldaer een ellendigh en jammerlijk leven, en worden met slaen en het opleggen van zwaren arbeit zeer ellendigh gehanthaeft en geplaeght, hoewel eenigen, dien ’t gelukt by goede Patronen of meesters te komen, veel zachter gehandelt worden.”

5 A second volume, by Simon de Vries, was published under the title *Handelingen en geschiedenissen, voorgevallen tusschen de staet der vereenighde Nederlanden en dien van de zeeroovers in Barbaryen, van ’t jaar 1590 tot op ’t jaar 1684*, Amsterdam 1684.

6 The etcher M. Schaep created a series comprised of twelve prints from drawings made by Cornelis de Wael in 1649, which also showed scenes from the daily life of slaves in Turkish captivity.

7 The Amsterdam lawyer and collector Laurens van der Hem obtained a copy of this report as well as drawings by Matham. Both the text and the drawings were used by Van der Hem in his atlas, which is now in the collection of the Austrian National Library in Vienna.

8 Also preserved from the collection of the Dordrecht notary Gerrit de Jager are a view of Algiers from the year 1663 (Museum Boijmans Van Beuningen, Rotterdam) and a view of Tripoli from 1665 (Huis Van Gijn, Dordrecht). Both are based on drawings of paintings by Reinier Nooms which are now lost. Cf. Friso Lammertse, “Reinier Nooms en notaris Gerard de Jager schilderen Algiers,” in *Vorm geven aan veelzijdigheid: Opstellen aangeboden aan Wim Crouwel ter gelegenheid van zijn afscheid als directeur van Museum Boymans-van Beuningen*, ed. Jeroen Giltay et al., Rotterdam 1993, 45–51.

9 For example, in the Statens Museum for Konst, Copenhagen, and the Herzog Anton Ulrich-Museum in Braunschweig. Thanks to Erik Spaans for this information.

10 Additional examples of paintings of battles between Barbary pirates and European ships were made by Aert Anthonisz. (National Maritime Museum, Greenwich, London), Andries van Eertvelt (National Maritime Museum, Greenwich, London), Gaspard van Eyck (Sotheby’s London, September 7, 2002, lot 357), Johannes Lingelbach (formerly John Mitchell and Son, Art Dealers, London), Gaspar van den Bos (private collection), Jeronymus van Diest II (Het Scheepvaartmuseum, Amsterdam), Jacob Gerritsz. Loef (Amsterdam Museum), Cornelis de Wael (Museo Nacional del Prado, Madrid, and Museo Poldi Pezzoli, Milan), Lieve Verschuier (National Maritime Museum, Greenwich, London), and an anonymous artist (Hofje van Aerden, Leerdam). Reinier Nooms and Willem van de Velde the Younger painted such battles (Prentenkabinet Universiteit Leiden and National Maritime Museum, Greenwich, London).

11 Regionaal Historisch Centrum Rijnstreek en Lopikerwaard, Rechterlijk Archief IJsselstein 644-1 (1573–1761).

12 A “piece of eight” was a Spanish real, a silver coin worth two guilders and eight stuivers. The man was ransomed for 420 guilders. The statement was put in writing as there were differences of opinion about the payment of the ransom. According to these files David Palache was the intermediary. Members of the Jewish family Palache maintained relations between Morocco, Algiers, and the Dutch Republic for several decades. This was done from locations in Livorno, Amsterdam, and The Hague. Since the ransom was usually paid after the return of the prisoner to the Republic, an advance was paid in Algiers or Salé. In the meantime there were other costs, including transportation, accommodation, commissions to middlemen such as guards, translators, and money changers. The ransomers, of course, ran a certain risk, for which reason they demanded a cut that sometimes amounted to as much as thirty percent.

13 For Geertje Dircx and her relation to Rembrandt, see Hendrik Frederik Wijnman, “Een episode uit het leven van Rembrandt: De geschiedenis van Geertje Dircks,” in *Jaarboek Amstelodamum* 60 (1968), 103–18.

14 Cornelis Jansz. married the widow Trijntje Lambertsdr. in 1639 (notice of marriage, November 20, 1639, Doop-, trouw- en begraafregisters van Edam, Waterlands Archief, Purmerend). In her last will and testament, dated April 25, 1656, Trijntje Lambertsdr. is identified as a widow; it can thus be assumed that Cornelis died sometime between 1643 and 1656 (Notary Houttuyn, April 25, 1656, Waterlands Archief, Purmerend, Oud-Notarieel Archief Edam, inv. 492).

Knowledge from the East
Collecting Oriental Manuscripts in the Dutch Republic in the Age of Rembrandt

Arnoud Vrolijk

The city of Leiden is the location of the oldest university in the Netherlands and the city where Rembrandt was born and trained. At the age of thirteen or fourteen, after he graduated from the Latin school, Rembrandt matriculated at the University of Leiden on May 20, 1620, as a student in the faculty of letters: "Rembrandus Hermanni Leydensis Studiosus litterarum annor[um] 14, apud parentes" (Rembrandt, son of Harmen, from Leiden, student of Letters, fourteen years of age, living with his parents).[1] It is impossible to establish what he had in mind. Was he planning to follow a career in academia? Did he want to drink tax-free beer, one of the privileges of students? Or did he need exemption from service in the local militia? That is not very likely for a boy of almost fourteen who still lived with his parents. His academic career lasted only briefly, but it should not be underestimated. Recently documents were discovered according to which he reentered the university in 1622 at the age of fifteen. But it still remains anybody's guess whose classes he attended and what he may have learned, so a great deal of caution remains in order.[2]

The same caution must be exercised in the question of Rembrandt's familiarity with the Muslim Orient, which is related to the "visibility" of the Orient and Oriental culture in seventeenth-century Amsterdam. There was a small colony of silk merchants from Persia, but as far as we know they were all Armenians. There were also foreign envoys from the East in the Republic, but the chance of meeting them in the street was not great. How many people would have actually met an Armenian silk merchant from Persia who was wearing the traditional garments of his native country when he left his house in Amsterdam? Nevertheless, it appears that Rembrandt grasped every opportunity that presented itself to draw a Moor, a Pole, or a Turk.[3] It has also been suggested that he met the Dutch painter Jan Lucasz. van Hasselt (see cat. 5), who was in the service of the Safavid Shah Abbas I and who in 1625 accompanied the Persian envoy Musa Beg to the Dutch Republic. If a very young Rembrandt had indeed met the envoy and his retinue, he would not only have been able to see Persian court garments at close range, but he would also have had the benefit of Van Hasselt's firsthand knowledge of the subject.[4] It is certain, though, that Oriental fabrics and—to a very limited degree—items of clothing were imported in the Dutch Republic, not only from the Middle East but also from India and Japan.

This essay will investigate how knowledge of the Middle East was gained and taught in the Netherlands in the seventeenth century and shows the role of the University of Leiden, the center of Arabic studies in the Netherlands, in the seventeenth century.

Illustrated Costume Books

From the inventory drawn up of Rembrandt's house on the occasion of his bankruptcy in 1656 we know that he possessed a collection of properties, including "Een pertije antieckse lappen van diversche coleuren" (one lot of antique pieces of cloth in diverse colors), which doubtless contained Oriental textiles.[5] Oriental garments are lacking in the same inventory, but this does not prove that Rembrandt never possessed them.[6] Apart from these considerations, it is more than likely that Rembrandt and his fellow artists also drew their inspiration from prints and costume books. If they actually borrowed from these works is quite another matter.[7]

The most sophisticated of these artistic approaches to the Orient date not from the seventeenth but rather the sixteenth century, when draftsmen and engravers accompanied the first embassies of France or the Holy Roman Empire to the *Grand Signor* (Ottoman Emperor) in Constantinople. Rembrandt may have seen an early example of this pictorial tradition in the library of Leiden University. It is an almost twelve-meter-wide panorama of Constantinople by the artist Melchior Lorck (Lorch, Lorichs) from Flensburg (1526/27–after 1583). An engraving from 1610 shows the panorama on the left wall of the library building (figs. 1–2). Lorck had spent the late 1550s in the entourage of the Imperial ambassador, the Fleming Ogier Ghislain de Busbecq (Busbequius). He also made drawings of the sultan, his courtiers, officials, and soldiers, and woodcuts made from these drawings were reprinted until the end of the seventeenth century (fig. 3).[8]

Rembrandt's inventory mentions a book (or more likely album) "full of Turkish buildings, Melchior Lorich, Hendrick van Aelst, and others, depicting Turkish life"—"Turkish" being a holdall term for any given Muslim people from the Ottoman Empire.[9] The Hendrick van Aelst mentioned is almost certainly identical with the Flemish artist Pieter Coecke van Aelst (1502–1550), who in 1533 visited Constantinople in the retinue of the Imperial ambassador Cornelis de Schepper. Coecke made a large, multipanel woodcut of the journey of the ambassadorial train from Serbia to Constantinople, which shows many Turks in their flamboyant costume from the lowliest servant to Sultan Süleyman I.[10] Another entry in Rembrandt's inventory is a book or album "full of curious miniature drawings, as well as various woodcuts and copper prints of miscellaneous costumes."[11] Such costume books invariably included "Turks" in their presumed native dress.

One of the great centers where illustrated costume books on the East were published was the city of Antwerp. It was part of the Holy Roman Empire, and Emperor Charles V had his court in nearby Brussels. But it was also close to France, another major European power. In 1553 Pieter Coecke van Aelst's large panorama was published posthumously in Antwerp by his widow. In 1576 the Antwerp printer Willem Silvius published the illustrated travels of Nicolas de Nicolay (1517–1583), who in 1551 joined the French embassy to the Sublime Porte headed by Gabriel d'Aramon. Nicolay's sketches were true to life, but in the case of high-ranking ladies from the Serail he had recourse to prostitutes, whom he had dressed up in costumes obtained from palace eunuchs (fig. 4).[12] His illustrations were also reissued in a larger format by Abraham de Bruyn in Antwerp in 1581.[13]

Closely associated with the Antwerp art scene was the Italian artist Antonio Tempesta (1555–1630, see cat. 108–09), whose etchings were also represented in Rembrandt's collection.[14] He had never been to the Orient, but included rather incongruous-looking Turkish characters with turbans and drooping moustaches in his scenes of the *Works of Alexander the Great* of 1608 (fig. 5),[15] and also illustrated a cavalcade of the Ottoman sultan, probably after the work of Pieter Coecke

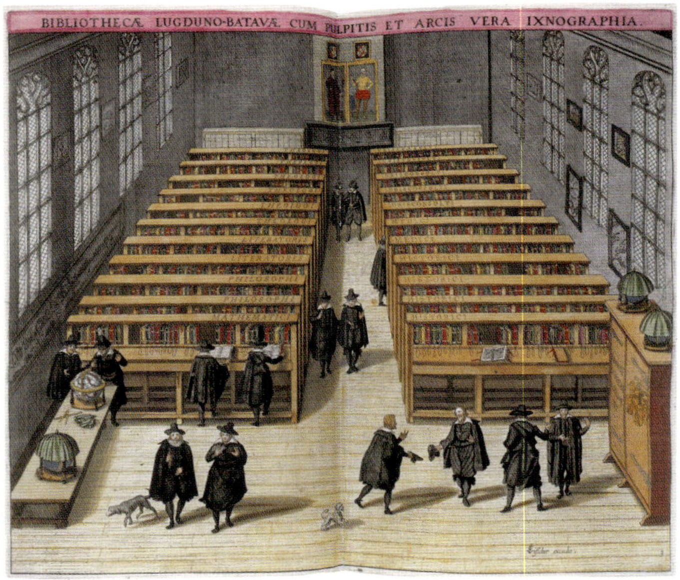

1 Willem van Swanenburg after Jan Cornelisz. van 't Woudt, *The Library of Leiden University,* colored engraving, 1610, Leiden University Libraries

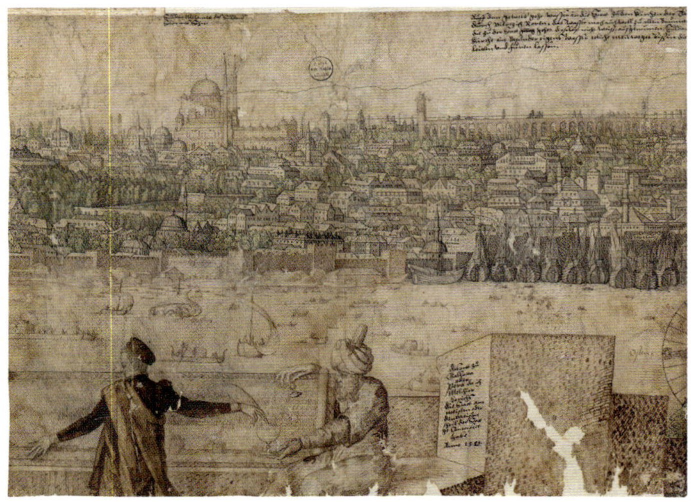

2 Melchior Lorck, *Prospect of Constantinople, Self-Portrait of the Artist with a Turk Holding an Inkwell* (detail), 1559, Leiden University Libraries

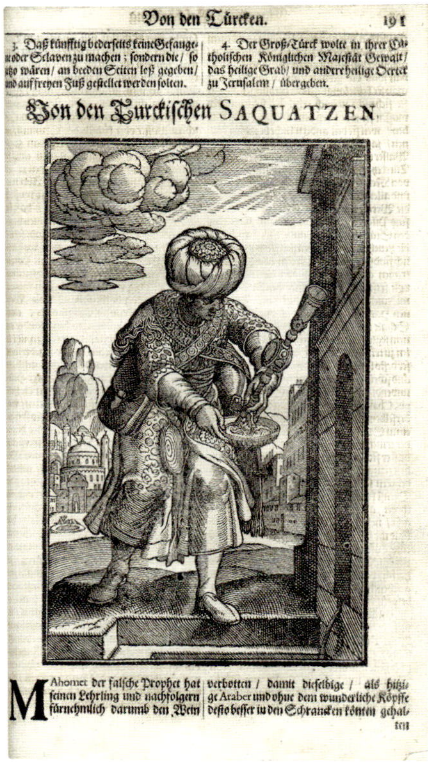

Von den Türcken. 191

3. Daß künfftig bederseits keine Gefange- ne oder Sclaven zu machen; sondern die/ so itzo wären/ an beeden Seiten leß gegeben/ und auf freyen Fuß gestellet werden solten.

4. Der Groß-Türck wolte in ihrer Ca- tholischen Königlichen Majestät Gewalt/ das heilige Grab/ und andere heilige Oerter zu Jerusalem/ übergeben.

Von den Turckischen SAQUATZEN.

MAhomet der falsche Prophet hat seinen Lehrling und nachfolgern fürnehmlich darumb den Wein verbotten / damit dieselbige / als hitzi- ge Araber und ohne dem wunderliche Köpffe desto besser in den Schrancken könten gehal- ten

3 Anonymous after Melchior Lorck, *A Turkish* Saka *or Water Seller,* in Everhardus Guernerus Happelius, *Thesaurus exoticorum . . . ,* Hamburg 1688, p. 191, Leiden University Libraries

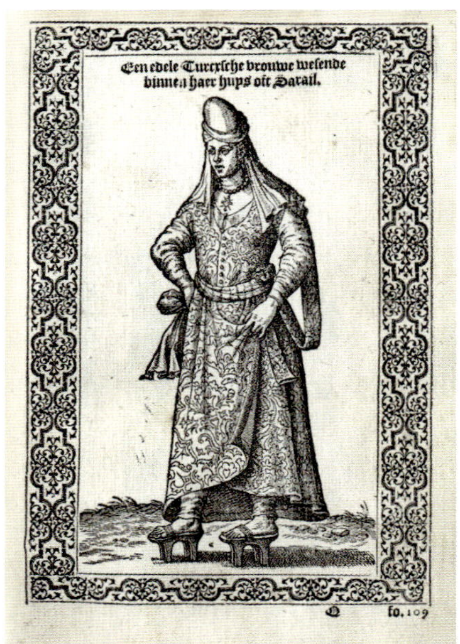

4 Anonymous after Nicolas de Nicolay, *A Noble Turkish Lady in Her Home or Serail,* in Nicolas de Nicolay, *De schipvaert ende reysen gedaen int landt van Turckyen,* Antwerp 1576, p. 110, Leiden University Libraries

van Aelst.[16] Not attested to in Rembrandt's inventory is the work of the Swiss-German woodblock engraver Jost Amman (1539–1591), whose popular depictions of Turks were published in Frankfurt am Main in the *Türckische Chronica* of 1577 and elsewhere. Like Tempesta, he never traveled to the Orient himself, so he must have based his work on earlier models. Nevertheless, his work is lively, elegant, and perfectly executed (fig. 6).[17]

Artists freely copied each other's work, and as a result the image of Turks developed into a genre of its own that did not necessarily realistically reflect sartorial culture in the Ottoman Empire. As an example, only the use of color shall be mentioned. A copy of Abraham de Bruyn's costume book kept in Antwerp shows two Turks, a woman from Syria, and a Persian in their native dress, dyed in subtle, natural hues (fig. 7), and these are the same colors one sees in the paintings of Rembrandt and his contemporaries such as Jan Lievens (cat. 58).[18] But original samples of Ottoman textiles in vibrant colors and strikingly bold designs show that the European interpretation was perhaps "pretty" but far from reality.[19] It may even be impossible to determine what a genuine "Oriental" textile looked like. As one of the most frequently traded commodities in the premodern world, textiles played a critical role in the transfer of motifs within the Islamic world and between it and its European and East Asian trading partners. In India, for example, there was both artisanal expertise as well as a willing ability to copy European and particularly English fabrics. As early as 1617 the English ambassador Sir Thomas Roe wrote of Indian artisans: "They imitate everything wee bring, and embroder now as well as wee."[20] On the other side of the globe a similar situation prevailed, for in the mid-seventeenth century thousands of Leiden weavers were employed in the manufacture of woolen camlets or "Turkish cloths" from imported Anatolian mohair (either raw wool or undyed yarn), which were dyed in the bright colors that appealed to Ottoman tastes and then exported to the Middle East.[21]

In contrast "Turkish" woodcuts and engravings from the sixteenth century onwards were the most widespread and cheapest images available to both artists and the general public, and they must have influenced the public's mindset as to what a Turk was supposed to look like. It is doubtful whether Rembrandt ever tried to render an authentic image of a contemporary Turk or Persian, since many of his Oriental paintings are devoted to Biblical subjects. More likely, it was quite enough for him to recreate the theatrical panache of a large turban with exotic feathers, flowing robes, and flashing scimitars (see cat. 60, 68, 73–75).

Pioneering Orientalists

The French and Imperial embassies to the Ottoman Empire not only indirectly underpinned the visual tradition of Rembrandt's Orient, but were also present at the cradle of Dutch Orientalism and its collections of relevant manuscripts and rare books. The origins of this new academic tradition in the nascent Dutch Republic go back to the year 1534, when King François I of France sent his ambassador Jean de La Forêt to Constantinople to negotiate a treaty or so-called Capitulations with the Ottoman Sultan Süleyman I the Magnificent. In the friction between the Ottomans and the Holy Roman Empire, the sultan granted both friendship and extensive trading privileges to France, the Empire's main contestant for supremacy in Catholic Europe.

A member of the ambassador's entourage was the French scholar Guillaume Postel (1510–1581), who had taught himself a smattering of Arabic.[22] He returned to France in 1537, after he had improved his Arabic, learned the rudiments of Turkish, and acquired a number of Oriental manuscripts. The following year he became the first professor of Arabic in Western Europe and wrote the first printed grammar of the Arabic language in the West. François I appointed Postel to his own Collège royal, not only for his prowess as a scholar but also because the knowledge of Oriental languages figured prominently on the political agenda. In 1550 Postel visited Constantinople a second time to join the entourage of Ambassador Gabriel d'Aramon.

Some of Guillaume Postel's pupils eventually made it to Leiden, where they founded Dutch Oriental studies and established collections of Oriental manuscripts. The ascendancy of these pioneers was linked to the political and economic circumstances in the Dutch Republic.

In 1568 Protestant forces in the Netherlands rebelled against the Catholic hegemony of Spain under King Philip II. This led in 1575 to the foundation of the first university in the new Republic in Leiden. Ten years later, in 1585, Spanish troops took the city of Antwerp, the greatest cultural and economic center of the Netherlands. One of the thousands who sought refuge in the Protestant North was Franciscus Raphelengius the Elder (Frans van Ravelingen, 1539–1597), a Flemish scholar who had studied Arabic with Arabist Guillaume Postel. Raphelengius was an employee and son-in-law of the Antwerp printer and publisher Christophe Plantin. He was welcomed, along with many other refugees, in Leiden, where he founded a branch of the Plantin printing business and was named professor of Hebrew at the university. He was also the first to teach Arabic at Leiden.[23] Raphelengius came into possession of a small but select collection of Islamic manuscripts—probably as a result of the hostilities between the Holy Roman Empire and the Ottoman Empire.[24]

In 1533 the Ottomans dispatched their admiral Khair ad-Din Barbarossa to capture Tunis from its ruler Mulay Ahmad, a vassal of Emperor Charles V. Two years later the emperor retaliated by retaking Tunis in a massive naval expedition. The city and adjoining regions were plundered, including mosques and libraries, and in this way a number of Islamic manuscripts found their way to the West. It is quite possible that one of these, an Arabic manuscript containing part of the Quran, eventually came into the possession of Franciscus Raphelengius. A note in Arabic at the beginning of the book informs us that in December 1505 it was the property of a mosque in Binzart (Bizerte), a coastal town not far from Tunis (fig. 8).[25]

The second example is an Ottoman compendium of Islamic law that was taken as spoils during the Battle of Lepanto on October 7, 1571, fought between the Holy League under Don Juan de Austria and the Ottoman fleet.[26] The manuscript contains an inscription in Spanish explaining the circumstances under which it was taken. Not long afterwards this manuscript came to Raphelengius, and in 1626 it was added to the collections of Leiden University Library. Nowhere is the antagonism between Islam and Christianity better expressed than in the unusual description of the provenance of this particular item in the Leiden catalog of 1674 where it states "this copy was wrested from the Turks in the famous naval battle that took place at Naupaktos [Lepanto] in AD 1571, where the Christians won the day."[27]

The first noteworthy Oriental manuscript collection entered the Leiden University Library in 1609 upon the death of the French Protestant scholar Joseph Justus Scaliger (1540–1609). Finding life in France increasingly difficult for Protestants due to the upheavals of the French wars of religion, he rather unwillingly emigrated to the northern Netherlands and in 1593 made his triumphant entry at Leiden as a celebrated universal scholar. In 1562, when he was a student in Paris, Scaliger had taken his first Arabic lessons from the aforementioned scholar Guillaume Postel, and until the last years of his life he dedicated himself to the study of this language.[28]

Like Raphelengius, he never traveled to the East, but nevertheless collected more than fifty Middle Eastern manuscripts, which reached him through a network of scholars and merchants that spread across Europe and beyond to Constantinople. At least one manuscript, containing the *Golestan* (Rose Garden), a book of popular wisdom by the Persian poet Saadi from Shiraz (1210–1291/92), is related to acts of war (fig. 9). It bears an annotation by a certain Carll Kuningk, a captain in the Imperial army, written in the citadel of Comorn (Komárno or Komárom) on the present-day Slovak-Hungarian border and dated July 31, 1566. The note explains that the manuscript was

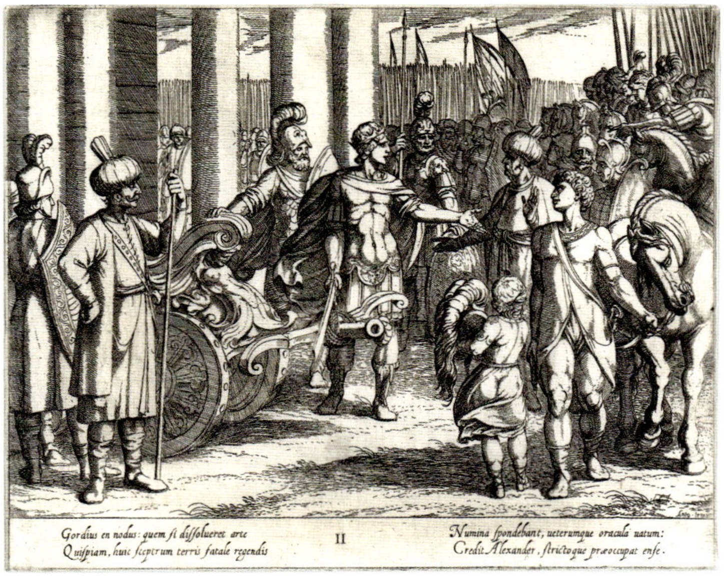

5 Antonio Tempesta,
Alexander the Great Cutting the Gordian Knot in the Presence of Turbaned "Turks," in *Alexandri Magni praecipue res gestae,* Antwerp 1608, plate 2, Leiden University Libraries

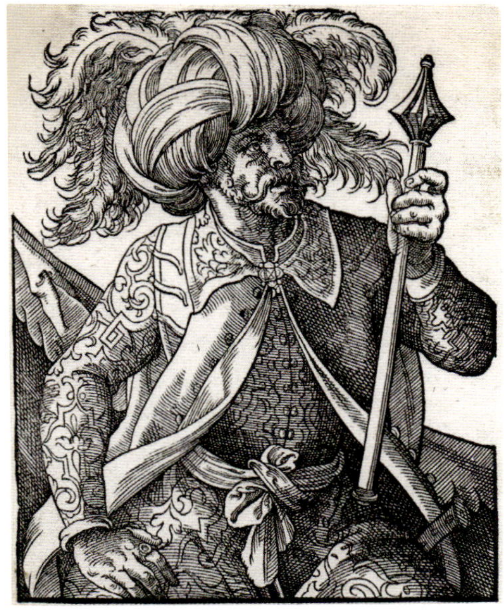

6 Jost Amman,
Ottoman Deli *or Member of the Irregular Light Cavalry,* in Vasco Díaz Tanco,
Türckische Chronica . . . , Frankfurt am Main 1577,
Leiden University Libraries

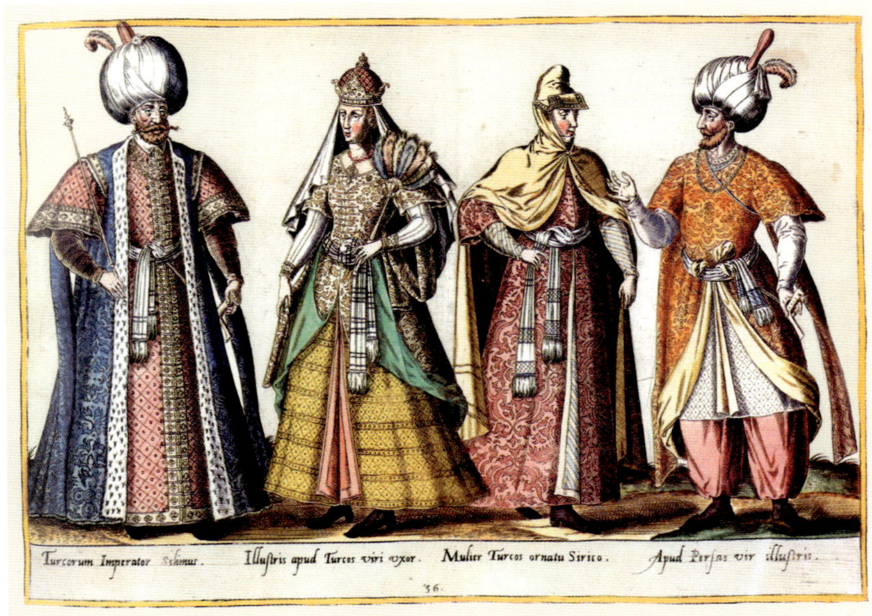

7 Anonymous after Nicolas de Nicolay,
Turkish, Arab, and Persian Costumes, in Abraham de Bruyn,
Omnium pene Europae, Asiae, Aphricae atque Americae gentium habitus . . . ,
Antwerp 1581, p. 36, Stedelijk Prentenkabinet, Antwerp

found in a fortress reclaimed from the Turks, and this circumstance would place the manuscript right in the middle of the endless border conflicts between the Holy Roman Empire and the Ottomans.[29]

Unexpected Business Opportunities

The Netherlands gradually carved out a position for itself and thus became independent of other nations in its political, mercantile, and academic relations with the East. In 1595, for instance, it embarked on the first Dutch expedition to the Indies. A little earlier Franciscus Raphelengius, who was still active as a printer, had presented his newly designed Arabic types, the first in Europe outside Rome. He used these types to print an Arabic translation of a letter from Stadtholder Maurits of Nassau, requesting a safe passage for the ships and crew of the expedition.[30] In 1599 the first Dutch ship sailed to the Levant, to be followed by countless others. Eleven years later, in 1610, the States General of the Republic concluded a treaty with the sultan of Morocco and in 1612 Sultan Ahmed I rounded off his ring of anti-Habsburg alliances by granting "Capitulations" to the Dutch Republic.[31] A Dutch ambassador, Cornelis Haga, was dispatched to Constantinople and consulates were established in major centers of commerce such as Smyrna, Aleppo, and Cairo.

The new treaty with the Ottomans opened up unprecedented business opportunities for the Dutch, and the revenues it yielded sustained the power and wealth of the Dutch Republic. Artists added Oriental or pseudo-Oriental elements to their work to emphasize their patrons' sudden rise to fortune. Scholarship contributed in a significant way by amassing texts on the history, geography, medicine, mathematics, and religion of the Orient as well as literature in the most important languages of the East. Among these languages, Arabic, the language par excellence of the Muslim world, played a dominant role, and the regions where this language was spoken naturally received more attention than others from Dutch scholars.

Diplomacy facilitated both trade and scholarship. The various interests of merchants and scholars resulted in collections with different emphases. Scholars amassed manuscripts written in languages that were inaccessible to nonspecialists and focused almost exclusively on texts. In contrast, merchants acquired Oriental manuscripts for their "exotic" incidentals, for example, if they contained interesting miniatures. In the age of chambers of curiosities, these were part of a fascination with the unknown.

On the cultural level, high-ranking Dutch diplomats were closer to the scholars than the merchants. In several cases they helped scholars acquire manuscripts, and the largest single collection of Oriental manuscripts in seventeenth-century Leiden was bequeathed by a diplomat who was educated as an Orientalist. Early Dutch diplomats in the Ottoman Empire such as ambassador Cornelis Haga and Cornelis Pauw, the first consul in Aleppo, also brought together collections of "souvenirs," paintings, and manuscripts.[32]

The Excellence and Dignity of Arabic

In 1613, only one year after the Ottoman "Capitulations" to the Dutch Republic, the first chair for Arabic and other Oriental languages was established at Leiden. In his public oration "On the Excellence and Dignity of the Arabic Language," the first incumbent, Thomas Erpenius (1584–1624),[33] summed up the traditional arguments for learning Arabic: the wealth of information in Arabic historical and scientific texts, the lost knowledge of Greek antiquity that was preserved only in Arabic, and the linguistic proximity of Arabic to biblical Hebrew that could be so useful in the interpretation of difficult passages in the Old Testament. But the main reason for studying Arabic, he claimed, was "to bring back to Christ all those who had been deceived by the Ishmaelite impostor Mohammed."[34]

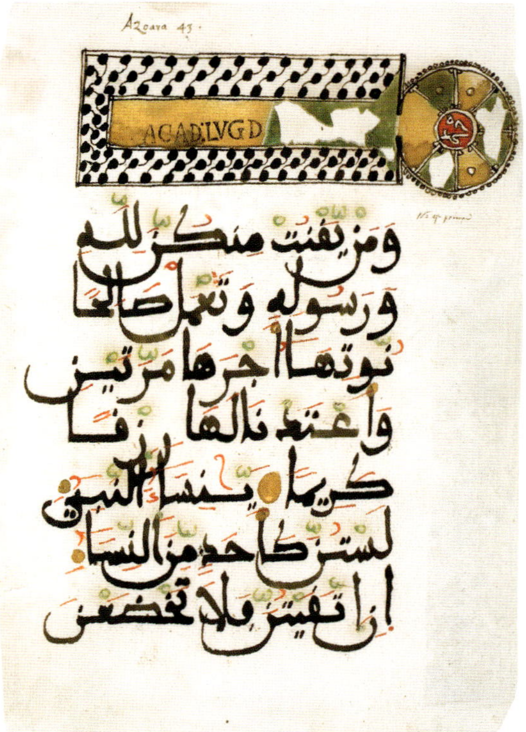

8 Opening page of a Quran fragment,
North African manuscript, probably 14th–15th century,
Leiden University Libraries, Or. 241

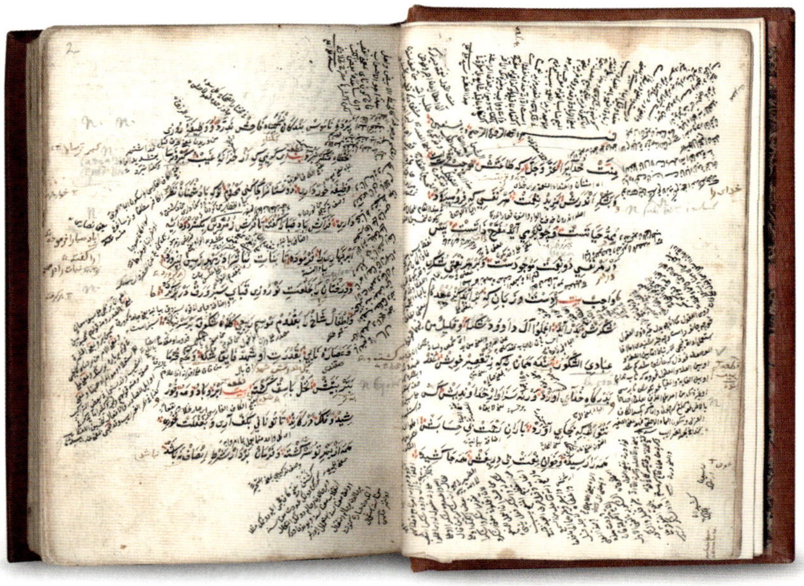

9 Saadi, *Golestan* (Rose Garden),
Persian manuscript with Turkish notes, 1566, fol. 1b–2a,
Leiden University Libraries, Scaliger collection, Or. 242

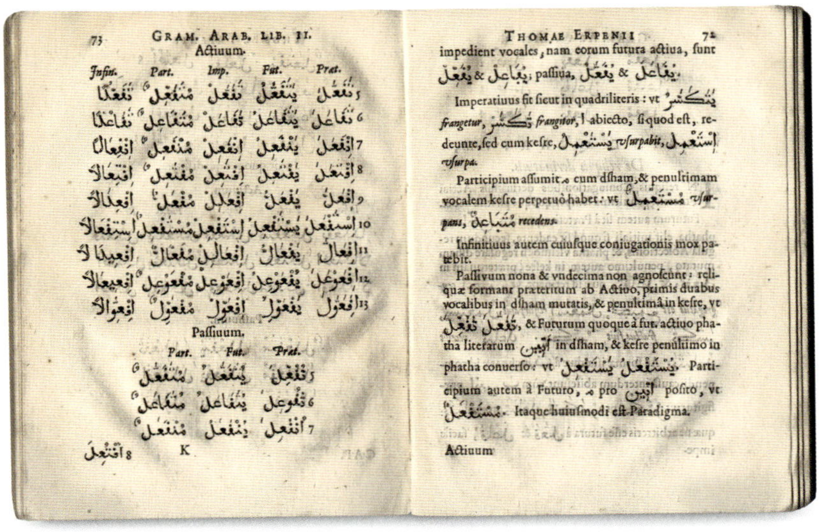

10 Examples of Arabic verbs,
in Thomas Erpenius, *Grammatica arabica,*
Leiden 1613, pp. 72–73,
Leiden University Libraries

The last-mentioned thesis was probably only meant to be understood rhetorically, for the board of governors of Leiden University do not seem to have shared the missionary fervor to convert the Muslims to Protestant Christianity. According to these gentlemen, Arabic would be "useful for the faculty of medicine and other faculties." There is, however, not a single word on the question of converting the Muslims. On an earlier occasion the Board had declared that the knowledge of Arabic would be "useful for the Asian trade." The Dutch had strong feelings against Islam, but among the elite of the Republic these feelings were restrained or played down for commercial gain.[35]

Erpenius was the first Dutch scholar who, upon his graduation in 1608, traveled to England and subsequently France to learn Arabic. In England he met the Arabist William Bedwell, and in Paris he was in close touch with Arabists such as Étienne Hubert, professor at the Collège royal, and Isaac Casaubon, custodian of the Bibliothèque royale. He intended to travel to the Orient, but never proceeded beyond Venice. In spite of this, he assembled a collection of more than eighty Oriental manuscripts, which after his death in 1624 were sold by his widow to the Englishman George Villiers, the first Duke of Buckingham. They are now in the Cambridge University Library.

The manuscripts were lost to Leiden, but Erpenius established a Dutch tradition of Arabic studies with his *Grammatica arabica*, first published in 1613 and a bestseller until the nineteenth century (fig. 10). He was professor at Leiden when Rembrandt was a student there, and they are likely to have seen one another. They were both in the same faculty, and the University was, after all, still a small school in those days, with an enrolment of little more than three hundred new students every year.[36] It cannot have escaped Rembrandt that a language such as Arabic was on the curriculum, but there is nothing to prove that he ever learned any of the language. In any case, it must have contributed to his awareness that the Orient was an integral part of academic life.

When Erpenius died in 1624 he was succeeded by his pupil Jacobus Golius (1596–1667), a scion of a prominent family from The Hague that was embedded in the government of the Dutch Republic.[37] When Erpenius was a student he had been obliged to travel to England and France to learn Arabic; Golius, on the other hand, could sit at the feet of a chaired professor at less than twenty kilometers from his hometown. Golius had started out as a student of mathematics, physics, and astronomy, but only after his graduation in 1616 did he realize that he needed to know Arabic to gain access to the source texts that were unavailable in translation. In 1618 he returned to Leiden University and studied Arabic with Erpenius until 1621. After that he enjoyed the full benefits of the Dutch diplomatic and commercial network in North Africa and the Levant. In 1622, for instance, he was added to a Dutch mission to Morocco, where he acquired his first Islamic manuscripts.[38] In 1624 Golius returned to Holland, in time to bury his professor and secure an appointment as his successor.

Scholarly Manuscripts

Before taking up his teaching duties, though, Golius obtained permission from the university to travel to the Orient one more time and received a generous budget of two thousand guilders—a small fortune in those days—to buy manuscripts. He left in 1625 and lived with the Dutch consul in Aleppo, Syria, where he bought manuscripts or arranged for copies to be made if the originals were unavailable. In 1627 he left for Constantinople, where he stayed as a guest of the first Dutch ambassador, Cornelis Haga. In both cities he performed translation work and other chancery services to earn his keep.

When he returned to the Dutch Republic in 1629, Golius turned out to have overspent his budget by an impressive twelve hundred guilders. Nevertheless, the governors of the university decided not only fully to reimburse these expenses, but also appointed him professor of mathematics. During his lifetime, Golius acquired more than two hundred Middle Eastern manuscripts for his university. Golius died in 1667, two years before Rembrandt, and like the painter he, with his activity as a collector, represents the heyday of the Dutch Republic.

Golius's choice of manuscripts was far from typical in terms of Middle Eastern *Schrifttum*, in which religious literature, the Quran and Quranic exegesis, prayer books, and other works of devotion, theology and mysticism, and Islamic law in all its varieties prevail. Golius's collection, though not entirely lacking in religious texts, is mainly devoted to secular subjects: algebra and geometry, astronomy, geography, medicine, history, lexicography, and belles lettres. Some manuscripts were already ancient when they were acquired in the second quarter of the seventeenth century; many stand out through their exceptional provenance. Some manuscripts are exquisite artworks, but none were chosen for their aesthetic value. Manuscripts with attractive and colorful miniatures are practically absent, but many contain well-made diagrams, tables, maps, or fine drawings of sophisticated machinery (figs. 11–12).

The manuscripts and Golius's letters reveal that he was in close touch with local scholars and scribes who generously shared their expertise with the foreign scholar from Holland. In addition to the manuscripts that Golius bought for Leiden University, he also assembled a private collection of roughly equal size and value, which was auctioned off in 1696—almost three decades after his death. Apart from some minor items, it is now in the Bodleian Library, Oxford.[39]

It was not only Golius's manuscript collection that brought him fame, but also his achievements as a scholar and teacher. The best proof of his didactic spirit is his *Lexicon Arabico-Latinum*, published in 1653. This dictionary is based on the classical lexicographical sources he unearthed in the Middle East. The huge and expensive folio edition was never reprinted but remained in use throughout Europe until it was finally replaced by a greatly expanded new edition by the German scholar Georg Wilhelm Friedrich Freytag in the 1830s.

Scholars from Germany and Switzerland

Golius was a gifted teacher who attracted many students from abroad, especially from the German-speaking lands. However, there were two sides to this influx. The Thirty Years' War, which raged from 1618 to 1648 in the Holy Roman Empire, caused many concerned parents to send their sons abroad for their personal safety. The Leiden matriculation records for 1626–50, for instance, show that one in every four students was a German. Some of them made their mark as Oriental scholars. They deserve our special attention, although none of them gained a foothold in Dutch academic life.

Christian Raue (Ravius, 1613–1677) was born in Berlin, studied with Golius in 1637–38 but then traveled onward to England, where he received financial support to visit the Orient.[40] He lived in Smyrna and Constantinople at the English legation and brought together a collection of some three hundred Oriental manuscripts, some of which he seems to have obtained by doubtful means. He was back in the Dutch Republic by 1642. Although Raue received permission to teach Arabic at the University of Utrecht and subsequently at the Athenaeum Illustre of Amsterdam, he failed to be appointed to a professorial chair in either place. He offered Utrecht a small collection of Oriental manuscripts that contain his elaborate dedications in bold flourishes, but this gesture did nothing to mollify his prospective employers, who seem to have had grave doubts about his qualifications. After leaving the Netherlands, Raue spent many years abroad before eventually becoming professor at Frankfurt an der Oder, where he died in 1677. His manuscript collection is now at the Staatsbibliothek in Berlin.

Another German Orientalist, Georg Gentze (Georgius Gentius, 1618–1687) from Dahme in Brandenburg, arrived in Leiden in 1638 and studied Arabic, Persian, and Turkish under Golius. In 1641 a grant from prominent Dutch merchants enabled him to travel to Constantinople in the retinue of an Ottoman envoy who had visited the Dutch Republic to renew the "Capitulations." In Constantinople he found lodging and employment at the Dutch legation. When the Dutch resident died in 1647, however, he lost his position and was forced to return to the Republic but remained unsuccessful in his efforts to find alternative employment. In 1651 he published the first Persian text edition with parallel Latin translation of the aforementioned *Golestan* of Saadi, entitled *Rosarium politicum* (Political Rose Garden), for which he used the manuscript from the battlefield that Scaliger had once possessed (figs. 9, 13). Gentze eventually returned to Germany, where he entered into the service of the elector of Saxony and other German princes.[41]

More than one Orientalist from the German-speaking lands was the victim of adversity, but none more so than the Swiss scholar Johann Heinrich Hottinger (1620–1667) from Zurich. He arrived in the Dutch Republic in 1638, studying in Groningen until 1640, when he moved to Leiden as a student of Golius. After returning to Switzerland in 1641 he became professor in Zurich, then in Heidelberg, and again in Zurich. While in Heidelberg in 1658, he published the first comprehensive Oriental bibliography of his age, the *Promptuarium sive Bibliotheca Orientalis* (The Storehouse, or Library of the Orient). Many of the Arabic entries were based on the information he had collected in Leiden under Golius's wing. Hottinger also enjoyed an excellent reputation as a Calvinist theologian, and in 1667 Golius and other scholars persuaded him to take up the chair of theology at Leiden. However, while Hottinger was traveling by boat to his estate to put his affairs in order, his vessel capsized. He drowned in the river Limmat in a desperate effort to save his fellow passengers.[42]

Levinus Warner, a German who is still remembered as one of the luminaries of Oriental studies in the Netherlands, was more successful.[43] Born around 1618 in the principality of Lippe, he received his education in Bremen, where he studied together with the aforementioned Georg Gentze. Because of Bremen's Calvinist allegiance it was quite natural for him to continue his education in the Netherlands, and on May 19, 1638, he matriculated at Leiden, where he learned Middle Eastern languages under Jacobus Golius as well as Hebrew. Upon graduation he received generous financial support from prominent scholars and other notables in the Dutch Republic to travel to the Orient. He departed in 1644, traveling overland round war-torn Germany through Poland, Ukraine, and the Balkans, as far as Constantinople (fig. 14). Warner entered into the service of Nicolaes Ghysbrechtsz., a jeweler from the southern Netherlands, and followed him as a secretary and interpreter when the latter was appointed "resident" (envoy) for the Dutch Republic in 1647. After the death of Ghysbrechtsz. in 1654 Warner received further marks of recognition when the States General in The Hague appointed him resident to the Sublime Porte. He kept this position for the rest of his short life.

Warner's salary as an envoy allowed him a lifestyle which was far beyond the expectations of any Leiden professor, but in addition he was entitled to a percentage of all Dutch trade entering or leaving the Ottoman Empire. Though living in the comfortable seclusion of the European diplomatic quarter in Pera on the other side of the Golden Horn, he sought the company of Ottoman men of letters and scribes, and his fellow Europeans accused him of living "entirely after the Turkish fashion." This reproach was accompanied, however, by a far more serious complaint from the Dutch merchant colony in Smyrna that he spent far too much of his time and money collecting Oriental manuscripts. This complaint appears to have been fully justified.

With the help of Syrian Christian intermediaries Warner skimmed the cream off the antiquarian book market and acquired over nine hundred manuscripts in the three major languages of the vast Ottoman Empire: Arabic, Persian, and Turkish, and an additional eighty manuscripts in Hebrew. He had not only a deep purse but also a discerning eye. His acquisitions include a copy of the *Shahnameh* (Book of Kings), the national epic of Persia, dated 1437 with many splendid miniatures in the Timurid style (fig. 15). He also purchased the unique manuscript of the *Tawq al-Hamama* (Ring of the Dove), a work on love and friendship by the Andalusian religious scholar Ibn Hazm of Cordoba, who died in 1064 (fig. 16).[44]

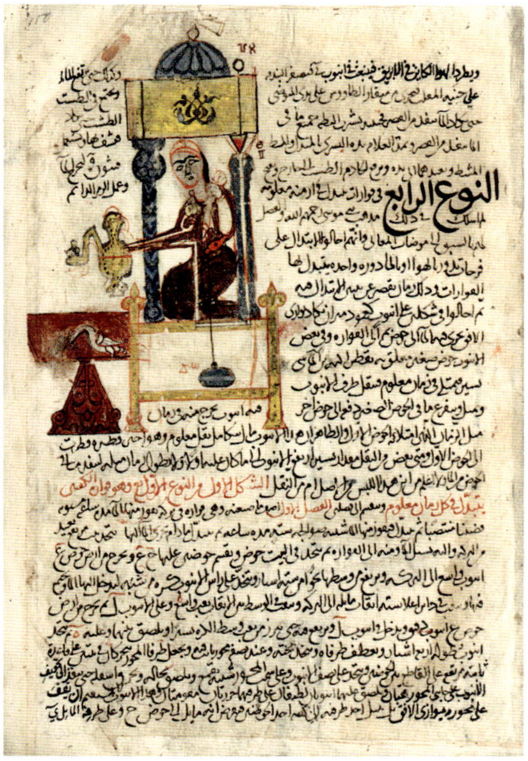

11 *Automaton Water Clock*,
in al-Jazari, *Book of Knowledge of Ingenious Mechanical Devices,* Arabic manuscript, ca. 1200, fol. 150a,
Leiden University Libraries, Golius collection, Or. 117

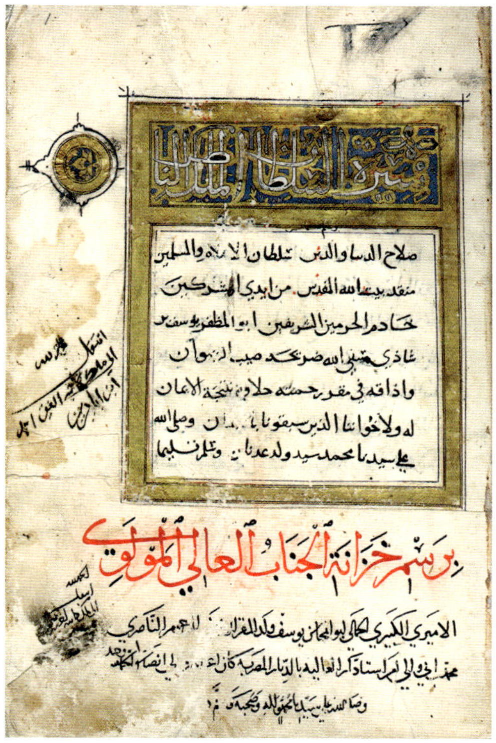

12 Title page, in Ibn Shaddad,
Biography of Sultan Saladin, Arabic manuscript, 1334,
Leiden University Libraries, Golius collection, Or. 9

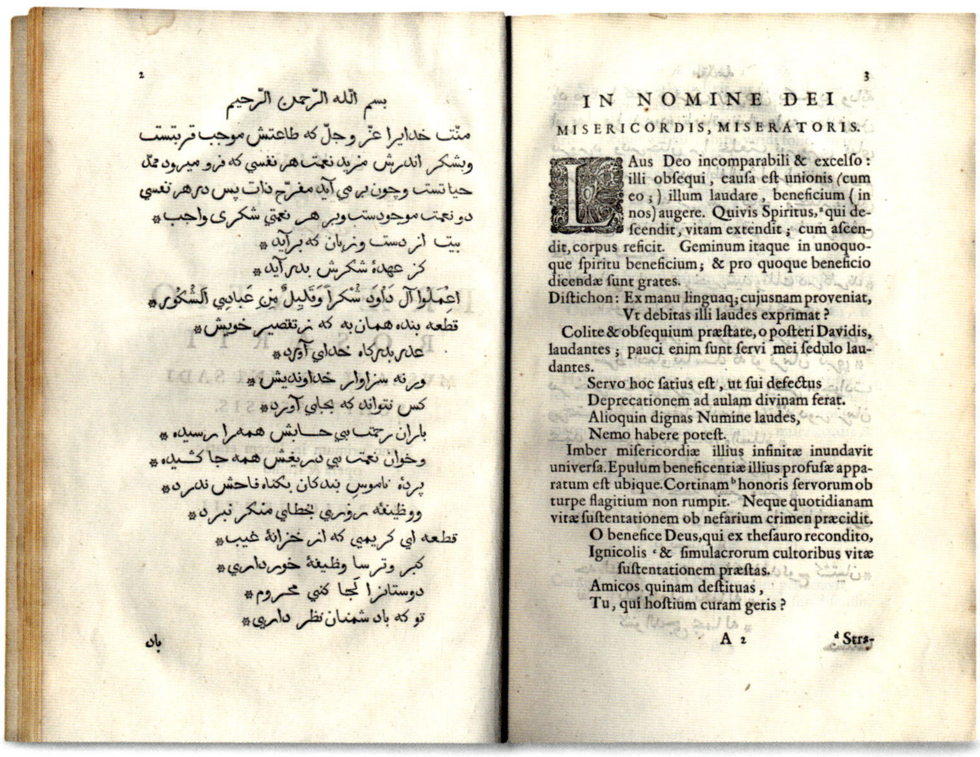

2

بسم الله الرحمن الرحيم

3

IN NOMINE DEI
MISERICORDIS, MISERATORIS.

LAus Deo incomparabili & excelſo: illi obſequi, cauſa eſt unionis (cum eo;) illum laudare, beneficium (in nos) augere. Quivis Spiritus,ª qui deſcendit, vitam extendit; cum aſcendit, corpus reficit. Geminum itaque in unoquoque ſpiritu beneficium; & pro quoque beneficio dicendæ ſunt grates.

Diſtichon: Ex manu linguaq; cujusnam proveniat,
Vt debitas illi laudes exprimat?

Colite & obſequium præſtate, o poſteri Davidis, laudantes; pauci enim ſunt ſervi mei ſedulo laudantes.

Servo hoc ſatius eſt, ut ſui defectus
Deprecationem ad aulam divinam ferat.
Alioquin dignas Numine laudes,
Nemo habere poteſt.

Imber miſericordiæ illius infinitæ inundavit univerſa. Epulum beneficentiæ illius profuſæ apparatum eſt ubique. Cortinam[b] honoris ſervorum ob turpe flagitium non rumpit. Neque quotidianam vitæ ſuſtentationem ob nefarium crimen præcidit.

O benefice Deus, qui ex theſauro recondito,
Ignicolis[c] & ſimulacrorum cultoribus vitæ
ſuſtentationem præſtas.
Amicos quinam deſtituas,
Tu, qui hoſtium curam geris?

A 2 [d] Stra-

13 Title pages in Persian and Latin,
in Georgius Gentius, *Rosarium politicum,* Amsterdam 1651,
Leiden University Libraries

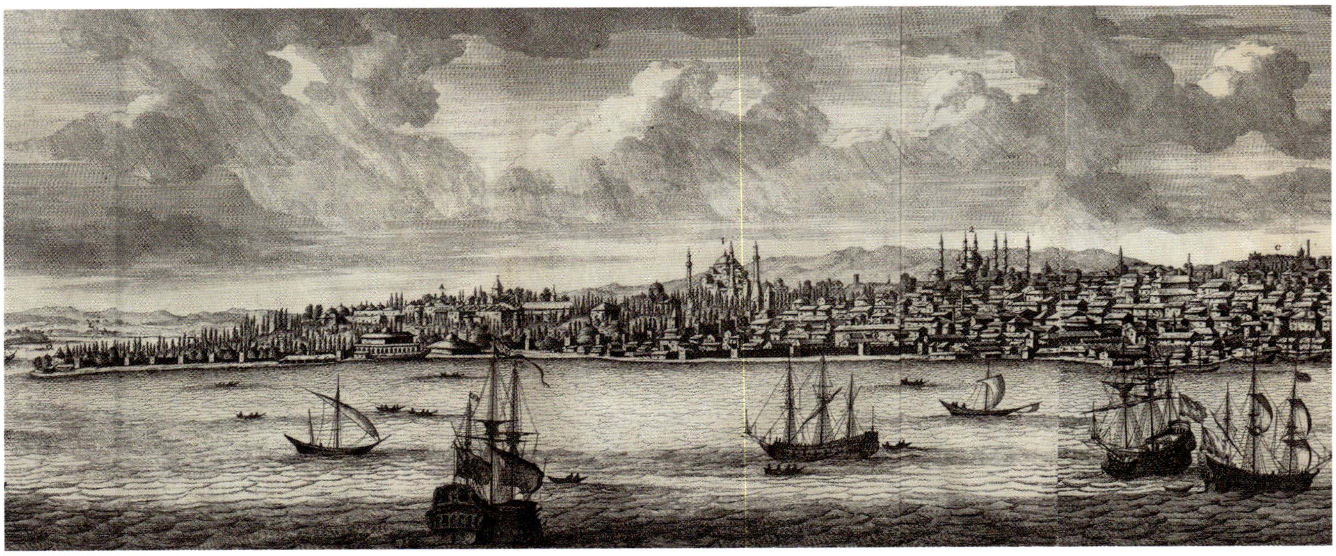

14 Anonymous after Cornelis de Bruyn,
View of Constantinople (detail), 1670s, in *Reizen van Cornelis de Bruyn . . .*,
Delft 1698, plate 22A, Leiden University Libraries

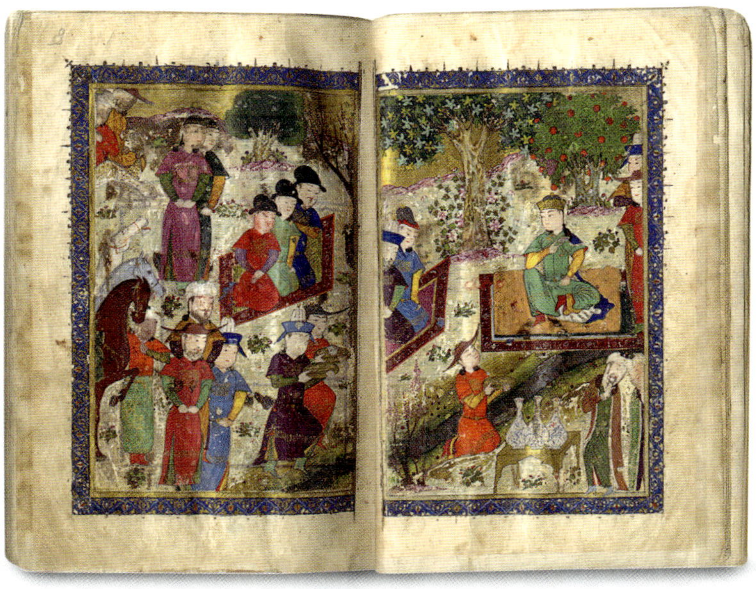

15 Anonymous,
Royal Audience, in Abolqasem Firdausi, *Shahnameh* (Book of Kings),
Persian manuscript, 1437, fol. 7b–8a, Leiden University Libraries,
Warner collection, Or. 494

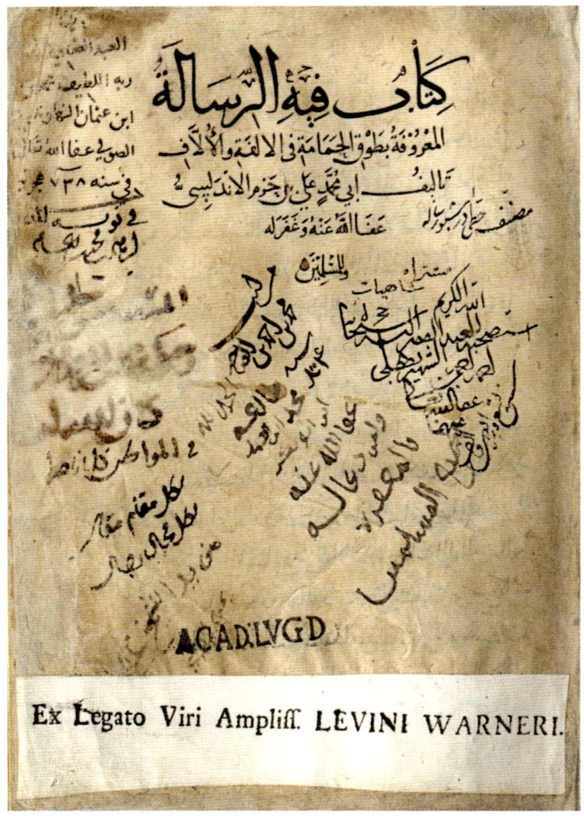

16 Title page, in Ibn Hazm,
Tawq al-Hamama (Ring of the Dove), Arabic manuscript, 1337,
Leiden University Libraries, Warner collection, Or. 927

Levinus Warner died in 1665 without ever seeing his home country again. As an act of recognition toward the country that had adopted him, he bequeathed his collection to the University of Leiden, where he had once been a student. It is still the largest and most valuable single Oriental collection that Leiden ever acquired and a veritable gold mine of knowledge for the international scholarly community. The importance of the manuscript collection also contributed to the fact that philology played a dominant role in Oriental studies at Leiden until nearly the end of the twentieth century. Afterwards, modern Middle Eastern studies with a social scientific focus took its place.

In conclusion, it can be said that although Rembrandt and the Dutch Orientalists of the seventeenth century belonged to different spheres of life, they profited, materially as well as culturally, from the emergence of the Dutch Republic as a global player in the mercantile expansion in Asia and the concurrent creation of a diplomatic network.

1 [Gulielmus Du Rieu], *Album studiosorum Academiae Lugduno-Batavae, MDLXXV–MDCCCLXXV: Accedunt nomina curatorum et professorum*, The Hague 1875, col. 147; MS Leiden University Libraries, Archief Senaat en Faculteiten 8, p. 45.

2 Jef Schaeps and Mart van Duijn, *Rembrandt en de Universiteit Leiden*, Leiden 2019, 25–31.

3 See Schwartz 2006, 296.

4 See Scarce 2013, 68. But please note that no such meeting between Rembrandt and Jan Lucasz. van Hasselt is mentioned in Schwartz 2013, 158–60.

5 Amsterdam 1999a, Appendix 2, no. 336.

6 See Schwartz 2006, 141.

7 See De Winkel 2006, 260.

8 On Lorck or Lorichs, see Amanda Wunder, "Western Travelers, Eastern Antiquities, and the Image of the Turk in Early Modern Europe," in *Journal of Early Modern History* 7, 1–2 (2003), 89–119, here 103–08; Wanda den Boer, "Oriëntalisme en het kostuum," in Schaeps/van Ommen/Vrolijk 2005, 31–48, here 38. For a late reissue of Lorck's images, see Everhardus Guernerus Happelius, *Thesaurus exoticorum, oder eine mit Ausländischen Raritäten und Geschichten wohlversehene Schatz-Kammer . . .*, Hamburg 1688.

9 Amsterdam 1999a, 150, Appendix 2, no. 234: "een boeck vol Turcxe gebouwen, Melchior Lorich, Hendrick van Aelst en andere meer, uytbeeldende het Turcxe leven."

10 On Pieter Coecke van Aelst, see Alastair Hamilton, *Arab Culture and Ottoman Magnificence in Antwerp's Golden Age*, London, Oxford, and New York 2001, 20, 27–33; Wunder 2003 (see note 8), 108–14.

11 Amsterdam 1999a, 149, Appendix 2, no. 203: "Een boeck vol curieuse minyateur teeckeninge nevens verscheyde hout en kopere printe van alderhande dragt."

12 Nicolas de Nicolay, *De schipvaert ende reysen gedaen int landt van Turckyen*, Antwerp 1576; Den Boer 2005 (see note 8), 37; De Winkel 2006, 260, acknowledges the popularity of De Nicolay's prints, but ignores the fact that they were based on firsthand observation; Charlotte Colding Smith, *Images of Islam, 1453–1600: Turks in Germany and Central Europe*, London 2014, 118.

13 Abraham de Bruyn, *Omnium pene Europae, Asiae, Aphricae atque Americae gentium habitus . . .*, Antwerp 1581.

14 Amsterdam 1999a, 130, Appendix 2, nos. 207, 210.

15 Antonio Tempesta, *Alexandri Magni praecipuae res gestae*, Antwerp 1608, plate II.

16 Hamilton 2001 (see note 10), 20, 22–26.

17 Smith 2014 (see note 12), 152–54.

18 Hamilton 2001 (see note 10), 26–27.

19 See Nurhan Atasoy et al., *İpek: The Crescent & the Rose: Imperial Ottoman Silks and Velvets*, London 2001.

20 Cited in Dede Fairchild Ruggles, *Islamic Gardens and Landscapes*, Philadelphia 2008, 121.

21 Arnoud Vrolijk, Jan Schmidt, and Karin Scheper, *Turcksche Boucken: The Oriental Collection of Levinus Warner, Dutch Diplomat in Seventeenth-Century Istanbul*, Eindhoven 2012, 65–70, with reference to Nicolaas Wilhelmus Posthumus, *De geschiedenis van de Leidsche lakenindustrie*, 3 vols., The Hague 1908–39, vol. 2, 272–79, 304–06, 324–27; vol. 3, 760, 767–68.

22 On Guillaume Postel see, for instance, William J. Bouwsma, *Concordia Mundi: The Career and Thought of Guillaume Postel (1510–1581)*, Cambridge MA, 1957; Marion L. Kuntz, *Guillaume Postel: Prophet of the Restitution of All Things: His Life and Thought*, The Hague and Boston 1981.

23 On Franciscus Raphelengius, see Wilhelmina Maria Cornelia Juynboll, *Zeventiende-eeuwsche beoefenaars van het Arabisch in Nederland*, Utrecht 1931, 36–45; Francine de Nave, "Franciscus Raphelengius (1539–1597): grondlegger van de Arabische studiën in de Nederlanden," in *Ex officina Plantiniana: Studia in memoriam Christophori Plantini (ca. 1520–1589)*, ed. Marcus de Schepper and Francine de Nave, Antwerp 1989, 523–55; Arnoud Vrolijk and Richard van Leeuwen, *Arabic Studies in the Netherlands: A Short History in Portraits, 1580–1950*, Leiden 2014, 17–20.

24 Alastair Hamilton, "'Nam tirones sumus': Franciscus Raphelengius's Lexicon Arabico-Latinum, Leiden, 1613," in De Schepper/De Nave 1989 (see note 23), 557–89, here 585–88.

25 Theodor Dunkelgrün, "The Hebrew Library of a Renaissance Humanist: Andreas Masius and the Bibliography to His *Iosuae Imperatoris Historia* (1574), with a Latin Edition and an Annotated English Translation," in *Studia Rosenthaliana* 42–43 (2010–11), 197–252, here 216–17. Dunkelgrün rejected the reading بنزرت (Binzart) on the flyleaf.

26 Leiden University Libraries, Or. 222.

27 *Catalogus Bibliothecae Publicae Lugduno-Batavae noviter recognitus: Accessit thesaurus librorum Orientalium praecipue MSS.*, Leiden 1674, 279: "Compendium Nomocanonis Obeidallah Arabice cum paraphrasi Turcica interlineari; Arabica vocalibus sunt insignita, non verò Turcica: hoc exemplar Turcis fuit ereptum in celebri illa navali pugna, commissa ad Naupactum A. 1571. ubi Christiani victoriam reportarunt." On this particular manuscript, see Robert Jones, "Piracy, War and the Acquisition of Arabic Manuscripts in Renaissance Europe," in *Manuscripts of the Middle East* 2 (1987), 96–110, here 100–01, with a facsimile of the letter in Spanish explaining the circumstances of the manuscript's forceful acquisition; Jones, "Learning Arabic in Renaissance Europe, 1505–1624," unpublished doctoral thesis, London 1988, 50–51.

[28] On Scaliger as an Orientalist, see Juynboll 1931 (see note 23), 45–51; Vrolijk/Van Leeuwen 2014 (see note 23), 20–27.

[29] Johannes T. P. de Bruijn, *Een Perzisch handschrift in Leiden*, Leiden 1996; Jan Schmidt, *Catalogue of Turkish Manuscripts in the Library of Leiden University and Other Collections in the Netherlands*, vol. 1, Leiden and Boston 2000, 33.

[30] Herman de Leeuw, "The First Indonesian Treaty," in *Manuscripts of the Middle East* 4 (1989), 115–22. For a comparable document from 1600, see Arnoud Vrolijk, "Scaliger and the Dutch Expansion in Asia: An Arabic Translation for an Early Voyage to the East Indies (1600)," in *Journal of the Warburg and Courtauld Institutes* 78 (2015), 277–309.

[31] For an edition and study of the Ottoman "Capitulations" awarded to the Dutch Republic, see Alexander H. de Groot, *The Ottoman Empire and the Dutch Republic: A History of the Earliest Diplomatic Relations 1610–1630*, Leiden and Istanbul 1978.

[32] Ibid., 224.

[33] On Thomas Erpenius, see Juynboll 1931 (see note 23), 59–118; Johann Fück, *Die arabischen Studien in Europa bis in den Anfang des 20. Jahrhunderts*, Leipzig 1955, 59–73; Vrolijk/Van Leeuwen 2014 (see note 23), 31–40.

[34] Thomas Erpenius, *Oratio de lingvae Arabicae praestantia & dignitate,* Leiden [ca. 1615], fol. E1.

[35] Arnoud Vrolijk and Joanna Weinberg, "Thomas Erpenius, Oriental Scholarship and the Art of Persuasion," in *Scholarship between Europe and the Levant: Essays in Honour of Alastair Hamilton*, ed. Jan Loop and Jill Kraye, Leiden and Boston 2020, 34–59, here 36–40.

[36] For matriculation figures at Leiden during the 1620s, see Du Rieu 1875 (see note 1), cols. 145–224.

[37] On Jacobus Golius, see Juynboll 1931 (see note 23), 119–83; Fück 1955 (see note 33), 79–84; Vrolijk/Van Leeuwen 2014 (see note 23), 41–48.

[38] On Golius's contacts with local Moroccan scholars, see Gerard Wiegers, *A Learned Muslim Acquaintance of Erpenius and Golius: Ahmad b. Kasim al-Andalusi and Arabic Studies in the Netherlands*, Leiden 1988.

[39] For a study of the Golius collection, see Jan Just Witkam, *Jacobus Golius (1596–1667) en zijn handschriften*, Leiden 1980; Marie Madeleine Viré, *Pierre Gassendi orientaliste, et sa publication du catalogue des manuscrits que Jacobus Golius amena d'Orient à Leyde en 1629: Avec une traduction annotée de ce catalogue*, Digne 2009. Golius's private manuscript collection was acquired by Archbishop Narcissus Marsh (1638–1713), Primate of Ireland, who bequeathed it to the Bodleian Library. The first catalog of the Golius manuscripts in the Marsh collection was published in 1697: "Bibliothecae Illustrissimi Domini Narcissi Archiepiscopi Dubliniensis nobile auctarium," in [Edward Bernard and Humphrey Wanley], *Catalogi librorum manuscriptorum Angliae et Hiberniae in unum collecti*, vol. 2, Oxford 1697, part 2, 61–65.

[40] Juynboll 1931 (see note 23), 217–22; Gerald Toomer, "Ravis [formerly Raue], Christian [Christianus Ravius] (1613–1677), Oriental and Biblical Scholar," in *Oxford Dictionary of National Biography*, Oxford 2004; http://www.oxforddnb.com/view/10.1093/ref:odnb/9780198614128.001.0001/odnb-9780198614128-e-23174 (accessed April 18, 2019). For Ravius and the Greek-Orthodox Arab from Aleppo Nicolaus Petri (arab. Niqula ibn Butrus), who accompanied Ravius to Europe, cf. Martijn Theodor Houtsma, *Uit de Oostersche correspondentie van Th. Erpenius, Jac. Golius en Lev. Warner: Eene bijdrage tot de geschiedenis van de beoefening der Oostersche letteren in Nederland*, Amsterdam 1887, 80–102; Hilary Kilpatrick and Gerald J. Toomer, "Niqūlāwus al-Ḥalabī (c. 1611–c. 1661): A Greek Orthodox Syrian Copyist and His Letters to Pococke and Golius," in *Lias* 43,1 (2016), 1–159. For the general context of Arabic studies in England and neighboring countries, with many references to visits to the Orient, see Gerald J. Toomer, *Eastern Wisedome and Learning: The Study of Arabic in Seventeenth-Century England*, Oxford 1996.

[41] Juynboll 1931 (see note 23), 215–17; Vrolijk/Schmidt/Scheper 2012 (see note 21), 34–35; Philip Christiaan Molhuysen and Petrus Johannes Blok, *Nieuw Nederlandsch biografisch woordenboek*, vol. 9, Leiden 1933, 277–79; Faramarz Behzad, *Adam Olearius' "Persianischer Rosenthal": Untersuchungen zur Übersetzung von Saadis "Golestan" im 17. Jahrhundert*, Göttingen 1970, 27–28.

[42] On Hottinger, see Jan Loop, *Johann Heinrich Hottinger: Arabic and Islamic Studies in the Seventeenth Century*, Oxford 2013.

[43] On Warner, see Juynboll 1931 (see note 23), 222–34; Vrolijk/Schmidt/Scheper 2012 (see note 21).

[44] Ibn Hazm, *The Ring of the Dove: A Treatise on the Art and Practice of Arab Love*, trans. A. J. Arberry (1951), London 1994. It has been translated into many languages including German; see Abu Muhammad Ali Ibn-Hazm al-Andalusi, *Halsband der Taube: Über die Liebe und die Liebenden*, trans. Max Weisweiler, Leiden 1941. The archive of the Arabist and librarian Max Weisweiler (1902–1968), otherwise known as an expert on Islamic bookbinding, is now in the Leiden University Library, see Beate Wiesmüller, *Das Max-Weisweiler-Archiv der Universitätsbibliothek Leiden*, Leiden 2007.

Turbans and Silk Robes: Bringing the Orient Home

The expansion of Dutch trade to different continents not only resulted in the acquisition of great fortunes for sections of the Republic's mercantile population. Owing to greater knowledge of the world and the availability of goods, faraway lands seeped into their lives—either intellectually through what they knew, or physically through the objects around them. Thus, developing a relationship to the Orient by no means required distant travel—which, in any case, was only undertaken by a very small proportion of the population. Back home, the presence of the exotic also influenced lifestyles, fashions—and painting. Motifs with origins in foreign cultures began to crop up in genre paintings, portraits, and *portraits historiés*. These motifs were status symbols articulating social rank and wealth.[1]

Turbans and Oriental carpets had previously featured in fifteenth-century Netherlandish art, including Jan van Eyck's *Portrait of a Man in a Red Turban* of 1433 (The National Gallery, London) and his *Virgin and Child with Canon van der Paele* of ca. 1434–36 (Groeningemuseum, Bruges). However, these works were exceptions. In the seventeenth century, by contrast, it was by no means unusual for Johannes van Swinderen to provide the subject of *An Artist of Antiquity* (cat. 2) with a magnificent turban, nor would it have struck contemporary viewers as odd that Govert Flinck adorned his *Lady in Oriental Costume* (cat. 3) with Eastern accessories such as the feather tucked into her headwear. Fantastical accoutrements such as these responded to the general allure of the foreign, to which even a genre scene such as Rembrandt's *Musical Company* (cat. 1) paid tribute.

The most characteristic exotic motif seen in portraits and interiors is the Oriental carpet,[2] which began to appear regularly in paintings during the Italian and Northern Renaissance. However, in a work like Van Eyck's *Virgin and Child with Canon Van der Paele,* the carpet decorates the floor in front of the Virgin's throne. In seventeenth-century paintings, by contrast, such carpets barely ever grace tiled floors but are instead conspicuously draped over tables. This is evidence of the prestige accorded to Oriental carpets, since their placement at eye level was certain to capture the viewer's attention. The Oriental carpet came to be such a standard decorative component of interiors during the seventeenth century that its appearance was even expected in so archetypically Dutch a genre as the group portraits of civic guard associations—as shown, for example, in Bartholomeus van der Helst's *The Headmen of the Arquebus Civic Guard House* (cat. 10). And as late as the last quarter of the seventeenth century, a courtier like *Don Francisco Lopes Suasso* (cat. 16), dressed in the very latest French fashions, rests his beribboned arm on a strikingly patterned Oriental carpet. The opulent piece also signals the sitter's wealth.

While this motif certainly documents the integration of foreign elements into the domestic realm, the personal connection to the wider world is even more manifest with such items of clothing as the *japonse rok* (Japanese robe). Nicolaes Maes's *Young Scholar in an Armchair* (cat. 11) is dressed in sumptuous silk, which is also how Jan Lievens (cat. 12) and Jürgen Ovens (cat. 13) chose to appear in their respective self-portraits. Even then, the garment may not have even originated in the Far East, since domestic demand was so high that East Asian-style housecoats were also produced in the Netherlands.

In his portrait of an unnamed governor of the Dutch East India Company (cat. 15), Gerbrand van den Eeckhout creates a biographical link between the sitter and his exotic clothing, which he possibly brought back from a faraway country. The same applies to Dirck van Loonen's portrait of *Assueer Jacob Schimmelpenninck van der Oye* (cat. 14), who presumably acquired his Oriental accoutrements on location while traveling in Asia. In this painting, the unusual costume not only serves as a mark of social status, but also attests to the sitter's education and worldliness.

Aelbert Cuyp's *Group Portrait of the Sam Family* (cat. 7) has an enigmatic quality: while some of the family members appear in Orientalized garb, the majority of the sitters are portrayed in the black suits and white collars typical of the period. It is unclear whether the sitter's choice of clothing was merely whimsical or intended to articulate a specific statement now lost to us.

In the *portrait historié*, one of the most popular genres in seventeenth-century Dutch painting, there was also profound significance attached to having oneself depicted in Oriental costume. It is the desire to make a profession of faith that links the bride and groom who had Jacob van Hasselt depict them in the roles of Esther and Ahasuerus, the Molenschot family portrayed by Aelbert Cuyp in a scene with David and Abigail (cat. 8), and the unknown family painted by Gerbrand van den Eeckhout in a recreation of the biblical scene *The Infant Samuel Brought by Hannah to Eli* (cat. 9). In these paintings, adopting items of clothing perceived as "Oriental" was about more than just donning fashionable costumes as escapism. The clothes offered a striking way for the sitters to display their identification with figures from the Bible and the values they connoted, while communicating to viewers their own aspiration to fulfill—or come close to—a biblical ideal.

Regardless of how common it became to integrate exotic elements into private, domestic environments during the seventeenth century, however much their striking aspect came to typify portraits of this period, their presence still reveals something about how sitters wished to be seen. For exotic motifs also symbolized an openness to the new, to modernity, erudition, and sophistication. Their significance derived from a projection of cultural capital typical of the age and did not necessarily denote a genuine interest in far-off countries and cultures. Nonetheless, the act of appropriation shows that elements of foreign cultures were not viewed negatively or with trepidation, but rather as something special and desirable. MPH

1 For more on this subject cf., among others, Kuipers 2014, Amsterdam 2002b, and Amsterdam 2015.

2 Cf. Ydema 1991.

1 Rembrandt Harmensz. van Rijn (1606–1669)
Musical Company, 1626

Oil on panel, 63.4 x 47.5 cm
Inscribed bottom left: RH 1626
Inv. SK-A-4674
Rijksmuseum, Amsterdam, purchased with the support of the Vereniging Rembrandt and the Stichting tot Bevordering van de Belangen van het Rijksmuseum
(Basel only)

Lit.
CRP, vol. 1, no. A 7; vol. 3, 784; vol. 4, 660–61; vol. 6, no. 11
Schwartz 1985a, 42–44
Berlin 2006, 205, fig. p. 207
Amsterdam 2008a, 96, 98, and passim
Van de Wetering 2016, 226
Amsterdam 2019, 776–77
Leiden 2019, no. 72

The man in the turban sitting on the left is playing the viola da gamba; the young man behind him is strumming the harp. They are accompanying the main figure in the painting, the young woman sitting at the table on the right. The old woman standing behind her seems to be listening to the concert. The picture hung on the wall in the back shows Lot and his family fleeing Sodom as it is destroyed and thus provides the first intimation of sinfulness. All in all, the iconography corresponds to that of a classic bordello scene. The communal music-making from a score symbolizes the arranged harmony of the feelings between the men and the young woman with the bold décolleté, whose breasts are more exposed than covered by a transparent veil. The old woman watching so attentively would assume the role of the procuress.

The feature that distinguishes this early work of Rembrandt's from other *bordeeltjes* (brothel scenes) is its profligate use of Oriental props. Complementing his glistening buttoned housecoat, the mustached gamba player wears earrings, a turban with a colorful pattern, and a matching sash in which a dagger is tucked. The singer's dress is sewn from fabric with a carpet-like pattern. She is wearing a diadem with a curved spur that with its veil hanging down in the back resembles the shape of a Phrygian cap. The tablecloth of luminous turquoise and the old woman's colorfully striped headscarf complete an almost orgiastic explosion of color.

It is apparent that Rembrandt is exploiting the exotic here. He presents it next to other pictorial elements in order to visualize excess. The protagonists are clothed much too colorfully, too strangely. There are too many instruments and too many pieces of sheet music—a viola and a lute lie unplayed in the foreground next to a pile of songbooks. The young man, clearly European and dressed in muted tones but historicized in the style of the sixteenth century, is wearing a beret with extravagant slits and enormous ostrich feathers. Rembrandt's message, or that of his client, could correspond to what Torrentius wrote twelve years earlier on his famous still life (Rijksmuseum Amsterdam): "Wat buten maat bestaat, int onmaats qaat verghaat" (That which goes beyond moderation, ends in immeasurable evil). BB

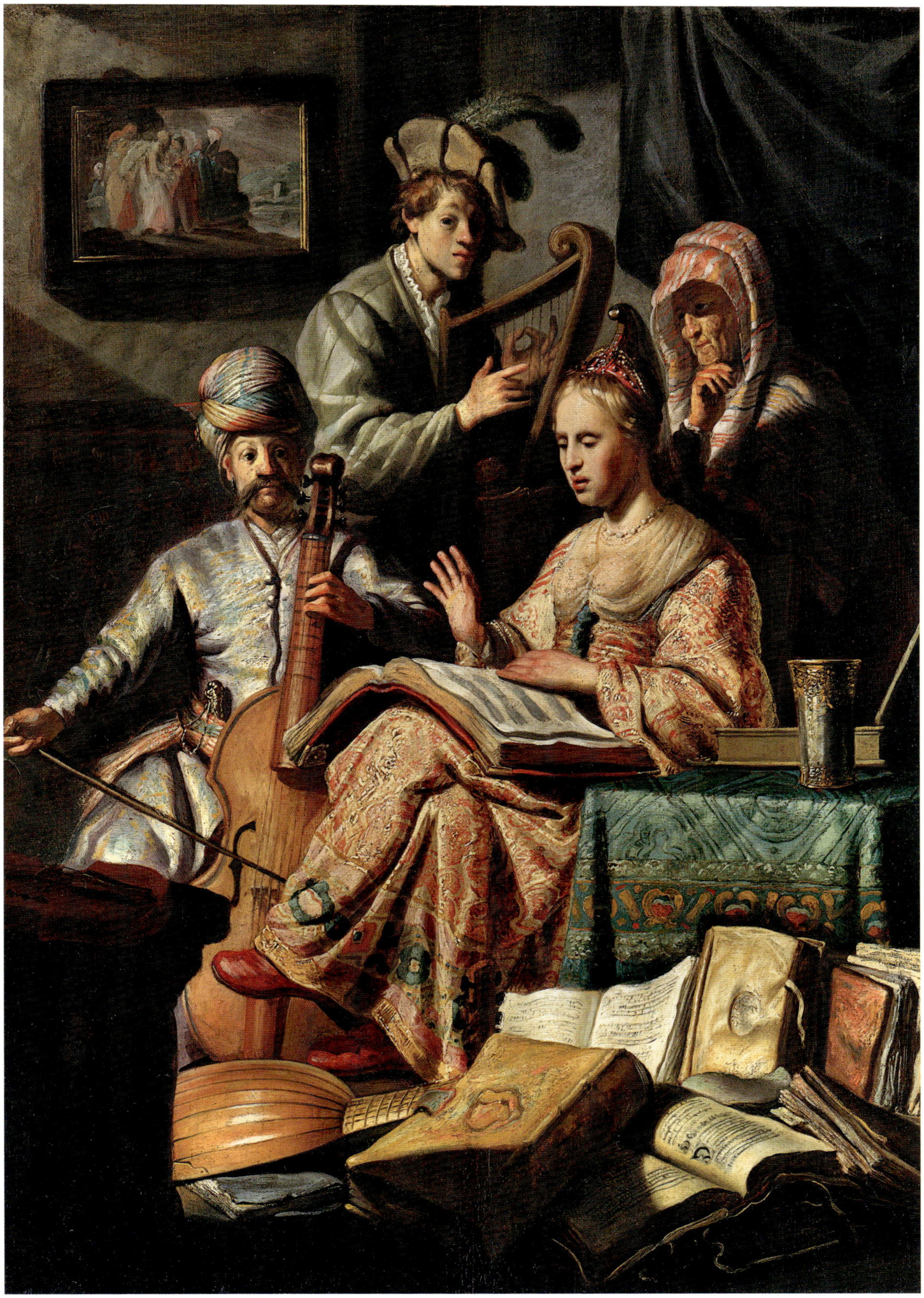

1

2 **Johannes van Swinderen** (1594–1636)

An Artist of Antiquity, ca. 1628–36

Oil on canvas, 103.3 x 89.3 cm
Inscription at bottom right: P. DG 1647
Inv. SK-A-2310
Rijksmuseum, Amsterdam

Lit.
Slatkes 1983a, 245–46
Amsterdam 2007b, no. 277
Dordrecht 2012, 286

Although the painting is inscribed at the bottom right with the monogram "P.DG," it is not a work by the Haarlem painter Pieter de Grebber (ca. 1600–1652/53); instead it is attributed to the little-known Johannes van Swinderen. Documents show that he was a court clerk and painter in Zutphen and in 1627 was paid for a picture depicting the Judgment of Solomon, which he had made for the council chamber of the local town hall (today Rechtbank Oost-Nederland, Zutphen). A comparison with that picture, Van Swinderen's masterpiece, suggests that the present work was made around the same time.

The artist who is the subject of the picture is given a distinctly Oriental look, sporting a white turban with an ornamental clasp and a feathered egret plume (*aigrette* in French), an attribute that in the Ottoman Empire was awarded as a valued medal of honor (see cat. 3, 6, 8, 14, 37, 54, 58, 60, 62, 69, 73–74, 99–100, 103, 119). This is capped by an overly long, imaginatively tied, colorful scarf, and a fur-like wrap. If this painting from the Rijksmuseum were a self-portrait, it would be an astonishing predecessor to Rembrandt's *Self-Portrait in Oriental Attire with Poodle* of 1631–33 (fig. p. 63). However, the head of the painter corresponds by and large to the type of young man in the *Judgment of Solomon* and lacks distinct individual traits.

In addition, the subject matter that is developed through the use of the still life on the right suggests that the artist was aiming to depict an idealized painter of the past. An open sketchbook hangs over the front edge of a covered table, revealing a page with a male nude in red chalk. The sketchbook is held in place by a skull and two bones. An hourglass tipped on its side and a flickering oil lamp behind emphasize the arrangement's reference to the transience of all earthly things. The powerful gesture with which the artist leans his clenched fist on the skull, his thumb gripping the palette, somewhat contradicts the melancholy *vanitas* motif. The frontal view of the slightly bent torso of a man with a hint of a loincloth depicted in the sketch recalls, perhaps not coincidentally, the main figure of Rubens's *Death of Seneca* of ca. 1612–13 (Bayerische Staatsgemäldesammlungen, Alte Pinakothek, Munich), which was based on an ancient statue. Seneca was the author of one of the key texts on the idea of *vanitas*, *De brevitate vitae* (On the Shortness of Life), the tenth of his philosophical dialogues. This work also includes "Vita brevis, ars longa" (Life is short, art is long), the aphorism attributed to Hippocrates, in its universally known Latin formulation.

The drawing departs in one respect from its presumed model: Seneca lectures with the orator's gesture of the open right hand, which in the sketch is clenched in a fist—duplicating the painter's energetic fist that rests on the skull directly above it. Perhaps he intended to reinterpret the resigned sigh of "Art is long, our lives are short" as the triumph of art, in its creation of eternity, over the transience of material things. In his court job Van Swinderen would have been acquainted with learned and well-read jurists, which makes such a sophisticated concept plausible.[1] BB

1 Another history painting by Van Swinderen deals with an event from Byzantine history that is extremely rarely depicted: *Emperor Theodosius II Banishes His Wife Athenaïs* (formerly Collection Jean Decoen, Knokke-Zoute).

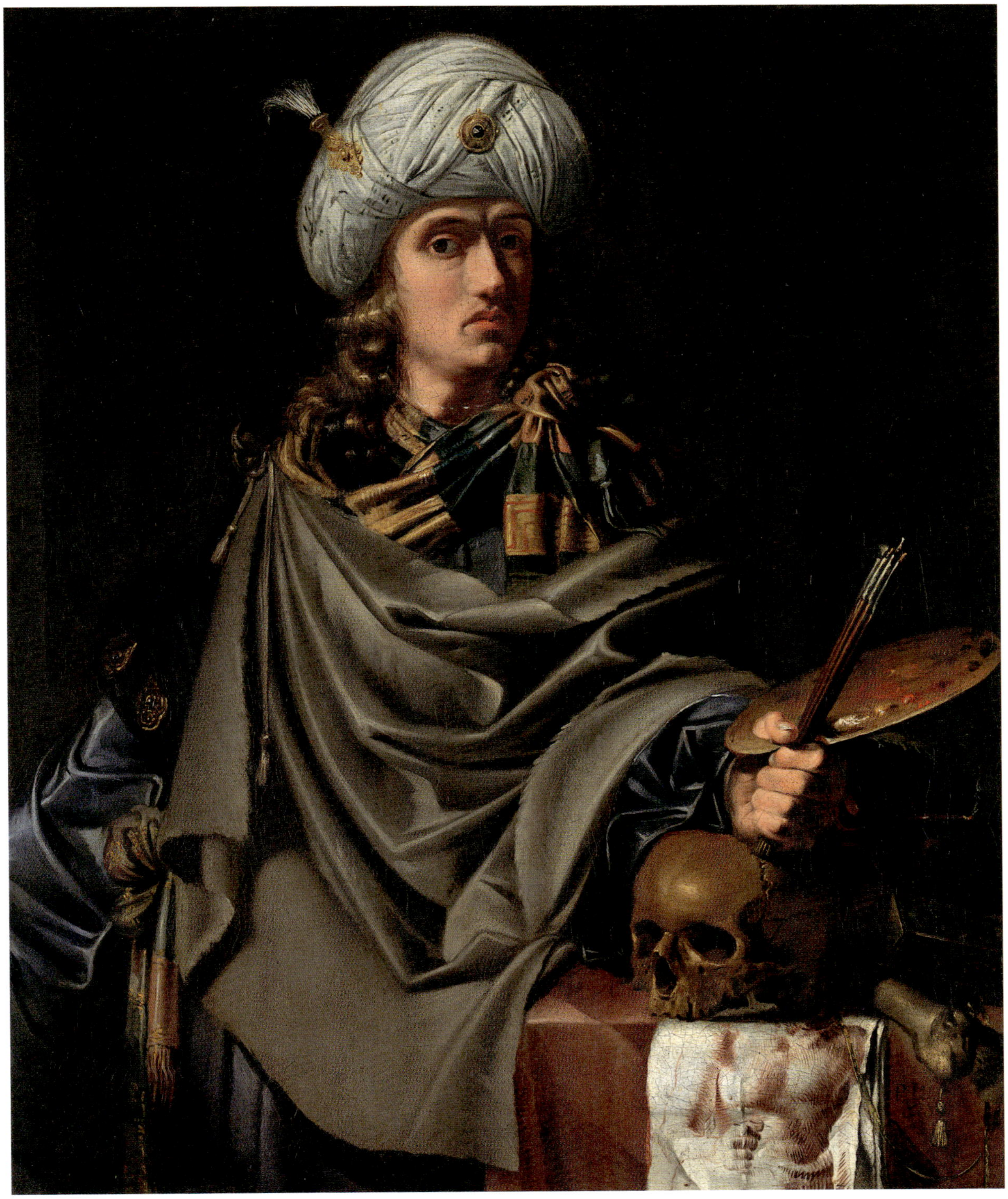

2

3 **Govert Flinck** (1615–1660)
Lady in Oriental Costume, 1636

Oil on canvas, 79 x 66 cm
Inscribed bottom right: Rembrandt f. 1636
Inv. 159
Emil Bührle Collection, Zurich

Lit.
Bauch 1966, no. 495
Bredius/Gerson 1969, 95, fig. 106
Zurich 2005, 108–09

This atmospheric *tronie* of a lady in an unusual costume, characterized by subtle lighting and harmonious tone-in-tone color, was long thought to be an original Rembrandt—not only because of its signature—before it was ascribed to his student and workshop assistant Govert Flinck. Like hardly any other member of Rembrandt's large circle of students, Flinck was able in the late 1630s to imitate the motifs and painting style of his teacher, which is the reason why many of his paintings—a large number of which were created in Rembrandt's workshop under his supervision—were considered authentic works by the teacher. In the 1640s Flinck was to break away from his close ties to Rembrandt's style and turn with similar skill to other models. This was not seen as a flaw during his lifetime. Flinck enjoyed a remarkable career as a sought-after and respected painter of the Amsterdam upper class, and the poet Joost van den Vondel even praised him as "Apelles of Cleves."[1]

Flinck took the greatest care in depicting the exotic costume his model is wearing. Similar to the cloak, the dress, which is held together below the bosom by a sash, is made of a kind of gold brocade, whose sumptuous structure is revealed by reflected light. The face, which looks candidly at the observer, is effectively framed by a delicate veil interwoven with gold. A magnificent cluster of feathers in an aigrette (see cat. 2) set with precious stones provides a further accent. The pearl earrings and the necklace, whose medallion rests on a finely pleated chemise, are also exquisite treasures. The imaginative mix of garments that were already antique and ahistorical when the painting was made, along with the veil and the superb details, must have evoked an impression of unusual exoticism and, inevitably, associations with Eastern cultures, such as Persia.

Although the sitter's facial features bear a certain resemblance to Rembrandt's first wife, Saskia van Uylenburgh, it is unlikely—contrary to what has long been assumed—that she was the model. Rather, Flinck's composition, of which a drawing exists (National Gallery of Art, Washington, DC), belongs to the genre of *tronies* with Oriental costumes, with which Rembrandt and Jan Lievens had played in numerous examples in the late 1620s and early 1630s (cat. 99–101, 103–04, 106). Flinck's adaptation makes clear the role the Rembrandt workshop had in the spread of this genre. Yet *Lady in Oriental Costume* is not an isolated case in Flinck's oeuvre. The type of the female *tronie* in fantasy garb based on Rembrandt's example is more frequently represented here, with the costume varied repeatedly but always based on the same patterns. In at least one case, the allusion to the Orient is immediately recognizable even for a present-day viewer, since Flinck used a turban instead of a veil (Chatsworth, Devonshire Collections).[2] GD

1 For Flinck, his relation to Rembrandt, and his evaluation during his life and after cf. De Witt 2017 and Lootsma 2017.
2 Cf. Sumowski 1983–94, vol. 2, no. 659.

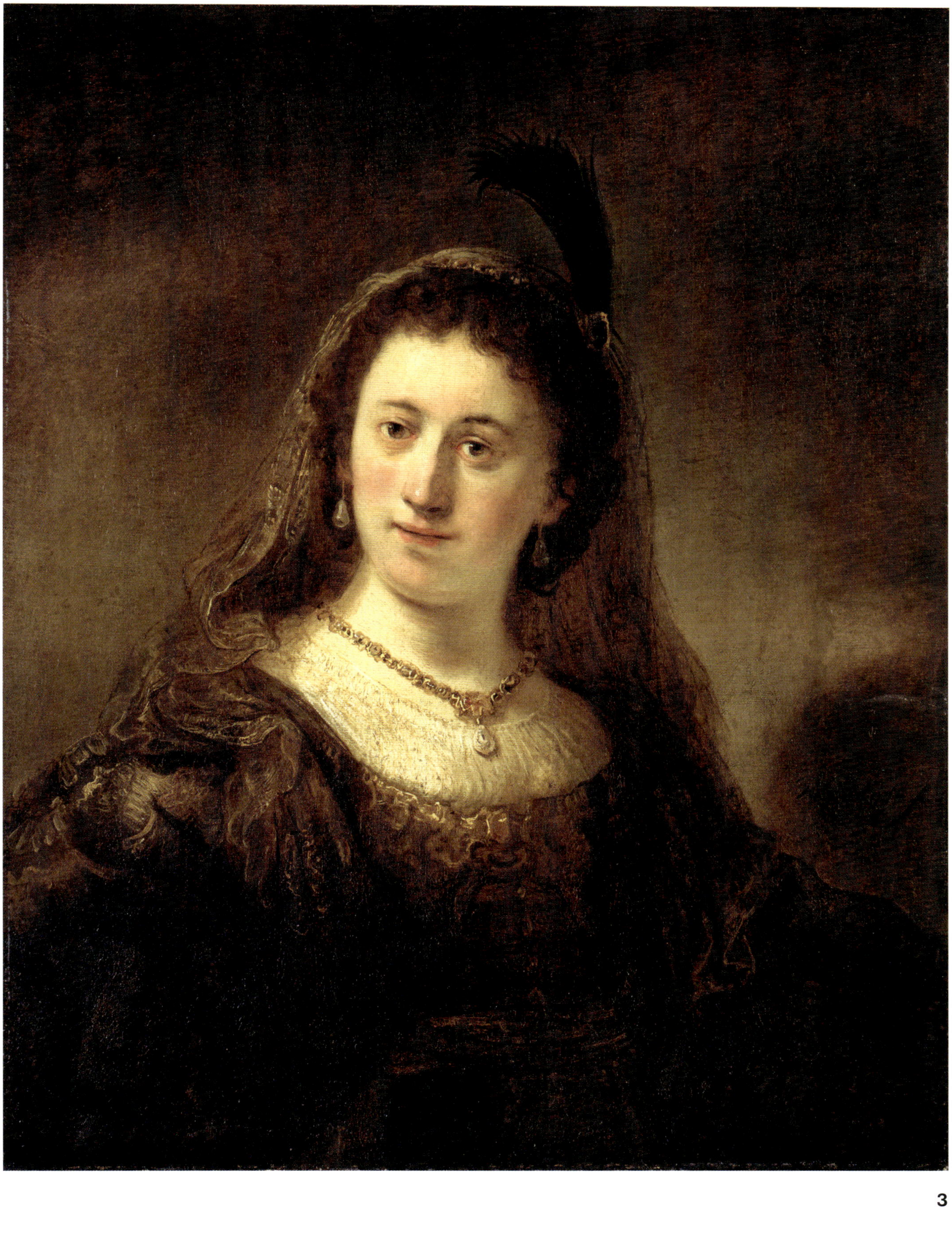

4 Jacob van Hasselt (1597–1674) (?)
The Wedding Feast of Grietje Hermans van Hasselt and Jochum Berntsen van Haecken, 1636

5 Anonymous after Jan Lucasz. van Hasselt (before 1600–after 1653)
Portrait of Sitti Maani Gioerida della Valle, 1627

4
Oil on canvas, 102.1 x 135.5 cm
Inscribed top left (on the curtain):
J. Hasselt fe 1636
Inv. 10046
Centraal Museum Utrecht

Lit.
Swillens 1946
Slatkes 1983b, 37–41
Utrecht 1999, vol. B, no. 254
Utrecht 2006, no. 48
Schwartz 2006, 111
Schwartz 2014, 53–54, fig. 1.10a
Van Leeuwen 2018, 555, 672, fig. p. 899

5
Engraving
In Girolamo Rocchi, *Funerale della Signora Sitti Maani Gioerida della Valle . . . celebrato in Roma* (The Funeral of Lady Sitti Maani Gioerida della Valle . . . Celebrated in Rome), Rome: Bartolomeo Zannetti, 1627, p. 4
HOTZ 330
Leiden University Libraries, Special Collections

Lit.
Baskins 2012

The party is dressed in fantasy costumes although the wedding took place in the Dutch city of Utrecht. Grietje Hermans van Hasselt and Jochum Berntsen van Haecken documented their wedding of May 15, 1636, in a painting that places the celebration in a biblical setting. It probably refers to the banquet mentioned in the Old Testament that was given by Ahasuerus, the king of Persia, on the occasion of his marriage to Esther. While the stars woven in the carpet pattern behind the bridal couple allude to the name Esther—in Persian she is called Stara (meaning "star")—the pearl necklace she is demonstratively fingering indicates the bride's first name. Grietje is a derivation of Margaret, which comes from *margarita,* the Latin word for "pearl." The man behind the bride might be a self-portrait of the painter, based on his positioning and facial expressions.

The genre of the *portrait historié,* in which real people are placed in a biblical or historical context, had its heyday in the Netherlands in the seventeenth century, when citizens had themselves portrayed in scenes from the Bible. This symbolic participation in sacred history replaced the donor portrait, which was widespread until the sixteenth century. In this way, representative manner could testify to personal religiousness. Thus, wedding depictions were suitable for family group portraits. The wedding at Cana, for example, where Jesus changed water into wine, could be considered a symbol of the sacrament or the granting of grace, depending on one's denomination, while the figure of Esther is generally regarded as a moral model of female virtue.

The occasion and subject of the painting can be deciphered, but the identity of its creator cannot be clearly established. The signature "J. Hasselt" can refer to two painters who can be traced back to seventeenth-century Utrecht: Jacob Claesz. van Hasselt, documented to have been there between 1636 and 1659, and Isaac Jansz. van Hasselt, who is reported to have been a student of Paulus Moreelse in 1619. However, the signature also fits Jan Lucasz. van Hasselt, although there is no proof that he was ever in Utrecht. Still he was one of the few Dutch artists of the seventeenth century who could have drawn from his own experiences. Jan Lucasz. van Hasselt worked for Shah Abbas I in Isfahan in the 1620s, until he took up residence once again in his home country from 1630 to 1653.[1]

Jan Lucasz. van Hasselt is also associated with a bizarre episode of the meeting of Western and Eastern cultures. In 1614 he accompanied the Italian pilgrim Pietro della Valle on a journey of several years to the Levant. Along the way Della Valle married the Syrian Christian Sitti Maani, of whom Van Hasselt painted a full-length portrait, which was sent to Rome. The sitter dressed in Syrian garb for the painting, although, according to one of Della Valle's letters, she hardly ever wore such clothing. Obviously, the emphasis on the exotic was important to him with respect to his family.

Based on this painting—which has not been preserved—an engraving was created, which shows Sitti Maani in half figure. It appeared in a publication on the occasion of her funeral in March 1627 in Rome. She had, however, already died in 1621—Della Valle had carried her mummified corpse with him for years on his journeys. It is impossible to say to what extent the engraving resembles the living person. According to Della Valle, even Van Hasselt's painted portrait possessed considerable flaws. The clothing, jewelry and the Arabic scimitar in the engraving correspond to Oriental stereotypes, as they were also disseminated by contemporary costume books. MPH

[1] Cf. Goetz 1938, 283–84.

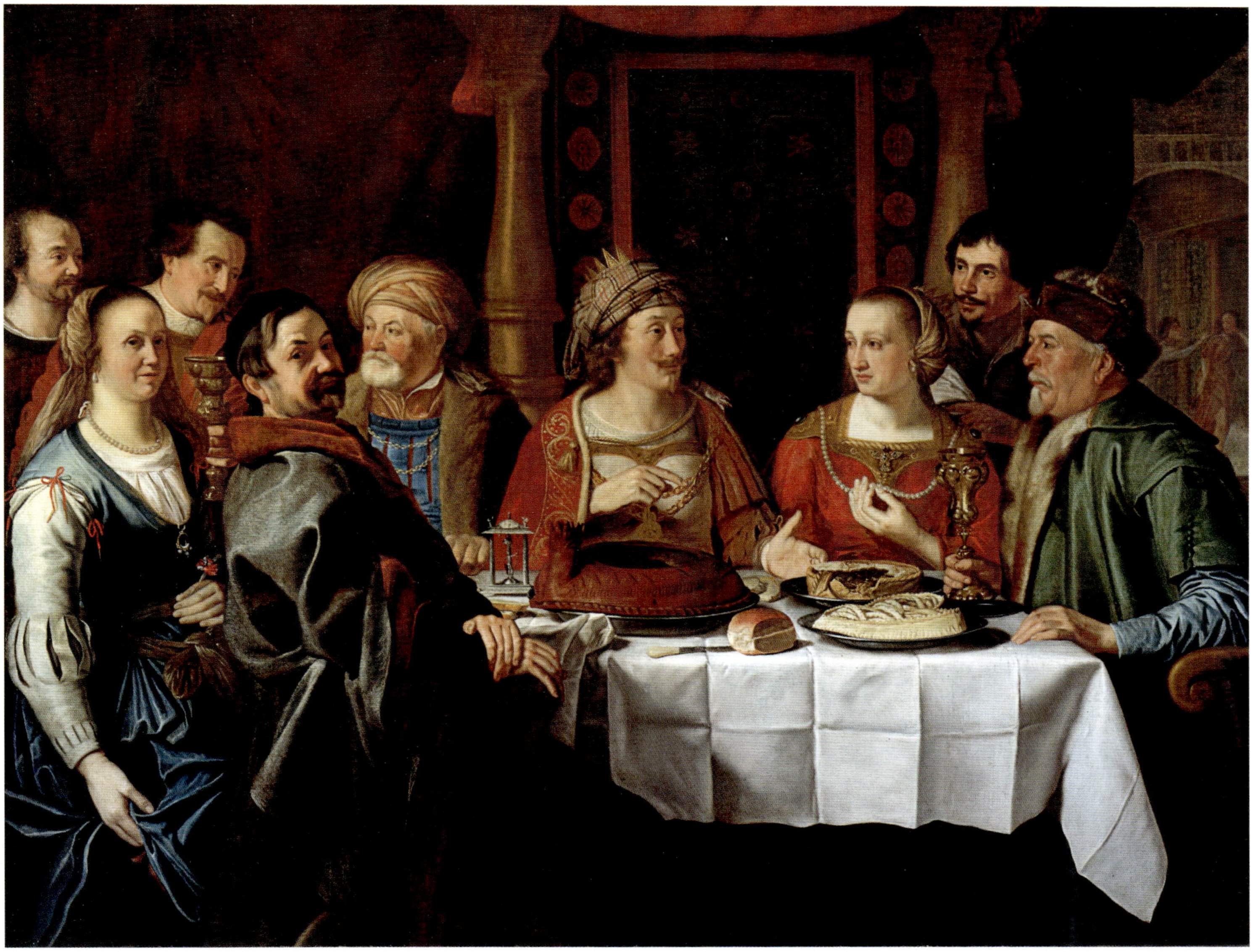

4

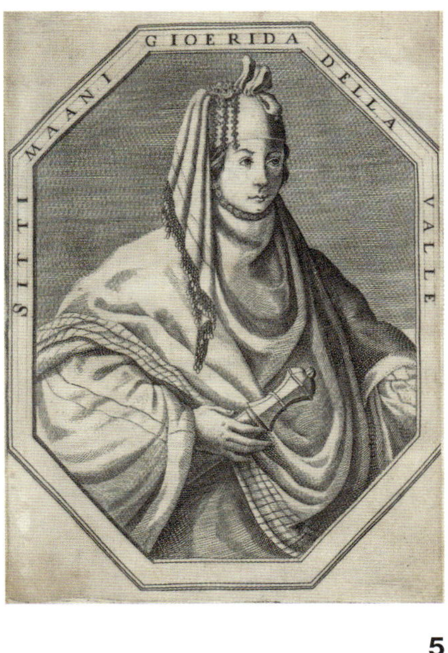

5

6 **Ferdinand Bol** (1616–1680)

Couple in a Landscape, ca. 1647–50

Oil on canvas, 103.2 x 91.8 cm
Inv. DM/948/126
Dordrechts Museum, loan of the Cultural Heritage Agency 1948

Lit.
Blankert 1982, 23, no. 167, fig. 178
Sumowski 1983–94, vol. 1, 285, no. 150
Bruyn 1994
Ekkart 2017, 149–50

An exotically outfitted couple stands in front of an Arcadian landscape bordering a forest on the left. The woman, richly draped with pearls, is wrapped in a magnificent, floor-length dress of iridescent silk. Her companion wears a fringed doublet with sash and a shoulder cloak of velvety shimmering fabrics along with an eccentric, multicolored turban with an aigrette (see cat. 2). The physiognomies of the couple, who are tenderly holding hands, suggest that these are not fantasy figures but individual portraits of a Dutch couple, even if the man has had a moustache painted on to match his costume. Accordingly, this is a role portrait in Oriental costume of the kind that enjoyed great popularity in the Netherlands around the middle of the seventeenth century (see cat. 4, 7–9).

Bol was active in Rembrandt's workshop from the mid-1630s on and, as was typical, had carefully appropriated Rembrandt's style (see cat. 119). Nevertheless, even later, when he had long worked on his own as a painter, he was still strongly influenced by this period.[1] The sitters' costumes correspond to the patterns Bol knew from Rembrandt's work, while the woman is reminiscent of the type of Rembrandt's *Flora* of 1634 (The State Hermitage Museum, St. Petersburg). The composition of the landscape is borrowed in mirror image from Rembrandt's 1635 *Sacrifice of Isaac* (The State Hermitage Museum, St. Petersburg), and other elements of the landscape as well as the use of light adopt motifs familiar from Rembrandt's work.

Such role portraits often illustrate biblical history (see cat. 4, 8–9). In this case, a contemporary source seems to document both the scene and the identity of the sitter. In the estate of Ferdinand Bol's second wife, Anna van Erckel, who was the widow of a rich merchant, there was a picture painted by Ferdinand Bol that depicted her and her first husband as Isaac and Rebecca. However, technical findings and another archival source have disproved this assumption. Because the painting is trimmed on all sides, it must be a fragment of a larger composition. An auction catalog from 1804 contains a suitable description of a lot in which, in addition to the couple in Oriental costume, a shepherd with sheep could be seen in the picture's left half. The Musée des Beaux-Arts in Lyon has preserved a fragment of such a shepherd painted by Bol, which matches the format as well as the scale of the figures and which, therefore, is probably the missing piece. Since the Lyon picture had already come into the museum's possession in 1841, the original composition would have been cut up, for unknown reasons, sometime between 1805 and 1841. The underlying mystery has, admittedly, not been solved. Who the couple and the shepherd in Lyon are, what their relationship to one another was, and how the original composition is to be interpreted in terms of content must remain an open question. GD

[1] For the life of Bol and his relation to Rembrandt cf. De Witt/Van Sloten 2017.

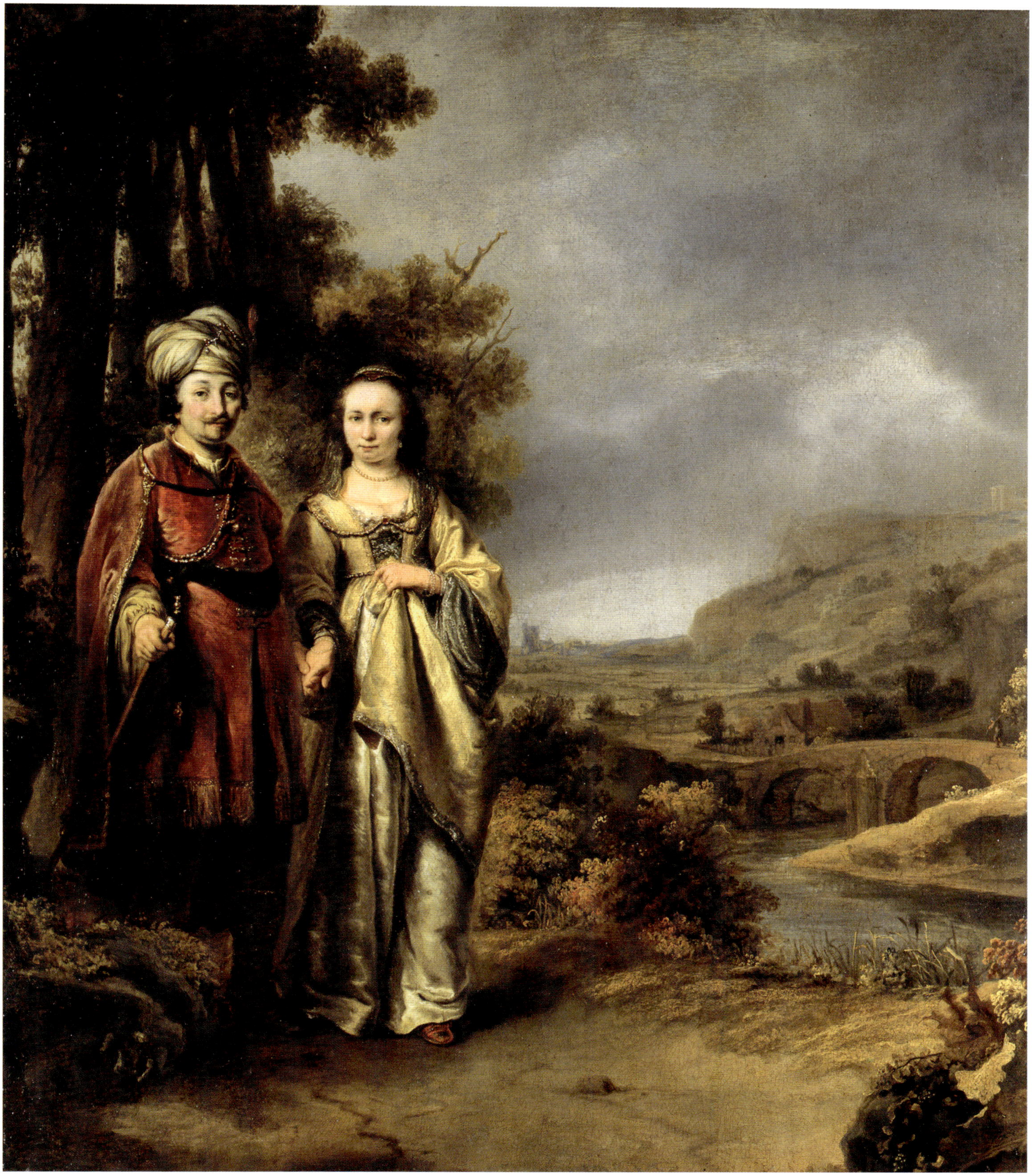

6

7 **Aelbert Gerritsz. Cuyp** (1620–1691)

Group Portrait of the Sam Family, ca. 1653

Oil on canvas, 168 x 240 cm
Inscribed bottom right: A : cuijp . fecit .
Inv. 398
Szépművészeti Múzeum, Budapest

Lit.
Loughman 2008, 586–91
Bonn 2016, no. 94

Divided into two groups corresponding to the trees to the left and right that frame a view of the landscape in the center, the family of the Dordrecht wine merchant Jan Jacobsen Sam poses here. The head of the family dominates the group on the left with his spouse, Catharina Wulfraets, at his side. The younger woman to their right may be a relative of Catharina's. The remaining figures are the couple's ten children along with Arent Huttenus, the husband of their oldest daughter, Catharina.

Huttenus is wearing a turban decorated with a feather and exotic-looking garments. With his wife, he occupies the most prominent position behind the family patriarch. A similar turban, in a child's size, adorns the head of the youngest brother, Abraham, who is dressed in an equally striking purple tunic. The squirrel that he holds on a leash and points at with his left hand symbolizes hard work and care. Next to him, the youngest daughter, Anneken, who is also colorfully dressed in yellow and blue, points toward the other side where the four middle brothers, Andries, Herbert, Willem, and Daniel are portrayed as returning hunters. Willem presents his take, a snipe, while little Daniel leads the dogs. The equestrian jackets of the two are based on the *dolman* worn by Hungarian hussars. Herbert too is wearing a turban with a feather and also has a scimitar.

The exotic dress of seven of the ten children contrasts starkly with the bourgeois Dutch garb of the others and with that of the parents' generation. Thus, on the one hand, it seems to be a matter of age; on the other hand, perhaps biblical ideals are being evoked. Does this express the wish that the married couple Catharina and Arent along with the youngest siblings harmonize with each other like Isaac and Rebecca (Genesis 24:67)? And does the bright vermilion that sets little Daniel apart from his brothers allude to one of the most famous late-born sons in the Old Testament, to Joseph, to whom Jacob gave a coat of many colors (Genesis 37:3)? Clearly there could be a warning here against envy, which gripped Joseph's brothers in the biblical story.

The Sam family business is alluded to abundantly. Anneken holds a grapevine in her hand. Immediately next to her, in the middle ground, agents seem to be negotiating a deal. This takes place on the banks of the Rhine, for the fortified city in the background is Bacharach, copied from an engraving by Matthäus Merian the Elder, which in addition to being published in Frankfurt am Main in 1633, also appeared in Amsterdam in 1642 in the Dutch edition of Merian's *Theatrum Europaeum.* Then as now, Bacharach was a famous wine-making town, and Dordrecht had held staple rights in Holland for wine imported from Germany since the Middle Ages. BB

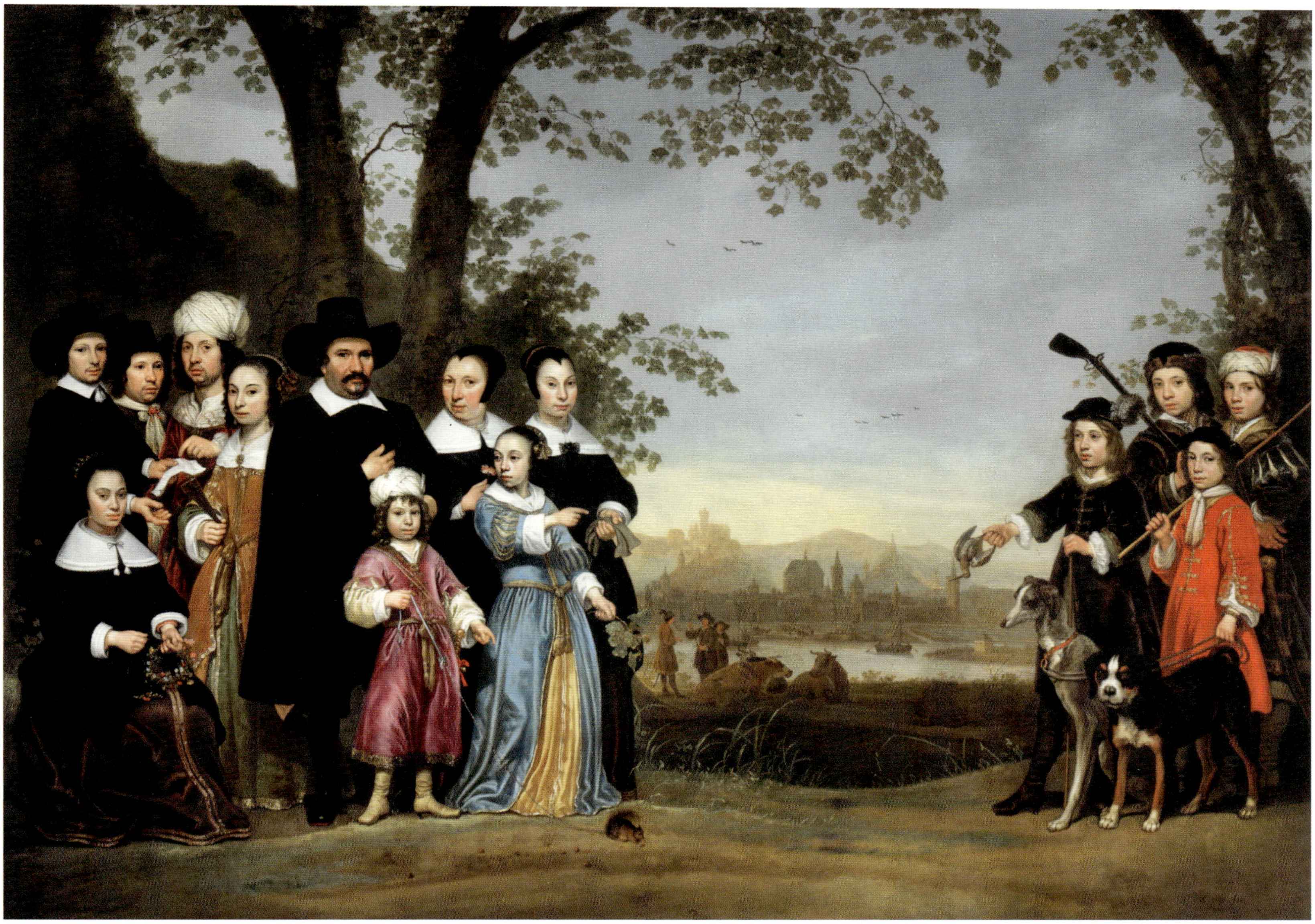

8 **Aelbert Gerritsz. Cuyp** (1620–1691)
The Encounter of David and Abigail: Portrait of the Family of Lowijs Jacobsz. Molenschot and His Wife, Janneken Jansdr. Rokus, 1655 (?)

Oil on canvas, 154.5 x 207.5 cm
Inscribed bottom right on rock: A. Cuyp.
Inv. 904
Kunstmuseum Basel,
Bequest of Hans Vonder Mühll 1914

Lit.
Pastoor 1991, 130–32
Basel 1995, no. 3
Loughman/Montias 2000, 45
Van Leeuwen 2018, 378–91

The painting is listed in the 1669 inventory of the estate of the Dordrecht cloth merchant Lowijs Jacobsz. Molenschot as "een extraordinaris groot stuck schilderij, sijnde de conterfeijtsels van den overleden, sijn huijsvrou, kinderen, ende andere van haer geslachte gefigureert als d'historie van Davidt ende Abiagael" (an extraordinarily large painting with portraits of the deceased, his wife, children, and other members of their family, portrayed as the story of David and Abigail).

Accordingly, Molenschot himself poses as King David, while his wife, Janneken Jansdr. Rokus († 1655), slips into the role of the wise and generous Abigail, whom the Old Testament ruler will soon take as his second wife (1 Samuel 25). The black veil worn by Abigail alias Janneken is just as striking as the hand of the maid pointing at her from behind. The work may have been painted on the occasion of her death.

Of the couple's five children, only two lived to be adults. Their son Rochus, born in 1629, would have been twenty-six years old the year his mother died. The standard-bearer behind David alias Lowijs might be him. The parallel position of their arms could be meant to emphasize a connection between father and son. We would expect to find Rochus's one-year-younger sister, Engeltgen, among Abigail's maidservants. Is she the one pointing at her mother from behind? Engeltgen's husband Abraham de Gelder appears in the uniform of a corporal on the left edge of the picture. The fourth male portrait head between Abraham and Rochus appears older than the latter and fits the style of Lowijs's beard. It could be Lowijs's brother, Christoffel, the only one who was still alive at the time. The group of women is probably completed by his wife, Geurtken Rouwers, and Rochus's young wife, Catharina Splinters.

Cuyp's work can be characterized as a synthesis of a group portrait, biblical history painting, and military group portrait. Molenschot did, in fact, hold the rank of a high officer in the civic guard in Dordrecht. Thus apparently he attached importance to the fact that the military element and the biblical exoticness were in balance in the picture, which is presumed to be a memorial for his wife. The main character reflects this dichotomy in exemplary fashion. In his role as the Old Testament king and commander of the army, Molenschot proudly wears a turban set with gold, pearls, and a feather—but at the same time, he bears his real officer's partisan with equal pride.

The curiously stocky proportions of the figures with their disproportionately large upper bodies, particularly pronounced in that of the head of the family, could indicate that Cuyp planned his painting from the outset to present a view from below. The inventory referred to above locates it in the rear Great Hall of the Molenschot house. It may have been placed there as a large-format piece for the fireplace placed up high as is often seen in interiors, like those by Pieter de Hooch (The National Gallery, London). BB

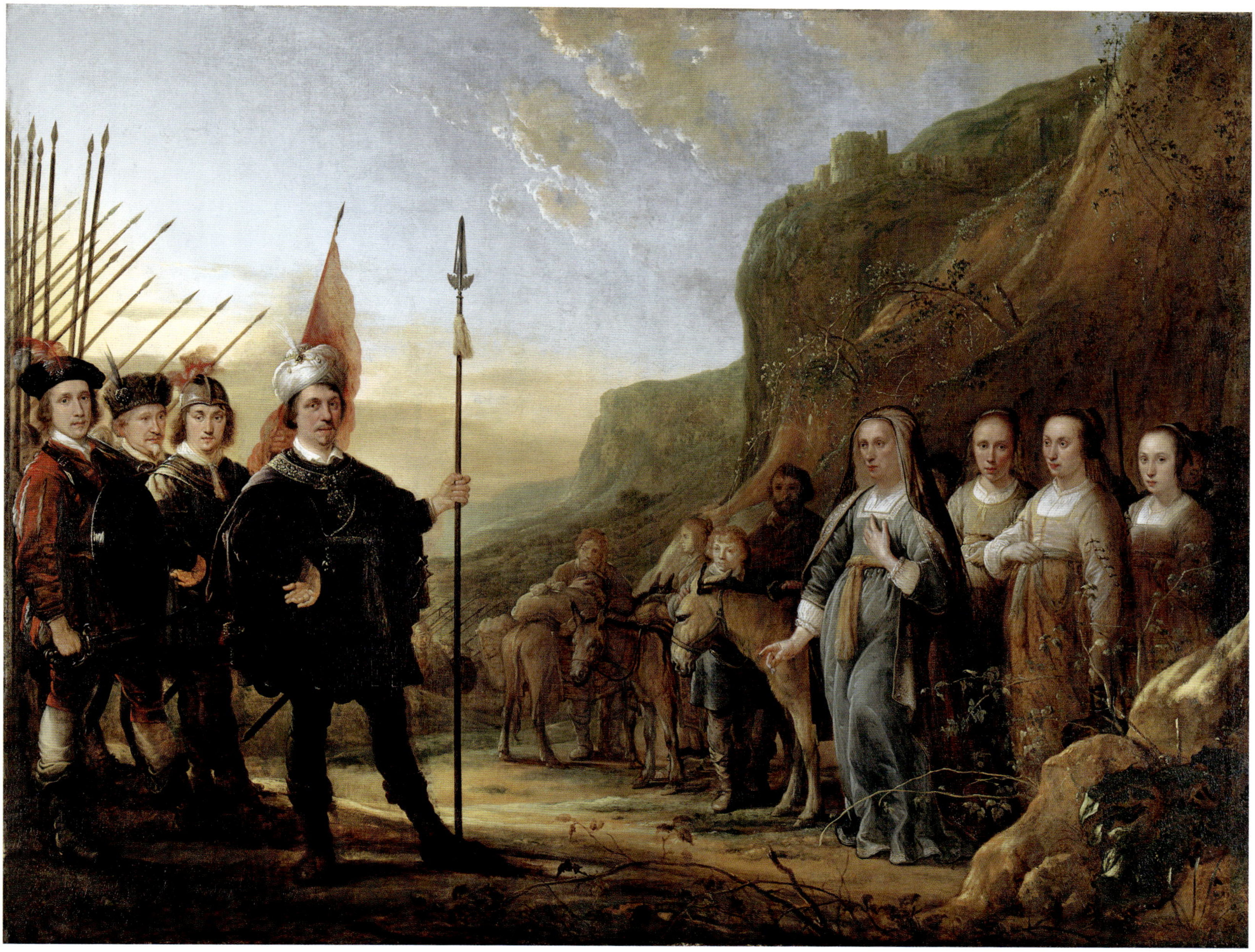

8

9 **Gerbrand van den Eeckhout** (1621–1674)

The Infant Samuel Brought by Hannah to Eli, ca. 1660–63

Oil on canvas, 110 x 135 cm
Inscribed bottom left: G.V: Eekhout
Inv. WA1945.73
Ashmolean Museum of Art and Archaeology—University of Oxford
(Basel only)

Lit.
Roy 1972, 65–66, no. 31
Oxford 1975, no. 29
Sumowski 1983–94, vol. 2, 722, 734, 796, no. 433; vol. 6, 3601
Oxford 1999, no. A 714
Van Leeuwen 2018, 367, 664, fig. p. 882

An event from the Old Testament is portrayed by Gerbrand van den Eeckhout in warm, muted tones. In fulfillment of a vow, Hannah gives her son, Samuel, into the care of the high priest Eli (1 Samuel 1:24). While, as judge of the people of Israel, Eli embodies the highest authority and resides in the temple of Shiloh, where the holy Ark of the Covenant is housed, the scene is extremely intimate. Old Eli, seated, stretches out his left hand to Samuel in a gesture of blessing. Hannah's husband, Elkanah, leans casually with his left hand on the table next to the Holy Book and the incense burner. Hannah's presenting right hand echoes Eli's hand. Little Samuel in a white gown turns and looks out of the picture, offering an apple. This inviting gesture, which involves the viewer, identifies the painting as a *portrait historié*. The popularity of the Eastern style of dress probably encouraged the sitters to identify with their painted roles. In contrast to Rembrandt, who showed only *tronies* (cat. 99–101, 103, 106) or himself (fig. 12, p. 63) but not other, real people in Orientalizing costumes, students of his, including Ferdinand Bol (cat. 6) and Gerbrand van den Eeckhout, accommodated the wishes of their clients.

The choice of a biblical theme for a *portrait historié* could be based on general moral statements—such as the reference to virtue in Jacob van Hasselt's *Wedding Feast* (cat. 4)—or biographical circumstances. This could also be the case with the story of Hannah and Samuel, for the Lord had first "shut up her womb" (1 Samuel 1:5) and only after long prayer, in which she promised to dedicate her child to the temple service, did the Lord heed her wish to have children. Thus, this subject can serve as an expression of trust in God as well as testimony to gratitude. That the occasion for this painting was connected somehow to the question of motherhood is also indicated by Hannah's positioning in the foreground, while the man assumes the role of an extra in the background.

The nonspecific clothing of the figures follows a typical vision of people from the Bible. This is also true of Eli, although the Old Testament provides detailed information about the high priest's clothing. How Van den Eeckhout portrayed this historical scene without reference to such descriptions is shown in a version of the same motif created around 1665 (Musée du Louvre, Paris). There, too, Hannah is kneeling, but with her back to the viewer, and Eli sits at a distance in sumptuous clothing on a high throne in an enormous hall. The high priest is wearing the breastplate described in Exodus with the twelve rectangular gems representing the twelve tribes of Israel (Exodus 39:8–14), as is also shown in a painting of this subject in 1668 by Rembrandt's student Lambert Doomer (Musée des Beaux-Arts, Orléans).[1] In the painting of 1665, Van den Eeckhout was more concerned with the painterly evocation of Oriental splendor and an orientation toward tradition than with the possibility for sitters to be identified with historical figures. MPH

1 Cf. Van Leeuwen 2018, 482–83.

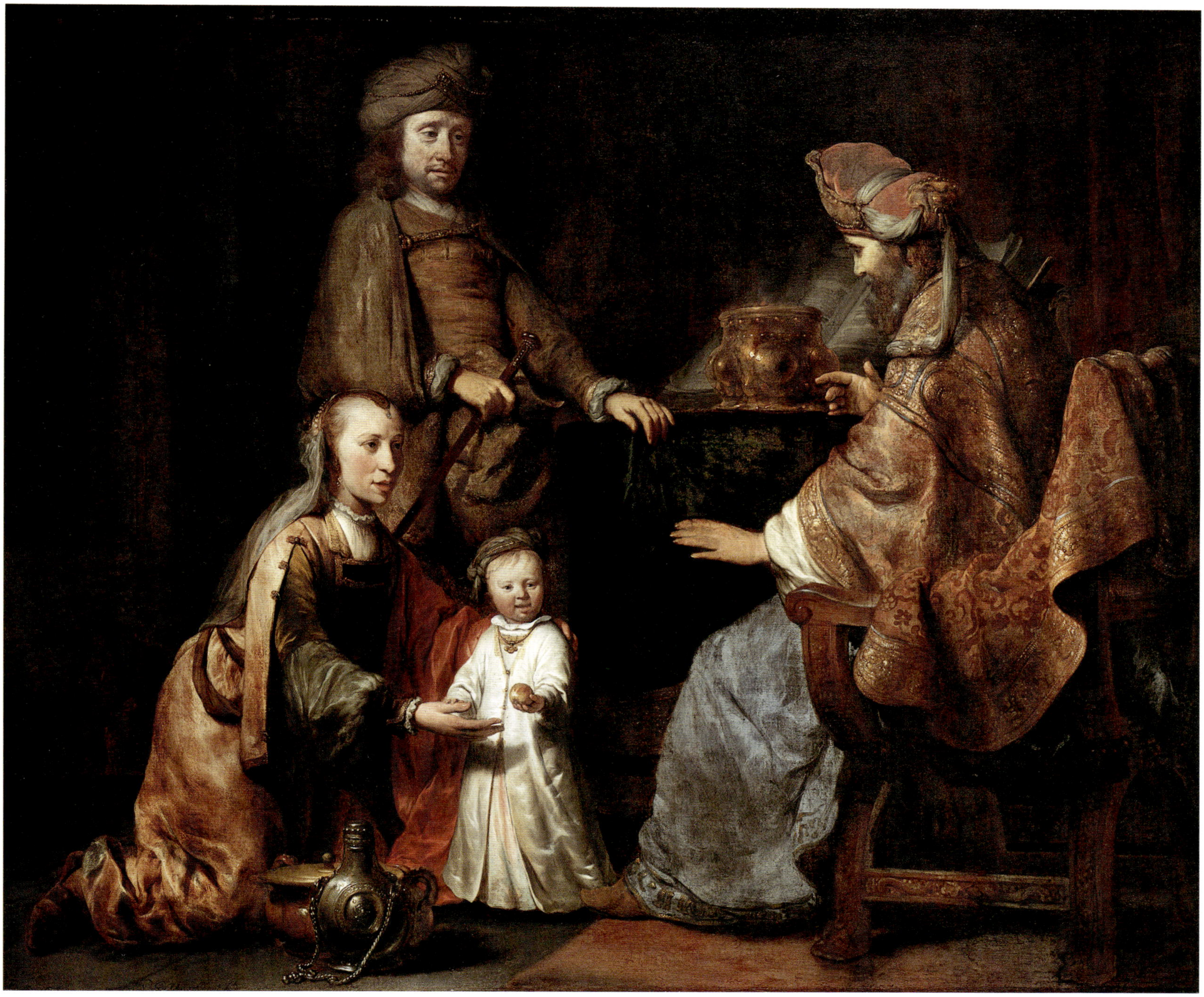

9

10 **Bartholomeus van der Helst** (1613–1670)
The Headmen of the Arquebus Civic Guard House, 1655

Oil on canvas, 171 x 283 cm
Inscribed on the left chair:
BARTHOLOMEUS.VANDER.HELST 1655
Inv. SA 2101
Amsterdam Museum

Lit.
Amsterdam 1975–79, no. 171
Ydema 1991, no. 413
Amsterdam 2002a, 209–10; no. 76
Amsterdam 2008b, 112–13.
Van Gent 2011, no. 76, fig. p. 100
Amsterdam 2014, 18

No other type of painting reflects the self-image of the Amsterdam elite of the seventeenth century more aptly than group portraits. In these portraits, the heads of the civic guards or charitable institutions had themselves depicted at their meetings. Bartholomeus van der Helst shows the leaders of the Amsterdam Kloveniersdoelen, the headquarters of the civic guard, eating a meal of oysters. In keeping with contemporary fashion, they sit in black clothing and wide-brimmed black hats around a table covered by a Persian carpet painted in detail. The placement of the Oriental material in a central position in this scene, which is creating a sense of identity, is here not primarily a status symbol as in the individual portraits of that time (cat. 16, 25, 34). Rather, it demonstrates how natural it had become in the seventeenth century to include exotic objects in the Dutch way of life.

The civic guard associations, which had existed since the Middle Ages, performed a function of social cohesion in addition to the practical task of protecting the general order. Their members—frequently only their leaders—were portrayed life-size in monumental paintings, which documented examples of civic virtue in practice in the assembly rooms and banquet halls of the clubhouse. The sitters paid for being included in a group portrait, and their placement in the composition often depended on the size of their contribution. The most famous civic guard painting is Rembrandt's *Night Watch* (fig. p. 18). Until the beginning of the eighteenth century, the painting hung in the clubhouse of the Amsterdam Kloveniers, named after the *klover*, an early kind of rifle.

In 1655 Cornelis Jansz. Witsen, Roelof Bicker, Gerard Reynst, and Simon van Hoorn were the heads of the Amsterdam Kloveniersdoelen. They had distinguished themselves as mayors, art collectors, or wealthy merchants. They are shown here in a staged conversation where wine and oysters are being served. The oyster meal was a popular subject in Dutch painting—and usually erotically charged. It was thus an unusual subject for a group portrait of a civic guard association.

Occasionally, attendants are also depicted in group portraits. Here it is probably Jacob Pietersz. Nachtglas, then castellan of the Kloveniersdoelen, and his daughter Geertruyd, whose husband may be portrayed in the doorway. Their simple clothing and serving function emphasize their social difference from the upper middle class.

Rembrandt too painted a group portrait in which a few gentlemen dressed in black sit at a table with an Oriental carpet: *The Sampling Officials of the Amsterdam Drapers' Guild,* known as *"The Syndics"* of 1662 (Rijksmuseum, Amsterdam). Unlike Van der Helst and most other contemporary painters, Rembrandt did not attach importance to a detailed reproduction of the carpet pattern. He was concerned with the atmospheric value of its red color, which he accentuated through the use of light. MPH

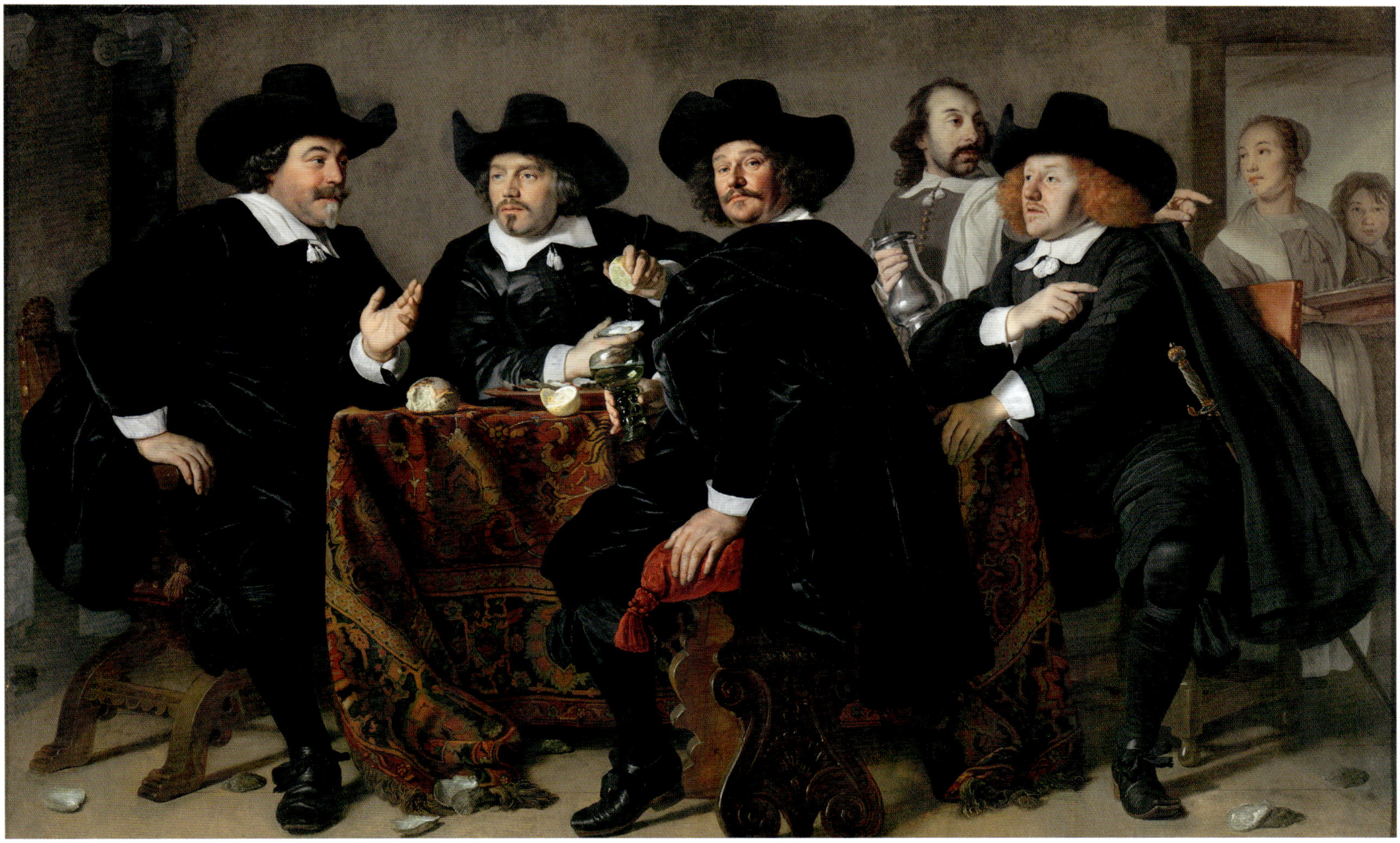

10

11 **Nicolaes Maes** (1634–1693)

Young Scholar in an Armchair, ca. 1655–60

Oil on panel, 39 x 31 cm
Inscribed on the globe frame: N. MAES
Inv. GG 265
Herzog Anton Ulrich-Museum, Braunschweig, Kunstmuseum des Landes Niedersachsen

Lit.
Valentiner 1924, 58, 60
Sumowski 1983–94, vol. 3, no. 1398
Robinson 1996, 119, note 68
Krempel 2000, no. D 14

Based on dendrochronological evidence, the painting was probably made around or shortly after 1658. It shows a remarkably young academic in his apparently monumental library consulting three tomes at the same time. The globe, standing to the left in the foreground and showing America, could indicate that he is a geographer. It is appropriate that he is wearing a brass-colored housecoat in the Japanese style with a bright red lining turned out to form a kind of lapel. Such an article of clothing in blue can also be seen in Vermeer's *Geographer* (fig. p. 18). In both paintings the robe, which is intended to be worn at home, indicates that this is the respective scholar's own study, where we have been invited to a rather intimate encounter with him.

The robe—known in contemporary sources as *japonse rok* (Japanese robe) due to its derivation from the Japanese kimono—enjoyed great popularity among the propertied upper class of the Netherlands beginning in the middle of the seventeenth century as an expensive and unusual luxury product and status symbol. It was worn as a housecoat (see the essay by Erik Spaans, pp. 12–23). At first such *japonse rokken,* like the originals that were presented to the representatives of the East India Company at their annual reception by the emperor of Japan, were made primarily of silk. Later, however, they were also made of Indian chintz, a similarly shiny and iridescent cotton fabric that often had colorful patterns. The company imported chintz especially for this purpose.[1] Japanese robes can be found in numerous representative portraits of the time, and artists also liked to portray themselves in this garment (see cat. 12–13, 15, 34). BB

1 For the *japonse rok* and its characteristics cf. Amsterdam 2015, 195–99.

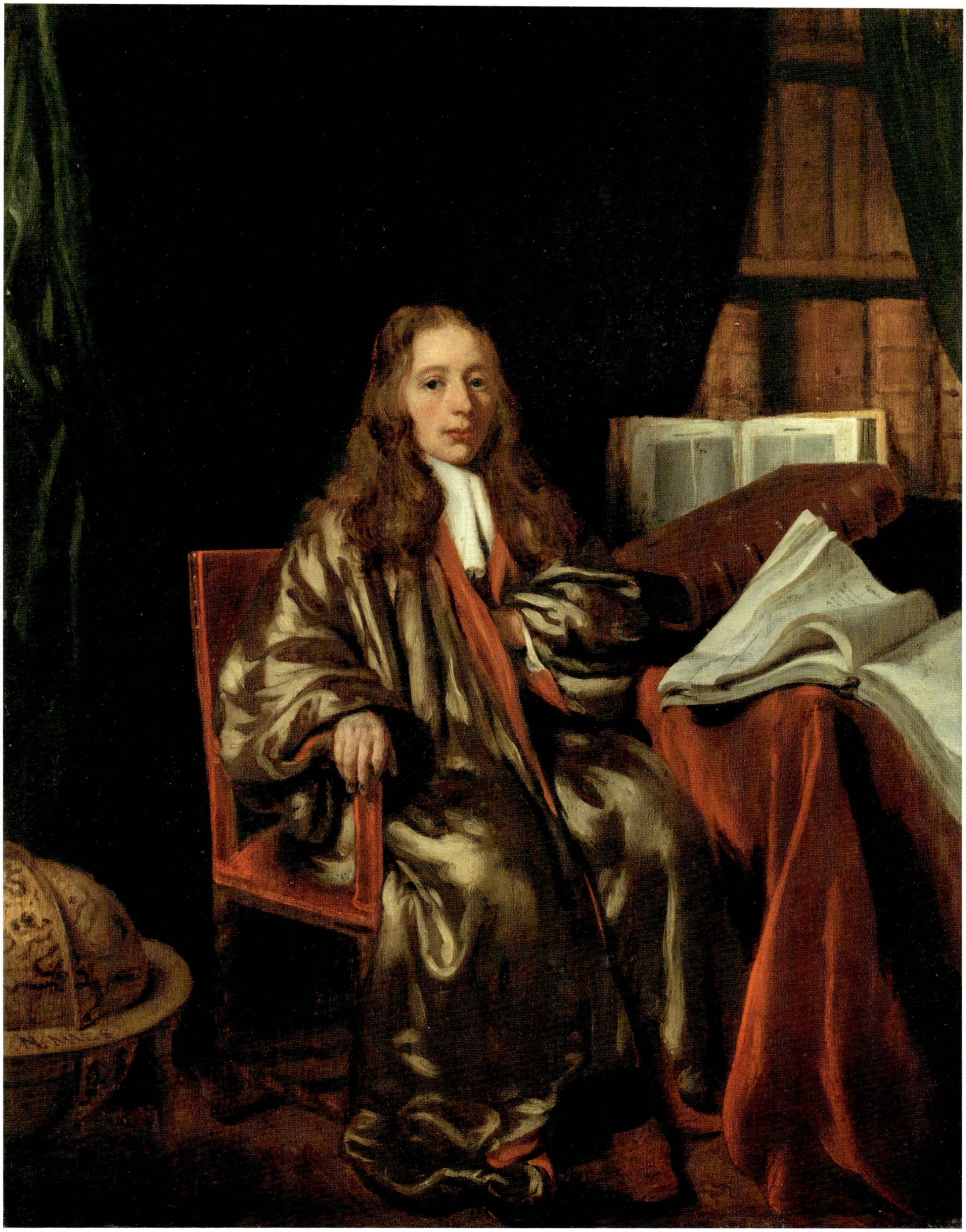

11

12 **Jan Lievens** (1607–1674)
Self-Portrait, early 1650s

Oil on canvas, 96.2 x 77 cm
Inscribed in center of wall: I.L.
Inv. NG2864
The National Gallery, London, presented by Charles Fairfax Murray, 1912

Lit.
Sumowski 1983–94, vol. 3, no. 1289
Gifford 2008, 50
Wheelock 2009, 20–21
Washington 2009, no. 48
Schnackenburg 2016, 454, no. A 16

The self-portrait, which combines provocative nonchalance with unshakable self-confidence and exudes aristocratic elegance through its distinctive coloring, shows Jan Lievens at the height of his career. There is little here, in terms of style or motifs, that would suggest the once close relationship to Rembrandt that had marked the work of both artists during their time together up to 1632 in Leiden (see the essay by Gary Schwartz, pp. 56–73; cat. 58, 103–04). In both London and Antwerp, where he worked successfully until 1644, Lievens had gradually adopted the Flemish models of painting established there and adapted his own painting style accordingly. Apart from Rubens and the Italian influences spread through Rubens's circle—which can be seen, for instance, in the Venetian-like colorfulness of the dusky background landscape—it was Anthony van Dyck who influenced Lievens. The London painting bears witness to this down to details of the painting technique.

In 1644 Lievens, following Rembrandt's example, moved to Amsterdam, where his career continued without interruption. In the next years he not only painted several portraits for a wealthy private clientele, but also received representative commissions for history paintings from the city government. His art was also regarded highly at the courts in The Hague and Berlin.

Thus, at the beginning of the 1650s Lievens had good reasons to present himself according to all the rules of his art as a recognized member of the better society. The Far East, whose exoticism had occupied him a quarter of a century earlier in other contexts (see cat. 58, 104), is also present here, albeit primarily as a status symbol. The precious garment, iridescent in various shades of gold, in which the artist wraps himself with such conscious carelessness, and dandyishly, with scarcely a hint of a body underneath, is a magnificent example of the *japonse rok*. In addition to members of the Dutch East India Company (cat. 15) and other official dignitaries as well as the financially powerful Dutch upper class (cat. 16, 34), other artists such as Jürgen Ovens (cat. 13) also used this costly accessory of East Asian provenance for self-dramatization. In contrast to Ovens, who for a time was thought to be portrayed in the London painting, Lievens did not depict himself at work in front of the easel, but for his portrait adopted those representational formulas including the correct dosage of *sprezzatura,* which he had got to know firsthand during his Flemish intermezzo and which was also to form the basis of his success in Amsterdam. The material prosperity thus expressed did not last. When he died, Lievens was so heavily in debt that his children rejected the inheritance. GD

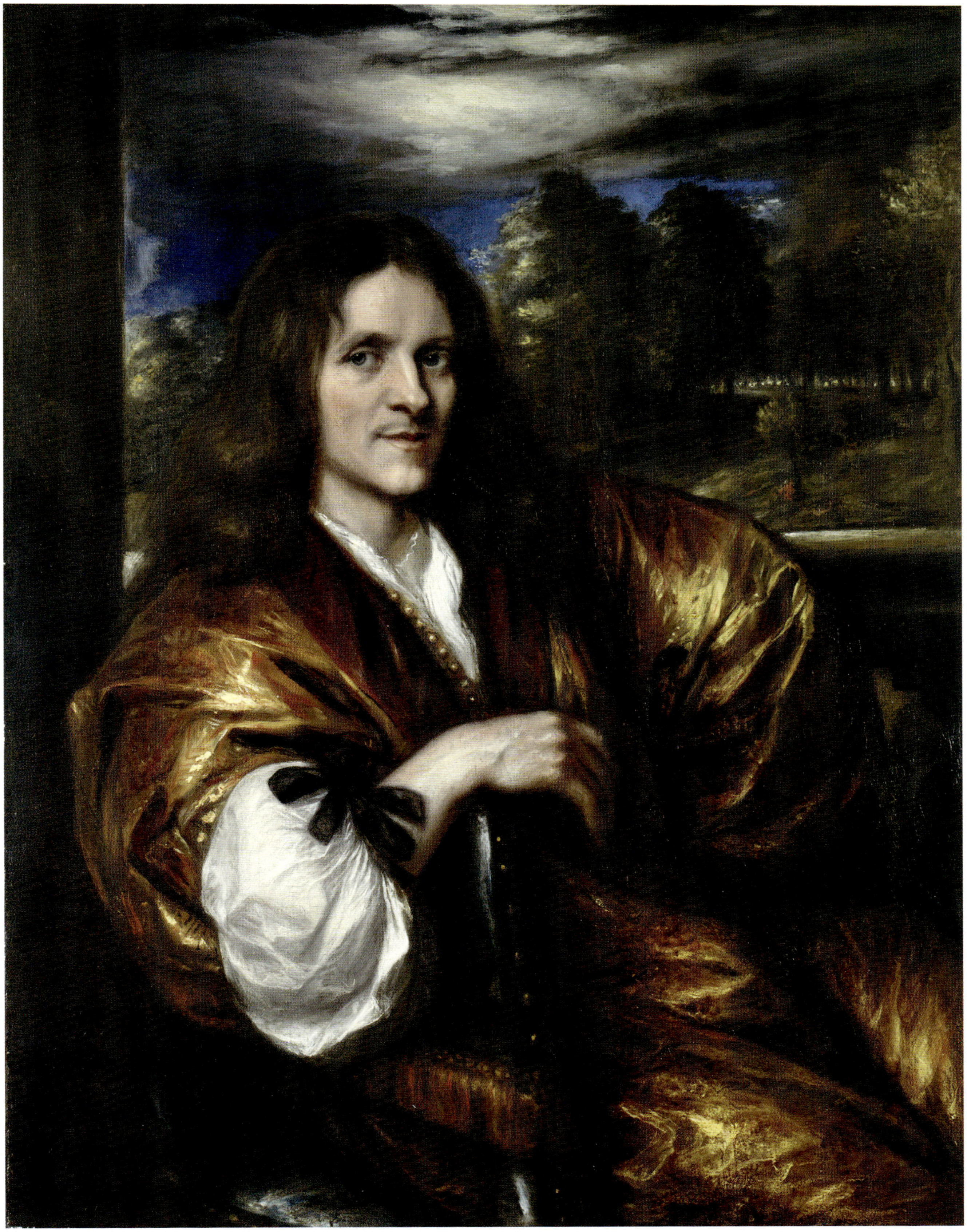

12

13 **Jürgen Ovens** (1623–1678) (?)
Self-Portrait with Easel, ca. 1670–75

Oil on canvas, 125 x 95 cm
Inv. GZ-2782
The State Hermitage Museum,
St. Petersburg

Lit.
Haak 2001, no. SB 5
Dordrecht 2012, no. 34
Köster 2017, 419

To the right in this nearly monochrome painting a half-length portrait of a woman in an oval is placed on an easel before a neutral, nearly black background. A chair stands in front of the picture and the artist is leaning on its back. He holds a brush and palette in his left hand; in his right, behind his back, he holds the mahlstick, which is thus more in the foreground than any other object in the painting.

Standing in front of his portrait, the painter has turned his head and looks over his shoulder at the observer. The fact that he is not using, indeed concealing, the conspicuously positioned mahlstick seems to be the key to the work's message. The stick, its tip covered with a soft knob of fabric or leather, is leaned on the painting's support during the work. Of all the tools of the painter's craft, it therefore indicates most clearly the material character of the work of art. Hence, its suspension negates the portrait's materiality, which at first glance could be mistaken for a real person in the dark composition. As a result, the picture evokes the Pygmalion motif of the true-to-life work of art that comes alive.

The myth implies intimacy in the relationship between painter and work, which is reinforced by the costume of the former. The artist wears a house coat of Japanese silk—common in other paintings (cat. 11, 12, 15, 34)—held together with a colorful cloth belt. A scarf is hung casually over his shoulder. The clothing, therefore, is more suited to a tête-à-tête with an intimate friend than to the daily work of a painter.

Born in Schleswig-Holstein, Jürgen Ovens spent some time in Amsterdam from 1640 onwards, before he returned to his homeland in 1651, bidden there by Friedrich III, duke of Holstein-Gottorp. At the ducal court he also represented the Amsterdam art dealer Gerrit van Uylenburgh, who was close to Rembrandt. Between 1657 and 1663 Ovens was back in Amsterdam working with Govert Flinck, whose workshop he took over after Flinck's death in 1660.

In her recently published catalogue raisonné, Constanze Köster removed the present painting from Ovens's oeuvre without further explanation. It had previously been considered a late work of the painter because of the airy and relaxed application of paint. If it must really be attributed to someone else, that artist would most likely be found in Govert Flinck's circle. BB

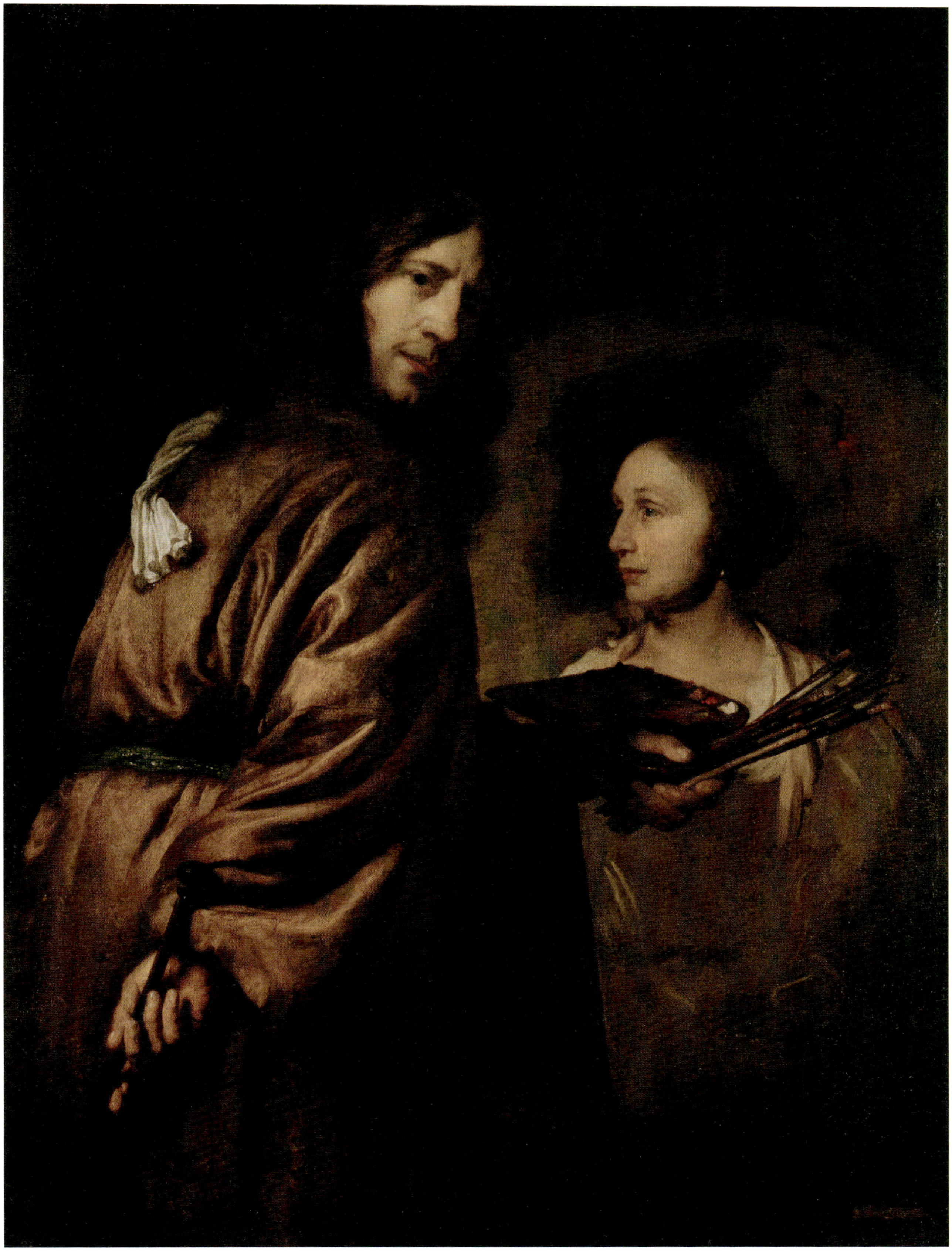

14 **Dirck van Loonen** (1619/20–1711)

Assueer Jacob Schimmelpenninck van der Oye (1631–1673) with Servant and Dog, 1660

Oil on canvas, 224 x 185 cm
Inv. DVS00402
Stichting Duivenvoorde, Voorschoten

Lit.
Franken 2002, 10–13
Nijmegen 2002, no. 32

[1] Cf. Schimmelpenninck van der Oye 1871.

In Dutch portraits of the seventeenth century, exotic clothing was a common element. While wearing a Japanese housecoat (cat. 11–13, 15, 34), for example, was a fashionable trend, Assueer Jacob Schimmelpenninck van der Oye had a personal motive to have himself painted in Oriental dress. He had just returned from a year-long trip to the Levant, from where he had presumably brought back the precious caftan, dagger, and saber as well as the turban decorated with a feather. He probably also brought back the monstrous dog. Whether this is true of the servant, too, who is also dressed in Oriental costume, is impossible to determine. The nobleman from Geldern staged himself in a self-confident pose as a cosmopolitan connoisseur of the foreign and lover of the unusual. From all his experiences in the Orient he could claim that his clothing was authentic and original. This, however, does not necessarily indicate any deeper interest in other cultures.

After attending university in Groningen and Utrecht, the twenty-seven-year-old Schimmelpenninck left his hometown of Zutphen in November 1657 on a pilgrimage to the eastern Mediterranean. He reached Jerusalem via Cyprus, Tyros, and Sidon, and then proceeded to Damascus, Tripoli, and finally to Aleppo, an undertaking that was by no means common at the time. His diary provides information about his route, by ship, on foot, and on horse or donkey.[1] He focused his attention on the biblical places that, according to the descriptions of his local guides, were believed to have remained unchanged since the days of Jesus—for example, the well from which the water was drawn that was supposed to have been turned into wine at the wedding in Cana. Occasionally, the traveler also recorded observations about local customs, but he only mentions encounters with priests or Western merchants, such as Havic Benningh, a resident of Aleppo from Amsterdam.

Schimmelpenninck's proud posture speaks of the self-confidence he felt after mastering the challenges of such a journey. His pride in his accomplishment is conveyed by his ornamental weapons and clothing, which are more than mere souvenirs. His claim to fame is underscored by the massive dog, which was apparently so large that the person portrayed had to stand on a stone step to be able to so casually lay his hand on its head. The diary does not mention at which point in his journey he found the unusual animal. Dogs appear frequently as status-enhancing accessories in portraits, but they are primarily lapdogs or hunting dogs. Rembrandt painted a self-portrait with a poodle around 1631–33 (fig. p. 63). Schimmelpenninck's animal companion, however, is extraordinarily dominant. With his enormous stature and red-hot eyes he may also be reminiscent of the dangers to be found in foreign lands and serve the clichéd idea of the absolute power of Oriental rulers. MPH

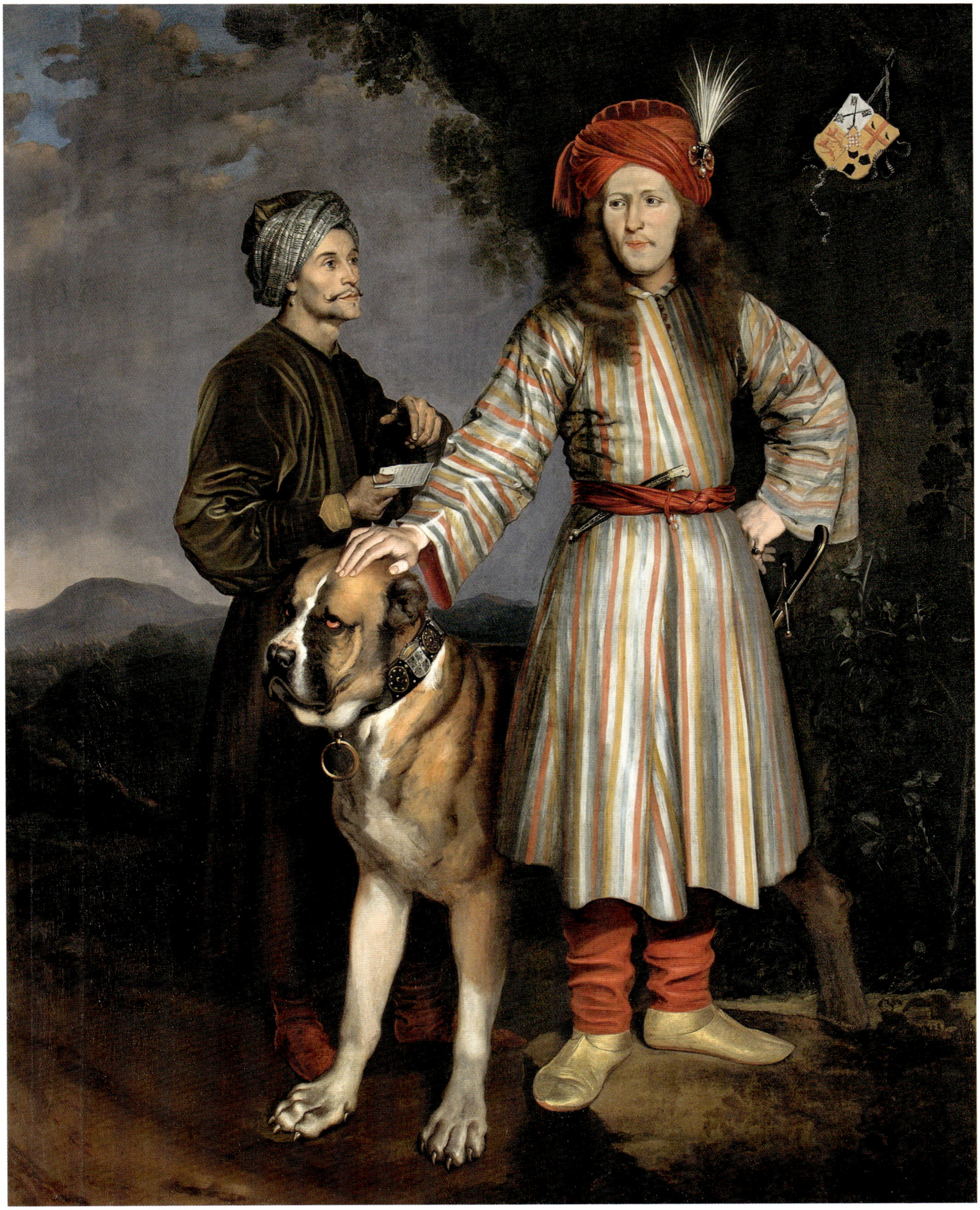

14

15 **Gerbrand van den Eeckhout** (1621–1674)

Portrait of an Unknown Governor of the Dutch East India Company, 1669

Oil on canvas, 111 x 90 cm
Inscribed bottom, left of center (on balustrade pillar): Aetatis 41 / [illegible] / G.Vanden.Eeckhout. f. / Aº 1669
Inv. MG 74
Musée de Grenoble

Lit.
Paris 1971, no. 71
Sumowski 1983–94, vol. 3, no. 534
Lyon 1992, no. 39
Grenoble 1994, 84
Chambéry 2001, no. 78

This representative painting shows the knee-length portrait of a man with loose, shoulder-length hair. According to the inscription he is forty-one years of age. He is standing on a narrow terrace that runs parallel to the picture plane and is closed off at the back by a low parapet wall. The front border is marked by a stone balustrade that enters the picture on the left and ends on a column. On the left an imposing red curtain, a motif of ennoblement, blocks the view; on the right, there is a view of a landscape that is clearly not to be found in Holland. On a flat spit of land with a sandy beach and rows of palm trees there are some fenced-in buildings of wooden construction over which the flag of the Dutch East India Company waves—thus, it might be one of the company's settlements in present-day Indonesia (see cat. 86) or some other area of East Asia, although precise identification is not possible.

The unknown sitter looks at the observer confidently, one hand resting on the column while the other holds his garment closed in front of his chest. This is just as exotic as the landscape. Over a snow-white shirt he is wearing a magnificent long cloak, whose shiny silk fabric shimmers in various shades of ochre and brown and which on the inside has a light-colored, finely patterned lining. This is a typical example of a *japonse rok* as it appears in numerous (self-) portraits (cat. 11–13, 34).

The sitter must have been one of the East India Company's high-ranking officials since, along with the great display of wealth and social status, and the Far East setting, the portrait has a direct connection to the Company that can hardly be overlooked. One name that has been suggested is Johan de Witt, who as grand pensionary of Holland beginning in 1653, was one of the leading political figures of the Republic for a good twenty years. This, however, has not been definitely established. GD

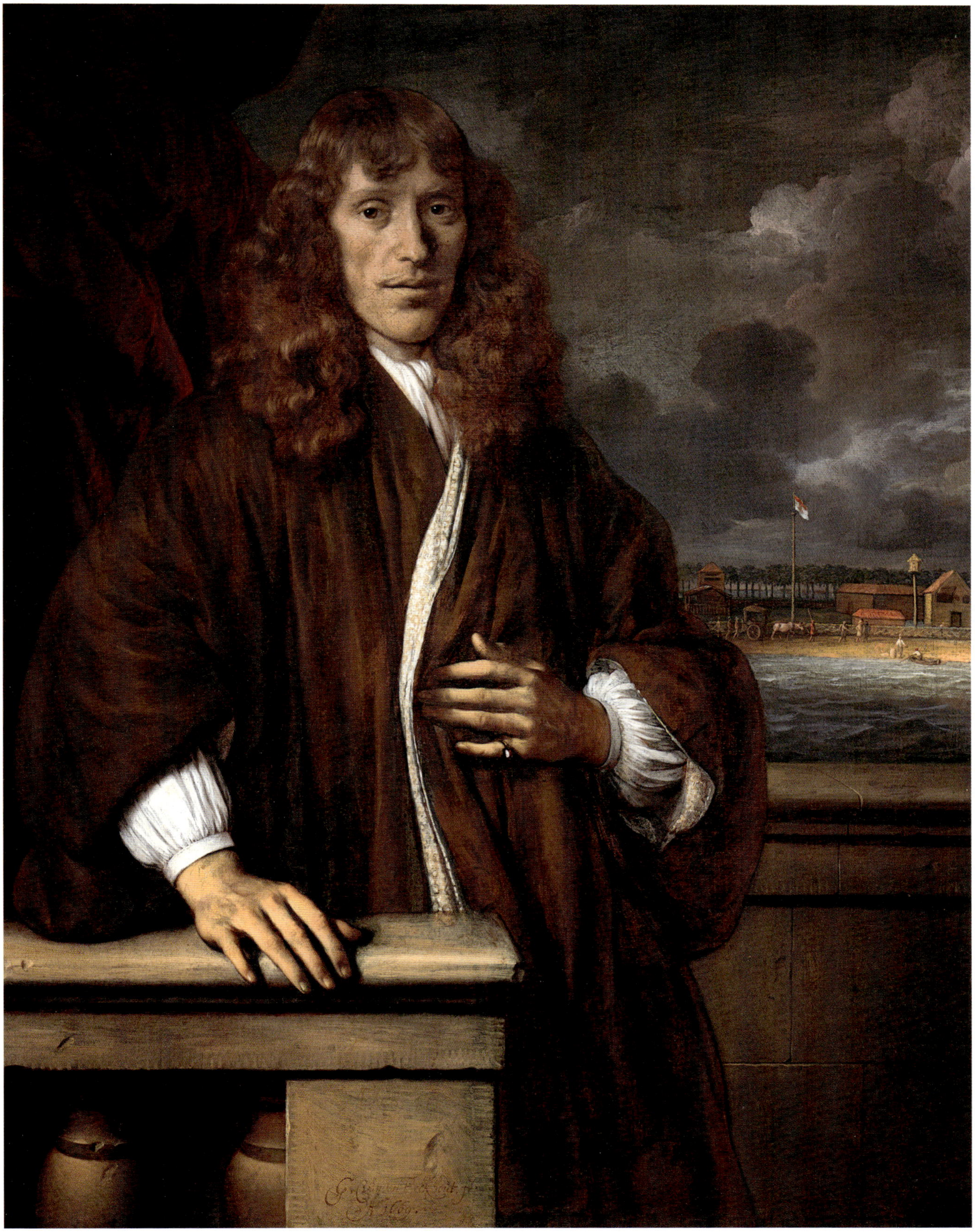

16 Anonymous

Don Francisco Lopes Suasso, ca. 1675–90

Oil on canvas, 144 x 120 cm
Inv. SA 487
Amsterdam Museum

Lit.
Amsterdam 1975–79, no. 563
Schönduve 1988, fig. 2
Ydema 1991, 89–90.
Amsterdam 2008b, 232, 261, 263

Sephardic Jews who had been expelled from Spain and Portugal played an important role in the Dutch economy as traders and bankers. With their multilingual ability, high level of education, and international family connections, they possessed important prerequisites for successful involvement in the burgeoning global trading power. One of the most important Sephardim in the Dutch Republic in the second half of the seventeenth century was Francisco Lopes Suasso, who had himself portrayed in contemporary courtly guise. The orange in his right hand indicates his personal closeness to Stadtholder Willem III, prince of Orange. His arm rests on the table, which is covered by a Persian carpet, which is prominently depicted in the picture—a contemporary status symbol (see cat. 10, 25, 34) and color counterpart to his clothing.

Suasso's wardrobe follows, in every detail, the latest fashion from the court of Louis XIV, which spread from France throughout Europe. The allonge wig, parted in the middle with curls falling far over the shoulders; the lace jabot with a bow around his neck; the hip-length black jacket with lace cuffs, red ribbons, and bows; the wide, gold-embroidered sash; the wrinkled, knee-length rhinegraves; silk stockings and shoes with high heels that are just as red as the soles. The column in the background, a traditional symbol of dignity, fits in well with this status-conscious staging, as, for example, the successful fleet commander Wollebrand Geleynsz. de Jongh had himself painted in his portrait (cat. 25).

Francisco Lopes Suasso was born in Amsterdam in 1657. His father, Antonio, came from Bordeaux and belonged to the Marranos, Spanish Jews who were forcibly baptized but who more or less adhered to the Jewish faith. Some of whom, including Suasso, later returned to Judaism.[1] Elevated by the king of Spain in 1676 to the rank of Baron of Averras le Gas, he was one of the richest Sephardic merchants in Amsterdam. He made his fortune trading in diamonds, Brazilian sugar, and Spanish wool and invested in shares in the West India and East India Companies. His son, Francisco, retired from trading and worked exclusively as a banker and investor. He settled in The Hague in a city palace near the seat of government. Suasso took part in court life and was in personal contact with Willem III, whose policies he supported with substantial sums of money. The orange, however, does not necessarily allude to the phrase "to have someone in hand"—in Dutch the expression *iemand op zijn hand hebben* means to support someone.

For all the religious tolerance toward Jews in the Netherlands, they were allowed to practice only a few professions and were not granted civil rights until 1796. Even though their number was not great in seventeenth-century Amsterdam—around 1700, with about ten thousand members of the community, they made up only about five percent of the population—they played an important role in the economic life of the city as traders and financiers and in its intellectual life as publishers and printers. They were a visible and active part of the internationally oriented Dutch society. Thus, they also appeared in paintings such as the harbor scene by Thomas Wijck (cat. 27) or the *Parody of Religious Tolerance* (cat. 46). MPH

1 Cf. Israel 2007, 107–08.

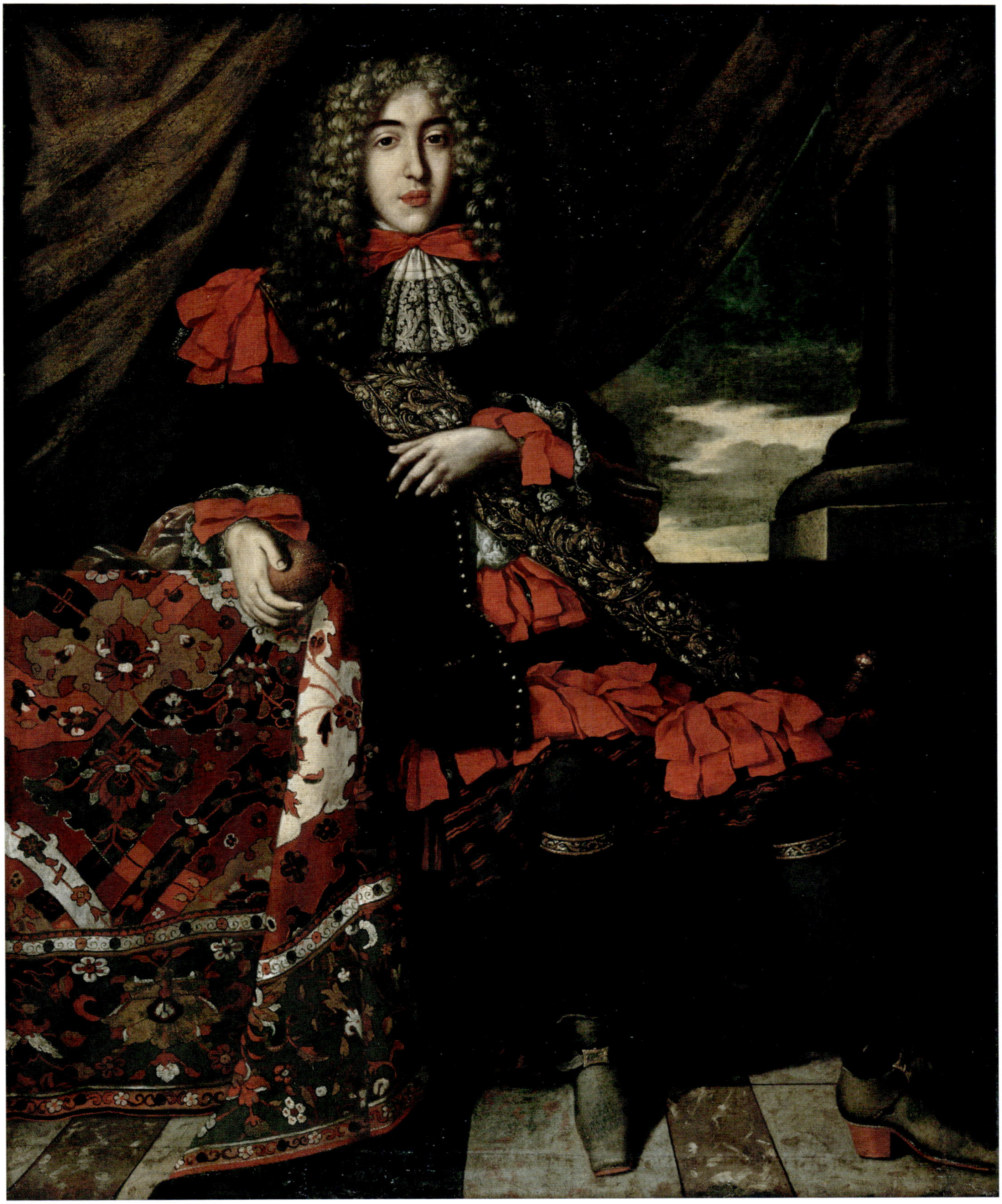

16

Paths to Prosperity: Trade and War

The global trade networks developed by the Dutch in the seventeenth century provided the basis for the interest in faraway lands and the availability of exotic objects. Visual representations on the theme of trade were typically neither realistic nor documentary in character, insofar as they made no claim to reproduce scenes faithfully or visualize episodes from history with scrupulous attention to facts. Rather, they were intended to convey prestige and fulfill a decorative function. This latter aspect even applied to depictions of the ongoing violent conflicts that formed one of the shadow sides of global trade. The Dutch Republic's wealth was also built on other devastating activities in East Asia such as slavery, economic exploitation, and violence—although negative topics such as these would at most be depicted in engravings in published works[1] and never received artistic treatment from painters of the era.[2]

The engraving *View of Amsterdam* by Claes Jansz. Visscher II and Pieter Bast (cat. 17) mixes an accurate panorama of the city with allegory. The silhouette of the city, though precisely rendered, merely serves as the backdrop to Amsterdam's symbolic elevation as the center of world trade. People of various ethnicities are shown peddling their wares. In reality, the exotic goods arriving in Amsterdam were already the property of Dutch merchants. Having purchased the goods in the Near or Far East, merchants had them transported to the Netherlands in their own ships, and so reaped the lion's share of the total value chain.

The engraving *The Headquarters of the Dutch East India Company in Amsterdam* by the workshop of Jacob van Meurs (cat. 18) is an architecturally accurate representation of the building. The depiction of the all-powerful trade organization's imposing headquarters was intended to convey the same sort of grandeur as Gerrit Adriaensz. Berckheyde's *The Town Hall on Dam Square in Amsterdam* (cat. 21). The latter work shows people milling on the square in front of the recently completed building, which was lauded by contemporaries as the eighth wonder of the world.[3] Among them are a number of men wearing turbans—a subtle reference to the presence of a delegation from the Orient. This anecdotal detail was possibly based on a moment from real life. It might well have been here that Rembrandt, who after all never set foot outside the Netherlands, saw and sketched such turban-wearing men (cat. 19–20).

Another work created to reflect the grandeur of its subject is Caesar van Everdingen's portrait of Wollebrand Geleynsz. de Jongh (cat. 25), which stylizes the merchant from Alkmaar as a successful negotiator in the Far East. The two Black pages function as attributes of the Dutchman's power. The painting shows nothing of the unscrupulousness of the man, who in real life did not shy from using force of arms to settle trade disputes. A similar story of commercial success is recounted in Elias Herckmans's poem *Der zee-vaert lof* (In Praise of Seafaring), which was published in 1634 as a book with a title page illustrated by Rembrandt (cat. 22). The hardship of down-at-heel sailors—precisely the sort of people whose toil contributed to such Dutch success stories—is embodied by Cornelis Dusart and Abraham Allard, albeit only with caricatural cursoriness (cat. 23–24).[4] The sailors' appearance is in stark contrast to the self-satisfied pride exuded by Wollebrand Geleynsz. de Jongh.

One of the very few paintings that refer to a concrete, historically attested event in trade history is Jan Baptist Weenix's *The Dutch Ambassador on His Way to Isfahan* (cat. 26). History records both the name of the envoy and the date of the voyage, although it seems unlikely that the group would have been welcomed by the waving group of friendly women dressed in European fashions. The large work may have been painted for a client who wished to commemorate his trade mission, although it would also have served as a decorative showpiece. Genre paintings of ports around the Mediterranean did not aspire to either historical or topographical accuracy. Important Levantine trading posts in this period were the port cities of Alexandretta (present-day Iskenderun) and Smyrna (now İzmir). Then located in the Ottoman Empire, both cities were home to populations of Armenians, Jews, Muslims, and Greeks. Featuring picturesque scenes populated with stock characters amid architectural set pieces, the paintings by Thomas Wijck, Abraham Begeyn, and Jacob Toorenvliet convey an aestheticized mood and an exotic atmosphere (cat. 27–29).

This sort of idealization even characterizes works that depict scenes of war. The Dutch East India Company had just as few scruples as its competitors when it came to enforcing monopoly interests, and thus found itself continually embroiled in armed conflicts with mercantile nations and great powers such as Portugal, Spain, England, and the Ottoman Empire. The decontextualized setting and aestheticization of the cannon painted by Leendert Maertensz. van Haestar (cat. 30) effectively obscures the weapon's lethal function. The paintings of battles on land and at sea by Philips Wouwerman, Jacques Muller, and Johannes Lingelbach (cat. 31–33), in which the fighting takes place beneath storm-filled skies, are aesthetically choreographed arrangements. While satisfying thrill-seeking viewers in the comfort of home, the battle scenes are packed with a broad sweep of figures that allow for the widest possible range of gestures and details—true to the principle of *Varietas delectat* (Variety is the spice of life). MPH

1 Numerous examples can be found in Schmidt 2015.
2 For more on this subject cf., among others, Amsterdam 2002b, Amsterdam 2011b, and Amsterdam 2015.
3 Cf. Gundolf Winter, "Sprechende Architektur: Jacob van Campens 'Neues Rathaus in Amsterdam,'" in Wilczek 1993, 213–36, here 214, and Hundertmarck 2010.
4 For sailors' living conditions, cf. Schmitt 2008.

17 Claes Jansz. Visscher II. (1586/87–1652) and **Pieter Bast** (ca. 1570–1605)
View of Amsterdam, Seen from the IJ, 1611

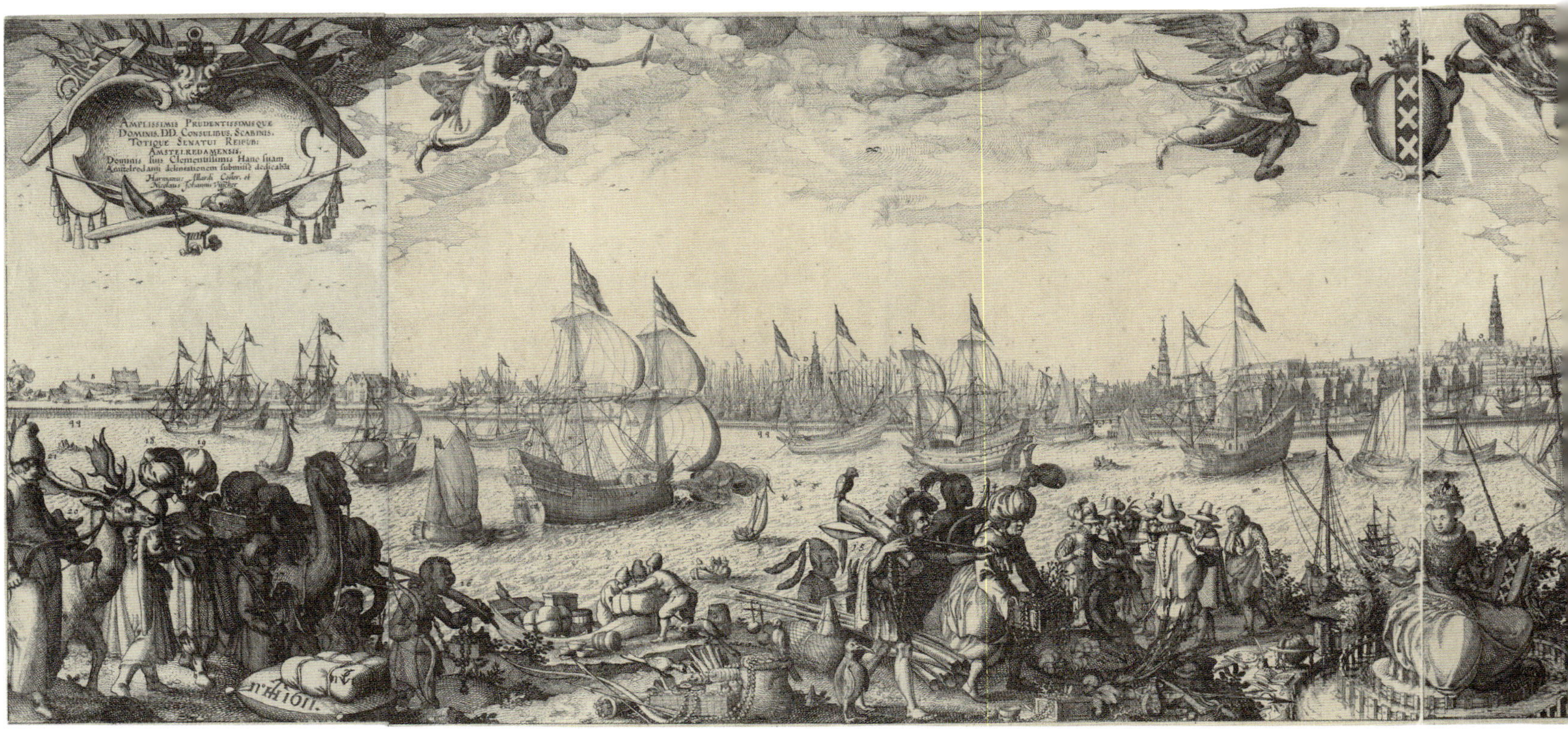

Engraving and etching, printed from four plates on two sheets, 26 x 112.2 cm
Inscribed on the bundles of merchandise to the left: n C [mirrored] IV [intertwined] 1 / n° HA [connected with a vertical line, monogram of publisher Herman Allertsz. Koster] 1611 •
Inv. RP-P-1884-A-7654
Rijksmuseum, Amsterdam, Rijksprentenkabinet

Lit.
Amsterdam 2007a, after p. 79 and no. 60
Amsterdam 2011a, 11–13
Kolfin 2011, 385–87
Swan 2013, 102–03
Leeflang 2014, 244–46
Amsterdam 2015, no. 2

Among the numerous seventeenth-century depictions of the city of Amsterdam as the center of world trade (figs. pp. 15, 26), this print by Claes Jansz. Visscher II occupies a special position. It combines an allegorical representation of goods and merchants from all over the world in the foreground with a realistic reproduction of the cityscape in the background. Prominent buildings like the stock exchange and the Nieuwe Kerk are not only recognizable but are also identified by letters and shown as separate illustrations in close-up along with a description in the text field of the engraving (fig. p. 31). The trade goods and their agents are situated on the north bank of the IJ, an inlet that connects the city with the North Sea and from there with the ocean. The countless sailing ships on the water and in the port provide evidence of the density of commercial traffic.

Pieter Bast engraved a view of Amsterdam on two printing plates in 1599; twelve years later, Claes Jansz. Visscher reworked them considerably with further engraving and etching, in addition to extending them laterally with impressions from two extra plates. In the process, he completely redesigned the foreground. While Bast restricted himself to a loose, genre-style image with costumed figures representing the city's inhabitants, Visscher developed what might be seen as an extensive program of visual propaganda.

At the center of the foreground is enthroned the figure of the *stedenmaagd,* the personification of the city of Amsterdam, like a profane Madonna of the *hortus conclusus*. In the sky above her, two winged figures bear the city's coat of arms. The *stedenmaagd,* dressed in contemporary style and wearing a crown, also holds a crowned city coat of arms in her left hand, together with the rod of justice, reminiscent of a scepter. Her right hand boldly raises the model of a merchant ship—the basis of the city's claim to both power and wealth. The *stedenmaagd*'s seat, built like the city of Amsterdam

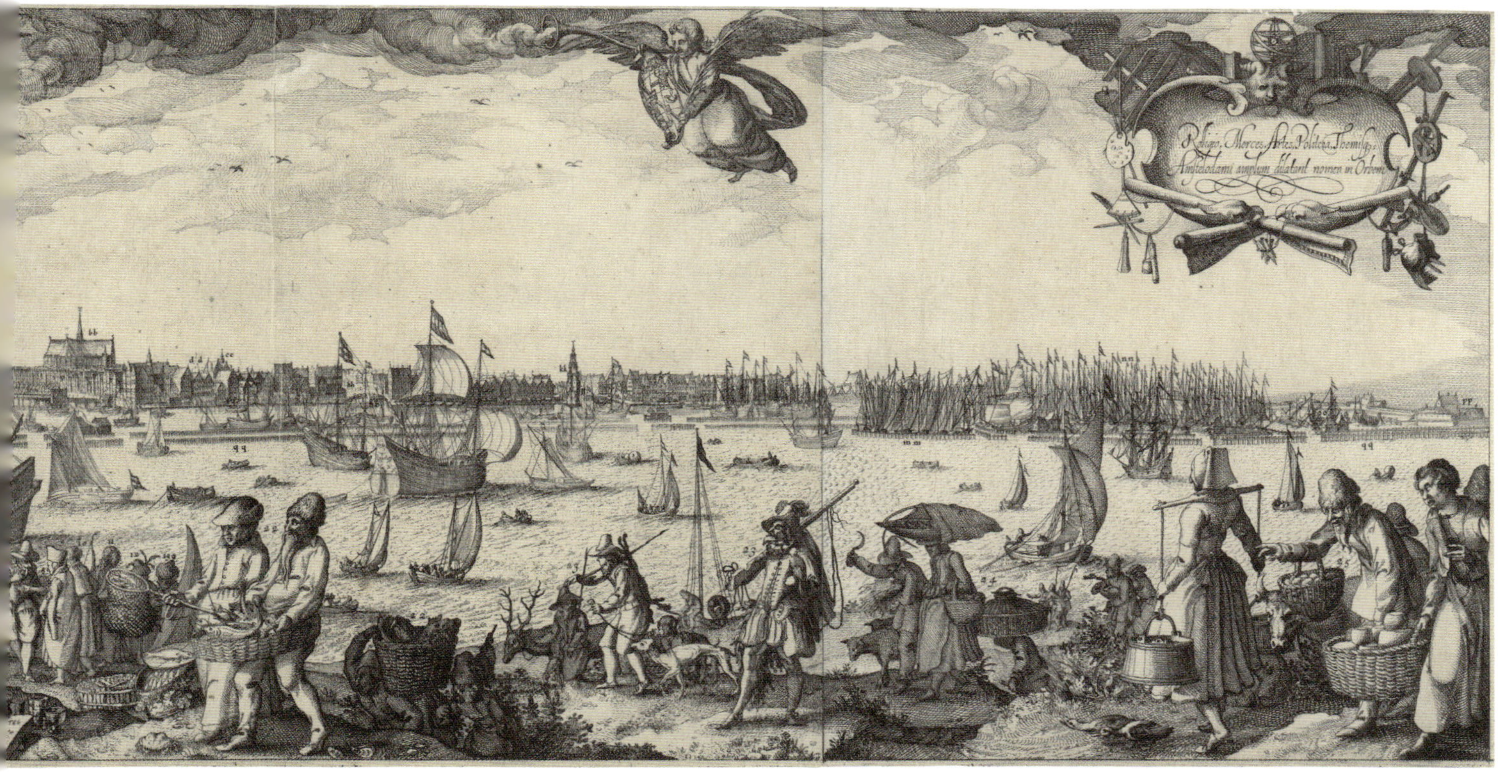

17

on stilts in boggy ground, is surrounded by grouped symbols of art and science such as books, a globe, a painter's palette, and a book of sheet music.

Merchants stream in from both sides, offering their goods in a gesture of homage. All of this, the text and images suggest, urges us to regard the "wijtvermaerde Hooft-Coop-Stadt des gantschen Weerelts" (the illustrious capital of trade with the entire world) as an honest broker for the exchange of goods. From the right, local fishermen, hunters, and farmers approach with baskets full of fish, eggs and cheese, game and chickens, geese and sheep. Among the figures on the left side, identified by numbers, are not only Europeans including an Englishman (4), a Pole (6), and a Hungarian (12) but also the inhabitants of such distant countries as East India (14), West India (15), Guinea (16), Persia (18), and China (20). Some of them are wearing turbans.

The "East Indians" bring pepper, cloves, precious stones, porcelain, nutmeg and mace, birds of paradise, silk, damask, parasols, and much else besides. From the opposite direction, the "West Indians" contribute sugar cane, gold and silver, precious woods, and tobacco; from China, in addition to porcelain, pearls, and silk, come musk, rhubarb, and the "very famous" China root, the root of the Chinese prickly bindweed used to treat syphilis. The scene also incorporates strange birds, a camel, exotic weapons, and natural objects like coral.

The world market staged here—this is the message of the engraving—is a fair one, and the economic success enjoyed by the metropolis on the Amstel is richly deserved—as promised by the Calvinist doctrine of predestination. It is hardly insignificant in this context that an open volume of the New Testament lies immediately to the right of the *stedenmaagd.* BB/MPH

18 Jacob van Meurs (ca. 1619/20–1679) or workshop
The Headquarters of the Dutch East India Company in Amsterdam ('T Oost-Indisch Huys), 1663

Engraving
In Olfert Dapper, *Historische beschryving der stadt Amsterdam . . .* (Historical Description of the City of Amsterdam), Amsterdam: Jacob van Meurs, 1663
Inv. RP-P-OB-102.062
Rijksmuseum, Amsterdam, Rijksprentenkabinet

Lit.
H 27
London 1990, no. 5
Amsterdam 1999a, 13
Outram 2006, 137

The Dutch East India Company was founded in 1602 by the government of the Republic to prevent competition between various Dutch expeditions to Asia and to channel their forces into a centralized structure. In economic terms, this move allowed it to develop into an unprecedented success story. The nongovernmental company, which operated as an independent commercial undertaking, was also appointed with extensive monopolies as well as both diplomatic and military authority. It was empowered to negotiate with rulers and governments on legal terms of its own (see cat. 26) and to act as a sovereign government both in the bases it established (see cat. 86) and the territories it administered as colonies.[1] However, the fact that it was also associated with bloody violence, oppression, exploitation, and the other negative effects related to early modern colonialism was hardly reflected in the general understanding or the visual arts of the time.

The company consisted of six chambers in the Republic's important port cities, and Amsterdam was its headquarters. In 1603, the year after its founding, it moved into a prestigious sixteenth-century building, previously used as an arsenal, on the centrally located Kloveniersburgwal. As this soon proved to be too small for the up-and-coming organization, a two-wing extension in the contemporary Mannerist style was built in 1606, probably designed by Hendrick de Keyser, the town architect of Amsterdam. In the 1630s and 1650s, additional wings were added to the complex known as the Oost-Indisch Huys (East India House), closing off with a façade the courtyard that had formerly been open to the Oude Hoogstraat.[2]

This engraving, which was published in 1663 in a history of Amsterdam by Olfert Dapper that includes views of the city's most important buildings, shows the last stage of construction as seen from Oude Hoogstraat. The bird's-eye view makes it possible to distinguish the various phases of construction: on the left, the old arsenal extends into the distance and one can see the inner façade of the rear courtyard and the first section of the right wing with its scrolled gables dating from 1606. The other sections represent later additions. The magnificence and imposing scale of the building are also quite evident. The fact that the engraving was included in Olfert Dapper's compilation demonstrates the significance attached to this building and, by extension, to its owner—an early example of corporate architecture.

The interior of the complex included not only offices, warehouses, and meeting rooms but also an extensive and publicly accessible collection of ethnographic and natural-history objects as well as maps (see cat. 40) and pictures from the West and East Indies. In the meeting room, for example, visitors were confronted with Andries Beeckman's monumental painting *The Castle of Batavia* (see cat. 86). The abundance of precious and exotic merchandise and luxury goods available here and elsewhere in the city offered artists like Rembrandt a convenient opportunity, unique in Europe, to view such objects without ever having to leave home. GD

1 For the history of the Dutch East India Company cf., among others, Bamberg 1988 and Gosselink 2015.
2 Cf. Kuyper 1994, 278.

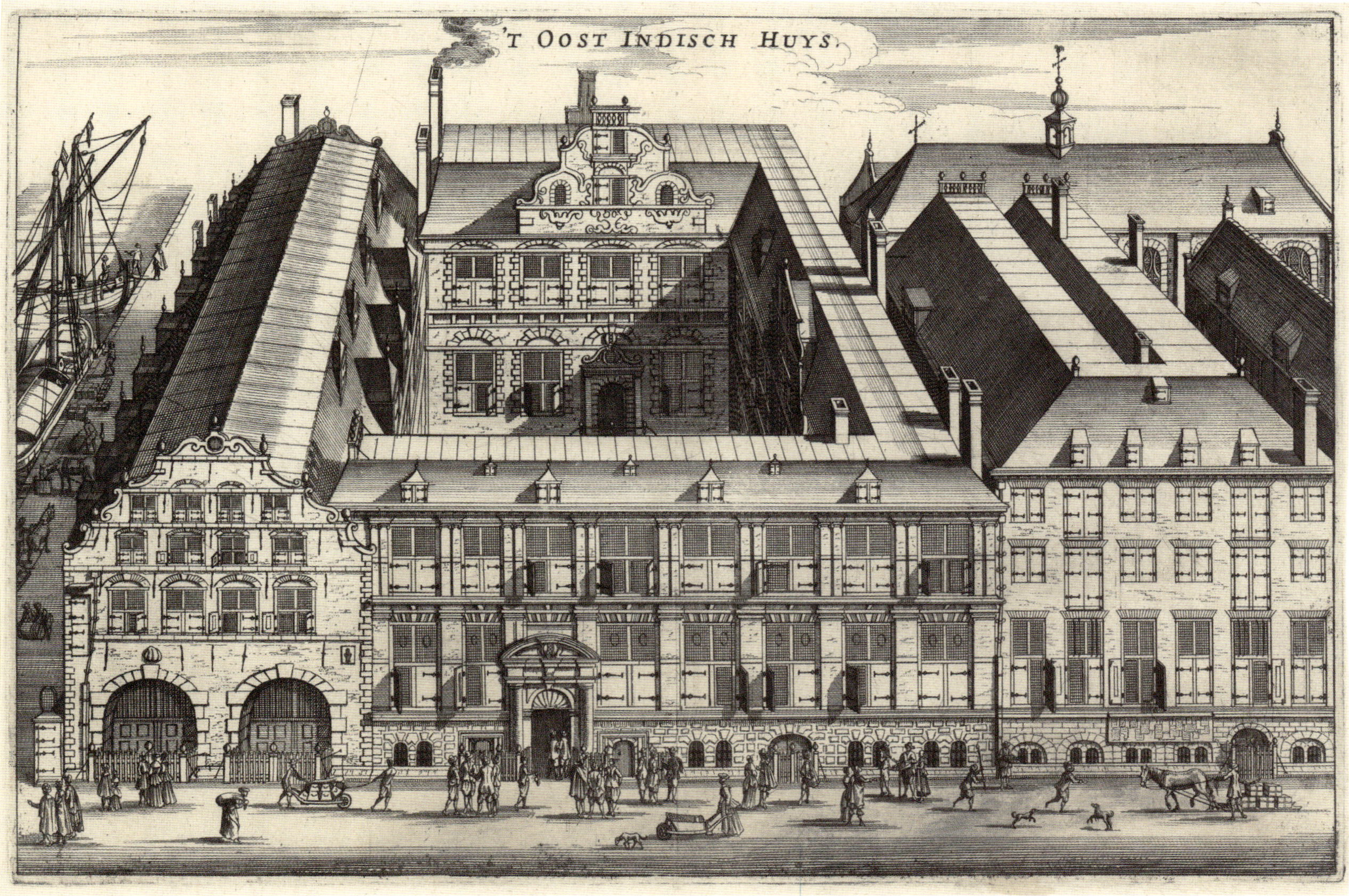
'T OOST INDISCH HUYS.

19 **Rembrandt Harmensz. van Rijn** (1606–1669)

Group of Men in Oriental Apparel and Two Half-Length Studies of a Beggar, ca. 1641–42

Pen, brush, brown ink, and wash,
14.3 x 18.6 cm
Inv. zb. d. 4285
University of Warsaw Library, Print Room

Lit.
Benesch 1954–57, vol. 4, no. 667, fig. 806
London 1992, with cat. 30, p. 86, fig. p. 88
Kansas City 1993, 101, no. 72, fig. p. 124
Schatborn 1999, 121, fig. 18
Warsaw 2004, 84–86, no. 5, fig.
Paris 2011, 91, pl. 3.11, 93, no. 22, 238
Warsaw 2019, 281–83, no. 130, fig.
(with a complete bibliography)

1 Cf. Benesch 1954–57, vol. 5, no. 914, fig. 124.
2 London 1992, no. 30, p. 86, fig. p. 88.
3 Cf. Sumowski 1979–92, vol. 9, no. 1052; Schatborn 1999, fig. p. 110, cat. 58, 255.

At the center of the drawing stand four men in conversation, dressed in Oriental clothing, flanked by two studies of the same beggar. A half figure, difficult to identify, appears at the lower right; it perhaps describes a man with a turban. It is reminiscent of the sphinx and the bust of a woman depicted by Rembrandt both in his drawing *Minerva in Her Study* in Jan Six's *Album amicorum* of 1652 (Six Collection, Amsterdam)[1] and, as early as about 1639, in the etching *The Artist Drawing from a Model*. The standing figure on the right is reminiscent of the man in Oriental dress in a drawing in the British Museum.[2] Similar compositions with Oriental figures can be found in other drawings by Rembrandt. Comparable types and arrangements of figures can also be seen in the sheet *Three Orientals Conversing* (cat. 20) as well as in several sketches by Rembrandt's pupil Arent de Gelder, such as the *Group of Oriental Figures* (Museum of Fine Arts, Boston).[3] The Warsaw sheet with the study of Oriental figures shown here might also have been one of the sources for the standing Pharisee on the left of the composition of *Christ Healing the Sick,* Rembrandt's *"Hundred Guilder Print"* of 1647–49.

This sheet documents the changes in Rembrandt's drawing style. His works from the 1640s show a combination of delicate brushstrokes and forceful, broad pen strokes that have gained in consistency and clarity; at the same time, the powerful expressiveness of earlier works has been reduced without actually diminishing the overall tautness of the composition. With just a few pen strokes, Rembrandt has detailed individual facial features with exceptional precision. This suggests a sketch quickly made from life.

Rembrandt made several such drawings, but we cannot assume that he faithfully recreated here a scene he had actually witnessed on the streets of Amsterdam, even though men dressed in Oriental clothing might occasionally have been seen there, as Gerrit Adriaensz. Berckheyde shows, for example, in his painting *The Town Hall on Dam Square in Amsterdam* of 1672 (cat. 21). It is much more likely that drawings such as this one feature a compilation of actual figures and genre types. Besides, the problem of Oriental stylization of this kind is more complex and reflected issues beyond the mere opportunity for direct observation. The biblical heroes in Oriental clothing masked important national ideas and the identification of the young Dutch Republic with the chosen nation, the so-called "New Israel." JT

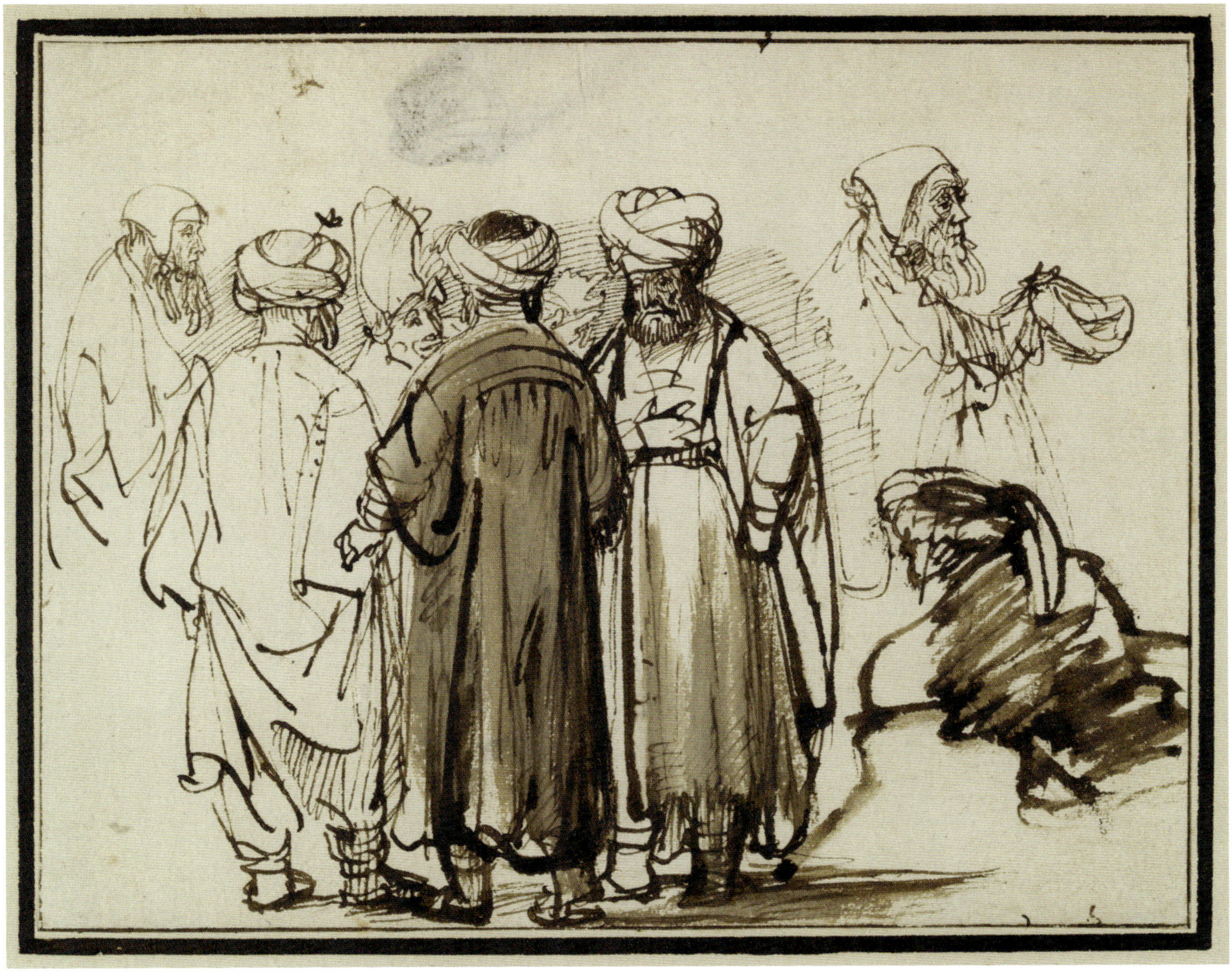

19

20 **Rembrandt Harmensz. van Rijn** (1606–1669)
Three Orientals Conversing, ca. 1645

Pen and brown ink, traces of framing line (left), 17.2 x 15.2 cm
Bottom right in old handwritten inscription: R
Inv. RP-T-1930-47
Rijksmuseum, Amsterdam, Rijksprentenkabinet, Gift of Cornelis Hofstede de Groot, The Hague
(Potsdam only)

Lit.
Benesch 1954–57, vol. 4, no. 682, fig. 821
Sumowski 1979–92, vol. 2, 1979, no. 368
Schatborn 2017
Amsterdam 2019, 664–65
Schatborn/Hinterding 2019, no. Z 387

Two men in exotic clothing are engaged in lively discussion. A man, wearing a turban and standing a little off to the side with his arms crossed behind him and an insinuating smile, seems to be casually following their exchange. The draftsman has, however, broken off in his drawing of this figure, describing it only from the head to the hem of the tunic. With his reed pen, Rembrandt was perhaps sketching here a street scene of the kind that he might have observed in cosmopolitan Amsterdam, for instance, on the square in front of the town hall that Gerrit Adriaensz. Berckheyde depicted (cat. 21). And because the group dispersed before his eyes, the sheet remained unfinished. On the other hand, it is also representative of the sort of genre sketch with Oriental figures that Rembrandt often produced anyway (cat. 19).

In any case, the configuration that Rembrandt captured here clearly expressed enough artistic eloquence to have a lasting influence. His student Lambert Doomer (1624–1700), who happily and frequently recycled material from Rembrandt's studio, was inspired by this group of three figures for those in the background of his painting *The Young Moses Steps on the Crown of Pharaoh* (Armand Hammer Museum, Los Angeles) and transformed the foreground figure seen from behind into a man leading a horse in his large drawing of *Rebecca and Eliezer at the Well* (The Metropolitan Museum of Art, New York).

These resemblances to details in works by Doomer led at a given point to the attribution of this sheet to Doomer himself. However, this does not really hold up to stylistic examination. As a draftsman, Doomer, who actually devoted himself almost exclusively to landscape subjects featuring small or large numbers of staffage figures, remains much more conservative and restrained, especially in contrast to the expressive strokes of the *Three Orientals*. The drawing fits better into the oeuvre of Rembrandt, especially a series of drawings, some of which are signed, from the 1640s. Thus, if the return of the sheet to Rembrandt's oeuvre is justified, it might be reasonable to assume that the artist was more interested in exploring an original motif than in creating a specific image. It was only in a second stage that his student was able to make use of it in biblical narratives. BB

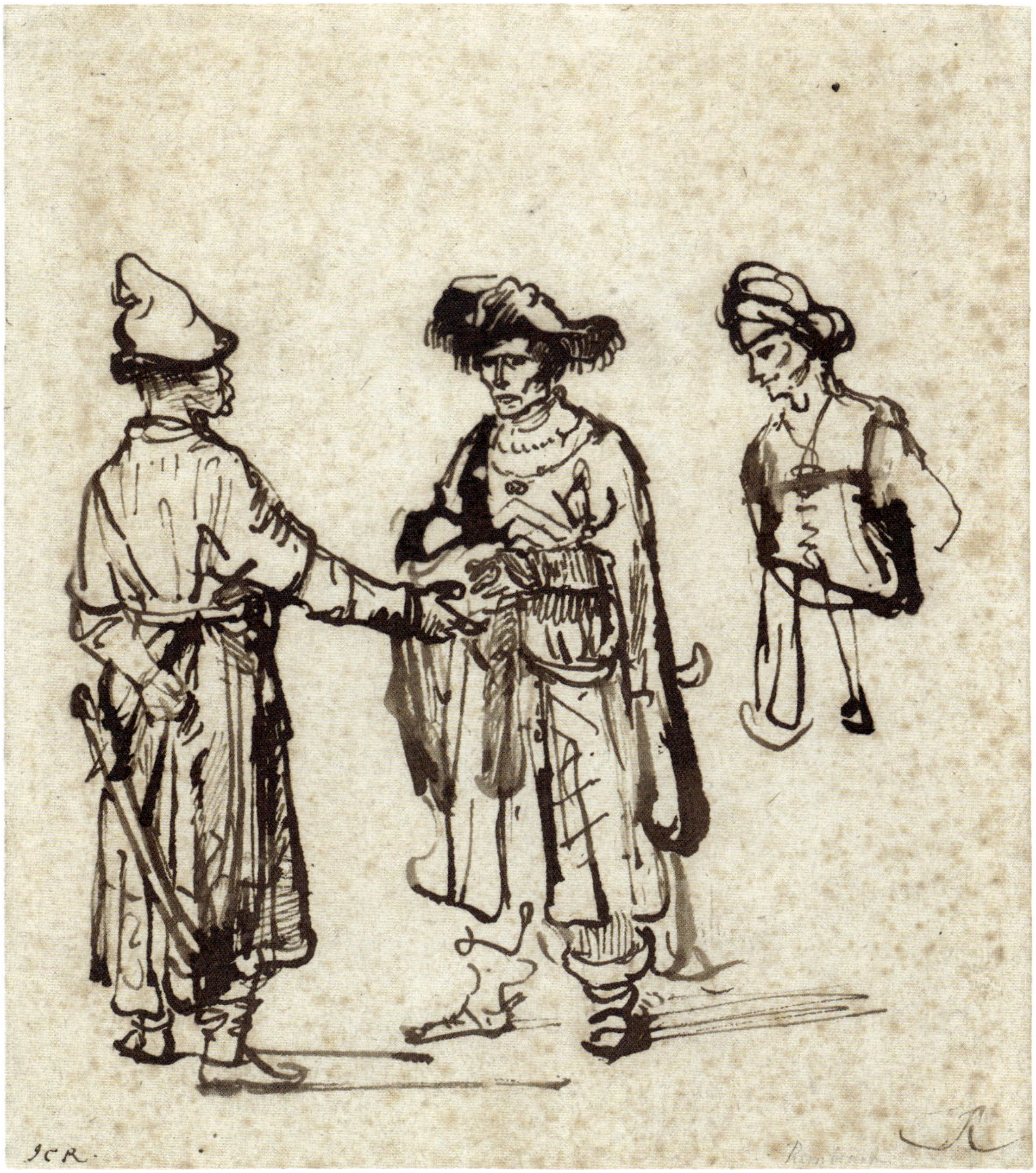

20

21 **Gerrit Adriaensz. Berckheyde** (1638–1698)
The Town Hall on Dam Square in Amsterdam, 1672

Oil on canvas, 33.5 x 41.5 cm
Inscribed bottom left: Gerrit Berck Heyde 1672
Inv. SK-A-34
Rijksmuseum, Amsterdam

Lit.
Lawrence 1991, 52–58, no. 49

[1] For the history of the planning and construction, cf. Hundertmarck 2010.

Within just a few decades at the beginning of the seventeenth century, Amsterdam developed into the most important trade city in Europe in the wake of the economic and political progress of the Dutch Republic, stimulated by two global trade organizations, the Dutch East India Company and the Dutch West India Company (see cat. 18). By the middle of the century, the city's population had climbed to two hundred thousand, more than tripling its size since 1600 (see the essay by Michael Philipp, pp. 24–39). Merchant ships with goods from all over the world anchored in the port of Amsterdam, and the prosperity of some of its inhabitants rose to hitherto unimagined heights. All this left its mark on the city, which was extended in several phases by a belt of canals running concentrically around the historic center.

At the same time, there was a growing need to give visual expression to the community's growing importance and to its supremacy among the Dutch provinces through the construction of prestigious public buildings. After the historic, late-medieval town hall was damaged by a fire, it was replaced by a new building on the Dam intended to reflect increased pretensions. Begun in 1648 after plans by the painter-architect Jacob van Campen as a monumental four-wing complex grouped around two inner courtyards, the town hall was considered the largest public building of its time. Even during its construction it astonished observers, and after its completion in 1665 it was praised as the eighth wonder of the world.[1]

Its main façade facing the Dam, with its corner pavilions and a central *avant-corps* crowned with a tower, has no fewer than twenty-three window axes, putting some princely residences in the shade. The grand effect is established by the elegant, classically inspired architectural vocabulary with two-story pilasters, set one above the other and arranged in a colossal order, together with the sophisticated iconographic program of the sculptor Artus Quellinus I that celebrates the city and its significance.

The building quickly became a favorite subject for painted cityscapes. The Haarlem painter Gerrit Berckheyde, one of the outstanding representatives of this genre, captured it from various perspectives, including a frontal view of the façade from the Dam Square. On the right, the transept of the Nieuwe Kerk, which had just been restored and modernized following a fire, is visible.

The square is bustling with activity: while on the right various goods are being loaded up, on the left is a large crowd. In the midst of the elegantly clad Dutch figures, a group of turban-wearing "Orientals" stands in a prominent spot. While their exotic clothing visually sets them apart from the rest of the crowd, they are by no means foreign elements; in fact, they are engaged in obviously animated conversations with the locals. The painting thus signals that in Amsterdam, trade delegations from distant corners of the earth were more or less part of daily street life. Rembrandt might have made his drawings of men dressed in Oriental costumes in such a setting (cat. 19–20). The fact that Berckheyde and other artists sometimes emphasize this aspect so obviously might indicate that the presence of members of non-European cultures was regarded with sympathetic curiosity, an occurrence naturally attendant on their own long-distance mercantile activities, and as an asset. GD

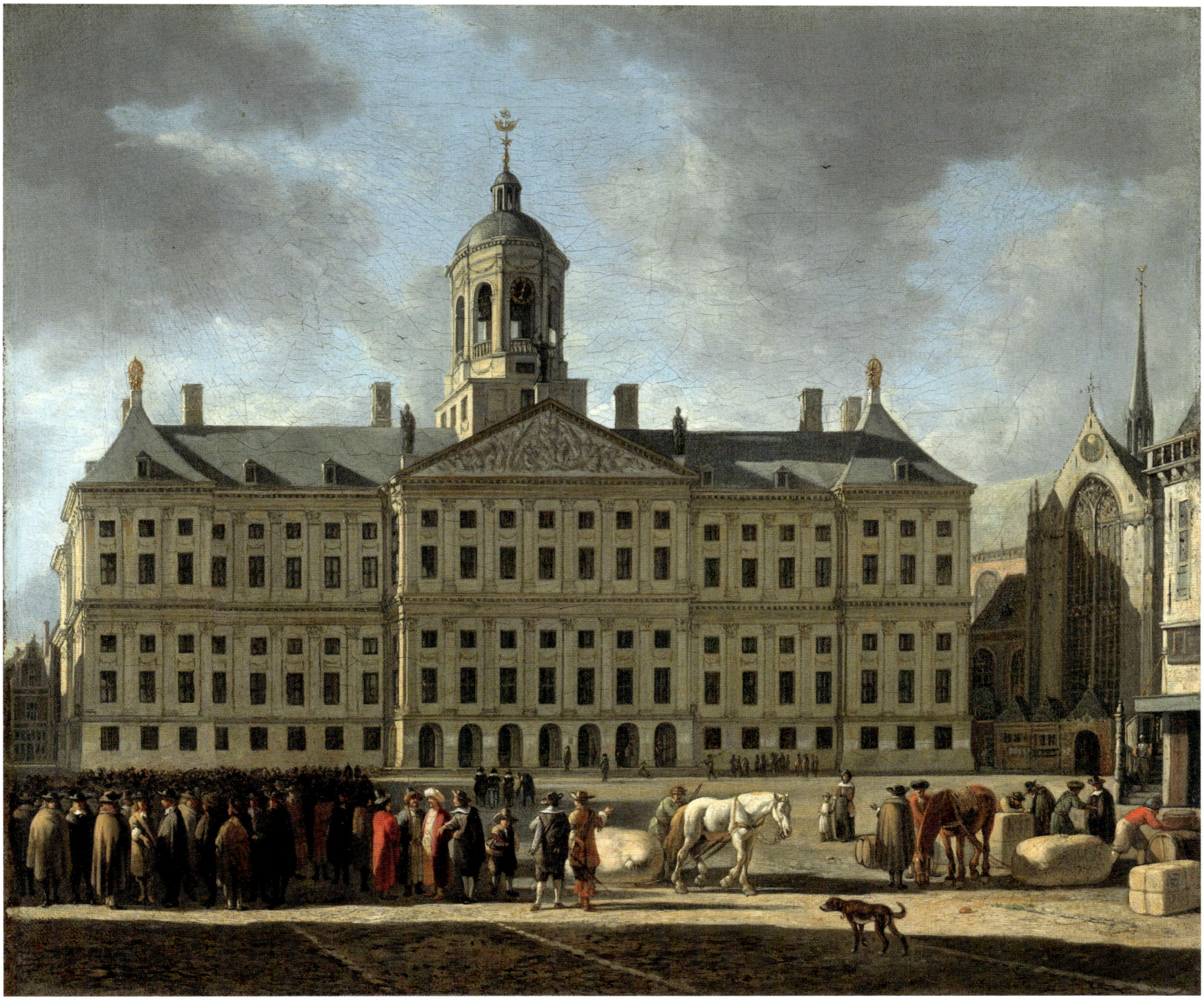

22 **Rembrandt Harmensz. van Rijn** (1606–1669)
The Ship of Fortune, 1633

23 **Cornelis Dusart** (1660–1704)
The Sailor to the East Indies, 1695

24 **Abraham Allard** (ca. 1676–1725)
East Indian Sailor, ca. 1690–1725

22
Etching, 11.3 x 16.6 cm
2nd state (of 2)
Inscribed on plate at right of center, on the bow of the ship: Rembrandt. f. 1633
In Elias Herckmans, *Der zee-vaert lof* (In Praise of Seafaring), Amsterdam: Jacob Pietersz. Wachter, 1634, p. 97
Inv. 2007.177
Kunstmuseum Basel, Kupferstichkabinett
Donation Eberhard W. Kornfeld, Bern

Lit.
B 111 (2/2)
NH 123 (2/2)
Basel 2005, no. 18
Schwartz 2006, 230–33, fig. 385
Van der Grind 2016
Cologne 2019, no. 63
Leiden 2019, no. 123

23
Sheet 6 from the series *The General Gladness about the Siege at Namur by William III, King of England, September 1695*
Etching, 24.8 x 17.9 cm
Inscribed on plate at bottom left: C.Dusart in J.Gole Exc. Amstelodami cum Privilegio.
Inv. RP-P-BI-7300
Rijksmuseum, Amsterdam, Rijksprentenkabinet

Lit.
H 37 (4/4)

24
Etching, 16.3 x 9.3 cm
Inscribed on plate at bottom: Te Amsterd : by A:Alard in de beurs straat m Pr:
Inv. 10097/0/010 097007076
Stadsarchief Amsterdam

Book illustration plays a minor role in Rembrandt's graphic oeuvre. Only four such projects are known. These include his allegorical depiction of the poem *Der zee-vaert lof* (In Praise of Seafaring) by the scholar, poet, and merchant Elias Herckmans. This vast epic tells the story of seafaring from its beginnings right up to the author's day—it ends in 1632, shortly before the volume went to press. The third book in the epic, with a title page illustrated by Rembrandt's etching, addresses the period of the Roman Empire from Augustus's *Pax Romana* until its decline with the Ottoman conquest of Constantinople.

Rembrandt's illustration trenchantly summarizes the text while building a bridge to the contemporary Netherlands, even if its precise meaning remains unclear in some respects. On the left, the temple of the two-faced god Janus, who sees both the warlike past and the more peaceful future (and who bears Rembrandt's features), has been closed on the orders of Bellona, the goddess of war. The goddess is probably depicted among the figures in the crowd, where she lays down her weapons and plays the peace pipes. On the right, a ship sets off with billowing sails, probably with Neptune at the helm, while the nude figure of Fortune, her back turned to the viewer as she looks out to sea, guarantees the success of the journey. It is to her that the print owes the title that was conferred on it by early collectors.

Figures in contemporary dress are seated in the bow of the *boeier*, a type of ship known in the seventeenth century. They seem to be joyfully celebrating their departure for new shores, an allusion to the present. Between the two scenes is the laurel-wreathed figure of a rider with outstretched arms whose horse is collapsing beneath him. This is probably a personification of the declining Roman Empire, since it would thus represent the entire period covered by the chapter. The celebration of the latest maritime activities of the Dutch Republic, thus declared the successor and heir to an illustrious tradition, relates to the author's hope that an early peace with Spain will open the way to a golden future, with general prosperity fostered by the shipping trade.

The downside of the seafaring glorified by Herckmans is shown by the two satirically exaggerated depictions of sailors returning from the East Indies. The sheet that was designed by Cornelis Dusart gives a good sense of the lowly social status of these men, who, through hard work full of privation, contributed to the advancement of overseas trade but had little advantage from its economic spoils, and whose lives were in constant danger due to such pervasive perils as shipwreck, illness, and piracy (see the essay by Roelof van Gelder, pp. 74–85).[1] As the crude caption explains, the drunken seafarer, scarred by life, will run through his wages with prostitutes and alcohol.

Abraham Allard's sailor, whose clothing and lit pipe resemble Dusart's, and who also has a bottle of liquor at his feet, is on the hunt for physical love. To this end, he is apparently offering for sale the exotic animals he has brought home with him—a cockatoo and a small monkey. The animals and other items indicate that sailors were allowed to transport exotic souvenirs in their luggage that they could use to make money upon their return.[2] The depiction of the sailors stands in stark contrast to the self-important splendor with which fleet commanders of the East India Company like Wollebrand Geleynsz. de Jongh typically had themselves portrayed (cat. 25). GD

1 A compilation of sources from the seventeenth and eighteenth centuries can be found in Schmitt 2008.
2 Van der Veen 2015, 138–39, note 21.

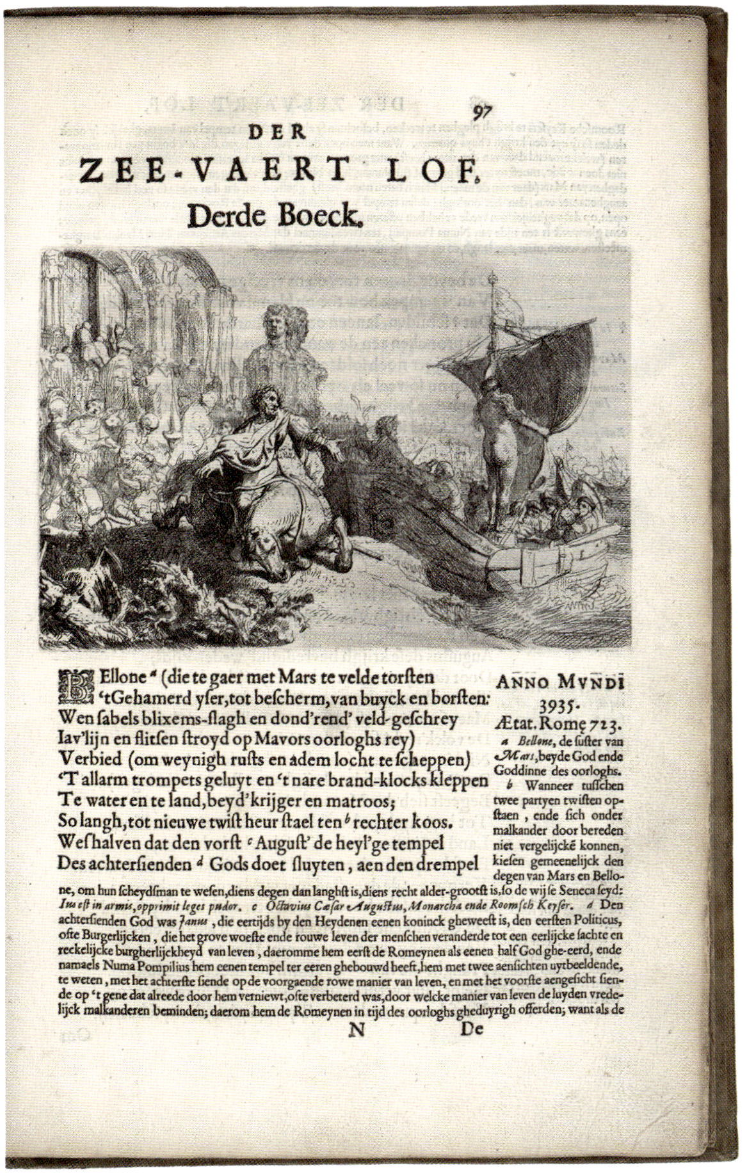

97

DER

ZEE-VAERT LOF.

Derde Boeck.

BEllone [a] (die te gaer met Mars te velde torsten
'tGehamerd yser, tot bescherm, van buyck en borsten:
Wen sabels blixems-slagh en dond'rend' veld-geschrey
Iav'lijn en flitsen stroyd op Mavors oorloghs rey)
Verbied (om weynigh rusts en adem locht te scheppen)
'T allarm trompets geluyt en 't nare brand-klocks kleppen
Te water en te land, beyd' krijger en matroos;
So langh, tot nieuwe twist heur stael ten [b] rechter koos.
Weshalven dat den vorst [c] August' de heyl'ge tempel
Des achtersienden [d] Gods doet sluyten, aen den drempel

ANNO MVNDI 3935.
Ætat. Romę 723.

a *Bellone*, de suster van *Mars*, beyde God ende Goddinne des oorloghs. b Wanneer tusschen twee partyen twisten opstaen, ende sich onder malkander door bereden niet vergelijcke konnen, kiesen gemeenelijck den degen van Mars en Bellone, om hun scheydsman te wesen, diens degen dan langhst is, diens recht alder-grootst is, so de wijse Seneca seyd: *Ius est in armis, opprimit leges pudor.* c *Octavius Cæsar Augustus, Monarcha ende Roomsch Keyser.* d Den achtersienden God was *Janus*, die eertijds by den Heydenen eenen koninck gheweest is, den eersten Politicus, ofte Burgerlijcken, die het grove woeste ende rouwe leven der menschen veranderde tot een eerlijcke sachte en reckelijcke burgherlijckheyd van leven, daeromme hem eerst de Romeynen als eenen half God ghe-eerd, ende namaels Numa Pompilius hem eenen tempel ter eeren ghebouwd heeft, hem met twee aensichten uytbeeldende, te weten, met het achterste siende op de voorgaende rowe manier van leven, en met het voorste aengesicht siende op 't gene dat alreede door hem verniewt, ofte verbeterd was, door welcke manier van leven de luyden vredelijck malkanderen beminden; daerom hem de Romeynen in tijd des oorloghs gheduyrigh offerden; want als de

N De

22

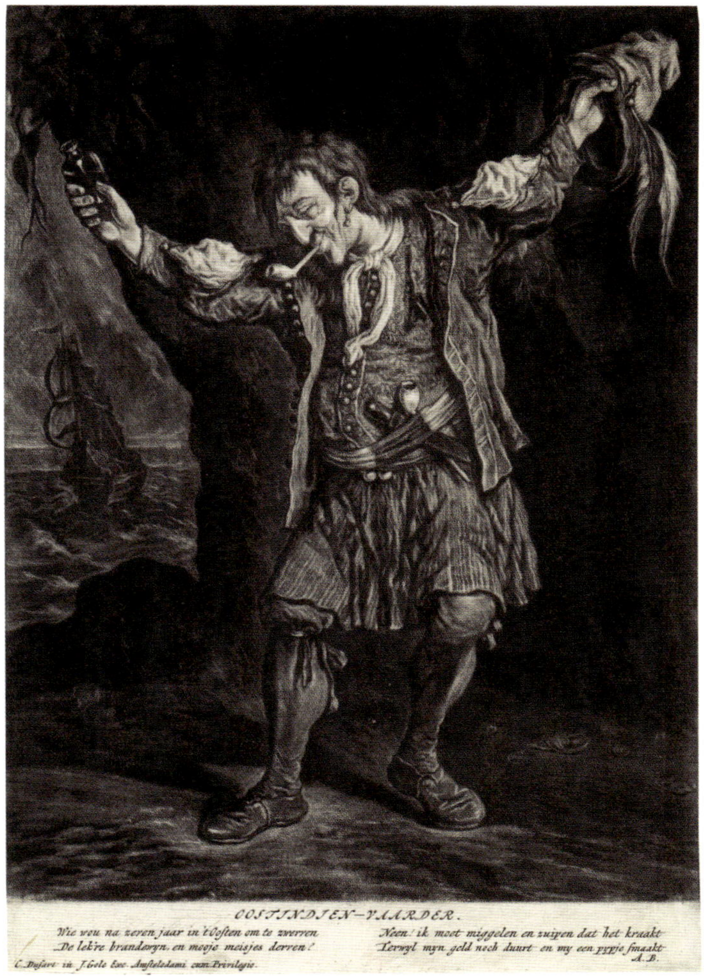

23

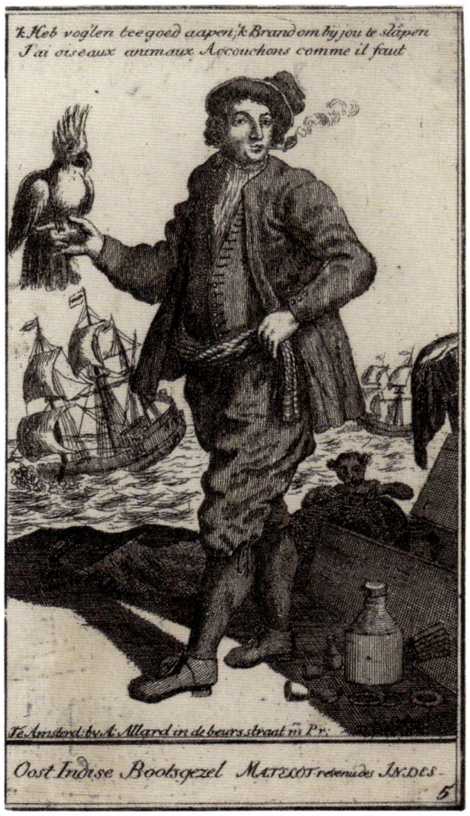

24

25 **Caesar van Everdingen** (ca. 1616/17–1678)

Wollebrand Geleynsz. de Jongh, 1674

Oil on canvas, 214.5 x 182.2 cm
Inscribed center left, on the baton: CVE; on the letter on the table: M[s]: W.G.D.J. Aetatis 54 Anno 1648
Inv. 20926
Stedelijk Museum Alkmaar

Lit.
Bamberg 1988, no. 10
Ydema 1991, no. 400
Alkmaar 1997, no. 29
Huys Janssen 2002, no. 15, fig. 66
Amsterdam 2015, no. 3
Haveman 2015, 12
Alkmaar 2016, no. 34

1 Cf. Kolfin 2020, 21.
2 Cf. Schmidt 2011.

Wollebrand Geleynsz. de Jongh, who had achieved wealth and prestige as a trade representative and fleet commander of the East India Company, presents himself here as proud, prosperous, and commanding. The setting of the portrait points to the source of his success—trade in the Far East. This is represented by the precious Persian carpet, reproduced in detail, and the clothing of fine blue-green shimmering silk with a gold floral pattern. The most striking prop is the red parasol held by a young Black man. This characteristic Asian national emblem is far more distinctive than the traditional European signifier of dignity, the pillar rising behind the sitter.

De Jongh did not owe his career to family fortune. Born in Alkmaar in 1594, he lost his parents in 1611 and was sent to the orphanage there. Two years later, at the age of nineteen, he entered the service of the East India Company. Over the next thirty-five years, he was appointed chief merchant in India, director of the Persian branch, and advisor to the Dutch government in Batavia (now Jakarta). In 1648 he went back to the Dutch Republic as commander of a return fleet of twelve ships. This event in the year of the Peace of Westphalia is alluded to by the gold medal (formerly in the Koninklijk Penningkabinet, Leiden) that De Jongh wears on a chain. It was also a mark of his unscrupulousness, which he demonstrated in 1645 when he led an armed attack on the Persian island of Qeshm in the Strait of Hormuz in order to obtain better trading conditions.

De Jongh commissioned this full-length portrait the year before his death. However, the seventy-nine-year-old did not have himself represented at his actual age at the time but as he would have looked in his mid-fifties after his return to the Netherlands, in full possession of his powers. He observes the viewer with a confident expression, his left hand resting on his hip in a typical gesture of authority while the right points with the commander's baton at the fortress of Batavia, which can be seen in the background. It was common for Europeans to keep slaves in Dutch trading centers in Asia. However, De Jongh probably did not take the two rather caricatured Blacks in the portrait to Alkmaar.

Black servants can be found in Dutch genre paintings of this period as well as in family portraits, where individual traits, sometimes recorded, suggest that they were based on actual people.[1] In any case, they were always also incorporated as status symbols. This is also true of De Jongh's portrait, where the exotic figures emphasize the lofty position of the successful trader. This applies equally to the *pajong*, the parasol that had quickly come to epitomize the Far East[2] and appears in such topographical depictions as Andries Beeckman's *The Market in Batavia* (cat. 86), such genre paintings as *Traders with Goods in a Levantine Harbor* by Thomas Wijck (cat. 27), and in Rembrandt's biblical history paintings, like the *Adoration of the Magi* (cat. 75).

De Jongh gave instructions that his portrait, with its extreme emphasis on wealth and self-confidence one of the most distinctive of its kind, should go to the orphanage in Alkmaar where he had spent two years of his youth. After his return from the East, he temporarily served as a regent there. Thus, the painting also represents the enormous economic rise of the Dutch Republic in the seventeenth century—progress which, according to the national self-image of the period, was achieved through its own efforts and after it had surmounted any number of challenges. MPH

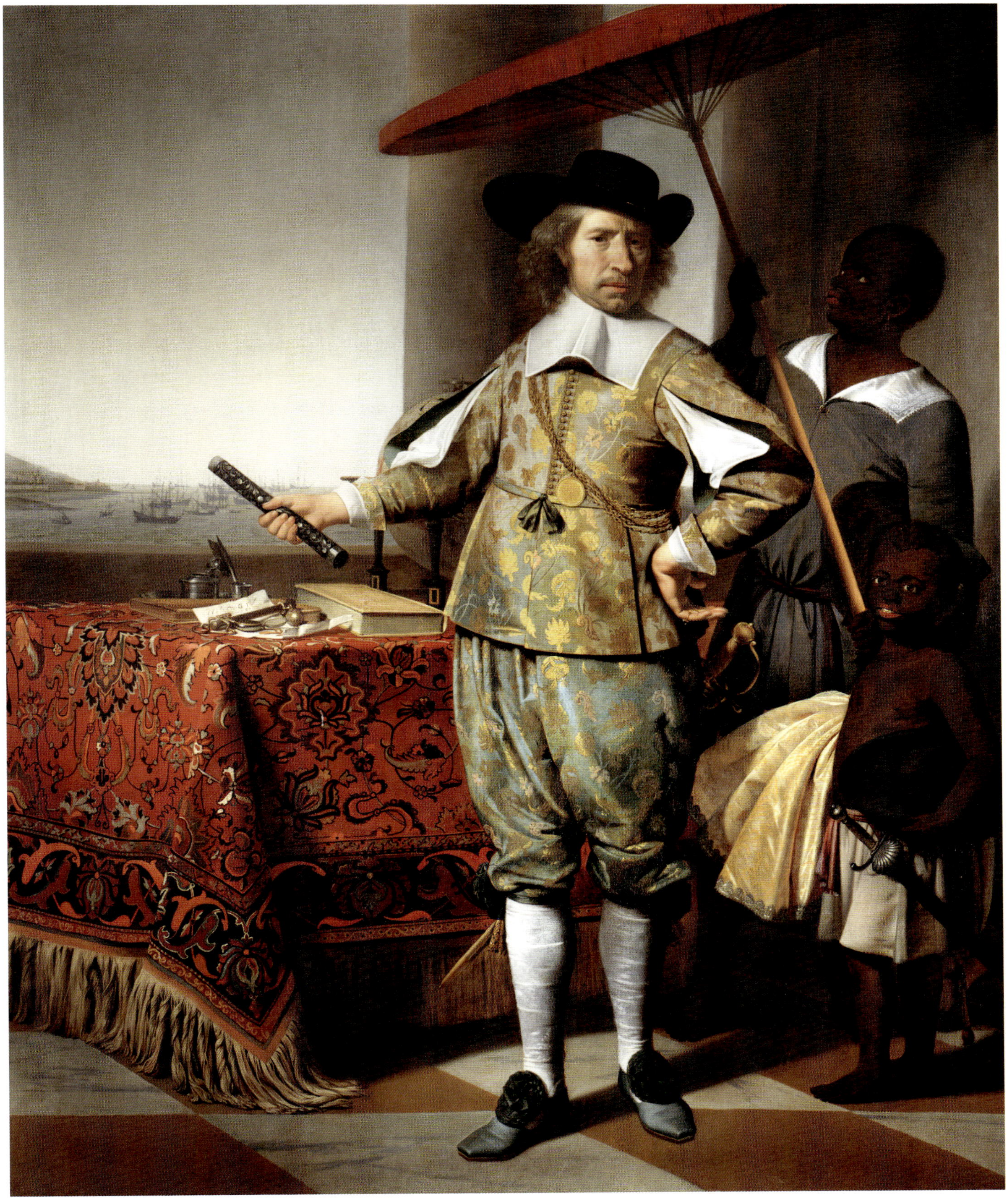

26 **Jan Baptist Weenix** (1621–1659)

The Dutch Ambassador on His Way to Isfahan, ca. 1653–59

Oil on canvas, 101 x 179 cm
Inscribed center right on the paper:
Gio Batt Weenix
Inv. SK-A-3879
Rijksmuseum, Amsterdam
(Basel only)

Lit.
De Groot 2009
Schwartz 2014, 53; pl. 1.9
Gommans 2016, 36, fig. 4; 38
Amsterdam 2018, no. 65
Van Wagenberg-Ter Hoeven 2018, no. 43

[1] For the relationship between the Dutch East India Company and the Persian shah, cf. Steensgaard 1975, 391–94, 406–11.

The monumental landscape format of *The Dutch Ambassador on His Way to Isfahan* is one of the largest paintings in the oeuvre of Jan Baptist Weenix and the only one that shows an actual historical event. It depicts the convoy of a legation of the Dutch East India Company traveling from the Persian port of Bandar Abbas, visible in the background, to Isfahan, the capital of the Safavid Empire, a good six hundred miles inland. The striking figure wrapped in the golden-silk robe and riding the Arabian white horse at the center of the composition is Joan Cunaeus, presumably also the patron of this official work. In 1651–52 he was the leader of a Company delegation to the court of Shah Abbas II, where he was supposed to negotiate improvements in the trade of silk and horses. The trip had also become necessary because the behavior of some Dutch merchants, seen as disrespectful by the shah, had disrupted the good relations between the two sides that had existed for a quarter of a century.[1] The painter Philips Angel (see cat. 44) also took part in the journey and drew the ruins of Persepolis (cat. 84) along the way.

In addition to Cunaeus, two other figures are highlighted here: the horseman in the turban on the black horse might be the governor of Bandar Abbas or another high official, while the man depicted behind Cunaeus is his young secretary, Cornelis Janz. Speelman. Speelman wrote a detailed report of the long journey that vividly describes numerous receptions and revelries as well as the court ceremonial in Isfahan. Weenix's account deviates from the chronology of the journey in one important point: Cunaeus was not given the previously mentioned silk robe, known as a *khilat*, until his audience with the shah, who received the legation with great honors. The ceremony, in which the recipient was presented with a robe previously worn by the shah himself, represented both a privilege and a gesture of submission to the Persian ruler.

For the figure of the presumed patron, Weenix was able to make a preparatory study of Cunaeus, who returned to Holland in 1653; horses and precious fabrics did not pose any great challenges for him either. But the position was rather different in the case of the landscape. Indeed, his coastal and harbor landscapes, influenced by a stay of several years in Italy, bathed in mild southern light and enhanced by set pieces of ancient architecture, were highly admired. This was possibly why Cunaeus considered him a suitable artist to sympathetically represent distant Persian lands. However, Weenix had never visited a country in the Middle East. For the outline of the port as well as the ship anchored under the Dutch flag to the left in the middle ground, he probably used illustrations from the travel report of the merchant Pieter van den Broecke, who had traveled to Bandar Abbas in 1629. For the rest of the painting, he relied on his own inventiveness and his training in numerous genre scenes. He also took the liberty of placing a group of women and girls, seen making music, dancing, and scattering flowers, in front of the cavalcade, leading it to resemble a triumphal procession.

Cunaeus's command of this diplomatic mission with the reception by the shah was the high point of his career, which explains the creation of this documentary image, unique in this form. His young companion went on to become the governor general of Dutch India, one of the highest offices of the Dutch East India Company. Speelman died in Batavia in 1684 during his tenure. GD

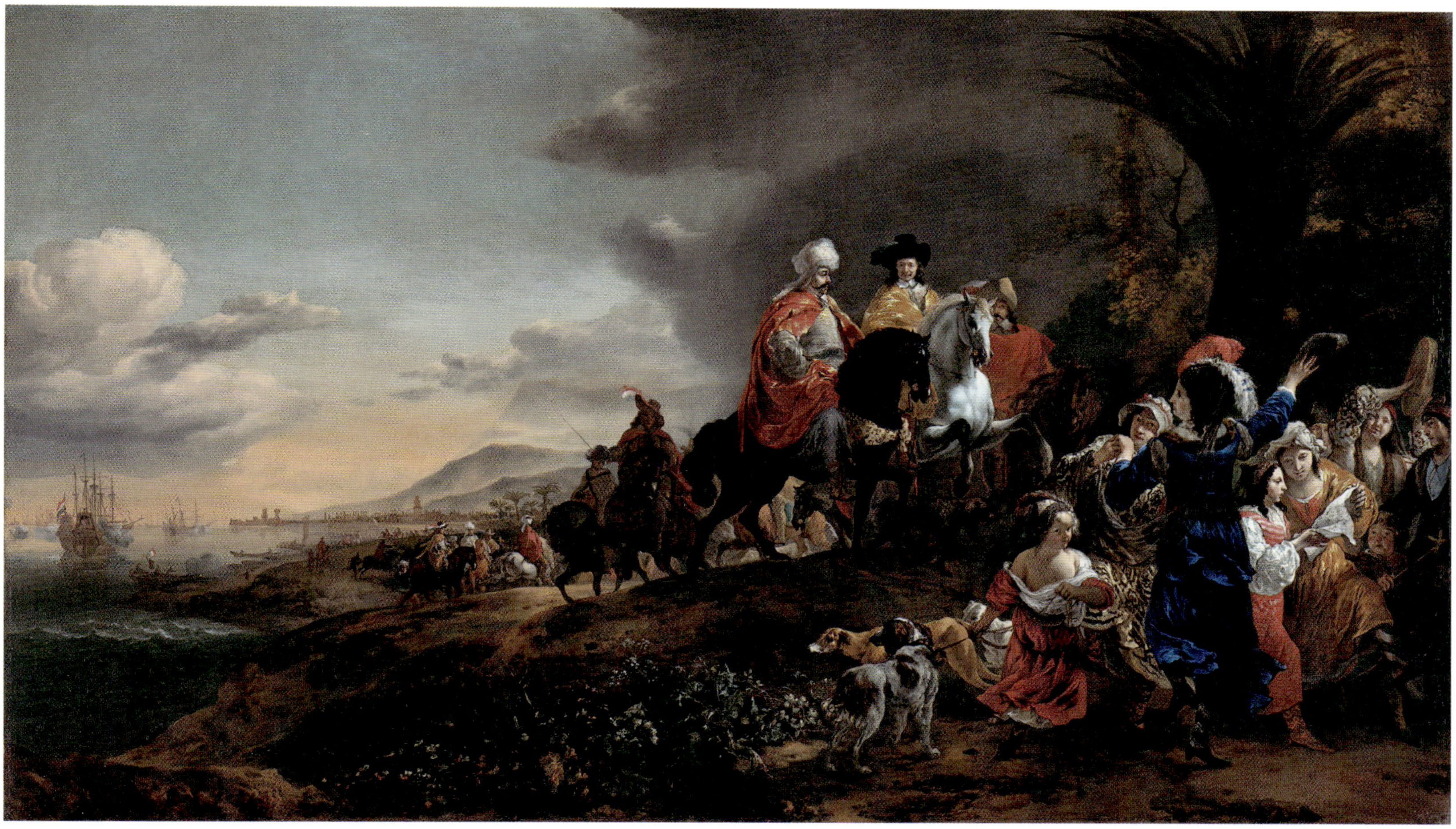

26

27 **Thomas Wijck** (ca. 1616/21–1677)

Traders with Goods in a Levantine Harbor, ca. 1660–70

Oil on canvas, 108 x 87 cm
Inscribed bottom center: Twijck.
Inv. 837.1.100
Musée Fabre, Montpellier

Lit.
Paris 1998, no. 67

In a southern port full of activity, merchants do business before a monumental architectural complex, and various goods are piled high. Thomas Wijck composed an idyllic, exotic scene whose foreign charm is underscored by the merchants. At its center is a stately man wearing a turban while at his feet sits a merchant, identifiable as a Jew by his tall, fur-trimmed hat. Next to him is a Dutchman dressed in contemporary clothing and a black hat. The variety of the figures introduces an element of the picturesque here, also evident in the seemingly random arrangement of the trade goods and in the charming floral tendrils in the archway.

Beginning in the 1620s, many Dutch painters traveled to Italy, sometimes staying in the south for several years. The works that these painters, who were known as the Italianates, made in Italy or after their return were popular on the Netherlandish art market. In addition to painting mainly sunlit Arcadian landscapes with ancient ruins, they produced genre pictures showing apparently genuine scenes of everyday life, conjured by an invented realism. Thomas Wijck, a pupil of Adriaen van Ostade, also spent time in Rome and Naples around 1640 before returning to his homeland in 1642. In the decades that followed, he produced several views of southern ports (such as Rijksmuseum, Amsterdam, fig. p. 21; Bayerische Staatsgemäldesammlungen, Alte Pinakothek, Munich; and Staatliches Museum Schwerin), each of which he set in contexts similar to the monumental archway in this painting.

While the depiction of a man with a turban in Dutch cities as in Gerrit Adriaensz. Berckheyde's *The Town Hall on Dam Square in Amsterdam* (cat. 21) was very much out of the ordinary, contemporary viewers probably expected to see such figures in southern settings. The precise role of the central figure here, whose depiction is as stately as it is clichéd, is not really clear. The negotiations seem to be happening between the Jew and the Dutchman. The man wearing the turban and his companion, who is conspicuously light-skinned, are set apart under a ceremonial parasol—a stereotypical symbol of the Far East that also occurs in the work of Rembrandt (cat. 75) as well as that of numerous other painters (cat. 25, 28, 62, 66–67, 75–76, 86, 94). The parasol is held by a young Black pageboy. This motif also reflects a cliché—Caesar van Everdingen, for example, used it in the portrait of Wollebrand Geleynsz. de Jongh (cat. 25), painted at about the same time.

Whether or not the combination here of members of different faiths—a Muslim, a Jew, and a Christian—can be interpreted as an expression of religious tolerance must be set aside for now (see cat. 46). Nonetheless, the message that business can be done, even when opinions on the path to salvation differ, is quite clear. In this sense, at least, this idealized depiction has some connection to the reality of Dutch international trade in the seventeenth century. But the picture of a peaceful exchange between cultures was by no means standard. Armed conflicts, like the *Sea Battle between Christians and Turks* by Johannes Lingelbach (cat. 33), were represented far more frequently. MPH

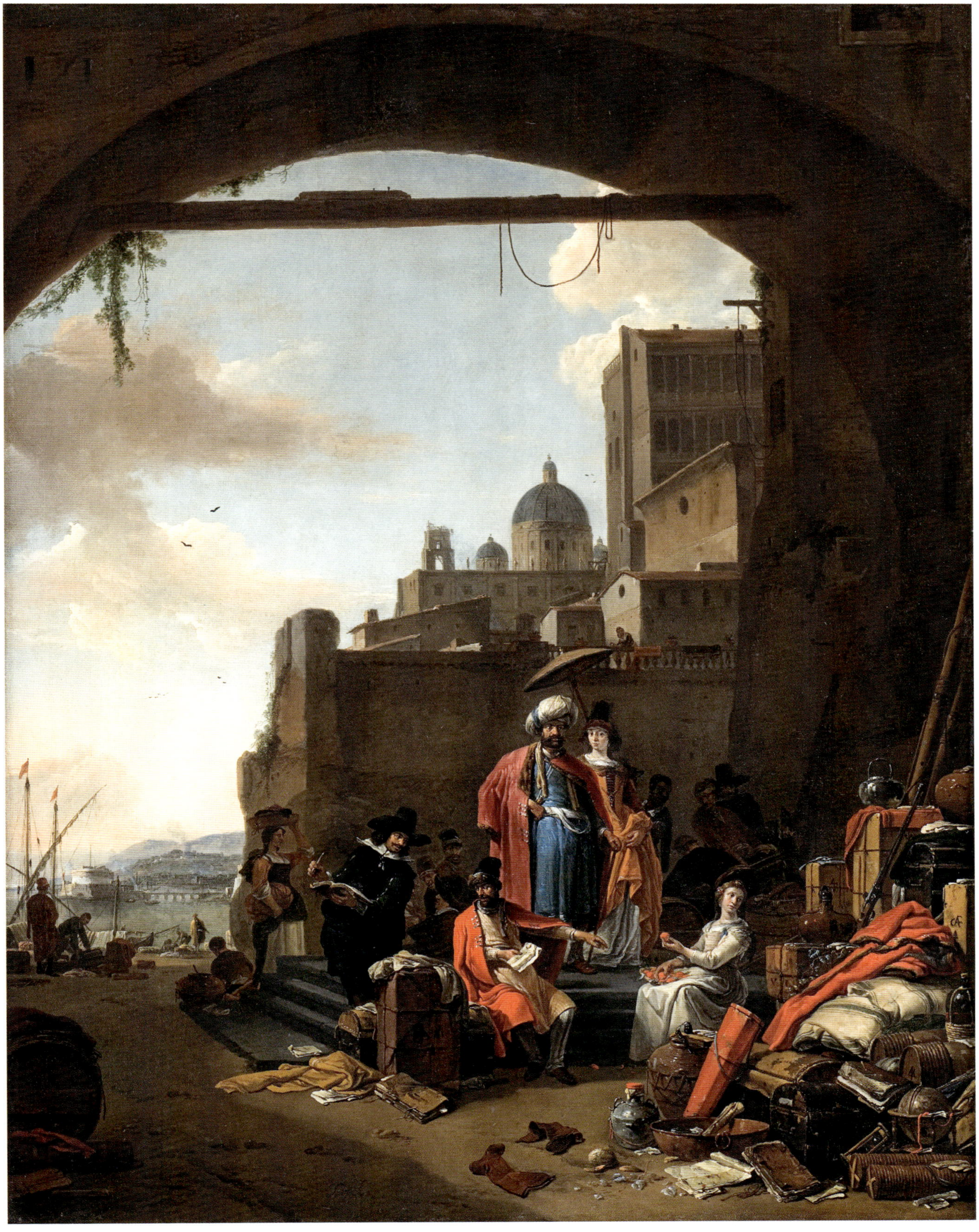

28 **Abraham Begeyn** (ca. 1637/38–1697)

Seashore, 1662

Oil on canvas, 90 x 118.5 cm
Inscribed bottom right (on rock):
A. Begein / 1662
Inv. GZ-3469
The State Hermitage Museum, St. Petersburg

Lit.
Skeeles Schloss 1982, 22, 42, fig. 37
Leningrad 1990, 332, 342

Around 1640 a group of Dutch painters in the circle of Jan Baptist Weenix (cat. 26), Johannes Lingelbach (cat. 33), and Nicolaes Berchem introduced a new subject into Dutch painting that swiftly met with considerable demand and was soon taken up by other painters: Mediterranean harbor scenes flooded with golden southern light, with various figure types that situated the pictures somewhere between genre, landscape, and marine painting. Although individual, identifiable buildings and landmarks were frequently incorporated, the works do not show real, topographically accurate ports, but fantasy places in which the artists freely combined impressions and motifs they had collected during their stays in Italy.

From the 1660s onwards, the genre-like scenes of daily life in the harbor increased in elegance and scenic detail; alongside merchants, ships' crews, and slaves from the Ottoman Empire or other parts of the Orient, courtly, elegantly dressed couples appeared, apparently using the harbor as the setting for a pleasant stroll. This category includes the work of Leiden-born artist Abraham Begeyn, characterized by harmonious effects of light. It is not clear, however, whether or not he actually traveled to the south; even if he did not, he nonetheless appropriated perfectly the typical stylistic elements used by the Dutch Italianate painters.

From a strip of shore parallel to the picture plane in the foreground, the view opens onto a wide bay lined with steep rocky cliffs with a large merchant ship anchored in the center. Apart from the cityscape, just about recognizable to the right of the background, and a Baroque fountain set on a stepped platform, Begeyn avoided any kind of architectural detail; instead, the foreground is occupied by various groups of people in addition to bales, boxes, and barrels of all kinds of merchandise scattered over the entire area. The figures here reflect a broad cultural and social range as well as stark social inequality: individuals in Dutch clothing are in the minority among the numerous merchants and shipowners who are supervising the transport of goods by local dock workers or conversing with each other; by contrast, most wear turbans and fur-trimmed, high caps, signifying their origins in different regions of the Orient. At the left foreground, two Black slaves with shaved heads, presumably from a ship's crew, are seated next to a fruit seller in Italian clothing, while in the other half of the picture an elegantly dressed Dutch couple with a parasol strolls through what, from their perspective at least, looks like a picturesque scene. Notably, here the parasol is not held by a servant, as so often (see cat. 27), but by the gentleman.

It is not clear if this couple is intended to allude to the kind of loose behaviors in Italian ports mentioned in contemporary travel reports—as we can assume in other paintings—and if there are other allusions in the scene that might have been decipherable for viewers of the period. Begeyn's harbor scene sketches out an idealized vision of the peaceful exchange of goods and cultures from all over the world, made possible by trade and shipping, with all negative side effects dissipated. At the same time, this fanciful representation satisfied a need for visual images of exotic southern landscapes and might be read as an illustration of the most important source of the viewer's own prosperity. GD

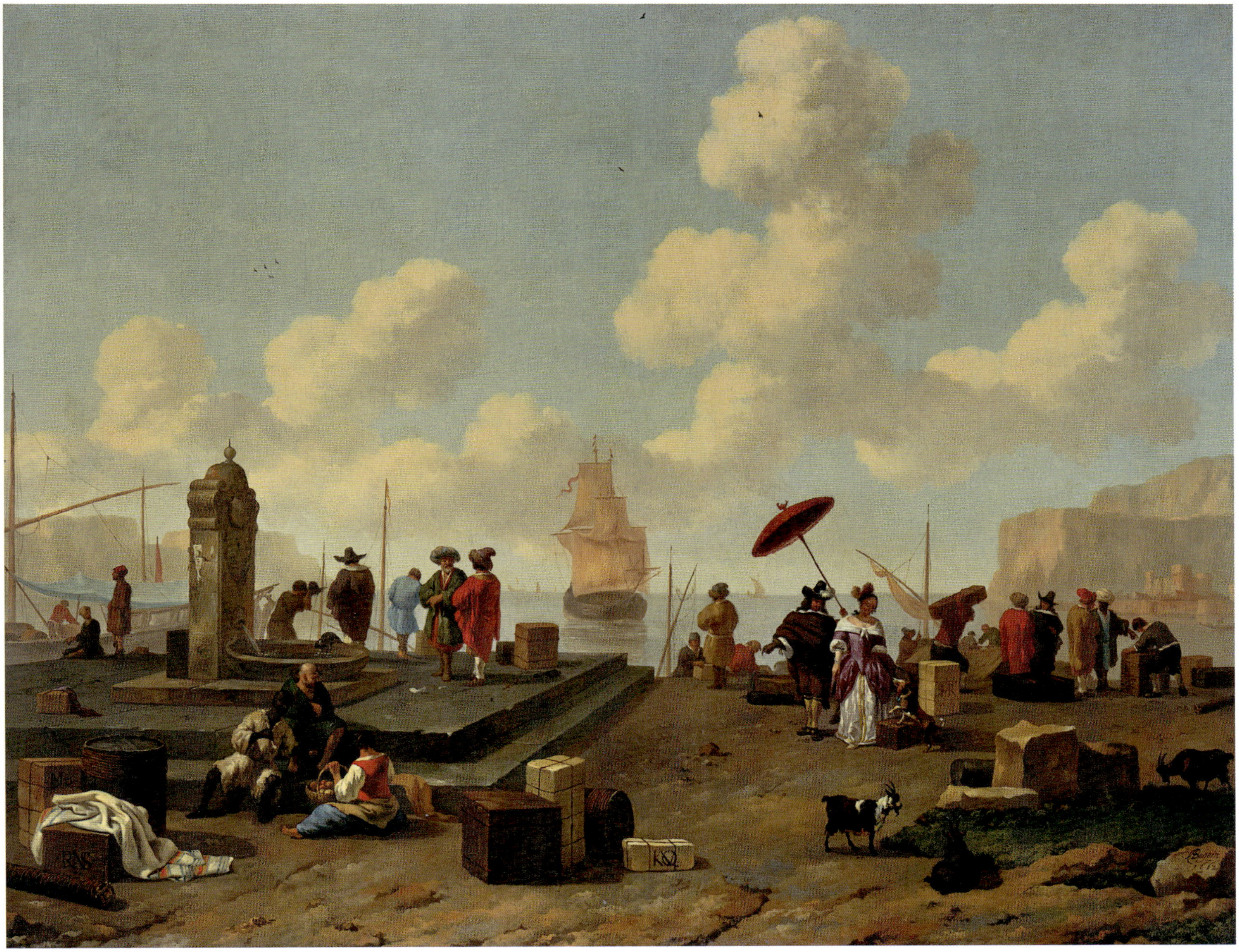

28

29 **Jacob Toorenvliet** (1640–1719)
Two Levantine Merchants in Conversation, 1660

Oil on panel, 49 x 36 cm
Inscribed bottom left: JT [in ligature] in. 1660
Private collection

Lit.
Karau 2002, vol. 1, 15–16; vol. 2, 3, no. A 5

Jacob Toorenvliet's *Two Levantine Merchants in Conversation,* showing the two merchants with their goods in a kind of courtyard, was made in 1660 at a time when Dutch enthusiasm for the Orient was at its height. The painter often drew from the works of his Dutch contemporaries, extracting from them individual figures or figure groups that he then staged in modified and greatly enlarged form. They thus effectively became Toorenvliet's own pictorial inventions and his *Levantine Merchants* are a good example of this.

The two men recall figures from paintings of the Bamboccianti, Dutch painters who lived in Rome and had a preference for genre-like scenes featuring character types from the lower classes. One was Thomas Wijck (fig. p. 21, cat. 27), who also painted many Mediterranean trade scenes. Wijck's paintings almost always show an "Oriental" with a colorful turban next to another "Oriental" with a shorter caftan and fur-trimmed hat, surrounded by such goods as bales of cloth and long rolls packed in rope, secured at their ends with strips of wood, in which carpets were probably transported. Toorenvliet adopts this motif here and the color scheme of the costumes to some extent, but his merchants are dressed in wide knee-length, fur-lined caftans, with decorative trims, buttons, and loops over the chest, each garment differing only in color. They also wear short, pointed leather boots. One particularly eye-catching detail is the wide patterned hem of the white tunic on the standing man, a detail that is somewhat reminiscent of the robes depicted in Rubens's *Adoration of the Magi* (Musée des Beaux-Arts, Lyon), known from the engraving made after it by Lucas Vorsterman (cat. 61).

Leiden, the painter's hometown, was the center of the Netherlandish cloth industry in the first half of the seventeenth century. Textiles with a wide variety of patterns and colors were produced there for both the domestic and the foreign markets. It might once actually have been possible to encounter an Oriental merchant there. However, Toorenvliet's merchants have European facial features. As for the caftans, he might have been inspired by a real garment or by prints and costume books (fig. p. 43, cat. 91). This also applies to the carpet shown here. Since no two carpets are alike in Toorenvliet's paintings, it is possible that the artist is describing actual pieces.

The painter depicted this subject only once, at the very beginning of his career. However, a few years later, probably in Vienna, he made several preparatory drawings for portrait engravings for Galeazzo Gualdo Priorato's *Historia di Leopoldo Cesare,* which included five images of Ottoman rulers, probably after paintings.[1] SHK

[1] Galeazzo Gualdo Priorato, *Historia di Leopoldo Cesare, contiente le cose più memorabili successe in Europa, del 1656 fino al 1670*, 2 vols., Vienna 1669–70. For Toorenvliet's share in the work, cf. Karau 2002, vol. 1, 44–47, and vol. 2, cat. nos. E2.20, E2.27, E2.33, E2.35, and E.2.37.

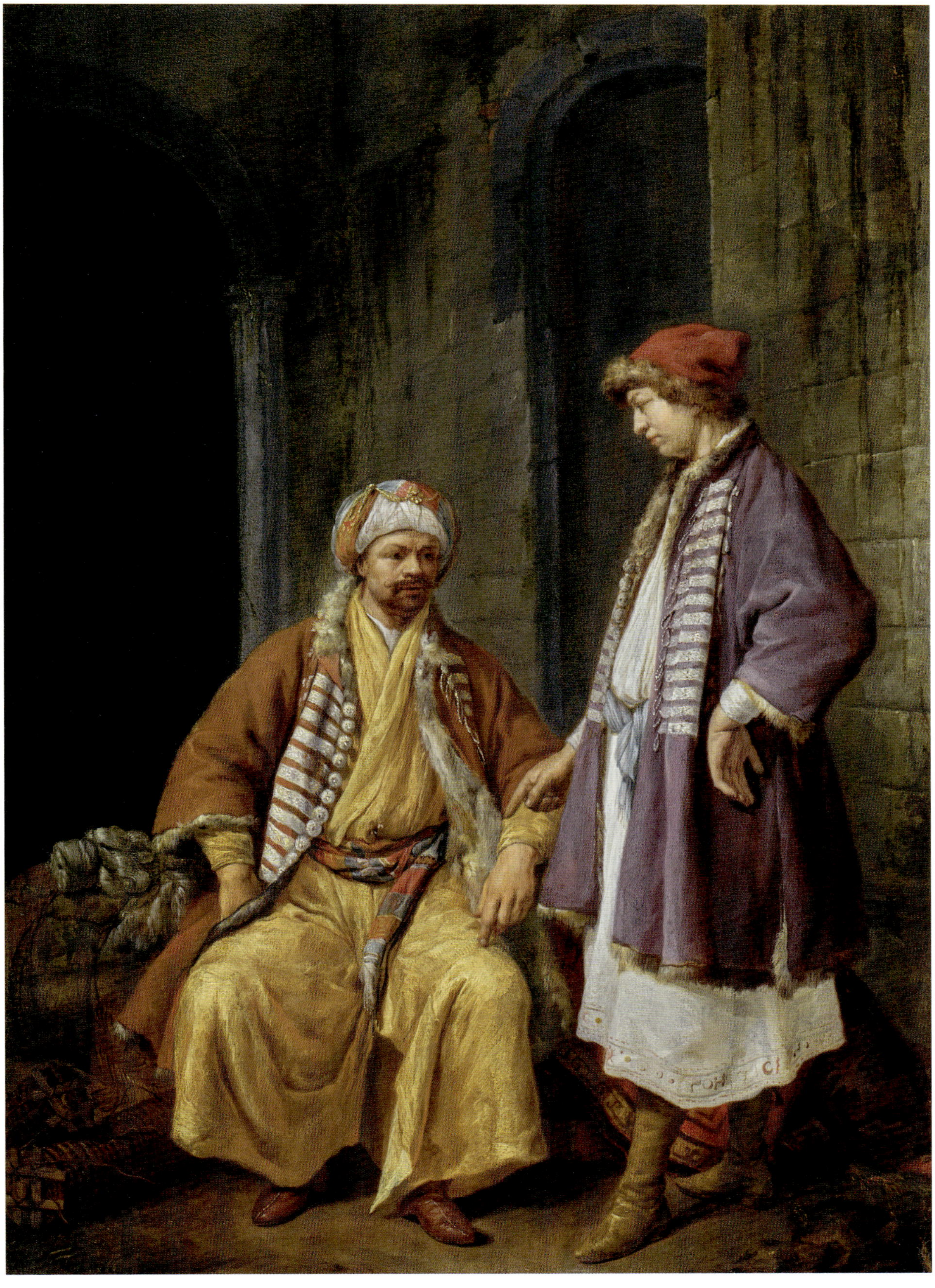

30 **Leendert Maertensz. van Haestar** (ca. 1610/15–1675)

A Cannon near a Guard Post, ca. 1640–45

Oil on panel, 50 x 65 cm
Private collection, Europe, by courtesy of the Hoogsteder Museum Foundation

Lit.
Guido M. C. Jansen et al., expert's report [unpublished] for Hoogsteder & Hoogsteder, ca. 2015

Van Haestar's painting is the only known "portrait" of a cannon in Netherlandish painting of the seventeenth century; the closest comparison is a late depiction of *Amsterdam's Bastion Blauwhoofd with a Cannon Post* by Ludolf Bakhuizen (1630–1708), dated 1705 (TEFAF 2020, Bijl-van Urk); in it, however, the artist gives the gun far less prominence. Around 1620, Maurits of Orange standardized Dutch artillery and officially restricted it to four types of cannon. Here we see a half-kartouwe, also known as a twenty-four-pounder, on an iron-mounted wall carriage. The cannon and carriage are precisely rendered down to such details as the coat of arms, which is visible but not actually identifiable.

In spite of his obvious infatuation with detail, the artist transports the viewer into what is ultimately a fantasy world. The cannon made of bronze has a golden shimmer; it would have been brand-new, perhaps even plated with gold—a completely unrealistic notion. A fuse glows near the front frame of the gun—the first shot might thus be imminent; a small powder keg lies next to it. A soldier in ancient-Roman armor oversees a larger supply of gunpowder behind the cannon. Figures in Oriental clothing approach from behind: one woman wearing a turban rides a donkey bridled in Eastern fashion. The mother holding a child in front of her also wears a turban and an exotic-looking, multicolored costume as she sits on an animal skin. Before her is a ceremonial sword of the Ashanti of modern-day Ghana (recognizable from the characteristic form of the handle) in its sheath and an Asiatic saddle. The collection of military objects spread out in the foreground, however, is European in origin.

The halberdier looking out of the picture might be Conraet Wegewaert, the proprietor of a cannon foundry in The Hague that was located in service buildings of the former Dominican monastery on Lange Voorhout. Leendert Maertensz. van Haestar was probably a parishioner of the former Kloosterkerk and might well have lived in the neighborhood. If the panel was commissioned by the bronze caster, the exotic and luxurious imported goods were perhaps intended to emphasize the value of his product or to demonstrate the full the range of his craftsmanship. Or could Wegewaert even have afforded a cabinet of curiosities containing such objects? BB

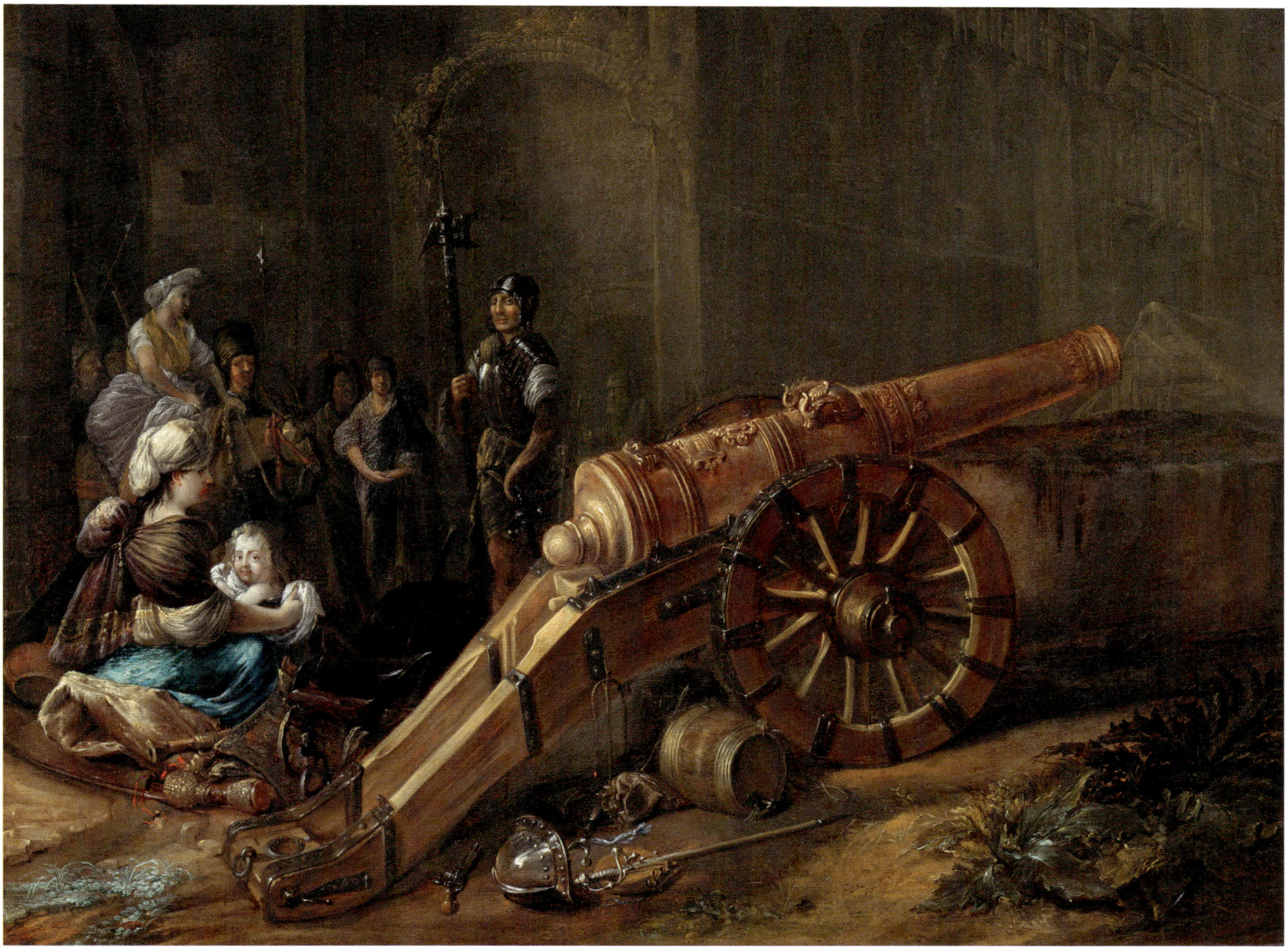

30

31 **Philips Wouwerman** (1619–1668)
Skirmish among Enemy Troops, 1648–49

Oil on canvas, 69.7 x 71.5 cm
Inscribed (bottom left): PHILS. W.
Inv. P002154
Museo Nacional del Prado, Madrid

Lit.
Schumacher 2006, no. A242, fig. 224
Madrid 2009, no. 65

Philips Wouwerman of Haarlem was one of the most productive and successful Netherlandish artists of the seventeenth century. More than 570 paintings by him have survived. The artist was already famous during his lifetime, and his works remained sought-after by aristocratic collectors in Europe until the eighteenth century. Although his oeuvre also includes landscapes and a small number of Christian and mythological history paintings and allegories, he was known as a painter of lifelike depictions of horses as well as scenes of soldiers, battles, and raids. Out of a good thirty images of cavalry battles, some show Oriental soldiers; the *Skirmish among Enemy Troops* is a good example of this. King Philip V of Spain acquired it as one of no fewer than nine works by the painter in his collection.

On stylistic grounds, this undated picture can be placed around 1648–49, when the painter, whose cavalry battles had previously closely followed the model set by the older Pieter van Laer, found his own distinctive style. This close-up battle scene shows in careful detail the stubborn fight of a few foot soldiers against charging cavalry troops. In each case, two or three fighters—as well as some of the horses—are connected to each other in complementary pairings so that the composition seems almost to consist of several individual studies.

In addition to the varied postures of the combatants, depicted on horseback, standing, or lying on the ground, Wouwerman also rendered their closely differentiated emotional expressions. He also took great care with the detailed depiction of costumes, gleaming armor, and shiny weapons. The fact that one of the groups of fighters is from the East is made clear by their conspicuously colorful clothing and exotic headgear, such as the feathered fur cap of the rider charging in from the far left in the background. Nonetheless, it is not always easy at first glance to figure out who belongs to which side of the battle. In general, the fighting seems confused, with such narrative elements as the half-overturned wagon on the right contributing to the sense that the action has been going on for some time and is now devoid of any coherent strategy. Neither side is presented as superior so that the outcome seems open, and, overall, the battle lacks any kind of triumphant gesture. It presents soldiers fighting with each other in a struggle for survival, with all the attendant physical and psychological consequences.

As a long-time member of Saint George's Civic Guard in Haarlem, Wouwerman knew about contemporary and historical weapons, but had probably never seen combat like this with his own eyes; after his home town of Haarlem was captured and occupied by the Spanish between 1573 and 1577, it was spared for the rest of the Eighty Years' War. His battle paintings cannot be connected to specific historical events. Rather, they are dramatically charged fantasy pieces in which he was able to deploy his exceptional ability as a painter of horses and of expressive figures in equal measure. It is not clear why he used Oriental motifs in some cases; perhaps this exotic element simply enhanced the paintings' appeal to contemporary buyers. GD

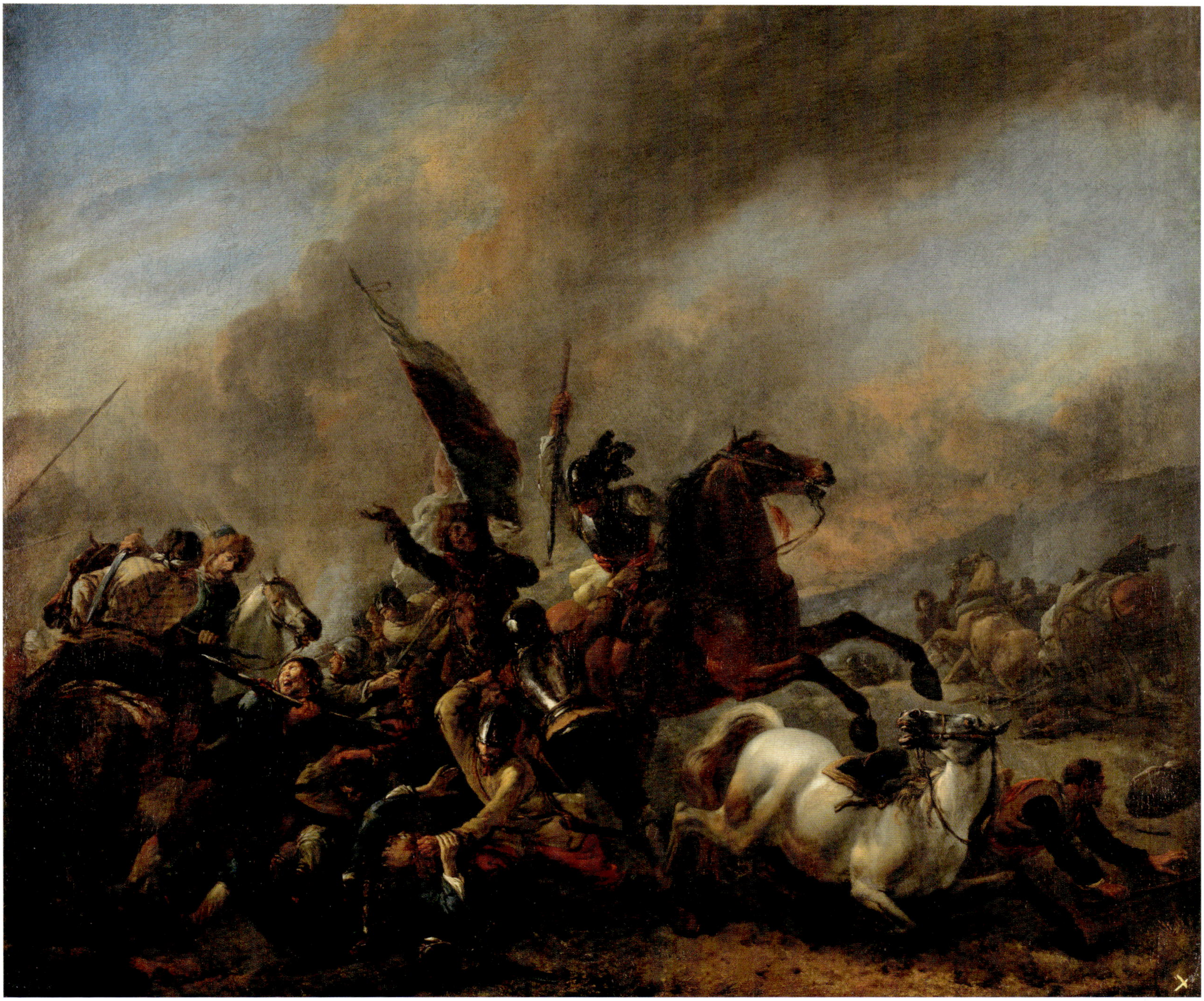

32 **Jacques Muller** (1620–1673)

A Cavalry Encounter between Turkish Troops and the Troops of the Habsburg Empire, ca. 1645–73

Oil on canvas, 72 x 88 cm
Inscribed (bottom left): J. Muller f.
Inv. SK-A-1445
Rijksmuseum, Amsterdam,
Gift of A. Bredius, The Hague

Lit.
Unpublished

This cavalry battle bears the signature of Jacques Muller, who was active in Utrecht from 1655 until his death. It can be compared in many respects to a cavalry battle with a similar theme by Philips Wouwerman (cat. 31) and, despite its uncertain date, is probably also based on prototypes like that one. There are certainly compositional similarities between the two: the dark mountain range in the background of the picture to the right; the white horse set in the foreground to provide a light accent (a motif that Wouwerman had already adopted from earlier examples); and the gunpowder vapor that seems to blend directly into the dramatically cloudy sky. But there are also differences that cannot be overlooked. Besides the different color palettes, there is also the less-convincing construction of perspective in the landscape here, the shifting of a large part of the fighting action away from the viewer into the middle ground, and, in direct comparison, the clumsier and more schematic depiction of both the figures and the psychological state of the fighters.

In addition to the painting style and composition, there are also differences in terms of content. The combatant groups here are not only more clearly and immediately distinguishable; the Oriental, or, more precisely, the Ottoman troops wear uniforms that from a distance are comparable to those worn by Rembrandt's "Orientals" and similar figures by those in his circle—robes tied with sashes and feathered turbans, one of which has landed decoratively in the foreground.

Muller's painting also lacks any reference to a specific event, especially since the exact date of the painting, which might provide clues, remains unknown. Nonetheless, in this case, unlike the general fray depicted by Wouwerman, the allusion to the rivalry between the Habsburg Empire and the Sublime Porte, which had a variety of associations for contemporary Dutch viewers, is obvious. Without a precise date for the painting, however, we can only speculate about possible references to contemporary events. If the picture was painted in 1664 or later, it might refer to the fourth Austro-Turkish War of 1663–64, which was fought on Hungarian territory and initially ended the period of peace between the two powers that had reigned since the conclusion of the Treaty of Zsitvatorok in 1606. The war was concluded by the Peace of Vasvár, which in power-political terms was not exactly advantageous for the Habsburg side but which did reflect the military exhaustion of both sides.[1]

In spite of the political differences, the painter in no way disparages the fighters of the Ottoman Empire, who appear so exotic to European viewers in contrast to their Christian counterparts. Instead, he uses artistic means to pay equal respect to both sides. GD

1 Cf. Karlsruhe 2019, 130–33.

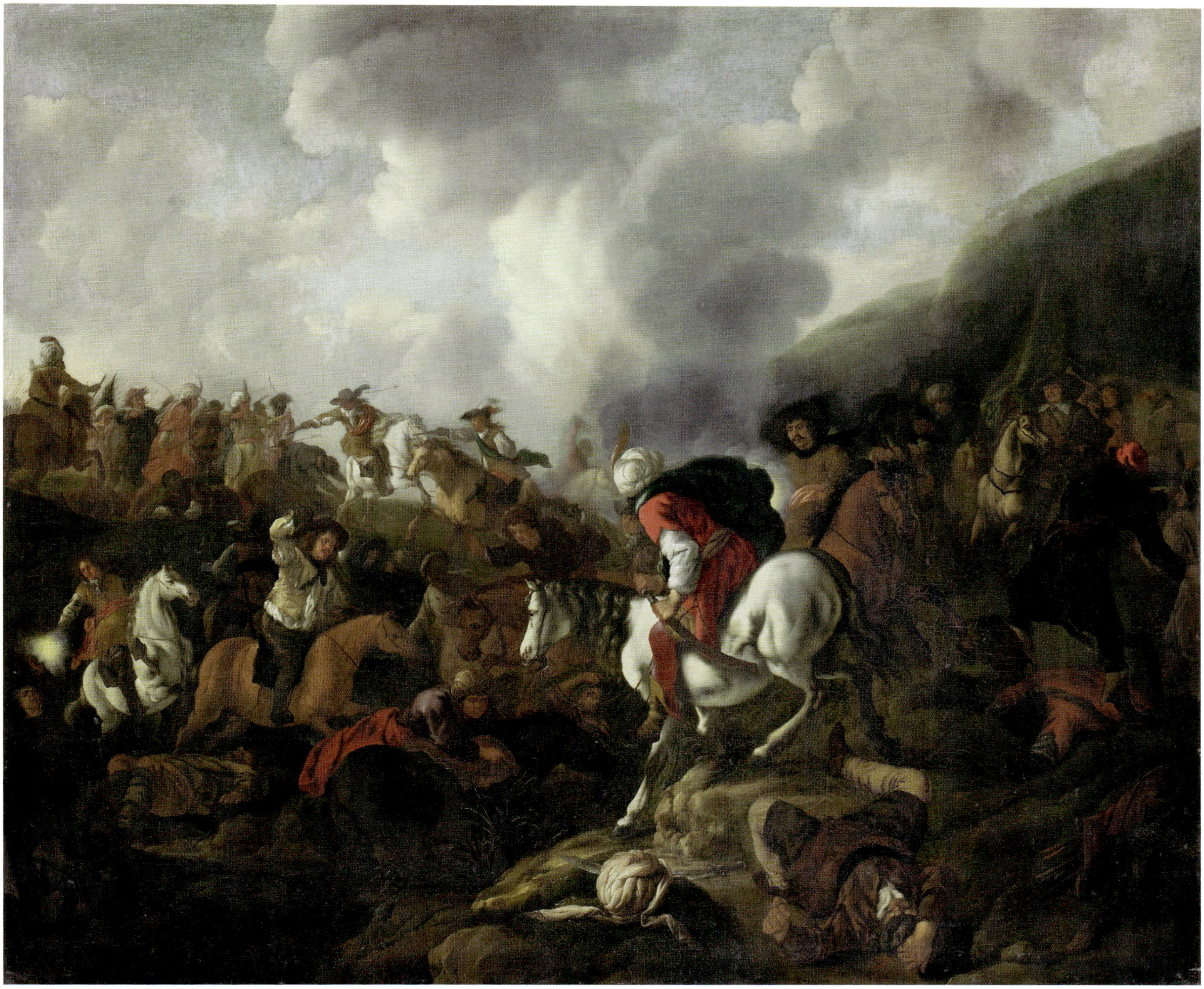

32

33 **Johannes Lingelbach** (1622–1674)

A Sea Battle between Christians and Turks, ca. 1670–74

Oil on canvas, 36 x 45.5 cm
Inscribed (right from center): JL
Inv. YORAG: 2001.40
York Museums Trust (York Art Gallery), purchased with the aid of grants from Art Fund and Museum Libraries and Archives / Victoria and Albert Museum Purchase Grant Fund, 2001

Lit.
Burger-Wegener 1976, 151–52, no. 230

1 For details on various aspects cf. Hamburg 2010.

At no other time and in no other country did the genre of marine painting with its numerous subcategories have greater significance than it did in the seventeenth-century Netherlands. Seafaring was the most important lifeline of the young Republic and was not only a guarantee of its economic prosperity but also of its continued existence, since many of its existential struggles for independence and free access to the world's oceans were fought on the water. Many paintings of this kind, therefore, also conveyed allegorical or political meaning.[1]

Sea battles were an important subject in marine painting. A subgenre emerged in the early seventeenth century dedicated to battles between Christian-European seafarers and their opponents, generally characterized as Oriental, or, more specifically, as representatives of the Ottoman Empire, by their clothing, weapons, and banners (see figs. pp. 80, 83). Johannes Lingelbach's painting also belongs to this category. However, the artist, who was born in Frankfurt and moved to Amsterdam at an early age, was hardly an established marine painter. Like Thomas Wijck (cat. 27) and Jacob Toorenvliet (cat. 29), he belonged to the circle of artists known as the Bamboccianti, a group of Dutch painters occasionally active in Italy and specializing in southern genre scenes. It was only in the last years of his life that he created a whole series of such pictures in a short period of time, works in which he repeatedly combined similar motifs in new ways.

Since Lingelbach's paintings, like those of related subjects by other artists, offer hardly any evidence that might connect them to identifiable historical conflicts, they are often associated with the Battle of Lepanto. In 1571, the Holy League, a united Christian naval power under Spanish leadership, destroyed the numerically superior Ottoman fleet, which had been considered invincible. This victory put a stop—for the time being—to the enemy's further expansion into the Mediterranean. Many of these paintings, however, show seventeenth-century ships (figs. pp. 80, 83); in such instances, the paintings probably refer to the danger of an attack by the Barbary pirates operating off the north coast of Africa, a situation that also affected Dutch ships and against which military expeditions were repeatedly organized (see the essay by Roelof van Gelder, pp. 74–85).

This is less likely to be the case with Lingelbach's painting and similar pieces created in the 1670s. Here, both sides are mostly fighting from galleys rather than from contemporary ships and the European participants in the conflict, in at least some cases, are identified as Maltese. For this reason, Lingelbach's sea battles—which focus more on the genre-like depiction of dramatic battle scenes, highly detailed and presented in close-up, along with desperate rescue efforts in the picture's foreground, than on any overarching narrative—are difficult to relate to events then taking place off the coast of North Africa. Nevertheless, they might have suggested such incidents to a contemporary buyer. GD

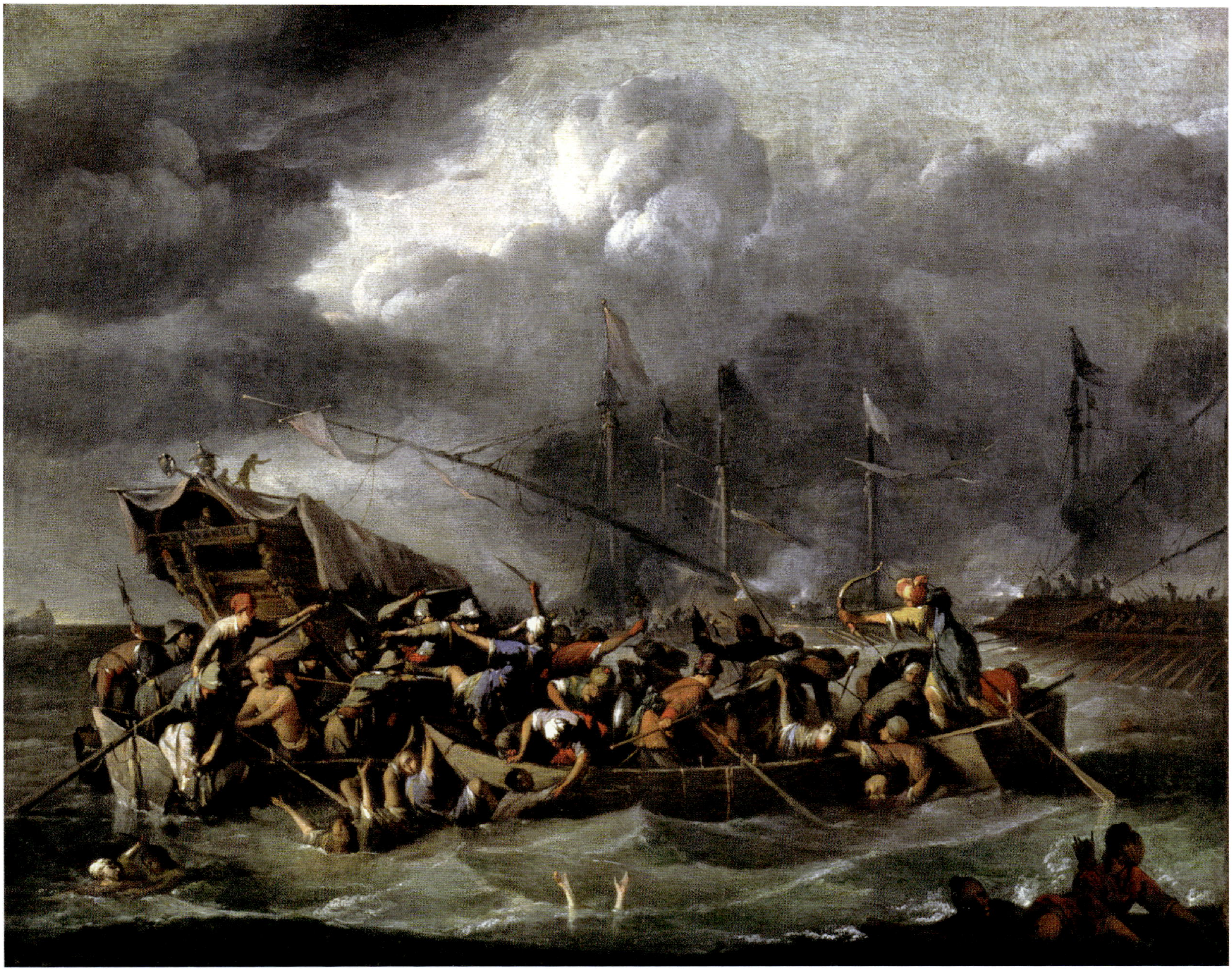

Understanding the World: Collections and Research

In the Netherlands, the spread of trade to all continents fostered greater knowledge of the world and an expansion in learning. A plethora of books and maps described and opened up faraway lands to domestic readers. Amsterdam developed into a center of publishing.[1] Portraits of scholars with books highlighted the idealization of learning that had emerged along with the ambition to pursue trade. The homes of wealthy burghers began to boast cabinets of curiosities for displaying prized objects such as exotic shells.[2] Still lifes and interior scenes lavished attention on exotic and valuable items.[3] This intellectual engagement with the world beyond Europe's shores assumed various forms, albeit sometimes superficial and—as exemplified by attitudes toward Islam—marked by intolerance. Furthermore, there were only a small number of documented occasions when scholars from different countries engaged in direct intellectual exchange.

The work of researching, sharing knowledge through writing, and accumulating learning through study, was symbolized in portraits of scholars with open folios. Examples of such paintings are Michiel van Musscher's portrait of Barend van Lin (cat. 34) and Rembrandt's etching of Abraham Francen (cat. 35). However, reflecting the preeminence of money and commerce in this period, such tomes might just as easily contain business ledgers or tax records, as with Rembrandt's etching of Joannes Wtenbogaert (cat. 36). Memories of the lofty heights achieved by Arab scholarship possibly still resonate in paintings with titles that refer to unspecified Oriental scholars. However, there is very little specific or individual definition about, for example, the generic representations created by Benjamin Gerritsz. Cuyp or the Monogrammist I. S. (cat. 38–39).

Dutch travelers and explorers eagerly collected manuscripts from the Orient written in Arabic, Syriac, and Hebrew (see the essay by Arnoud Vrolijk, pp. 86–101). Their interest in owning such works did not signify, however, that they engaged in personal interactions or knowledge transfer with representatives of different cultures. Drawn by an anonymous artist, the small-scale work *Three Men with a Folio in an Office* (cat. 37) depicts a conversation in which the participants could equally be discussing scholarly or business-related matters. Either way, the pointing gesture and posture of the European figure suggest that the encounter is undercut by an unequal power dynamic.

This accumulation of learning about the world was also reflected in cartography, which for a maritime nation had the practical benefit of aiding navigation, while also serving as an instrument for organizing geographical knowledge. The Dutch were world leaders in this field during the seventeenth century, the era of cartographers like Jodocus Hondius, Johannes Janssonius, and Willem Jansz. Blaeu. The latter published *Theatrum orbis terrarum sive Atlas novus* (Theater of the World or New Atlas), comprising more than two hundred maps embellished in a manner befitting the Baroque era's taste for ornamentation (see cat. 40).

Dutch publishers produced countless works about the lands of the Far East—travel reports, depictions of local customs, and scientific compendia (cat. 41–43). The authors of these works were often in fact talented compilers: armchair travelers who relied on existing publications and written travels for their source material. Second or even third-hand texts such as these would inevitably confirm and so sustain existing clichés.[4] The imperative for painters to closely study sources in order to create suitable representations of historic scenes is highlighted in *Lof der schilder-konst* (Praise of the Art of Painting) by Philips Angel, who cited Rembrandt as a model for others to follow (cat. 44). However, this in itself raises the question of just how thorough Rembrandt's study of ancient texts actually was and what this brought to bear on his compositions.

The intellectual engagement with foreign cultures also included an interest in Islam. In a society shaped by Christianity, which had in the previous century seen rival denominations descend into bloody conflicts, there was little chance of Islam finding acceptance. The various Christian denominations and Judaism were tolerated following the Union of Utrecht, signed in 1579, which guaranteed a certain level of religious freedom. However, while by seventeenth-century standards this equated to an unusual degree of religious tolerance,[5] such rights were not extended to followers of Islam. The anonymous Haarlem painter of *Parody of Religious Tolerance* (cat. 46) takes a satirical slant on the community of religious leaders, by showing various Christians and one Jewish representative standing alongside one another as equals, each holding the text of their respective dogmas. Implacable hostility is reserved, however, for the Muslim figure. Even Dutch translations of the Quran, of which there were at least several versions in the seventeenth century, are not characterized by their unprejudiced faithfulness to the original text (cat. 47–49).

Of the luxury goods brought to the Netherlands through global trade, not all were foodstuffs such as spices and tea or consumer goods such as fabrics, porcelain, and carpets. For while many products were imported to Europe for their luxury or utility value, other items were never intended to be eaten or used, but were instead coveted for their rarity and beauty. These items might take the form of valuable craft objects (*artificialia*) or natural objects such as shells, rocks, and zoological specimens (*naturalia*). Like the princes and aristocrats of the previous century, wealthy citizens in the Netherlands took to collecting such rarities and displaying them in cabinets of curiosities.[6] Sometimes collections had encyclopedic ambitions, serving as a microcosm showing the diversity of all natural forms and man-made design. Thus, while documenting humanity's real-life appropriation of the natural world, the collections also served to praise the wonders of God. In his interiors, Jan van der Heyden depicts stylized cabinets of curiosities (cat. 52–53) that showcase objects from different continents. Paintings like these indicated the owners' wealth, refinement, modernity, and intellect. The same was true of still lifes, such as the arrangement of precious objects painted by Willem Kalf (cat. 50–51), which revels in the possession of the foreign and valuable. As emblems of transience and vanity, however, the objects also evoke a preoccupation that was ubiquitous in the seventeenth century. MPH

1 Cf. Jos van Waterschoot, "Publizistisches Zentrum Amsterdam: Eine gelungene Symbiose von Geld und Buchstabe?," in Wilczek 1993, 120–35, and Pettegree/Der Weduwen 2019.
2 Cf., for example, Amsterdam 1992.
3 Cf., for example, Hochstrasser 2007.
4 Cf., for example, Schmidt 2015, 25–81.
5 Cf., for example, Bernd Wilczek, "Die offene Stadt: Toleranz als Regulator des öffentlichen Lebens," in Wilczek 1993, 60–73, and Manuth 2006.
6 Cf. Amsterdam 1992.

34 **Michiel van Musscher** (1645–1705)

Barend van Lin with His Younger Brother and His Future Brother-in-Law, 1671

Oil on canvas, 59.5 x 51.5 cm
Inv. SA 35787
Amsterdam Museum

Lit.
Ydema 1991, 86, fig. p. 88
Amsterdam 1992, 182–83, no. 402
Amsterdam 2008b, 145, 229
Van der Veen 2008
Amsterdam 2012, 36–37
Dekker 2002

The master of the house donning a fashionable dressing gown, an Oriental rug draped over the table, and lying open on top of it a copy of Ptolemy's *Geographia* surrounded by assorted astronomical instruments invented in the Netherlands—Michiel van Musscher's *Portrait of Barend van Lin* is a marriage not only of privacy and prestige, but also of the knowledge and accomplishments of Occident and Orient. The astronomical model forges the connection with the cosmos. Thus a study on Amsterdam's Herengracht becomes an expression of erudite cosmopolitanism.

The age of the millstone collar was long since over by the second half of the seventeenth century and Barend van Lin is portrayed here wearing a garment then very much en vogue: an eye-catching dressing gown made of exquisite light red silk with a blue lining. Positioned at the center of the composition, its expanse greatly enlarged by the wearer's outstretched arms and legs, this *japonse rok* with its multiple layers of cloth and smooth, shiny surface is the dominant visual element here (see cat. 11–13, 15). The red velvet beret, long white stockings, and light red slippers further enhance the impression of extravagance. So powerful is Van Lin's presence that it condemns the two younger men, both of them more soberly dressed and traditionally identified as his brother and future brother-in-law, to a minor role.

Barend van Lin (ca. 1641–1705) earned his living as a tax collector, although he also worked as a cartographer and surveyor for the Raad van Holland, a consultative body that advised the stadtholder. At the time of this portrait he lived on Herengracht, Amsterdam's most expensive address, which he relinquished only after being appointed professor of mathematics at the University of Utrecht. Van Lin was just thirty when he had this portrait of himself as a scholar painted. The open cabinet full of tomes and the huge bookcase in the background tell of his erudition, while the books and instruments in the foreground are an allusion to his activities as a geographer.

Lying on the table are a copy of Ptolemy's *Geographia,* an ancient cartography textbook, and a Bible. The latter is opened at the Book of Joshua, which contains the verse: "And the sun stood still and the moon stayed" (Joshua 10:13). With his right hand Van Lin is pointing at a tellurium, an astronomical model for demonstrating the motion of the Earth and Moon. Now in Amsterdam's National Maritime Museum, this particular tellurium was designed by the publisher and cartographer Willem Jansz. Blaeu (see cat. 40), who died in 1638. Lying on the floor on the right at Van Lin's feet is a *Hollandse Cirkel,* an instrument for measuring land area invented by Jan Pietersz. Dou in 1610, and next to it a quadrant such as Ptolemy himself would have used along with another instrument that he described: an aid to navigation called an astrolabe, which was developed and refined by Arab scholars of the ninth century.

The painter Van Lin commissioned with his likeness was Michiel van Musscher. He had arrived in Amsterdam only three years before, but had already become the portraitist of choice for Amsterdam's aspiring middle class. His fondness for incorporating Oriental motifs into his portraits is also apparent in that of *Thomas Hees with His Nephews Jan and Andreis Hees and a Servant* of 1687 (Rijksmuseum, Amsterdam). MPH

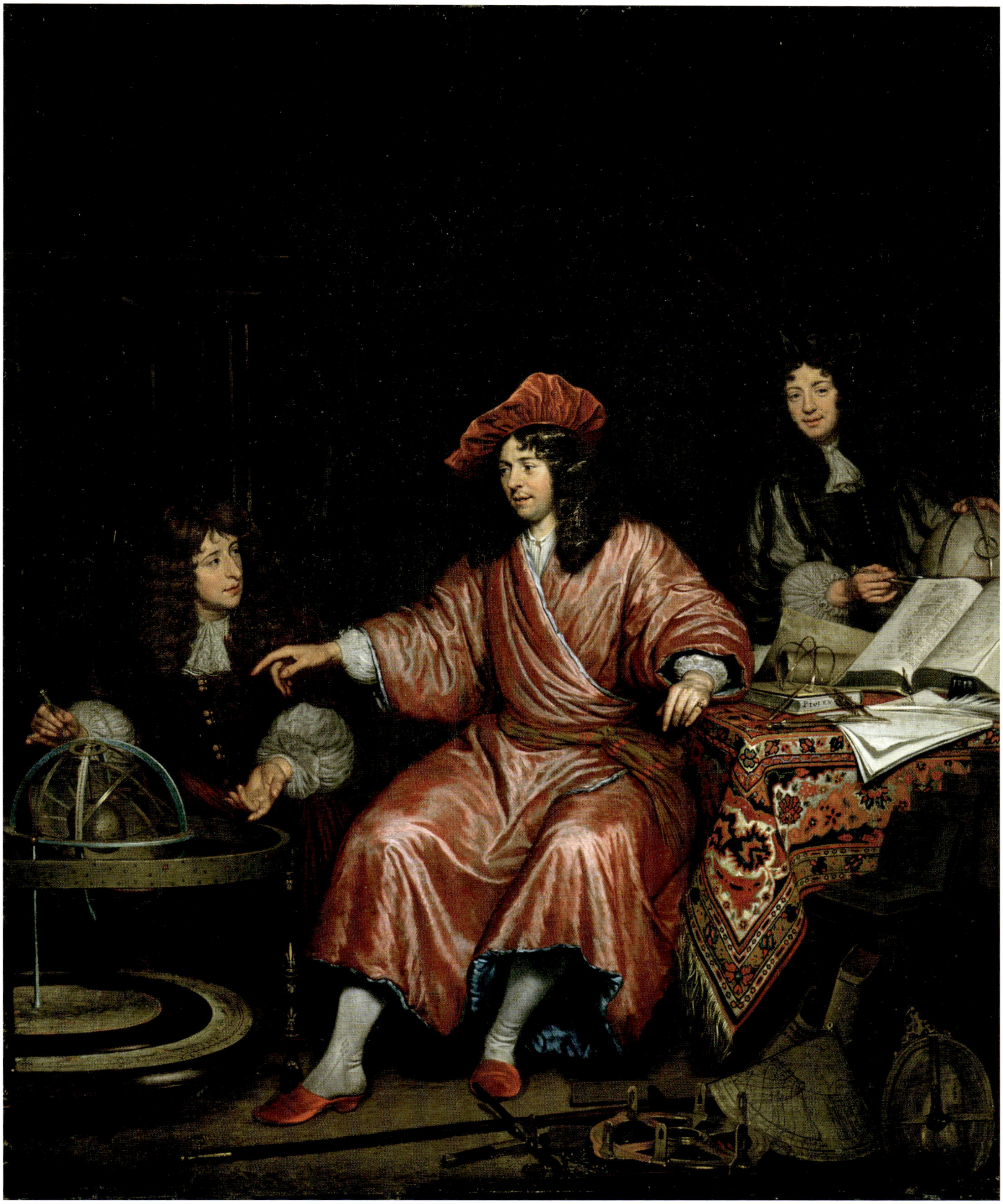

35 **Rembrandt Harmensz. van Rijn** (1606–1669)

Abraham Francen, ca. 1657

Etching, drypoint, and burin on paper,
15.8 x 20.9 cm
7th state (of 12)
Inv. 2007.264
Kunstmuseum Basel, Kupferstichkabinett,
Donation Eberhard W. Kornfeld, Bern

Lit.
B 273 (7/10)
NH 301 (7/12)
White 1999, 162–65, figs. 213–16
Basel 2005, no. 97
Schwartz 2006, 223–27, fig. 375
Peters 2019

Among the objects on the table, including an open book, is the single most complete image of an Oriental objet d'art that Rembrandt ever created. It is a statuette of a seated person holding a talisman on his lap. In China images of this kind served as meditation objects in the house altar of an adherent of the Taoist way of life. It has not been possible to identify the figure depicted. It could be a deity, a ruler, or a sage, such as Lao-tzu, whose teachings underpin Taoism.

A folding triptych of a type that served for private Christian meditation hangs on the back wall of the room. While the central position of the *Crucifixion* makes it clear that no equivalence between the two faiths was intended, the placing of the sculpture suggests that it had particular meaning for the sitter. It is possible that it served as an object of contemplation if not meditation. The skull next to the statuette is a highly suggestive detail. It is reminiscent of the skull on the desk of Saint Jerome in prints and paintings of the sixteenth century. This brings the portrait of Abraham Francen at his own desk into the realm of Christian humanism. In Dutch art and culture, this often devolved into the concept of *vanitas*—that all earthly striving is vanity. Whatever specific meaning might be implied by the Oriental figure in the etching, just finding it this domestic environment tells us that exotic objects like it could be integrated into Dutch households.

In the eighteenth century, the sitter was identified as the Amsterdam apothecary Abraham Francen, who was also a physician. Francen was one of Rembrandt's most faithful friends of his later years, witnessing family papers and even serving after the artist's death as guardian of his orphaned daughter, Cornelia. He was connected by family ties and network relations to high-standing figures in Dutch society and the arts. Although there is no documentation concerning his art collection, Francen is said to have been an extremely passionate print collector. Rembrandt memorializes this aspect of his friend's persona by showing him holding up a print or drawing to the light. GS

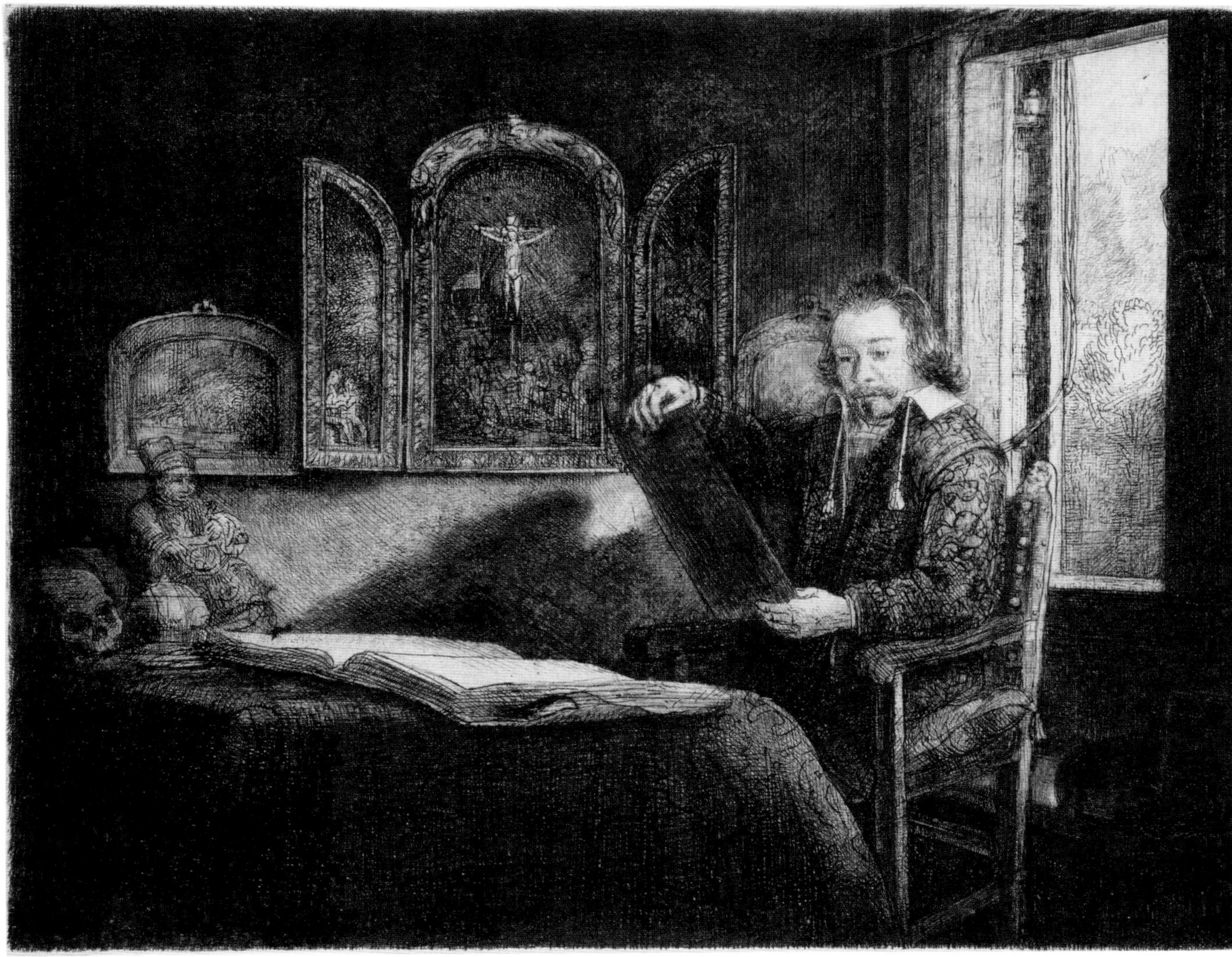

35

36 **Rembrandt Harmensz. van Rijn** (1606–1669)

Jan Wtenbogaert (The Gold Weigher), 1639

Etching and drypoint on Japanese paper,
24.8 x 20.3 cm
2nd state (of 3)
Inscribed on plate at bottom left:
Rembrandt. f. / 1639
Inv. 2007.191
Kunstmuseum Basel, Kupferstichkabinett,
Donation Eberhard W. Kornfeld, Bern

Lit.
B 281 (2/2)
NH 172 (2/3)
Dudok van Heel 1978, 154–55
White 1999, 136–37, fig. 174
Dickey 2004, 79
Basel 2005, no. 31
Schwartz 2006, 224–27, fig. 376
Tuynman 2006, 155–68

In July 1638 the thirty-year-old Joannes Wtenbogaert was appointed by the province of Holland to the office of tax receiver for Amsterdam and surroundings. He was a committed member of the Remonstrant church, a liberal alternative to strict Calvinism. When Wtenbogaert studied law in Leiden University in the 1620s he lodged with a relative of Rembrandt's, and the two seem to have known each other since then.

When in 1639 Rembrandt was having trouble collecting payment for two paintings he had made for Stadtholder Frederik Hendrik, the prince of Orange, Wtenbogaert intervened and actually advanced payment out of tax money he had collected. All of this background plays a role in Rembrandt's remarkable allegorical portrait of his friend. The print of the following year has been interpreted as a vocational portrait in his new function. It also has an allegorical dimension: the rich young man in the foreground stands for the youthful, rapidly growing city of Amsterdam while the peasants in the background would then represent the countryside, the other component of his district.

The large picture behind Wtenbogaert depicts the brazen serpent spoken of in both the Old and New Testament. Having been punished for their ingratitude by the Lord with a plague of deadly serpents, the Israelites were saved by a bronze statue of a serpent put up by Moses, of which God said "that every one that is bitten, when he looketh upon it, shall live" (Numbers 21:8). The miracle was cited by Jesus when he said to Nicodemus: "As Moses lifted up the serpent in the wilderness, even so must the Son of man be lifted up: That whosoever believeth in him should not perish, but have eternal life" (John 3:14–15). The underlying message—that sinners can be saved—lends support to the Remonstrant belief in justification by faith, as opposed to the predeterminism of the Calvinists. An artist and art collector would also have been touched by the power of the sheer gaze in the story. One can also wonder whether the positive role assigned to a precious metal by God himself could have served to assuage in Wtenbogaert's mind any qualms he may have had about collecting lucre for the common good.

This intriguing print is thought to have been made by Rembrandt not as a commission but as a gift to the sitter, a gesture of friendship and thanks for Wtenbogaert's help in getting payment from the prince. Although it does not contain Oriental elements, it is included here because of the sitter's documented ownership of a rare album of Mughal portraits, and its possible importance for Rembrandt (see the essay by Gary Schwartz, pp. 56–73).

This impression of the etching has a material connection to the Orient: it is printed on Japanese paper. Steeped in tradition, this silky, shiny paper, which is made from the fibers of various types of Japanese wood, was an exquisite import product that was used as a support for images in Europe for the first time in the seventeenth century in the Netherlands. Rembrandt's drawings after Mughal miniatures, one of which is in the exhibition (cat. 97), are his only drawings on Asian paper. GS

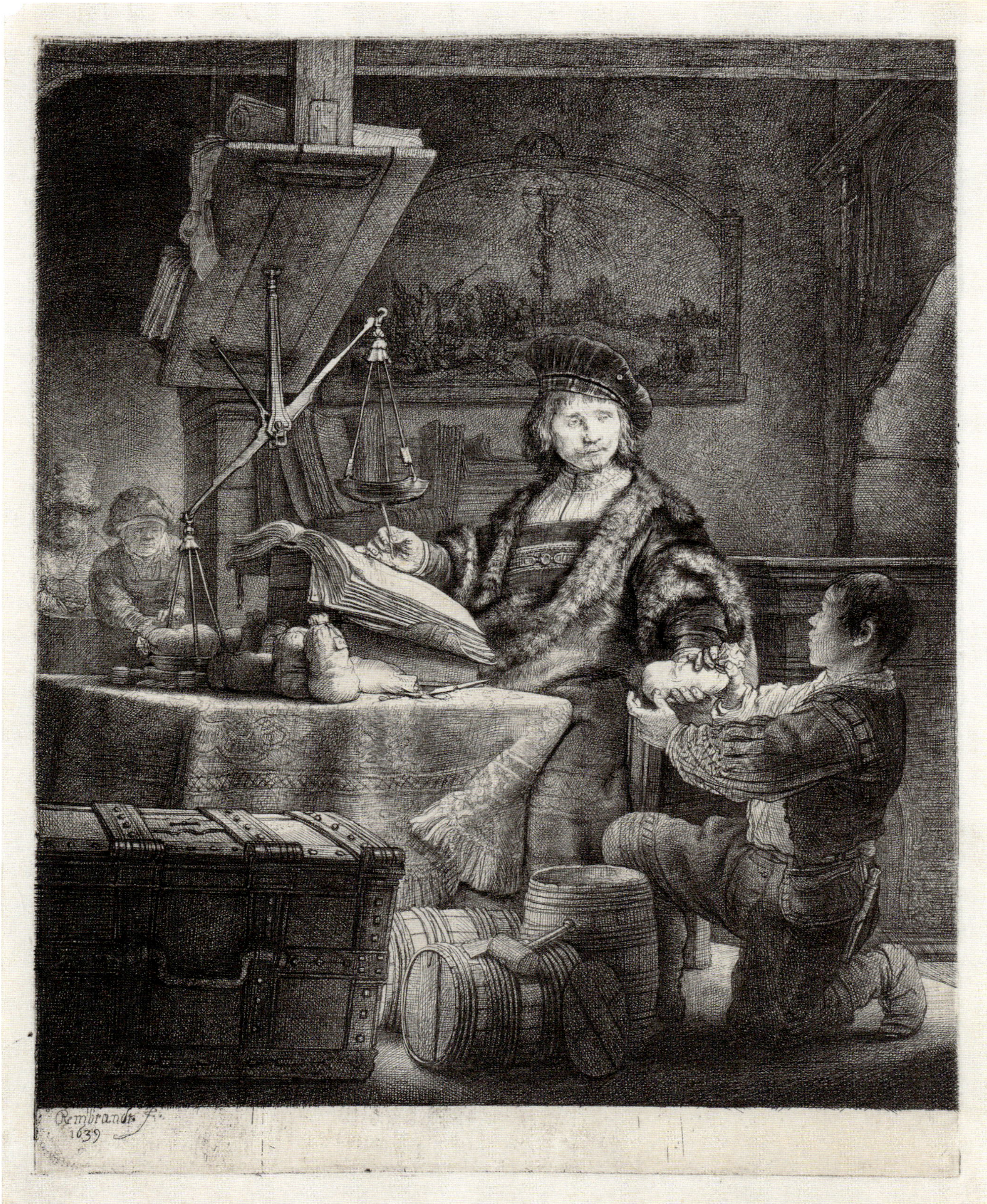
Rembrandt f.
1639

37 **Anonymous** (formerly attributed to Cornelis Visscher II [ca. 1628/29–1658])
Three Men with a Folio in an Office, 17th century

Etching, 6.1 x 8.9 cm
Inv. RP-P-1897-A-19543
Rijksmuseum, Amsterdam,
Rijksprentenkabinet, Gift of H. P. Gerritsen,
The Hague, 1897

Lit.
Unpublished

The object preoccupying the three gentlemen in this tiny print is the open tome that lies on the table, propped up by another such volume. Standing in the right foreground is a man with a mustache sporting a turban with an aigrette pinned onto it (see cat. 2) as well as a cloak, and a robe belted with a sash. He could be an envoy of the Sublime Porte. With his arms folded behind his back, he cuts a dignified figure as he listens attentively to the Dutchman standing next to him. While the latter has turned to face the guest with whom he is conversing, he is also pointing at the left-hand page of the aforementioned book. Behind him is a third man, hunched over the opposite page. What the two gentlemen are clearly fascinated by is the illustration the Dutchman is pointing at, presumably a map or nautical chart. The globe in front of the books on the left supports this association with geographical discourse. Are they discussing the guest's faraway homeland? Or are the two Europeans the travelers here?

The furnishings, which call to mind a stereotypical Dutch interior, would speak against any localization of this work in the Orient. On the left behind the curtain is a bookcase, in which the books are lined up with the fore edge and clasps facing outward—a contemporary custom that has been observed elsewhere. Lying on the shelf above them is what appears to be a stack of albums or portfolios, while leaning against the shelf below is a painting showing a frontal view of several bare-headed men. Hanging on the wall to the right of the bookcase is a large map and next to it a wall clock with weights. The almost identical selection and arrangement of props in this work and in the still life in Jan van der Heyden's *Corner of a Library* (cat. 52) is astonishing; except that in the latter work the books in the bookcase have their spines facing out and the rolled-up wall charts are leaning against the bookcase.

Both the authorship and the theme of this etching remain a mystery. Yet there can be no doubt that it is about the exchange between Occident and Orient, whatever the occasion for that might have been. BB

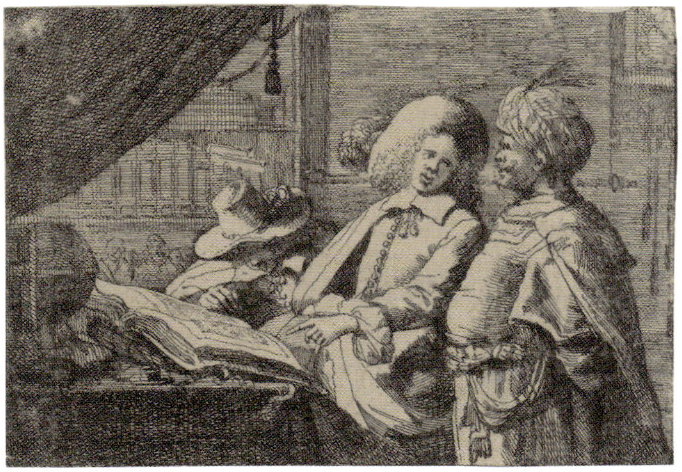

37

38 **Benjamin Gerritsz. Cuyp** (1612–1652)
Oriental Writer Cutting His Pen, ca. 1640–50

Oil on panel, 27.5 x 22.5 cm
Inscribed top left: CUijP
The Kremer Collection—
www.thekremercollection.com

Lit.
Christie's New York, December 1, 1996, lot 427

[1] On this category, cf. Hirschfelder 2008, 205.

The painting owes the title it is known by today to the turban made of olive-green cloth shot through with white and gold thread worn by the bearded old man with pince-nez, who is busy sharpening his quill pen. Supplementing his headgear is a leather cap worn underneath the turban that covers the nape of the neck, but leaves the ears exposed. The unusual cut of this leather helmet resembles that worn by the ancient Roman priesthood, the *galerus* or *apex,* images of which can be seen, for example, in the procession of pontifical priests—the *flamines*—in a relief on the Ara Pacis in Rome.

The sandals on the old man's feet might equally well count as an Oriental or *all'antica* accessory, whereas his robe and cloak are simply generically exotic. Both the book lying open on his knees and the loose leaves on the lectern draped with a rug on the left are blank, as far as we can see, and his right foot hovers over another loose leaf lying on the floor. The drawing (?) pinned to the side wall seems to show a draped figure seated outdoors, a subject most closely associated with scenes from classical antiquity or the Bible.

The costume assembled out of different items of dress gives the impression that this figure, like the one in the work by Johannes van Swinderen (cat. 2), is not a specific individual, but rather an ideal type of the "wise old man" from time immemorial, in which case the work itself would be a *tronie* of a scholar.[1] BB

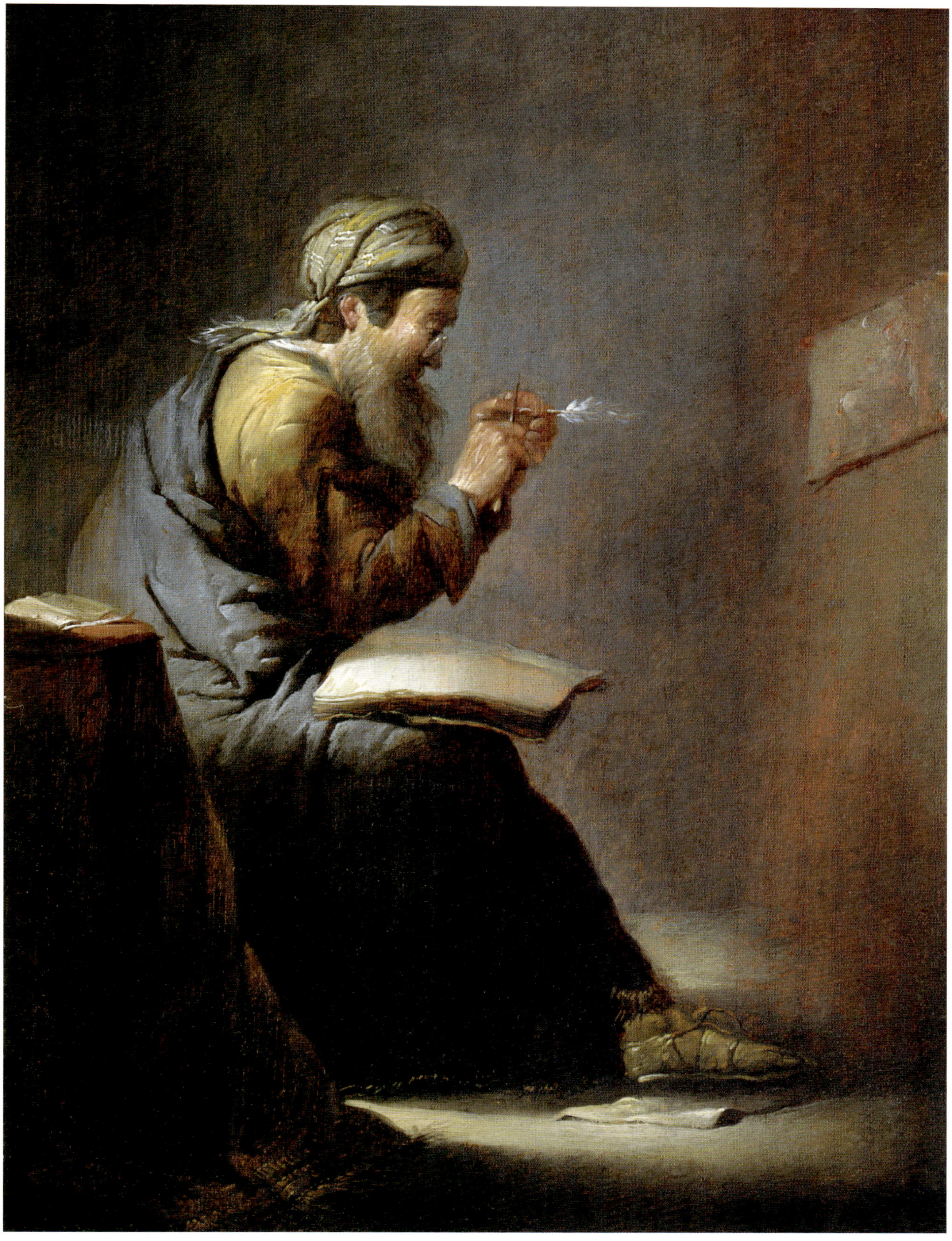

39 **Monogrammist I. S.** (active 1633–1658) (?)

An Oriental Scholar, Half-Length (King Solomon Studying for the Construction of the Temple?)

Oil on panel, 55 x 41 cm
Inv. M 166
Kunstpalast, Düsseldorf,
M. J. Binder Donation 1947

Lit.
Düsseldorf 2002, 20

1 Sumowski 1983–94, vol. 4, 2548–49.
2 Examples include Herzog Anton Ulrich-Museum, Braunschweig; and Sotheby's London, April 26, 2001, lot 48, monogrammed and dated 1651.

The oeuvre attributed to the Monogrammist I. S.,[1] formerly erroneously identified as the Leiden painter Jacob van Spreeuwen (1609/10–after 1658), is a slim one, consisting of genre scenes, *tronies*, and portraits. While the scholars in their studies stand out among the artist's genre scenes,[2] they are very different, being more finely observed and composed with more conspicuously arranged still lifes on the desk. The monogrammist also excelled at haunting representations of the heavily wrinkled faces of elderly men and women. The recent attribution to him of this unsigned panel therefore seems wrong, so that earlier attempts to link it to names such as Salomon de Bray (1597–1664) or Pieter de Grebber (ca. 1595/1605–1652/53) should perhaps be reconsidered. The connections to the latter's oeuvre are legion and include the somewhat cursory treatment of the subject's facial features and the material properties of the dark cloth in which he is swathed.

No less open to speculation than its attribution is the meaning of the work. A young man is consulting a book, on whose right-hand page is a whole-page illustration of a column on a pedestal, such as might be found in an architectural treatise. In his left hand he holds a scroll, on which another fluted column and a study for a capital can be made out. Lying further back, next to his right hand with raised index finger, is a folded sheet of paper and behind that a turban. It is this exotic head covering made of a cloth with colored stripes woven into it that has earned the figure wearing a scarf in matching colors the designation "Oriental scholar." Yet neither the young man's looks nor his coat made of heavy black velvet have anything Oriental about them.

Here we encounter the same eclectic combination of traits both Occidental and Oriental as in the *tronies* and portraits in Oriental costume of Rembrandt and his pupils (see cat. 99–101, 106, 119). Yet the turban in this painting differs from the accessories typically deployed in those genres in one key respect: it is topped by a little golden crown. In history paintings crowned turbans often function as a badge of identity—for the three Magi of the New Testament, say, or for the rulers of the Old.

The most probable classification of this work is therefore that of *portrait historié*, here of an artist or scholar cast in the role of King Solomon studying the plans for the temple in Jerusalem that was to bear his name. Perhaps some aspiring young architect wanted the biblical reference to ennoble his métier. For this he was able to avail himself of the account in the Old Testament, according to which Solomon was still just a "little child" when he became king and began building the temple in the fourth year of his reign (1 Kings 3:7, 6:1, 6:37, and 1 Chronicles 29:1); hence the departure from the usual iconography and the depiction of the scholar as a beardless young man. According to 1 Chronicles 28:11, Solomon was guided by a "descriptio" (Vulgate) or "voorbeelt" (Statenbijbel 1637) of the temple architecture provided by his father. Perhaps those are the materials that the young king is poring over here. BB

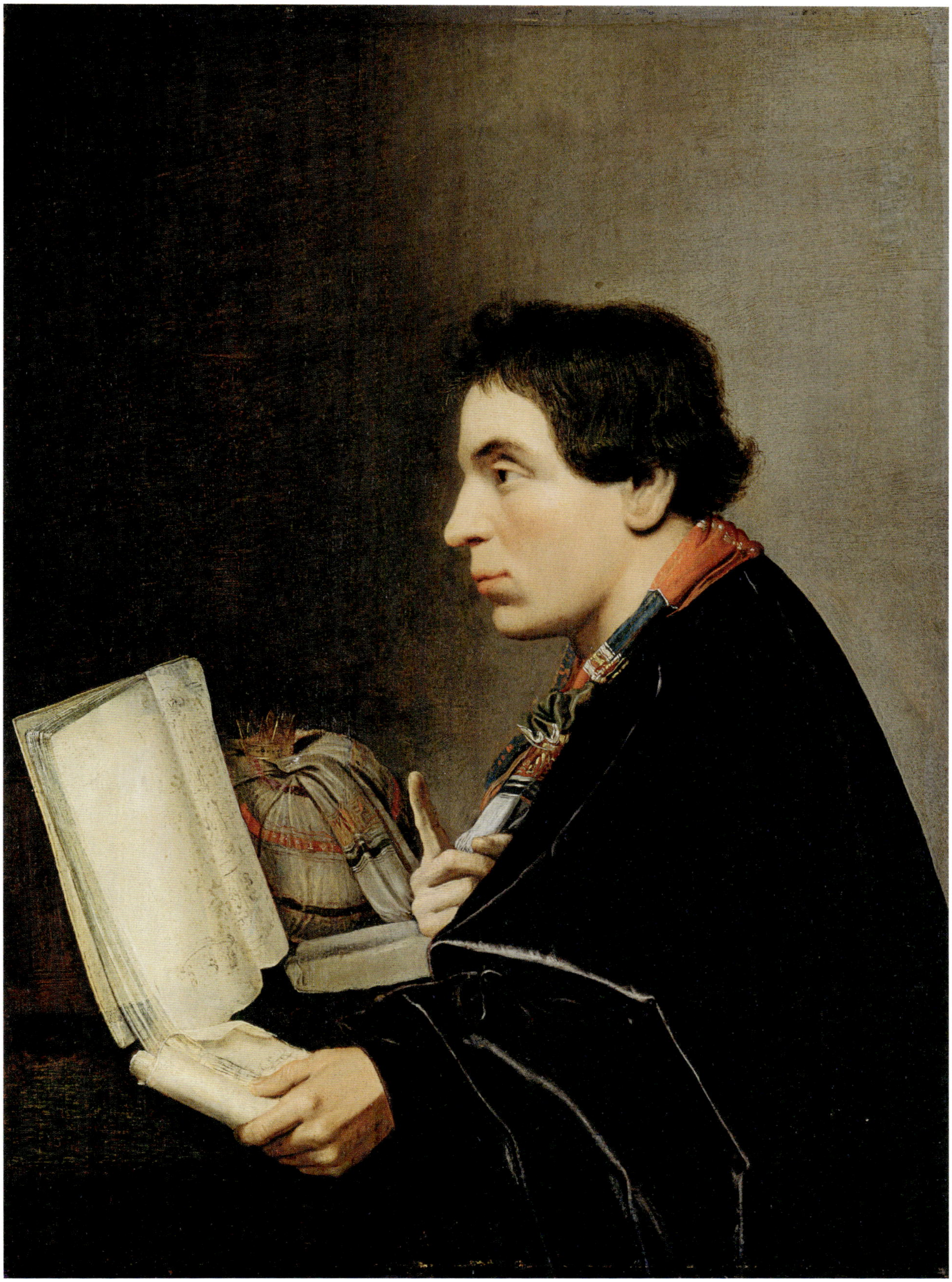

40 **Willem Jansz. Blaeu** (1571–1638)
Asia noviter delineata, ca. 1630

Colored engraving, 51.5 x 60 cm
HB-KZL 33.12.41 (Potsdam)
HB-KZL 33.12.42 (Basel)
Allard Pierson, University of Amsterdam
COLLBN Port 172 N 11
Leiden University Libraries
(Basel only)

Lit.
Goss/Clark 1990, 190–91

Indispensable to the pursuit of global, transoceanic trade was an extensive knowledge of geography and navigational skills, both fields in which the Dutch were world leaders in the seventeenth century. One of their best cartographers was Willem Jansz. Blaeu, who studied astronomy with Tycho Brahe in Denmark.[1] In Amsterdam Blaeu made globes (the first of them in 1598), designed a tellurium (see cat. 34), and in 1633 won the crucial appointment of cartographer to the Dutch East India Company, which kept its maps and charts at the Oost-Indisch Huys in Amsterdam (see cat. 18). Blaeu designed his first wall map as early as 1604 and in the 1630s turned his printing shop into Europe's leading publisher of maps and atlases.

His map of Asia, which he published separately in 1617, later formed part of the *Theatrum orbis terrarum sive Atlas novus* (Theater of the World or New Atlas) of 1635, a work comprising at first two, and in later editions six, volumes. At bottom right is the Island of Java, now part of Indonesia, on the northwestern corner of which the capital of the Dutch East India Company was situated. The Dutch began calling it Batavia in 1619 (see cat. 86), although on the Latin map it bears its former name Jacatra (now Jakarta).

As was standard practice in those days, Blaeu endowed the vast expanses of water on his land maps with images of ships, a whale, and the mythological figure of a Triton. On the landmasses there is a lion, an elephant, and, above the very detailed rendition of the Great Wall of China, a camel. Blaeu's maps derive much of their decorative charm from the illustrations in the margins. These might be allegorical representations of the four elements, the four seasons, the Seven Wonders of the World, or the seven planets, as is the case on the world map.[2] On the maps of the continents of Europe, Africa, America, and Asia, the top margin is filled with images of the major cities, while the left and right margins feature representatives of the various countries or regions, always arranged in pairs.[3] The map of Europe, for example, shows Englishmen, Frenchmen, Germans, and Hungarians wearing costumes typical of both social class and country. The same is true of the map of Asia, which introduces Syrians, Arabs, and Persians. Most of these figures wear turban-like head coverings. The Javans are shown bare-chested and the native of the Moluccan Banda Islands carries the sword and long shield believed to be typical of his people, as seen in Andries Beeckman's *Dancing Ambonese Warriors Dressed in Yellow* (cat. 87). The figures in these illustrations might also have been drawn from contemporary costume books (fig. p. 43) or ethnographic works such as Joannes de Laet's *Persia* (cat. 91).

The map was published unchanged in the *Atlas Maior*, the largest and most ambitious book project of the seventeenth century, which Blaeu's son Joan (1596–1673) pieced together out of older maps. The ten years between 1662 and 1672 saw the publication of Latin, French, Dutch, German, and Spanish editions, each comprising between nine and eleven volumes with nearly six hundred maps and three thousand pages of text. When the Ottoman sultan received a copy of the *Atlas Maior* as a gift of honor in 1668 the project also attracted notice in the Ottoman Empire, and in 1685 the Ottoman cartographer and professor in Istanbul, Ebû Bekir b. Behrâm ed-Dımaşkī (died in 1691) translated the whole work into Turkish. His manuscript, which was never printed, also contained land maps, of which 246 were labeled with Turkish place names. MPH

1 Wawrik 1982, 94–99; on the *Atlas Maior* in general, cf. also Koeman 1970; Wawrik 1982, 110–16; and Pettegree/Der Weduwen 2019, 110–15.
2 Illustrated in Goss/Clark 1990, 24–25.
3 On the design of the margins, cf. Schneider 2004, 136–37.

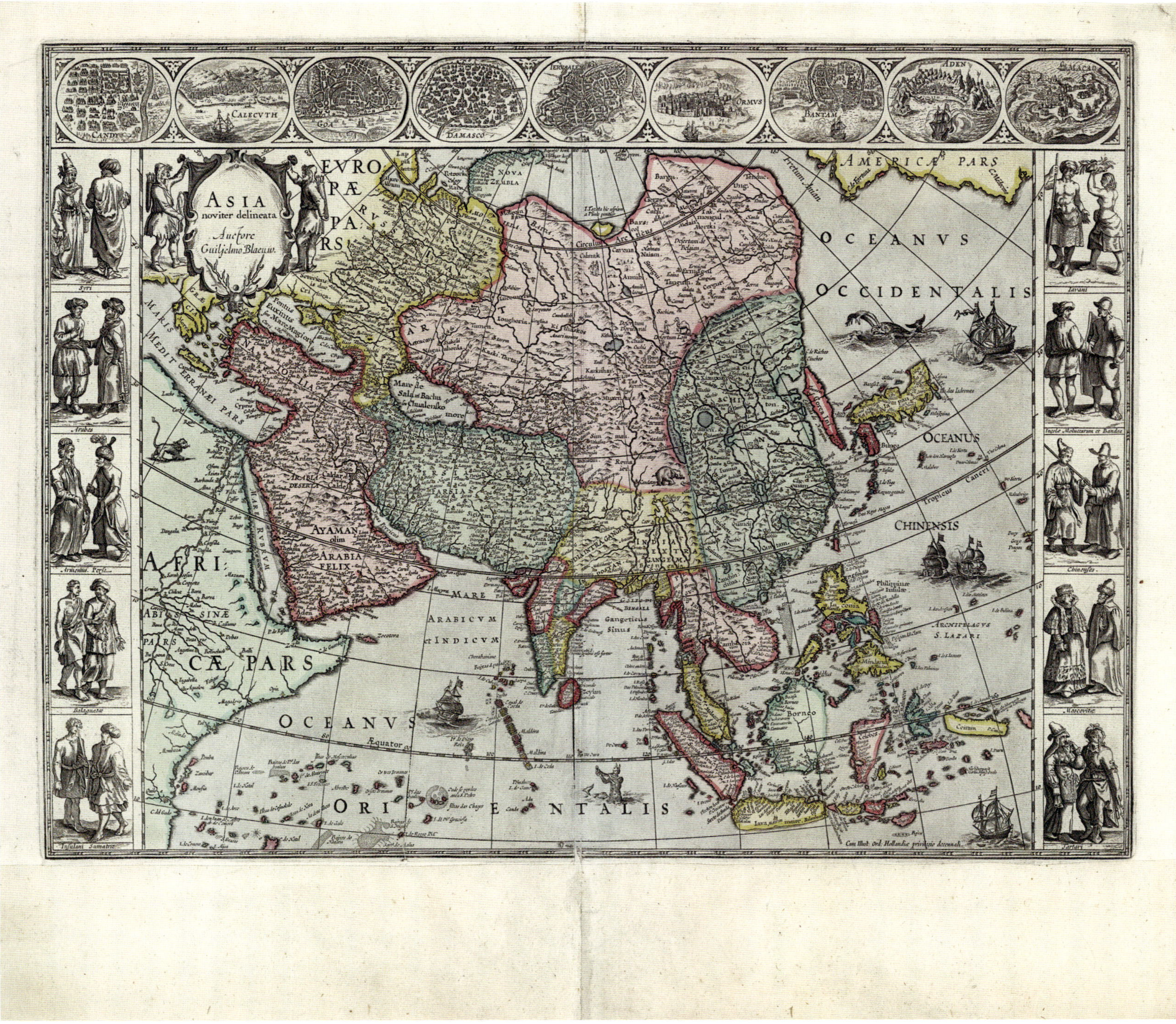
Asia
noviter delineata
Auctore
Guiljelmo Blaeuw.
Calecuth
Goa
Damasco
Ormus
Bantam
Aden
Macao
Candy
Nova Zembla
Evropæ pars
Americæ pars
Oceanvs Occidentalis
Oceanus Chinensis
Tropicus Cancri
Mare Arabicvm et Indicvm
Gangeticus Sinus
Archipelagus S. Lazari
Philippinæ Insulæ
Borneo
Oceanvs Orientalis
Æquator
Afri cæ pars
Arabia Felix
Arabia Deserta
Syri
Arabes
Armenini. Persæ
Javani
Chinenses
Moscovitæ
Tartari
Cum Illust. Ord. Hollandiæ privilegio decennali.

41 Jacob van Meurs (ca. 1619/20–1679)
Asia, 1672
42 Romeyn de Hooghe (1645–1708)
Title page*,* 1682

41
Engraving
Frontispiece in Olfert Dapper,
Asia, of Naukeurige beschryving van Het Rijk des Grooten Mogols, en een groot gedeelte van Indiën . . .
(Asia, or Precise Account of the Empire of the Great Mogul and Large Swathes of India . . .), Amsterdam: Jacob van Meurs, 1672
OTM: OM 63-115
Allard Pierson, University of Amsterdam
(Potsdam)
UBH EUU I 66
Basel University Library,
Department of Manuscripts and Early Printed Books
(Basel)

42
Engraving
In Simon de Vries,
Curieuse aenmerckingen der bysonderste Oost en West-Indische verwonderens-waerdige dingen . . .
(Curious Observations on the Most Remarkable and Astonishing Things from East and West India . . .), 4 vols., Utrecht: Johannes Ribbius, 1682, vol. 2
347 C 12
Leiden University Libraries,
Special Collections

Lit.
Roeper/Wildeman 1996, 48
Schmidt 2015, 25–47

Starting in the late sixteenth century, Europe was bombarded with stories, information, and objects from parts of the world about which Europeans had never before heard. Much of these material and immaterial goods came first to the Netherlands, from where they were packaged and marketed in the rest of Europe. Part of that packaging took the form of book publishing. Building on Dutch dominance in the graphic arts, the publication of maps and atlases (see cat. 40), and the commercial channels through which they were distributed throughout Europe, publishers brought out increasingly sumptuous volumes intended to exploit existing curiosity and spark interest without satiating it.

The leading figure in this development was the Amsterdam printer-publisher Jacob van Meurs, who in 1664 acquired state license to bring out a canonical text on China, which he provided with elaborate illustrations. Numerous books about other overseas regions of the world followed (see cat. 43), and readers were amazed by the presentation. Meurs was unembarrassed about purveying cliché images that had little or nothing to do with the text. The frontispiece to his edition of Olfert Dapper's book on Asia (where the author had never been; all his information is secondhand) is a case in point.

Another compendium of the kind was a four-volume set of *Curieuse aenmerckingen der bysonderste Oost en West-Indische verwonderens-waerdige dingen* . . . (Curious Observations on the Most Remarkable and Astonishing Things from the East and West Indies . . .). The author, Simon de Vries, was a tireless producer of works of this kind. In 1671 he had brought out *Oude en nieuwe-tijds wonder-toneel* (A Wondrous Theater of Old and New Times), the sources for which have been found in no less than eighty earlier publications by others.[1]

The artist who made the illustrations for the book was no less prolific. No one has yet succeeded in producing a complete catalog of the graphic production of the phenomenal Romeyn de Hooghe, by whom the Rijksmuseum has some 1,500 prints.[2] He dedicated his immense talents and energies to the glorification of princes and politicians, but also of exotic locales. The frontispiece to the second volume of Simon de Vries's book overflows with products of De Hooghe's graphic imagination and learning, in a more serious mode than the Dapper print.

A commanding Western figure in a plumed turban, his hand on a scepter, stands in front of two dark-skinned representatives of peoples dominated by Europeans. At the bottom left is a similar trio in the water, with shells in hand, raising the suggestion that the group above is illustrative of conquests on land, that below at sea. In the center is a dark figure with a shovel, placed to look like a mine worker. In the upper center and right are tropical plants and a palm tree. We are put in mind of horticultural and mining products from land and sea and under the ground. In the lower right are a writer and an artist with images of exotic birds on his panel—the creators of the kind of book we have in hand. Western commentators are infiltrated into the depiction of the objects they are describing. GS

1 Roeper/Wildeman 1996, 48.
2 Cf. Van Nierop 2018.

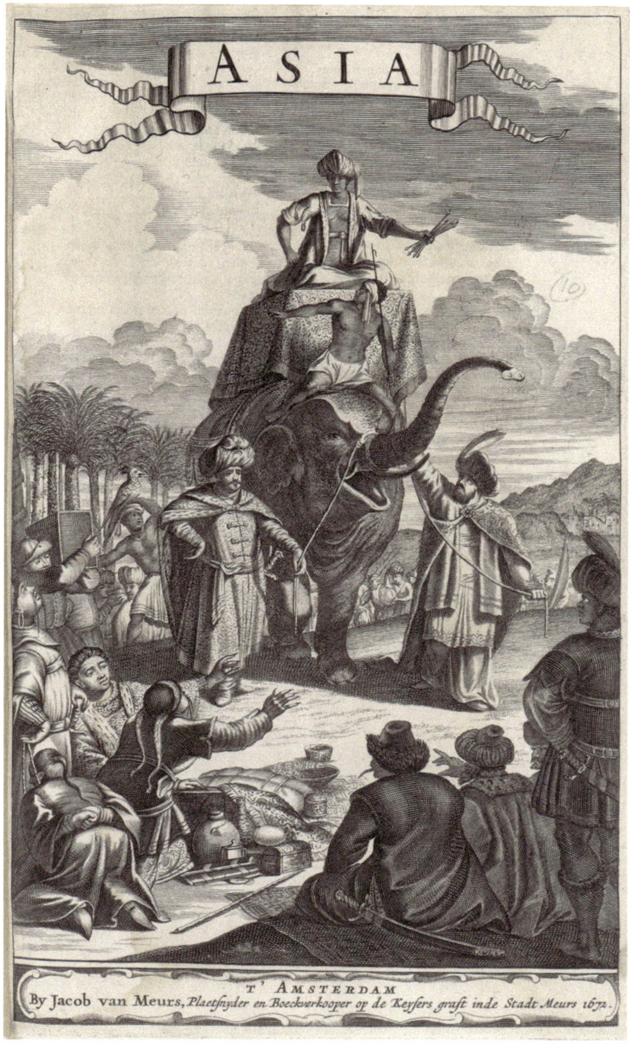
ASIA
T' AMSTERDAM
By Jacob van Meurs, Plaetsnyder en Boeckverkooper op de Keysers graft inde Stadt Meurs 1672.

41

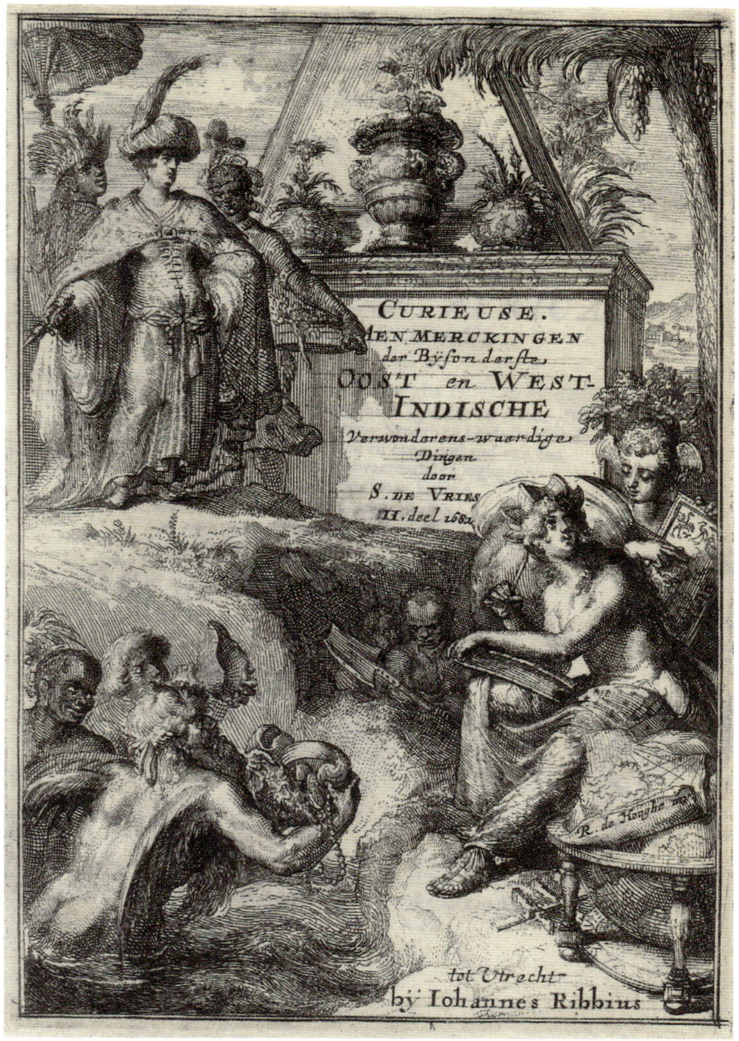
CURIEUSE.
EN MERCKINGEN
der Bÿsonderste
OOST en WEST-
INDISCHE
Verwonderens-waerdige
Dingen
door
S. DE VRIES
II. deel 168
tot Utrecht
by Iohannes Ribbius

42

43.1–2 **Jacob van Meurs** (ca. 1619/20–1679) and workshop
Different Types of Head Coverings, 1670
Mandarin Insignia, 1670

43.1
Engraving
In Olfert Dapper, *Gedenkwaerdig Bedryf Der Nederlandsche Oost-Indische Maetschappye, op de kuste en in het Keizerrijk van Taising of Sina . . .* (Memorable Activities of the Dutch East-India Company at the Shores of and within the Empire of Taising or China), 2 vols., Amsterdam: Jacob van Meurs, 1670, vol. 1, after p. 460
OTM: KF 61-3979
Allard Pierson, University of Amsterdam (Potsdam)
Inv. 1926/0312
Rijksmuseum, Amsterdam, Rijksprentenkabinet
(Basel)

43.2
Engraving
In Olfert Dapper, *Gedenkwaerdig Bedryf Der Nederlandsche Oost-Indische Maetschappye, op de kuste en in het Keizerrijk van Taising of Sina . . .* (Memorable Activities of the Dutch East-India Company at the Shores of and within the Empire of Taising or China), 2 vols., Amsterdam: Jacob van Meurs, 1670, vol. 1, p. 459
OTM: OM 63-124
Allard Pierson, University of Amsterdam (Potsdam)
368 A 3

Lit.
Schmidt 2015, 94–98; plate 3 (*Verschiedene Arten von Kopfbedeckungen*)

[1] Illustrated in Schmidt 2015, 98.

Artists found ideas and models for their exotic motifs not just in the imported objects that they themselves possessed or were able to study in the cabinets of curiosities amassed by the wealthy, but also in the illustrations of travelers' accounts of their journeys to distant lands, large numbers of which were published in the seventeenth-century Netherlands. One of the most productive authors was Olfert Dapper (1636–1689) of Amsterdam, who studied medicine in Utrecht, but probably never practiced as a physician. Having in 1663 published a detailed account of his native city (fig. p. 26) and having in 1665 translated the *Histories* of Herodotus, he threw himself into the work of describing faraway places. He started with Africa and continued with China, India, Syria and Palestine, Asia Minor, and finally the Mediterranean lands. Dapper's books were soon translated into French, English, and German and hence widely circulated.

Like Rembrandt and most of those artists who made use of exotic motifs in their works, Dapper never actually left the Netherlands. Yet he was still able to fill hundreds of pages with descriptions of the remotest corners of the world. His sources included published books, like those of the Jesuit missionary to China, Nicolas Trigault, as well as information gleaned from manuscripts and from traveling merchants and members of the Dutch East India Company with whom he had contact.

Dapper's report on China begins with a very detailed and long-winded account of Dutch trading activities in the year 1665, followed by an encyclopedic exposition of Chinese geography. The second volume even has an alphabetical index that starts with *Ananas* (pineapple) and ends with *Zee-paert* (seahorse). The text is illustrated with thirty-nine fold-out, double-page engravings along with fifty-six additional illustrations. There are no names on these, although they are known to have been produced in the workshop of the Amsterdam publisher, Jacob van Meurs. Most of the engravings show views of cities and of the coast, or are anecdotal scenes presented in a contemporary style.

Among them, however, are also four whole pages presenting systematic compilations of the garments and accessories worn by the Mandarins, the caste of Chinese public servants and scholars. Two of these show *Verscheiden slagen van Bonetten* (Different Types of Head Coverings), and two more the *Mercken der Mandaryns* (Mandarin Insignia). The images probably derive from drawings done in the 1620s by the Jesuit Adriano de las Cortes.[1]

The objects are lined up as if in a catalog and thus divorced from their original context, although the letters alongside them refer to the explanations of them in the text. Readers interested in the head coverings, for example, learn that models F, G, and H were worn by the most venerable Mandarins only after setting aside their insignia, and hence mostly at home. As for the insignia themselves, the object identified with an H is apparently a branching bamboo tube onto the end of which an iron tip was mounted. These exotic items must have fascinated contemporary readers, irrespective of the author's ethnological approach, while artists might well have used these pages as a pattern book for all sorts of motifs. MPH

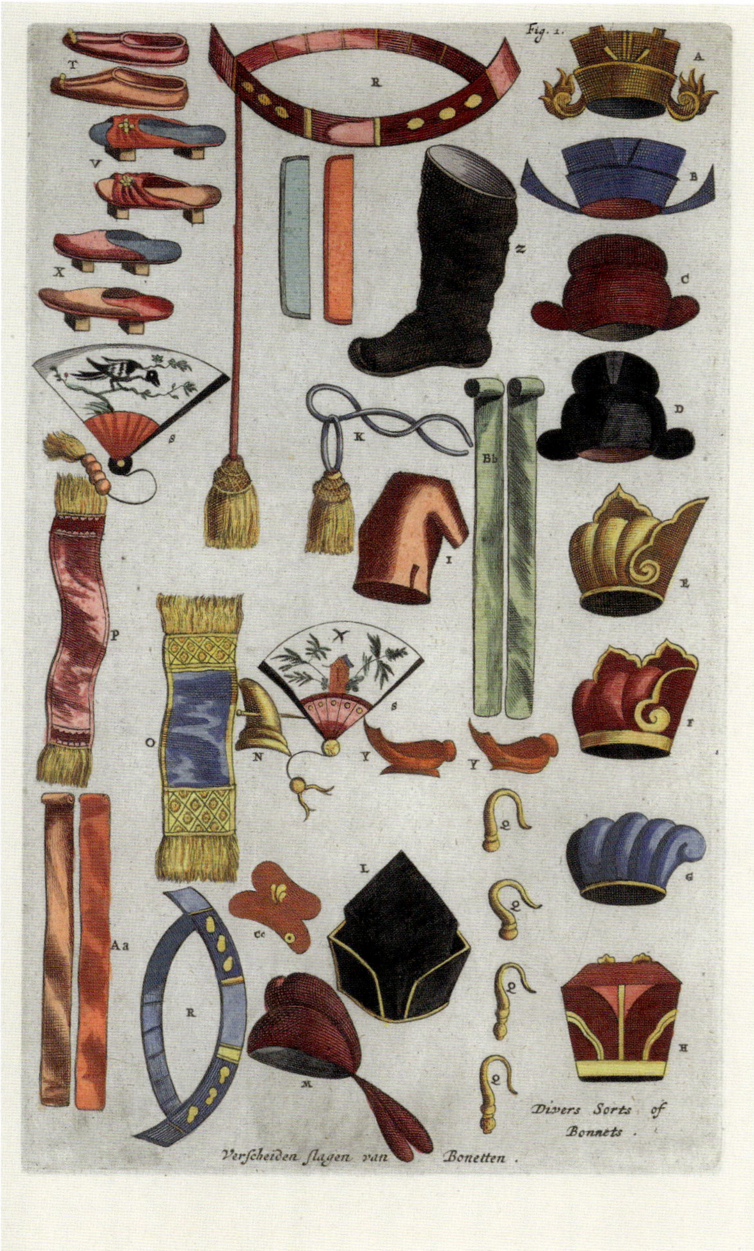
Fig. 1.
Divers Sorts of Bonnets.
Verscheiden slagen van Bonetten.

43.1

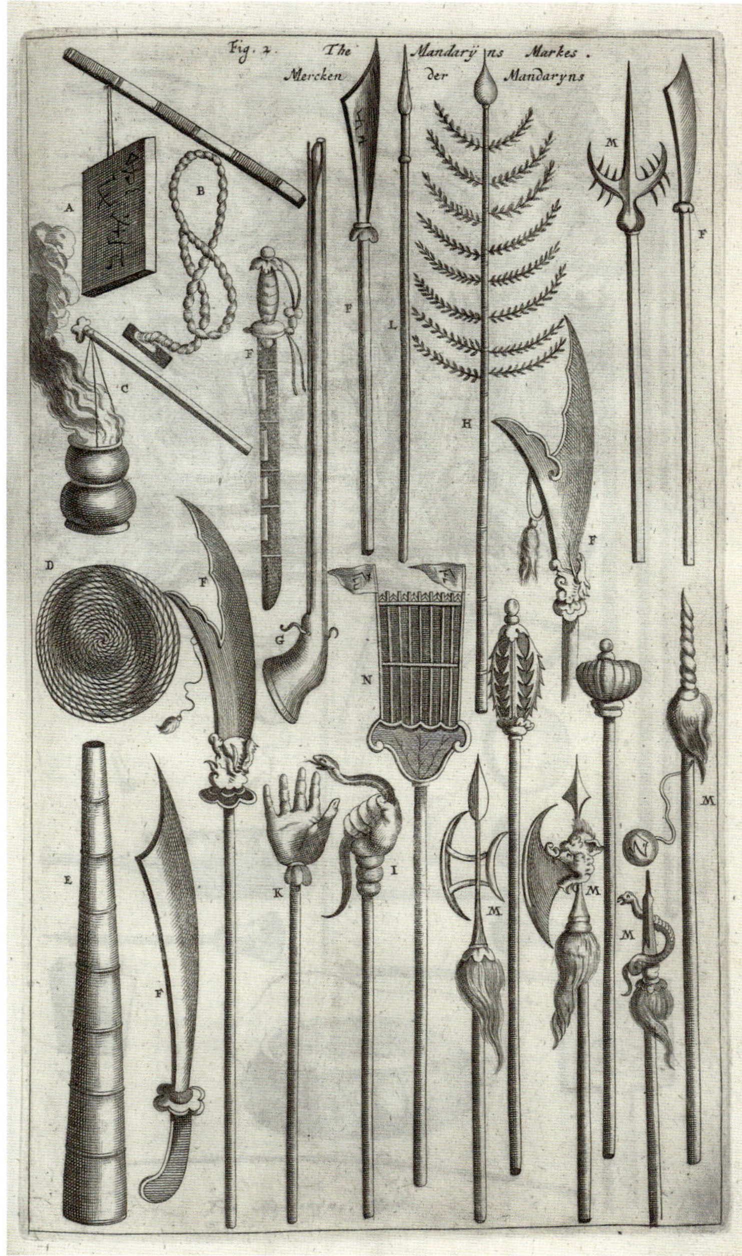
Fig. 2.
The Mandarÿns Markes.
Mercken der Mandaryns

43.2

44 **Philips Angel** (ca. 1618–after 1664)
Lof der schilder-konst (Praise of the Art of Painting), Leiden: W. Christiaens, 1642

45 **Philips Angel** (ca. 1618–after 1664) after **Jan Lievens** (1607–1674) or **Rembrandt** (1606–1669)
Bust of an Old Man with a Beard, 1637

44
21220 F 38
Leiden University Libraries,
Special Collections

45
Etching, 5.5 x 5.3 cm
Inscribed on plate at top left: P. Angel 1637
Inv. RP-P-BI-84
Rijksmuseum, Amsterdam, Rijksprentenkabinet

Lit.
Schwartz 2013, 160–62

1 Philips Angel: *Lof der schilder-konst,* Leiden 1642, 47; translated by Gary Schwartz.
2 Speelman 1908 gives an account of this journey.
3 Cf. Aqajani Isfahani/Javani 2007, 5, 86.

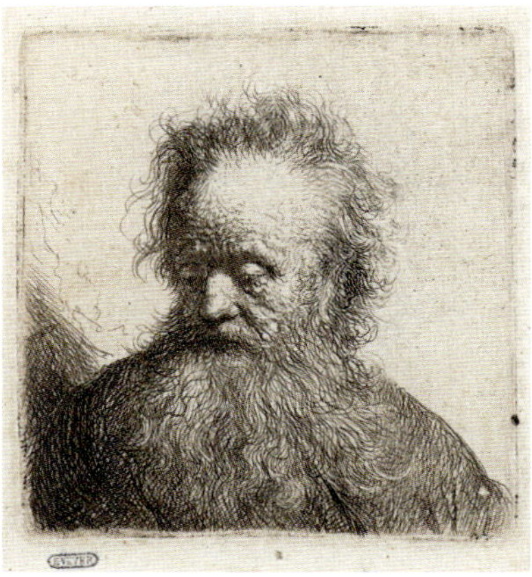

Rembrandt,
Old Man with Flowing Beard, 1631

The one essential text linking Rembrandt to the Oriental motifs that are the subject of this exhibition is contained in this rare volume. On the day of Saint Luke in 1642, when the painters of Leiden gathered to honor their patron saint, Philips Angel delivered an oration in praise of the art of painting. In it, he encouraged painters to take seriously their responsibility for correctness as well as decorum. His main example for historical accuracy was Rembrandt's painting *Samson Proposing the Riddle at the Wedding Feast* (cat. 73), painted just four years earlier: "I once saw a depiction by Rembrandt of the Wedding of Samson, of which we read in Judges, chapter 14, verse 10. You can see in it how that keen intelligence, by thinking hard about the actual way the guests sit (or in this this case recline) at table—since the ancients used small beds on which to lie, not sitting at table the way we do today, but lying on their elbows the way the Turks still do in that part of the world—showed it very nicely." Angel specified that a thorough study and contemplation of literature were the prerequisites for this precision: "These fruits of natural representation, true to the subject, come into being by reading the story well and analyzing it in lofty and wide reflections."[1]

Philips Angel, having praised Rembrandt's knowledge of the Orient in the quotation above, went on to become dean of the Leiden Guild of Saint Luke, to work as an art dealer, and then, in 1645, to take ship to the Indies with the Dutch East India Company, the Vereenigde Oostindische Compagnie (VOC). In 1646 he served as a merchant and member of the justice council in Batavia (now Jakarta), the headquarters of the VOC on the island of Java (see cat. 86). In 1651–52 he took part in the mission of the Dutch emissary Joan Cunaeus to the court of Shah Abbas II in Isfahan (see cat. 26). En route, he made drawings of the ruins of Persepolis (cat. 84).[2]

Angel experienced difficulties with the East India Company when he was accused of ignoring the regulations against engaging in private business in Persia. He was saved from being sent back to Batavia for trial by Shah Abbas II, who took him on as court painter. In that capacity, he is thought to have designed and perhaps even painted a number of wall paintings in the Chehel Soutun pavilion in Isfahan.[3] As the traveler and art dealer Jean-Baptiste Tavernier noted in a diary entry in 1657, Angel was said to have given drawing lessons to Shah Abbas II in his youth. While the Persian ruler paid considerable honor to Angel, the East India Company continued to cast aspersions on him.

In 1655 Angel returned to Batavia and was again active in local government. However, the old accusations were revived in 1661; he was arrested, and his property was sold at auction. He is mentioned for the last time in a document of July 1664. Of his work in Batavia the only surviving remnant is a remarkable illustrated manuscript on the avatars of the Hindu god Vishnu (fig. p. 260). The only surviving work of his made in the Netherlands is a single impression of the etching of an old man, a feeble adaptation of a motif popularized by Rembrandt and Jan Lievens (fig. on left). GS

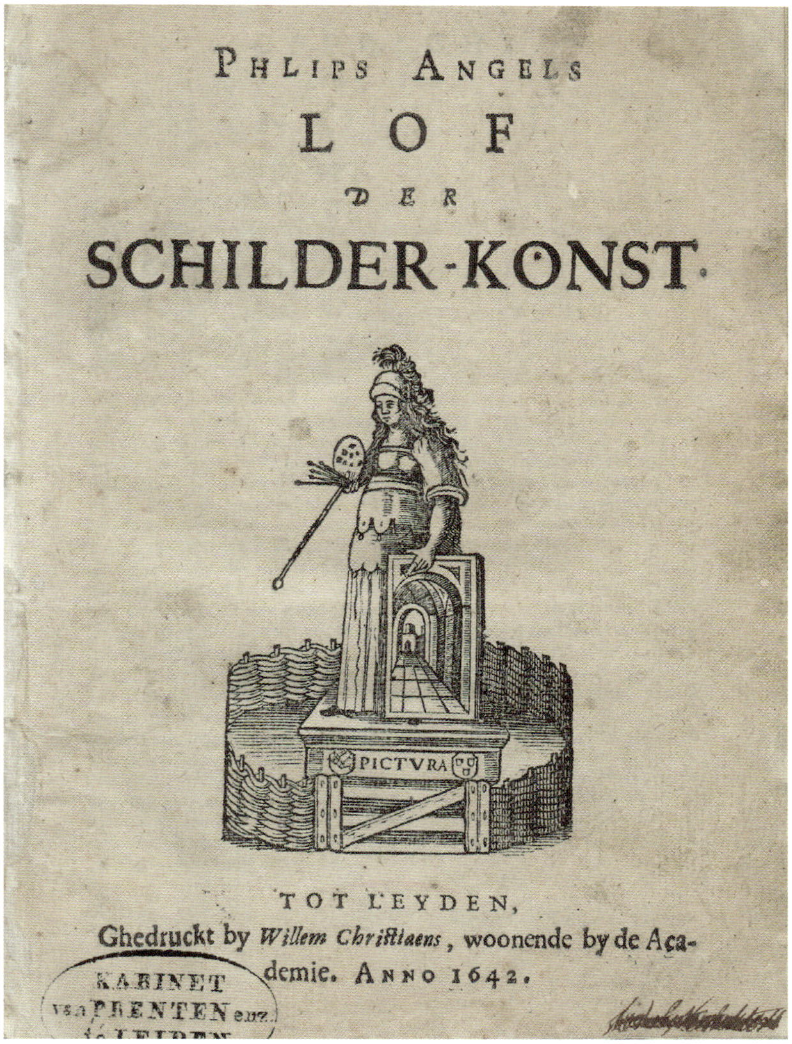
PHLIPS ANGELS

LOF

DER

SCHILDER-KONST.

PICTVRA

TOT LEYDEN,

Ghedruckt by *Willem Christiaens*, woonende by de Aca-
demie. ANNO 1642.

44

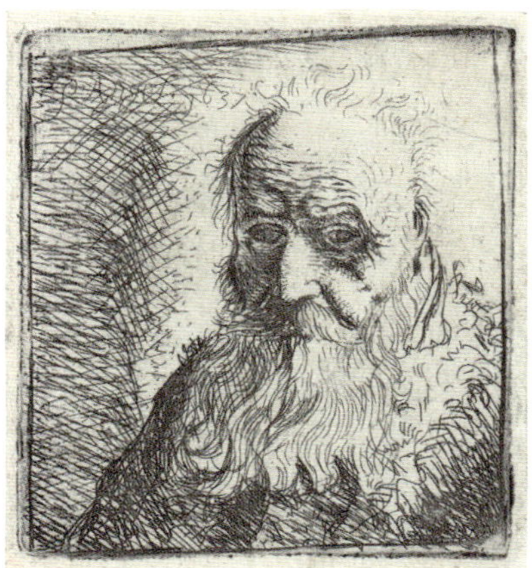

45

46 Anonymous

Parody of Religious Tolerance, 1659

Oil on panel, 46 x 43.5 cm
Inv. os 1-552
Frans Hals Museum, Haarlem

Lit.
Haarlem 1969, 40, no. 500
Münster/Osnabrück 1998, no. 901
Haarlem 2006, 674–77, no. 607
Nieuwenhuizen 2006

The Chamber of Rhetoric "Trou moet Blycken" is the title by which this painting is most commonly known. The scene is a large hall with twelve men either seated at a table or standing elsewhere in the room, as well as a servant. *Rederijkerskamers,* or chambers of rhetoric, which in the Netherlands can be traced back to the fifteenth century, were middle-class confraternities that composed poems and plays for religious or civic festivities as well as staging poetry contests both among their own members and in competition with rival chambers. The location evoked in this painting, dated 1659, has been identified as Haarlem. The little coat of arms on the right wall supports this, as are the large escutcheons belonging to the city's three known chambers of rhetoric: from left to right the *Pelicanisten* (Pelicanists), whose motto was "Trou moet blycken" (Loyalty must prove itself), the *Wijngaertrancken* (Vineyard Vines) with their motto "Liefd boven al" (Love conquers all), and the *Witte Angieren* (White Carnations) with their "In Lief'd getrauw" (True in love).

The figures, however, are certainly not ordinary burghers of Haarlem, but are rather the famous founders of the main Protestant confessions of the sixteenth century along with representatives of other religions. Seated at the table, therefore, are (from right) John Calvin, Jacobus Arminius as the man behind the Remonstrant movement, Martin Luther, and Menno Simonsz., who gave his name to the Mennonites. Standing in front of the fireplace is a Jew on the right and a Muslim on the left. Also present are representatives of Socianism, Libertinism, and the Collegiants as well as a Sophist and a Catholic, each of whom has a book title or written tablet to indicate his confessional identity. The man whose turban marks him out as a Moslem is holding a tablet blazoned with the words: "The Quran, left to us by Mohammed, disputes Christian law; it dulls and destroys it to the detriment of those who hate it."

Sentences like that are not exactly proof of a liberal mindset in matters of faith. Yet the seventeenth-century Netherlands did in fact allow religions of all kinds, even if its tolerance was closer to sufferance than acceptance. Overt hostility to those of a different faith would also have been bad for business. That this parody of religious concord includes a Muslim at all is noteworthy, even if it is unlikely that he actually lived in the Netherlands—unlike the representatives of the other denominations shown here. The inclusion of a Muslim even in stylized works such as this was anything but common; Gerrit Adriaensz. Berckheyde's work, *The Town Hall on Dam Square in Amsterdam* (cat. 21), painted not long after this work, is a notable exception in this respect.

That the never-ending doctrinal disputes—which in the previous century had occasioned numerous executions and atrocities—had lost much of their erstwhile importance is evident from the inscriptions on the wall, which besides telling of the chambers' boozy social events can also be read as an ironic commentary on religious debates generally. They are headed with the motto "Door der druiven soetheijt Rapen wij solaes" (From the sweetness of grapes we derive solace) and under it "Retorica seer aerdich, wort door Bacchus weer onwaerdich" (Rhetoric is very nice, but Bacchus turns it into a vice). MPH

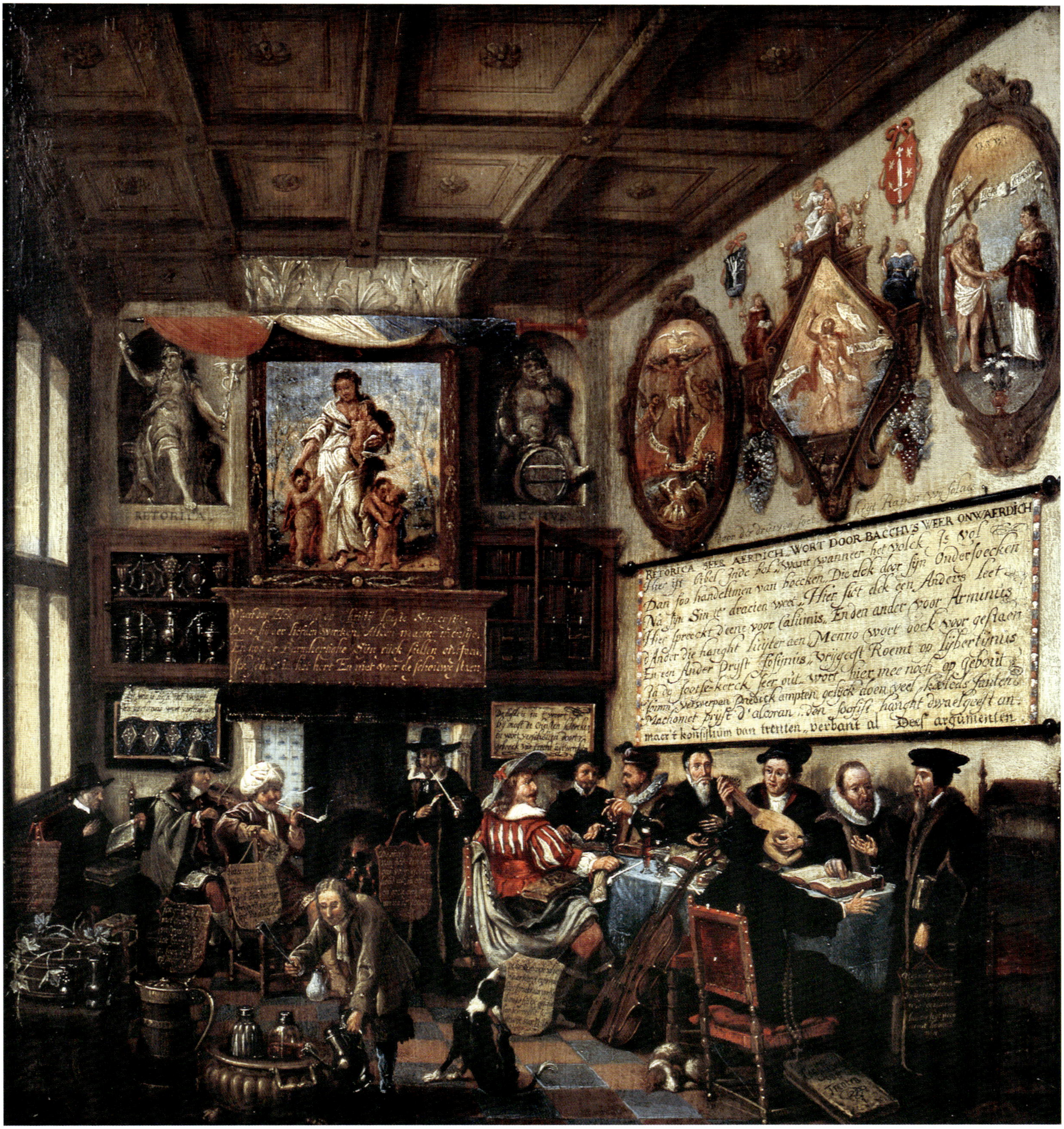
RETORICA SEER AERDICH WORT DOOR BACCHVS WEER ONWAERDICH

47 Anonymous
Historie, Van den Oorsprongh, Geslacht, Geboorte, Opvoedinge, en Leere des grooten valschen Propheets Mahomets . . . (History of the Origins, Family, Birth, Education, and Teaching of the Great False Prophet Muhammad . . .),
Amsterdam: Broer Jansz., 1640

48 Anonymous
De Arabische Alkoran, door de Zarazijnsche en de Turcksche Prophete Mahometh, In drie onderscheyden deelen begrepen . . . (The Arabic Quran, by the Saracen and Turkish Prophet Muhammad, Divided into Three Discrete Sections . . .),
Hamburg: Barent Adriaensz. Berentsma, 1641

49 Jan Hendrik Glazemaker (ca. 1619–1682)
Mahomets Alkoran, door de hr. Du Ryer uit d'Arabische in de Fransche taal gestelt . . . , Alles van nieuws door J. H. Glasemaker vertaalt, en te zamen gebracht (Muhammad's Quran, Translated by Mr. Du Ryer from Arabic into French . . . , Newly Translated and Edited by J. H. Glasemaker), 2nd ed.,
Amsterdam: Timotheus ten Hoorn, 1696

47
OTM: O61-1420 (1)
Allard Pierson, University of Amsterdam
(Potsdam)
1144 A 46
Leiden University Libraries
(Basel)

48
OTM: O 63-894
Allard Pierson, University of Amsterdam
(Potsdam)
877 D 16
Leiden University Libraries
(Basel)

49
Six etched illustrations by Caspar Luyken
Private collection

Lit.
Van Gent 2013

Christian antagonism against Islam dates from the very start.[1] Muhammad was regarded by Christians as a false prophet, and the Quran, which to Muslims is the word of God himself, as a literary concoction written by Muhammad (ca. 570–632). The life of Muhammad, which formed part of Muslim tradition from the start, was seen by Christians as a disqualification for his prophecy. In 1618–19 the Calvinist Council of Dordt resolved not only to impede the dissemination in the Republic of heretical books, of which the Quran was the first example on the listing, but also to destroy existing copies.

That medieval prejudices and reservations persisted into the seventeenth century is shown by the very titles of two of the books in this entry. The book of 1640 on Muhammad calls him a false prophet (cat. 47), and the translation of 1641 calls the Quran a writing by Muhammad, which no Muslim can accept. This first Dutch Quran was translated not from Arabic, but from a German edition of 1616, translated by Salomon Schweigger. The Dutch publisher took various measures to protect himself against prosecution for furthering heresy. In the first place he falsified the city of publication as Hamburg, whereas the book was printed in Amsterdam. He also covered himself by taking over from the German edition heavy-going disclaimers, full of insults to Muhammad, the Quran, and Islam, by which he distanced himself from the contents of the book. Nonetheless, the appearance of this edition attests to interest in Islam.

In 1657 the more authoritative Dutch Quran by Jan Hendrik Glazemaker saw the light, based on a 1647 French translation. The 1696 edition of Glazemaker's translation with etchings by Caspar Luyken is the first Quran—perhaps the first in any language—to be illustrated (cat. 49).

The first four illustrations are an impression of how Muslims pray. None of these images is based on firsthand observation of Muslim practices. The pose of prostration by which Muslims touch their foreheads to the ground, for example, is not rendered accurately. Yet these images attest to a certain respect. The fifth and sixth etchings however depict anti-Muslim stories that had been in circulation since the Middle Ages. One shows Muhammad flat on the ground on his back, in an epileptic fit. The other exposes Muhammad as an impostor, who declared the Quran a gift from heaven that had been brought by a wild bull, although he had actually trained the bull beforehand. In this unfortunate way the advancement of knowledge concerning Islam was contaminated by old calumnies. GS

[1] Cf. Daniel 2000.

47

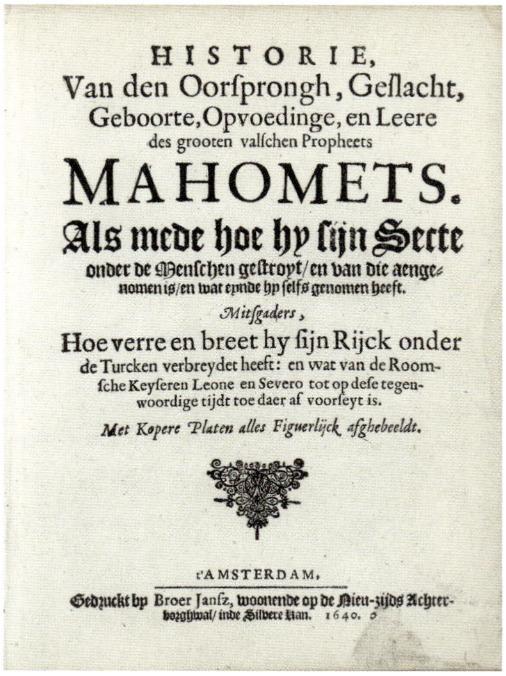

HISTORIE,
Van den Oorsprongh, Geslacht,
Geboorte, Opvoedinge, en Leere
des grooten valschen Propheets
MAHOMETS.
Als mede hoe hy sijn Secte
onder de Menschen gestroyt/ en van die aenge-
nomen is/ en wat eynde hy selfs genomen heeft.
Mitsgaders,
Hoe verre en breet hy sijn Rijck onder
de Turcken verbreydet heeft: en wat van de Room-
sche Keyseren Leone en Severo tot op dese tegen-
woordige tijdt toe daer af voorseyt is.
Met Kopere Platen alles Figuerlijck afghebeeldt.

t'AMSTERDAM,
Gedruckt by Broer Jansz, woonende op de Nieu-zijds Achter-
borghwal/ inde Silvere Kan. 1640.

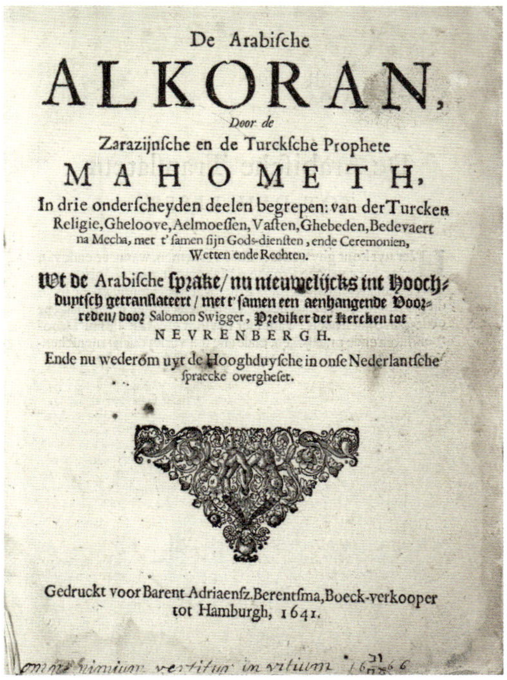

De Arabische
ALKORAN,
Door de
Zarazijnsche en de Turcksche Prophete
MAHOMETH,
In drie onderscheyden deelen begrepen: van der Turcken
Religie, Gheloove, Aelmoessen, Vasten, Ghebeden, Bedevaert
na Mecha, met t'samen sijn Gods-diensten, ende Ceremonien,
Wetten ende Rechten.
Wt de Arabische sprake/ nu nieuwelijcks int Hooch-
duytsch getranslateert/ met t'samen een aenhangende Voor-
reden/ door Salomon Swigger, Prediker der Kercken tot
NEVRENBERGH.
Ende nu wederom uyt de Hooghduysche in onse Nederlantsche
spraecke overgheset.

Gedruckt voor Barent Adriaensz. Berentsma, Boeck-verkooper
tot Hamburgh, 1641.

48

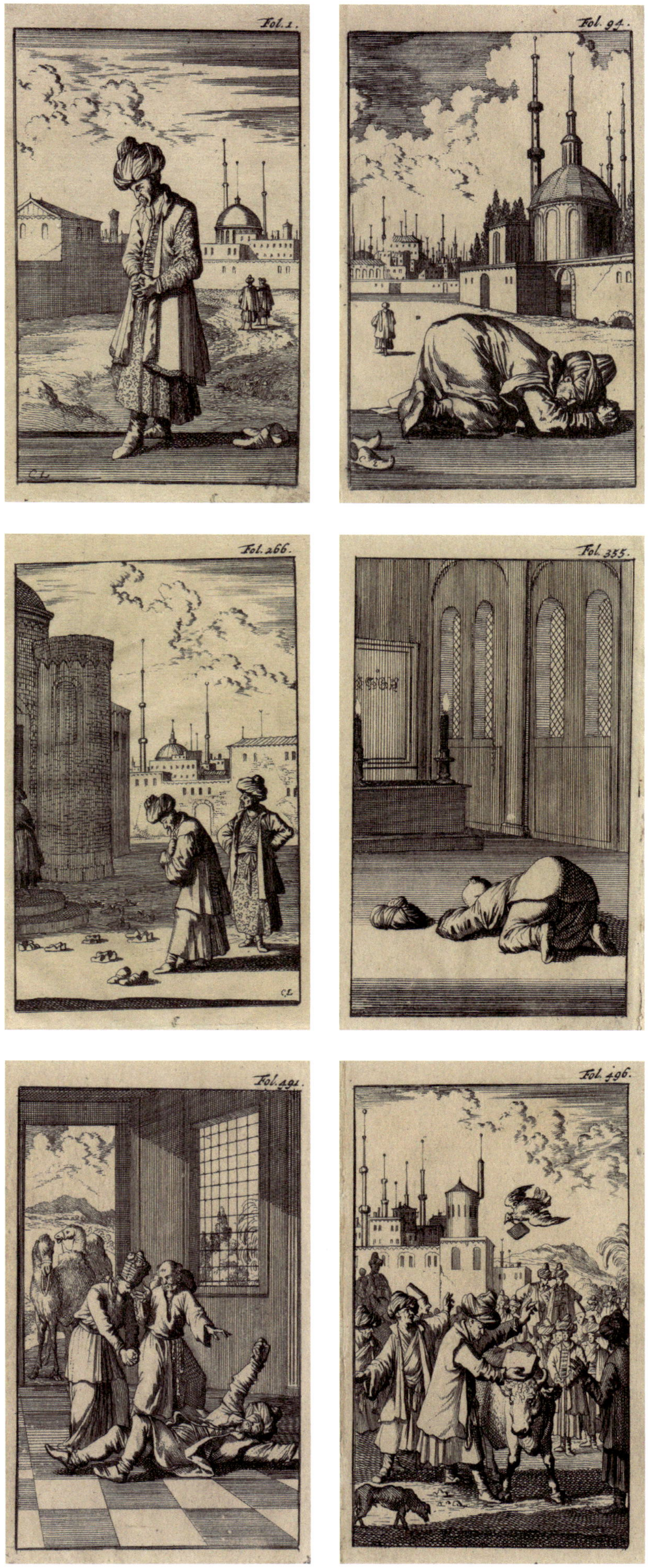

49

50 **Willem Kalf** (1619–1693)
Still Life with Nautilus Cup, ca. 1660 (?)

51 **Willem Kalf** (1619–1693)
Pronkstilleven, 1678

50
Oil on canvas, 66.5 x 56 cm
Inv. 153
Emil Bührle Collection, Zurich
(Basel only)

Lit.
Grisebach 1974, no. 118
Ydema 1991, no. 471
Amsterdam 1999b, 218, note 1
Zurich 2005, 122–24; no. 14

51
Oil on canvas, 68 x 56 cm
Inscribed left under the tablecloth:
W.KALF 167.
Inv. KMS1531
Statens Museum for Kunst—National
Gallery of Denmark, Copenhagen

Lit.
Grisebach 1974, no. 138, figs. 146–48;
126–27, 160–62
Ydema 1991, no. 469
Rotterdam 2006, no. 36

Willem Kalf visualized the wealth being amassed by Dutch merchants of the seventeenth century as did no other painter. The *pronkstilleven* presenting artful arrangements of luxury objects was a type of still life of his own invention. Alongside Venetian glassware, crystal bowls, and silver ewers, exotic objects such as Oriental rugs, Chinese porcelain, and exquisite nautilus cups played a crucial role in these works. Far more than just merchandise from the Far East, they delivered tangible proof of commercial success. That they were quite naturally combined with European arts and crafts shows how readily such foreign objects were appropriated and underscores their role as status symbols. The exotic curiosities themselves, and Kalf's still lifes too, reflect the proprietary pride and desire for prestige felt by their owners as the successful protagonists of world trade.

Kalf himself was the scion of a wealthy family of merchants from Rotterdam. He began his oeuvre with rustic interiors in the manner of David Teniers the Younger and Adriaen van Ostade in which vegetables and everyday objects such as pots, pitchers, and brooms were grouped together like a still life in the foreground. He began painting still lifes proper even before he left for Paris for several years in 1642. While these belonged to the Dutch tradition of monochrome breakfast scenes known as *banketjes,* he included exquisite silver ewers and Chinese porcelain bowls even then. This love of luxury became all the more pronounced after 1653, when Kalf left the West Frisian port of Hoorn and settled permanently in Amsterdam. The city was then at the height of its powers as a flourishing center of world trade, and Kalf witnessed with his own eyes both the unstoppable influx of goods from faraway places and the amassing of vast fortunes and luxury possessions by Amsterdam's bourgeoisie. The painter first took lodgings with Johan le Thor, a wealthy merchant and one of the directors of the Dutch West India Company, who already possessed a major collection of paintings, silverware, porcelain, Turkish carpets, and assorted rarities. Some of the valuable objects that Kalf painted might therefore have belonged to him.

There were innumerable still-life painters in seventeenth-century Amsterdam. Thus Kalf was able to build on the works of Jan Jansz. den Uyl, Jan Jansz. Treck, and Simon Luttichuys, who had already shown an interest in light reflecting off metal or glass against a dark background, though he enriched their repertoire by adding still more exquisite collectibles. Many of the still lifes from his Amsterdam period are organized along similar lines. Heaped on a marble table, of which often no more than a corner is visible, is an arrangement of objects bathed in light against what is always a dark background. Kalf used the same motifs over and over again: an Oriental carpet patterned with flowers, "casually" rumpled often with its fringes clearly visible, a large silver charger with an ornate floral rim, a knife whose agate haft points beyond the table top, and Mediterranean fruits such as peaches and boldly colored oranges. Unusually, Kalf painted the latter complete with leaves on the stalks, which has the effect of lending his paintings freshness and immediacy. The fruits are frequently piled up in a bowl made of Chinese porcelain, whose inside surface is often a pool of light. While such bowls were widespread in bourgeois households and hence a common feature of the still lifes of the age, Kalf also painted an exquisite lidded bowl made of Chinese porcelain of the 1620s, which was exceptionally decorated with sculptural figures (Gemäldegalerie, Staatliche Museen zu Berlin; Museo Nacional Thyssen-Bornemisza, Madrid).

Most striking of all, however, are the nautilus cups. As luxurious as they were exotic, the sole purpose of these decorative cups made out of the shell of a nautilus set in an artfully worked silver-gilt mount was to betoken the prestige of their owner. Rembrandt included one in his 1634 painting *Judith at the Banquet of Holofernes* (formerly called *Artemisia*; Museo Nacional del Prado, Madrid). The cup in the Zurich painting features a Triton shouldering the nautilus shell that in its turn is crowned with the head of a sea monster, on top of which stands a figure of Neptune. The gaping maw and razor-sharp teeth inject an element of alarm into the work. While there is a known nautilus cup that might have served as the model here—made in 1596 by the silversmith Jan Jacobsz. van Royesteyn of Utrecht (Toledo Museum of Art)—the cup with a figure of Neptune riding a mythical seahorse in the Copenhagen painting cannot be linked to any specific object. This cannot be said of the cup made of rock crystal, the "Holbein Cup" (Schatzkammer der Residenz, Munich), which until 1649 belonged to the English Royal Collection and in Kalf's day was probably in Amsterdam, although by 1711 it had passed into the hands of the Counts Palatine in Düsseldorf. This choice collector's item, which was made in Venice in the fourteenth century, derives its name from the silver mount designed for it by Hans Holbein the Younger in ca. 1540. In his painting of it, Kalf emphasizes its uniqueness by applying the inscription "HoLBeen Fe" (Holbein fecit) to the stem, even though there is no such inscription on the original.

For all their splendor and superfluity, Kalf's still lifes, like the works of Jan van der Heyden (cat. 52–53), also include elements that recall another important seventeenth-century theme: *vanitas*. The precarious angle of the delicate porcelain bowls, for example, perhaps underscores the fragility of their momentary state, while the little pocket watch, whose gold-rimmed glass case has been left open, serves as a subtle way of alerting us to the clock key dangling off the table on the end of a ribbon. The message is clear: its dial is not legible, since no one can know his appointed hour. And time is the one commodity that is limited for everyone—as should never be forgotten, even when celebrating material wealth. MPH

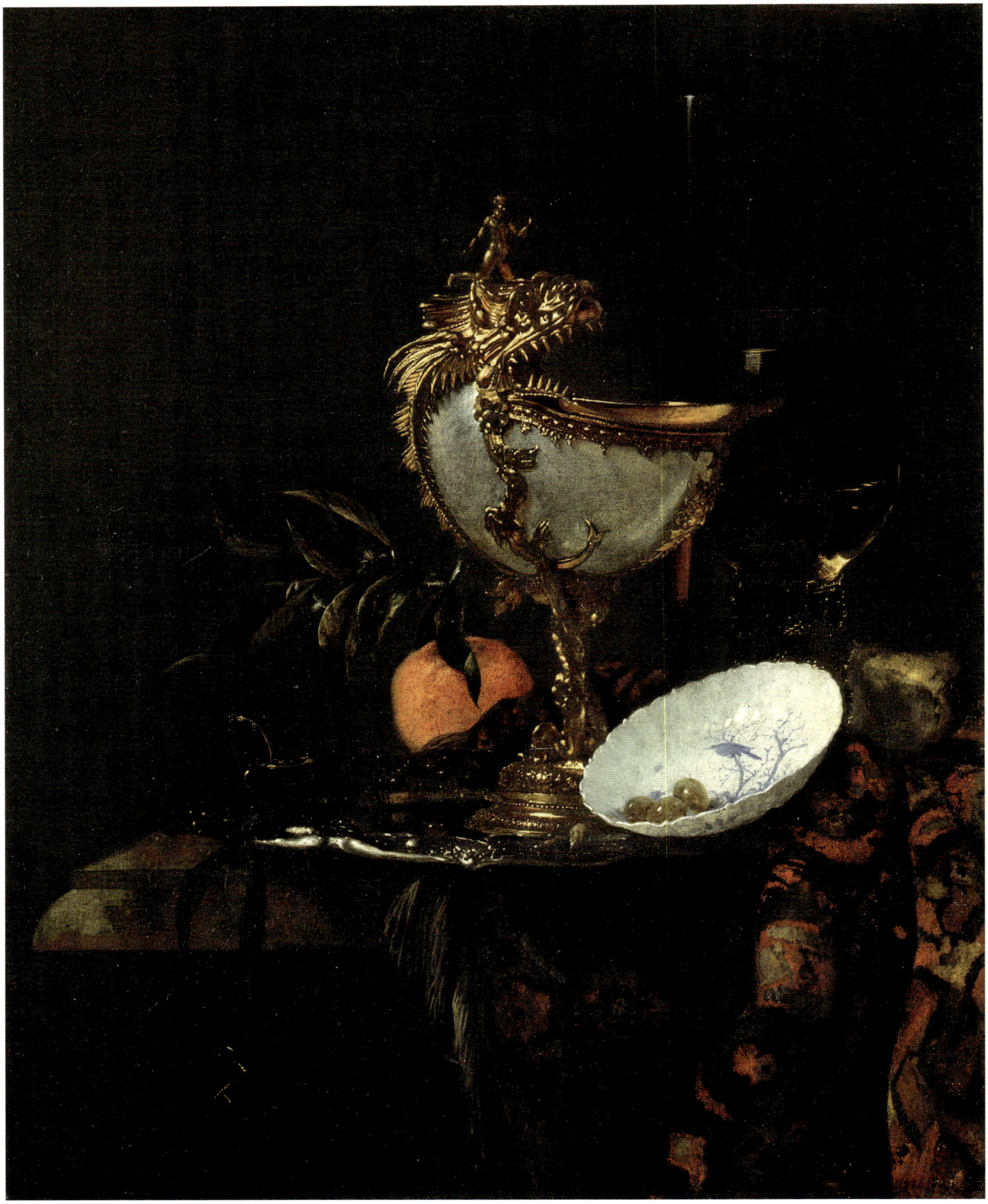

50

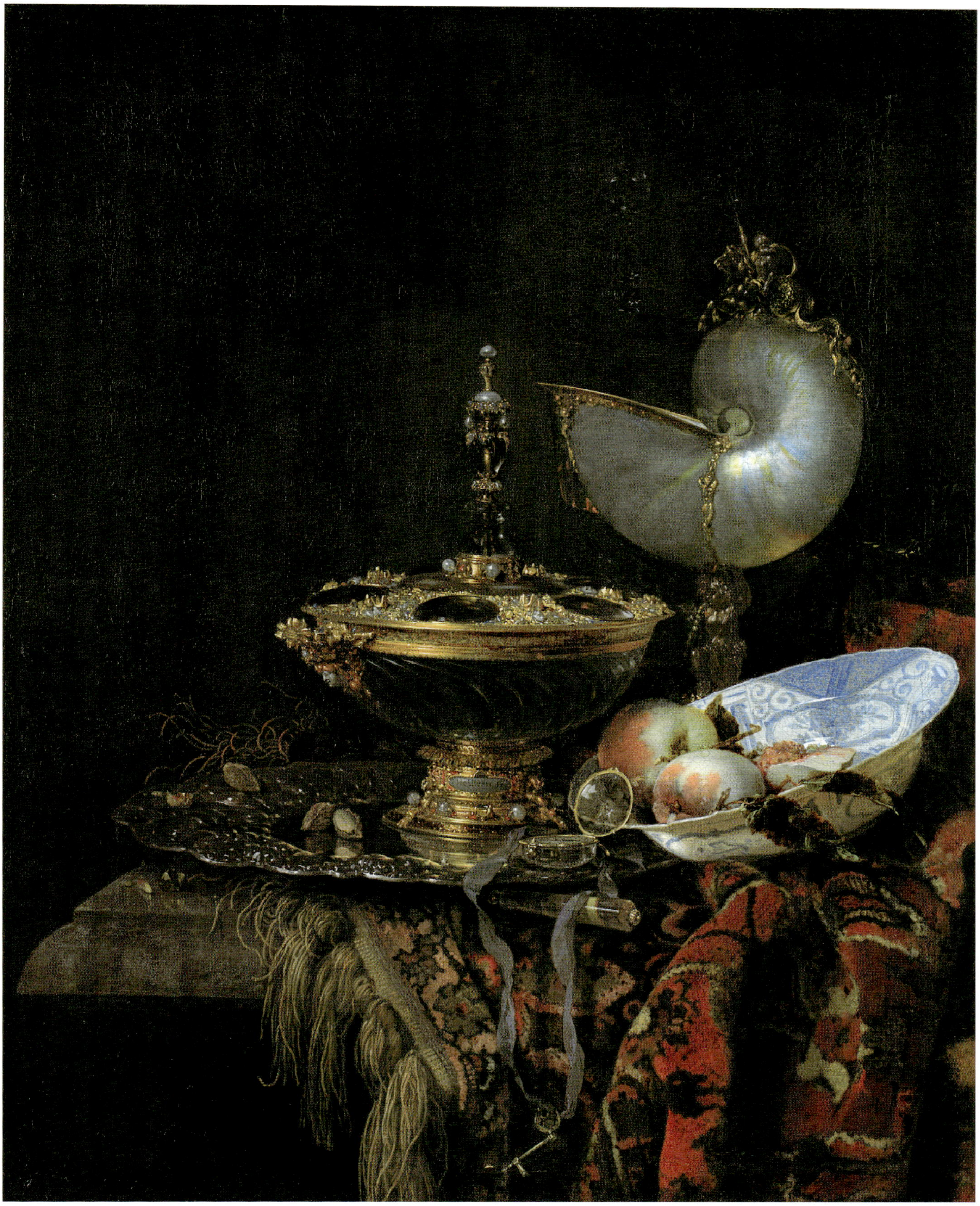

52 Jan van der Heyden (1637–1712)
Corner of a Library, 1711
53 Jan van der Heyden (1637–1712)
Room Corner with Curiosities, 1712

52
Oil on canvas, 77 x 63.5 cm
Inscribed top on pedestal capital:
JvdHeyden oud 74 ja
Inv. 186 (1981.40)
Museo Nacional Thyssen-Bornemisza, Madrid
(Potsdam only)

Lit.
Wagner 1971, no. 219
Greenwich 2006, no. 38

53
Oil on canvas, 75 x 63.5 cm
Inscribed bottom right on chair upholstery:
oud J.v.d.H. 75 jar
Inv. 201
Szépművészeti Múzeum, Budapest

Lit.
Wagner 1971, no. 217
Wasau 1989, no. 21
Amsterdam 1992, text volume, 78, fig. p. 204; catalog volume, no. 2
Greenwich 2006, under no. 38
Cologne 2006, no. 21
Budapest 2011
Amsterdam 2015, no. 4a

Jan van der Heyden's still lifes enlarged to an interior stage the theme of mortality as a view of a scholar's study full of books, globes, and exotic objects. Unlike Willem Kalf, whose depictions of Chinese porcelain and exotic rarities such as nautilus cups generate an atmosphere of affluence and splendor (cat. 50–51), Van der Heyden's still lifes emanate serene restraint. This also sets them apart from the paintings of galleries and cabinets of curiosity that were popular in Flanders (fig. p. 31), many of which turn on the presentation of rare and exquisite objects in abundance. The measured, yet emphatic, demonstration of wealth, knowledge, and cosmopolitanism of Van der Heyden's still lifes, by contrast, epitomizes how the bourgeois elite of the Dutch Republic perceived itself in the late seventeenth and early eighteenth century.

Jan van der Heyden painted mainly atmospheric cityscapes, in which he reproduced the architecture with painstaking attention to detail. Only nine still lifes by him have survived. They each show a stylized study or cabinet of curiosities—a theme that had not yet been introduced in the northern provinces and was no more than touched on in sixteenth-century paintings such as Marinus van Reymerswaele's *Saint Jerome* (Museo Nacional del Prado, Madrid) and the works of Joos van Cleve (Kunstpalast, Düsseldorf). While cabinets of curiosities and the collecting of exotic objects were widespread in the Dutch Republic, no matching subgenre of painting evolved.

Unlike Van der Heyden's views of Amsterdam and other Dutch cities, in which the soft contours of the clouds, trees, and reflections in the *grachten* make for a bright and cheerful overall impression, his still lifes are painted with the utmost technical precision. The meticulousness recalls the finely done works of the painter Gerrit Dou of Leiden. The accuracy Van der Heyden brought to bear on his reproduction of objects is also apparent in a book about firefighting, published in 1690, which he illustrated with engravings of water hoses and nozzles of his own invention in use.

Van der Heyden died in Amsterdam, aged seventy-five, and the still lifes *Corner of a Library* and *Room Corner with Curiosities* date from the last two years of his life. They were painted over a hundred years after the founding of the Dutch East India Company and hence at a time when natural wonders and finely crafted objects from distant lands had long since become a fixture in the reception rooms and cabinets of curiosities of bourgeois households. As widespread as they may have been, exotic objects like those painted by Van der Heyden were much admired and coveted. He stages them so as to generate an atmosphere of the exceptional, which is further enhanced by bright, overhead light, which is unusual for still lifes. Also atypical is the absence of people in such an interior. Collectors or scholars sitting for their portraits generally liked to surround themselves with priceless objects signifying both ownership and knowledge, as did Barend van Lin for the likeness of himself painted by Michiel van Musscher (cat. 34). By dispensing with any representation of the possible owner of the rarities here on display, however, Van der Heyden is able to emphasize the objects' symbolic meaning instead.

Both works show a marble tabletop, only a corner of which is visible, draped with a sumptuous bright red tablecloth that is almost certainly made of Chinese silk, lavishly embroidered with flowers. Both also feature a *naginata*, a Japanese pole weapon fitted with a long blade, the tip of which is curved.

The walking cane with ivory pommel features only in *Corner of a Library.* The objects in *Room Corner with Curiosities* are significantly more exotic: there is an Oriental carpet as well as a Japanese bowl made of Kakiemon porcelain displayed on top of an Augsburg collector's cabinet made of ebony inlaid with ivory and tortoiseshell. While these materials were imported from the regions in which the Dutch East India Company operated, the stuffed armadillo that has pride of place in front of the chimneypiece comes from America and hence from the trading zone of the Dutch West India Company. The globes on the table, the rolled-up map leaning against the wall, and the *Atlas Maior* by the cartographer Joan Blaeu (see cat. 40) lying open on the table make the connection between the *Kunstkammer* and the globalization of trade.

The emphasis on possessions, on the thirst for knowledge, and on good taste, however, here come with a reminder of the transience of all things, which was a key theme of Dutch still lifes of the seventeenth century. The two paintings nevertheless manage without the motifs traditionally used for this message—the hourglass, the snuffed candle, the death's head, or wilting flowers. One explicit pointer to the relative unimportance of all earthly goods in *Room Corner with Curiosities* is the Bible in the right foreground. Significantly, it is lying open at the Book of Ecclesiastes, which famously opens with the lamentation that "all is vanity." The globes and books can thus stand for knowledge, the Japanese lance for power, and the luxury collectibles for property—all of which are ephemeral values. As is love, represented here by the painting *The Death of Dido*—a composition modeled on a print after Pietro Testa—hanging above the fireplace. Viewed in this light, the armadillo likewise takes on the character of a memento mori. Yet for all Van der Heyden's efforts to remind his contemporaries of the transience of all things, nothing could deter them from amassing riches in abundance and displaying them for all to see. MPH

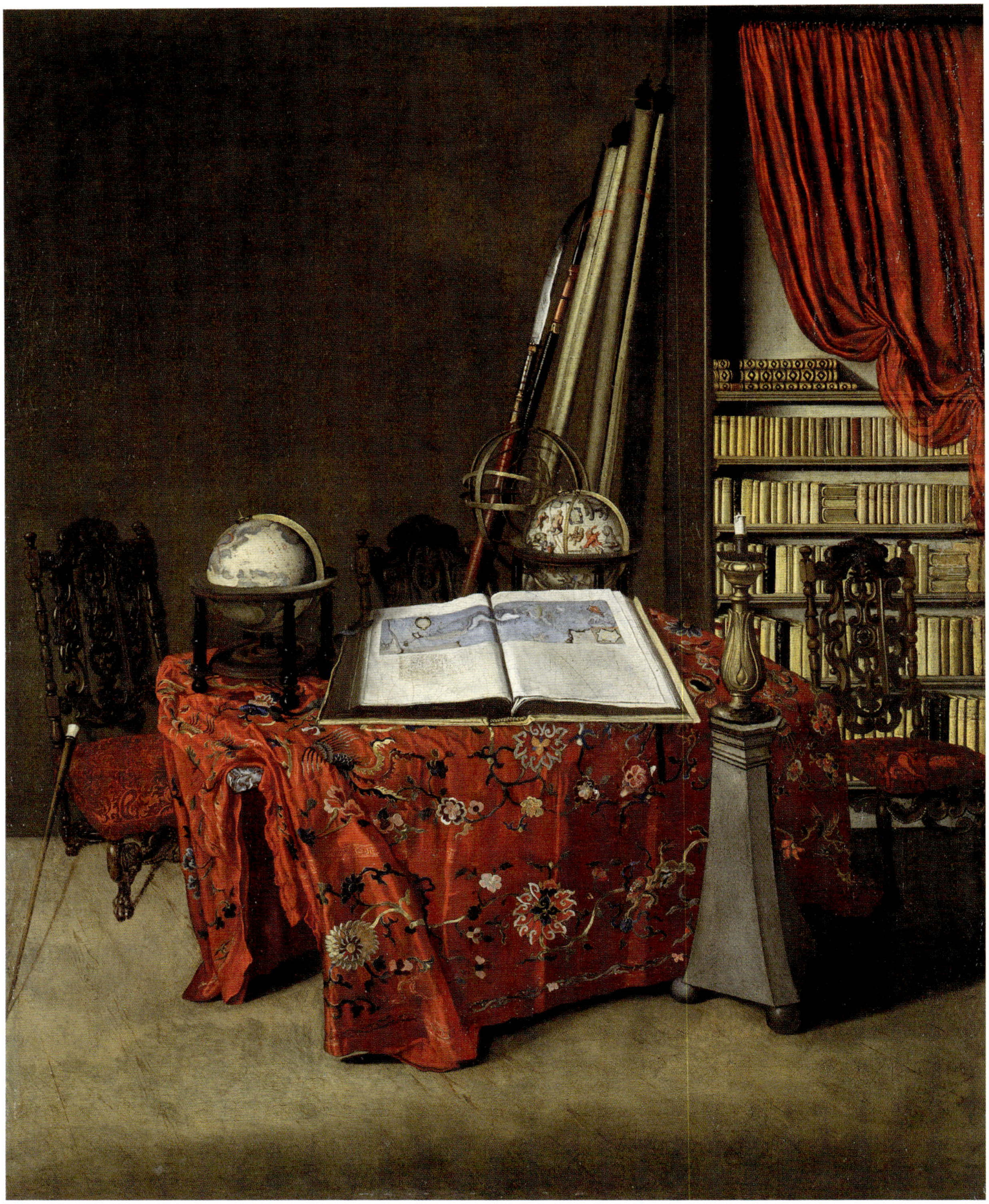

52

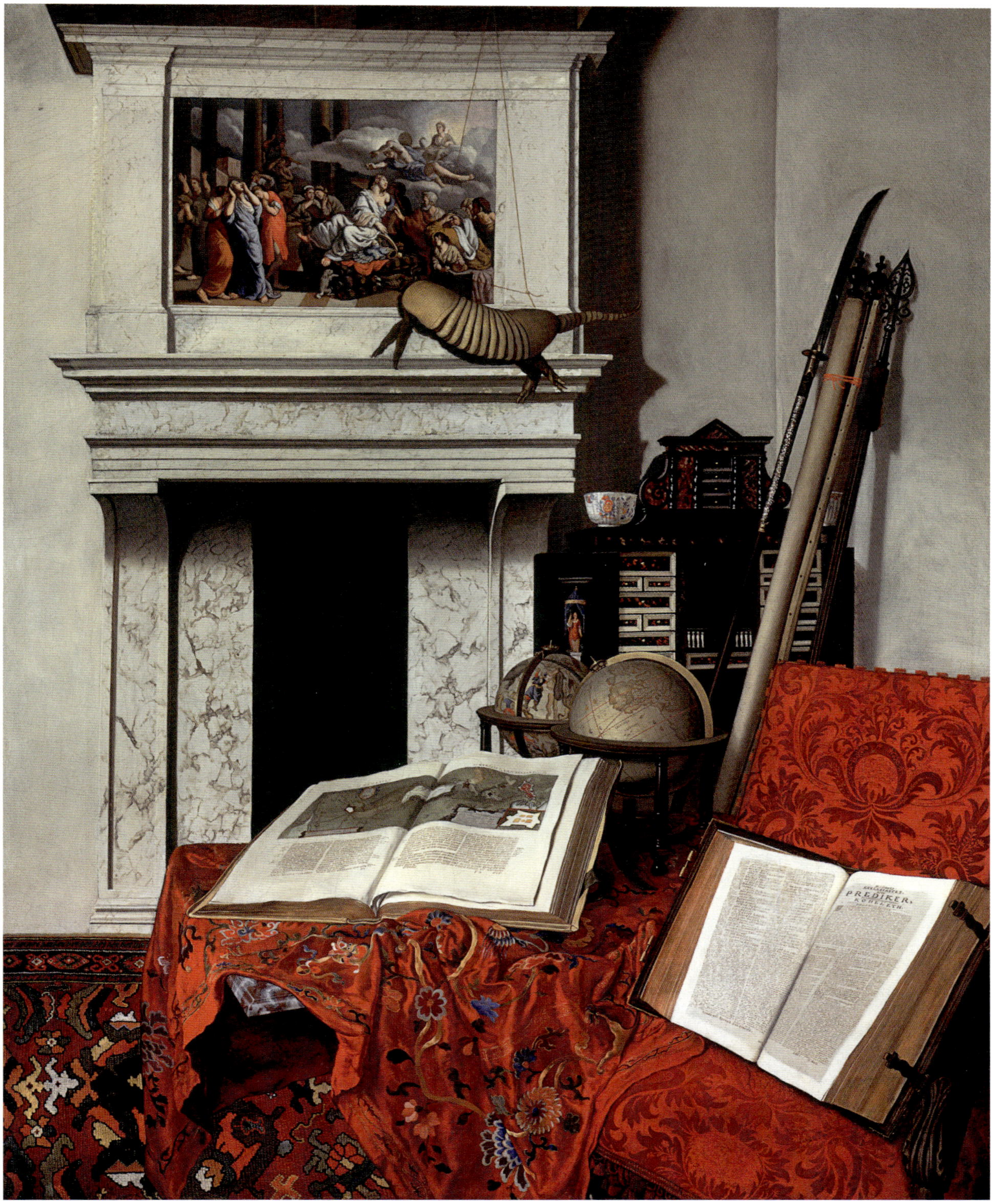

The Landscape of the Bible: Early Rembrandt and His Influences

In the seventeenth century, books on foreign cultures and reports by pilgrims and travelers returning from expeditions to the Middle and Far East were readily available in the Netherlands. However, very few Dutch had actually seen the Orient with their own eyes or had any idea of the prevailing conditions there. For most, the Orient was rather vaguely the place where the events of the Bible had occurred. Rembrandt and his contemporaries staged their depictions of stories from the Old and New Testaments in landscapes of rocky scrubland and grayish-brown hills that were very different from the verdant green plains of the northern Netherlands. The artists populated these pictorial settings with men wearing turbans and women in colorful, often lavish costumes. Although they were largely figments of the artists' imaginations, the colors and patterns of some of the silks, for instance, may have resembled actual seventeenth-century imported fabrics.[1]

In about 1565 Pieter Bruegel the Elder set his version of *The Massacre of the Innocents* (The Royal Collection, Windsor Castle) in a Flemish village covered in a blanket of snow. By the seventeenth century, however, art theory prescribed that representations of biblical subjects should incorporate Orientalized motifs, primarily in the landscape and architecture. Trees bearing little resemblance to the vegetation of the Levant were valued for their decorative qualities, and when buildings were required for particular scenes, such as palaces or temples, they were generally rendered after ancient Roman models. At best, these structures demonstrated only a very loose connection with the architecture of the Holy Land. A true representation of the local topography was clearly not considered necessary, or even desired.

The generation of painters preceding Rembrandt, such as Pieter Lastman, Jacob Pynas, and François Venant, depicted the Orient with the help of stock motifs that were accepted as authentic, but were generally based on clichés—and in doing so, they further reinforced and perpetuated them. Artists were also catering to an aesthetic that demanded beauty, variety, and vitality from a painting.

In the Netherlands of the seventeenth century, Amsterdam was the center of history painting, the most respected of all genres at that time. The themes depicted in religious paintings were not only derived from the Scriptures, such as the New Testament parables of *The Good Samaritan* by Pieter Lastman (cat. 55) or *The Baptism of the Eunuch* by Rembrandt (cat. 62). In *The Stoning of Saint Stephen* (cat. 59), Rembrandt also depicted the death of the first Christian martyr in history. This was an unusual subject in the pictorial canon of the Protestant Netherlands, being, as it was, closer to the veneration of saints practiced by the Roman Catholic Church.

The artists frequently painted scenes from the Old Testament, which relates the history of the people of Israel in a series of dramatic accounts.[2] Citizens of the northern Netherlands, still marked by the war of independence from the Spanish Empire, identified with the struggles of the Israelites against occupiers of their country such as the Assyrians and imperial Rome. The notion of the Dutch Republic as a "new Israel" that emerged in the sixteenth century was still regarded as a legitimate model for state and society in Rembrandt's day and most likely influenced how paintings depicting episodes from Jewish history were appreciated at the time.

The scenes artists selected from the Old Testament were either full of drama and emotion or served as exemplary depictions of a virtuous life, and could thus be understood and accepted by all Christian denominations. Often the aim was not to illustrate religious doctrine but to portray an exceptional moment in a historical narrative. In addition to emotionally charged scenes such as *David's Parting from Jonathan* by François Venant (cat. 57), these included heroic tales celebrating the triumph of the individual over a seemingly invincible opponent, like *Samson Destroying the Temple of Dagon* by Salomon de Bray (cat. 67), *David with the Head of Goliath before Saul* by Rembrandt (cat. 60), or *Joseph Distributing Corn in Egypt* by Bartholomeus Breenbergh (cat. 66), which clearly portrays Joseph in a better light than his brothers, who had betrayed him and sold him into slavery.

A number of history paintings taken from the Old Testament show situations in which the subjects remain ignorant of the significance of other figures or the narrative unfolding around them. For example, in *Scene from the Old Testament (Judah and Tamar?)* by Arent de Gelder (cat. 64) and from the circle of Rembrandt (cat. 63), the figure of Judah has no idea who the woman beside him is. And in Jacob Pynas's version of *Abraham Receiving the Three Angels* (cat. 56), Abraham is unaware of the true identity of his divine visitors.

Capturing the exact moment of realization was also popular, for instance, when the judge and general Jephthah first becomes aware of the fatal consequences of his vow in Pieter Lastman's *Jephthah and His Daughter* (cat. 54) or when Tobit suddenly recognizes the heavenly nature of his companion in *The Angel Taking Leave of Tobit and His Family* by Jan Victors (cat. 65). Another example is Jan Lievens's painting *The Feast of Esther* (cat. 58), which depicts the moment when Esther reveals to King Ahasuerus the murderous intentions of his adviser Haman.

By honing in on the pivotal moment of realization or the emotional peak of a narrative situation, these paintings aimed to appeal to an erudite audience that was well-practiced in the social self-restraint demanded of them, by holding an alternative mirror up in which they could see their own inner desires, needs, weaknesses, and personal indulgences reflected, but cast in an Orientalizing scene. MPH

[1] For more on this subject, cf. Bahre 2006.
[2] Cf. Tümpel 1994.

54 **Pieter Lastman** (1583–1633)

Jephthah and His Daughter, 1611

Oil on panel, 122.5 x 200 cm
Inv. G.2018.49
Kunst Museum Winterthur, Donation of the Jakob Briner Foundation, 2018

Lit.
Schwartz 1983, 2–4, figs. 1–2
Schwartz 1985a, 31, fig. 10
Amsterdam 1991a, no. 1
De Winkel 2006, 220
Winterthur 2006, 64–66
Seifert 2011, 4–5, 35, 79, 81–83, 107, 134–35, 140, 155, 253 (note 549), fig. 67
Seifert 2014, 100, fig. 36

The unusually grand format of this panel painting, Pieter Lastman's largest-known work, tells the gruesome story of the unfortunate commander Jephthah (Judges 11:29–40). He had promised God before the battle with the Ammonites that if he were victorious he would sacrifice the first living being he laid eyes on upon his return. After the battle, he was greeted by his only daughter; full of pain and realizing the horrible consequences of his ill-considered vow, Jephthah nonetheless kept his word.

Lastman—the most influential history painter in Amsterdam during the first third of the seventeenth century, in whose studio Jan Lievens and Rembrandt were also to complete part of their artistic training—represented the dramatic climax of the event in monumental widescreen format, the emotions of the protagonists clearly readable in their gestures and postures. From the right, the triumphal procession of the victorious army streams into the picture, interspersed with narrative details such as jubilant soldiers, bound prisoners, and numerous animals. From the left, Jephthah's daughter, playing the tambourine, rushes over with two companions; their joy is underscored by the flowers scattered on the ground. Like the celebrating warriors, she does not yet have any awareness of the sudden reversal of fate, from the highest feelings of joy to those of deepest horror, of the kind that has already gripped Jephthah at the sight of them. Standing on his chariot high above the crowd, her father rends his robe in despair and raises his eyes to the sky, where dark clouds are gathering from behind.

For the composition of this rarely depicted theme, Lastman looked to an engraving by Hans Bol, which he nevertheless altered in essential details by adopting a closer perspective and enlarging the scale of the figures. The painter took special care to imbue the event with a sense of historical authenticity. The Middle Eastern setting is established by the commander's magnificent Oriental costume as well as by the *nimcha*, an Arabic scimitar with a forward-curved, multipart cross guard, that hangs on a trophy next to Jephthah. The pattern on the daughter's clothing, the many turbans, and the exotic elephant on the right edge of the picture also reinforce the effect. Other motifs, however, refer to Roman antiquity; in addition to the architectural backdrop and the sequence of figures suggesting a relief, these include the numerous trophies Jephthah carries with him that Lastman based on Andrea Mantegna's series of paintings of *The Triumphs of Caesar*, widely available as prints. The impaled head, which also appears around the same time in Lastman's *Orestes and Pylades Disputing at the Altar* (Rijksmuseum, Amsterdam), is a traditional triumphal symbol that had already been mentioned by Herodotus in his *Histories*. Lastman, who, as a *pictor doctus*, frequently used texts as sources, was probably familiar with the corresponding section in the book on this treatment of defeated enemies by the Taurians, especially given his preoccupation with the Iphigenia theme. Finally, the two companions of Jephthah's daughter are derived from Hendrick Goltzius's engraving *The Judgment of Midas.*

The story of Jephthah and his sudden change of destiny was also seen on theatrical stages in Amsterdam when the picture was painted, and in 1615, Abraham de Koning published the tragedy *Iephthahs Ende zijn eenighe dochters* (Jephthah and His Only Daughter). So the subject was ubiquitous and might be interpreted as a warning to the Dutch Republic not to be lulled into a false sense of security in spite of the twelve-year armistice with Spain that had been in place since 1609.

Lastman, with his effort to establish historical accuracy and his Orientalizing motifs, was an important model for Rembrandt's staging of the Orient in biblical histories, works that were nonetheless far more ambitious than those of his teacher (cat. 59, 60, 62). GD

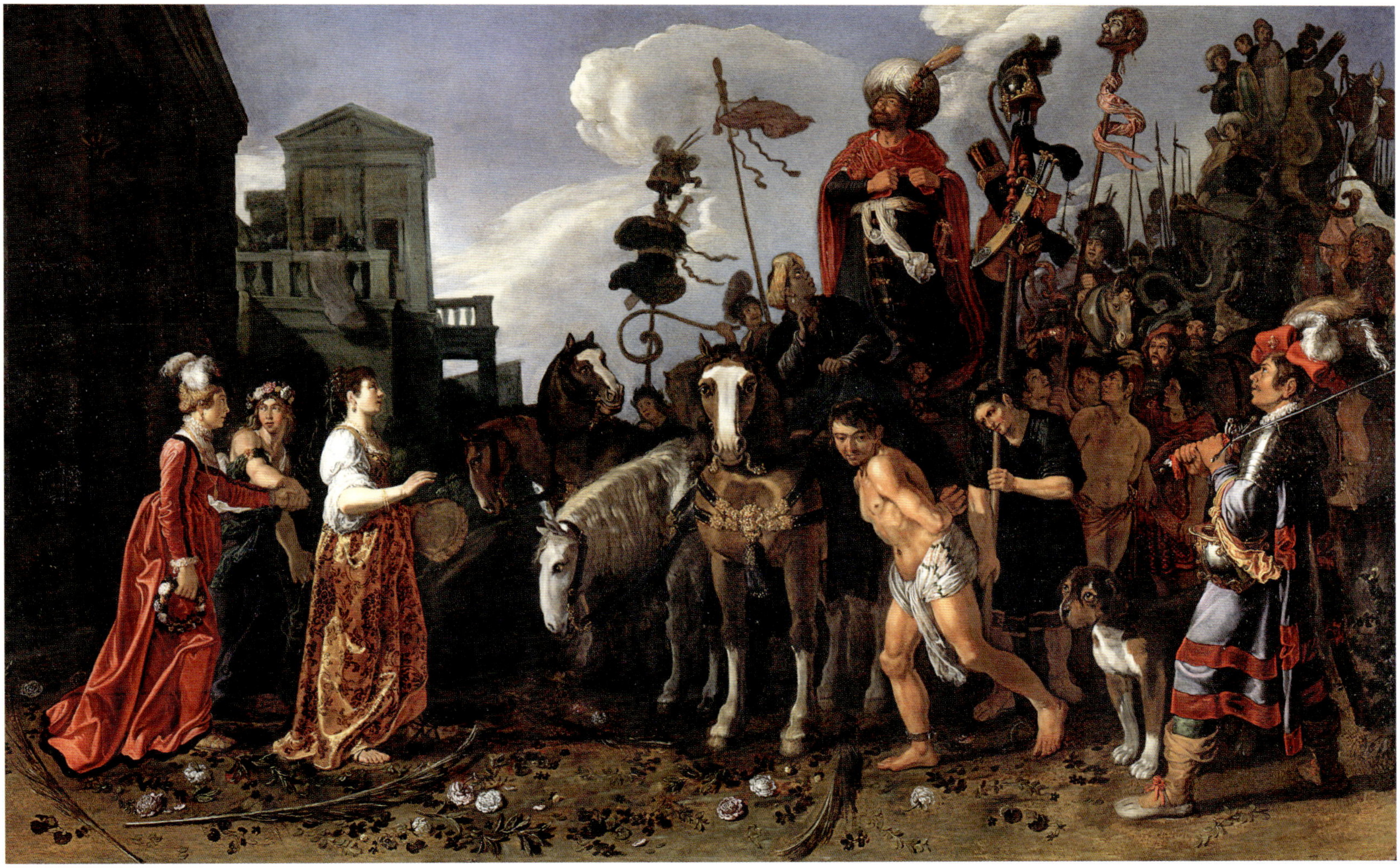

54

55 **Pieter Lastman** (1583–1633)

The Good Samaritan, ca. 1613–15

Oil on canvas, 102 x 128 cm
The Kremer Collection—
www.thekremercollection.com

Lit.
Seifert 2014
New York (n. d.)

1 De Winkel 2006, 252–54.

This unsigned painting, rediscovered a few years ago, can be attributed to Pieter Lastman on the basis of both stylistic similarities and common motifs. In addition to comparable compositions with two large main figures set against a landscape, the horse also relates to the one in Lastman's *Jephthah and His Daughter* (cat. 54). It is, therefore, reasonable to assume that the painting was probably made in the second decade of the seventeenth century.

Lastman had spent several years in Italy and had come into contact with Venetian painting as well as current developments including the art of Caravaggio and the artists around Adam Elsheimer. Soon after his return, he emerged as Amsterdam's leading painter of biblical narratives and those borrowed from ancient mythology. He often chose subjects that had hitherto rarely or never been the subject of paintings, as in the case of the New Testament story of the Good Samaritan (Luke 10:25–37). A priest and a Levite thoughtlessly pass by a seriously injured traveler who has been the victim of a brutal robbery. A Samaritan who comes by later, however, tends to the traveler's wounds, takes him to an inn, and pays for his further care. With this parable, Jesus gave a scribe an example of the virtues of mercy and charity essential to the attainment of eternal life.

As so often, here Lastman borrowed motifs from other artists. The body of the naked traveler, distorted by pain as he lies injured on the ground, references Titian's depiction of the bound giant Tityus from around 1565 (Museo Nacional del Prado, Madrid). Since the famous image was also known north of the Alps through prints, an art connoisseur might have noticed the connection. The artist's lighting effects, with their juxtaposition of bright light and deep shadow, effectively model the figures, reflecting the influence of Caravaggio. At the same time, Lastman was keen to represent his interpretation of the location of the event as authentically as possible. While the landscape, where the priest and the Levite can be seen going their way in the background, features vegetation from north of the Alps, the sloping topography might also suggest the steep descent from Jerusalem to Jericho.

Lastman also invoked a stereotype of the Middle East of ancient times with the Samaritan's costume; along with his imposing turban, he wears a colorful garment with a hem rather like a carpet and that would have seemed Oriental, given the viewing habits of the time. In contrast to the clothes, which incorporate common motifs, he is also wearing a surprising Far Eastern accessory that reflects a specific prototype: in his belt he wears a *wakizashi*, a short Japanese sword. Lastman evidently had some knowledge of exotic weapons because in the *Jephthah* panel (cat. 54) he shows an Arabic *nimcha*, an equally unusual type of weapon, and Javanese *kris* daggers can also be found in his work, as later in that of Rembrandt (see fig. p. 15).

Rembrandt would hardly have overlooked such details in his teacher's paintings, and they might have inspired similar motifs in his own art (cat. 107); Lastman's paintings also provided an important source for Rembrandt's Orientalizing costumes (see the essay by Gary Schwartz, pp. 56–73).[1] Rembrandt might even have seen *The Good Samaritan* when he was staying with Lastman; the inventory of Lastman's possessions, drawn up in 1632, lists a "Samaritiaen Lastman," which might be identified with this painting. If so, it would have been in the painter's home until the end of his life. GD

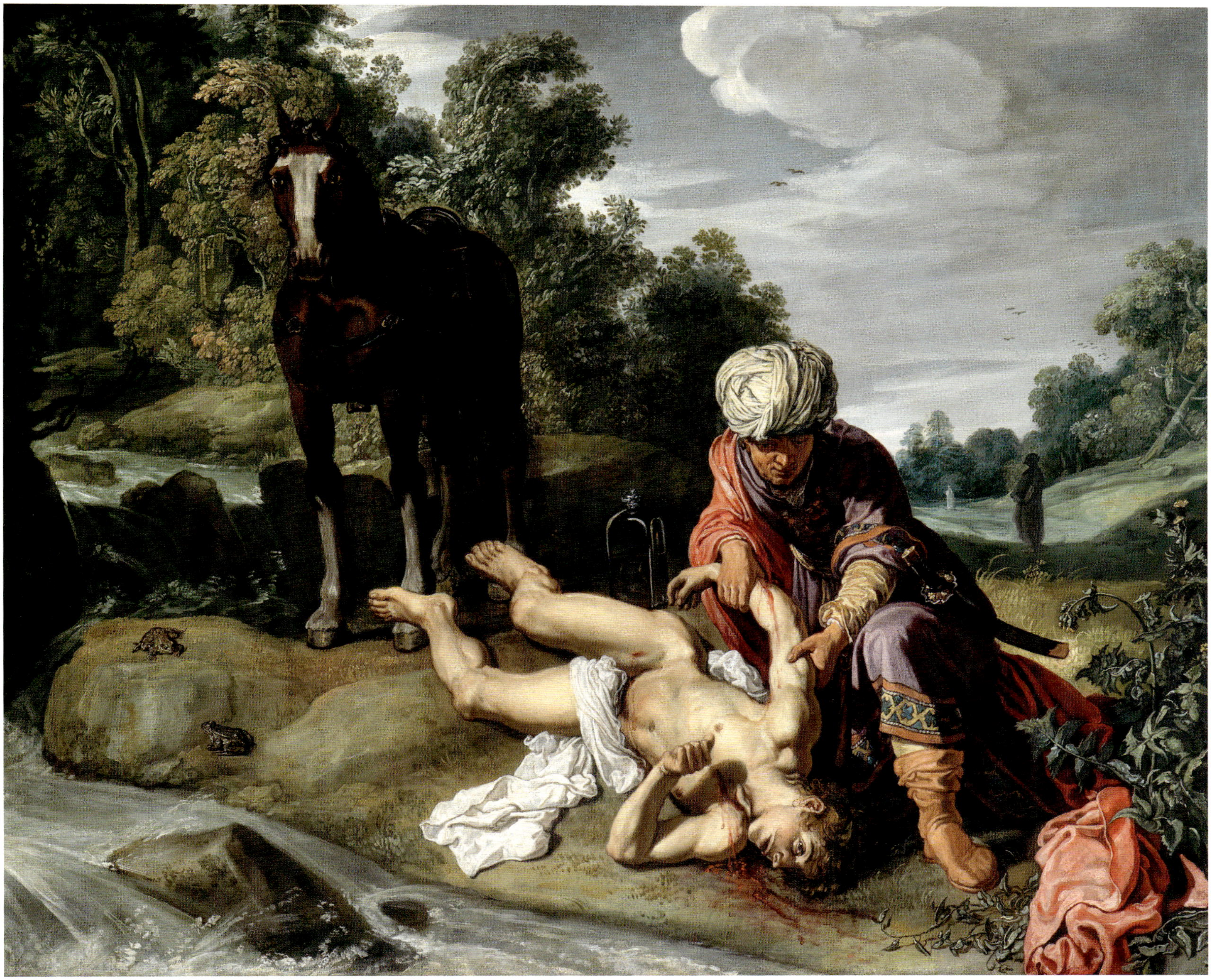

56 **Jacob Pynas** (1592–1650)

Abraham Receiving the Three Angels, ca. 1618

Oil on panel, 27.4 x 39.7 cm
Private collection

Lit.
Christie's Amsterdam, May 6, 2008, lot 69, attributed to Jacob Symonsz. Pynas

Arnold Houbraken, in the first biographical dictionary of Dutch painters of the seventeenth century, gives Jacob Pynas a special place in Rembrandt's training. After his apprenticeships to Jacob Isaacsz. van Swanenburg and Pieter Lastman, Houbraken said that Rembrandt had stayed for several months with Jacob Pynas, "until he decided to practice the art [of painting] on his own, in which he was wonderfully successful from the start. Others say that Pynas was his first master in the art."[1] Pynas is indeed documented as present in Leiden in 1626. Like Lastman, he was one of the Dutch artists who worked for a while in Italy.

Jacob had an older brother, Jan, whose work is difficult to distinguish from Jacob's. Houbraken had an unkind remark about the presumed relationship between Rembrandt and Jan Pynas. "His brushwork tended toward the brownish side, leading many to believe that Rembrandt imitated him in this regard."[2] One marked preference of Jan and Jacob Pynas that was shared by Lastman and his Amsterdam contemporaries was for narrative subjects from the Bible, staged in Italianate landscapes. The inclusion of the so-called Temple of Vesta in Tivoli, near Rome, in the background of this painting is a characteristic touch also employed by Lastman but never by Rembrandt, who invented his own backgrounds. Like other painters, Rembrandt also dressed Abraham in an Oriental mode.

The story of Abraham Receiving the Three Angels (see cat. 118), which is related in Genesis 18, has three narrative lines: Abraham extending hospitality to "three men," one of whom he recognized as God; the announcement by the men that Abraham's aged wife, Sarah, was going to bear him a son, and the couple's frightened reaction; and the negotiations between Abraham and God concerning the destruction of Sodom, in which Abraham bargains God down from fifty to ten righteous souls for whose sake the city would be spared. The "two angels"—God did not join them—who went to Sodom in Genesis 19 did not even get around to counting. Only Abraham's reception of the men is shown in the painting. GS

1. Arnold Houbraken, *De groote schouburgh der Nederlantsche konstschilders en schilderessen*, vol. 1, Amsterdam 1718, 254–55; translated by Gary Schwartz.
2. Ibid., 214–15.

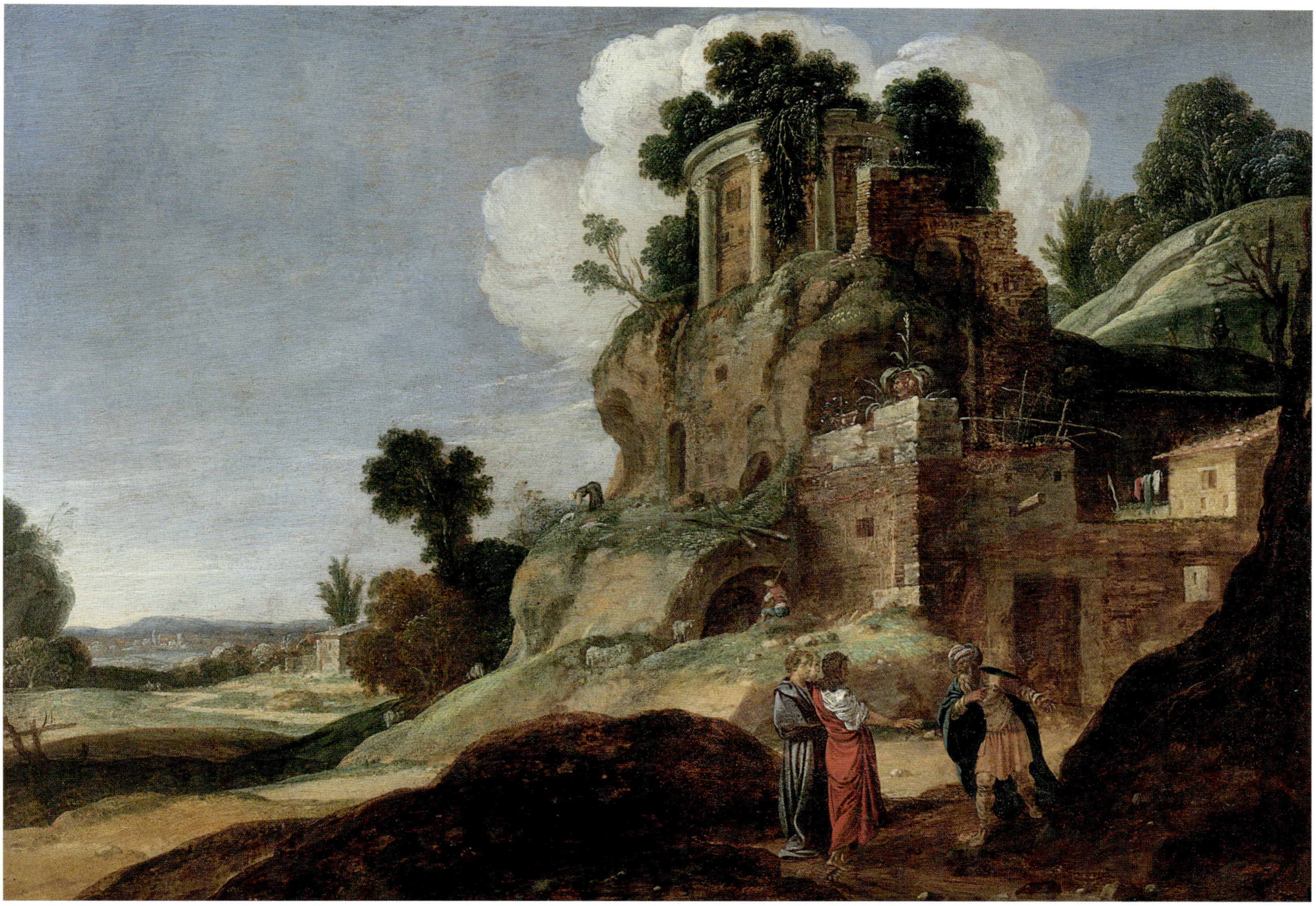

56

57 **François Venant** (1591/92–1636)
David's Parting from Jonathan, 1630 (?)

Oil on panel, 30 x 47 cm
Inscribed bottom left: FV [monogram]
Inv. 5497
Fondation Custodia/Collection Frits Lugt, Paris

Lit.
CRP, vol. 3, 540–41
Van Gelder 1937
Bruyn 1997, 163–67

The subject here is the tearful forced farewell of two friends, as recounted in the first book of Samuel. The aging king Saul, filled with jealousy, tries to kill the young David, but this does not undermine his friendship with Saul's son, Jonathan. For his own protection, however, David must flee abroad for a period (1 Samuel 20:41–42). According to the Bible, David throws himself to the ground and bows three times before the king's son, gestures that François Venant translates here into an elegant bow.

In 1937 Jan Gerrit van Gelder took this rather small monogrammed panel as the starting point for a reconstruction of Venant's oeuvre. At this date, biographical data on Venant had already been established but no works by the artist were known. The attribution is based on the fact that Venant married Pieter Lastman's sister, Agnieta, in 1625, and on the close connection between this picture and some of the paintings being produced by Lastman at the time. As a result, it seems likely that Venant was apprenticed to his future brother-in-law. The relationship between the depictions of David and Jonathan's farewell created by the two artists—Lastman's painting of the subject dates to 1620 (Pushkin Museum, Moscow)—is also clear. For the figure of Jonathan, the two artists might have sketched the same model from different angles, although one of them must have reversed his study. The composition of the landscape is also similar in both panels, with each featuring the same dominant motifs of a rocky wall on the left with hanging vines and the ruins of an ancient round building on the right.

Three drawings currently attributed to Ferdinand Bol (Département des Arts graphiques, Musée du Louvre, Paris; sale, Amsterdam, October 25, 1933, lot 36; Rijksprentenkabinet, Rijksmuseum, Amsterdam) might occupy an intermediary position between Venant's composition and the St. Petersburg painting of the same subject by Rembrandt (cat. 74). BB

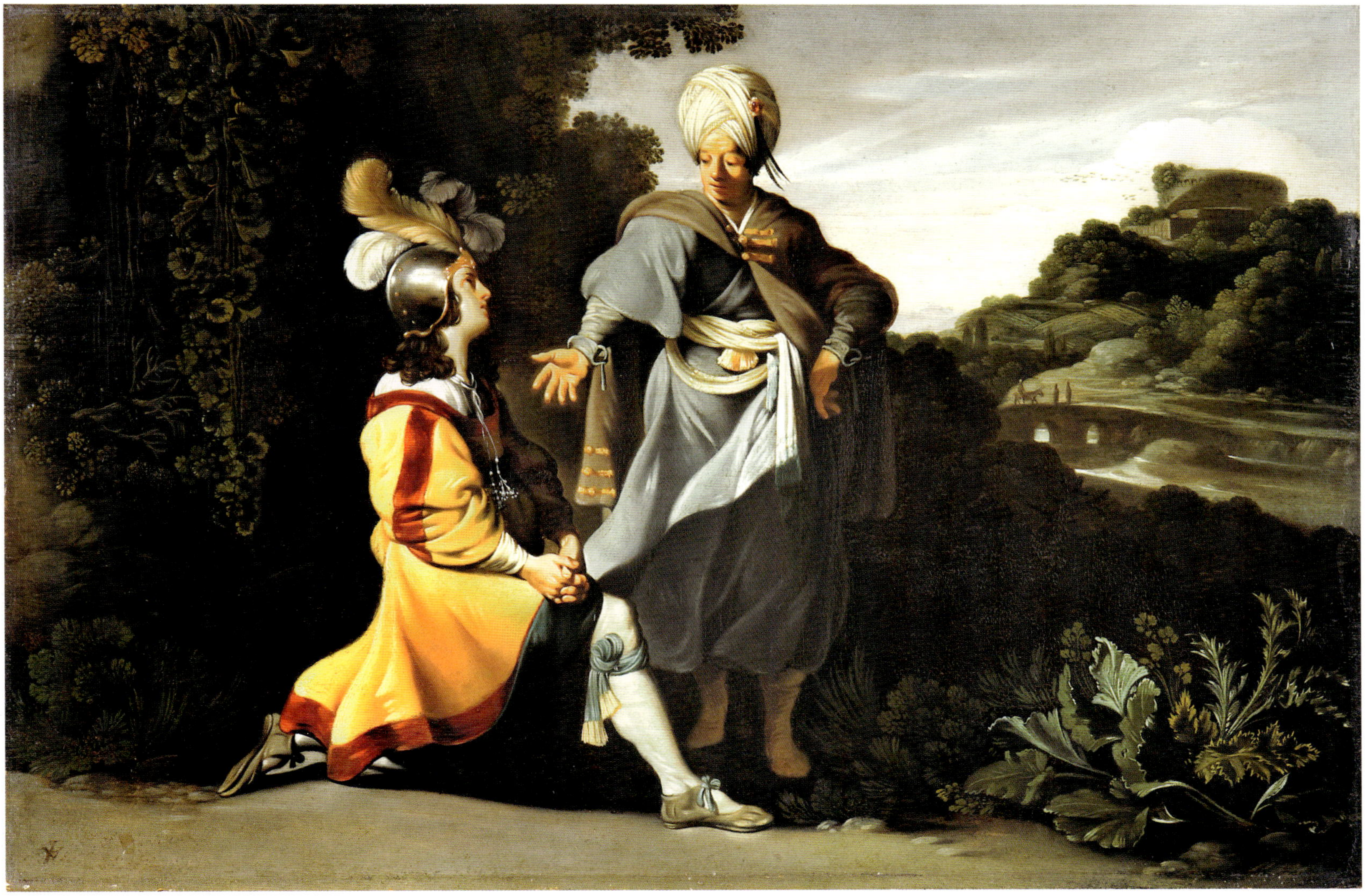

58 **Jan Lievens** (1607–1674)
The Feast of Esther, ca. 1625

Oil on canvas, 130.8 x 163.8 cm
Inv. 52.9.55
North Carolina Museum of Art, Raleigh, purchased with funds from the State of North Carolina

Lit.
CRP, vol. 1, no. C2
Sumowski 1983–94, vol. 3, no. 1181
Gutbrod 1996, 115–26
Kassel 2001, 192–95
Washington 2009, no. 6
Schnackenburg 2016, 48–51, no. 26

This large, imposing work depicts the rescue of the Jews from their threatened annihilation as related in the book of Esther (Esther 7:1–10). The Persian king Ahasuerus had chosen Esther as his queen because of her beauty, unaware of her Jewish identity. When Esther's Jewish stepfather, Mordecai (see cat. 81), refuses to kneel as required before Haman, Ahasuerus's highest government official, Haman plans in revenge to have all Jews murdered by royal decree on a predetermined day. Esther devises a rescue plan. She invites Ahasuerus and Haman to a banquet where she reveals herself to be Jewish and thus also condemned to death. She truthfully answers the king's question about who is responsible for the conspiracy, and Ahasuerus then becomes angry with Haman. When a servant announces that the gallows erected for Mordecai is ready, the king orders Haman to be hanged instead. Since Haman's decree cannot be revoked, however, the Jews are given the right to defend themselves against their enemies and kill them, which is what they do.

The attribution of this early work, painted around 1625, which is also Lievens's first multifigure history painting, has long been disputed; in addition to an attribution to Rembrandt, a collaboration between the two painters has been suggested.

While still at the beginning of his career, Lievens absorbed various influences, which he combined here to create a psychological showpiece par excellence. Esther, set at the center of the composition, turns to the king and points to the shadowy figure of Haman, who sits opposite her with his back to the viewer. Ahasuerus, his fists clenched in anger, then pronounces his judgment on the horrified, unfortunate man, while the servant looks on with interest from the background. The picture shows a space bordered by a curtain in which the three-quarter-length figures are gathered around a table, connected by glances and gestures; with its bright lighting and powerful chiaroscuro effects it also indicates the artist's familiarity with the latest works from the circle of Utrecht Caravaggisti such as Gerrit van Honthorst. The evocative gestures of the figures, on the other hand, point to Lievens's teacher Pieter Lastman, from whom he had also learned to conjure up an appropriate Orientalizing atmosphere by incorporating exotic, fanciful garments with turbans and veils (see cat. 54–55).

Lievens, however, supersedes such prototypes with his splendid display and the range of iridescent fabrics in the clothing. Haman's boldly striped costume, on the other hand, is borrowed from the Utrecht Caravaggisti, in whose pictures dandies of questionable character appear in similar clothing. This iconographic device reinforces his separation from Esther and Ahasuerus, already established by the composition and effects of light. Rembrandt's *Stoning of Saint Stephen* (cat. 59), painted around the same time, shows a similar *repoussoir* figure in the horseman at the left margin of the picture, suggesting that the artists might actually have influenced each other. *A Musical Company* of 1626 (cat. 1), with its profusion of precious fabrics, also seems to compete with Lievens's history painting. GD

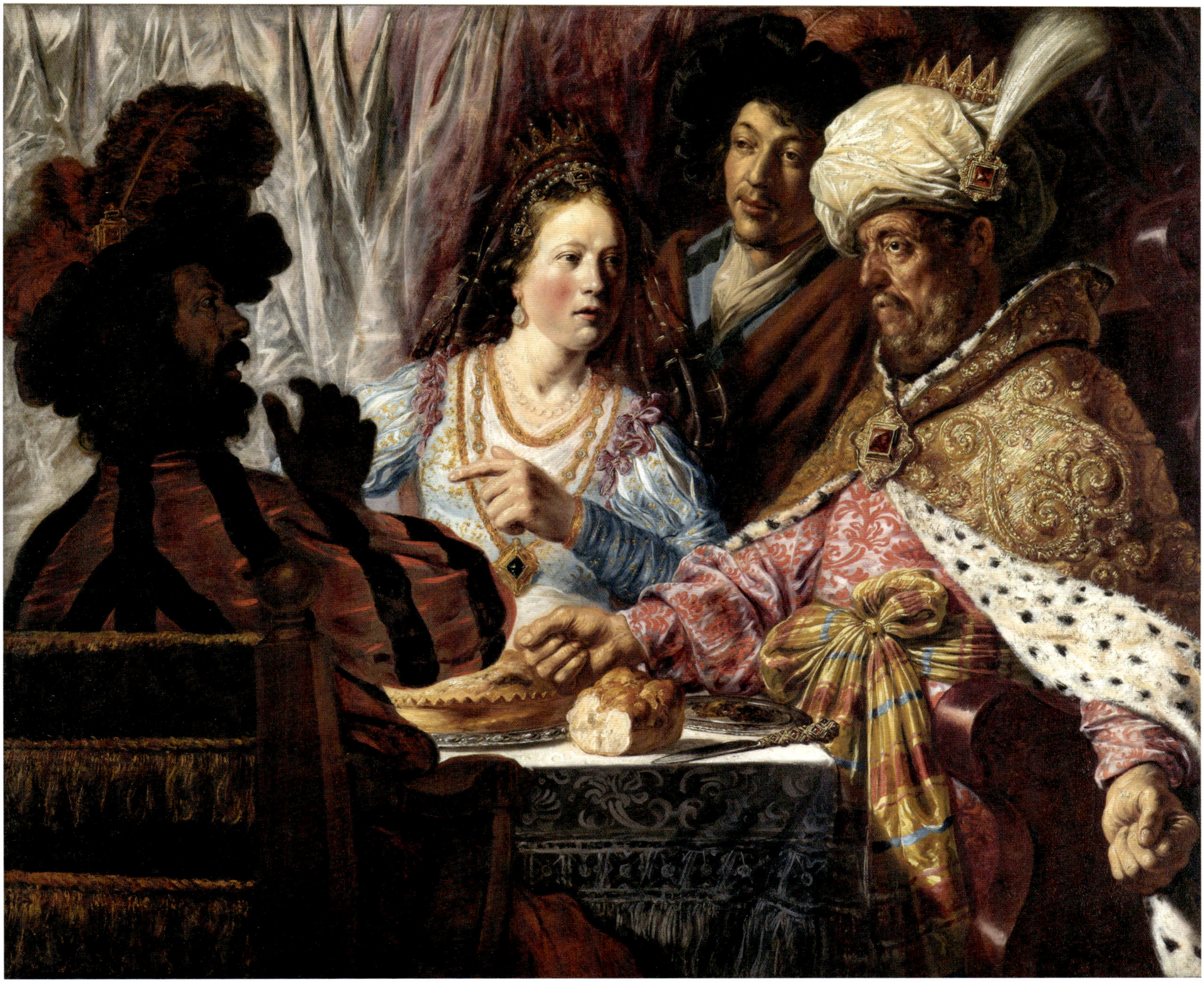

59 **Rembrandt Harmensz. van Rijn** (1606–1669)
The Stoning of Saint Stephen, 1625

Oil on oak panel, 89.5 x 123.6 cm
Inscribed top left: R f. 1625
Inv. A 2735
Musée des Beaux-Arts, Lyon
(Basel only)

Lit.
CRP, vol. 1, no. A 1, vol. 6, no. 5
Karlsruhe 2015, no. 6
Paris 2016, no. 1
Van de Wetering 2016, 63, 134
Leiden 2019, no. 58

The nineteen-year-old Rembrandt undertook his first intellectual excursion to the Orient of biblical history—figuratively speaking—as part of a travel group, in the company of several artist colleagues. There was a broad pictorial tradition for the stoning of Saint Stephen (Acts 7:54–60), a deacon of the original congregation in Jerusalem, showing the first Christian martyr in a magnificent dalmatic, the liturgical vestment worn by deacons, in the midst of the lynch mob that was stoning him.

Rembrandt took the basic structure of the composition and the beam of light falling sharply from the upper left from Adam Elsheimer's painting on copper (ca. 1603–04, Scottish National Gallery, Edinburgh) that Paul Bril might have brought back from Rome to the Netherlands. Jacob Pynas's version of the theme from 1617 (Agnes Etherington Art Centre, Queen's University, Kingston, Ontario) provided Rembrandt with the stone thrower seen from behind in the right foreground, using him in the same place as Pynas had done and then again in the center of the foreground, with his legs mirroring the position of the other one. While the artist bathed the first figure in the brightest light, the latter is cloaked in deep shadow. He thus alludes to the principle of *gemini* (twins) from Italian art theory, demonstrated by Antonio Pollaiuolo in 1475 in *The Martyrdom of Saint Sebastian* (The National Gallery, London). Rembrandt based the high priest riding a horse in the left foreground on a rider from *Coriolanus and the Roman Matrons*, painted by his teacher Pieter Lastman in 1625 (Trinity College, Dublin). Lastman's work is also the source for a member of the High Council—seen meeting in the middle ground of the picture—who rests his left arm on his hip.

In spite of all this borrowing, the young Rembrandt was quite proud of his composition, and he indicated this by inserting a portrait of himself as well as one probably showing Jan Lievens, who worked in his studio, immediately to the left and right of the dramatically raised left hand of the saint. And justly so: the focus here on a pivotal moment a mere split-second long, freezing it for an instant, is probably unique in the pictorial tradition of this subject. The thug with a yellow turban at the center of the picture appears to have just thrown a stone from the second row, seen in flight to the right of his victim's hip. According to every law of ballistics, the missile must have missed the saint, who remains unharmed, or, at most, only grazed. He will not get off so lightly from the attacks of the other, better-equipped thugs hurling stones right behind Stephen, like those standing immediately on his left and right. Paradoxically, the missed first shot makes it perfectly clear how deadly this threat really is. It radically extends the tension of the narrative. BB

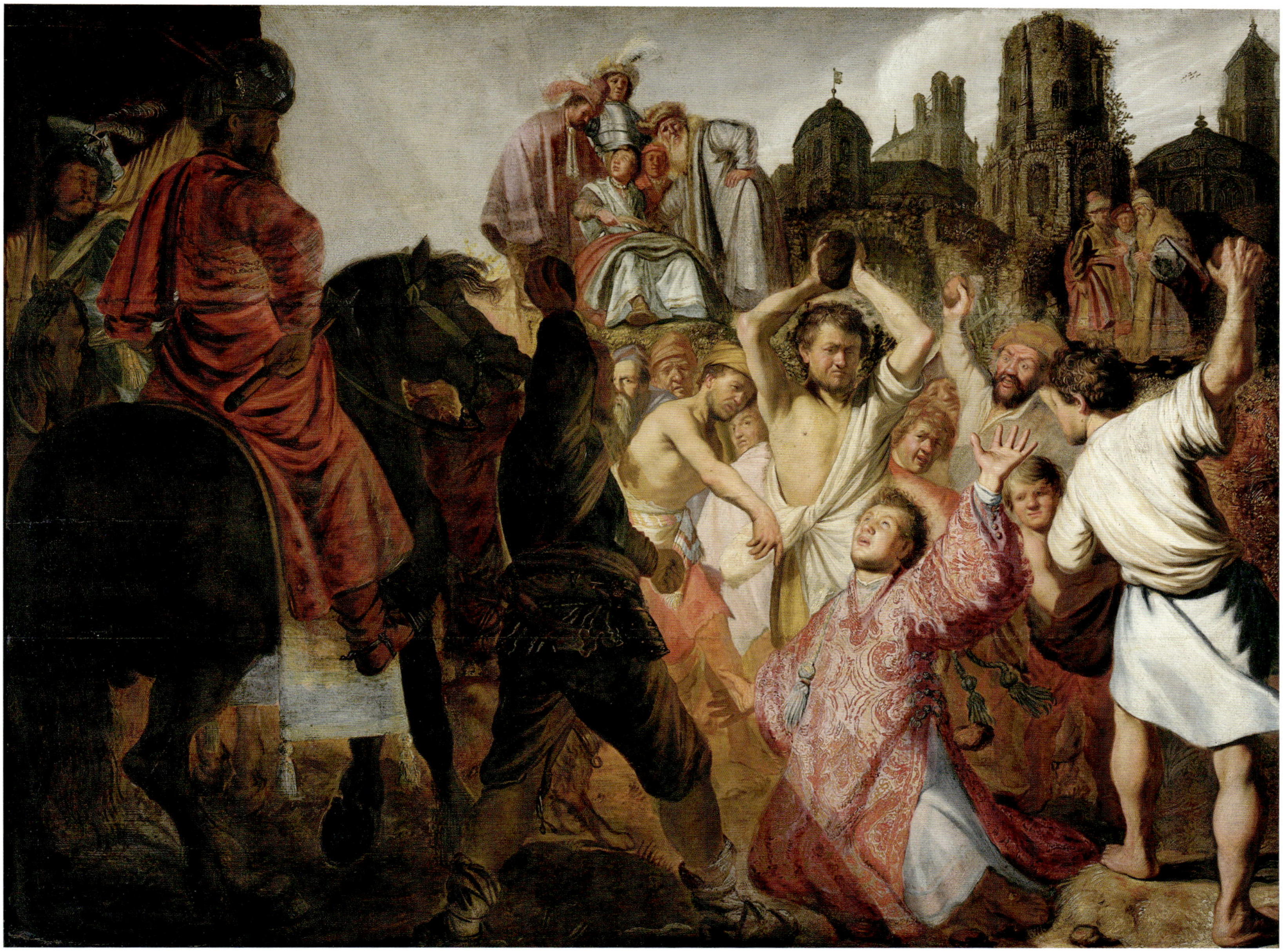

60 Rembrandt Harmensz. van Rijn (1606–1669)
David with the Head of Goliath before Saul, 1627
61 Lucas Vorsterman (1595–1675) after **Peter Paul Rubens** (1577–1640)
The Adoration of the Magi, 1621

60
Oil on oak panel, 27.4 x 39.7 cm
Inscribed bottom center: RH. [in ligature] 1627.
Inv. G 1958.37
Kunstmuseum Basel, Max Geldner Bequest, Basel

61
Engraving from two plates on two sheets of paper, 57 x 73.6 cm
Inscribed bottom left and right:
P. P. Rubens pinxit. / Lucas Vorsterman sculp. et excud. A.° 1621.
Inv. X.2529
Kunstmuseum Basel, Kupferstichkabinett

Lit.
CRP, vol. 1, no. A 9
Basel 2000, no. 7
Baer 2003, 30–31
Bürgi/Zimmer 2011, no. 27
Basel 2017, 46–48
Leiden 2019, 41

[1] De Witt 2008, 32–33, no. 12.

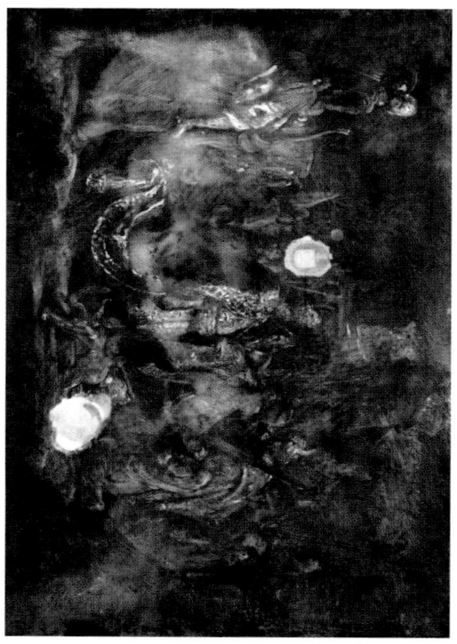

X-ray of cat. 60

Rembrandt's small-format panel portrays a rarely depicted episode from the Old Testament (1 Samuel 17:57–58). After his victory over the gigantic Philistine, Goliath, the shepherd boy David presents the severed head of the defeated man to Saul, king of the people of Israel, whom he would later succeed. The painting is often considered Rembrandt's earliest oil sketch, but its strong coloration as well as the signature and date set it outside the normal range in this category of the artist's work. The extremely loose brushwork, however, remains surprising in a work from his early period. Curiously, a partial copy, dated after 1639 through dendrochronology, and painted *en brunaille*, a monochrome style of painting in brown tones, is of the same size as this one but shows a somewhat tighter close-up; it is even more sketchy than the model with an even more open style (Bader Collection, Agnes Etherington Art Centre, Queen's University, Kingston, Ontario).[1]

Rembrandt actually used the panel of the Basel painting twice. Beneath the layer of paint that we see now, the X-ray reveals a *tronie,* perhaps even a self-portrait with a turban, apparently well advanced (fig. on left). If this work had been completed, it would have been the earliest dated example of an Oriental head known to be in Rembrandt's hand.

Turbans and precious fabrics give the biblical setting an Oriental touch. During this period, Rembrandt drew his motifs primarily from the latest works of his older contemporaries. He borrowed the main character of the aged king from Peter Paul Rubens's *Adoration of the Magi* (Musée des Beaux-Arts, Lyon) of 1617–18, probably as translated by Lucas Vorsterman's engraving after it. The standing figure, the gesture of the left hand, and the train, whose folds have been reproduced in almost identical detail, as well as the striking motif of the childlike train bearers together leave no doubt about the original source of the image. Rembrandt might have used the clothing of the third Magus, seen from the front in Rubens's work, as the model for the sash around Saul's waist. Both groups of figures feature the hand extended toward a figure bowing down in deep devotion—in Rubens's case, the oldest king and in Rembrandt's, the prophet Samuel.

Rembrandt situates this central group of figures inspired by Rubens in a composition generally based on *Coriolanus with the Roman Women* painted by his teacher Pieter Lastman (Trinity College, Dublin) in 1625. The placement and shape of the mighty commander's tent in the background, and the rider seen at an angle from behind in the left foreground, originate in this work. Rembrandt moved the lance bearer, seen in shadow, to the right edge of the picture, showing him in profile. And he seems to have drawn ultimate inspiration from Lastman's definition of the pictorial space through starkly contrasting areas of light and shade. BB

60

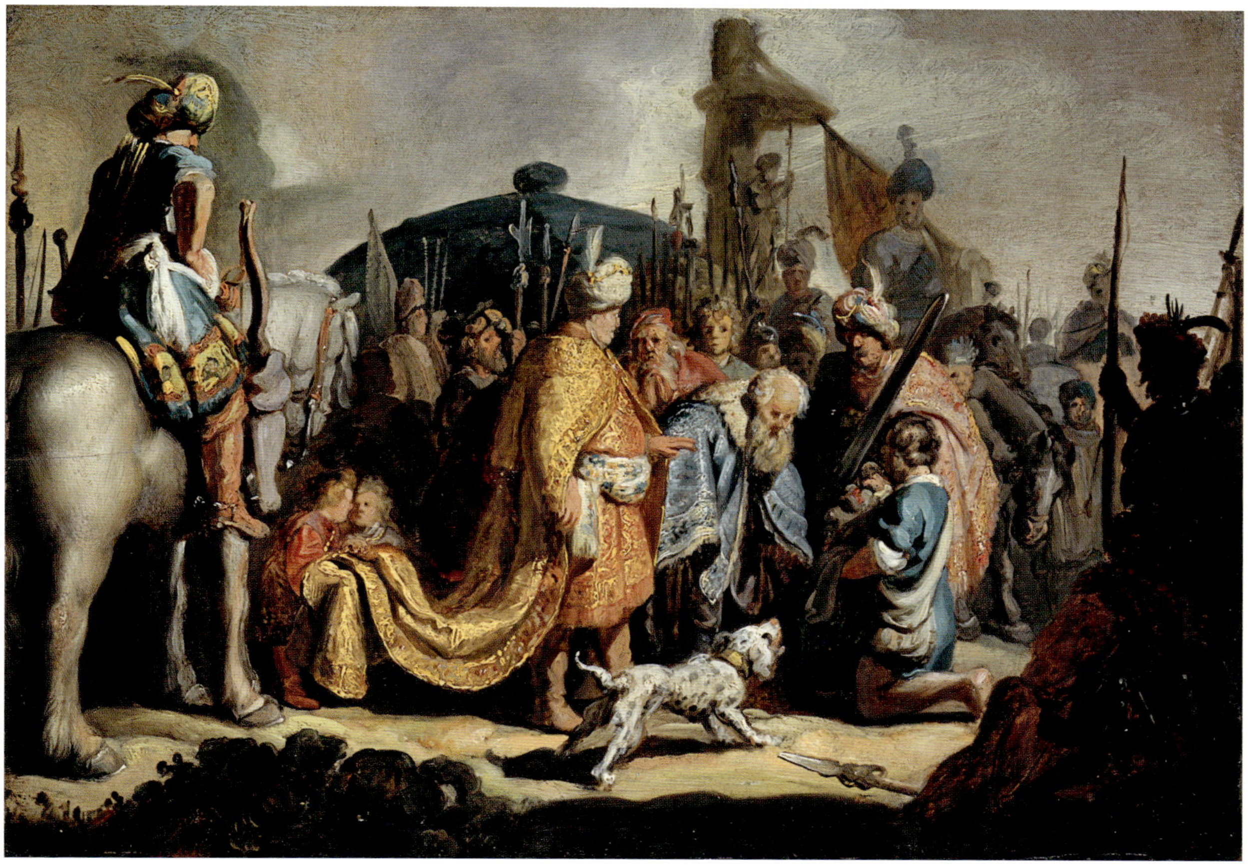

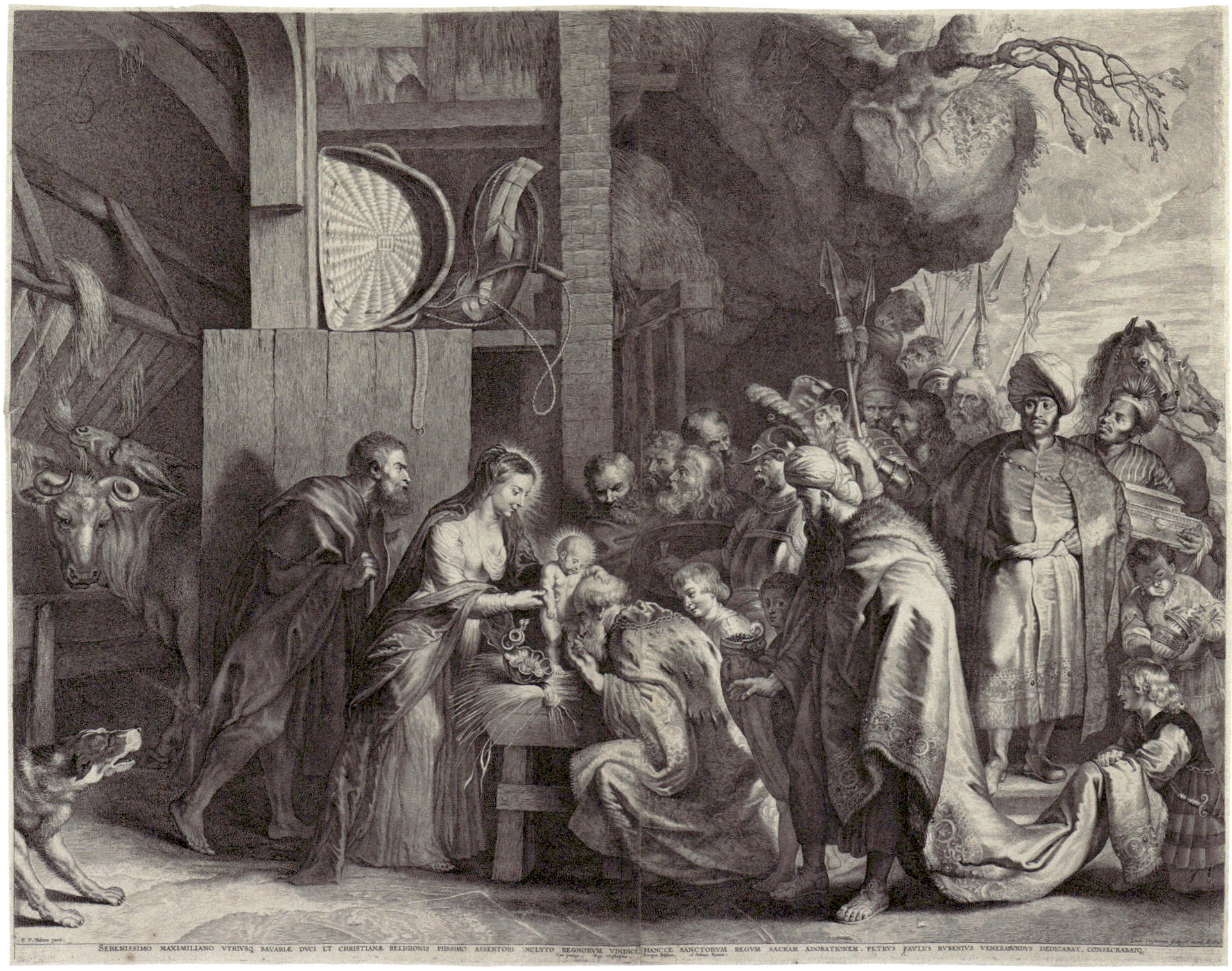
SERENISSIMO MAXIMILIANO VTRIVSQ. BAVARIÆ DVCI ET CHRISTIANÆ RELIGIONIS PIISSIMO ASSERTORI INCLYTO REGNORVM VINDICI HANCCE SANCTORVM REGVM SACRAM ADORATIONEM. PETRVS PAVLVS RVBENIVS VENERABVNDVS DEDICABAT, CONSECRABATQ.

61

62 Rembrandt Harmensz. van Rijn (1606–1669) and workshop
The Baptism of the Eunuch, ca. 1631

Oil on canvas, 64.8 x 95.3 cm
Private collection

Lit.
Bonebakker 1998, 59
Kolfin 2010, vol. 3, 271–307
Amsterdam 2020, 91 (as lost)
Schwartz 2020

The phenomenon of conversion is a central element of Christianity. At its birth, Christianity was reserved to people of the Jewish faith. The expansion of the base beyond the Jewish world was a key moment in the history of the faith. Two stories in the book of Acts vie for precedence as being the first conversion of a non-Jew to Christianity. The one that is usually assigned this role is the conversion by Saint Peter of the Roman centurion Cornelius in Acts 10. As important as the theological significance ascribed to that event was, it was seldom depicted in art. Instead, the iconography of a conversion of a non-Jew was monopolized, especially in Dutch art, by an earlier event described in Acts 8:26–38.

An angel of the Lord visited Philip, one of the first deacons of the early church. He was told to go to the road descending from Jerusalem to Gaza. When he got there, Philip was instructed to approach a man riding in a chariot. The man was a high official in the court of Ethiopia, identified in some Bible translations as a Black eunuch. He was reading a passage in the book of Isaiah that he was struggling to understand. At his request, Philip explained it to him, apparently as a prediction of the divinity of Christ. Accepting the interpretation, the eunuch asked Philip to baptize him in a body of water they had come to. The two men stepped into the water, Philip performed a baptism, and he then was taken off by the angel.

The iconography that found its way into seventeenth-century art reduces the story to the act of baptism. For unknown reasons, artists never showed the deacon and the eunuch standing in the water together, as Scripture says they did. This peculiarity reveals to us that artists looked more at each other's work for visual inspiration than to the text they were depicting. This is certainly true of Rembrandt's *The Baptism of the Eunuch*, which depends heavily on the example of his master Pieter Lastman (Staatliche Kunsthalle Karlsruhe). Rembrandt's earlier depiction of the subject (Museum Catharijneconvent, Utrecht) from 1626 is also indebted to Lastman.

Religious meanings played less of a role in seventeenth-century depictions of the Baptism of the Eunuch than the narrative and emotional facets of the story. One particular feature of the story was particularly appealing: the "whitening" through baptism of the soul of a man whose skin remains black. The iconography was hallmarked by that paradox, which was built into the imagery. To artists it held irresistible attraction. That is surely one of the main reasons for its great popularity as a subject in print and painting.

In the middle of the seventeenth century Rembrandt's *The Baptism of the Eunuch* served as the model for an engraving by Claes Jansz. Visscher II showing the same composition. The Latin caption reads: "Here Philip washed the Black Ethiopian, dispels the color not of his skin but of his soul, after having explained the prophecies."[1] The print is inscribed "Rembrandt invent.," meaning that Rembrandt was the author of the model after which the print was made. Rembrandt's art has far more images of Blacks than one would think (see cat. 72),[2] a fair number of whom lived in Rembrandt's immediate environment in Amsterdam: enslaved and indentured household servants as well as free Blacks, seamen, hostel keepers, and others.[3] GS

1 Bonebakker 1998, 59.
2 Cf. Kolfin 2010; Amsterdam 2020.
3 Cf. Ponte 2020, 44–57. In 1644 slavery was outlawed in Amsterdam; see ibid., 52.

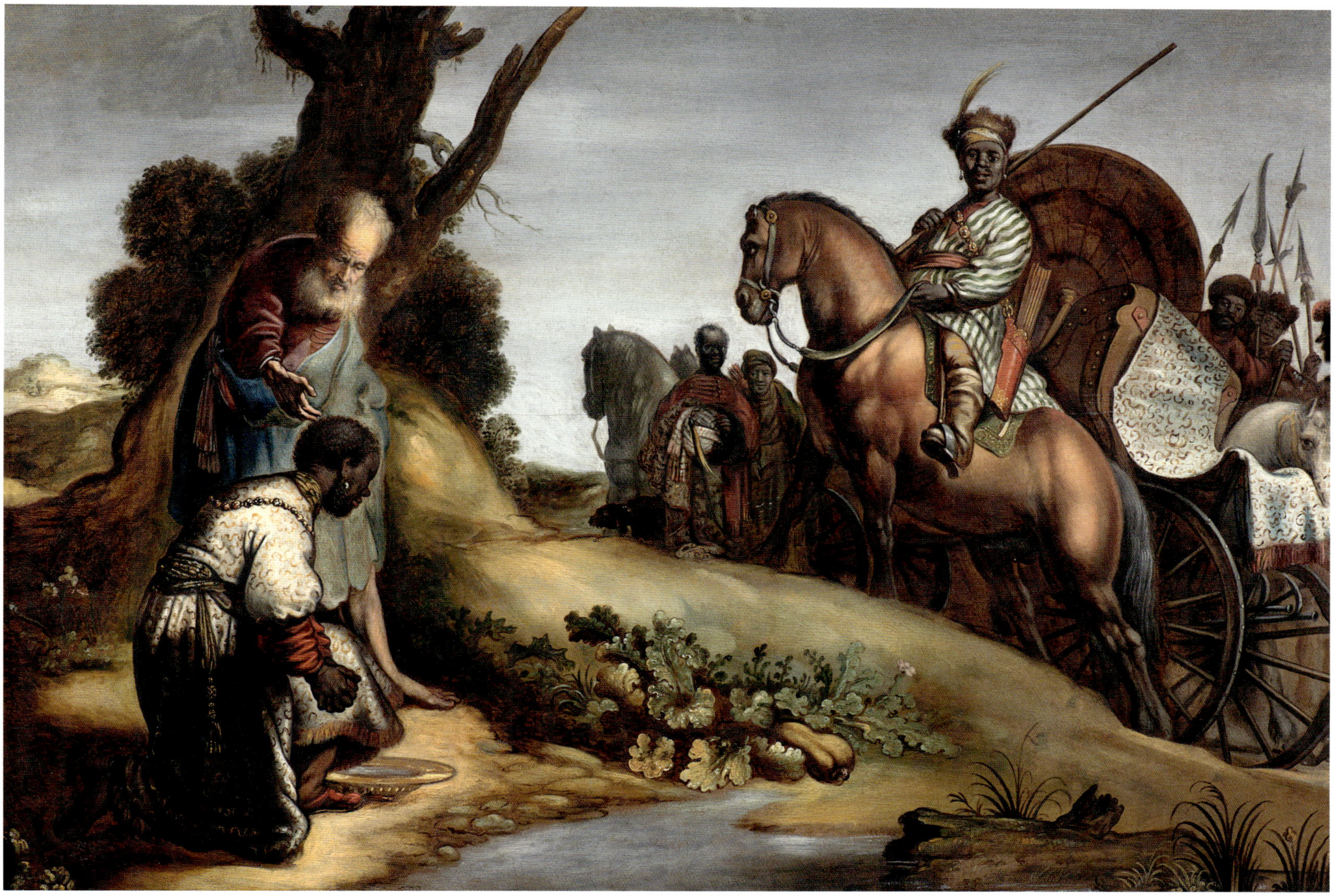

62

63 School of **Rembrandt Harmensz. van Rijn** (1606–1669)
Judah and Tamar, ca. 1650–1700

Oil on canvas, 108.5 x 130 cm
Inv.-Nr. 570
Residenzgalerie Salzburg

Lit.
Salzburg 1993, 73–75
Salzburg 2001, 26–27

Judah wears a towering turban while Tamar wears a headpiece that resembles a greatly enlarged *agal*, the ring of cord familiar traditionally in the Arab world and still in use today. It is worn on the head to secure the headscarf known as the *kufiya*, replaced here by a black veil. The *agal* can be worn with a cap, like the gold one on Tamar's head. All of this represents Arabic *male* clothing. Oriental costume is thus combined here with a Western pictorial tradition. For since the early sixteenth century, numerous images show decidedly masculine head coverings like the ostentatious feathered berets worn by flamboyant women of easy virtue, especially prostitutes. In this respect, the artist hits the nail on the head in his treatment of the subject: while the noble and clever Tamar is by no means a prostitute, at this particular moment her male counterpart nonetheless mistakes her for one (Genesis 38:15–19).

Judah, a son of Jacob, arranges for his firstborn son, Er, to marry Tamar, but Er dies soon afterward. Following the principle of levirate marriage law (Deuteronomy 25:5–10), Judah delegates his second son, Onan, to marry and have sexual relations with the young widow. Onan resists, because any son thus conceived will be considered his dead brother's, and breaks off the act. Yahweh, displeased with this behavior, punishes him with death. Judah, fearing he will also lose his last son, Shela, this time refuses his widowed daughter-in-law sexual relations with him. The clever widow then disguises herself and intercepts her father-in-law on the side of the street; believing her to be a prostitute, he impregnates her. As a pledge for the promised whore's wage, she obtains Judah's signet ring, bracelet—which she holds here—and staff. Her illegitimate pregnancy becomes public, and for this Judah wishes her to be put to death. But Tamar reveals the pledges, and her father-in-law realizes the injustice of his position.

It is one of the most astonishing aspects of Orientalism in the Netherlands during the seventeenth century that a subject based on such an alien social construct was so popular in art: Pieter Lastman, Ferdinand Bol, Gerbrand van den Eeckhout, Jan Victors, and Arent de Gelder are among the many artists to address it.[1] This Rembrandt School painting sensitively indicates Tamar's status: the black covering over her face suggests a widow's veil, but, like her red coat, it might also be read as part of the masquerade: "And she put her widow's garments off from her, and covered her with a vail [*sic*], and wrapped herself" (Genesis 38:14). BB

1 Lastman: Christie's, London, December 12, 1959, lot 83. Bol: 1644, Museum of Fine Arts, Boston; 1653, Pushkin Museum, Moscow. Eeckhout: 1645, Gemäldegalerie, Staatliche Museen zu Berlin. Victors: ca. 1650, Lempertz, Cologne, May 19–21, 2016, lot 1267. De Gelder: 1681, Agnes Etherington Art Centre, Queen's University, Kingston, Ontario; Mauritshuis, The Hague; Akademie der bildenden Künste, Vienna.

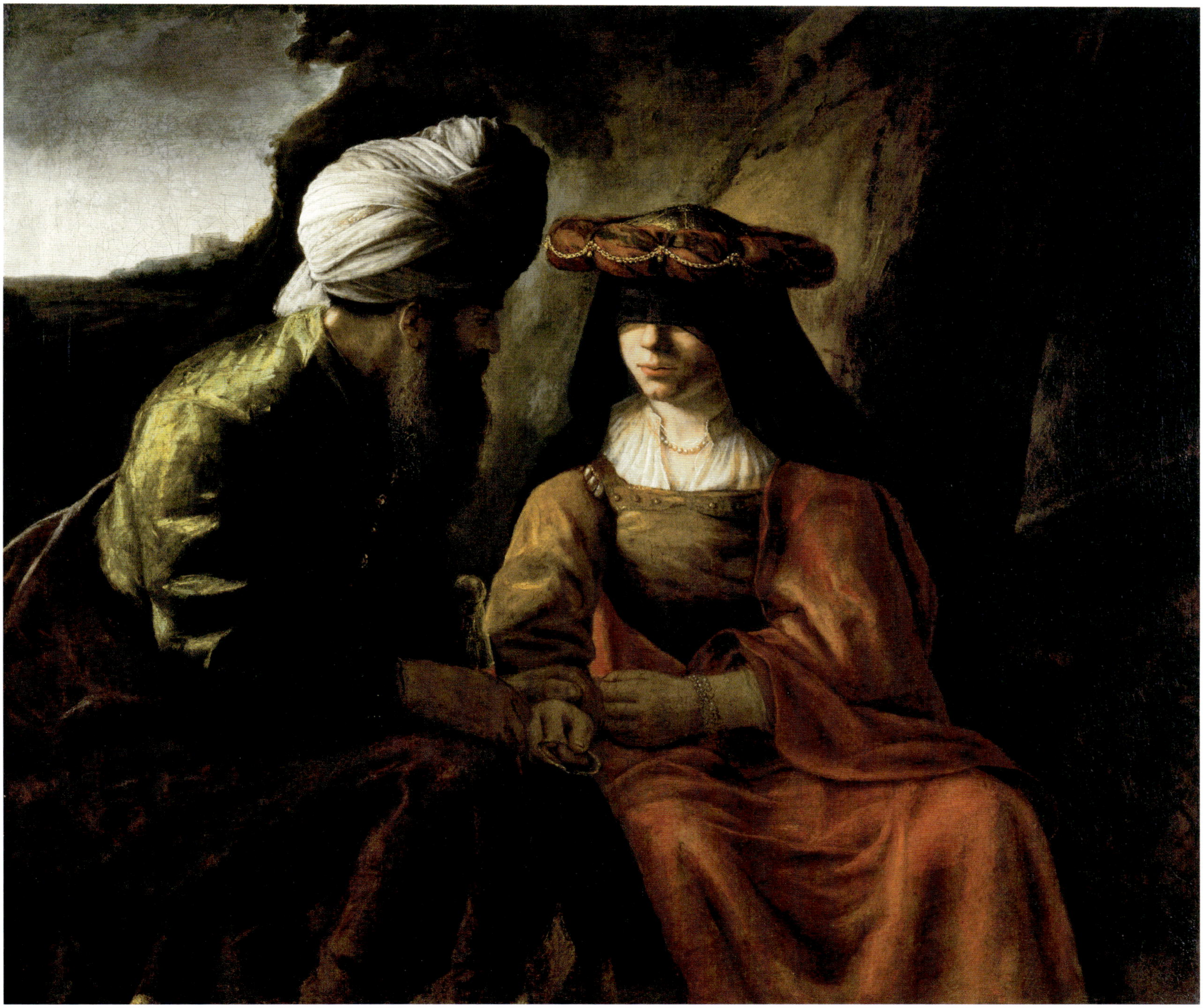

64 **Arent de Gelder** (1645–1727)

Scene from the Old Testament (Judah and Tamar?), ca. 1680–83

Oil on canvas, 97 x 129.5 cm
Inscribed (bottom right, fragmentary):
. . . [Gel]der f.
Inv. GG-817
Gemäldegalerie der Akademie der bildenden Künste, Vienna

Lit.
Cologne 1998, no. 10

It is unlikely that this painting, as generally assumed, is about the Old Testament story of Tamar (Genesis 38), the young widow who tries to assert the principle of levirate marriage law by tricking her father-in-law, Judah. Certain objects that Judah gives her as pledges when the two of them meet, and which he must therefore have on hand, play a key role in her scheme: a signet ring, a bracelet, and a staff. De Gelder included at least the latter in his other versions of the subject (private collection; Bader Collection, Agnes Etherington Art Centre, Queen's University, Kingston, Ontario;[1] The Leiden Collection, New York; Mauritshuis, The Hague). In his painting of the subject, Ferdinand Bol chose the moment when the last pledge, the ring, is handed over, while Tamar holds the other two objects in her hand (Museum of Fine Arts, Boston). In a version from the School of Rembrandt (cat. 63), the bracelet is just changing hands.

In Arent de Gelder's Vienna painting, however, not one of the pledges can be made out, and the rather rough grasp of the man does not relate to the mood of the other versions, which tends to oscillate between seduction and negotiation. Might the man seen here grabbing the woman so recklessly actually be intoxicated? In which case, the scene might be interpreted as one showing the drunken Lot with one of his daughters (Genesis 19:30–38), although the absence of the sister and of the wine vessels significantly undermines this notion.

The lady's outer garment, which looks both sumptuous and comfortable with its loose belt and the wide cut of its short sleeves, is based on the *japonse rokken* that had become a fashionable import to the Netherlands (see cat. 11–13, 15, 34). The material seems to be silk—as, incidentally, in Bols's *Tamar*—a fabric that had Eastern connotations, although it had been produced in Byzantium since late antiquity and in Italy since the high Middle Ages. Samuel van Hoogstraten recommended in 1678: "Do you wish to depict the Turkish Sultan in all his splendor? Then paint him in white satin or silver cloth [*wit Satijn of zilver laken*]."[2] BB

1 Cologne 1998, nos. 2, 9.
2 Samuel van Hoogstraten, *Inleyding tot de hooge schoole der schilderkonst . . .*, Rotterdam 1678, 229; cited in Cologne 1998, 89 with note 17.

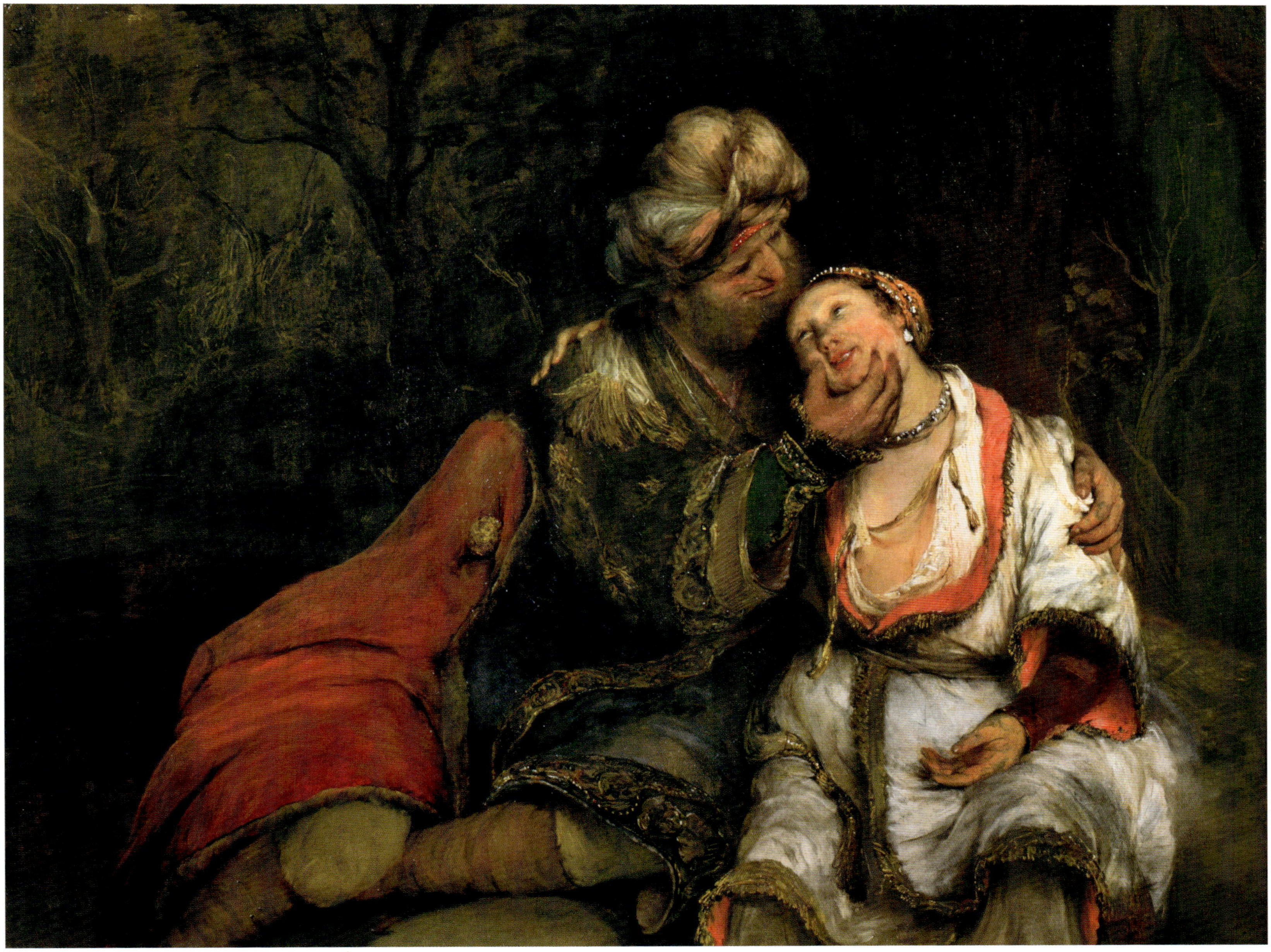

64

65 **Jan Victors** (1619–1677)

The Angel Taking Leave of Tobit and His Family, 1651

Oil on canvas, 163.3 x 206.5 cm
Inscribed center left on the slip of paper on the ground: Jan • Victoors f. / 1651
Inv. 1031
Bayerische Staatsgemäldesammlungen, Alte Pinakothek, Munich

Lit.
Munich 1983, 553–54

Jan Victors was first mentioned as a student of Rembrandt rather late, in a source from 1722. However, this information is generally considered to be accurate. He is supposed to have been in the master's workshop around 1630. There he learned at first hand how the enormous range of topics in the Old Testament, along with its rarely depicted incidents, could be effectively represented in art. Religious history became an important mainstay of Victors's work.

The painting does not show, as is common, Tobias's adventure-filled journey from Nineveh to Media in the company of the Archangel Raphael, who performs miracles with the innards of a fish; instead, it depicts the happy ending of the apocryphal book. Tobias has not only survived the dangers of the journey, but along the way he has also found a longed-for wife in Sarah, and is returned to his aged parents, Tobit and Hannah; he has also cured his father's blindness with the gall of the miraculous fish.

All of this was orchestrated by the angel, acting incognito, who at the end reveals his true identity, exhorts them in praise of the Lord, and ascends to heaven (Tobit 12:14–22). Victors illustrates these verses with the surprised newlyweds and the pious parents in the foreground; the bride's entourage, just arrived in Nineveh, can still be seen below the ascending angel.

With this subject, the artist established a direct connection to Rembrandt, who had depicted the scene in 1637 in a painting (Musée du Louvre, Paris) and in 1641 in an etching. Victors made use of both models in 1649 in his first picture of the subject, quoting them verbatim in some details (The J. Paul Getty Museum, Los Angeles). Two years later in the Munich painting, however, he emancipated himself from these sources. Here clouds hide the angel's legs, which are exposed in Rembrandt's version and in Victors's own painting in the Getty; further, the latter introduces a new element with his depiction of Sarah's entourage. The clothing of the newlyweds, which now has an Oriental look, is also an innovation. BB

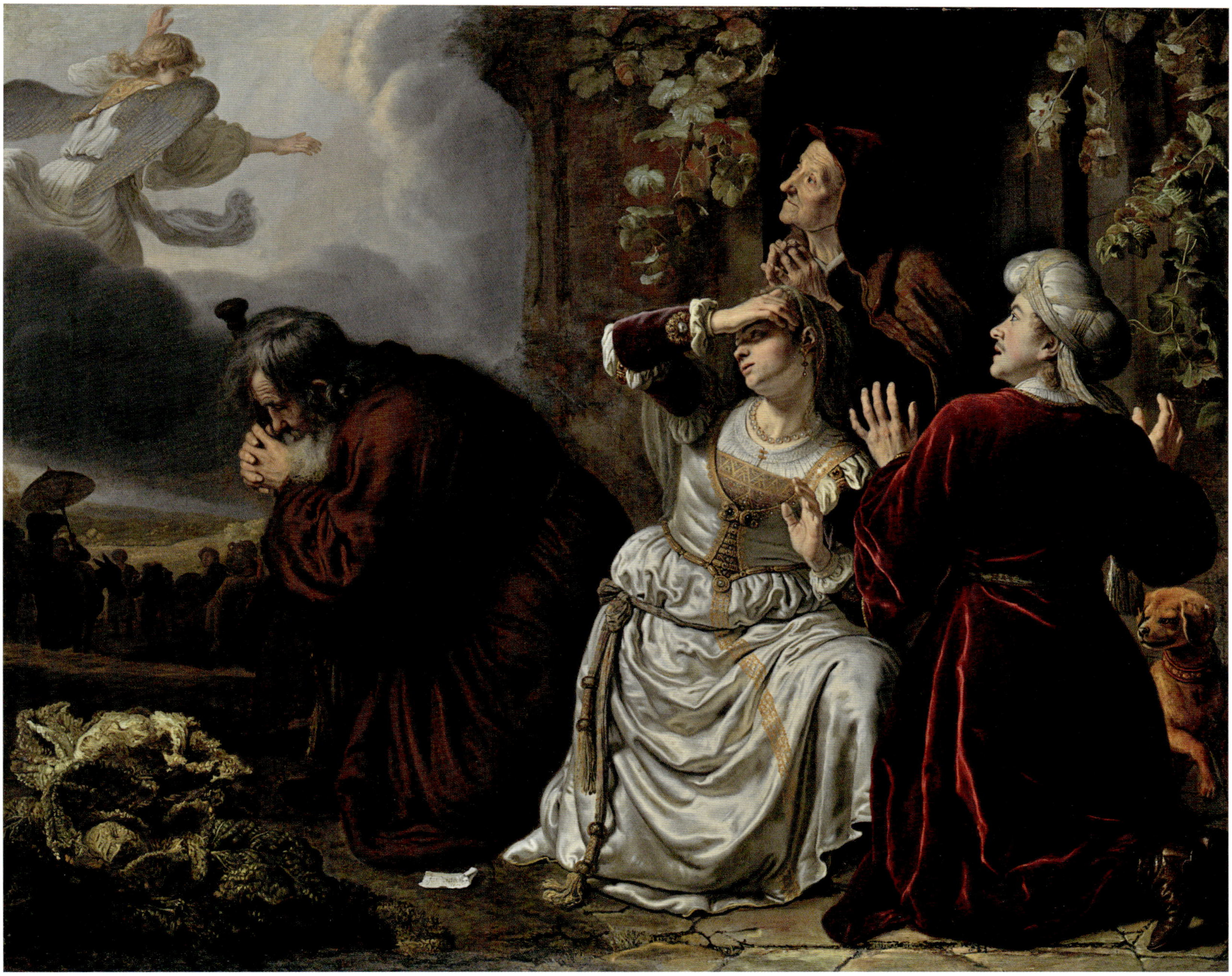

66 **Bartholomeus Breenbergh** (1598–1657)
Joseph Distributing Corn in Egypt, 1655

Oil on canvas, 110.5 x 90 cm
Inscribed bottom left: Bart.s Breenbergh.Fecit / A° 1655
Inv. 63.1
The Barber Institute of Fine Arts, Birmingham

Roethlisberger 1981, 1, 19, no. 231
London 2002, no. 11
Birmingham 2004
Sluijter 2015, 144, 146, fig. 95
Birmingham 2017, 59
Van der Molen 2017, 88–89.

In 1619 twenty-one-year-old Bartholomeus Breenbergh left for Rome, where he would spend more than ten years. Around 1630 he returned to Amsterdam, where he created paintings that pushed the boundaries of established genres and combined Italianate landscape painting, architectural capriccios, and mostly biblical history painting, in an inventive way. In the last years of his life, when his production of images noticeably declined, Breenbergh turned to more classical forms of Amsterdam history painting. Among these works *Joseph Distributing Corn in Egypt,* a very late painting, is reminiscent of the art of Pieter Lastman in the bold gestures of the figures, the magnificent costumes, and the construction of the architectural backdrop (see cat. 54–55).

The subject comes from the story of Joseph (Genesis 47:16–17); it relates how, in Egypt, Joseph has risen to become Pharaoh's steward and, according to his instructions, distributes grain that has been collected in storehouses during seven fruitful years to the buyers flocking in during the subsequent drought. Among them are Joseph's brothers, whose resentment led them to sell him as a boy, and who do not recognize him at first; later they will fall on their knees before him just as in his youth Joseph had foretold they would.

Although Breenbergh's pictorial language, with its light-flooded landscape, architectural backdrop, genre-like staffage figures, and bright colors, is very different from Rembrandt's painting style, he used comparable artistic methods to impart a sense of historical coherence to the events in ancient Egypt. These include the numerous turbans and magnificent Oriental costumes like those worn by Joseph, seen standing on a high platform at the upper right, and Pharaoh, who looks down from a terrace on the opposite side. They show characteristics that can also be found in Rembrandt's work. In addition, the camel on which a young man with a bright red cap is enthroned, and a number of Black figures in the crowd, provided Dutch viewers of the seventeenth century with some idea of the distant location.

Like most Netherlandish painters of his time, Breenbergh was not concerned with historical accuracy but rather with creating an atmospheric image, as demonstrated by the architectural view, resembling a stage set, and bathed in mild, southern sunlight (see cat. 26–28). Although an Egyptian obelisk rises up at the center of the scene, the relief on its base points to Rome, the source of the other motifs too. While the house fronts on the left incorporate generally antique-style forms, a fantasy city appears in the background, which combines motifs from ancient Roman monuments and is surmounted by a gigantic Pantheon. The granary behind Joseph was inspired by the Romanesque façade of the church of Santa Maria in Aracoeli. Breenbergh's Egypt thus lies less on the Nile than on the Tiber, where he had lived for a long time. The steep staircase construction on the right side is reminiscent of the spectacular composition by Jacopo Pontormo in *Joseph with Jacob in Egypt* from around 1518 (The National Gallery, London). The female figure in the left foreground is borrowed from a fresco by Guido Reni in San Gregorio Magno al Celio in Rome.

The picture, which recreates an existing painting dated 1654, is the only known second version of a work in Breenbergh's oeuvre. It might be connected to a series of scenes from the story of Joseph in the same format painted by other Amsterdam artists in 1655, which might have been inspired by a popular play by the poet Joost van den Vondel. GD

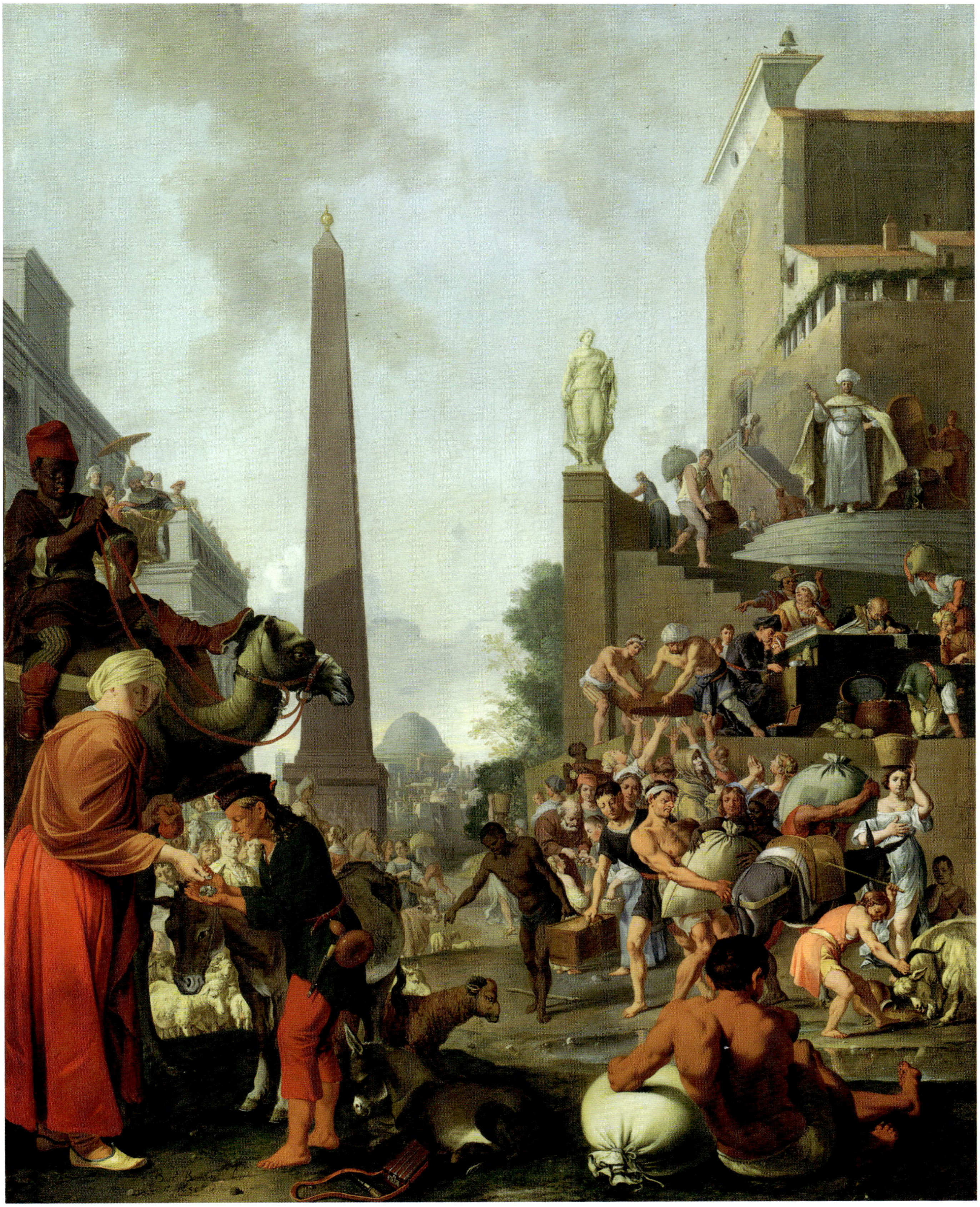

67 Salomon de Bray (1597–1664)
Samson Destroying the Temple of Dagon, 1659

Oil on oak panel, 65.2 x 51.1 cm
Inscribed on the fountain basin: D BrAY 1659
Inv. G 2009.14
Kunstmuseum Basel, purchased with funds from the Fonds Alte Meister

Lit.
Von Moltke 1938–39, no. 16
Brinkmann 2010

In addition to his signature and the date on the basin of the fountain, Salomon de Bray put the inscription “58 12/20 59 1/9” on the lower-left edge of the panel. This indicates that he began the painting on December 20, 1658, and completed it on January 9 of the following year, thus working on it for just under three weeks.

The subject is an Old Testament event in the city of Gaza: the death of Samson (Judges 16:21–31). The Jewish hero, blessed by Yahweh with superhuman strength, had fought all his life against the Philistines who ruled over the people of Israel. His lover, Delilah, elicited the secret of his strength from him—his hair should never be cut—and betrayed him to the Philistines, who stood ready while she cut off the curls of the sleeping Samson. Samson was overpowered, blinded (see fig. p. 15), and imprisoned. Many years later, the Philistines are celebrating a festival in honor of their god Dagon. A boy is sent out to fetch the blind prisoner, who is to perform music. In the meantime, however, Samson’s hair has grown back. He feels the supporting columns of the festival building, cracks them with the miraculous power he has regained, and once again causes the deaths of countless Philistines.

In contrast to most other artists, De Bray shows the moment immediately before the collapse of the building. The oblivious Philistines are celebrating on the upper floor of the building. The viewer can immediately relate to their ignorance—for we, too, must take a second look to make out Samson in the shadow of the arcades behind the already damaged columns. The harp on which he played lies on the ground; the boy who brought him here is fleeing.

De Bray’s vision of Gaza is a potpourri of styles: Italian palace architecture with columns in the Tuscan order is decorated with Oriental carpets, most often found outdoors like this in Venetian Renaissance paintings such as Antonello da Messina’s *Saint Sebastian* (Gemäldegalerie Alte Meister, Staatliche Kunstsammlungen, Dresden). Turbans and cone-shaped parasols, a common detail in Oriental scenes, give the celebrating Philistines a foreign veneer (see cat. 27). In one respect, however, the educated painter and poet excelled in the context of biblical philology and archaeology. Dagon was considered a fish god according to the interpretation of Saint Jerome, who believed the name derived from the Hebrew word *dag* (fish).[1] In contrast, in the first book of Samuel there is a description of an idol figure of Dagon as showing a head and hands (1 Samuel 5:4). De Bray solved the problem by crowning the fountain in the courtyard of the palace dedicated to Dagon with one of the tritons popular in the Baroque period. This fish-tailed hybrid from Greek mythology stands in here for the Levantine deity. BB

1 John F. Healey, “Dagon,” in *Dictionary of Deities and Demons in the Bible*, ed. Karel van der Toorn, Bob Becking, and Pieter W. van der Horst, Leiden 1999, 216–19.

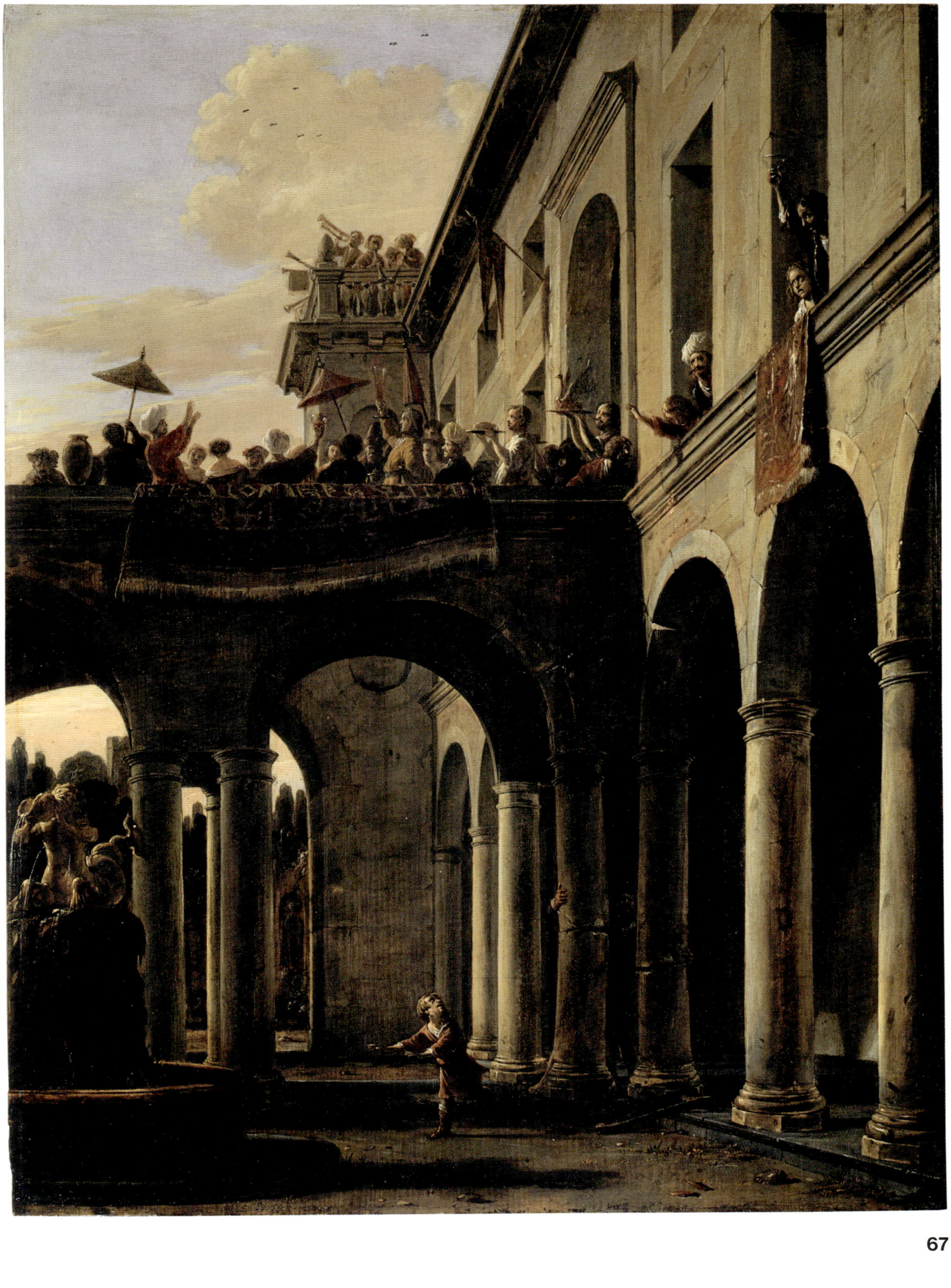

Light in the Temple: Rembrandt in Amsterdam and His Followers

In the 1630s Rembrandt and other painters often depicted biblical stories set in dimly lit interiors, be it the stable in Bethlehem or a temple. Exotic motifs such as turbans, robes, and swords were again used to lend authenticity to the scenes. Rather than being a magnificent fairy-tale backdrop, however, the Oriental setting envisioned in these paintings was usually a sacred site—the place where God's wisdom was revealed to the Israelites or where the miraculous events of Christian salvation unfolded. Rembrandt was able to demonstrate his deft command of light in the dark arches of the buildings, with beams of light reflected on metallic surfaces. As well as enhancing the impression of spatial recession and pictorial depth, they also emphasized the meaning of the work.[1]

The otherworldly atmosphere of these dark interior views contrasted starkly with the Reformed churches of the Calvinist Netherlands as painted by Hendrick van Vliet and Pieter Saenredam. Flooded with light, their white painted interiors were largely void of images of saints, retables, and other ornamentation. The central dogma of the Roman Catholic Church—the mystery of the Eucharist as the real presence of Christ—had no place there. By visualizing the mystical—while at the safe remove of far-away lands—Rembrandt and others were able to slake their clients' unabated natural desire to see or imagine miraculous wonders. And the degree of separation from the viewer's everyday environment would no doubt have further increased the sensual appeal of these paintings.

Placing the scenes in dark interiors allowed the artists to experiment with sophisticated contrasts of light and dark that heightened the sense of drama and underlined the meaning of the works. In the 1620s the Utrecht Caravaggisti around Gerrit van Honthorst and Dirck van Baburen introduced spectacular lighting effects to Netherlandish painting in their life-sized depictions of half-length figures; Rembrandt and others later incorporated these effects into their small-scale cabinet paintings of biblical themes.

Similar to the earlier history paintings (see "The Landscape of the Bible: Early Rembrandt and His Influences," pp. 200–227), a number of works from the 1630s also take up themes that center on the ability or failure to recognize a crisis situation. *Daniel and Cyrus before the Idol Bel* by Rembrandt (cat. 68) focuses on the strange events at the temple, while a dream has to be interpreted in *Daniel before Nebuchadnezzar* by Salomon Koninck (cat. 69), and in Rembrandt's *Samson Proposing the Riddle at the Wedding Feast* (cat. 73) a difficult question needs to be answered. The plot is revealed through a few telling gestures, while the psychological depth that permeates each scene is a source of dramatic tension. The same applies to the display of anger in *Samson Threatening His Father-in-Law* by Rembrandt (cat. 72) and the emotional intensity of *David and Jonathan*, also by Rembrandt (cat. 74).

Rembrandt staged *The Presentation in the Temple in the Dark Manner* (cat. 82), *The Circumcision of Christ* (cat. 78), and *The Woman Taken in Adultery* (cat. 77) within spectacular temples of which we only catch glimpses in the background. Mystical introspection dominates the paintings of the *Adoration of the Magi* by Rembrandt and Salomon Koninck (cat. 75–76). Completely absent in their works is the wealth of Oriental attributes common in seventeenth-century paintings of the same subject by Flemish workshops in the Catholic city of Antwerp. Instead of visually overwhelming viewers, the aim was to deeply move them in thought.

Among the Orientalizing paintings that Rembrandt drew on for inspiration were the works of his teacher Pieter Lastman. The monumental stained-glass window *Cyrus Restores the Treasures of the Temple* was designed by Lastman in 1611 for the Zuiderkerk in Amsterdam, and Thomas de Keyser reproduced the composition in an easel painting in 1660 (cat. 79). Rembrandt would have been familiar with the church window, which was close to where he lived. Around 1641 he incorporated the central element of Lastman's composition, namely the view of a domed building seen through a large archway, in his etching *The Triumph of Mordecai* (cat. 81), an episode from the Old Testament. Lastman's building was not even based on ancient architecture but was an adaptation of the dome of Saint Peter's, which he had seen on his travels through Italy. Rembrandt's inclusion of this pictorial invention shows how he creatively appropriated motifs from other artists, but also indicates that he was unconcerned with the issue of authenticity as long as the motif in question corresponded with what he and his contemporaries imagined the Orient to be. Such motifs were also used for ancient mythological subjects, as in the etching *Medea, or The Marriage of Jason and Creusa* (cat. 80). MPH

1 For more on this subject, cf., among others, Tümpel 1994, Bahre 2006, and Swan 2013.

68 **Rembrandt Harmensz. van Rijn** (1606–1669)

Daniel and Cyrus before the Idol Bel, 1633

Oil on panel, 23.5 x 30.2 cm
Inscribed bottom right on ledge of dais:
Rembrandt f •• 1633
Inv. 95.PB.15
The J. Paul Getty Museum, Los Angeles

Lit.
CRP, vol. 2, no. A 67; vol. 3, no. A 67; vol. 6, no. 102
Los Angeles 1997, no. 31
Frankfurt am Main 2003, no. 18
Woollett 2009, no. 5

The Persian king Cyrus asked his trusted friend, the Jewish prophet Daniel, why he did not venerate the idol of the god Bel as everyone else did. Daniel replied that he worshipped the living God, not a sculpture fashioned by humans out of bronze and clay. Cyrus objected that Bel was given quantities of meal, wine, and sheep every day as a sacrificial offering, which the idol consumed by the next morning, demonstrating that it must be a living entity. To prove this, the doors of the temple containing the idol were sealed overnight after the offerings had been brought in. But Bel's priests had built a secret entrance, which they used to carry off the victuals during the night. Consequently, on the following morning, the table of offerings was bare. However, before the temple was sealed and in the presence of the king, Daniel had had the floor strewn with ashes, which now bore traces of the footprints of the fraudulent priests, who were thereupon condemned to death. The prophet, meanwhile, was given leave by the king to destroy the sanctuary (Daniel 2:1–21).

Rembrandt depicts the beginning of the dispute between the prophet and the king. Cyrus indignantly points to the gleaming golden vessels that contain the offerings, while Daniel protests with an appropriate degree of deference. The matter in question, idolatry, was inevitably of interest to artists, and it is not clear whether Rembrandt himself takes sides here. If the ashes that were to settle the deadly dispute had already been scattered—they may be there at the ready in the urn standing between the king's feet and the table—the artist's signature etched prominently into the floor would be inscribed in them, akin to the telltale footprints in the biblical story and every bit as significant.

A shiny silver robe—perhaps made of silk—and a gold brocade cloak whose pattern is suggested but cannot be clearly determined lend an exotic air to the Persian king. His sumptuous turban with miniature crown is borrowed from the iconography of the Magi, as can be seen, for example, in the king at the center of the group in Abraham Janssens's *Adoration of the Magi*, painted in around 1616 (Koninklijk Museum voor Schone Kunsten, Antwerp). BB

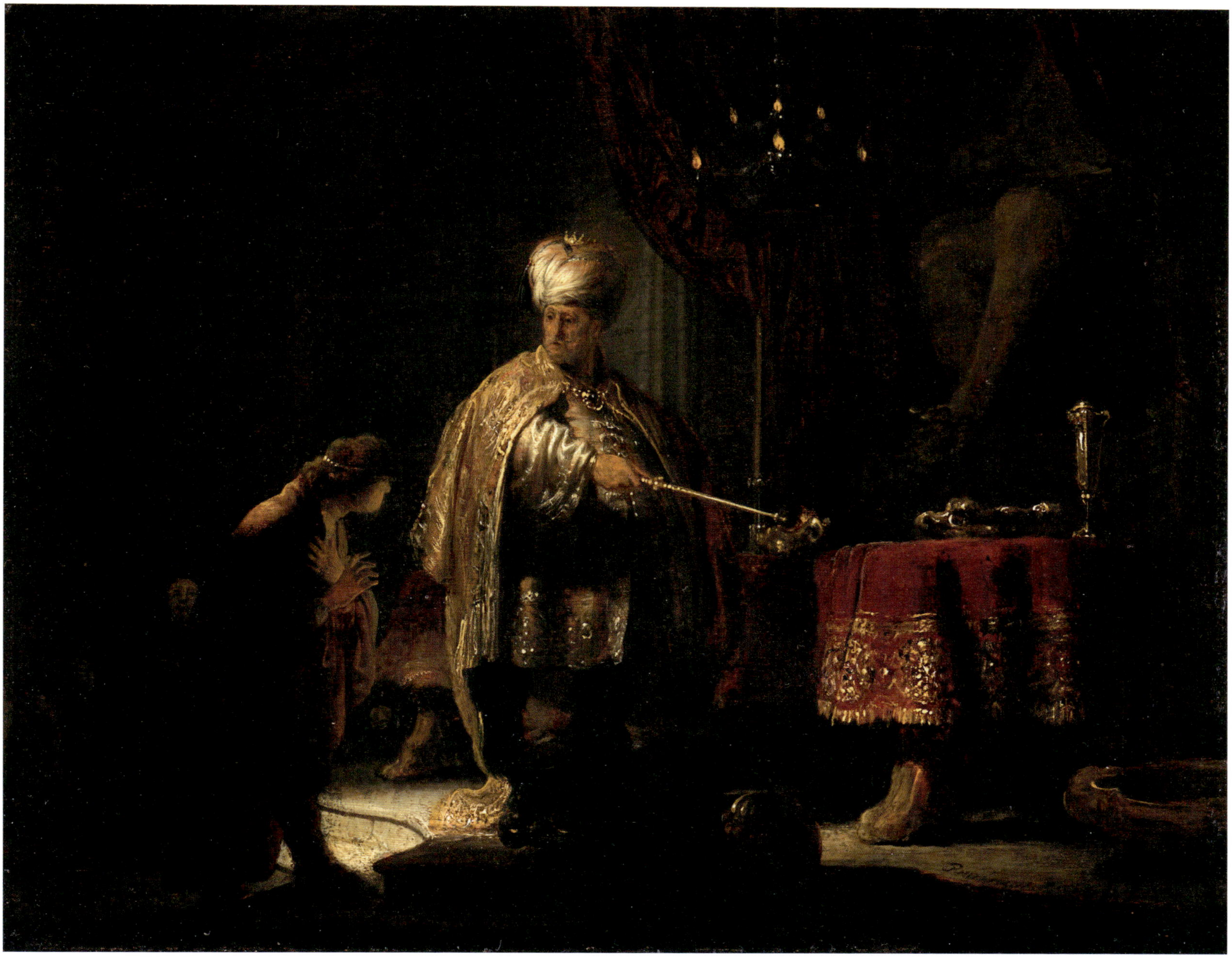

68

69 **Salomon Koninck** (1609–1656)

Daniel before Nebuchadnezzar, ca. 1630–56

Oil on canvas, 165 x 165 cm
Inv. NT 108892
Kedleston Hall, The Scarsdale Collection, acquired with the help of the National Heritage Memorial Fund and transferred to The National Trust in 1987

Lit.
Sluijter 2015, 202

After conquering Jerusalem and bringing the Jewish elite, including the prophet Daniel and three of his friends, to his court, the Babylonian king Nebuchadnezzar had a terrible dream, which he was unable to recollect, however, when he awoke. He called upon the wise men of his kingdom to divine his dream and interpret it. But only Daniel was able to achieve this impossible feat, aided by God. In a vision he saw the colossal statue dreamed of by the king, crafted in several different materials, which in the end was broken into pieces. Daniel interpreted this as a symbol of a declining series of world empires that are doomed to fall. Their disintegration goes hand in hand with the establishment of the kingdom of God; the dream is thus an injunction to convert (Daniel 2:1–45).

In Koninck's painting, the young prophet kneels reverently before the king and proceeds to count the four empires on his fingers.[1] Nebuchadnezzar is so mesmerized by what he hears that he half rises from his magnificent throne. The wise men and scribes of Babylon on either side of the throne are equally attentive to Daniel's explanation—the king has already condemned them to death should the riddle of the dream remain unsolved.

The fantastical two-story apse divided up by half pillars and alcoves, with statues occupying the upper level, constitutes a distinctive architectural backdrop to the throne room in the Babylonian king's palace. The same display of splendor is evident in the throne itself and its style of construction, crowned with an enormous gold-framed mirror hung in front of a green velvet arras. Nebuchadnezzar's costume is also luxuriant, with the extravagantly long aigrette plume of his turban catching the eye (see cat. 2). Writing in 1678, Samuel van Hoogstraten highlighted this particular accessory in the regalia of the Oriental potentate: "Do you wish to portray the Turkish sultan in all his magnificence? . . . Then set the lofty turban with painted feathers on his head."[2] BB

1 This is an argument against Sluijter's interpretation of the painting as *Joseph Interpreting Pharaoh's Dream*.
2 Samuel van Hoogstraten, *Inleyding tot de hooge schoole der schilderkonst*, Rotterdam 1678, 229; cited in Cologne 1998, 89, note 17; translated here by Simon Cowper.

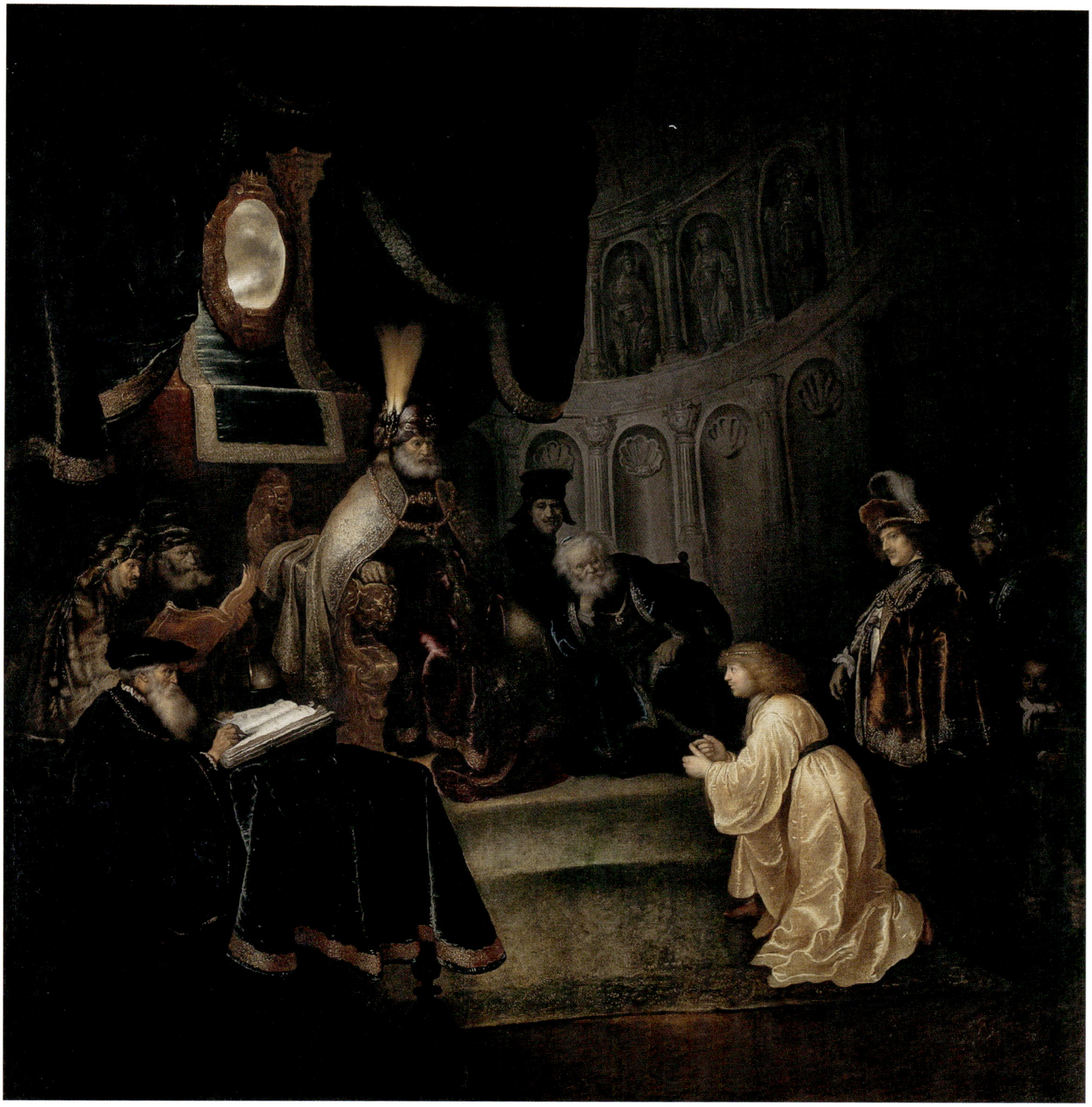

70 **Rembrandt Harmensz. van Rijn** (1606–1669)
The Tribute Money, ca. 1634

71 **Jan Gillisz. van Vliet** (ca. 1600/10–1668) and
Rembrandt Harmensz. van Rijn (1606–1669)
Christ before Pilate: Ecce Homo, 1636

70
Etching, 7.4 x 10.4 cm
1st state (of 3)
Inv. 2007.185
Kunstmuseum Basel, Kupferstichkabinett,
Donation Eberhard W. Kornfeld, Bern

Lit.
B 68 (2/2)
NH 138 (1/3)
Basel 2005, no. 25
Amsterdam 2019, 510–11
Schatborn/Hinterding 2019, no. R 32

71
Etching, with touches in drypoint,
55.2 x 44.5 cm
4th state (of 5)
Inscribed on plate at bottom left of center:
Rembrandt f. 1636 cvm privile[gio]
Inv. 2007.188
Kunstmuseum Basel, Kupferstichkabinett,
Donation Eberhard W. Kornfeld, Bern

Lit.
B 77 (4/5)
NH 155 (4/5)
Boston 2003, 33, no. 49
Basel 2005, no. 28
Amsterdam 2019, 530–31
Schatborn/Hinterding 2019, no. R 37
Schwartz 2019

The Tribute Money is a title given to depictions of an incident that occurred when Jesus returned to the Temple in Jerusalem (Mark 12:13–17). When bystanders asked him how his message related to the obligation to pay taxes, he asked them to bring him a coin. Pointing to the image and name of the emperor that it bore, he said, "Render to Caesar the things that are Caesar's, and to God the things that are God's." The Pharisees and Temple servants in the etching wear turbans and long cloaks. This garb brings to mind the warning uttered by the Savior in the very same chapter of the Gospels: "Beware of the scribes, which love to go in long clothing" (Mark 12:38).

In *The Tribute Money* we see only a bare hint of the architecture of the Second Temple, while in the *Ecce Homo* Rembrandt goes all out to reconstruct what the Jerusalem headquarters of Pontius Pilate might have looked like. He pictures it as a large semicircle with recesses and passageways, girting a pillar crowned by the bust of an emperor with a laurel wreath. The emperor of the day was Tiberius, who reigned from the year 14 to 37, but the face on the bust, with its impressive moustache, is pure fantasy.[1]

This etching had an unusual genesis. In 1634 Rembrandt started on the composition with an oil sketch (The National Gallery, London), giving it the same dimensions as those intended for the print. That was produced in the following year by Jan Gillisz. van Vliet, who left a blank space for the main group of Jews in heated discussion with the ruler. After going over the results with Rembrandt, who might have marked some of the areas needing corrections with oil paint on a proof (The British Museum, London), van Vliet and Rembrandt finished the print, with minor corrections by the latter, who also added his signature and the date 1636.

Filling in the gap that was still left open in 1635, Rembrandt made a point of indicating the individual features of the four figures disputing with Pilate. The two foremost of them are given the exotic appearance of Temple priests, with clothing suggestive of the tallit, a shawl worn by Jewish men at prayer. The markings on the headdress of the foremost figures are apparently intended to look like Hebrew. BB

1 Evidently Rembrandt was not yet in the possession of the numerous representations, probably busts, of Roman emperors listed in the inventory of his insolvent estate in 1656, see Amsterdam 1999a, appendix 2, 149, nos. 147, 149 (Tiberius), 151, 152, 156, 160, 170–73.

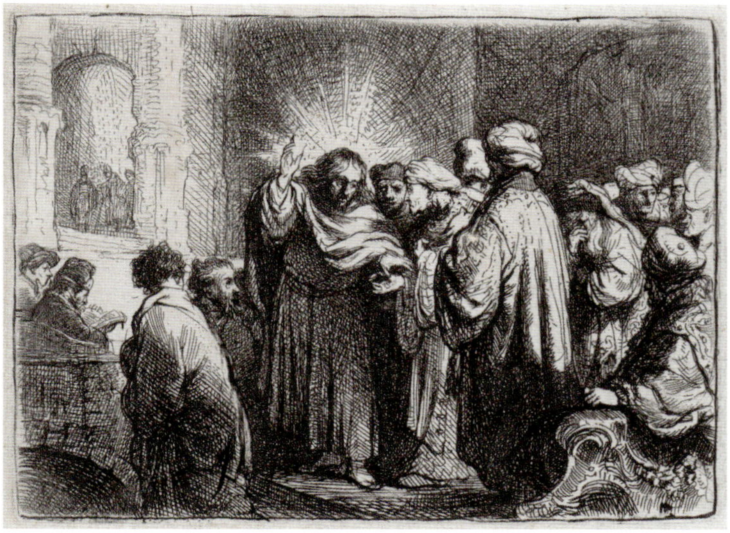

70

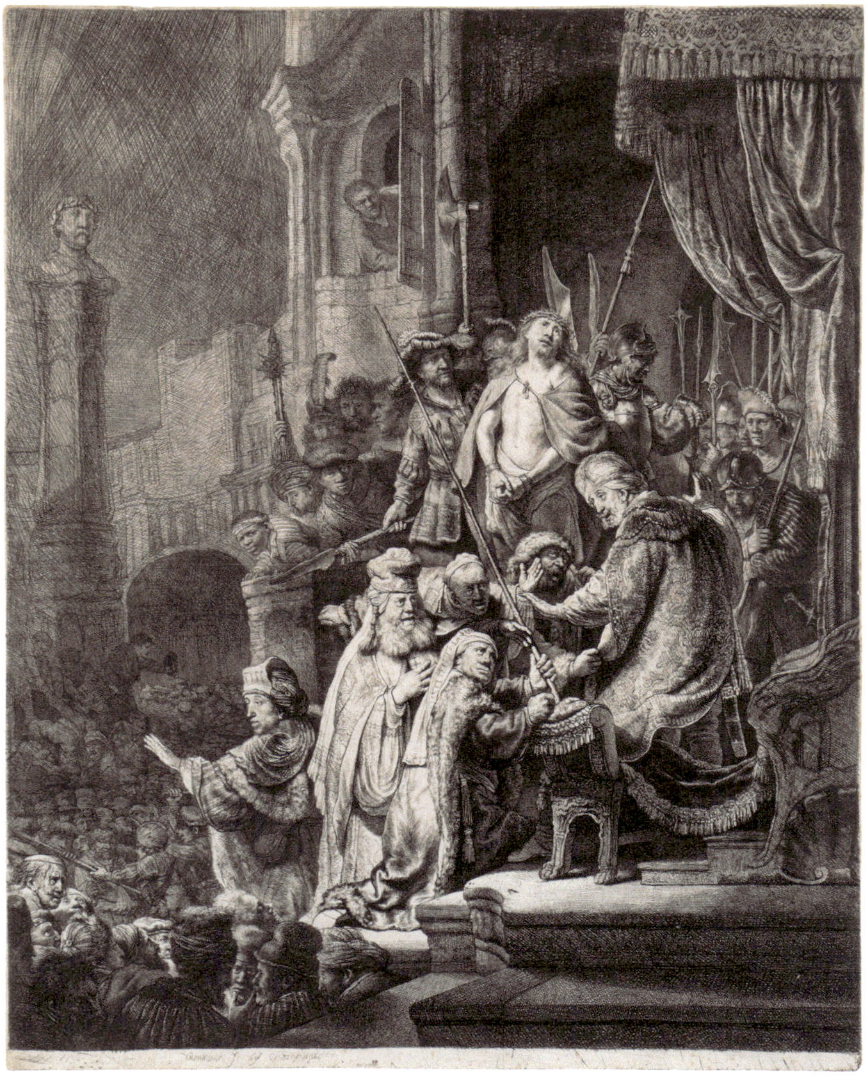

71

72 **Rembrandt Harmensz. van Rijn** (1606–1669) and workshop

Samson Threatening His Father-in-Law, ca. 1635

Oil on canvas, 162.3 x 174.8 cm
Natan Saban Collection, Israel

Lit.
CRP, vol. 3, no. A 109, copy no. 1; vol. 6, 231
Schwartz 1987, 177
Berlin 2006, 117–18; no. 21

In the Old Testament scene, which shows an enraged Samson face to face with his father-in-law (Judges 15:1–3), Rembrandt has costumed the hero standing in the center of the picture with a lavish outfit in an Oriental style. The gold of his tunic glints in the light shining down from above. The artist has placed a band of cloth around Samson's waist, and hanging from it at his side is a short, curved sword that calls to mind an Arab *saif*. His long hair, the source of his strength, is adorned with a bejeweled frontlet. Of the two young Black pages attending him, the one in front is wearing a bright red beret with a white ostrich feather, providing a striking dash of color. Unlike the young goat in the foreground on the left in the painting, the two attendants are not mentioned in the biblical text. Rembrandt uses them to give an exotic feel to the scene, which plays out in front of an architectural backdrop whose details cannot be precisely determined. In a number of his renderings of biblical stories, such as the etching *Christ before Pilate: Ecco Homo* from 1636 (cat. 71), Rembrandt integrated Black figures who were extraneous to the plot; he probably supposed that Black people lived in Palestine too.[1] At the same time, the pages are a token of Samson's power—a formula that Wollebrand Geleynsz. de Jongh used in 1674 in his portrait (cat. 25) as a metaphor drawn from reality.

After the wedding feast at which he had set the Philistines his riddle—an episode also painted by Rembrandt in Oriental style (cat. 73)—Samson wishes to visit his wife and bring her a kid goat. But his father-in-law refuses him entry to the house, which is secured here with a strong, ironbound door, and tells him that he has given his daughter to another man. In the book of Judges, Samson gives notice of the vengeance he will wreak in a few brief words (Judges 15:3). Rembrandt, by contrast, shows him here with his fist theatrically raised. His execution of this seldom painted scene can also be regarded as a "pathos formula" for depicting anger: an etching by Cornelis Massys—engraved in 1549 and thus dating from almost a century earlier—shows all the elements of the story without expressing any of the emotional drama.

The painting is considered to be a workshop copy, presumably carried out with Rembrandt's involvement. There is a signed autograph version of it dating from 1635 (Gemäldegalerie, Staatliche Museen zu Berlin). It is of approximately the same height but around forty centimeters narrower, and the goat, which is key to identifying the subject matter, is not included. Technical studies of the two canvases concluded not only that the Berlin version was not, for instance, cut down at a later date but also that the enlarged version of the copy was carried out later, although still in Rembrandt's studio. The studies also showed that the copy and the expanded version were worked on by different people. On the basis of this, it has been assumed that Rembrandt wanted to experiment with a different composition after completing the picture. Accordingly, the portrait format of the Berlin work was turned into an almost square painting, and the focus on the two main figures with their animated dialogue and expressive gestures—Samson's threatening fist contrasts with the defensiveness evident in his father-in-law's hand movement—becomes an embellished narrative composition that not only made space for the goat but also gave more prominence to the two Black pages. MPH

1 See De Witt 2020, 97.

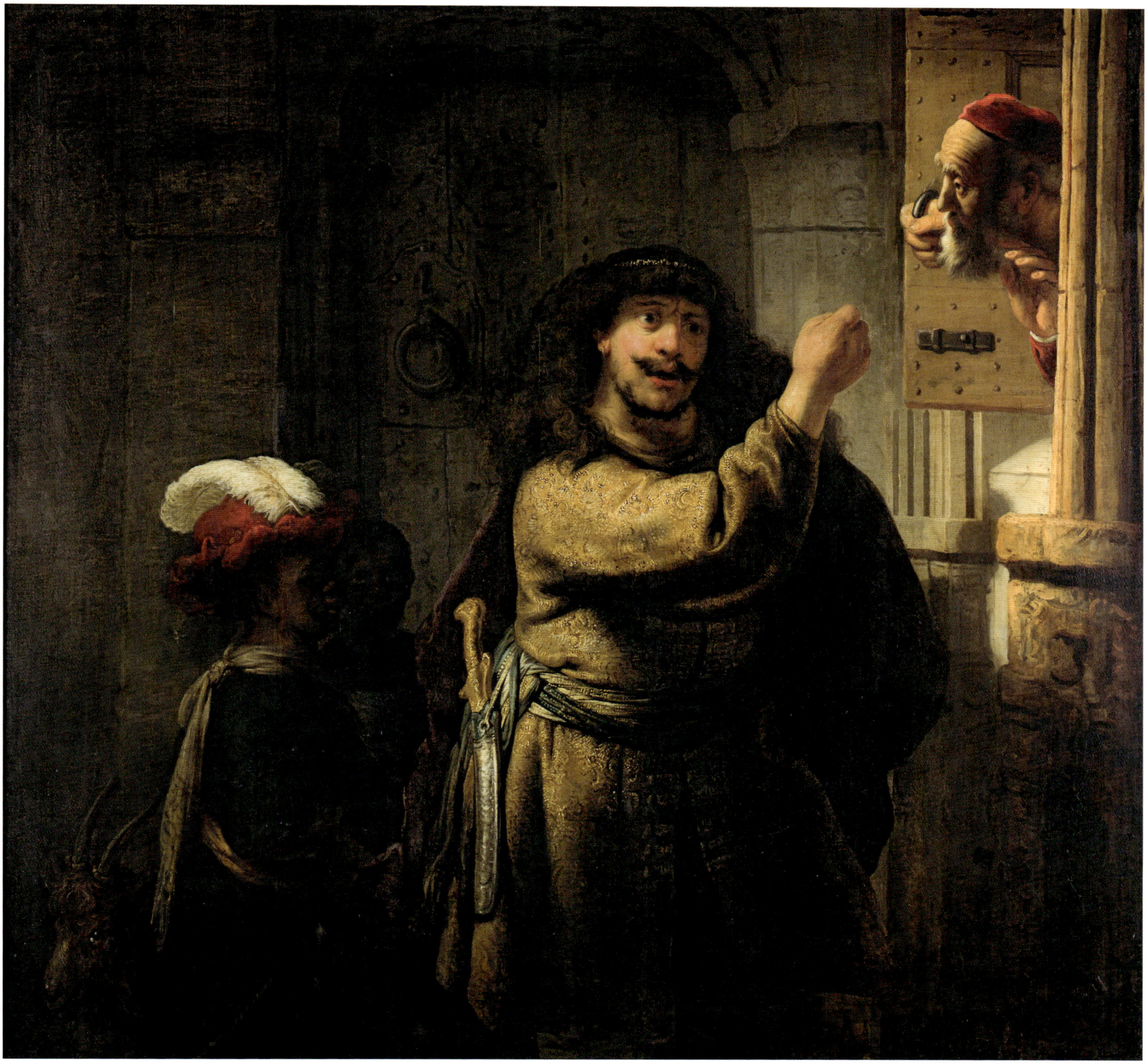

72

73 **Rembrandt Harmensz. van Rijn** (1606–1669)

Samson Proposing the Riddle at the Wedding Feast, 1638

Oil on canvas, 126 x 175 cm
Inscribed bottom center: Rembrandt. F. 1638
Gal. no. 1560
Gemäldegalerie Alte Meister,
Staatliche Kunstsammlungen Dresden
(Potsdam only)

Lit.
CRP, vol. 3, no. A 123; vol. 6, no. 160
Slatkes 1983b, 13–58
Schwartz 1987, 178–80
Golahny 2003, 35, 167, 169, 220–21; pl. 5
Berlin 2006, 38, fig. p. 36; no. 24
Schwartz 2006, 110–11
Seifert 2009
Schwartz 2014, 54–55, fig. 1.10b
Sluijter 2015, 64–65, fig. p. 62

Rembrandt's contemporaries considered the Oriental staging of his biblical histories to have a high degree of authenticity. Such were the sentiments, at least, of Leiden painter Philips Angel with regard to *Samson Proposing the Riddle at His Wedding Feast,* which he praised in a lecture in 1641 for its apt presentation of a historical theme based soundly on the sources (cat. 44). Angel singled out the attitude of the figures reclining around the banquet table as well as Samson's long hair, which accorded with the biblical injunction against shaving his head. In his view, Rembrandt also used the exuberance of the scene to focus attention on the difference between this and a Dutch wedding celebration. However, as Angel had as little direct experience of the Orient as Rembrandt himself,[1] his praises merely imply that Rembrandt was drawing on stereotypes that had already established themselves in the Dutch imagination. These included the recumbent posture at table, because, in Angel's words, "the ancients used small beds, which they lay upon, and did not sit at table as we do, but reclined on one elbow, as is still customary in those countries under the Turks."[2]

In his lecture *Lof der schilder-konst* (Praise of the Art of Painting), Angel urged artists to occupy themselves "by diligently scouring the musty old books" in order to be able to paint historical stories in the proper way. For him, the naturalness of Rembrandt's depiction is the product of careful reading and reflection. The episode is only accorded a brief description in the Old Testament book of Judges and by Flavius Josephus in his *Antiquities of the Jews*—a copy of which was in Rembrandt's possession. However, no mention is made there of a reclining posture at table. Samson married a Philistine woman. At the wedding, according to Josephus, "as they were drinking merrily and playing . . . as was usual at such times,"[3] Samson posed a riddle to the Philistines. After the bride had revealed the solution, he slew thirty Philistines. The Jewish hero is one of the Old Testament's more ambiguous figures, combining sagacity and violence, strength and weakness. The moral of this episode is a warning against indulgence, which here consisted in Samson submitting to his wife's entreaties to reveal the answer to the riddle.

Rembrandt devoted several canvases to the story of Samson, including *Samson Threatening His Father-in-Law* (cat. 72). His choice of Samson's riddle as his subject was a novel one, as he was the first to depict this scene. He drew inspiration from Leonardo's *Last Supper* (Santa Maria delle Grazie, Milan), which he knew from an engraving. An indirect model for the bride beneath the baldachin can be found in an etching by Jan Wierix after Pieter van der Borcht, printed in a 1571 breviary. Rembrandt may also have been familiar with the wedding picture that had been painted two years earlier in Utrecht by an artist who signed "J. Hasselt" (cat. 4). None of these works can lay claim to a sense of authenticity in the depiction of an Oriental atmosphere.

By contrast, Rembrandt most likely had no knowledge of a drawing by the Flemish artist Jan van der Straet, called Stradanus (1523–1605), who lived in Florence. *Abishai Bringing Water to David from the Well at the Gate of Bethlehem* (1595–99, Albertina, Vienna) shows the king lying on a *klini* or couch. Van der Straet added the inscription "convivio di ansuero alla Anticha" (the Banquet of Ahasuerus in the antique style) to a preliminary drawing (Cooper Hewitt, Smithsonian Design Museum, New York). The idea that festive meals were eaten lying down in the Orient was a cliché that was prevalent in Europe prior to Rembrandt's time. MPH

1 It was only later, from 1651 to 1656, that Angel is said to have taken up residence in Isfahan as court painter to Shah Abbas II.

2 Philips Angel, "Praise of Painting," trans. Michael Hoyle, *Simiolus: Netherlands Quarterly for the History of Art* 24, no. 2/3 (1996): 246. Originally published as *Lof der schilder-konst,* Leiden, 1642.

3 Flavius Josephus, *The Antiquities of the Jews*, trans. William Whiston, Project Gutenberg, 2009, book 5, chapter 8, paragraph 6.

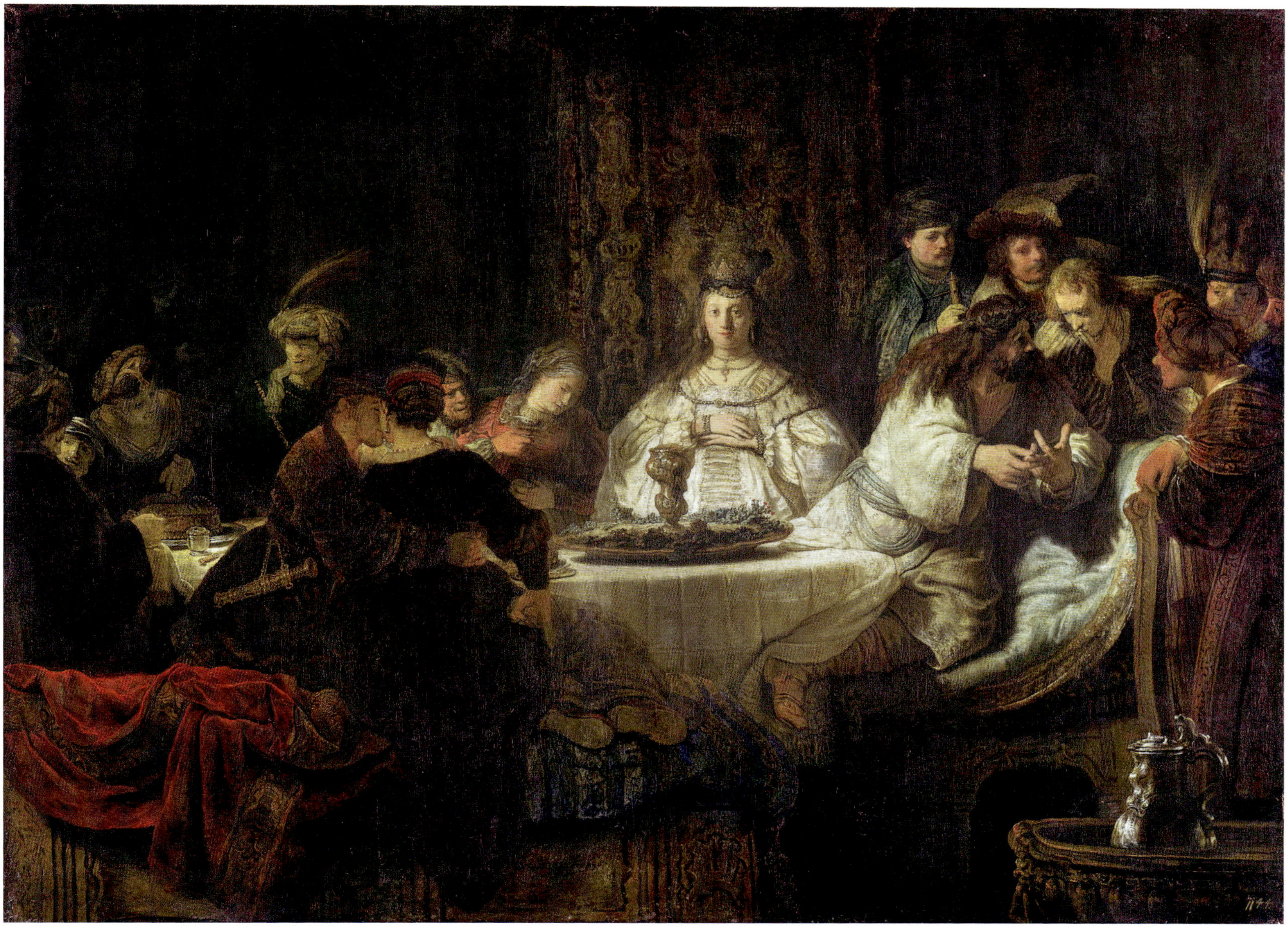

74 **Rembrandt Harmensz. van Rijn** (1606–1669)
David and Jonathan, 1642

Oil on panel, 73 x 61 cm
Inscribed bottom center: Rembrandt: f 1642
Inv. GZ-713
The State Hermitage Museum, St. Petersburg
(Potsdam only)

Lit.
CRP, vol. 3, no. C 84; vol. 5, 220–21;
vol. 6, no. 188
Schwartz 1985b
Schwartz 1987, 224–25
Perlove/Silver 2009, 118–20
Sluijter 2015, 65, 67, fig. p. 69
Burnet 2018

Two men stand close to one another as if on a theatrical stage; one has his face buried against the other man's chest. The latter, evidently the elder of the two, embraces the younger man tenderly. The plumed turban and rich Oriental costuming reveal the scene to be an enactment of a biblical story. This is also suggested by the city in the background, above which towers a large temple, recalling the Dome of the Rock in Jerusalem. The action can thus be placed in the Holy Land, without certainty, however, about which story from the Bible is being depicted. The most plausible subject is an episode from the book of Samuel in which the bosom friends Jonathan and David must bid farewell to one another (1 Samuel 20:41–42; see cat. 57). The attitude of the two figures expresses pain and sorrow, and their foreground placement focuses on the emotional drama of the event.

The scene has been variously identified, with suggestions ranging from the Return of the Prodigal Son (Luke 15:11–32), which Rembrandt painted in 1666–69 (State Hermitage Museum, St. Petersburg), to Jacob's Reconciliation with Esau (Genesis 33:3–4) or David's with Absalom (2 Samuel 14:33), to a depiction of David and Mephibosheth, an episode from the second book of Samuel. This final option is made more attractive by the fact that it ties in with a tragedy by Joost van den Vondel, one of the most important Dutch writers in Rembrandt's time. On April 8, 1641, in the year before the picture was painted, the play *Gebroeders* (Brothers) was premiered at Amsterdam's municipal theater, the Stadsschouwburg. The closing scene describes how Mephibosheth, his eyes full of tears, thanks King David for saving his life. While this reading would explain the difference in age between the two protagonists—as the son of Jonathan, who is the same age as David, Mephibosheth would have to have been considerably younger—it raises other questions: why would Mephibosheth, who had been lame in both feet since childhood, be carrying a large sword with him, and what need does he have of spurs when he is riding a donkey? The stonelike form at left in the foreground might, in fact, relate to a stage direction noted down by Van den Vondel for the performance, although it might also be the "stone Ezel" (1 Samuel 20:19) where Jonathan and David agreed to meet. Likewise, the sword that the younger man has at his side is mentioned in the book of Samuel—David received it as a gift from Jonathan along with his costly garments (1 Samuel 18:4). The spurs might betoken his imminent departure.

The great intimacy evident in the scene suggests a close attachment between the two men. The book of Samuel records that Jonathan loved David "as his own soul" (1 Samuel 18:3), and later, after Jonathan's death, David says, "Very pleasant hast thou been unto me: thy love to me was wonderful, passing the love of women" (2 Samuel 1:26). The forced leave-taking, made necessary by the murderous intentions of Jonathan's father, King Saul, shook them both: ". . . they kissed one another, and wept with one another, until David exceeded" (1 Samuel 20:41). The varying intensity of their grief can be seen in the postures of the two figures.

If Rembrandt's depiction were of David and Jonathan, the obvious difference in their ages, which is evident in the painting and does not tally with the biblical narrative, would remain a mystery. However, at the time, Rembrandt would have had an acute personal connection to this theme, which demonstrates the pain of loss and the forced separation of two lovers: on June 14, 1642, the year with which he dated the painting, his wife Saskia died—an event that shook him to the core. MPH

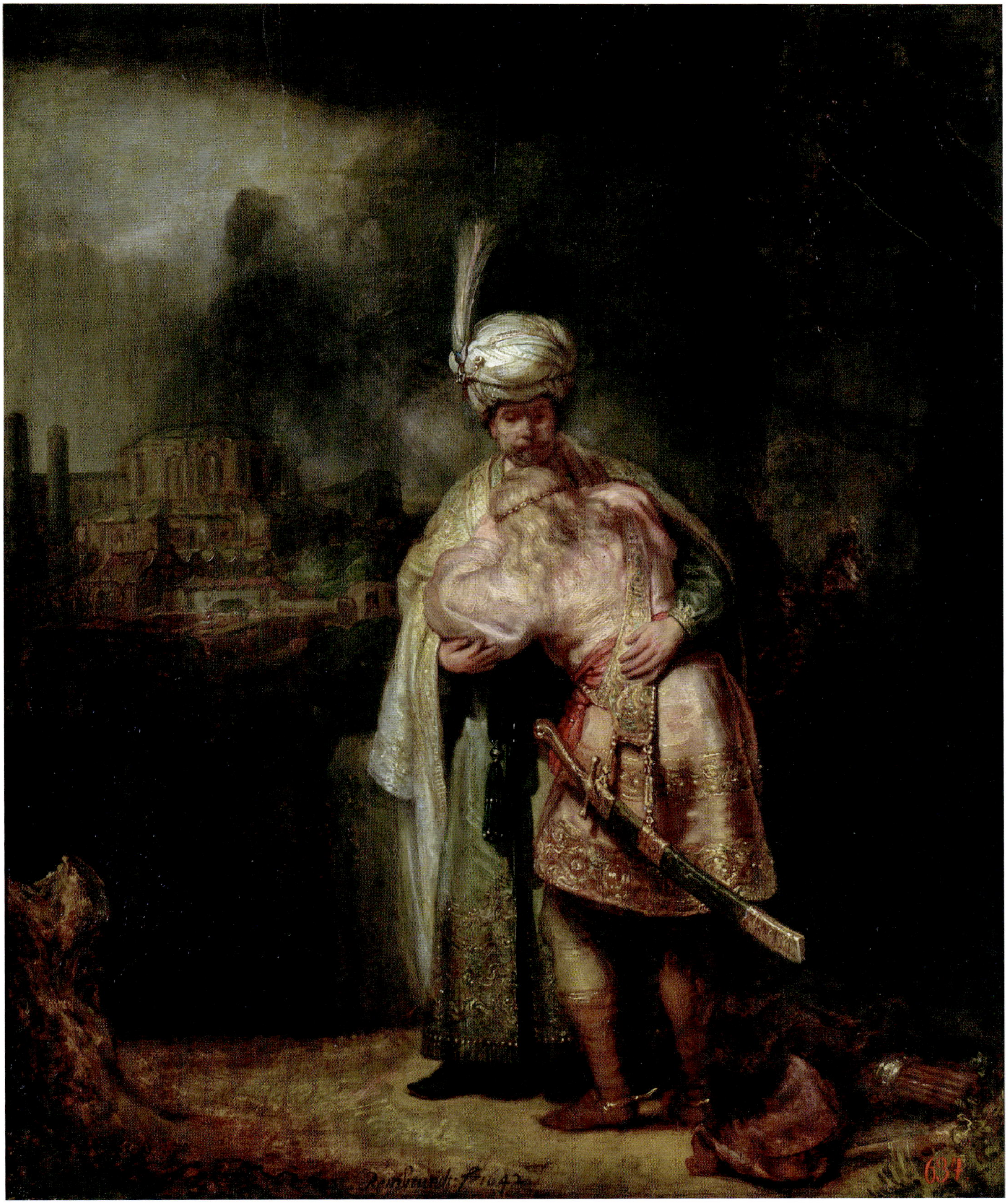

74

75 **Rembrandt Harmensz. van Rijn** (1606–1669)
Adoration of the Magi, ca. 1633

76 **Salomon Koninck** (1609–1656)
The Adoration of the Magi, ca. 1644–54

75
Oil on paper, pasted on canvas,
44.8 x 39.1 cm
Inv. GZ-7765
The State Hermitage Museum, St. Petersburg

Lit.
CRP, vol. 2, no. C 46; vol. 6, no. 109
Sluijter 2015, 64, fig. p. 61

76
Oil on canvas, 81 x 66 cm
Inv. 36
Mauritshuis, The Hague

Lit.
CRP, vol. 2, under no. C 46
Duyvené de Wit-Klinkhamer 1966, 89
Sumowski 1983–94, vol. 3, no. 1085
The Hague 1993, no. 19

No biblical subject lends itself better than the *Adoration of the Magi* for painting a scene featuring Oriental motifs. As is plainly stated in the Gospel according to Saint Matthew, the Three Wise Men came "from the East" (Matthew 2:1). Turbans, camels, and a king with dark skin had cropped up regularly in this scene since the sixteenth century. Peter Paul Rubens, for example, depicted the splendor and abundance of the Orient as he imagined it in his monumental *Adoration of the Magi* of 1609 (Museo Nacional del Prado, Madrid). Rembrandt and Koninck took a different approach. While they, too, used Oriental accoutrements, they set the story in a mysterious semidarkness in which mother and child are illuminated in a radiant light from an unknown source. The mystical mood conjures up an image of the Orient as a place of divine salvation. The palette of warm brown tones and the lighting lend the scene an intimate quality, which comes across even in the small format of their paintings.

Rembrandt placed the simply clad Mother of God with the Christ child on a pile of straw in the foreground on the right. Beside them, the oldest of the kings is kneeling in an attitude of worship. He has removed his turban and laid it on the ground. This is the group on which the beam of light is shining. Outside of this, in deep shadow on the left edge of the picture, stands the second king. On his head he wears a decorated turban, and he carries a sword with a curved blade, which could be an Ottoman saber. While this arrangement corresponds with the traditional composition of paintings depicting this subject, the third king has adopted a rather unusual pose. Magnificently dressed, he is standing on a platform, his right hand leaning on a staff, his left extended in the direction of mother and child as if in a gesture of blessing. This imposing figure is reminiscent of Rembrandt's *Man in Oriental Costume (The Noble Slav)* of 1632, painted around the same time (fig. p. 63). A servant is holding a parasol over this king—a customary emblem in seventeenth-century paintings referring to the Orient (see cat. 27), but rather at odds with the atmosphere of this painting, for it conjures up an image of a powerful Oriental potentate. The king's grand gesture and dominant position form a contrast to the intimacy of the scene of worship in the foreground.

Other exotic features include the enraptured priest with the incense vessel—the resin for the incense, which was no longer used in Protestant churches in the Netherlands, came from the Middle East—and the camel in the background. Camels were occasionally seen in Amsterdam (see cat. 17), and Rembrandt also used them in his paintings of Bible stories such as *John the Baptist Preaching* from ca. 1634 (Gemäldegalerie, Staatliche Museen zu Berlin) and in the print *Christ Healing the Sick,* known as *"The Hundred Guilder Print,"* from 1649.

There is one Oriental element that Rembrandt left out, however, even though this had become established in art-historical tradition, namely, the portrayal of one of the kings as Black, as, for example, in Hans Memling's *Adoration of the Magi* painted around 1470–72, or Hieronymus Bosch's late fifteenth-century depiction (both Museo Nacional del Prado, Madrid). Whereas in *Samson Threatening His Father-in-Law* (cat. 72) Rembrandt gives his main protagonist two Black pages—even though there is no mention of this in the Bible nor does their presence add anything to the narrative—in the present painting none of the three kings is depicted as Black. And indeed, in the chiaroscuro of the painting a Black figure would have been difficult to make out.

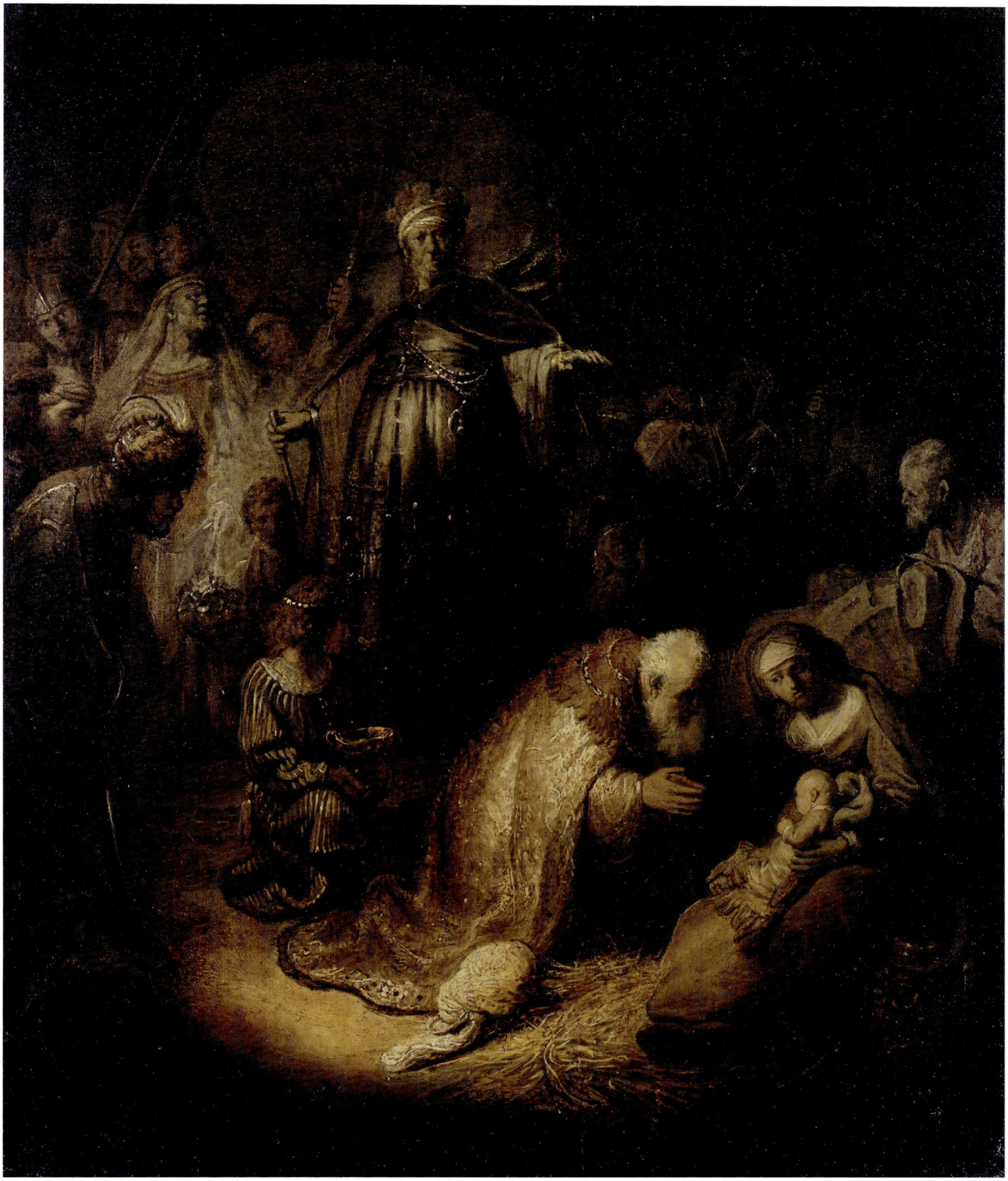

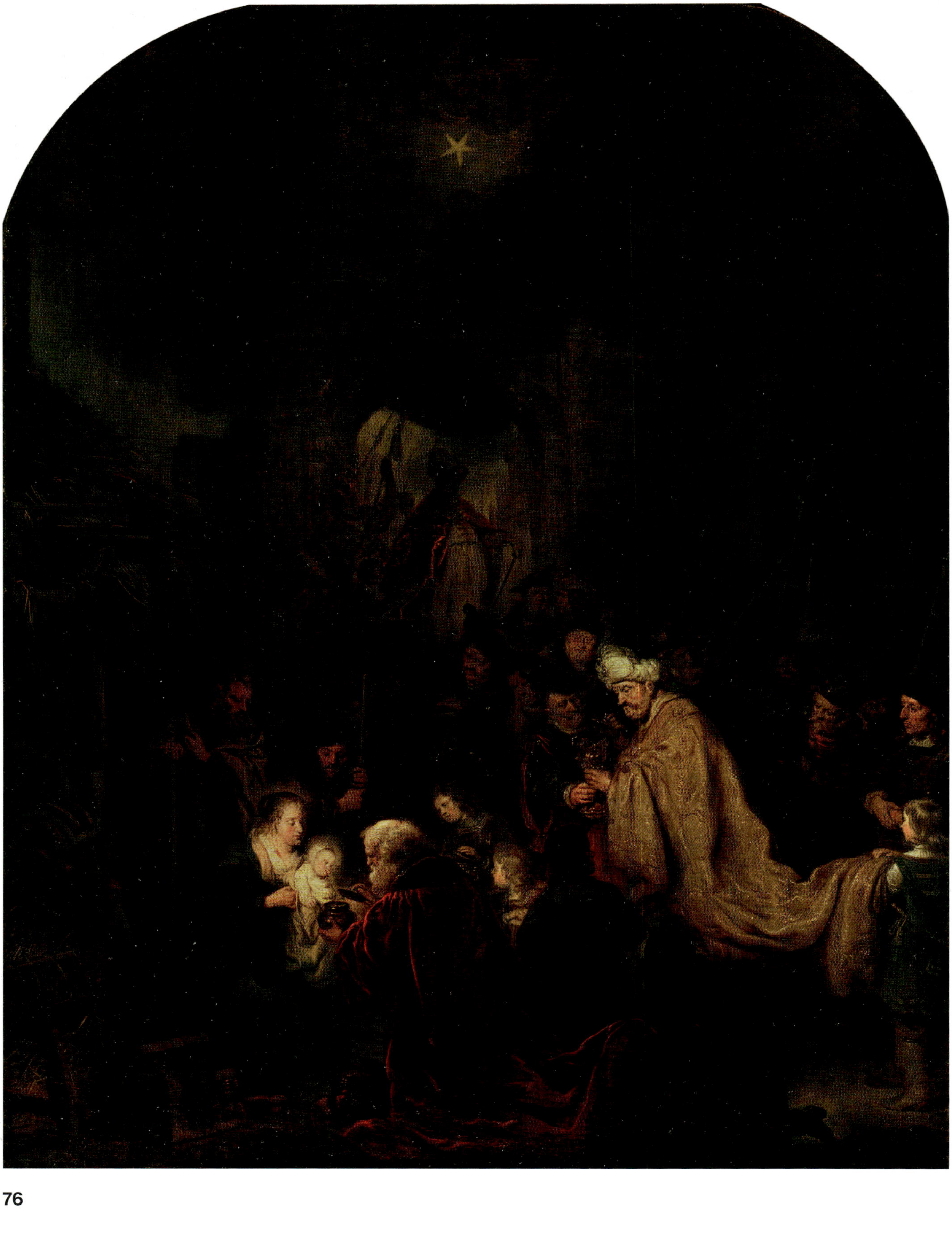

76

Rembrandt conceived his painting as a *brunaille,* using the various brown tones to achieve a variety of lighting effects. Salomon Koninck, by contrast, used strong colors—red and gold—to depict the kings, who thus stand out from the surrounding darkness. Koninck was three years younger than Rembrandt and had been a member of the Guild of Saint Luke in Amsterdam since 1632. Although he was not a pupil of Rembrandt's, many of his paintings show the latter's influence. In the present case he borrowed from Rembrandt the raised, central position of the third king and the parasol as his attribute as well as the stringent lighting scheme.

Whereas Rembrandt foregrounded his protagonists, Koninck's much larger painting includes atmospheric surroundings: on the left the straw roof of the manger, in the background the skyline of an ancient city. Koninck also included a rather crucial element of the narrative that Rembrandt had left out: the star that guided the kings to Jerusalem (Matthew 2:2), which is what tells us the scene takes place in the East. The Greek original of the gospels described the kings as *mágoi*, Zoroastrian priests with astrological connections.

Koninck drew his inspiration not only from Rembrandt but also from Peter Paul Rubens—via the engraving after the latter's *Adoration of the Magi* by Lucas Vorsterman (cat. 61). It was from Rubens/Vorsterman that Koninck took the page carrying the middle king's magnificent train. Koninck thereby gave this figure a significance that is suggested neither by the Bible story nor by art-historical tradition. The king's golden cloak radiates out of the semidarkness, and his face is as sharply illuminated as the mother and child. Perhaps Koninck decided to make this figure stand out in order to draw attention to the strangely shaped vessel he is holding in his left hand.

The magnificent covered goblet is not a product of artistic imagination to show the wealth of the Orient, but an object that really existed. It was made in 1614 by the Utrecht silversmith Adam van Vianen and was in the possession of the Amsterdam silversmiths' guild. It is unclear what Koninck's intention was in displaying this vessel in his painting. At any rate, it became a popular accessory among Rembrandt's emulators—Jacob Backer, Govert Flinck, and Gerbrand van den Eeckhout all painted the goblet as did Koninck, who used the motif in several paintings. MPH

77 **Rembrandt Harmensz. van Rijn** (1606–1669)

The Woman Taken in Adultery, 1644

Oil on oak panel, 83.8 x 65.4 cm
Inscribed (bottom right): Rembrandt f 1644
Inv. NG45
The National Gallery, London,
purchased in 1824

Lit.
CRP, vol. 5, 222–23, no. 3; vol. 6, no. 196
London 1988, no. 9
London 1991, no. 45
Schwartz 2006, 280, fig. 464
Paris 2011, 84–88, fig. 3.6, no. 25
Manuth/De Winkel/Van Leeuwen 2019, no. 66

This painting, dated 1644, illustrates the well-known scene from the Gospel according to Saint John (John 8:3–11) where a woman caught committing adultery is brought by the scribes and the Pharisees to Jesus while he is addressing his followers in the Temple. Instead of condemning her to death by stoning, as stipulated by law, or openly opposing that law (what the scribes hoped he would do), Jesus says to her accusers: “Let he among you who is without sin be the first to cast a stone at her,” whereupon they all slink away in shame. Rembrandt stages the events in the Temple of Jerusalem in front of a raised platform where a sacrifice is being made.

Whereas large parts of the Temple’s interior are immersed in semidarkness, Jesus is illuminated by a bright light, which also falls onto the adulteress kneeling before him. In keeping with the biblical text, she is standing in the center, while her opponents are assembled around her in a semicircle. Jesus stands out not least due to his towering stature. Behind him to the right stand the group of accusers, who, alongside exotically clad scribes and Pharisees, also include a soldier whose armor glitters in the light. He is firmly grasping the adulteress’s dress, while the leader of the group, dressed in black, lifts her veil and presents her defiantly to Jesus. In a departure both from the biblical text and art-historical tradition, Jesus is not shown writing with his finger on the ground while speaking his proverbial words; instead, Rembrandt chose the moment at which he is confronted with the decisive question, while the opponents wait with gloating contempt for his reply.

The small scale of the figures and the colored elements link the painting with works like the Braunschweig *Circumcision of Christ* (cat. 78), where the truncated Temple interior likewise has towering pillars. Even more similar is *Simeon in the Temple* (Mauritshuis, The Hague), painted earlier, in 1631. The London painting echoes other works by Rembrandt from this decade as well.

While elements like the two metal Temple pillars Jachin and Boas as well as the Temple curtain hanging on both sides of the imposing back wall—worked in gold in imitation of the contemporary ornamental Kwab, or auricular style—are historically accurate, the exotic and Oriental elements are intended not merely to locate the action convincingly in a particular time and place. Rather the elaborate costumes of the accusers, high priests, and Temple servants identify their wearers as members of the Old Covenant and thus of the age *sub lege* (under the law), while Jesus—immediately distinguishable from them by his bare feet, long flowing hair, and plain garment—stands for the New Covenant, which formed the foundation for the age *sub gratia* (under grace) when the prevailing religious laws and codes of behavior were annulled. By granting the genuinely repentant sinner clothed in gleaming white forgiveness and God’s grace without the need for good works such as a ritual sacrifice, Jesus is cast as the antithesis of the high priest celebrating diagonally above him.

Here Rembrandt uses darkness and light to contrast the splendor and luxury of the Pharisees and scribes and their stringent code of behavior with the morally superior carpenter’s son from a simple background who defies the prevailing order and who will even describe himself as the light of the world in the next moment. At the same time, this is a clear allusion to the insurmountable line of conflict that will bring Christ to the cross. GD

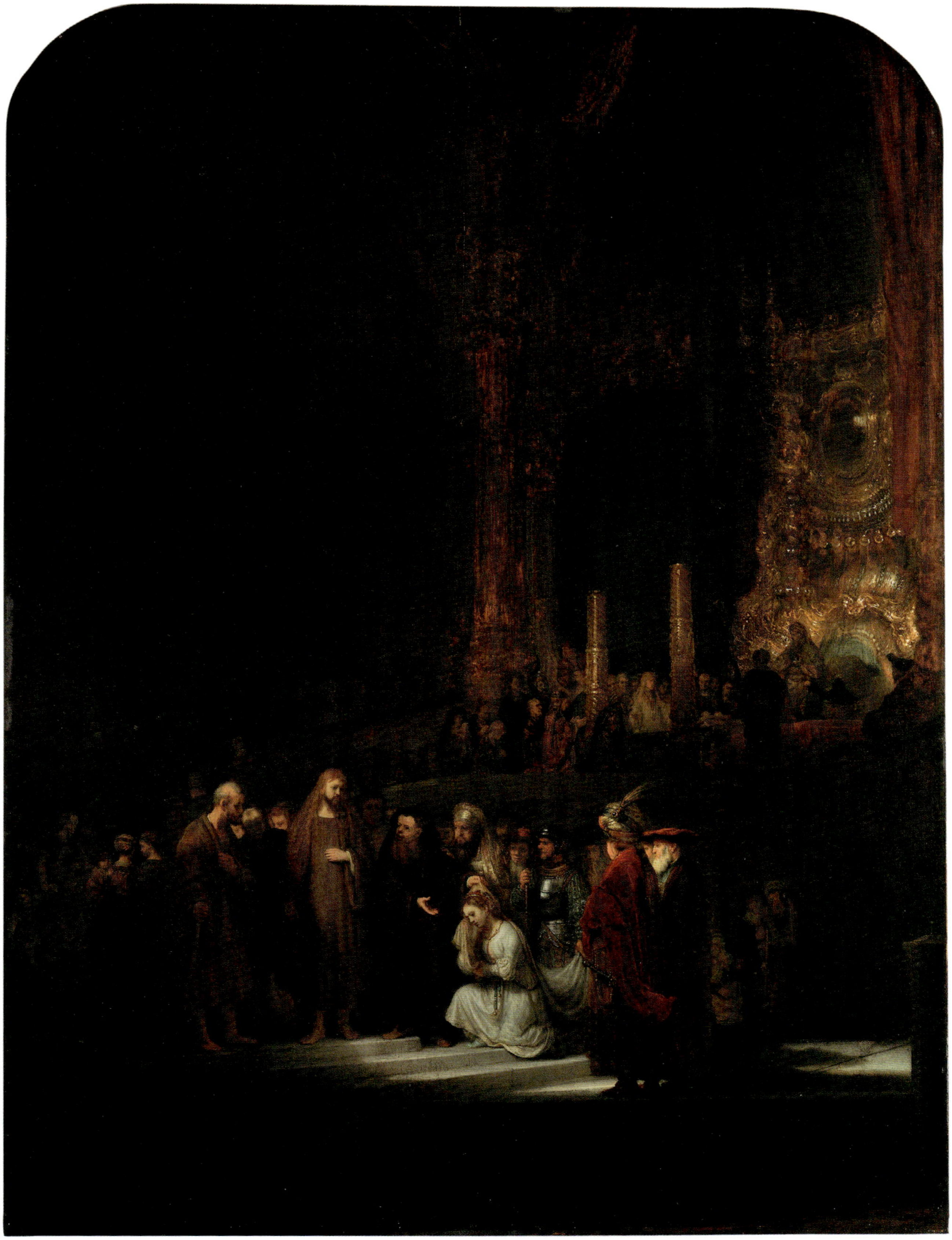

78 **Rembrandt Harmensz. van Rijn** (1606–1669) and workshop (?)

The Circumcision of Christ, ca. 1646 or later

Oil on canvas, 97.8 x 72 cm
Inv. GG 241
Herzog Anton Ulrich-Museum, Braunschweig, Kunstmuseum des Landes Niedersachsen

Lit.
CRP, vol. 5, no. 10
McNamara 2015, 4, 183–87

In the early 1630s Rembrandt painted a Passion cycle for Stadtholder Frederik Hendrik of Orange. In 1646 he added to it an *Adoration of the Shepherds* (together with the five actual Passion scenes: Bayerische Staatsgemäldesammlungen, Alte Pinakothek, Munich) and a *Circumcision of Christ*. The latter has been lost since the eighteenth century. The Braunschweig painting has the same dimensions as the Munich cycle and likewise a semicircular top edge. It is probably a replica of the version from 1646 produced in Rembrandt's workshop. Replicas of this kind were stored in artists' studios as *ricordi* (reminders) to be used at a later date. And indeed, Rembrandt's bankruptcy inventory from 1656 lists a depiction of the same theme, which may well be the painting in question here. At any rate, it was evidently executed by one of Rembrandt's pupils in his studio and probably communicates the pictorial ideas of the master very accurately.

The painting reveals a certain familiarity with the Jewish rite of circumcision but also a penchant for the fantastic. Unlike many of his predecessors, Rembrandt knew that the act of circumcision is performed not, as one might think, by the high priest but by a *mohel* employed especially for the purpose assisted by a *sandek,* who is holding the child. Here, however—unlike in his small etching on the same theme from around 1630—he painted each of them in the clothing normally worn by the other. The *sandek,* who was really a kind of godfather, is wearing a lengthy coat made of gold brocade over his white tunic; on his head is a turban with a gold chain. By contrast, the figure actually performing the circumcision is inconspicuously and plainly dressed. Furthermore, Rembrandt adhered to art-historical tradition and dressed the high priest watching over the ceremony with strangely exotic pontifical vestments in an approximation of the clothing regulations described in the Old Testament (Exodus 28:4–39, 29:5–9, and 39:1–31). To the articles of clothing described there—the headdress called a *mitznefet* and the breastplate called a *hoshen,* gleaming out of the picture, he added a freely invented staff, which in his etching resembles the Staff of Moses with the bronze serpent (Numbers 21:8–9). In the painting, by contrast, we see a staff modeled on that of a bishop with a closed crozier forming a circle. BB

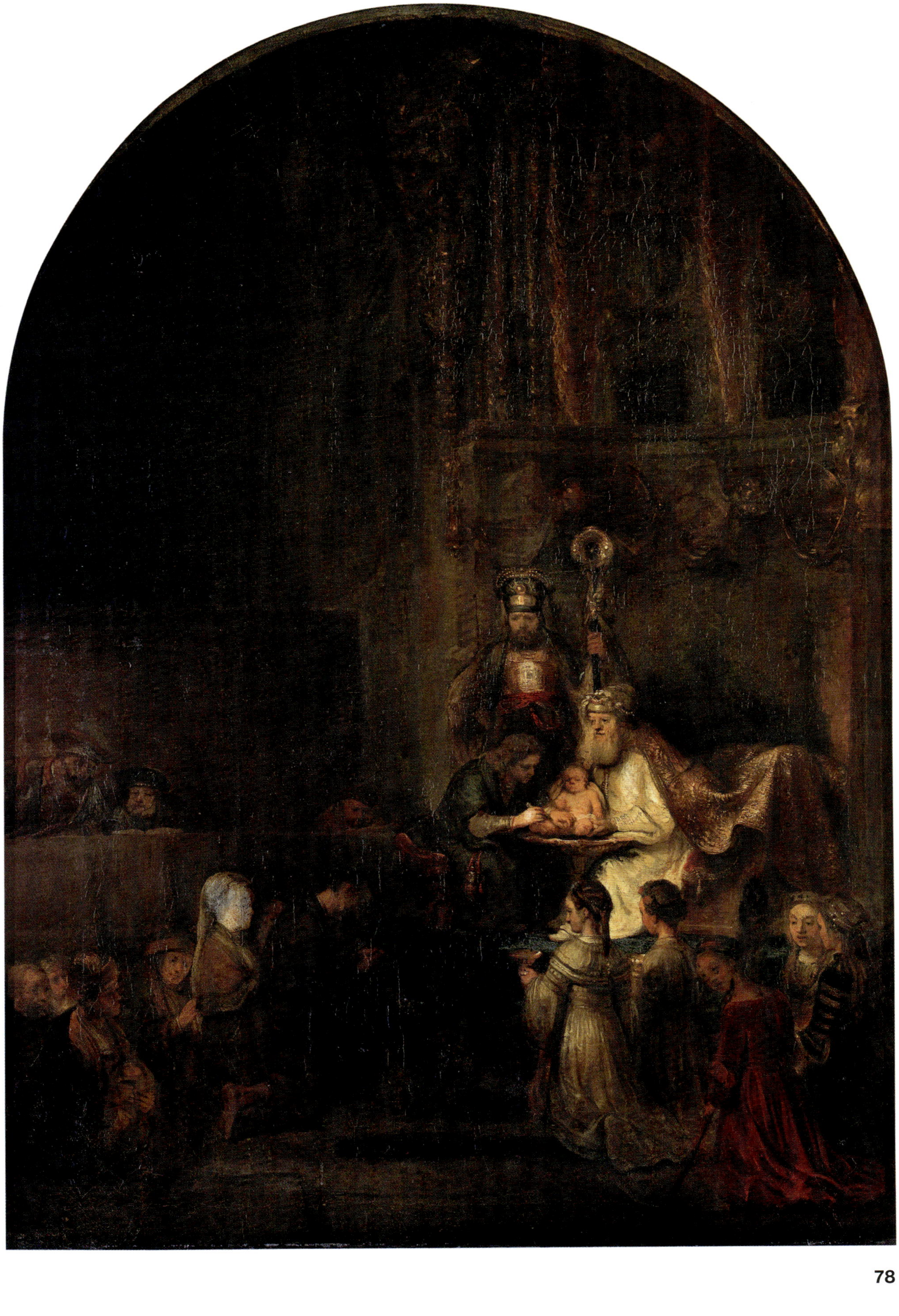

78

79 **Thomas de Keyser** (1596–1667) after **Pieter Lastman** (1583–1633)
Cyrus Restores the Treasures of the Temple, 1660

80 **Rembrandt Harmensz. van Rijn** (1606–1669)
Medea, or The Marriage of Jason and Creusa, 1648

81 **Rembrandt Harmensz. van Rijn** (1606–1669)
The Triumph of Mordecai, ca. 1641

79
Oil on canvas, 118.8 x 92 cm
Inscribed center on top step:
PL [in ligature] ASMAN INVENTOR. /
Tka [in ligature] IYSER PINXIT. 1660.
Inv. 6781
Fondation Custodia/Collection Frits Lugt, Paris

Lit.
The Hague 2002, no. 17
Amsterdam 1993, 572

80
Etching with touches of drypoint, 24 x 17.6 cm
5th state (of 5)
Inscribed on plate at bottom right:
Rembrandt f. 1648
Inv. 2007.217
Kunstmuseum Basel, Kupferstichkabinett, Eberhard W. Kornfeld Donation, Bern

Lit.
B 112 (4/5)
NH 241 (5/5)
Golahny 2003, 39–42
Basel 2005, no. 57
Denver 2018, no. 77
Amsterdam 2019, 294–95
Schatborn/Hinterding 2019, no. R 85

81
Etching and drypoint, 17.4 x 21.4 cm
3rd state (of 4)
Inv. 2007.200
Kunstmuseum Basel, Kupferstichkabinett, Donation Eberhard W. Kornfeld, Bern

Lit.
B 40 (1/1)
NH 185 (3/4)
Basel 2005, no. 40
St. Gallen 2005, 70–71
Denver 2018, no. 58
Amsterdam 2019, 446–47
Schatborn/Hinterding 2019, no. R 8

The background of Thomas de Keyser's painting *Cyrus Restores the Treasures of the Temple* is rather curious. In December 1658 the parish council of the Zuiderkerk in Amsterdam decided to remove all the stained glass from the church in order to let in more daylight. This included a glass window designed by Pieter Lastman for the church in 1611 that had been donated by the Amsterdam goldsmiths' guild, headed at the time by Lastman's brother Seeger. The window has been lost since then, but Lastman's sketch for it is preserved in the Kupferstichkabinett in Berlin. It corresponds largely with the painting, and the two-part signature of the latter that expressly mentions Lastman as the inventor and De Keyser as the painter testifies to the high esteem in which the composition was held, even half a century later.

Among the few differences between the window sketch and the painted copy are some alterations to the goldsmith's objects in the foreground, where a nautilus cup was originally planned instead of the jug at front right. Understandably, the clients wished to use this section of the image for the purpose of self-promotion, so the objects depicted here were almost certainly well-known to the public of the time. The *tazza* at front left, for example, which has fallen over, is the dish with a depiction of Susanna and the Elders by the goldsmith Paulus van Vianen (Museum Boijmans Van Beuningen, Rotterdam). Since it is dated 1612, the stained-glass window must have been executed the year after Lastman implemented his design.

The client's métier is probably what determined the choice of the rather unusual theme from the book of Ezra (1:2–11). The Persian King Cyrus II orders the Temple in Jerusalem to be rebuilt and personally restores the treasures stolen by Nebuchadnezzar during the destruction of its predecessor, the Temple of Solomon. His treasurer, Mithridates—shown on the right holding a book—has Cyrus count the vessels one by one and then hand them over to Sheshbazzar—seen kneeling on the left—the governor of Judah. The Persian king is wearing a turban with a small crown; his leading official is distinguished by an aigrette stuck into his turban (see cat. 2), a back projection of an Ottoman custom into biblical times. Lastman also furnished the royal palace of the ancient Persian Empire with a souvenir from his journey to Italy several years previously: a view of the dome of Saint Peter's in Rome. Here it serves as the upper floor of a central building and is spectacularly displayed in the view through a hall of pillars with barrel vaulting.

Rembrandt returned to this staging in his 1641 etching showing the *Triumph of Mordecai*. In the opening of the shadowy archway with deep recesses a central building appears in the middle of the print, gleaming in the light; this time, however, in a late Romanesque style. It represents the palace of the Persian King Ahasuerus in Susa. The scene is taken from the book of Esther (6:6–13) (see cat. 58): Haman, the adversary of the Jewish people, is ordered by the king to lead the Jew Mordecai, Esther's adoptive father, in splendid vestments on the king's horse in a triumphal procession through the city. Departing from the biblical text, Rembrandt's Mordecai does not wear a crown, but instead a cap decorated with a long ribbon; his regalia is limited to a scepter, which is not mentioned in the Bible.

The different head coverings serve to underscore that Mordecai is the confessional counterpart to the turbaned Haman. His portrayal on horseback echoes in mirror image the main group in Lastman's

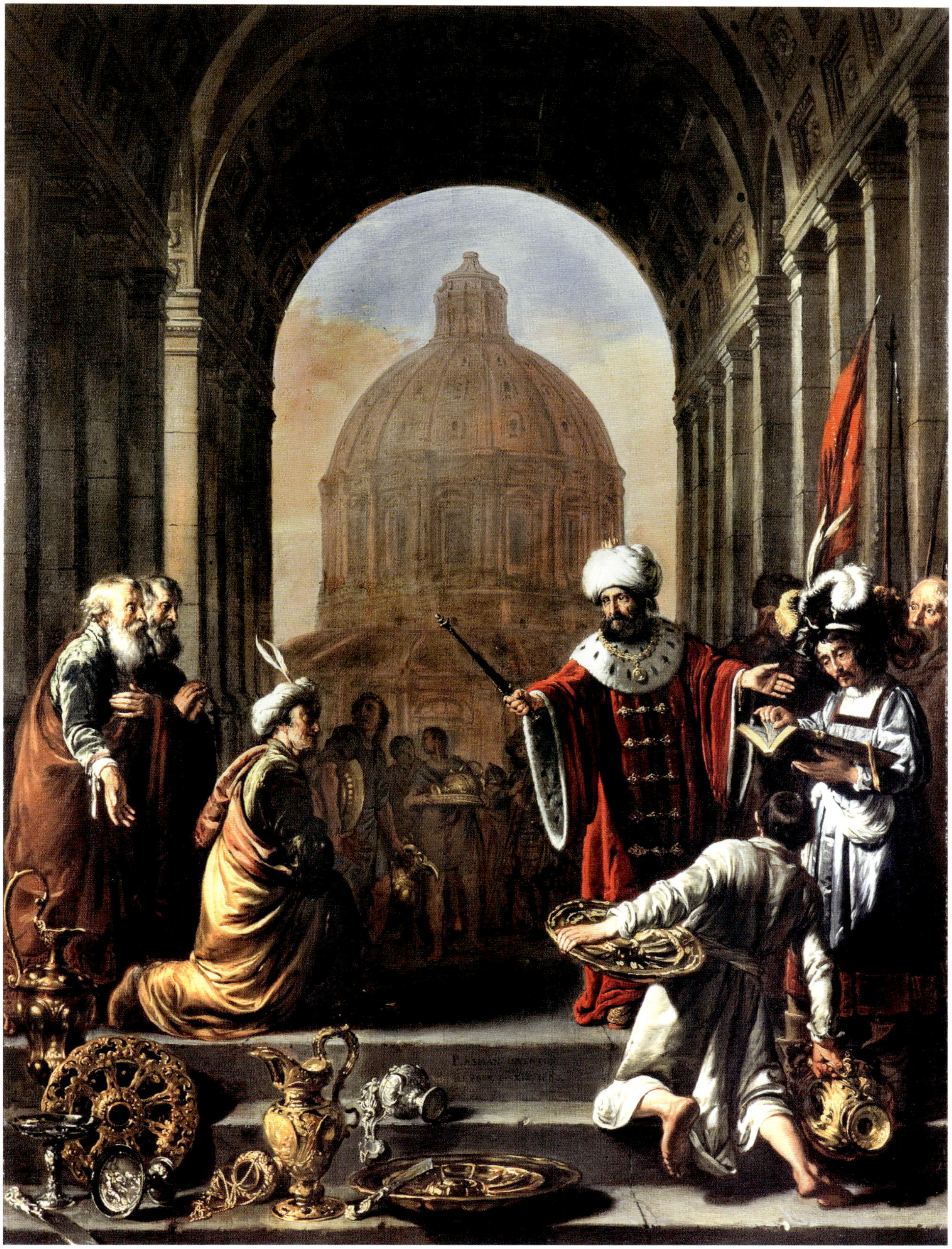

painting of the same subject of 1624 (Museum Het Rembrandthuis, Amsterdam). In that historically more plausible work, both protagonists are wearing turbans, and Mordecai is correctly depicted with a crown on top of his; as here, he is nonchalantly carrying the scepter before his chest. Like in Rembrandt's version, he is wearing a *collane*, alluding to the chain worn by the Order of the Golden Fleece. However, Rembrandt's teacher placed a different famous Roman monument in the background: the Pantheon. In the etching his pupil corrects this with reference to the stained-glass design of his teacher.

In Rembrandt's etching *Medea*—an ancient Greek subject—one protagonist in the front row towers over the crowd of people. The figure of the ruler whose train is being carried by two child pages was based on a painting by Rubens (see cat. 61). We first encounter him on an earlier panel of Rembrandt's in the Basel *David with the Head of Goliath before Saul* (cat. 60). In the etching the turban of this figure is decorated with a small crown of the same kind that the artist gave the king of Persia in his painting *Daniel and Cyrus before the Idol Bel* (cat. 68). The etching shows that Rembrandt and his clients had no problem transferring the configuration from a biblical setting to one of antique mythology. Here the crowned figure with a train is the Corinthian King Creon who is attending the marriage of his daughter Glauce (or Creusa) to the hero Jason, the leader of the Argonauts. The couple kneels before the priest, who most closely resembles Rembrandt's idea of a high priest from the Old Testament (see cat. 82). On the right an enthroned and, surprisingly, naked statue of Hera, wearing a crown and accompanied by her attribute, a peacock, marks the temple precinct.

Unfortunately, however, Jason is already married to Medea, a princess from Colchis with magical powers, who has brought him the Golden Fleece and bore him two sons. Abandoned by her husband in favor of his new lover, she appears in the foreground out of the darkness. The fact that her train is also being carried by a servant and she is wearing a *collane* identifies her as Creon's antithesis and this is further underlined by the contrast of light and shade. She will subsequently send his daughter Glauce a poisoned piece of fabric (in some versions a robe, in others a veil) to which both father and daughter will fall victim. We already see her holding it in her right hand while in her left hand she clasps a dagger with which Medea, mad with jealousy, will stab her own children.

Medea's madness also formed the subject of a tragedy written by Rembrandt's friend and patron Jan Six (1618–1700), which had its first performance in Amsterdam's municipal theater, the Stadsschouwburg, in 1647. Six had commissioned the print as the frontispiece for the first printed edition of his play; his star-shaped monogram modestly adorns the center of the lower edge between the explanatory verses. Although Six's drama begins at a later point in the story and does not include the marriage scene, Rembrandt nonetheless stages his painting unmistakably as a scene in a play, as clearly indicated by the theater curtain drawn back in the foreground and the contemporary architecture. The latter, however, bears no resemblance to the Stadsschouwburg, but instead takes as its model Hendrick de Keyser's Zuiderkerk inaugurated in 1611. BB

80

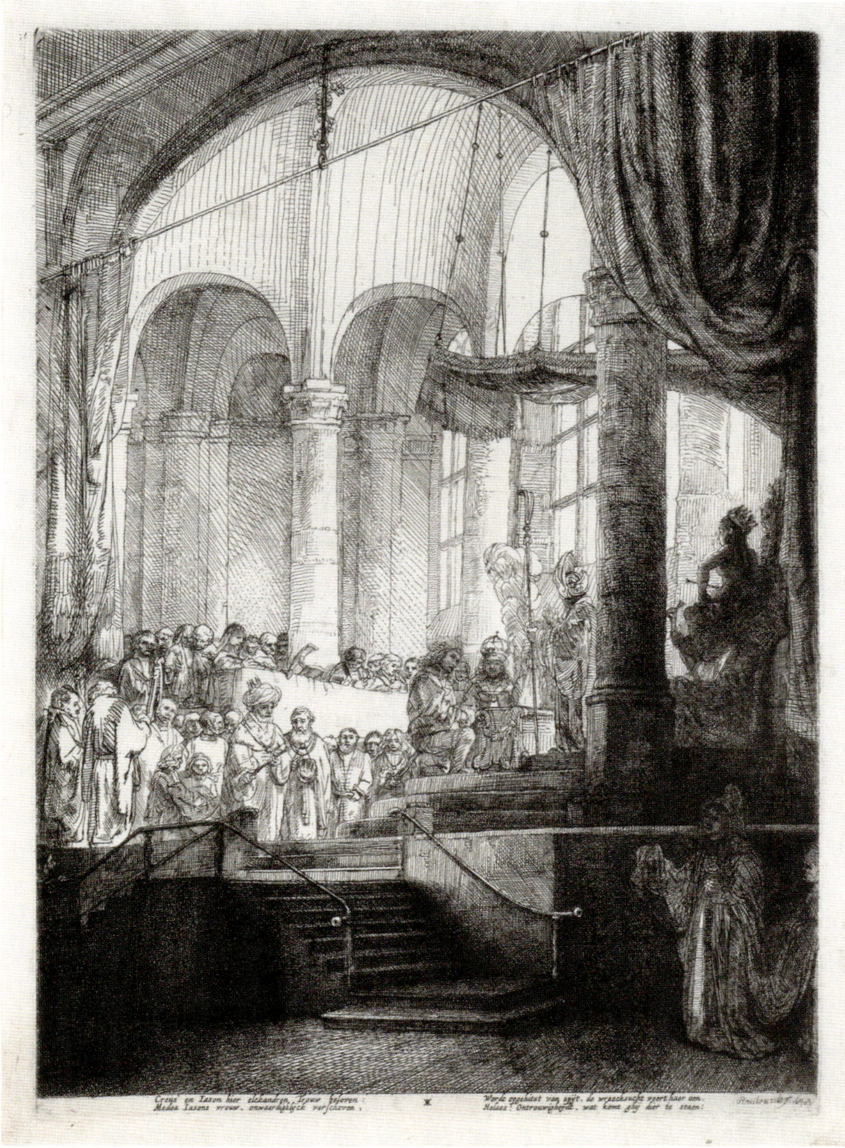
Creüs en Iason hier elckandren, Trouw beloven:
Medea Iasons vrouw, onwaerdighlijck verschoren,
Wordt opgehitst van spijt, de wraecksucht voert haer aen.
Helaes! Ontrouwigheijt, wat komt ghy dier te staen:

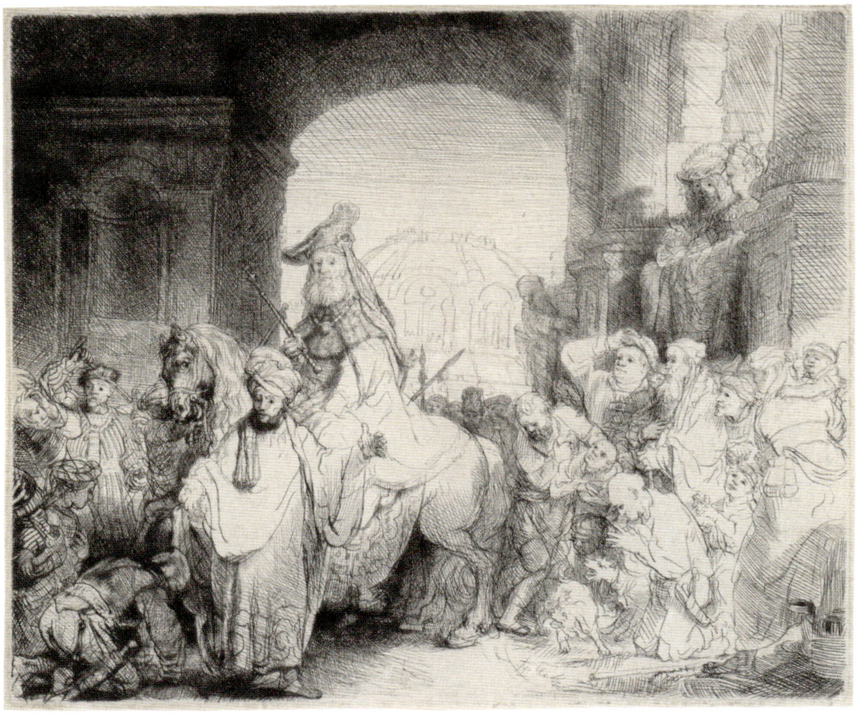

81

82 **Rembrandt Harmensz. van Rijn** (1606–1669)

The Presentation in the Temple in the Dark Manner, ca. 1654

Etching and drypoint, 20.9 x 16 cm
Inv. 2007.252
Kunstmuseum Basel, Kupferstichkabinett,
Donation Eberhard W. Kornfeld, Bern

Lit.
B 50 (1/1)
NH 285 (1/1)
Zell 2002, 99–123
Basel 2005, no. 85
Perlove/Silver 2009, 217–24
London 2014, no. 77
Amsterdam 2019, 476–77
Schatborn/Hinterding 2019, no. R 63

Rembrandt's depiction of the purification ceremony according to the law of Moses (see, for example, Numbers 18:15–16), to which the infant Jesus was subjected, focuses on the miracle that occurred during the ritual as told in the Gospel according to Saint Luke (Luke 2:22–40): the revelation by the old man Simeon that the child was the Messiah. In paintings from around 1627–28 (Hamburger Kunsthalle) and 1631 (Mauritshuis, The Hague) as well as in three etchings from 1630, ca. 1639–40, and ca. 1654 (the one shown here), Simeon, who has received a prophecy that he will not die without having seen the savior, is holding the infant Jesus in his arm and recognizes this as the fulfilment of the prophecy. His open mouth on the painting in The Hague and the later etching indicates that he is starting to sing *Nunc dimittis,* known as the Canticle of Simeon, one of the great liturgical songs of praise. Rembrandt's dramatic lighting effects in all his versions of this subject do justice to the metaphor in the third verse of the Canticle, in which Christ is praised as "a light to illuminate the heathens." Here, the artist broke with the medieval and early modern tradition of depicting Simeon as the high priest of the temple, instead following the Gospel of Saint Luke and depicting Simeon as an ordinary person "pious and God-fearing" (Luke 2:25), whose sudden epiphany is ignored, doubted, or plainly rejected by the Jewish clergy.

In his latest etching Rembrandt took this confrontation to extremes, showing Simeon presenting the child to two priests, whom, in keeping with the *Mishnah* of the Talmud, he casts as *Kohen Gadol*, the high priest, and his deputy, the *Segan*. The former watches the ritual in the background and is identified by his head covering *mitznefet*, the faceplate *ziz*, and the breastplate *hoshen*. Since the seated man at the front leafing through a text is wearing the *ephod*, the tunic of the high priest—recognizable by the alternating pomegranates and little bells hanging from the hem (Exodus 39:24–26)—he must be the second man, the *Segan*, heading the temple servants. The balconies to the right and left of the aisle in the background are surely reminiscent of the galleries reserved for women on both sides of the Nikanor Gate between the Court of the Women and the Court of the Priests in the Second Temple. Hence it is fitting that we see Anna, the prophet, who likewise recognizes the Messiah (Luke 2:36–38), looking down on the scene from the balcony on the right.

A unique feature of the etching from ca. 1654 are two spectacular artistic devices: the deep darkness into which the events are plunged and the increasing scale of the figures—like a persiflage of the hierarchical scale common in the Middle Ages and known as *Bedeutungsperspektive*—ranging from the tiny parents of Jesus on the left, followed by Simeon and the *Segan*, to the gigantic high priest who appears like a colossal statue towering over the scene. BB

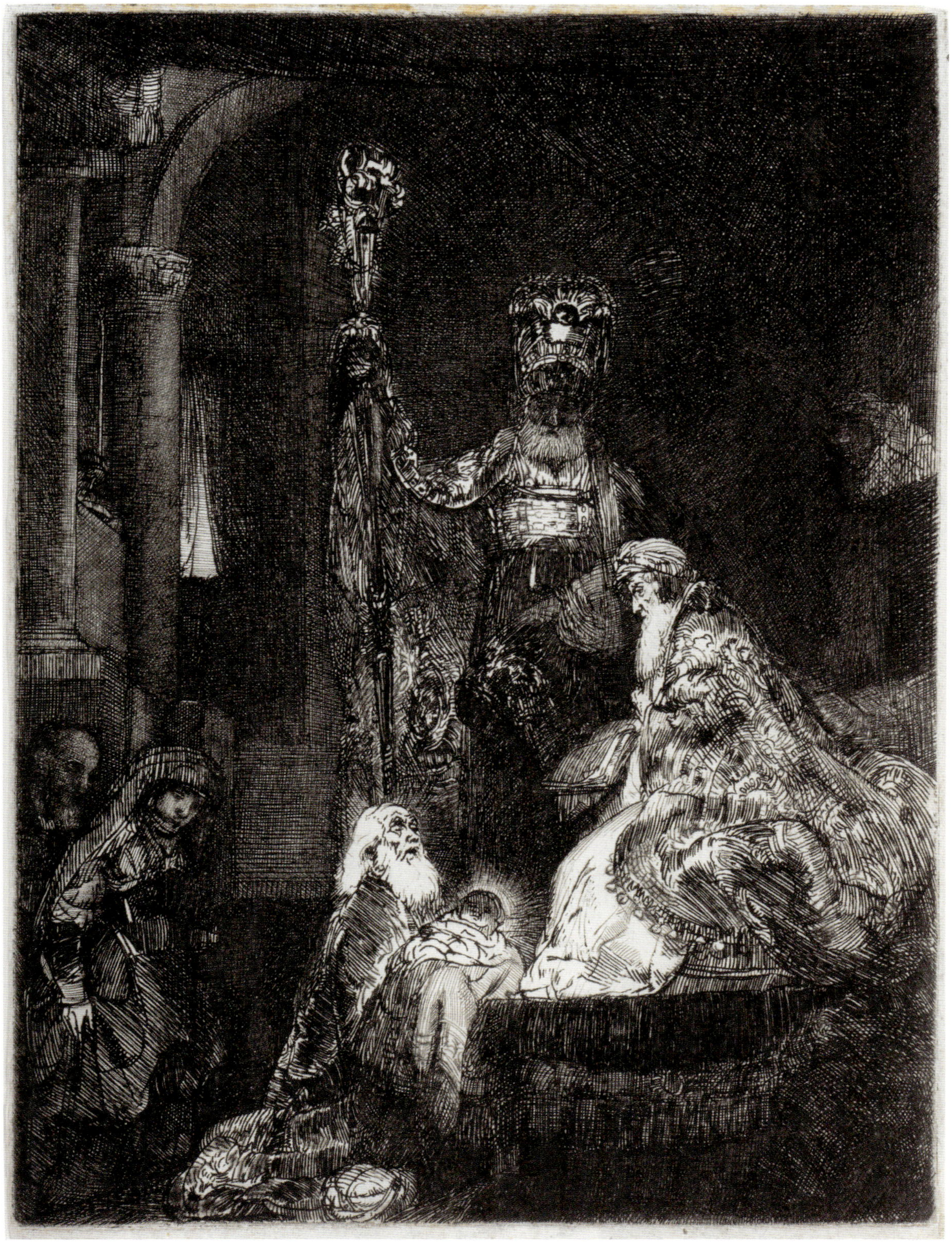

82

True to Life? Or Mere Convention?

Orientalizing costumes and settings were used to create an atmospheric backdrop for biblical narratives. In those paintings, the question of the reality behind such Orientalizing motifs was of little concern. But this was not the case for portraits and landscapes that claimed to represent a real place or person. However, only a few Netherlandish paintings from the seventeenth century aimed to provide a reliable representation of far-off lands and their inhabitants. There was clearly no interest in creating authentic images of different regions and peoples. Many works simply confirmed existing clichés and stereotypes. Original artworks from East Asia, such as miniatures from India and Persia, were given scant attention. They were rarely collected and only a small number of Dutch painters—among them, notably, Rembrandt—studied them in any greater detail.

One of the few artists to actually travel to the Far East was Andries Beeckman, who, on behalf of the Dutch East India Company, completed the topographically accurate view of *The Marketplace of Batavia*, which was copied a short time later (cat. 86). The archetypal figures were taken from his own sketches, in which he recorded the features and traits of subjects that were supposed to epitomize different ethnic groups (cat. 87). It is not known whether Hans de Jode ever saw the city of Constantinople that he painted in his large-scale *View of the Tip of the Seraglio with Topkapı Palace* (cat. 83)—he could just as easily have borrowed from earlier depictions of the view, such as engravings. Most contemporary viewers of the painting had of course never visited the Bosporus or seen the real view either and were thus not in a position to judge. The drawings of Egypt by Johan Teyler (cat. 85) and of Persepolis by Philips Angel, the latter surviving only in an engraving after the original (cat. 84), were indeed drawn from direct observation. However, as these were architectural studies and archaeological records, they would have hardly been suitable models for a painting.

Even in the case of portraiture, artists did not always meet the person who ultimately became the subject of their works. The likeness of Mehdi Quli Beg by Aegidius Sadeler II (cat. 89) is inscribed with the note "ad vivum" (from life). When the Persian envoy arrived in Prague in 1604, Sadeler had been working there as the court engraver for seven years. He made a portrait of the envoy in a similar manner to those of numerous other guests of Emperor Rudolf II, regardless of where they came from: in an oval framed by an inscription. Sadeler also made likenesses of Mehdi Quli Beg's companions Zaynal Khan Shamlu and the Persian envoy in Vienna, Cuchein Ali Beg, in the same way. These portraits are a sign of recognition and respect that was independent of the sitters' religious or geographical origin.

By contrast, in Wallerant Vaillant's portrait of a man, possibly identifiable as Sultan Süleyman II, we cannot even be certain whether it is actually a portrait or a character study of a man with a turban (cat. 90). The image could also belong to the popular genre of Orientalizing *tronies* (see "Familiarizing the Exotic: Rembrandt's Adaptation of the Orient," pp. 284–311). Vaillant was active in Antwerp, Frankfurt am Main, Paris, and Amsterdam, but his biography does not mention a trip to the Middle East; possibly he met someone wearing a turban in one of the above cities. Sometime around 1655–60, he even donned one of these headdresses himself for his *Self-Portrait with Turban* (Gemäldegalerie, Staatliche Museen zu Berlin).

The scene from Ceylon (modern-day Sri Lanka) drawn by Esaias Boursse in his *Scene with a Party in a Sinhalese Tavern or Living Room* (cat. 88) is presumably authentic. In contrast, the woodcuts of Persian costume studies in Johannes de Laet's book on the region are lacking in detail and variety (cat. 91). Perhaps they were derived from authentic sources, but they nevertheless share similarities with the stereotypical Oriental dress commonly seen in woodcuts. The author of the book was an armchair geographer who rarely left the city of Leiden, and as such was most definitely not able to judge how realistic these illustrations were.

Another approach to authenticity can be seen in the artistic response to original artworks from foreign cultures. Looking at Willem Schellinks's enthusiastic homage to Indian art (cat. 92), we have to ask how extensive the author's knowledge of it actually was. Although he had traveled to many countries in Europe, he had in fact never made it beyond Malta. When his eulogy to Indian art was printed in 1657, Schellinks had been living in Amsterdam for ten years. We can only conjecture how many Indian paintings he would have been able to lay his eyes on there, but it cannot have been many. What is certain however is that he must have seen examples of Mughal miniature paintings with his own eyes. They inspired such works as the *Parade of the Sons of Shah Jahan on Composite Horses and Elephants* (cat. 94), which in terms of form and content was perhaps the most substantial adaption of East Asian art in the Netherlands of the seventeenth century.

Schellinks's models were possibly the same miniatures that Rembrandt copied (cat. 97) and that later adorned the walls of Schönbrunn Palace in Vienna in the eighteenth century (cat. 95). Out of the many thousands of Netherlandish paintings from this time, those made in response to authentic originals remained the exception. Whether they were made because of a deeper artistic interest or for a specific commission can no longer be determined. Still, it bespeaks a certain appreciation of the foreign, as demonstrated too by the Persian miniature owned by Gesina ter Borch (cat. 98). Its reworking and subsequent addition to an album that otherwise exclusively contains works of Dutch provenance show, however, that it was more an exercise in appropriation than a tribute to an artwork in its own right. MPH

83 **Hans de Jode** (ca. 1630–after 1663)

View of the Tip of the Seraglio with Topkapı Palace, 1659

Oil on canvas, 135 x 221 cm
Inscribed (bottom right): Seraglio del gran signor 1659; below: H. de Jode
Inv. 2945
Kunsthistorisches Museum Wien, Vienna, Gemäldegalerie

Lit.
Brussels 2015, 278–79
Messling 2015

This unusually large landscape painting shows one of the most famous vistas of the early modern age and with it a spectacle that was sure to fire the imagination. Looking across the Golden Horn in the foreground, the viewer's gaze falls on the headland that in modern-day Istanbul is called Seraglio Point, on the crest of which stands the majestic Topkapı Palace. Until the mid-nineteenth century this was the residence and seat of government of the Turkish sultan and hence the nerve center of the Ottoman Empire. As the vantage point is at the foot of the formerly autonomous district of Galata, this haunting view of the old city of Constantinople is also the one that the merchants and diplomats from all over Europe who had been based there since the late Middle Ages would have had.

The painting, whose painted *cartellino* in the lower right-hand corner once recorded not just the date and name of the artist, but also its title, *Seraglio del gran Signor*, was acquired in the year of its creation by Archduke Leopold Wilhelm of Austria, in whose inventory it is listed as "Burg desz grossen Türckhen," that is to say, as the "Fortress of the Great Turk." The younger brother of Emperor Ferdinand III was Governor of the Spanish Netherlands from 1647 to 1656, and while resident in Brussels had had to suffer seeing the independence of the Dutch Republic recognized by the powers of Europe. But it was also while there that he had laid the groundwork for his extensive art collections.

The painter Hans de Jode was born in The Hague, but he left that city at a young age and went first to Venice and Rome and then finally to Vienna, where this painting was perhaps commissioned, either by Leopold Wilhelm himself or as a gift intended for him. Whether De Jode had any firsthand knowledge of Constantinople, as one contemporary source surmises, is questionable. The view is certainly accurate in a number of respects: the palace roof with its plethora of little domes, the Hagia Irena rising up out of the dip in the terrain to the right of it, and the minaret of the former church of Hagia Sophia that had already been converted into a mosque are all faithfully reproduced, as is the angle and general topography of the headland. On the other hand, the difference in height and gradient between the palace and the shoreline seems somewhat exaggerated, just as the two structures below it, the Waterfront Pavilion and Basketmakers' Kiosk, do not properly reflect their actual appearance.

The landscape beyond, by contrast, obviously belongs in the realm of fantasy. The ornamental-looking mountain range on the Asian side of the Golden Horn is just as much pure invention as the majestic, snow-capped peaks towering over the palace and conspiring with the bizarre cloud formations and light to lend the work the highly charged, dramatic atmosphere of a monumental veduta. The idyllic scene at the quayside in the foreground is a set piece that can be found in other paintings by the same artist. Veduta painters were not necessarily expected to have seen a place at first hand, and in the mid-seventeenth century there were multiple sources available for De Jode to consult.

The work's illustrious Habsburg provenance raises the question of what the painting might have meant to its first owner. That it was acquired during the fifty-year-long period when the Habsburg Monarchy and Sublime Porte were at peace—an intermezzo that was shortly to end with the fourth Austro-Turkish War of 1663–64—does not make that question any easier to answer. The fascination of the glory and grandeur of the near-legendary seat of a rival superpower must have been just as much a factor as the burgeoning enthusiasm for the Orient in general and the Ottoman Empire in particular, almost invariably accompanied by romantic fantasies of exotic traditions and alien rituals and customs that to the European imagination seemed more like the stuff of fairytales. GD

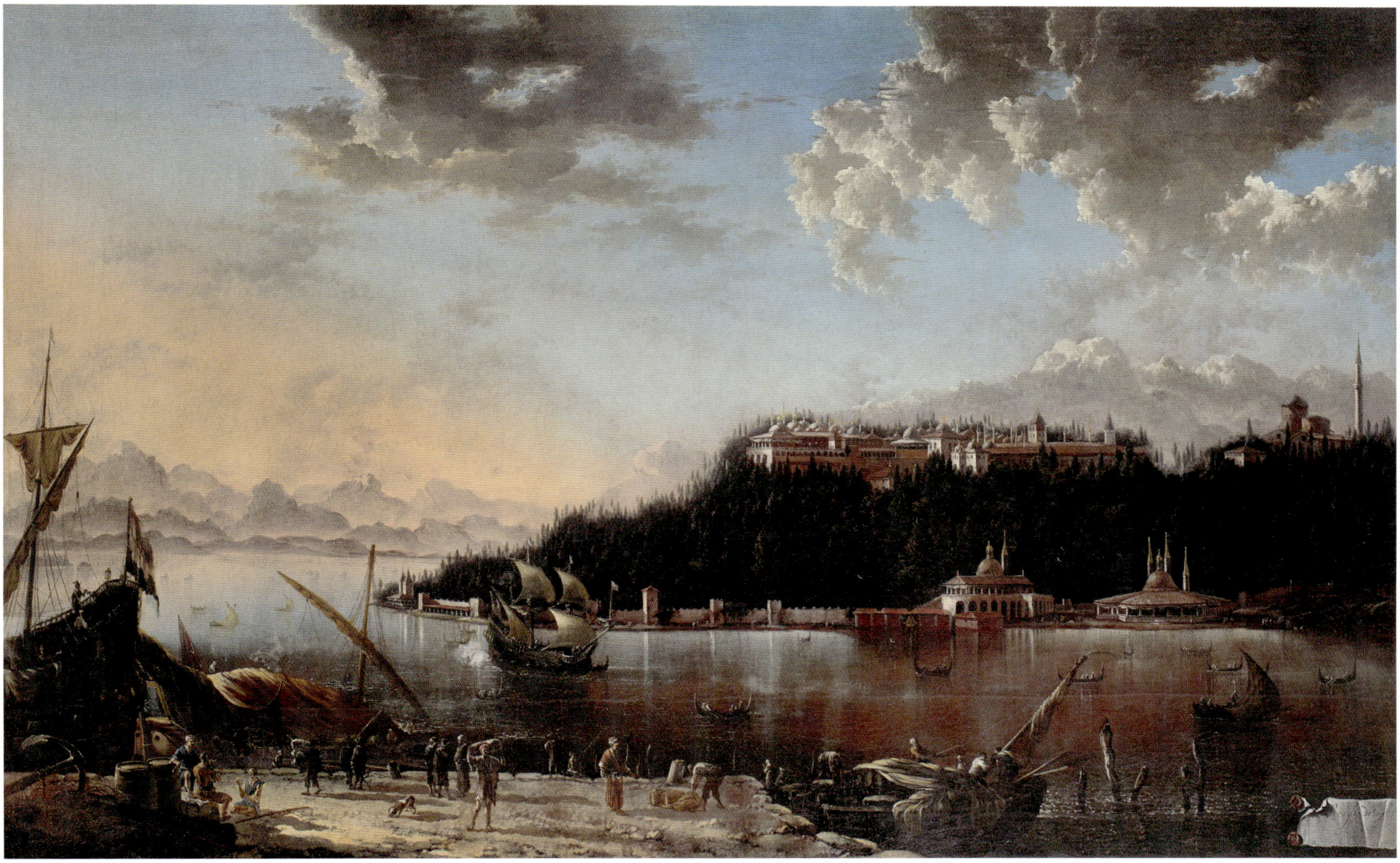

84 **Jan Caspar Philips** (1690–1775) after **Philips Angel** (ca. 1618–after 1664)

The Ruins of the Palace of Darius, Situated in Old Persepolis, Destroyed by Alexander the Great, 1726

Etching and engraving
In François Valentijn, *Oud en nieuw Oost-Indiën, vervattende een naaukeurige en uitvoerige verhandelinge van Nederlands mogentheyd in die gewesten . . .*
(The Old and New East-India, Repeated Precise and Detailed Treatise about the Dutch Power in Those Regions . . .),
5 vols., Dordrecht: Joannes van Braam / Amsterdam: Gerard onder de Linden, 1724–26, vol. 5.1, foldout between pp. 220 and 221
KF 62-4438 (Potsdam), KF 62-2874 (Basel)
Allard Pierson, University of Amsterdam

Lit.
Kratzsch 2007

1 Cf. Speelman 1908, 121.
2 Cited in Schwartz 2014, 36.
3 Cf. Stolte 2012.

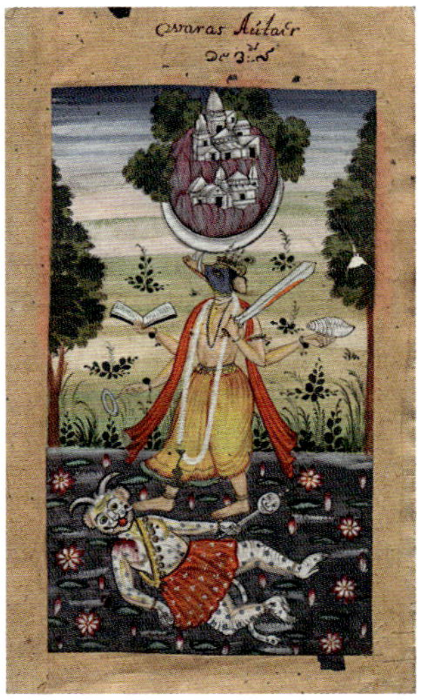

Philips Angel,
Illustration in the copy of a Hindu manuscript, 1650s, Postel Abbey, Belgium

The Leiden artist Philips Angel was one of the few seventeenth-century Netherlandish painters who actually traveled to the Orient. In 1651–52 he took part in a mission of the Dutch East India Company to Isfahan (see cat. 26, 44, and pp. 66–67). During the journey he made one of the first drawings ever done by a European artist of one of the great sites from classical antiquity in the Orient. In the journal of the embassy kept by the secretary, Cornelis Speelman, we read that on February 16, 1652, Joan Cunaeus, the leader of the mission, was led by Mahomet Isoffbeek, the provisioner, to see the ruins of Persepolis. There follows a long and detailed description, including many measurements, that could not have been made in the few hours that the delegation spent in Persepolis. Angel, who is identified in the report as a senior trader, stayed in Chelmenar to complete an accurate drawing of the location.[1]

Persepolis—the city of the Persians, as the Greeks called it—was built by Emperor Darius I of the Achaemenid Empire toward the end of the sixth century BC to serve as his capital. It exercised a magical hold on the imagination that was only enhanced when Alexander the Great demolished it in 330 BC. The actual ruins were not identified until the beginning of the seventeenth century. As renowned as it was, its spell was not sufficient to induce the commercially minded personnel of the Dutch East India Company to take a deeper interest in the ancient site.

Angel was no exception to this rule. One would think that his drawings of Persepolis were inspired by the scholarly interests that were manifest in his Saint Luke's Day lecture in praise of painting (cat. 44). There is however evidence to the contrary. The French traveler and art dealer Jean-Baptiste Tavernier claims to have met Angel at Persepolis, and that Angel had told him "that he had spent his time poorly, and that the thing [that is, Persepolis] was not worth the effort of being drawn, nor to oblige the interested traveler to take a detour of as much as a quarter of an hour from his route."[2]

After leaving Persia, Angel made a further contribution to knowledge of the ancient East by copying an illustrated Hindu text on the ten avatars of Vishnu, in a manuscript he presented in 1658 to the director-general of the Dutch East India Company in Batavia, Carel Hartsinck (fig. on left).[3] These two achievements—creating an accurate view of Persepolis on the spot and producing a valuable document of Hindu belief (which found its way back to Europe and became a source for Athanasius Kircher)—give Philips Angel unique significance. An artist who in the Netherlands had little of worth to his name became in the Orient the single most significant artistic transmitter of ancient history and religion of any European artist of the seventeenth century.

The print by the prolific Amsterdam engraver Jan Caspar Philips, who often collaborated on book projects in the eighteenth century, was made for a publication that appeared sixty years after the death of Philips Angel. The drawing from which he worked has not been preserved. GS

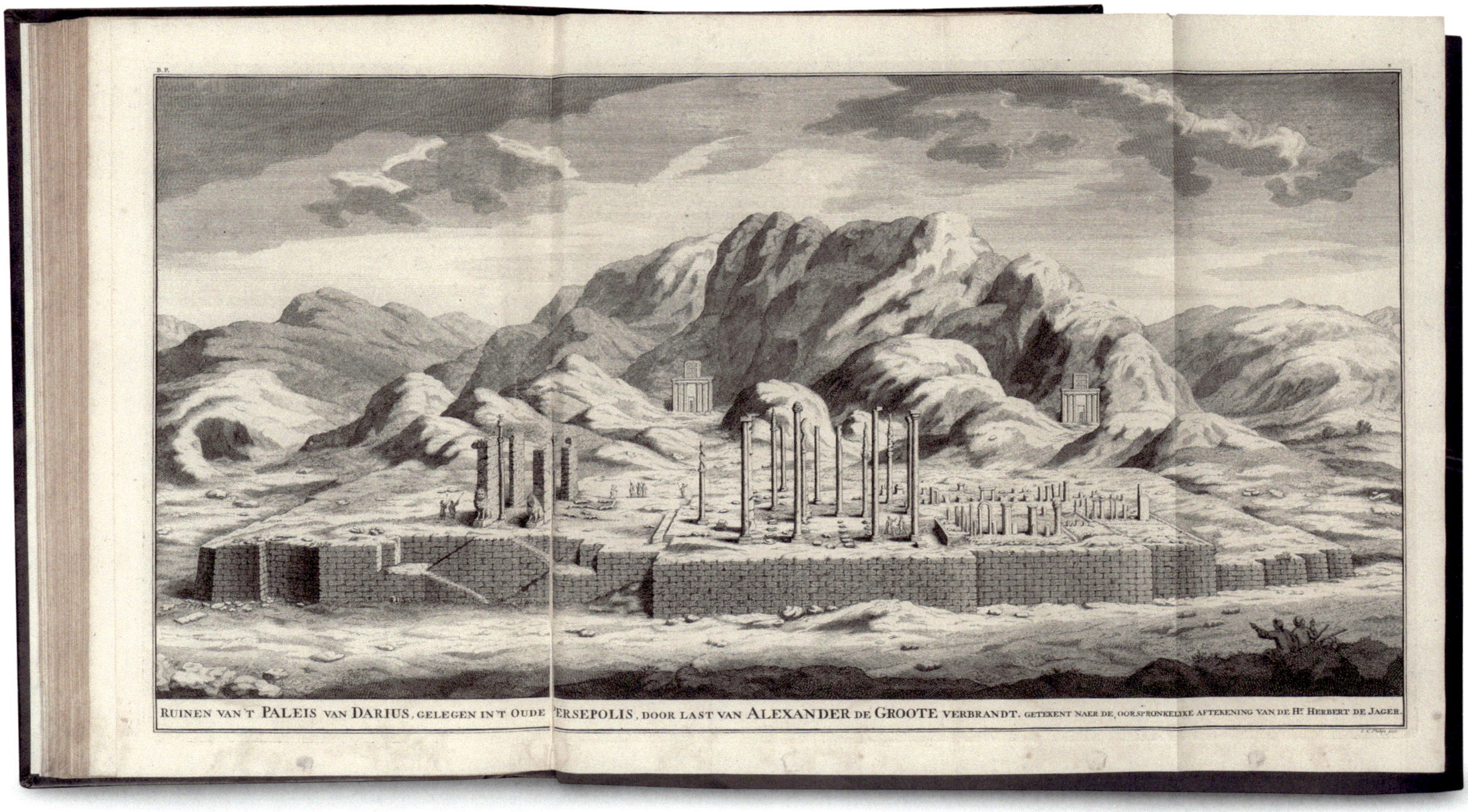
RUINEN VAN 'T PALEIS VAN DARIUS, GELEGEN IN 'T OUDE PERSEPOLIS, DOOR LAST VAN ALEXANDER DE GROOTE VERBRANDT. GETEKENT NAER DE OORSPRONKELYKE AFTEKENING VAN DE Hr. HERBERT DE JAGER.

85.1–4 **Johan Teyler** (1648–ca. 1709)

Four drawings from the series *Views of the Mediterranean,* 1679–83

85.1
Nile Landscape with a Sailboat
Pen and brown ink, 11.7 x 23.1 cm
Inv. RP-T-1935-59
Rijksmuseum, Amsterdam,
Rijksprentenkabinet, F. G. Waller Bequest,
Amsterdam
(Potsdam only)

85.2
View of the Nile at Saqqara Looking North
Pen and brown ink, 11.9 x 23.2 cm
Inv. RP-T-1935-63
Rijksmuseum, Amsterdam,
Rijksprentenkabinet, F. G. Waller Bequest,
Amsterdam
(Basel only)

85.3
Mosque on the Citadel in Cairo
Pen and brown ink, 12.1 x 23.4 cm
Inv. RP-T-1935-78
Rijksmuseum, Amsterdam,
Rijksprentenkabinet, F. G. Waller Bequest,
Amsterdam
(Basel only)

85.4
View of Alexandria
Pen and brown ink, 11.8 x 23.2 cm
Inv. RP-T-1935-75
Rijksmuseum, Amsterdam,
Rijksprentenkabinet, F. G. Waller Bequest,
Amsterdam
(Potsdam only)

Lit.
Henkel 1938, 574

Johan Teyler was a professor of philosophy and mathematics in Nijmegen as well as an inventor—of a method of color printmaking, for example—and a military engineer. It was in this last capacity that in 1677–78 he served at the court of Friedrich Wilhelm, elector of Brandenburg, in Berlin. In 1679 he set off on a four-year-long journey to Italy, Sicily, Malta, Egypt, and the Holy Land, one purpose of which was to study the military architecture of the Mediterranean. Teyler kept a record of many of his ports of call in meticulously executed ink drawings. Their standardized format and the care taken with their picturesque compositions perhaps indicate an intention to reproduce them as prints at some point.

To judge by the numerous views of the Nile drawn from the middle of the river it seems likely that Teyler toured Egypt by boat. In Alexandria he climbed the Round Tower and from there drew a view of the city with one of the obelisks—in those days erroneously called "Cleopatra's Needles"—then still in the country. At the Cairo Citadel his curiosity was piqued by the old mosque known as the "Divan of Joseph," in those days in a ruinous condition.[1] BB

[1] Cf. *Description de l'Égypte . . . État moderne,* ed. Edmé François Jomard, plates, vol. 1, Paris 1906, pl. 70. The localizations are by André Wiese, Basel.

85.1

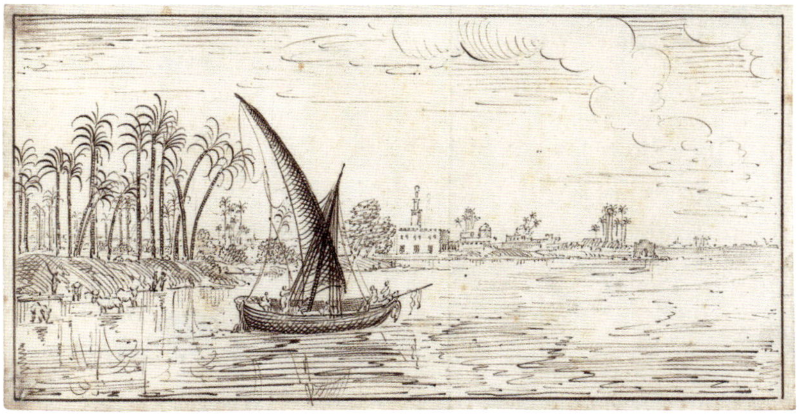

85.2

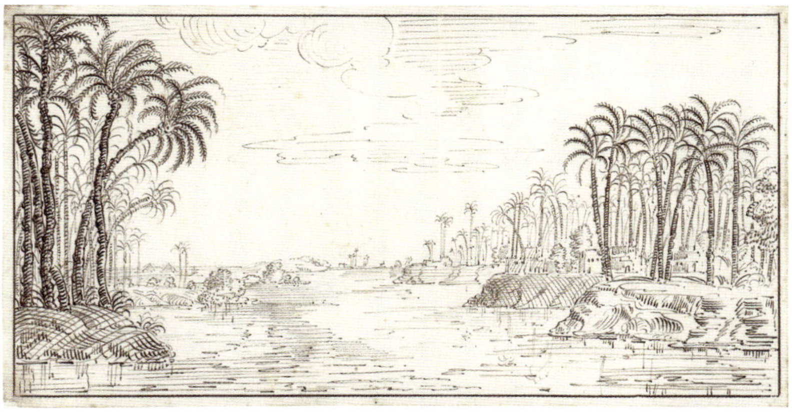

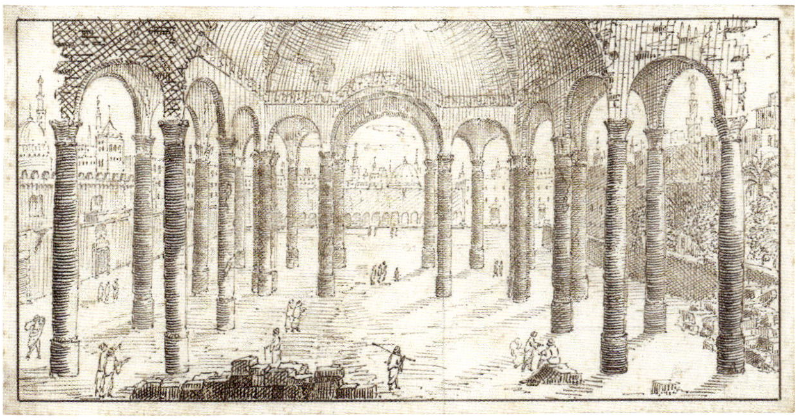

85.3

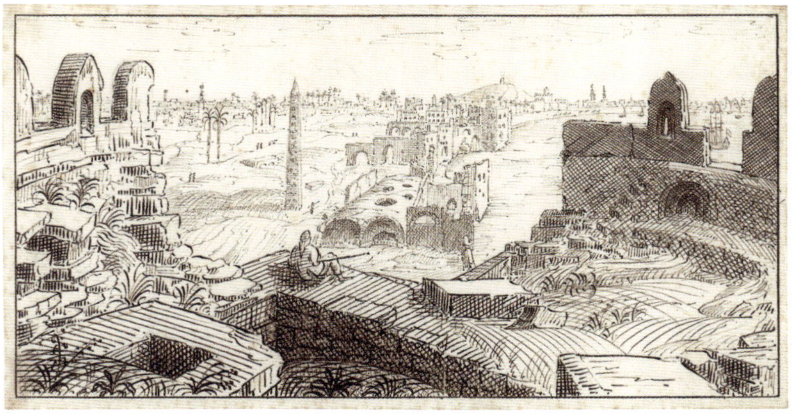

85.4

86 **J. F. F. after Andries Beeckman** (1628–1664)
The Marketplace of Batavia, after 1688

87 **Andries Beeckman** (1628–1664)
Dancing Ambonese Warrior Dressed in Yellow, 1658–64

86
Oil on canvas, 144 x 209 cm
Inscribed top right: J.F.F.; bottom right on the boat: De Marckt van Batavia.
Inv. TM-118-167
Tropenmuseum, Amsterdam

Lit.
Paris 1967, no. 389
Amsterdam 1972, under no. 1
Bamberg 1988, no. 45 (version formerly in the Museum Nusantara, Delft)
Amsterdam 1998, 26–27, 146
Amsterdam 2002b, 34–36 (version in the Rijksmuseum, Amsterdam)
London 2004, 141 (version in the Rijksmuseum, Amsterdam)
Rotterdam 2014, 22–23, 41, 49, ill. pp. 24–25; 9, 38 *passim*, ill. pp. 10–11, 53 (detail) (version in the Rijksmuseum, Amsterdam)
Amsterdam 2015, no. 6 (version in the Rijksmuseum, Amsterdam)
Mostert/Van Campen 2015, 128, 131; fig. p. 128 (version in the Rijksmuseum, Amsterdam)

87
Watercolor, 36.6 x 24 cm
Coté Est-389, no. 11
Bibliothèque de l'Arsenal, Bibliothèque nationale de France, Paris
(Basel only)

Lit.
Rotterdam 2014, 41–42; no. 16a

Among the very few artists of the seventeenth century who actually spent time in the regions in which the Dutch East India Company operated was the painter Andries Beeckman of Hasselt. He entered the company's service at the age of twenty-five in 1652–53 and remained in Asia for about five years. He was therefore able to draw on personal experience for his scenes of life in the Far East. Beeckman did not use exotic motifs merely as atmospheric props for biblical history paintings (see. cat. 4, 9). He rather produced studies of different ethnic groups as well as this view of Batavia, the Dutch East India Company's headquarters in Asia, whose apparent verisimilitude makes it a truly exceptional work. The painting, which was commissioned by the Dutch East India Company itself around 1661—that is, four years after Beeckman's return—enjoyed pride of place on the chimneypiece of the conference room at the Oost-Indisch Huys (cat. 18) in Amsterdam. Here is a copy of the work, also called *The Castle of Batavia* (Rijksmuseum, Amsterdam) by the otherwise unknown copyist J. F. F., that is significantly larger than the original and deviates from it in certain points of detail.

On conquering Jacatra (now Jakarta) on the north coast of the Indonesian island of Java, in 1619, the Dutch destroyed the city, drove out its inhabitants, and established the new settlement of Batavia in its stead. The new city grew fast and soon became the nerve center of the precolonial system of rule established by the Dutch in East Asia. Not only did they settle countless Chinese and Bantanese there, initially against their will, but they also imported thousands of slaves from India, Bali, and today's Myanmar, all of whom had to live alongside the Mardijkers, former slaves of the Portuguese, as well as the various ethnic groups who populated the Indonesian archipelago.

The scene depicted by Beeckman can be located very exactly. The market under the coconut palms, here doubling as emblems of the exotic, was situated on the west bank of the River Ciliwung. Looking north there is a row of typically Chinese houses on the left, while the middle ground is dominated by the Castle of Batavia itself, an enormous fortress proclaiming the military might of the Dutch.

Although the spatial situation by and large matches the reality on the ground, the market scene is less a reproduction of an actual market day than an ideal gathering of the different ethnic groups then resident in Batavia. Among the easiest to identify are the Chinese fishmonger on the right and the man in a blue robe next to him, who is presumably Japanese; promenading in the left foreground are an imperious-looking Dutchman and his indigenous partner, who are followed by a slave to hold the ceremonial parasol (see cat. 27). Further back is a group of Javans—recognizable by their white head coverings—playing ball.

On the far left are two Ambonesian warriors who, armed with sword and shield, are performing the traditional Moluccan war dance called the *cakalele*. These two figures are not included in the original painting. They were taken from an album, now in Paris, containing watercolors of the various ethnic groups that Andries Beeckman painted on his return to Amsterdam after sketches made in situ. The copyist J. F. F. must have known that album or have based his work on a different, presumably since lost, version of the painting. The sketches in the album show what an acute observer Beeckman was and attest to his interest in the many different peoples of Indonesia. But his compendium also follows the tradition of costume albums, which European artists in the Ottoman Empire and in Persia (cat. 91) had been compiling since the sixteenth century (see the essay by Jan de Hond, pp. 40–55). MPH

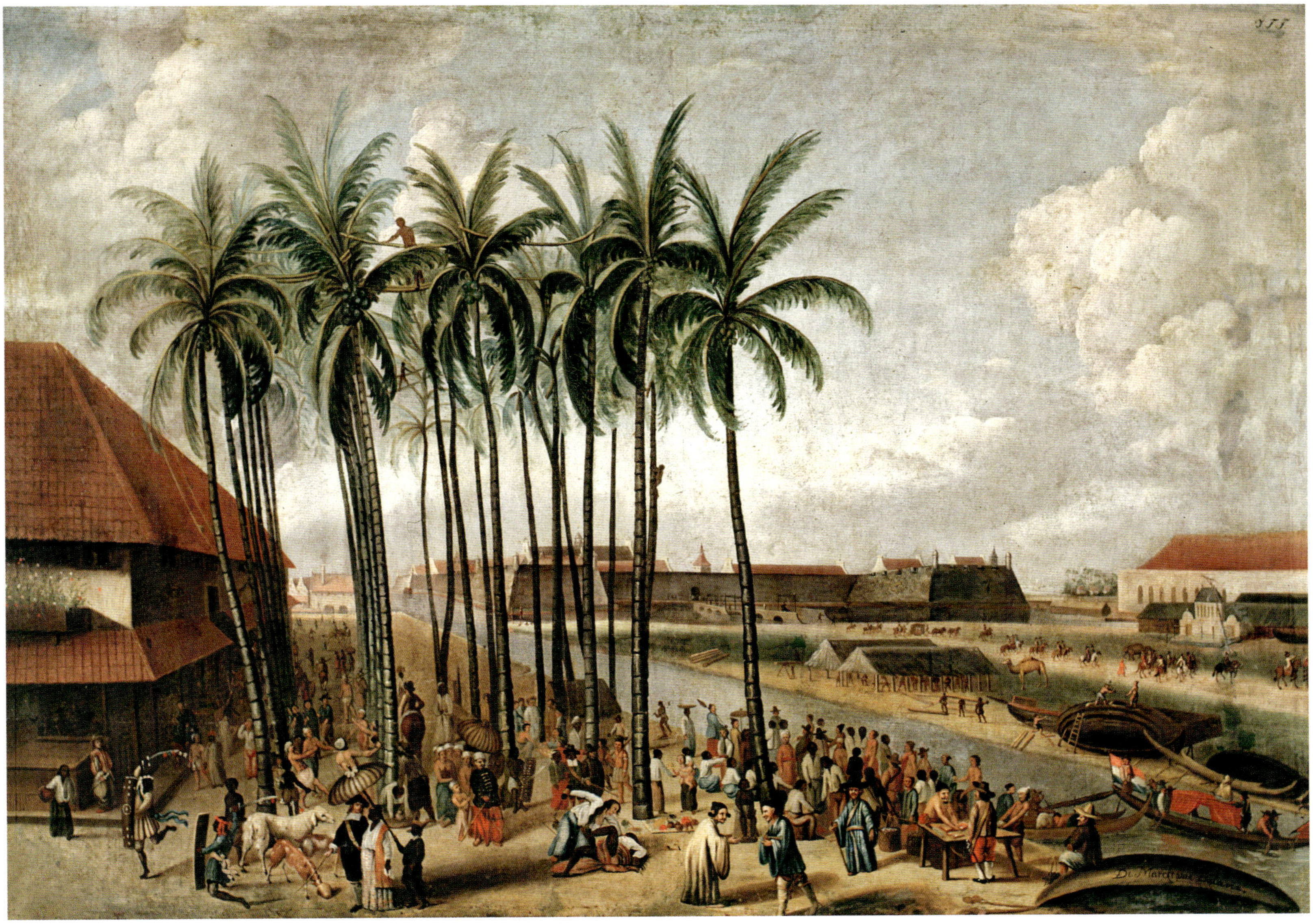

86

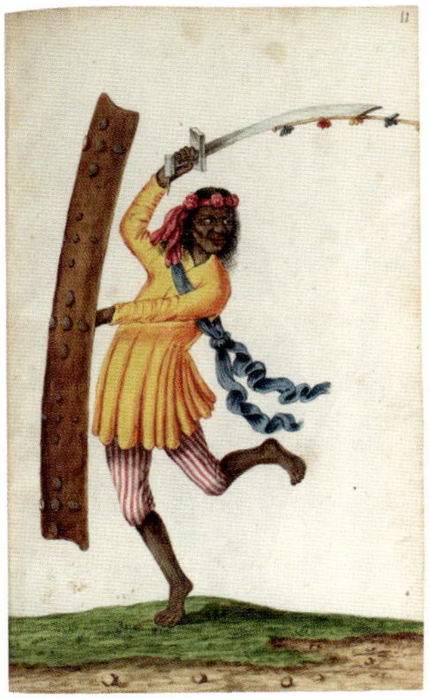

87

88 Esaias Boursse (1631–1672)
Scene with a Party in a Sinhalese Tavern or Living Room, 1662

Brush in gray, 14.8 x 19.6 cm
Inv. NG-1996-6-116
Rijksmuseum, Amsterdam,
Rijksprentenkabinet

Lit.
De Silva/Beumer 1988
Wagenaar 2016, 4

This work belongs to an album of 116 drawings, the first page of which, added at a later date, is inscribed as follows: "ik onder geschreven hebbe dit / tijken boeck, op Silon getijkent, / en verkocht aen mijn broeder / tot mijn contentement den / 1 Jannewarij 1671 / esias boursse" (I, the undersigned, drew this book of drawings on Ceylon and to my satisfaction sold it to my brother on January 1, 1671: Esaias Boursse). Boursse, a gifted genre painter, in 1661 enlisted in the service of the Dutch East India Company as a sea cadet on the *Amersfoort* that was sailing to Ceylon, in those days a Dutch colony. The voyage included a brief sojourn on the Cape of Good Hope. He returned to Amsterdam in 1663.

The last scene in the album shows a group of Dutch colonial masters in a high-ceilinged, sparsely furnished room with bare walls and what looks like a rammed-earth floor. On the left is a doorway to the outside, apparently without a door. Two European women are sitting opposite each other. One is viewed en face, the other from behind. Leaning on the backrest of the chair occupied by the latter is a man with a sword slung into his sash. The man standing to the left of the group is similarly armed, and with his wine glass raised is toasting the third European man present, who is seated in a chair on the right.

Standing in front of the rear wall and in the right foreground are two indigenous women wearing traditional Singhalese dress: the one further back is clad in a *redda* and *hatte*, a wrap-around skirt and blouse, while the one at the front wears only a *lungi*, while her upper body is bare, as are her feet. Also striking are the large heavy rings elongating her earlobes. The two women's stiff, attentive posture marks them out as servants. Although the occasion for the toast remains unclear, the depiction of the scene with its emphasis on the stark contrast between two cultures seems to capture a moment in the life of the Dutch colonialists in an authentic way. BB

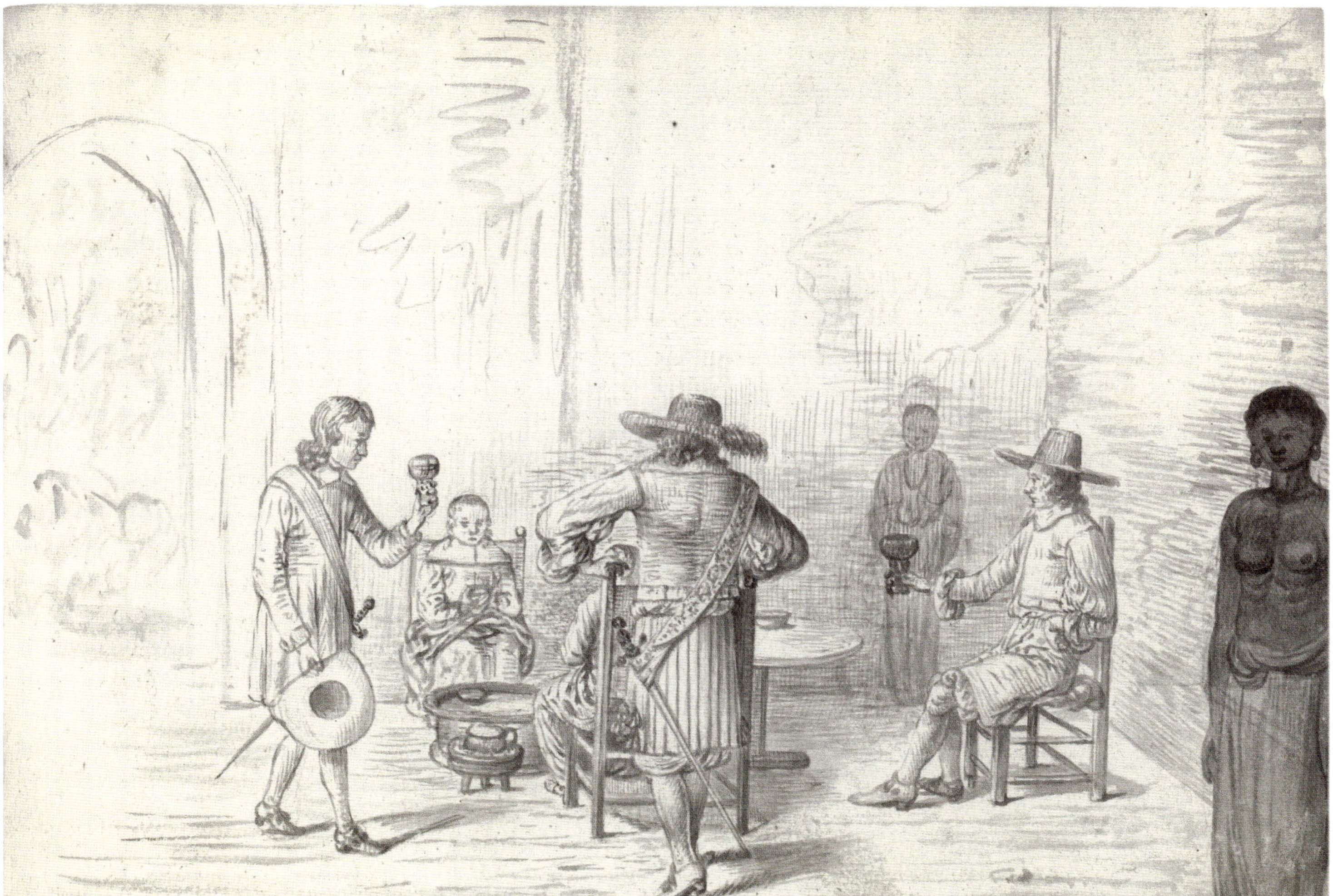

88

89 **Aegidius Sadeler II** (ca. 1570–1629)

Portrait of Mehdi Quli Beg, Persian Ambassador at the Imperial Court in Prague, 1605

Engraving
25.7 x 18.7 cm
3rd state (of 5) (Basel),
24.9 x 18.9 cm
3rd state (of 5) (Amsterdam)
Inscribed on plate at bottom left:
S . Caes . M^{tis} . Sculptor AE[in ligature]gidius Sadeler ad vivum / delineavit Cum Privil . S. Cae. M^{tis} . Anno . Pragae . 1605 .
Inv. X.1294
Kunstmuseum Basel, Kupferstichkabinett (Basel)
Inv. RP-P-1896-A-19007
Rijksmuseum, Amsterdam, Rijksprentenkabinet
(Potsdam)

Lit.
H 275 (1/3)
Schwartz 1985a, 46
Bonn 1995, no. 133 a
Kappel 1995, 129–30
Deluga 2008, 424, 426
Zurich 2013, no. 1
Niayesh 2016, 216–17

1 For a detailed account of the missions, cf. Steensgaard 1975, 230–44.

Safavid Persia enjoyed a period of consolidation and rising prosperity during the reign of Shah Abbas I from 1587 to 1629. He had the capital moved to Isfahan, which became an important political and economic center, and in 1600 established diplomatic ties to the Christian powers in Europe. The Shiite leader was looking for allies against the Ottoman Empire on Persia's western border, military conflicts with which had become a recurrent problem. Another purpose of his overtures, besides the discussion of possible military alliances, was to shift the export of Persian silks from the overland route, which crossed Ottoman territory, to the overseas route, which promised to be more profitable and would have the added benefit of weakening the enemy economically.

The first Persian mission arrived at the court of Emperor Rudolf II in Prague in 1600 and hence in the middle of the long-drawn-out military conflict with the Ottomans that has gone down in history as the Long Turkish War (1593–1606). The delegation was received with all due honors, although no treaties were signed; nor did subsequent meetings with representatives of other powers such as Venice and the Spanish crown yield anything other than well-meaning declarations of intent. The Safavids initiated a second attempt three years later, by which time Shah Abbas had launched a military offensive against the Ottomans and succeeded in reclaiming previously lost territory. This time, several envoys were dispatched from Isfahan, among them two destined for Prague, which they reached in the spring and December of 1604. The results of this second mission were similarly disappointing.[1]

The leader of the third—and for many years final—mission was the man depicted on this print, Mehdi Quli Beg, who while in Prague followed the example of his predecessors and his companion Zaynal Khan Shamlu, and had himself portrayed by Aegidius Sadeler II of Antwerp, then artist to the imperial court. With its inscription around the niche containing the bust recording the subject's name and position, the portrait follows a type that was standard at the Rudolfine court, but elaborates on it by adding a text in Persian.

Alongside the reference to his imperial privilege—the engraving might have been commissioned by Rudolf himself in token of his esteem—Sadeler also claims that the likeness was drawn "ad vivum," that is, after life. Even if there is no proof of this in this particular case, the portrait can certainly be considered realistic. The silk of the sitter's robe is adorned with figures resembling a contemporary Persian pattern; his mustache is in keeping with the current courtly fashion, and even his turban with its extravagant plumed jewel is a recognizable type: such turbans were coiled around a stabilizing structure, the tip of which, called the *taj-i Haydari* (Haydar crown), pokes out of the turban at the back of the head. This ancient headdress had been reintroduced by Shah Abbas and hence signaled the wearer's loyalty to the Safavid Dynasty. The falcon is an allusion to the courtly tradition of falconry, thus adding further weight to the subject's aristocratic bearing.

This portrait of an emissary from the Orient, or to be more exact from the Persian Empire, by an artist to the court of the Holy Roman Emperor tells of the two parties' mutual esteem and interest in each other's culture. Although the portraits were produced at the imperial court in Prague, they nevertheless provided Dutch and other European artists with an authentic impression of how high-ranking Persian dignitaries actually looked and what kind of attire they wore. Prints of the portraits of Mehdi Quli Beg and his predecessors are known to have featured in Amsterdam collections just a few years after they were made. GD

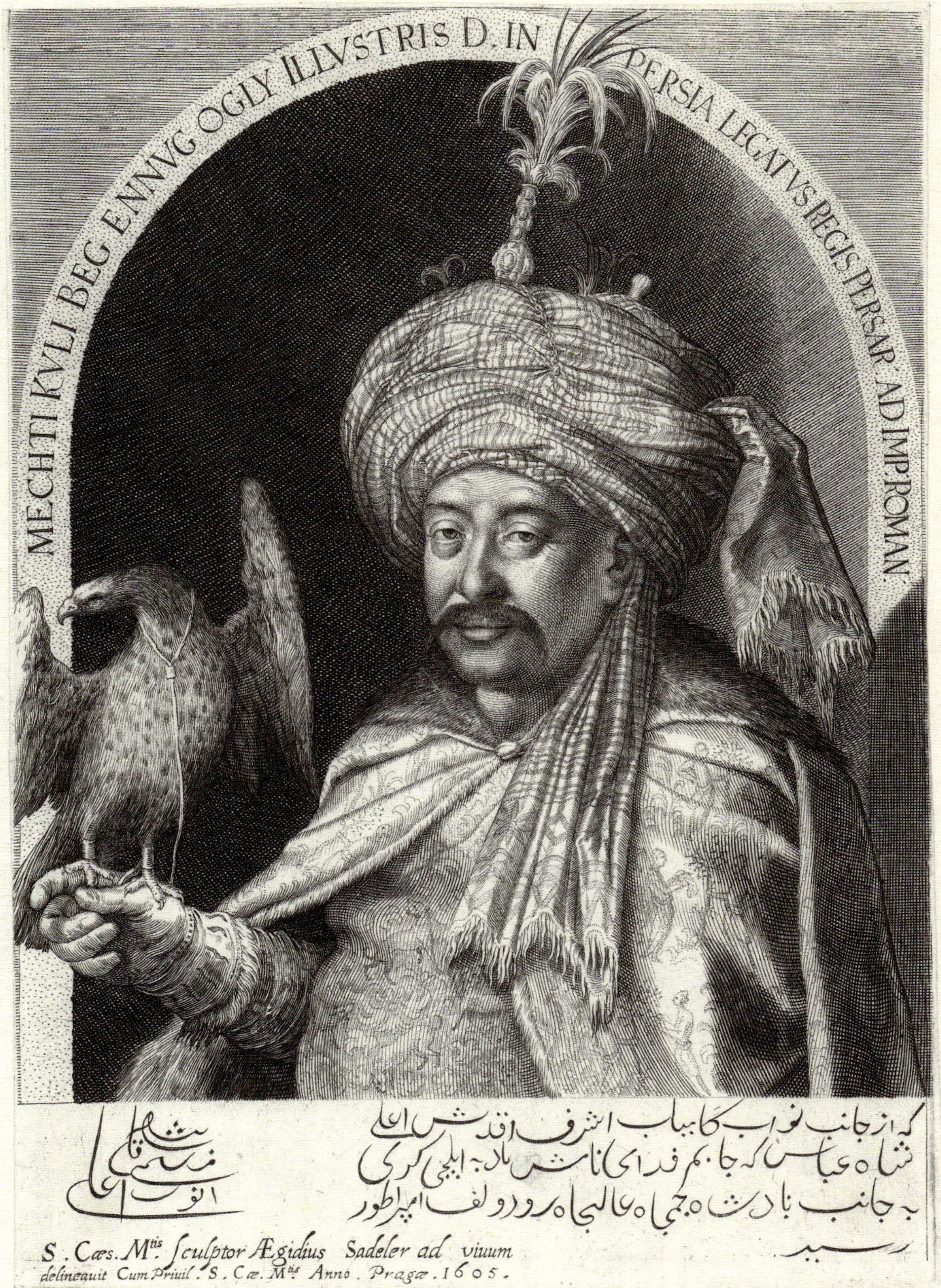
MECHTI KVLI BEG ENNVG OGLY ILLVSTRIS D. IN PERSIA LEGATVS REGIS PERSAR AD IMP. ROMAN.
که از جانب نواب کامیاب اشرف اقدس اعلی
شاه عباس که جانم فدای نامش باد به ایلچی گری
به جانب پادشاه جم‌جاه عالیجاه رودولف امپراطور
رسید
S. Cæs. Mtis. Sculptor Ægidius Sadeler ad viuum
delineauit Cum Priuil. S. Cæ. Mtis Anno. Pragæ. 1605.

90 **Wallerant Vaillant** (1623–1677)

Portrait of Sultan Süleyman II (?), ca. 1658–77

Mezzotint, 22.5 x 18.3 cm
2nd state (of 4)
Inscribed on plate at bottom right:
W. Vaillant fec. / et Pinx.
Inv. RP-P-1911-77
Rijksmuseum, Amsterdam,
Rijksprentenkabinet

Lit.
H 196 (2/3)
Wuestman/Webb 2006, 65

Wallerant Vaillant was the first artist to employ the newly invented technique of mezzotint on a large scale. He had first been introduced to it by Prince Rupert of the Rhine during a sojourn in Frankfurt am Main from 1656 to 1658. The prince was experimenting with the method at the time and with Vaillant's help hoped to perfect it.[1] Mezzotint entailed roughening the copper printing plate with a mechanical rocker, which made for soft, deep shades of black as ground, while subsequent smoothing with the appropriate tools enabled a vast array of gray tones. Painterly effects that had hitherto been unattainable in printmaking were thus now possible. The technique, which permitted print runs of only a hundred copies and hence far fewer than conventional engraving was used principally for portraiture and the reproduction of paintings.

Among Vaillant's numerous mezzotint portraits is this bust of a seated man sporting an Oriental mustache and turban, four states of which have been preserved. Only the third of these, a probably posthumous state with what is generally a rather weak impression, features the legend "Soliman III. Empereur des Turcs." inscribed in the lower edge of the plate to the left of the artist's signature. For the fourth state this legend was removed.

Presumably it had been added in response to a political change: Süleyman II[2] became sultan at the age of forty-five after his brother Mehmed IV was deposed in 1687, a decade after Vaillant's death. Until then he had spent his entire life in the *kafes,* a prison for princes of the blood inside the Topkapı Palace (see cat. 83) in which half-brothers of the reigning sultan sired in the harem were locked up to keep them out of politics. The circulation of portrait prints of Süleyman before he acceded to the throne would have undermined that strategy.

Vaillant must therefore have intended either to depict a different ruler, be it the reigning sultan Mehmed IV (r. 1648–1687), or even Süleyman the Magnificent (r. 1520–1566), who as the greatest of all the previous sultans was still considered eminently portrait-worthy. But perhaps what Vaillant really wanted was to produce an anonymous character head, a *tronie,* in Oriental style. The rededication in the third state might have been occasioned by rising public interest in the Ottoman Empire, which in the West was fueled—somewhat paradoxically—by the military successes of Ludwig Wilhelm, margrave of Baden-Baden (1655–1707), popularly known as "Türkenlouis." BB

1 Cf. Wuestman 1995, 66–67.
2 Identical with Süleyman III. Both regnal numbers exist; the canonical one is II.

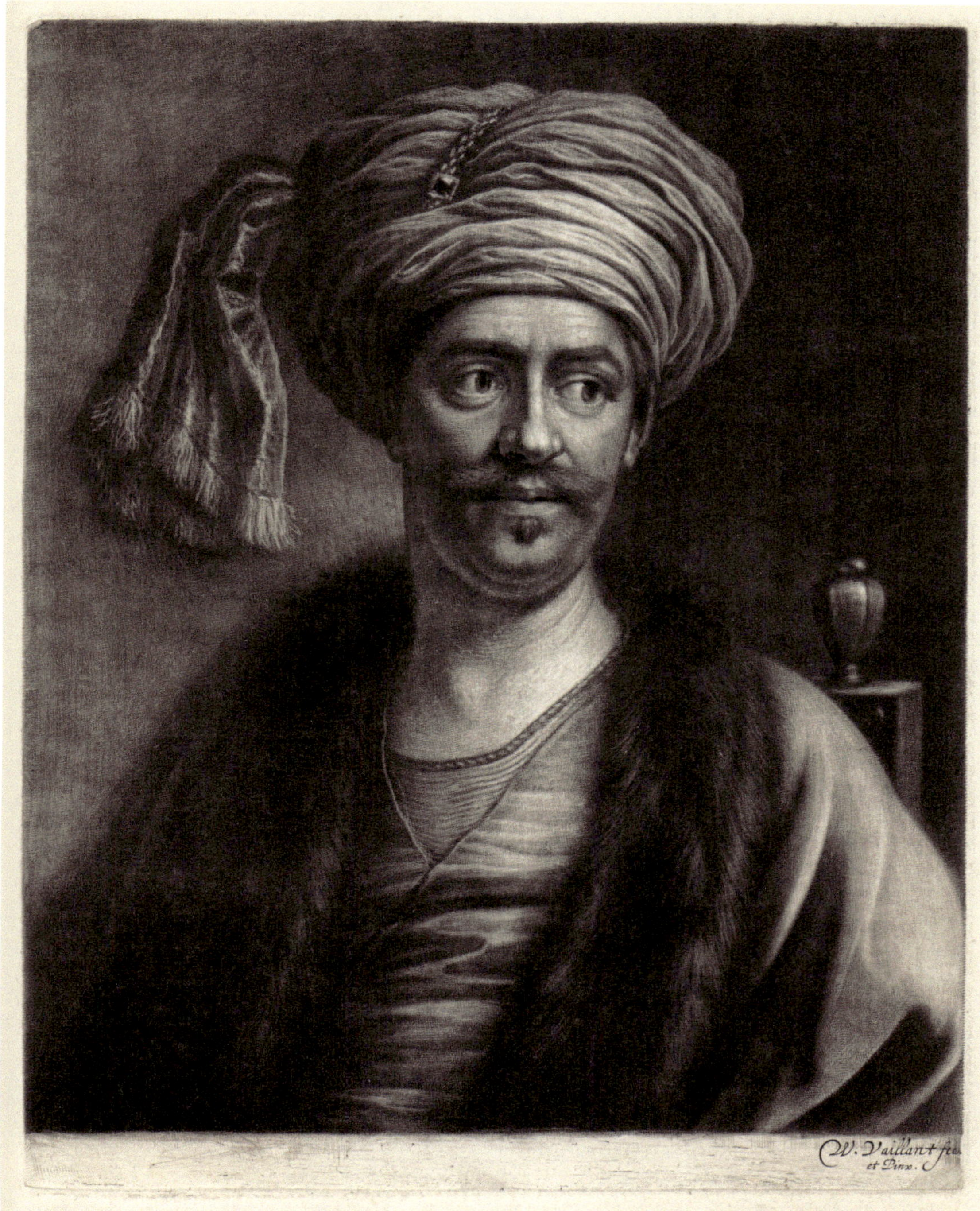

90

91.1–2 **Cornelis Claesz. Duysend** (active from 1630)

Two Inhabitants of Isfahan, 1633

Tatarean and Usbek, 1647

91.1
Woodcut
In Johannes de Laet, *Persia seu Regni Persici Status: Variaque Itinera in atque per Persiam: cum Aliquot Iconibus Incolarum* (Persia, or the State of the Persian Empire, as well as Various Itineraries to and through Persia; with Several Pictures of its Inhabitants), Leiden: Elzevir, 1633, pp. 138–39
OK 61-311 (Potsdam)
OK-62-1721 (Basel)
Allard Pierson, University of Amsterdam

91.2
Woodcut
In Johannes de Laet, *Persia seu Regni Persici Status: Variaque Itinera in atque per Persiam: cum Aliquot Iconibus Incolarum* (Persia, or the State of the Persian Empire, as well as Various Itineraries to and through Persia; with Several Pictures of its Inhabitants), 2nd expanded edition, Leiden: Elzevir, 1647, pp. 120–21
OK 62-6327 (Potsdam)
OK 61-304 (Basel)
Allard Pierson, University of Amsterdam

Lit.
Schwartz 2014, 28–29

[1] Cf. Rauschenbach 2013, 84; on De Laet cf. Bremmer/Hoftijzer 1998.

Johannes de Laet became a model for the new Dutch elite of learned merchants.[1] He was born into a Calvinist family from Louvain that fled to the northern Netherlands after the fall of Antwerp in 1585. At Leiden University he studied under the foremost humanists in the country, building a basis for intellectual independence and wide interests. De Laet was a successful businessman, a highly productive writer, and a correspondent with many other scholars.

In 1621 De Laet became a founder of the Dutch West India Company, a pendant to the Dutch East India Company that was vested with a monopoly on trade with America and West Africa. This entailed armed conflict with other expansive European powers, especially Portugal and England. In addition to being one of its nineteen directors starting in 1622, he was also the company historian. In 1644 his five-hundred-page history of the Dutch West India Company was published in Leiden.

De Laet's writings covered a wide range of topics, from church history to editions of ancient texts. He was a mainstay of one of the great book-publishing ventures of early modern times. From 1625 through 1649 the Elzevir publishing house of Leiden brought out the first series of books in paperback format, thirty-five volumes on the countries of the contemporaneous world and three of ancient times. The series is known as the Elzevierian Republics. The books were published in Latin, making them available throughout the learned world of Europe. They were solid digests of existing knowledge, augmented by travelers' reports.

In addition to his Elzeviers on the Moghul Empire (1631) and Turkey, Algeria, and Tunisia (1634), Johannes de Laet wrote a volume on Persia, published in 1633. For this book De Laet was able to provide eight woodcuts based, as he says in the introduction, on drawings procured by his friend Nicolaus Hemmius. The drawings reflect contemporaneous images by the foremost court painter to Shah Abbas I, Riza Abbasi (see the essay by Jan de Hond, pp. 40–55).

Even if these images have a measure of authenticity, they amount to a very meagre representation of foreign peoples. The same can be said of the figures in the cartouches of the map of Asia in Blaeu's *Atlas maior* (cat. 40) and other Dutch books of the time. This record compares very poorly with sixteenth-century publications such as the over one hundred authentic images of Turkish persons and locations published in 1575 by the Danish artist Melchior Lorck or the extensive production of the Flemish artist Jean-Baptiste Vanmour at the Ottoman court in the early eighteenth century. It remains a paradox why Dutch artists of the seventeenth century, with so many opportunities at their disposal, created so few images of "Orientals."

De Laet's books rank high among the contributions of Dutch writers to the ideal of the *mercator sapiens,* the "wise merchant," made immortal in 1632 by Caspar van Baerle, one of the founding professors of the Amsterdam institution of higher learning, the Atheneum Illustre. As the business-people of Amsterdam took upon themselves political, administrative, confessional, and diplomatic responsibilities formerly exercised by royal and princely courts and ecclesiastical bodies, they are called upon to furnish their children with the intellectual and spiritual background to fulfill these tasks adequately. De Laet himself shone in this regard. His book on Persia excels both as chorography and as a handbook for traders wishing to deal with the Safavid court. GS

91.1

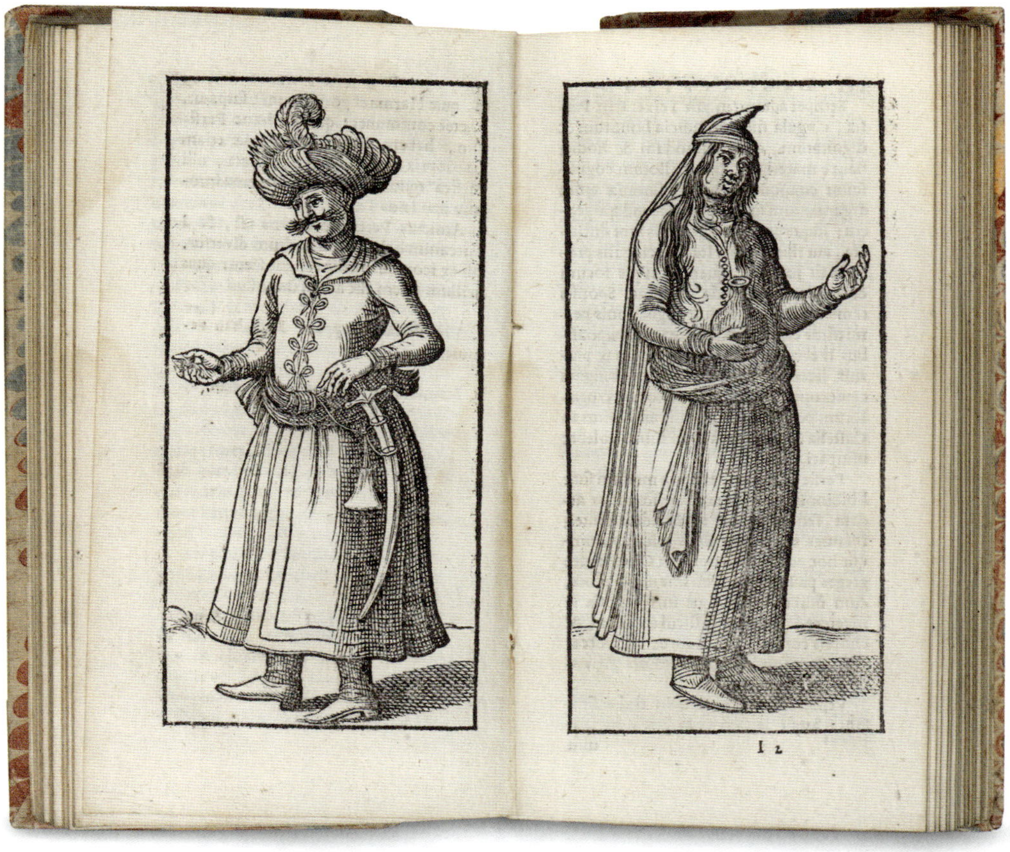

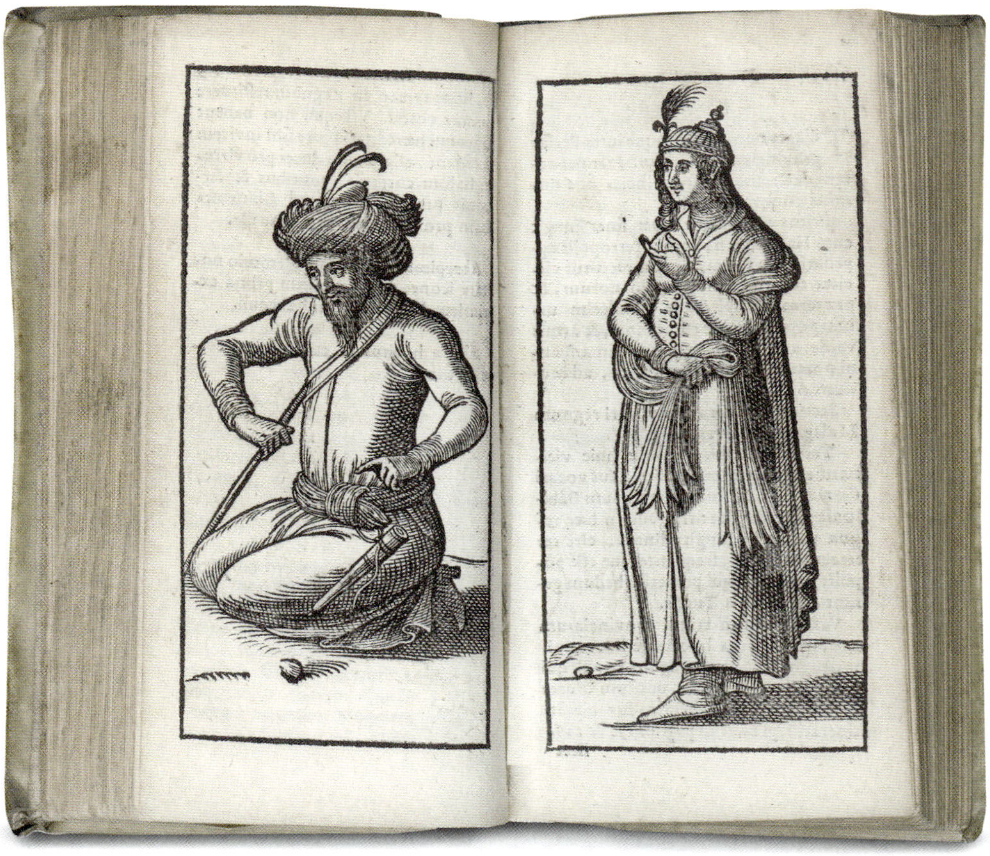

91.2

92 **Willem Schellinks** (1623–1678)
Op de schilder-konst der Benjanen (On Benjan [Indian] Painting),
in *Klioos Kraam . . .* (The Muse of History Gives Birth . . .),
Amsterdam: Henrik Rintjus, 1657, pp. 351–53

Private collection

Lit.
Schwartz 2014, 55
Gommans 2018, 215–19

Willem Schellinks was an accomplished draftsman and painter of town and country views. He distinguished himself through his cosmopolitanism, his wide travels, and his poetry. Although his written work never came out in a collected volume, occasional verse by him was included in a number of anthologies in the mid-seventeenth century.

Schellinks was associated with an Amsterdam enterprise of global breadth, the map and drawing collection of the Catholic attorney Laurens van der Hem (1621–1678). Van der Hem made use of the world atlas published in eleven volumes from 1649 on by Joan Blaeu, the *Atlas Maior* (see cat. 40), as a portmanteau for the additional materials from around the world in his possession. Some of these were commissioned, and that was the nature of Schellinks's relation to Van der Hem. The attorney was one of the sponsors of a European grand tour of no less than four years (1661–65) for the education of a youngster named Jacob Thierry, under the tutelage of Schellinks. Of the drawings he made on the road, Schellinks made large-scale copies of 120 of them for inclusion in Van der Hem's atlas. The ensemble of forty-six volumes was taken up in the UNESCO Memory of the World Register (Austrian National Library, Vienna; see figs. pp. 79, 80).

Through his tie to Laurens van der Hem, and perhaps other collector friends of his, Schellinks made the acquaintance of the world beyond Europe. To cite the most spectacular instance, the Van der Hem Atlas included four volumes of confidential manuscript maps of African and Asian lands made for the Dutch East India Company. Whether or not this was the decisive link that introduced Schellinks to Indian art, we find him expressing keen admiration for Indian art in his poem *Op de schilder-konst der Benjanen* (On Benjan [Indian] Painting), published in 1657. The year before, Rembrandt revealed in his etching of *Abraham Entertaining the Angels* admiring knowledge of Indian art (cat. 118), followed by his twenty-five copies of Mughal portraits (see the essay by Gary Schwartz, pp. 56–73).

That Schellinks and Rembrandt had access to the same models is clear from a comparison between the heavenly apotheosis in Schellinks's *Parade of the Sons of Shah Jahan* (cat. 94) with a drawing by Rembrandt of the same motif (Museum Boijmans Van Beuningen, Rotterdam). As fragmentary as they are, these indications point to close contacts in the mid-1650s between Schellinks, Rembrandt, and one or more Amsterdam collectors in possession of Indian miniatures. The rather hyperbolic praise of Indian art in Schellinks's poem is unique in the appreciation of Oriental art in Europe of the time. GS

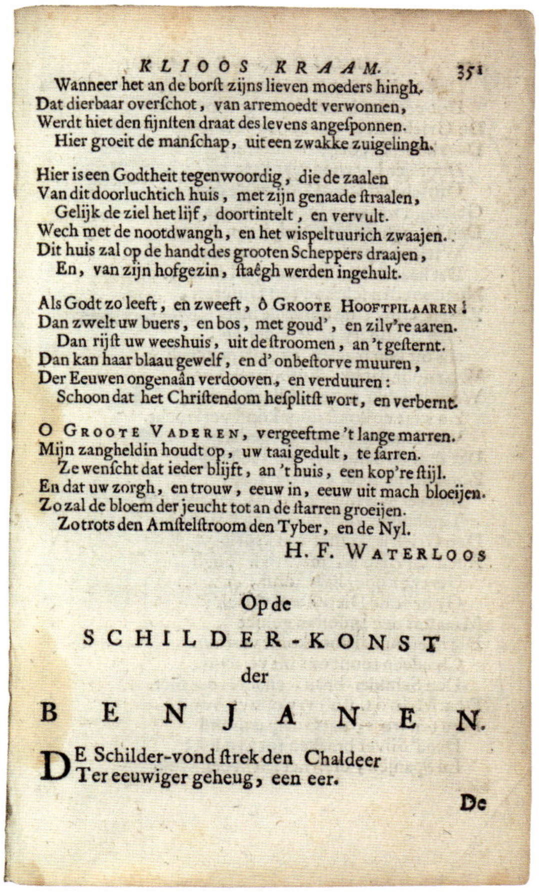

Wanneer het an de borst zijns lieven moeders hingh,
Dat dierbaar overschot, van arremoedt verwonnen,
Werdt hiet den fijnsten draat des levens angesponnen.
Hier groeit de manschap, uit een zwakke zuigelingh.

Hier is een Godtheit tegenwoordig, die de zaalen
Van dit doorluchtich huis, met zijn genaade straalen,
Gelijk de ziel het lijf, doortintelt, en vervult.
Wech met de nootdwangh, en het wispeltuurich zwaajen.
Dit huis zal op de handt des grooten Scheppers draajen,
En, van zijn hofgezin, staêgh werden ingehult.

Als Godt zo leeft, en zweeft, ô Groote Hooftpilaaren!
Dan zwelt uw buers, en bos, met goud', en zilv're aaren.
Dan rijst uw weeshuis, uit de stroomen, an 't gesternt.
Dan kan haar blaau gewelf, en d' onbestorve muuren,
Der Eeuwen ongenaân verdooven, en verduuren:
Schoon dat het Christendom hesplitst wort, en verbernt.

O Groote Vaderen, vergeefs me 't lange marren.
Mijn zangheldin houdt op, uw taai gedult, te tarren.
Ze wenscht dat ieder blijft, an 't huis, een kop're stijl.
En dat uw zorgh, en trouw, eeuw in, eeuw uit mach bloeijen.
Zo zal de bloem der jeucht tot an de starren groeijen.
Zo trots den Amstelstroom den Tyber, en de Nyl.

H. F. Waterloos

Op de
SCHILDER-KONST
der
BENJANEN.

DE Schilder-vond strek den Chaldeer
Ter eeuwiger geheug, een eer.

De

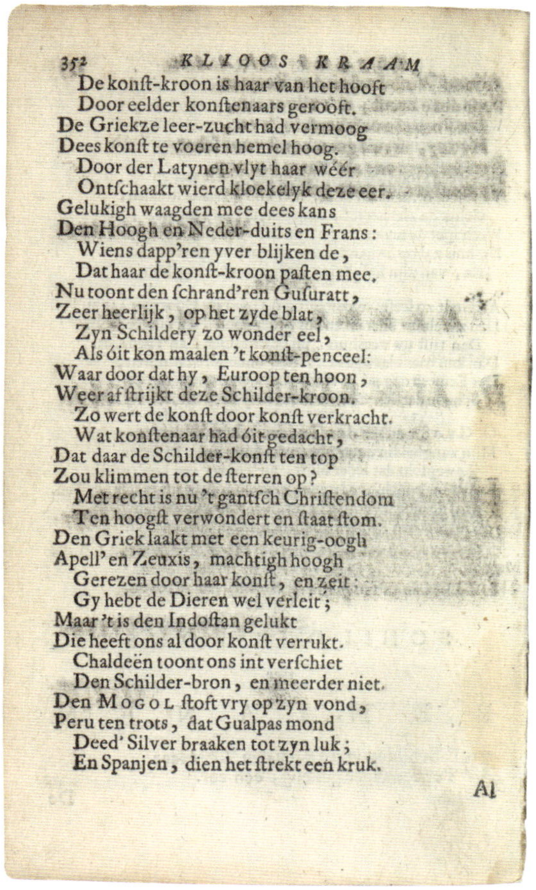

De konst-kroon is haar van het hooft
Door eelder konstenaars gerooft.
De Griekze leer-zucht had vermoog
Dees konst te voeren hemel hoog.
Door der Latynen vlyt haar wéér
Ontschaakt wierd kloekelyk deze eer.
Gelukigh waagden mee dees kans
Den Hoogh en Neder-duits en Frans:
Wiens dapp'ren yver blijken de,
Dat haar de konst-kroon pasten mee.
Nu toont den schrand'ren Gusuratt,
Zeer heerlijk, op het zyde blat,
Zyn Schildery zo wonder eel,
Als óit kon maalen 't konst-penceel:
Waar door dat hy, Euroop ten hoon,
Weer af strijkt deze Schilder-kroon.
Zo wert de konst door konst verkracht.
Wat konstenaar had óit gedacht,
Dat daar de Schilder-konst ten top
Zou klimmen tot de sterren op?
Met recht is nu 't gantsch Christendom
Ten hoogst verwondert en staat stom.
Den Griek laakt met een keurig-oogh
Apell' en Zeuxis, machtigh hoogh
Gerezen door haar konst, en zeit:
Gy hebt de Dieren wel verleit;
Maar 't is den Indostan gelukt
Die heeft ons al door konst verrukt.
Chaldeën toont ons int verschiet
Den Schilder-bron, en meerder niet.
Den Mogol stoft vry op zyn vond,
Peru ten trots, dat Gualpas mond
Deed' Silver braaken tot zyn luk;
En Spanjen, dien het strekt een kruk.

Al

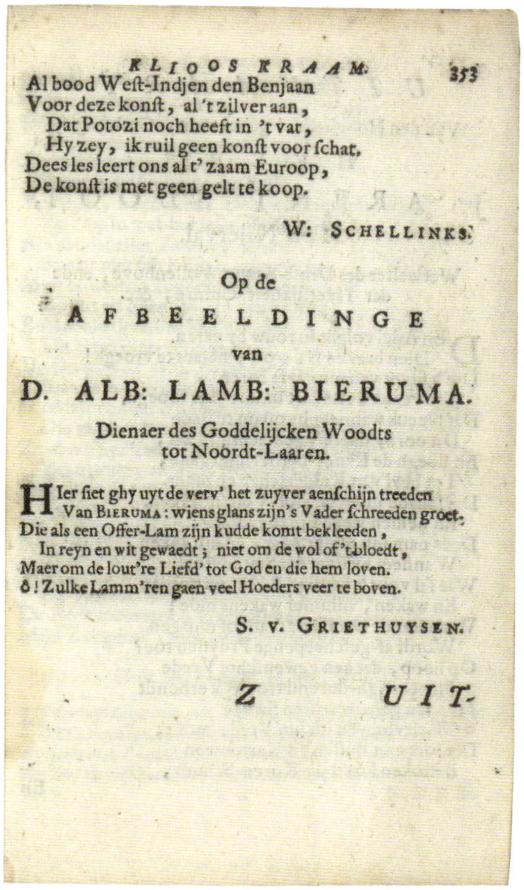

Al bood West-Indjen den Benjaan
Voor deze konst, al 't zilver aan,
Dat Potozi noch heeft in 't vat,
Hy zey, ik ruil geen konst voor schat.
Dees les leert ons al t' zaam Euroop,
De konst is met geen gelt te koop.

W: Schellinks.

Op de
AFBEELDINGE
van
D. ALB: LAMB: BIERUMA.
Dienaer des Goddelijcken Woodts
tot Noordt-Laaren.

HIer siet ghy uyt de verv' het zuyver aenschijn treeden
Van Bieruma: wiens glans zijn's Vader schreeden groet.
Die als een Offer-Lam zijn kudde komt bekleeden,
In reyn en wit gewaedt; niet om de wol of 't bloedt,
Maer om de lout're Liefd' tot God en die hem loven.
ô! Zulke Lamm'ren gaen veel Hoeders veer te boven.

S. v. Griethuysen.

Z UIT-

On Benjan [Indian] Painting

The invention of painting lends the Chaldeans honor to be remembered forevermore.
The crown of art was stolen from their head by artists elsewhere.
The eagerness of the Greeks to learn brought with it the ability to raise this art sky-high.
The honor was unflinchingly stolen again by Roman diligence.
Fortunately, the challenge [to win] this prize was also taken up by the Germans, Dutch, and French,
Whose valiant perseverance proved that the crown of art fitted them as well.
Now the clever Gusuratt [Indian] shows most delightfully on the silken sheet
His painting, as marvelously noble as artist's brush could ever paint.
So that he scorns Europe and makes off with the crown of painting.
Thus is art despoiled by art. What artist ever thought
It would be there that the art of painting would climb to the heights, to the very stars.
Rightfully, all of Christendom is now totally astonished and stands speechless.
The Greek, with a discerning eye, admonishes Apelles and Zeuxis, who rose
To great heights through their art, saying: You may have deceived animals
But the Hindustan has succeeded in enthralling us all with art.
Chaldeans show us at a remote distance the source of painting, and nothing more.
The Moghul boasts of his discovery, braving Peru, which caused Gualpa's mouth
To spew up silver, to its good fortune; and Spain, for which it serves as a crutch.
Were the West Indies to offer the Benjan for its art all the silver that Potozi
Still has in store, he'd say "I'll not trade art for treasure."
Which teaches all of us in Europe this lesson: "Art is not for sale for any amount of money."

W. Schellinks (translated by Gary Schwartz)

93 Indian

The Emperors Akbar and Jahangir in Apotheosis, from the Shah Jahan period (1628–1658)

94 Willem Schellinks (1623–1678)

Parade of the Sons of Shah Jahan on Composite Horses and Elephants, ca. 1665–70

93
Opaque watercolor, ink, and gold on paper, 22.2 x 14.6 cm (image) / 38.2 x 22.5 cm (page)
From an album of 41 Mughal Indian paintings and calligraphy, India, 17th century
MS. Douce Or. a. 1, fol. 19a
Bodleian Library, University of Oxford
(Potsdam only)

Lit.
Glynn 2018, 34–36; no. 36

94
Oil on canvas, 78 x 83.8 cm
Inv. IS.30-1892
Victoria and Albert Museum, London

Lit.
Schwartz 1985a, 55; pl. 1.11
Forberg 2015, 46–63, fig. 39
Gommans/De Hond 2015
Forberg/Lunsingh Scheurleer 2018

The Dutch painter Willem Schellinks produced two drawings and five paintings inspired by Indian miniatures. One of these is the *Parade of the Sons of Shah Jahan on Composite Horses and Elephants.*[1] Shown here as a fantasy spectacle is the warlike confrontation of four brothers vying for the throne. The mounts and the litters are just as much a borrowing from Indian miniatures[2] as are the figures of the princes and their attire. The orchestra playing on the gallery on either side of the baldachin is segregated so that the men are seated on the right and the ladies on the left. Their Oriental garb is modeled on both Turkish and Persian fashions.

The struggle for power depicted here took place between 1658 and 1660 and was won by Aurangzeb (r. 1658–1707), who slew his brothers and took his father Shah Jahan (r. 1628–1658) captive. Schellinks therefore shows him on top of the most powerful beast of all, the elephant. Shah Jahan's helplessness is translated into the figure of the spectator seated on the stage, who has to watch the spectacle without being able to intervene. Hovering above the action is a cloud containing the princes' illustrious ancestors, Akbar and Jahangir, who as in dynastic group portraits are included here as witnesses to lend legitimacy to Aurangzeb's accession.

The motif of the apotheosis of Akbar and Jahangir is also to be found among Rembrandt's drawings after Indian miniatures. The exact model has not yet been identified, although there are parallels with works in the Bodleian Library in Oxford (cat. 93) and in a private collection, both of which originate in the St. Petersburg Album of ca. 1640.[3] The latter work contains an inscription that identifies it as a gift for Akbar and hence as a form of reparations to the father, against whom Jahangir had rebelled.

But what would be the point of such a work if it were commissioned by Jahangir's son, Shah Jahan, after his father's death? The many audience scenes showing Shah Jahan receiving one of his sons emphasize the prince's loyal devotion to his father. The same attitude informs the apotheosis of Akbar and Jahangir. Images like this one were circulated at court and within the family and should be understood as part of Shah Jahan's efforts to preempt a violent war of succession. It was all in vain, however, for his death sparked the bloodiest civil war in the whole history of the Mughal Empire. CF

1 The other paintings are in the Musée Guimet, Paris; Orientalist Museum, Doha; The British Museum, London; The Metropolitan Museum of Art, New York; and two private collections.
2 Cf. Del Bontà 1999.
3 Ill. in Los Angeles 2018, no. 36.

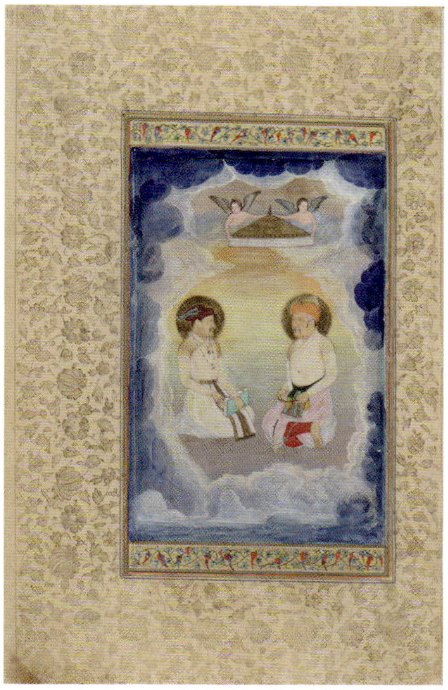

93

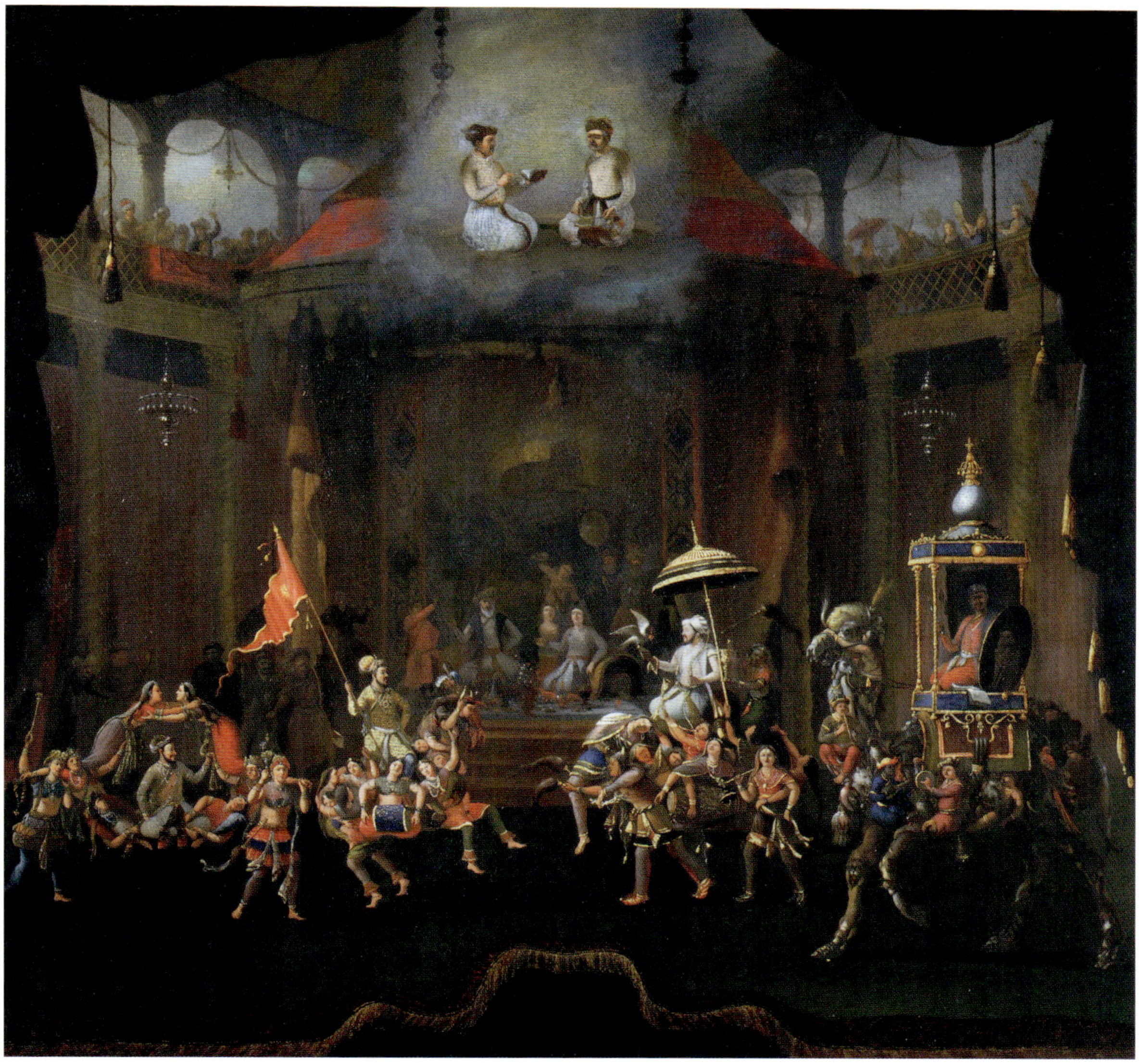

94

95.1–2 **Indian,** mounted in Vienna in the 18th century
Large Cross, Panel of Six Miniatures, ca. 1600/1720
Long Panel of Five Miniatures, ca. 1600/1720

95.1
From the Millionenzimmer
Ink, opaque watercolor, and gold on paper, mounted on a wooden panel, 93.4 x 55.9 cm
Inv. SKB 002655
Schönbrunn Palace, Vienna

95.2
From the Millionenzimmer
Ink, opaque watercolor, and gold on paper, mounted on a wood panel, 77.6 x 39 cm
Inv. SKB 002605
Schönbrunn Palace, Vienna

Lit.
Vienna 1923
Duda 1984
Duda 1997
Koch 2004

The *Large Cross* and the *Long Panel* are two of sixty collages that adorn the Millionenzimmer ("Millions Room") at Schönbrunn Palace in Vienna. Furnished with opulent rocaille frames made of rosewood, they occupy panels 55 and 5 respectively. The collages are pieced together out of countless Indian miniatures belonging to Empress Maria Theresia. To decorate her audience chamber they were cut up, reassembled, and in places even overpainted. The decoration of the room was completed in the year 1762.

Most of the miniatures used date from the seventeenth and early eighteenth century and belong to the Mughal and Deccan Schools. While they vary in quality, some exhibit the kind of exquisite workmanship that was to be found only in the workshops of the Grand Mughal. The inscriptions in Dutch on the verso of some of them attest to their having been imported via Amsterdam.

The *Long Panel* is composed of five miniatures with different motifs: single, double, and group portraits, supplemented by landscapes added by a painter in Vienna. Clearly visible in the lower middle register is the Mughal Emperor Jahangir (r. 1605–1627), seated on his throne and receiving a missive from a courtier. The same motif can be found among Rembrandt's drawings after Indian miniatures (The British Museum, London).

The *Large Cross* was pieced together out of six different works and shows picnics and wrestling matches as well as the women of the harem enjoying the luxuriant palace gardens. One miniature in the lower third of the cross was cut in two and another miniature inserted between the two halves.[1] The two half miniatures show a dynastic group portrait of the Timurids from Tamerlane himself to Jahangir,[2] which is another motif that Rembrandt copied in the 1650s (Musée du Louvre, Paris).

Ten of the miniatures used for the collages of the Millionenzimmer contain motifs that Rembrandt, too, copied in his drawings after Indian miniatures.[3] Also to be found there are three set pieces from Indian miniatures that Willem Schellinks (see cat. 92) integrated into his fantastical, pseudo-Indian painting (cat. 94) and drawings.

Quite apart from their role as a possible source of material for Rembrandt and Schellinks, the collages can be appreciated as works of art in their own right. The practice of cutting up and even overpainting Indian miniatures was for a long time decried as a barbaric act that destroyed some of the great works of classical Indian art. As regrettable as the loss of so many of these miniatures is, their recycling in a completely different cultural context is unique and intriguing. CF

1 The work in question shows Prince Murad Bakhsh (1624–1661) listening to music, cf. Duda 1997, 38.
2 Only the plumes on Jahangir's turban can still be made out. There is an inscription on verso with the names of all six Timurids present, cf. Duda 1997, 39.
3 On the question of whether the Schönbrunn miniatures were also used as a source by Rembrandt, cf. Benesch 1973, 318–25; Broos 1980; Duda 1997; Forberg 2015, 22–23; Amsterdam 2015, no. 80; and Schrader 2018, 11–12.

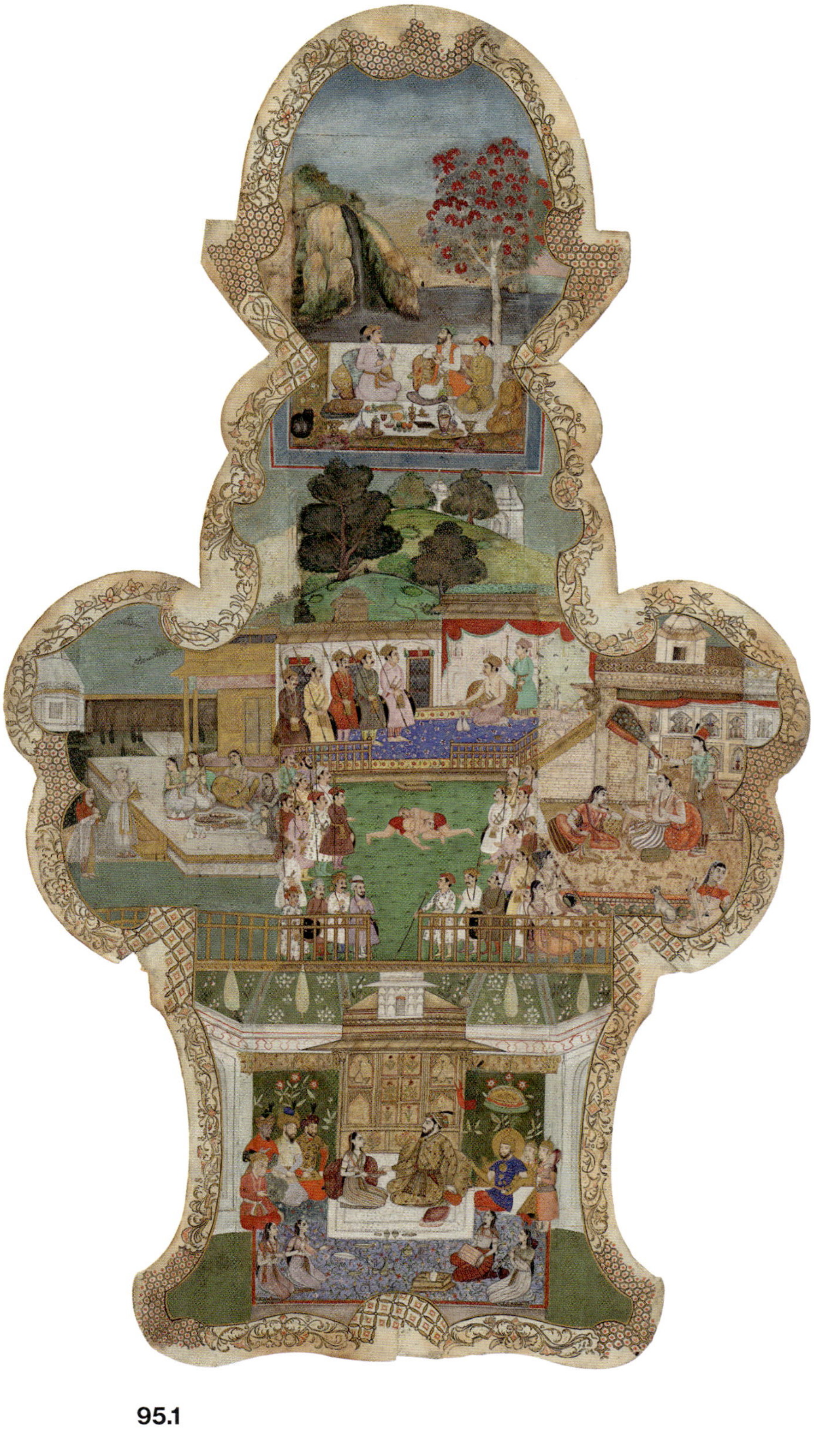

95.1

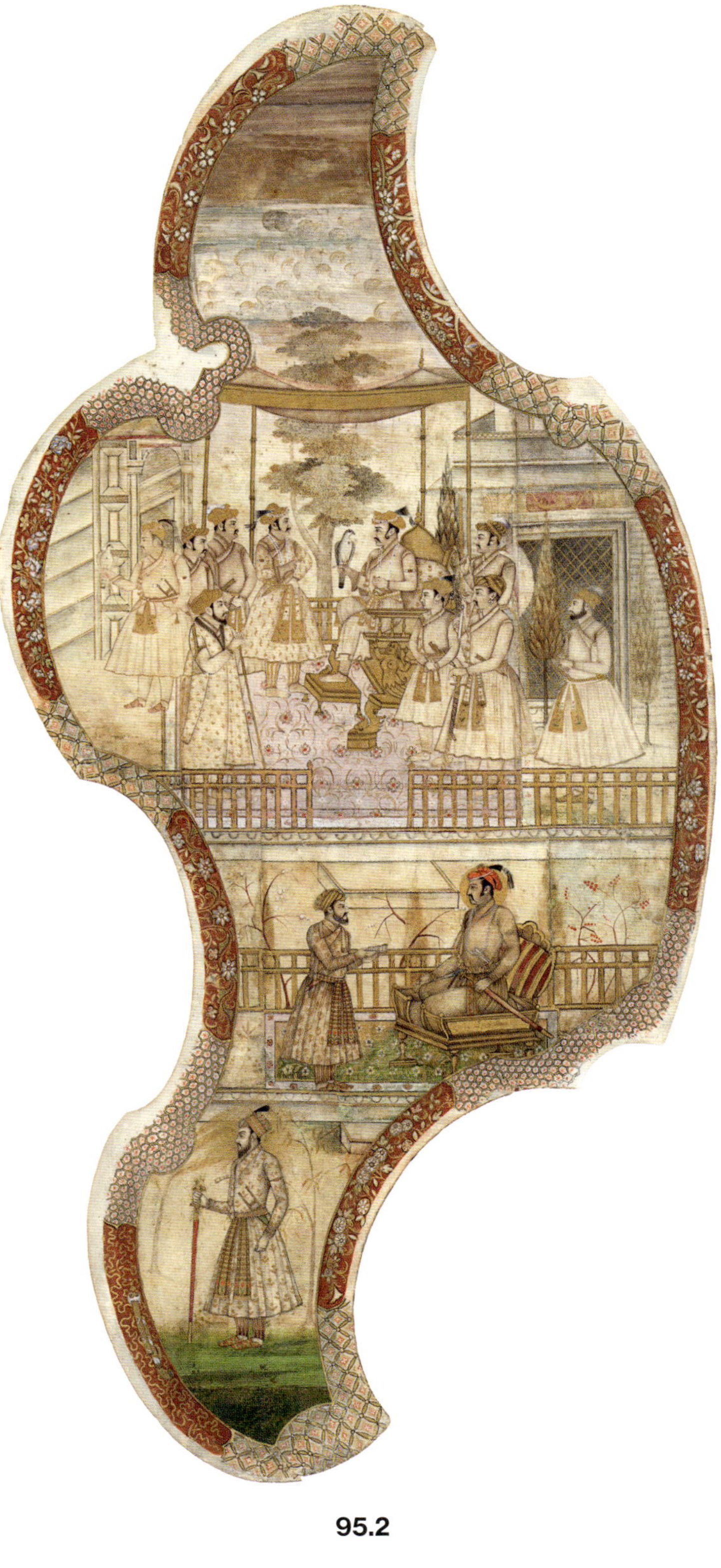

95.2

96 **Bichitr** (active ca. 1615–1650)
Raja Jujhar Singh Bundela Kneels in Submission to Shah Jahan, ca. 1630–40

97 **Rembrandt Harmensz. van Rijn** (1606–1669)
Moghul Prince, Presumably Shah Shuja, ca. 1656–61

96
From the *Minto Album*
Opaque watercolor and gold on paper, 26.4 x 16.2 cm (image), 39 x 27 cm (page)
Inv. CBL In 07A.16
Trustees of the Chester Beatty Library, Dublin
(Potsdam only)

Lit.
Verma 1994, fig. XXI
Dublin 2008, no. 51 A
Los Angeles 2018, no. 2

97
Pen and gray-brown ink, gray-brown wash, on brown prepared Japanese paper, 22.9 x 17.8 cm
Inv. 24471
Albertina, Vienna

Lit.
Benesch 1973, vol. 5, no. 1192, fig. 1490
Los Angeles 2018, no. 14

The imperial portrait of Shah Jahan (r. 1628–1658) contains a secondary scene showing the rebel Raja Jujhar Singh Bundela genuflecting before the emperor atop the globe. The subjugation of insurrectionists and other enemies of the state had been a widely used motif in Mughal painting ever since the reign of Akbar (r. 1556–1605).[1] Here, however, it takes place during an audience, and the rendition of it by court painter Bichitr combines three distinct genres—the depiction of a historical event, an allegorical scene, and a portrait—in a most innovative way.

Shah Jahan, the name Prince Khurran gave himself on his accession, means "King of the World." He is therefore portrayed with his feet firmly planted on a globe, on which his vast empire is roughly mapped out. Lying together at his feet in perfect harmony are a lamb and a lion, a pairing that in the Persian tradition served as a symbol of the just, peace-loving ruler, and had previously been used as such by Jahangir (r. 1605–1627). Shah Jahan stands tall with his head, offset against a nimbus, in the celestial sphere. In his left hand he holds a precious turban jewel, while his right rests on his sword. Two angels hold a crown above his head and floating on a band of clouds on either side of him is a host of Islamic saints, their arms raised in a gesture of adoration. According to Islam, saints and wise men are chosen by God and endowed with special gifts; hence their unshakable conviction that after death they would go to paradise, advancing even as far as the throne of God himself.

Raja Jujhar Singh Bundela kneels in front of the globe in the attitude of a penitent rebel submitting to a ruler on his throne. Shah Jahan's throne is thus the earth itself, whence he rules over the whole world. Thus he upholds the tradition of his ancestors, Akbar and Jahangir, who likewise presented themselves as rulers over both this world and the next.[2]

Rembrandt's portrait (cat. 97) shows a young Mughal prince, whose many necklaces and extravagant turban jewel mark him out as a member of the royal family. Identifying him nevertheless remains difficult as the original on which the drawing is based has not been found.

For all the artistic license he allowed himself in the position of the figure's legs and the shadow he casts, for example, Rembrandt followed his Indian models quite closely. This is especially true of the canonical posture with the head in profile and the upper body in three-quarter profile.[3] The figure is staring straight ahead with motionless facial features. Unlike Rembrandt's portraits of the Mughal emperors Jahangir and Shah Jahan (both Rijksmuseum, Amsterdam), this prince is shown without a nimbus, which in Mughal painting was reserved for emperors only. Rembrandt seems to have observed this practice and adopted it in his own drawings.

Similar to Rembrandt's engraving of Joannes Wtenbogaert (cat. 36), this drawing was made on precious Japanese paper. The material also adds a Far Eastern touch to the work. CF

1 Cf. Mukund, *Rai Surjan Hada Making Submission to Akbar*, ca. 1590–95, a page from the *Akbarnama* (Book of Akbar), and the *Maharana of Mewar and Prince Khurram*, ca. 1615–18, both in the Victoria and Albert Museum, London.
2 Cf. Franke 2014 and others.
3 Cf. Filipczak 2007–08; Forberg 2015, 15–45; Forberg 2016, 215–22.

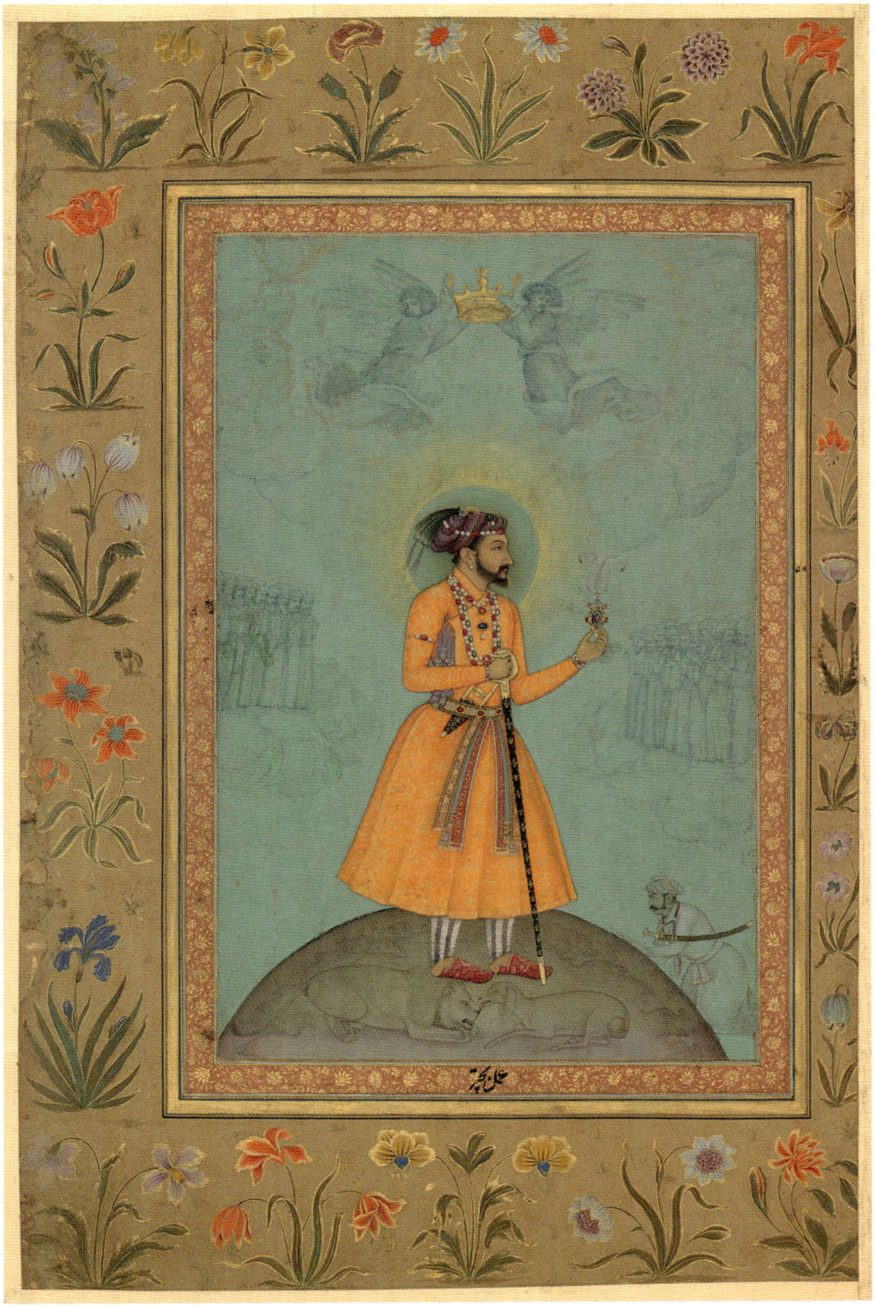

96

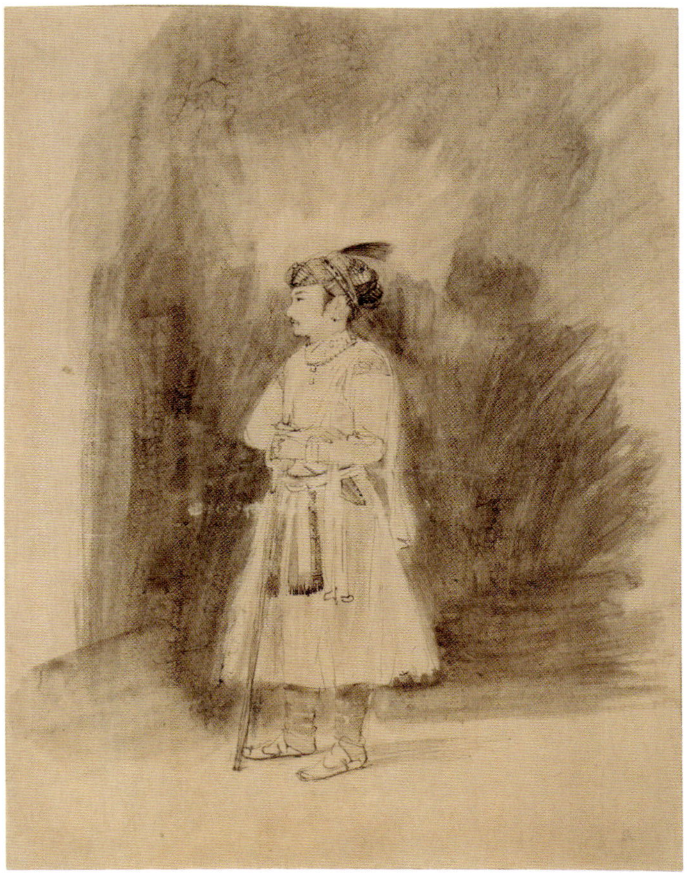

97

98 **Isfahan School** (17th century) and **Gesina ter Borch** (1631–1690)

Persian Youth, ca. 1650–80

Black and colored opaque watercolor on paper heightened with gold and silver paints
36 x 24.3 cm (page)
From the family scrapbook of Gesina ter Borch, fol. 40
Inv. BI-1887-1463-40
Rijksprentenkabinet, Rijksmuseum, Amsterdam, purchased with the support of the Vereniging Rembrandt

Lit.
Kettering 1988, vol. 2, 632
Christie's London, October 24, 2019, no. 54
De Hond et al. 2020

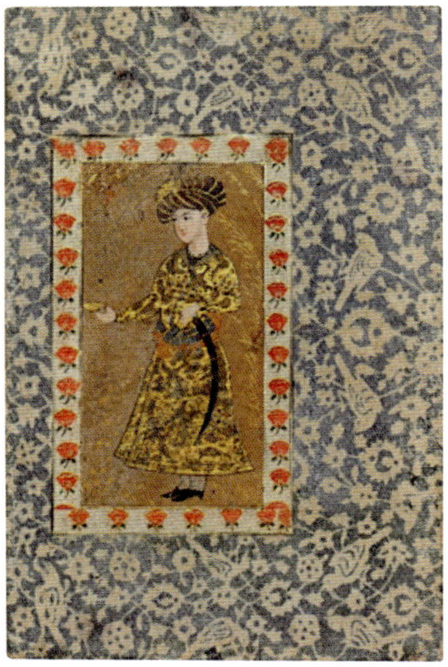

Isfahan School,
Youth with a Wine Cup in His Hand,
1650–70, private collection

This drawing of a Persian youth is to be found in a most surprising place: in a seventeenth-century album belonging to Gesina ter Borch. This Dutch artist from the provincial town of Zwolle kept a family album in which she collected not only her own drawings, but also works by other family members, copies after other masters, and even bits and pieces by her nephews and nieces. This *Persian Youth* is the only drawing with a non-European motif.

The composition matches exactly that of a Persian miniature recently sold at auction in London (fig. on left and p. 51). That Safavid drawing is thought to have been executed by an artist in the Isfahan School between 1650 and 1670. But the composition of the turbaned young man holding a drinking cup in his right hand and resting his left hand on his sword is probably older.

Close scrutiny by art historians and technical analyses reveal that the miniature in the album has been heavily reworked. That the solid black background is a later addition can be seen even with the naked eye, and the same is true of the colored sash, the coat collar, the plume, and other parts of the turban. Not only are these painted more freely and with three-dimensional modeling, but the colors are bolder than the original Persian illumination and there is white highlighting. It was also discovered that the sheet of the original miniature was rounded along the upper and lower edges and that at bottom right a piece of it is missing.

X-ray fluorescence revealed that in the original Persian miniature there were gaps in the pattern of the robe. The miniature, it seems, was already damaged in these places when Ter Borch added it to her album. The damage to the original gold paint had already been overpainted with a different, bolder shade of gold. The pattern of the robe was once finer and easier to discern, and as the birds and some of the leaves and rocks were executed in silver, they would have stood out more clearly from the gold background. The original lead white of the face has also been retouched. The analysis also brought to light the original gold background under the black one added later. The stylized vegetation is comparable with the landscapes of Safavid miniatures dating from the same period. To cap things off, an analysis of the lead white of the original hands and face revealed that the lead it contained was different from that in the lead white customarily used in the Netherlands. This lent weight to the hypothesis that lurking underneath the later overpainting was an original Persian miniature.

These investigations eventually yielded the following reconstruction: Between 1660 and 1680 Gesina ter Borch acquired a partially damaged miniature painted by a Safavid painter of the Isfahan School between 1650 and 1670. This miniature she pasted into her album. For aesthetic reasons, however, she blacked out the background and gave the work a rectangular format with a simple drawn frame, such as she had used for other works in her album. In doing so, she was careful to follow the outline of the figure's body, although certain projecting parts like the fluttering sash and the turban plume were also covered with black and had to be reinserted later on. Presumably Ter Borch herself restored parts of the damaged robe and retouched the face at the same time. Thus the original miniature was fundamentally reworked, making it difficult for us to judge the quality of the original. As much as Ter Borch's "restoration" of this work of art warrants criticism from today's perspective, it is impossible not to wonder at the lengths to which this Dutch artist went to preserve a severely damaged Persian miniature, even endeavoring to retain the original style. JH

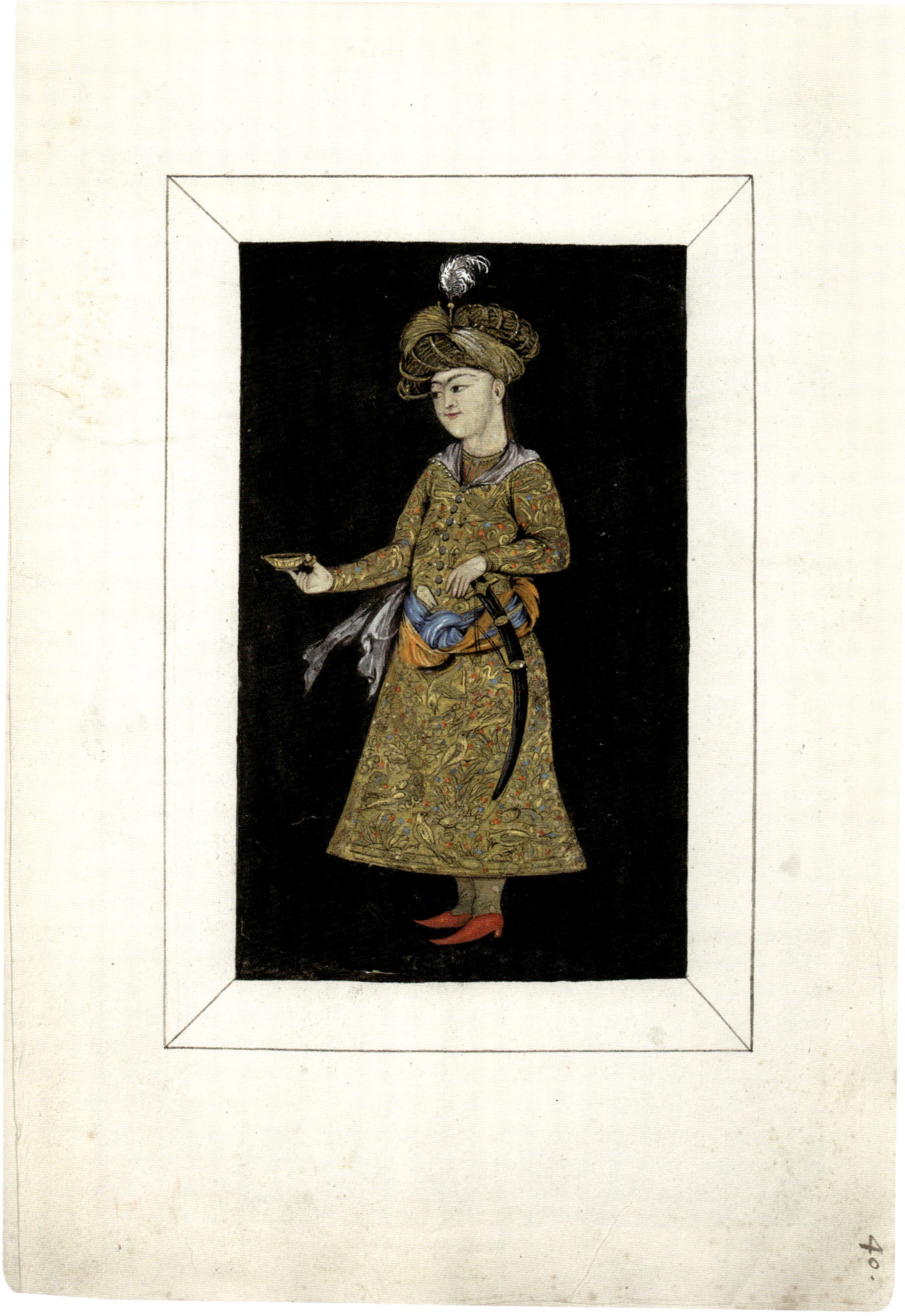

98

Familiarizing the Exotic
Rembrandt's Adaptation of the Orient

Fascination with the Orient in the Netherlands of the seventeenth century stemmed not only from the aesthetic pleasure to be attained from beautiful and luxurious objects. It was also linked to the positive associations of the imaginary world of the Bible, as represented in Rembrandt's paintings. One essential aspect of the enthusiasm for these sumptuous images can be explained by the contemporary mindset. The lavish opulence of the clothing and precious items in Orientalizing paintings contrasted starkly with the puritan sparseness of Calvinism. Interest in these exotic scenes was spurred by the desire for the unusual and the extraordinary. The "Orient" was the other, an abstraction of what was possible, a surface on which to project personal desires that had no place in the rationalistic worldview of the West, as epitomized by Protestantism.[1]

While Orientalizing motifs such as turbans and colorful robes may have been used as supposedly authentic elements to add credibility to biblical paintings, a new type of picture had emerged by the end of the 1620s which placed a special emphasis on the aesthetic value of fantasy costumes that could be associated with the East. Known as the "Oriental" *tronie*, this type of portrait study usually depicted an unknown person with striking facial features dressed in sumptuous robes and often wearing a turban.

Freed from the narrative of a story from the Old or New Testament, they made no attempt to dictate morals or provide instruction on virtuous behavior. These paintings were generalized character studies, but were also intended as an aesthetic expression of luxury and extravagance. The Oriental stylization was not coincidental or decided spontaneously for a particular scene. *Tronies* in costumes from other regions of the world did not exist. This suggests that the exoticism of the East was evidently familiar enough that people felt comfortable with believing in the role-play.

Staged in opulent costumes and precious jewelry, the "Oriental" *tronies* of the seventeenth century aimed to titillate the senses of the viewer, which Rembrandt further achieved through his precise rendering of the different materials, such as the brocades and silks of the robes, and the gold and pearls of the jewelry. His "Oriental" *tronies* from 1627 to 1637 exude elegance, dignity, and thoughtfulness, or self-confidence (cats. 99–101, 106).

Rembrandt was certainly not the only Dutch artist to produce Orientalizing *tronies*. A series of etchings by his friend and rival Jan Lievens, who also made the *Bust of an Oriental, in Profile to Left, Bearded and Wearing a Loosely Tied Turban* (cat. 104), was the inspiration for his etching known as *The Third Oriental Head* in 1635 (cat. 103). A few years earlier, in 1632, he made the etching of *The Persian* (cat. 105), which portrays a full-length figure of a man wearing a turban decorated with feathers, supporting himself with a stick, reminiscent of the posture of the figure in his painting *Man in Oriental Costume (The Noble Slav)* (fig. p. 63).

Rembrandt even depicted himself as an "Oriental." Indeed, over the years he assumed many roles ranging from soldier to burgher in roughly eighty self-portraits, among them his *Self-Portrait in Oriental Attire with Poodle* from 1631–33 (fig. p. 63) and again as an Asian ruler in the etching *Self-Portrait with Raised Sabre* (cat. 107). Here the artist looks out at the viewer with a grim demeanor, the unsheathed saber raised as if ready to strike. This empowering pose could be an expression of his inner desire for a position of power or simply be meant ironically.

Another theme found among Rembrandt's repertoire of Oriental motifs was the lion hunt (cat. 110–12). The subject offered the promising combination of a dramatic narrative and an exotic atmosphere. Rembrandt must have seen a real lion in Amsterdam, where he drew it from life (fig. p. 83). He also owned two lion skins which he kept in his cabinet of curiosities.[2] Also, the influence of the engravings of lion hunts by Antonio Tempesta (cat. 108, 109) cannot be denied. Rembrandt clearly drew inspiration from the works of the Italian engraver, as he did in other cases, too, which only underscores that his sources certainly did not have to be firsthand.

Even after 1640 Rembrandt continued to expand his collection of Oriental motifs. He not only copied the Mughal miniatures in Amsterdam (see "True to Life? Or Mere Convention?," pp. 256–83), but on at least one occasion took inspiration for a composition from Indian models. The composition of the etching *Abraham Entertaining the Angels* (cat. 118) is based on a Mughal miniature that Rembrandt had copied (fig. p. 69).

Rembrandt stopped producing Oriental *tronies* after the 1630s, but this type of image remained popular. Around 1665 Rembrandt's student Ferdinand Bol painted the *Portrait of an Oriental*, which displays all the characteristic traits of these studies, such as the flamboyant turban with a peak of heron feathers (cat. 119). The fascination with the East showed no signs of dissipating and persisted in the Netherlands throughout the second half of the seventeenth century. MPH

1 For more on this subject, see, among others, Tümpel 1994, Bahre 2006, and Swan 2013.

2 The bankruptcy inventory of Rembrandt's assets lists under no. 346 "Een leeue- en een leeuwinnenhuyt met twee bonte rocken" (Skins of a lion and a lioness, with two many-colored gowns); see Amsterdam 1999a, 151.

99 **Rembrandt Harmensz. van Rijn** (1606–1669)

Bust of an Old Man with Turban, ca. 1627–29

Oil on oak panel, 26.7 x 20.3 cm
Inscribed bottom left: RHL [in ligature]
The Kremer Collection—
www.thekremercollection.com

Lit.
CRP, vol. 4, addendum 3; vol. 6, no. 21
Frankfurt am Main 2003, no. 4
Berlin 2006, 131
Van Straten 2006, 77–78
Budapest 2014, no. 85

For a long time there was doubt about the attribution of this *tronie* to Rembrandt, but today it is acknowledged as an authentic work. The signature in the artist's own hand may have tipped the scales, as well as the fact that a second picture is present beneath the top layer of paint. In his early oeuvre, Rembrandt frequently reused panels whose subject was incomplete (see cat. 60). This work, which closely resembles works by Jan Lievens, is Rembrandt's earliest character study in the Oriental style.

An unusually strong light from the left shines flatly upon this bust-length portrait of an old man, who is shown in three-quarter profile to the right. Perhaps Rembrandt made a detour to Utrecht in 1627 to visit the Caravaggisti who were active in the town, and took the opportunity to study their similarly dramatic treatment of light: the old man's chest and face are hidden in shadow here, while intense light surrounds his right cheek and ear. The contrast between light and dark has a profound effect on the turban; the gold threads interwoven in the white strips of cloth truly seem to glisten where the light is strongest at left, and even shimmer in the partial shade at the front and across the right half of the forehead.

Rembrandt's treatment of the aigrette (see cat. 2) affixed to the right of the turban is spectacular. One ray of light just touches the tip of the plume of feathers, while another surrounds the rim of the gold setting—although this is not entirely consistent with the laws of light reflection known as catoptrics—and makes it possible for its ruby to glow from the shadows. The effects being tried out here prefigure the staging of the still life with a turban in the Amsterdam *tronie* (cat. 101), which was created six to eight years later. BB

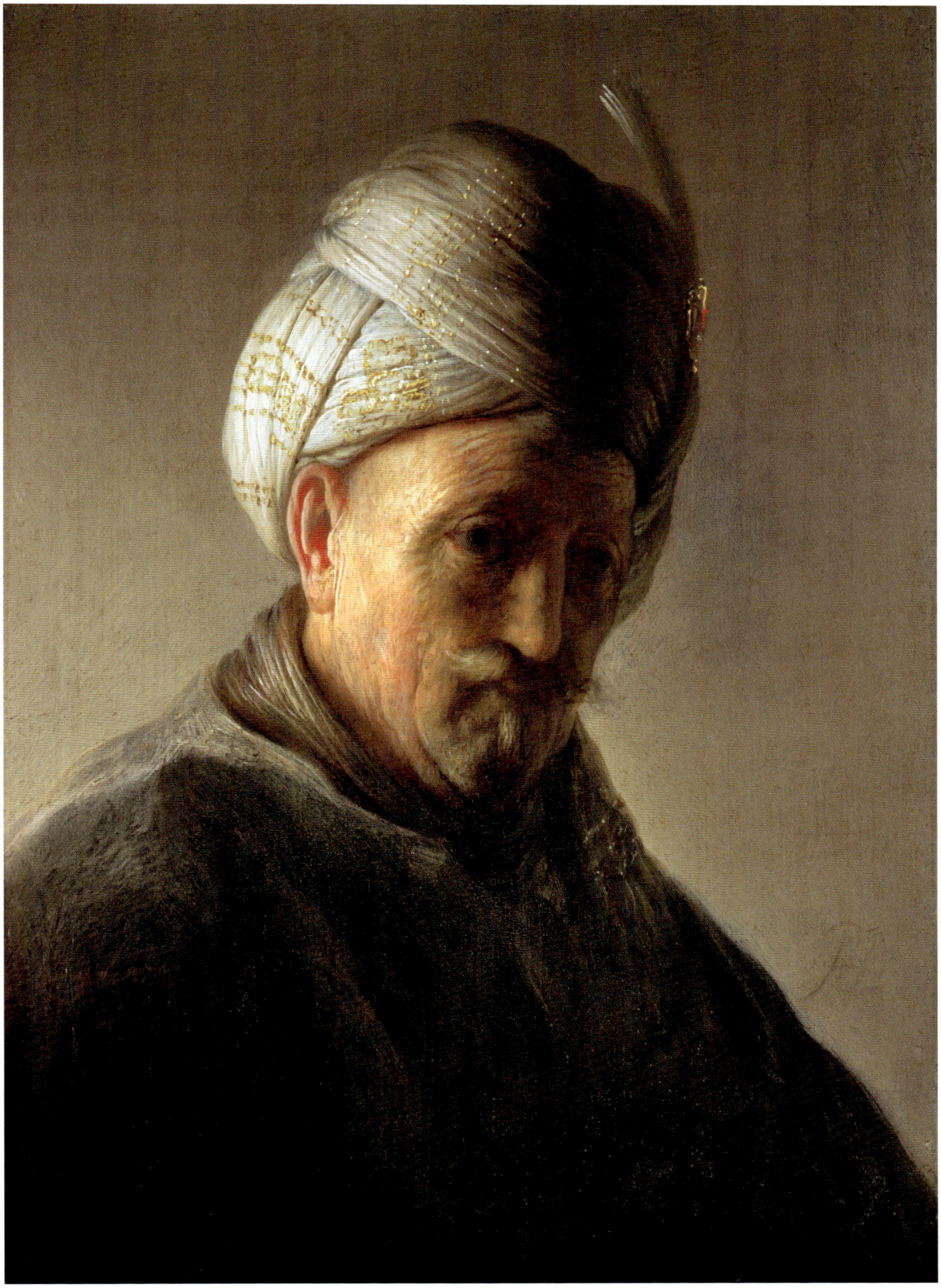

100 **Rembrandt Harmensz. van Rijn** (1606–1669) and workshop

Man in Oriental Costume, ca. 1635

Oil on canvas, 98.5 x 74.5 cm
Inscribed center left: [R]embrandt ft
Inv. 1940.1.13
National Gallery of Art, Washington, DC,
Andrew W. Mellon Collection
(Potsdam only)

Lit.
CRP, vol. 2, no. B 81; vol. 6, no. 99
Schwartz 1985b, no. 218
Tümpel 1986, no. A 38
Frankfurt am Main 2003, no. 20
Wheelock 2014

This painting, which may have been created with the assistance of Govert Flinck (see cat. 3), could feature the same model that posed in profile for the main character in Rembrandt's *Belshazzar's Feast* (The National Gallery, London). Here, however, the man's turban is not white and decorated with just a few interwoven gold threads as it is in London. Instead it is colorful, with fabric that has been dyed turquoise, violet, gold, and silvery gray. A gold chain adorned with gemstones is positioned around the turban, and the links bearing stones appear to be pinned to the cloth.
An ornament set with a ruby and an aigrette (see cat. 2) is placed at the front of the forehead.

In his right hand, the subject is gripping his black fabric sash, which he has used to gird his purplish-red skirt. His armless brown cape with fur trim on the collar is reminiscent of a hussar's fur-lined cloak called a *pelisse,* but it is held together by a gold chain serving as a tassel on the man's chest. The buttoned slit on the right side extending to the hem is rather peculiar. The sitter's left hand rests on a knotted stick. BB

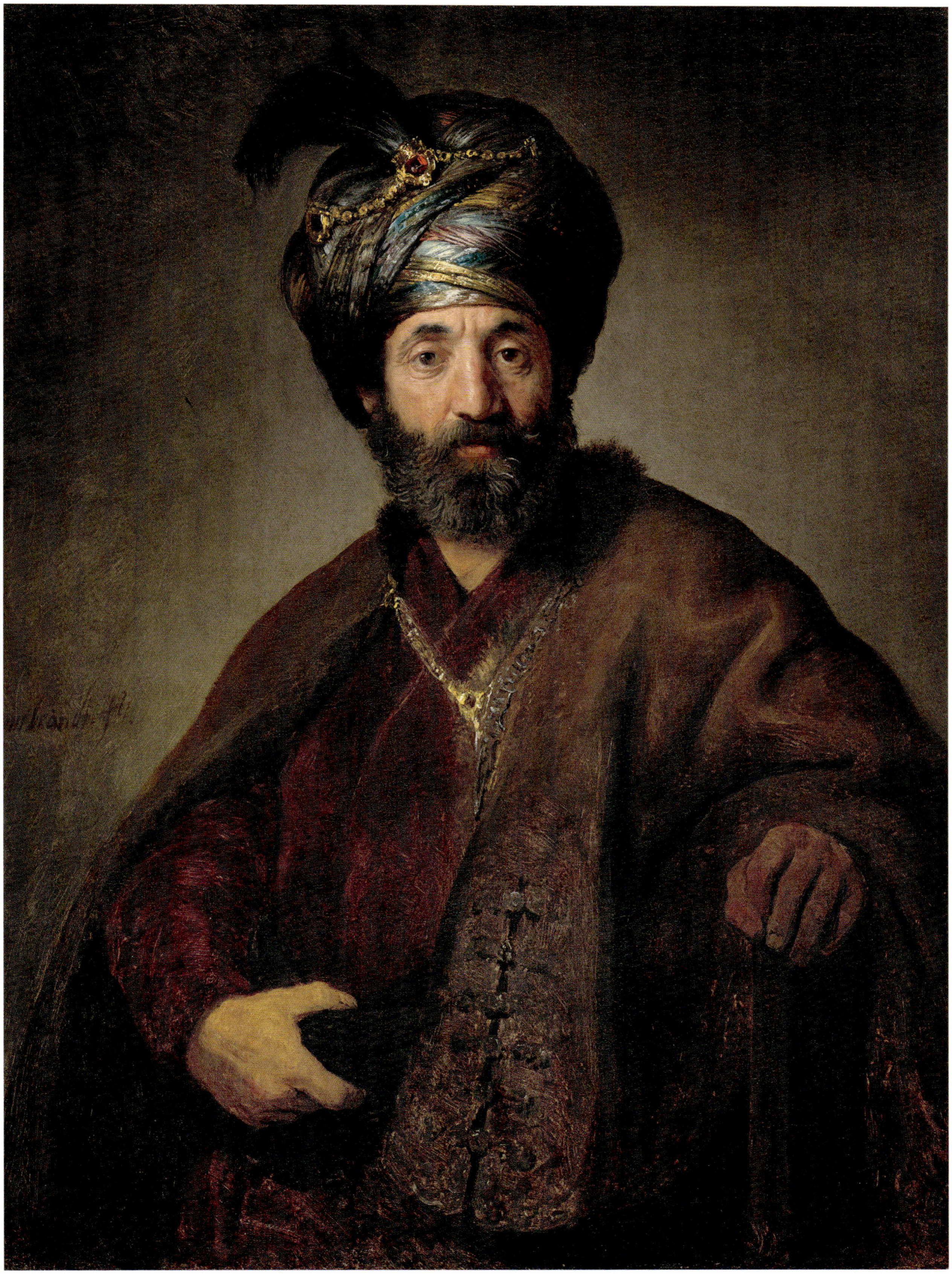

101 **Rembrandt Harmensz. van Rijn** (1606–1669)

Man in Oriental Clothing, 1635

Oil on oak panel, 72 x 54.5 cm
Inscribed center right: Rembrandt • ft • 1635
Inv. SK-A-3340
Rijksmuseum, Amsterdam, Gift of Mr. and Mrs. Kessler-Hülsmann, Kapelle-op-den-Bos
(Basel only)

Lit.
CRP, vol. 3, no. C 101; vol. 4, 635–36; vol. 6, no. 141
Sumowski 1983–94, vol. 6, no. 2280
Hirschfelder 2008, 256, 423, no. 429
Amsterdam 2019, 772–73

The principle of the *tronie*—the character study that oscillates between individuality and type—is perfectly illustrated by Rembrandt's portrait from 1635. The remarkably vivid reproduction of the face of an unknown bearded man in his mature years—undoubtedly a local, not an Oriental—occupies the center of the picture almost exactly. The man portrayed is wearing a pearl necklace on a black shirt with a coat of heavy gold brocade thrown on over it. The coat buckle set with a gemstone dangles down from the right collar. The hair on the man's head is almost completely hidden by an enormous turban, which towers up for almost a third of the picture's height. Wound from a long, intricately intertwined, white band, the turban is held together by a strap in the style of a golden chain belt. In the front it has a clasp with a sparkling silver stone setting; on the left side in the shadow, a huge, drop-shaped pearl hangs down from another setting in the strap.

The way that the band of the turban protrudes from the wrap at its bottom and falls over the left shoulder is more reminiscent of late medieval fashion than of Oriental: similarly, the *cornette* falls from the *chaperon*, which can be seen in numerous Early Netherlandish portraits. In addition, the end of the fabric band has an utterly fantastic form—it seems to fan out into an animal paw, as if the material were fur.

Strong light from the left captures all pictorial elements equally, ensures that the composition of turban still life, portrait study, and bust holds together, and, with the shadow of the figure on the implied wall in the background, even evokes a hint of spatiality.

The painting used to be attributed to the Rembrandt School, tentatively to Govert Flinck. One of the factors that speak for its creation by the master himself, however, is the wood used for the support: it comes from the same tree as the wood of Rembrandt's self-portrait dated 1634 (Gemäldegalerie, Staatliche Museen zu Berlin), another self-portrait that is thought to be somewhat later (The Wallace Collection, London), and the *Stormy Landscape* (Herzog Anton Ulrich-Museum, Braunschweig), all of which are regarded as almost certainly authentic. BB

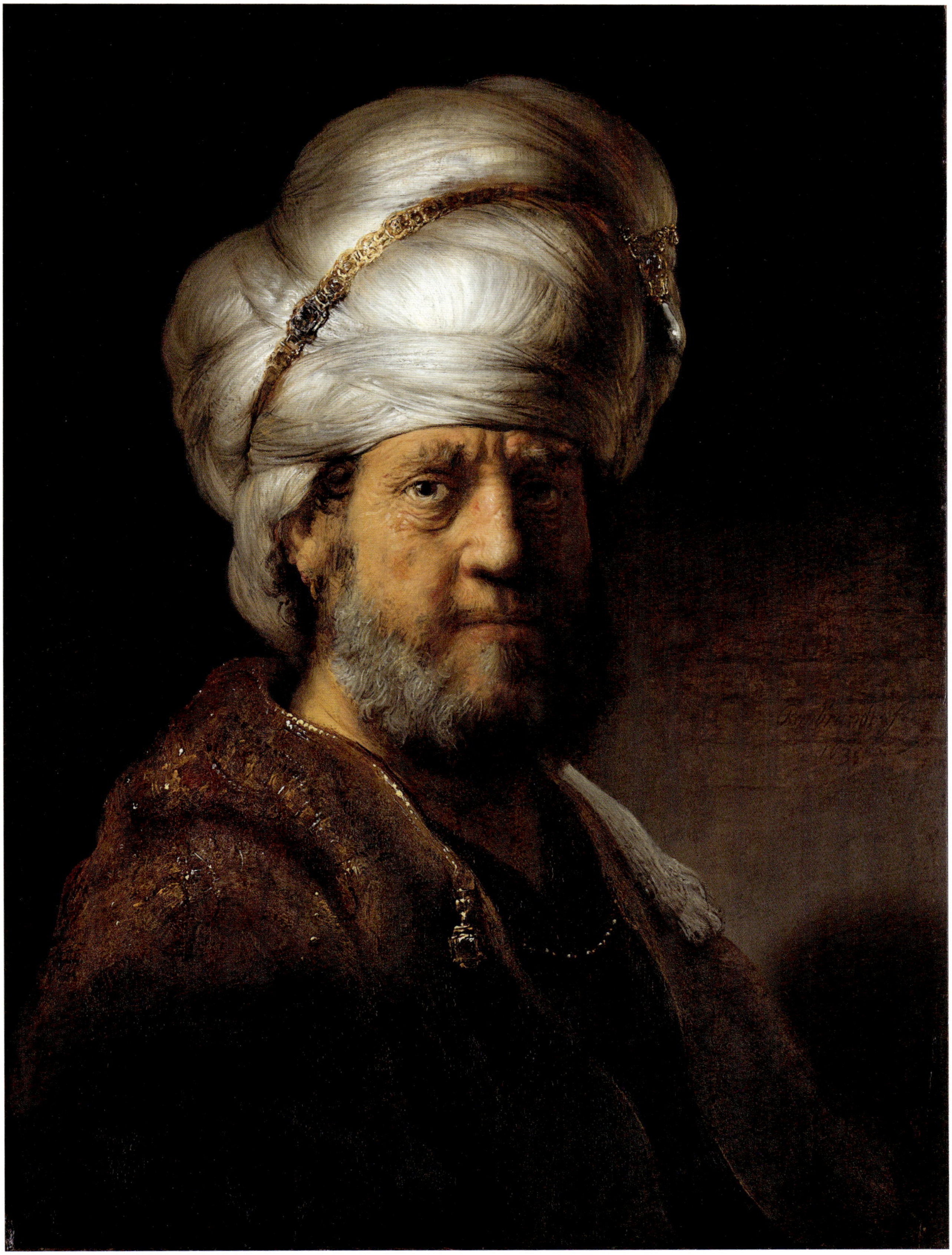

102 **Isaac de Jouderville** (ca. 1612–1648)
Young Woman in Profile, ca. 1632

Oil on panel, 40.5 x 31.1 cm
Natan Saban Collection, Israel

Lit.
CRP, vol. 2, no. A 49, copy no. 2
Sumowski 1983–94, vol. 5, no. 2104a
Broos 2009, 48 (version in the Museum Het Rembrandthuis, Amsterdam)

1 See Leeuwarden n.d.

This barely idealized portrait of a young woman with red hair, short nose, and double chin is traditionally believed to depict Maria van Eyck, the wife of art dealer Hendrick Uylenburgh. The hair clasp with a flower and the bejeweled trim along the edge of the dress are unusual for Netherlandish clothing of that era; the embellishment is reminiscent of the figures shown in Oriental style in Rembrandt's *Belshazzar's Feast* of 1635 (The National Gallery, London) and his 1633 *Portrait of a Man in Oriental Costume* (Bayerische Staatsgemäldesammlungen, Alte Pinakothek, Munich).

The picture, by Rembrandt's pupil Isaac de Jouderville, is a partial copy of Rembrandt's *Young Woman in Profile* (Nationalmuseum, Stockholm). It was possibly the copy that was described in a 1637 inventory of an estate as "cleine oostersche vrouwen troni het conterfeisel van H. Ulenburgs huijsvrouwe nae Rembrant" (A small *tronie* of an Oriental woman, the likeness of H. Uylenburgh's wife, after Rembrandt).[1] This would mean that according to contemporary perception, even a touch of exotic adornment in a Rembrandt picture would be sufficient for it to be labeled Oriental. Thus, Rembrandt would have introduced Orientalism not only into his self-portraits (cat. 107, fig. p. 63) but also his family surroundings. Hendrick Uylenburgh, who was born in Kraków but had settled in Amsterdam around 1625, was the cousin of Saskia van Uylenburgh, who was to become Rembrandt's wife in 1634.

Rembrandt had a close and successful business partnership with Uylenburgh, an art dealer who also ran a studio. After Rembrandt's early success, he lent his partner one thousand guilders, and in 1631 he moved into the latter's house on Jodenbreestraat in Amsterdam and took charge of the studio there. It may well have been in Uylenburgh's house that Rembrandt met the twenty-two-year-old Saskia in the spring of 1633. Like Hendrick Uylenburgh's parents she came from the town of Leeuwarden in Friesland. Hendrick Uylenburgh had a branch there that belonged to the business owned by painter and art dealer Lambert Jacobsz. The above-mentioned inventory was compiled after the latter's death on June 27, 1636.

It is entirely possible that the copy of a Rembrandt painting by Isaac de Jouderville existed among these holdings. Jouderville was one of Rembrandt's first pupils, dating back to his Leiden days, and he followed his teacher to Amsterdam. He also painted a *Portrait of Rembrandt in Oriental Dress* (The Leiden Collection, New York), copying his teacher's 1631–33 *Self-Portrait in Oriental Attire with Poodle* (fig. p. 63) that does not include the poodle later added by Rembrandt. This work is one of the few surviving examples of the practice of copying, which Rembrandt regarded as an important teaching method. Jouderville's copy of the *Young Woman in Profile* also documents this process, which had been a common feature of workshop practice since medieval times. MPH

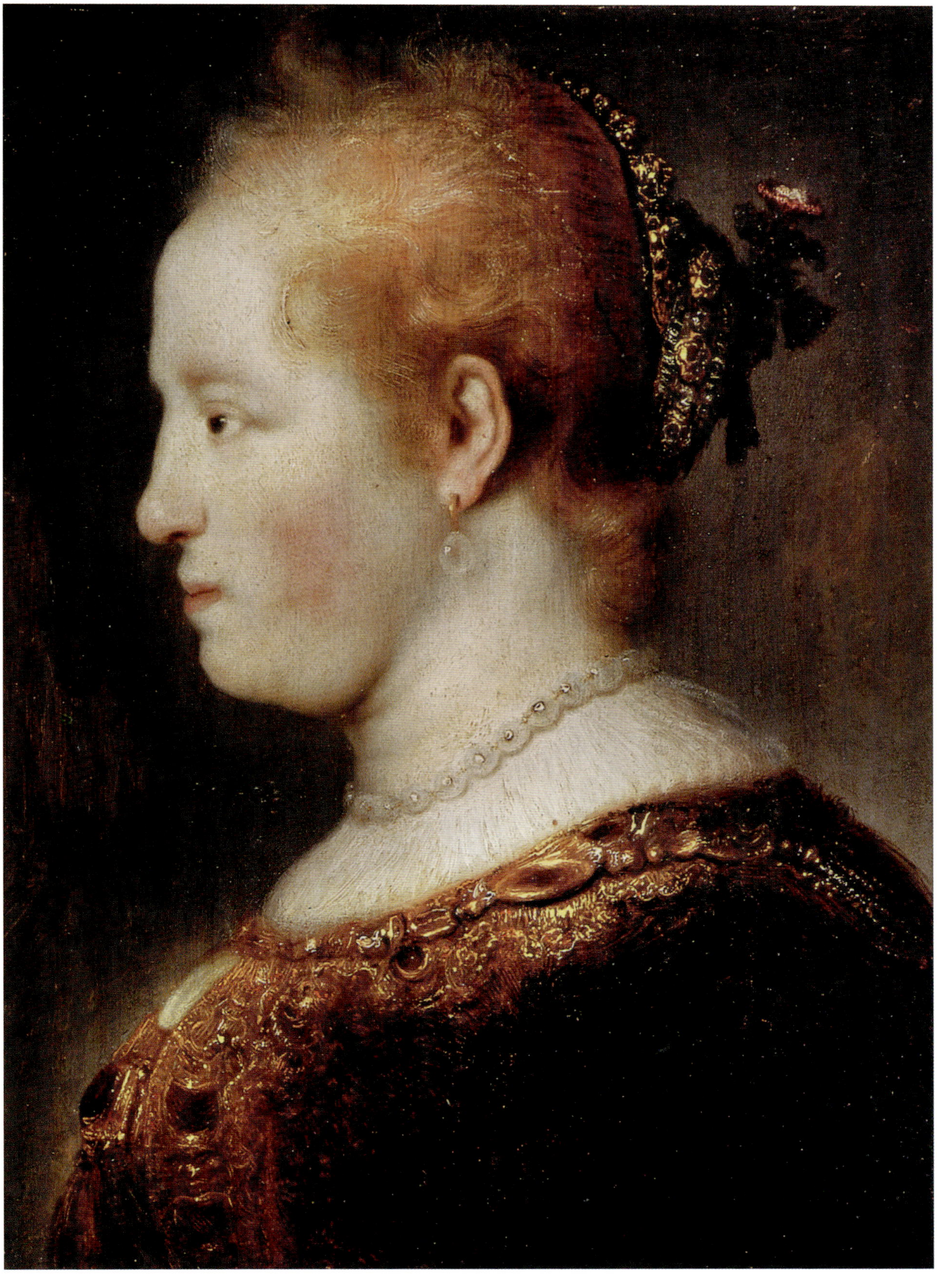

103 **Rembrandt Harmensz. van Rijn** (1606–1669)
The Third Oriental Head, 1635

104 **Jan Lievens** (1607–1674)
Bust of an Oriental, in Profile to Left, Bearded and Wearing a Loosely Tied Turban, ca. 1630–32

105 **Rembrandt Harmensz. van Rijn** (1606–1669)
The Persian, 1632

103
Etching, 15.5 x 13.4 cm
Inscribed on plate at top left:
Rembrandt / geretuck / .1635.
Inv. DG1926/484
Albertina, Vienna

Lit.
B 288 (1/1)
NH 151 (1/1)
Gutbrod 1996, 288–91
Washington 2009, 198–99
Swan 2013, 107, fig. 50
Leiden 2019, no. 139

104
Etching, 16 x 14.3 cm
2nd (?) state (of 5)
Inscribed on plate at center left: IL
Inv. X.900
Kunstmuseum Basel, Kupferstichkabinett

Lit.
B 18
H 35 (2/5) (?)
Gutbrod 1996, 288–91
Van Straten 2006, 180–81, fig. 302
Hirschfelder 2008, 31, 108, 256, 332, 417, no. 324
Washington 2009, no. 68
Schnackenburg 2016, 110, 112, 290, no. 210
Leiden 2019, no. 138

105
Etching, 10.6 x 7.9 cm
1st state (of 3)
Inscribed on plate at bottom center:
RHL 1632 [3 and 2 mirror-inverted]
Inv. X.1122
Kunstmuseum Basel, Kupferstichkabinett

Lit.
B 152 (1/1)
NH 110 (1/3)
Van Straten 2006, 231–32
Swan 2013, no. 38
Leiden 2019, no. 135

Around 1630–32 Jan Lievens made seven identically sized etchings of *tronies*, which were probably conceived as a group, even though they were only published as a series a decade later in Antwerp. Four of them show character heads of older men in exotic Oriental costumes. Lievens and Rembrandt exerted a mutual influence on each other as they simultaneously explored this motif in paintings (cat. 99–101, 106) as well as in etchings. Lievens's sheet on display (cat. 104) is one of the four prints by him that later became known as *Oriental Heads*.

The bust-length portrait of a full-bearded man facing left in profile, wearing a patterned turban and coarse garments, is presented in energetic strokes against a schematically indicated landscape. An effective contrast between the shaded sections with parallel hatching and the exceptionally bright yet less differentiated areas give the figure a sculptural quality, while the ornamental appearance of individual features, such as the untamed bristles of the beard, lends a sense of vibrancy. These characteristics also distinguish the other sheets in the series.

Lievens's inventiveness with costumed *tronies,* which was also apparent in his prints, did not go unnoticed by his former companion Rembrandt, and this spurred the latter into an artistic competitiveness even though the two had long since parted ways—Lievens had temporarily moved to London in 1632, while Rembrandt had left Leiden for Amsterdam in 1631–32. In 1635 Rembrandt was inspired by the series to produce his most thorough exploration of works by one of his fellow artists, with four copies of Lievens's *Oriental Heads* that were almost identically sized but laterally reversed. For three of them he added the comment "geretuck[eert]," meaning reworked or retouched, thereby taking responsibility for borrowing the motif while at the same time pointing to his own improvements.

There are striking variations that illustrate how the styles of the two artists differ. Rembrandt's denser and richly animated pattern of lines with multiple overlapping establishes not only a characteristically velvety impression of depth but also, in combination with his subject's more resolute facial characteristics, a higher degree of dramatic tension and psychological insight. Moreover, the material nature of his costumes is more differentiated, and he adds an extravagant aigrette with feather adornment (see cat. 2).

The Lievens reworkings are among Rembrandt's final explorations of the "Oriental" *tronie,* a theme with which he had concerned himself for over a decade. The collection of Eastern accessories he had established in the process would continue to find a use elsewhere: as early as 1632 he had already created *The Persian*, an imposing full-length figure of a man with Oriental attributes. Using elements such as a fur-trimmed cloak with chain, an undergarment with sash, and an exotic headdress with feather, this character brings together all the features that would continue to shape Rembrandt's Oriental-style figures in his biblical histories (see cat. 60, 68, 73–75, 77, 113–14, 116) and genre scenes (see cat. 117). GD

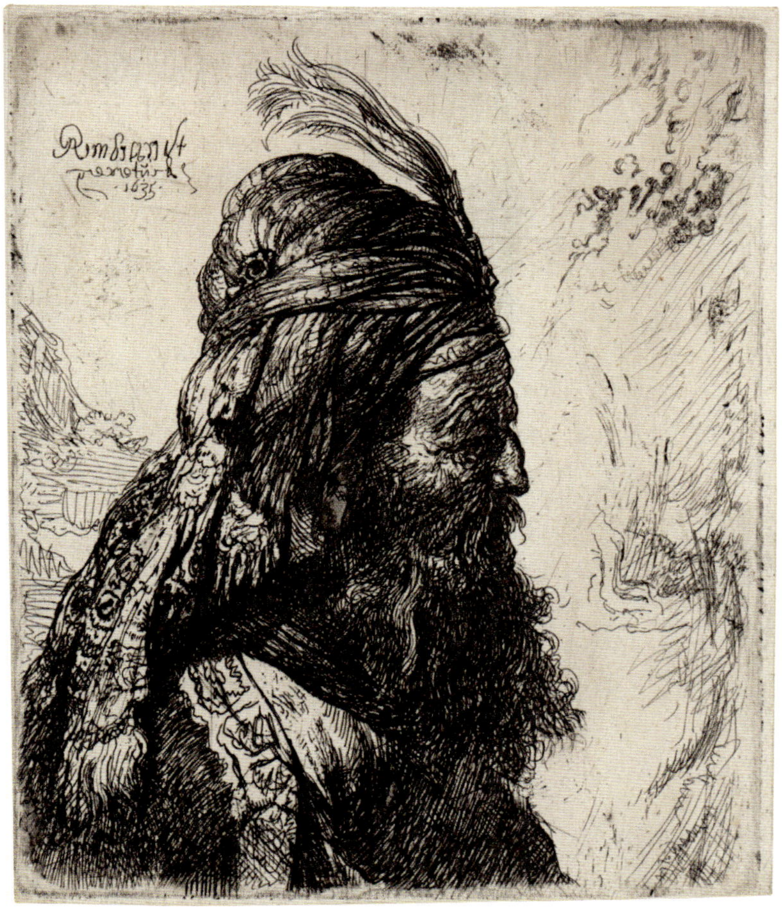

103

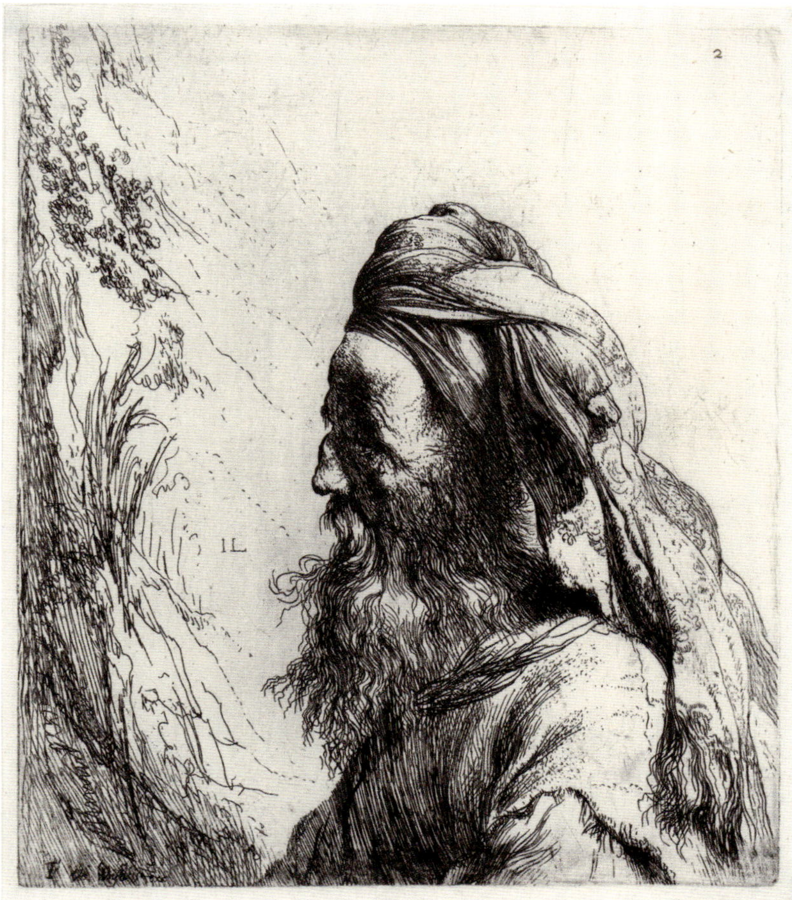

104

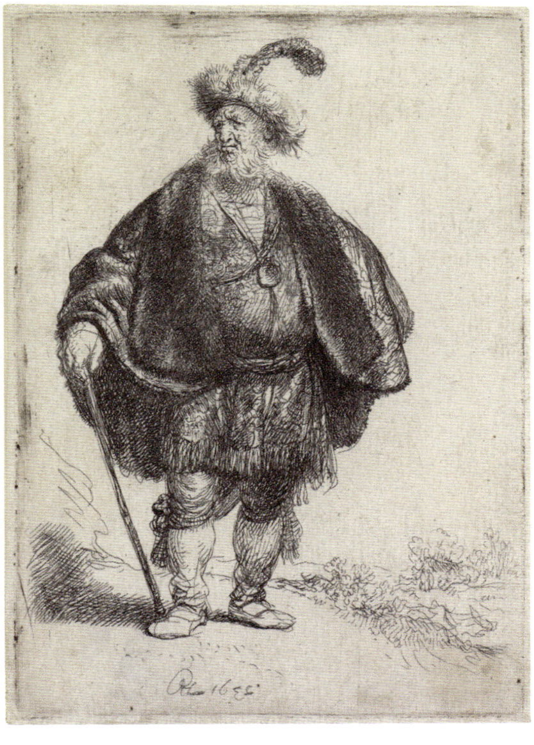

105

106 **Rembrandt Harmensz. van Rijn** (1606–1669) and workshop

A Tronie of a Bearded Old Man in Middle Eastern Dress, ca. 1635

Oil on oak panel, 74.7 x 54.5 cm
Inscribed: Rembrandt f / 163[6 or 7]
Inv. K023
Lent by the Earl of Derby

Lit.
Bauch 1966, no. 169
Bredius/Gerson 1969, fig. p. 169, no. 208
Lloyd 2019

1 See Leeuwarden n.d.
2 Ibid.
3 It is also possible that this comment refers to Rembrandt's painting *Portrait of an Old Man* of 1632 (Fogg Museum, Harvard Art Museums, Cambridge, Massachusetts); see London 2006, 183–84.

For a brief period of some ten years, Rembrandt created a small number of paintings and etchings showing studio models dressed in Eastern attire. As limited as the number of works may be, this group of images makes an outsized impression in his oeuvre. For one thing, it includes several unique works. The painting of 1632 with the sobriquet *The Noble Slav* (fig. p. 63) is the largest non-portrait figure painting Rembrandt ever made. With its commanding presence and glowing color, this painting alone has been enough to establish Rembrandt's reputation as a creator of Orientalizing images.

His fascination with the Oriental *tronie* went so far that in his only full-length (but far under life-sized) self-portrait, dated 1631, he shows himself in Oriental attire (fig. p. 63), not very different from that of the *Noble Slav*. Three years later, in a self-portrait etching, he once more chose, for reasons at which we can only guess, to take on the guise of an Oriental, this time a ruler with the power of life and death over his subjects (cat. 107). A further unparalleled gesture dating from this period are Rembrandt's copies of a number of etchings by his companion Jan Lievens (cat. 103–04). These have been known since the eighteenth century as *Oriental Heads,* further hammering home the association of Rembrandt with the East.

In addition to large figure paintings and etchings of heads, Rembrandt also painted *tronies* of "Orientals." Some are known only from documentary evidence. The 1637 estate inventory of the Leeuwarden painter Lambert Jacobsz., a relative of Rembrandt's Amsterdam business partner Hendrick Uylenburgh, included "A fine young Turkish prince, after Remb[randt]" and "A small *tronie* of an Oriental woman, the likeness of H. Uylenburgh's wife, after Rembrandt."[1] Paintings that answer roughly to this description and attribution are *Young Man in Turban* in the Royal Collection (rejected by most Rembrandt experts, but perhaps by him after all) and *Young Lady in Oriental Costume* in the Bührle Collection, Zurich (cat. 3). The latter is now attributed to Govert Flinck, who was a pupil of Lambert Jacobsz. before moving on to Rembrandt's studio.

Other *tronies* of the 1620s and 1630s by Rembrandt and/or workshop are in the Kremer Collection (cat. 99), the Rijksmuseum in Amsterdam (cat. 101), the Alte Pinakothek in Munich, and the National Gallery of Art, in Washington, DC (cat. 100). The Oriental *tronie* in the Derby Collection fits seamlessly into this set of paintings, to which it adds an element of depth, personal emotion, and life experience that is not found in the other *tronies*. A dating of 1636 or 1637 would allow us to regard the painting as the climactic conclusion of Rembrandt's ten-year preoccupation with the Oriental *tronie*. The dendrochronology of the panel supports this hypothesis, which also agrees with the painted date on the panel.

That Rembrandt painted at least one *tronie* resembling the one in the Derby Collection is documented by a record from the period describing a work that matches the Derby *tronie* very well. Lambert Jacobsz.'s inventory of October 2, 1637 (the artist died on June 27, 1636) lists in addition to six paintings after Rembrandt one by the master himself: "Een outmans troni met een lange bredebaert van M. Rembrant van Rijn selfs" (A *tronie* of an old man with a long, full beard by Master Rembrandt van Rijn himself).[2] The proposition that this entry refers to the Derby painting requires a dating preceding the demise of Lambert Jacobsz., which is not impossible.[3] Until now, no evidence has emerged concerning the subsequent fortunes of the paintings in his estate. GS

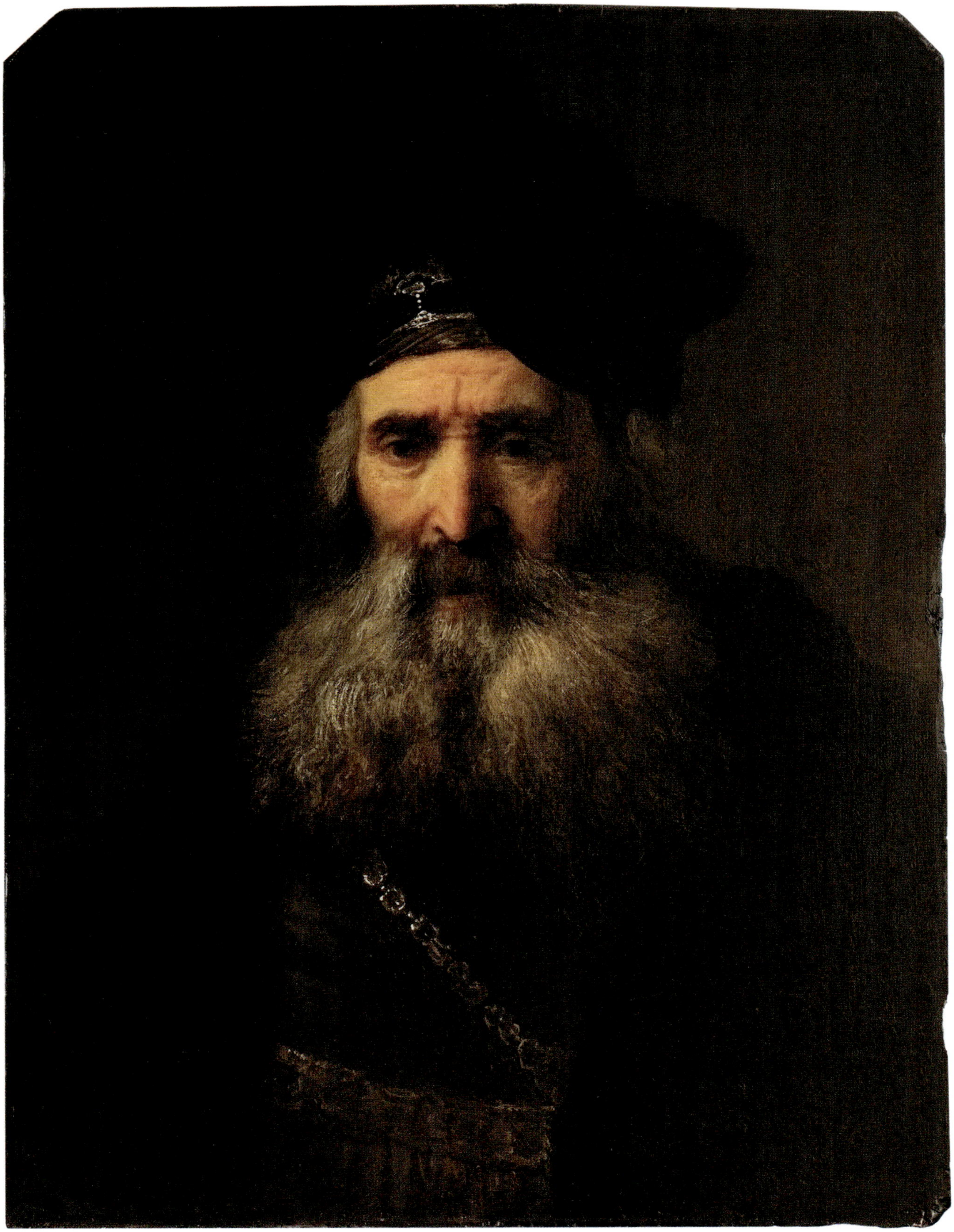

106

107 **Rembrandt Harmensz. van Rijn** (1606–1669)

Self-Portrait with Raised Sabre, 1634

Etching, with touches of burin, 12.4 x 10.2 cm
2nd state (of 2)
Inscribed in plate (top left):
Rembrandt f / 1634
Inv. 2007.180
Kunstmuseum Basel, Kupferstichkabinett,
Donation Eberhard W. Kornfeld, Bern

Lit.
B 18 (2/2)
NH 134 (2/2)
Chapman 1990, 43, fig. 58
London 1999, no. 41
De Winkel 1999, 61
Basel 2005, no. 20
Schwartz 2006, 196, fig. 334
Amsterdam 2015, no. 81
Cologne 2019, no. 75
Leiden 2019, no. 142

1 On the spread of the *kris* in Europe and its representation in paintings, see Göttler 2016.

2 "60 stucks soo Indiaens hantgeweer, pijlen, schichten, asegayen en bodgen" (sixty items including Indian handguns, arrows, spears, assegais, and bows); cited in Amsterdam 1999a, 151.

In the years around and after 1630, Rembrandt completed several self-portraits with military accessories such as gorgets, helmets, and assorted edged weapons. It was during this period that the artist also depicted himself in historical and Oriental costumes (fig. p. 63), and also created a series of etchings in the style of *tronies*, for which he used his own physiognomy to try out various facial expressions and states of mind.

Self-Portrait with Raised Sabre, dated to 1634, combines all these features. It was created in a year of significant personal and professional milestones for Rembrandt, with his entry into the painters' guild in Amsterdam and his marriage to Saskia van Uylenburgh. Displaying a mixture of fierce self-confidence and quiet melancholia—comparable to the *Man in Oriental Clothing* from Amsterdam (cat. 101) that he created a year later—the painter is facing us in this bust-length portrait. Despite the small format, an almost threatening presence is conjured up by the close-up composition, cropping the figure on both sides. The magnificent robe, a heavy, high-necked coat made of fabric with an intricate pattern, featuring an imposing ermine collar and wide chain resembling a livery collar, is reminiscent of traditional portraits of sovereigns. Rembrandt's head is covered with a beret adorned with an ostrich feather, which is also found in other self-portraits; here it extends until just over the eyebrows, and the close-fitting feather curling around the central axis appears like a lordly insignia complementing the robe.

Unlike his archaic and exotic costume, which belongs to the realm of fantasy, in front of his left shoulder Rembrandt is wielding a real weapon with an undulating edge and asymmetric blade that has its origins in Far-Eastern culture. It displays the characteristic elements of a *kris*, a kind of showpiece dagger rooted in the territory of what is now Indonesia that was used for ceremonial purposes and to convey prestige, but it also possessed spiritual significance. In Rembrandt's day it found its way into numerous European collections as a sought-after exhibit for cabinets of curiosities.[1] A one-sided undulating edge is not typical for a *kris*, so this may well not be a representation of a concrete item but rather a free copy; moreover, the handle should actually be held the other way around so that it protects the hand (which would have affected the composition).

It is uncertain how much Rembrandt knew about the function and meaning of the *kris*, just as nobody can be sure if he personally possessed one. There is reason to believe he may have done so, for the inventory of his possessions compiled in 1656 lists no fewer than sixty weapons of "East Indian" origin.[2] Its prominent use in paintings such as the 1636 work *The Blinding of Samson* (fig. p. 15) shows the fascination that this weapon from the Orient exerted on the artist. It remains unclear how this representation should be interpreted—possibilities range from a self-confident new image for the artist at a transitional point in his life, to a portrait of him playing a role due to his exuberant pleasure in experimentation, through to the idealized picture of an Oriental ruler bearing Rembrandt's facial features. GD

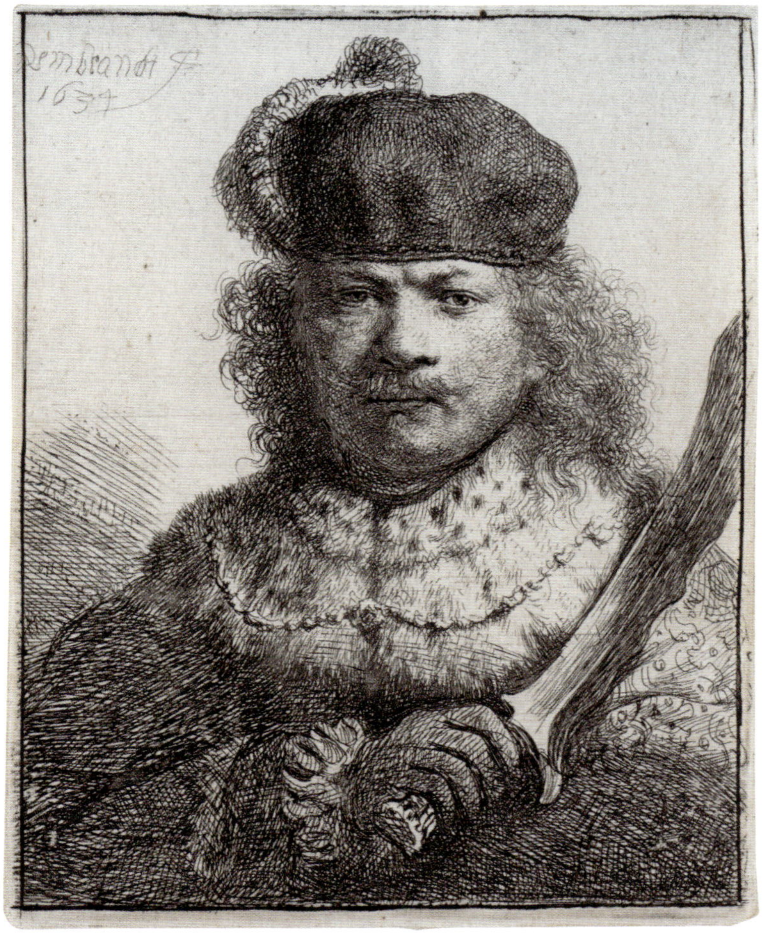

107

108 **Antonio Tempesta** (1555–1630)
A Lion Hunt, 1595

109 **Antonio Tempesta** (1555–1630)
A Lion Hunt, 1608

110 **Rembrandt Harmensz. van Rijn** (1606–1669)
The Small Lion Hunt with One Lion, ca. 1629

111 **Rembrandt Harmensz. van Rijn** (1606–1669)
The Small Lion Hunt with Two Lions, ca. 1629

112 **Rembrandt Harmensz. van Rijn** (1606–1669)
The Large Lion Hunt, 1641

108
From the series *Hunting Scenes IV*
Etching, 13.3 x 20 cm
Inscribed bottom left: AT [monogram] . F
Inv. RP-P-H-H-679
Rijksmuseum, Amsterdam, Rijksprentenkabinet, on loan from the Rijksakademie van Beeldende Kunsten

Lit.
B 1123

109
From the series *Hunting Scenes VII*
Etching, 20 x 28 cm
Inscribed bottom left: AT [monogram] . F .
Inv. 1848,1125.70
The British Museum, Department of Prints and Drawings

Lit.
B 1149

110
Etching, 15.8 x 11.7 cm
Inv. X.1105
Kunstmuseum Basel, Kupferstichkabinett

Lit.
B 116 (1/1)
NH 29 (1/1)
St. Gallen 2005, 46–47
Amsterdam 2019, 284–85
Schatborn/Hinterding 2019, no. R 111

The depiction of hunting in seventeenth-century Europe draws on various strands of tradition. The first dates back to the Middle Ages, where the art of hunting was explored in both literary and pictorial contexts, as practical instruction as well as courtly eulogy and allegorical idealization. Frederick II's *De arte venandi cum avibus* (On the Art of Hunting with Birds) from the thirteenth century and the *Livre de la chasse* (Book of Hunting) by Gaston Phoebus from roughly one century later deserve a mention here just as much as the panoramic courtly panel paintings by Lucas Cranach the Elder and many tapestries of the fifteenth and sixteenth centuries. All of these featured large game such as deer, wolves, wild boar, and bears, but no animals that were not native to Europe.

On the other hand, the creation account in Genesis contributed to the interest in exotic fauna, some of which were known only through hearsay, in medieval bestiaries and any attempts to depict paradise. Thus hippopotamuses and crocodiles found their way into the depiction of imaginary hunting scenes by Peter Paul Rubens, for example. Italian theory was particularly important in preparing the ground for the latter, with treatises based on Xenophon about the idealized hunt—as successfully practiced by the *uomo universale* as the ideal training for war, rather than for any purposes related to food or pleasure. For this reason, a noble and exotic animal such as a lion or tiger constituted the ideal prey, or rather, the ideal opponent, and indeed the depicted scenes resemble cavalry battles against a formidable enemy.

The literary culmination of this strand of tradition was the treatise on hunting published in 1616, *Il Simoncello o Vero della caccia* by the chamberlain to Cosimo II, the Grand Duke of Tuscany, Baldovino di Monte Simoncello, its pictorial counterpart being Rubens's large-format *Lion Hunt* of 1621 (Bayerische Staatsgemäldesammlungen, Alte Pinakothek, Munich).[1] Its creator was clearly aware of the various categories into which his hunting scenes fell. When, in 1618, Rubens was trying to encourage Sir Dudley Carleton, who already owned one of his hunting scenes, to accept a lion hunt, he wrote: "They would complement one another perfectly, because that one shows big cats and European hunters, and this one here shows lions and Moorish and Turkish riders, very exotic [*molto bizzara*]."[2]

Thus the tone was set for Rembrandt's exploration of the theme. His bankruptcy inventory of 1656 might have listed an album featuring sketches of animals drawn from life, but a more important source for his etchings of hunting scenes were Antonio Tempesta's prints, four albums of which Rembrandt listed in his possession.[3] Tempesta produced several series of hunting scenes of which the lion hunts, composed in the *grande maniera,* are almost contemporaneous visual equivalents of Simoncello's idealized hunting theory. Rembrandt used the main group of the horse and rider in Tempesta's etching from the fourth series, for example, in the same function in his *Large Lion Hunt.* In the print the group appears as a mirror image, so it would have been transferred directly and unreversed to the plate by the master.

1 Cf. Rosand 1969.
2 Letter of May 12, 1618; *Correspondance de Rubens et documents épistolaires concernant sa vie et ses œuvres,* eds. Max Rooses and Charles Ruelens, 6 vols., Antwerp 1887–1909, vol. 2, 1898, 149–50, no. 168; Rosand 1969, 36 and note 55.
3 Basel 2005, 72.

111
Etching, 15.4 x 12.3 cm
2nd state (of 2)
Inv. 2007.173
Kunstmuseum Basel, Kupferstichkabinett, Donation Eberhard W. Kornfeld, Bern

Lit.
B 115 (1/1)
NH 28 (2/2)
Basel 2005, no. 14
Amsterdam 2019, 282–83
Schatborn/Hinterding 2019, no. R 110

112
Etching and drypoint, 22.5 x 30 cm
2nd state (of 2)
Inscribed top right: Rembrandt f / 1641
Inv. 1851,0530.2
The British Museum, London, Department of Prints and Drawings

Lit.
B 114
NH 187 (2/2)
Amsterdam 2000, no. 42
Amsterdam 2019, 280–81
Schatborn/Hinterding 2019, no. R 147

The same etching by Tempesta informed the rear view of the horse, toppled to the ground by the leaping lion, in Rembrandt's *Small Lion Hunt with One Lion.* The *Small Lion Hunt with Two Lions* is dominated by the frontally viewed horse jumping out of the image, its rider holding the reins in one hand and preparing to hurl a spear with the other. Rembrandt took this motif—albeit exchanging the positions of the left and right arms—from Tempesta's etching in the series *Hunting Scenes VII,* in which the horse leaping off to the right also has no rider. In the prints by the Roman artist, the exotic setting is complemented by large palm trees, their waving fronds arching in the background. Their distinctive forms are also hinted at in two of Rembrandt's three etchings of lion hunts. BB

108

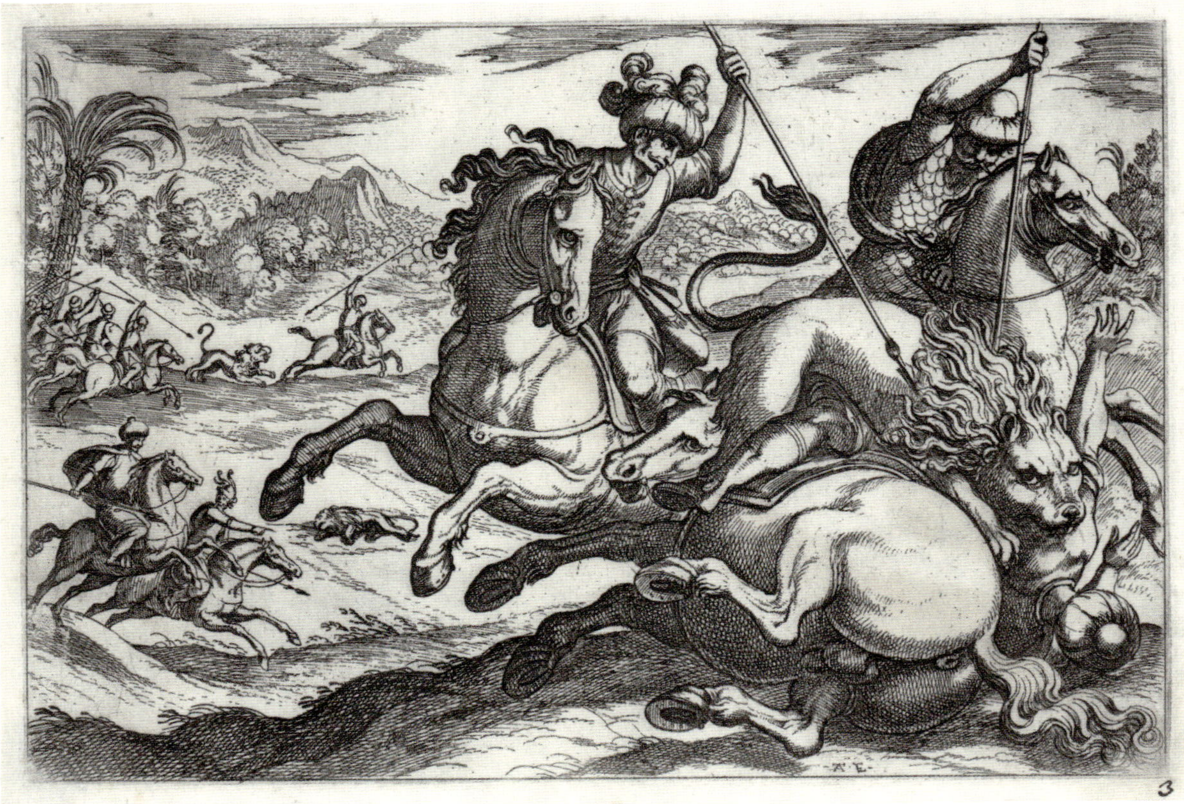

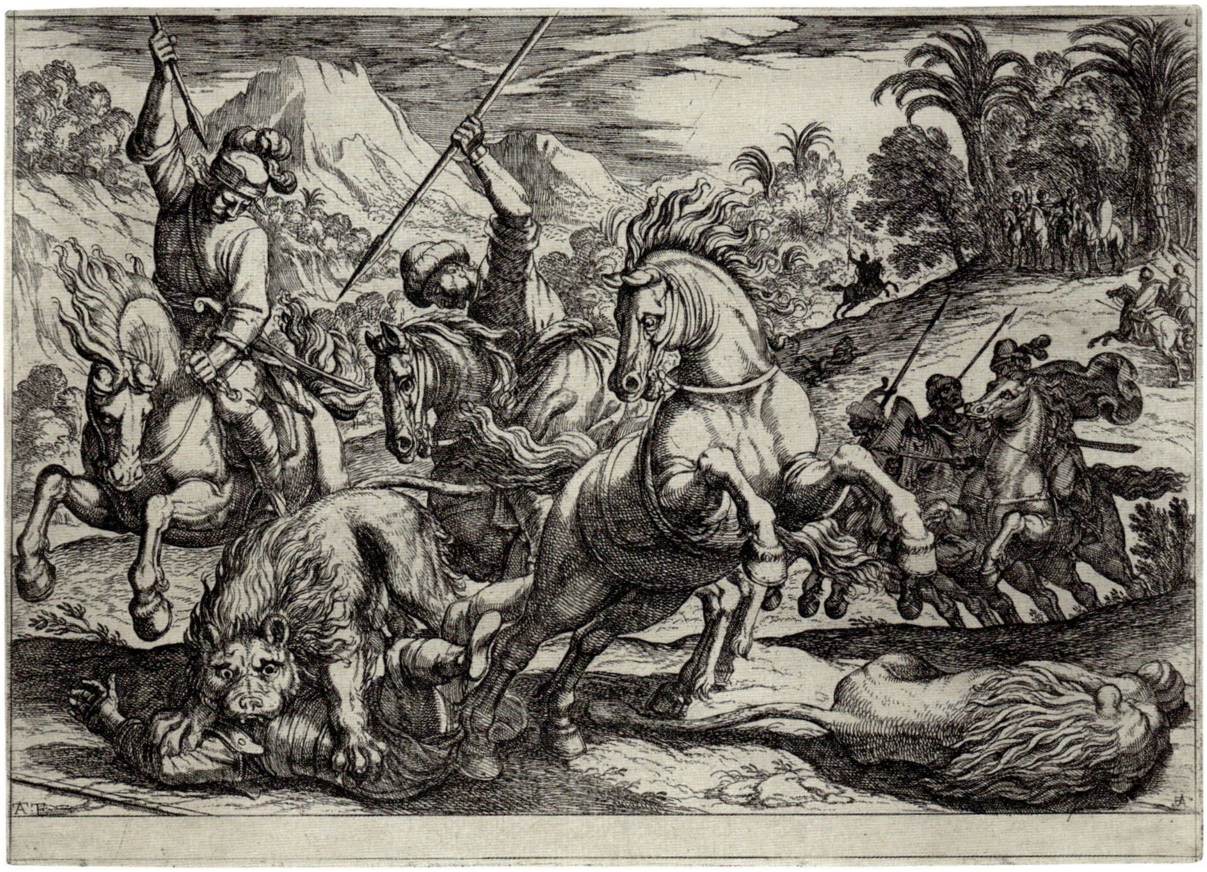

109

110

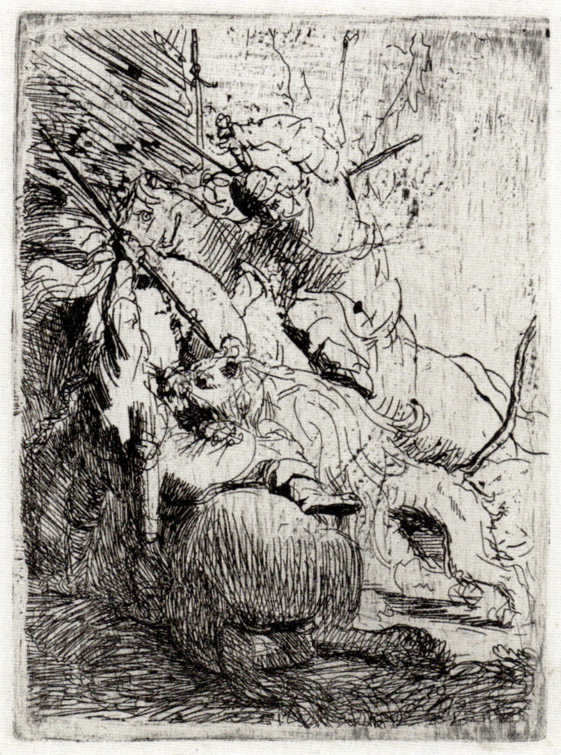

111

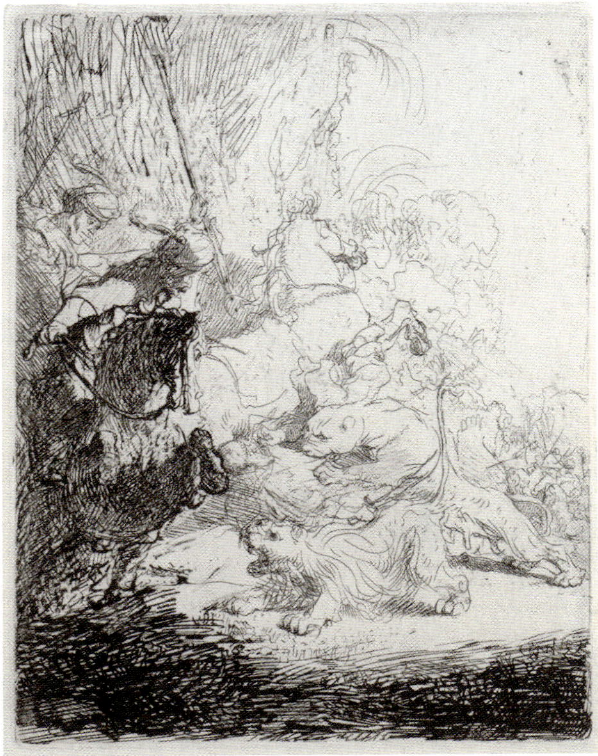

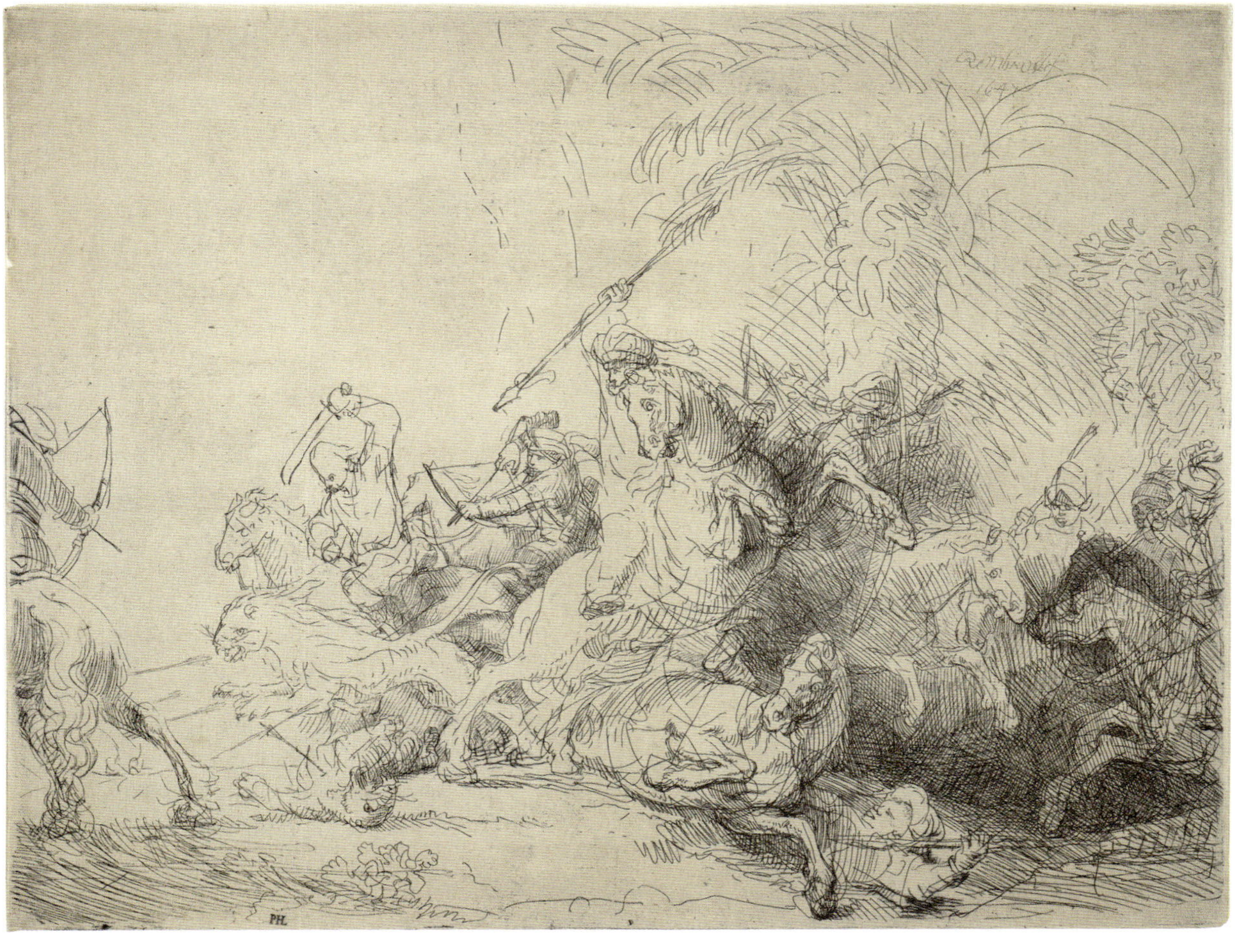

112

113 **Rembrandt Harmensz. van Rijn** (1606–1669)
Joseph Telling His Dreams, 1638

114 **Rembrandt Harmensz. van Rijn** (1606–1669)
Joseph Telling His Dreams, 1638

115 **Rembrandt Harmensz. van Rijn** (1606–1669)
Study for Joseph Telling His Dreams, ca. 1638

There were two reasons why Joseph, Jacob's favorite son, attracted the hate of his jealous brothers, so that they plotted to kill him, only deciding at the last moment to sell him into slavery in Egypt instead. The first of these was his "coat of many colors," a gift from their father. In his etching, Rembrandt interprets this as a half-sleeved fur coat, worn exlusively by Jacob and Joseph, but none of his brothers. Then, when the young man recounts his dream to the family circle, describing how his brothers' sheaves of corn bowed down to his own, and how even the stars bow down to him, it becomes actually too much for the father, too, who rebukes the boy (Genesis 37:3–11). The prophecy of Joseph's glorious ascent is ultimately fulfilled nevertheless (see cat. 66); for this reason his eventful life has often been interpreted christologically since the Middle Ages.

Rembrandt had already touched on the subject of Joseph's dream narration in an oil sketch in grisaille on paper from 1633 (Rijksmuseum, Amsterdam); its composition formed the starting point for the etching five years later. The comparison of the oil sketch with the laterally reversed counterproof of the etching shows that the spatial structure, with the four-poster bed on the right and the table on the left, as well as the group of figures remains the same, as does the posture of the individual figures—that of the seated patriarch, for example, or of the brother at the table who is leaning to one side.

One key difference between the oil sketch and the etching, however, lies in the more pronounced accentuation of the Oriental tone in the later one. Standing behind both Joseph and Jacob are men wearing turbans. These two secondary figures tower not only over the boy and his seated father, but also over Joseph's other brothers, restructuring the whole composition of the group. Rembrandt had recorded his idea for the man behind Joseph in the drawing shown here, in which details such as the turban's contours, the angle of the head, and the position of both arms were already established. The second figure in the drawing, that of a seated young woman with a book viewed at an angle from behind, also found its way into the etching. The iconography of this figure is unique; she must represent Dinah, Jacob's only daughter (Genesis 34:1). While Rembrandt was able to base his portrayal of Jacob's wife, Rachel, lying in bed in the background, in an engraving of 1532 by Heinrich Aldegrever,[1] the appearance of the daughter in this scene apparently has no pictorial precedent and is solely indebted to Rembrandt's in-depth study of the scriptures. And yet Aldegrever's engraving could have provided indirectly a point of departure for this novelty: in his print Jacob's chair stands in the same spot used by Rembrandt for Dinah's chair, right at the front in the bottom right-hand corner. BB

113
Etching and drypoint, 11 x 8.3 cm
3rd state (of 6)
Inscribed on plate at bottom left: Rembrandt f 1638
Inv. 2019.172
Kunstmuseum Basel, Kupferstichkabinett, Donation Eberhard W. Kornfeld, Bern

Lit.
B 37 (3/3)
NH 167 (3/6)
CRP, vol. 2, 295
Boston 2003, no. 52
St. Gallen 2005, 66–68
Van de Wetering 2009, 81
Amsterdam 2019, 440–41
Schatborn/Hinterding 2019, no. R 6

114
Etching and drypoint, 11 x 8.3 cm
3rd state (of 6), counterproof
Inv. F,4.67
The British Museum, London, Department of Prints and Drawings, bequeathed by Felix Slade in 1868

Lit.
NH 167 (3/6)
Amsterdam 2000, no. 31

115
Pen and brown ink with brown wash, heightened with white on pale brown prepared paper, 13.9 x 12.5 cm
Private collection, New York

Lit.
Benesch 1954–57, vol. 1, no. 168, fig. 186
CRP, Bd. 2, 295
Boston 2003, no. 53
Schatborn/Hinterding 2019, no. Z 52

[1] The Bible text is contradictory here. According to Genesis 35:19 Rachel dies while giving birth to Benjamin, yet in Genesis 37:10, Jacob refers to her as still alive: "Shall I and thy mother and thy brethren indeed come to bow down ourselves to thee to the earth?"

113

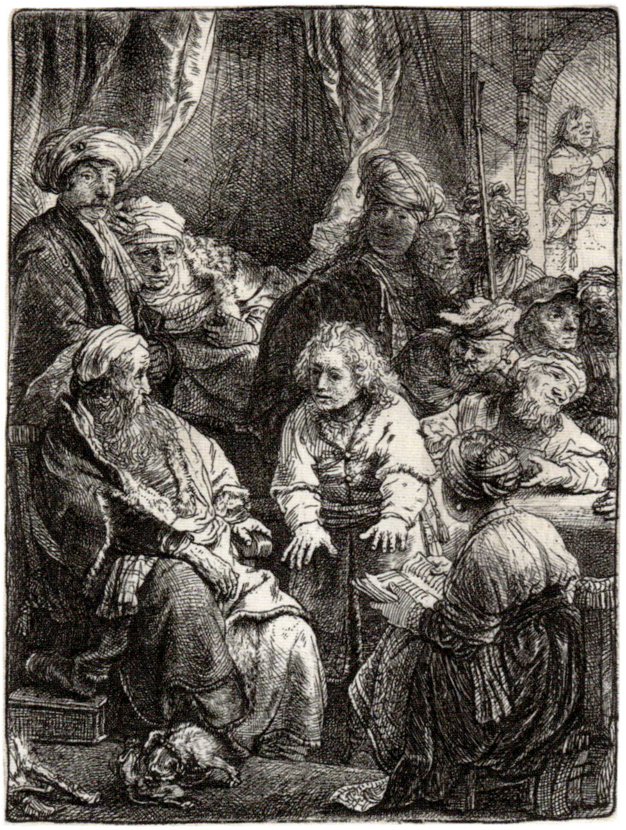

114

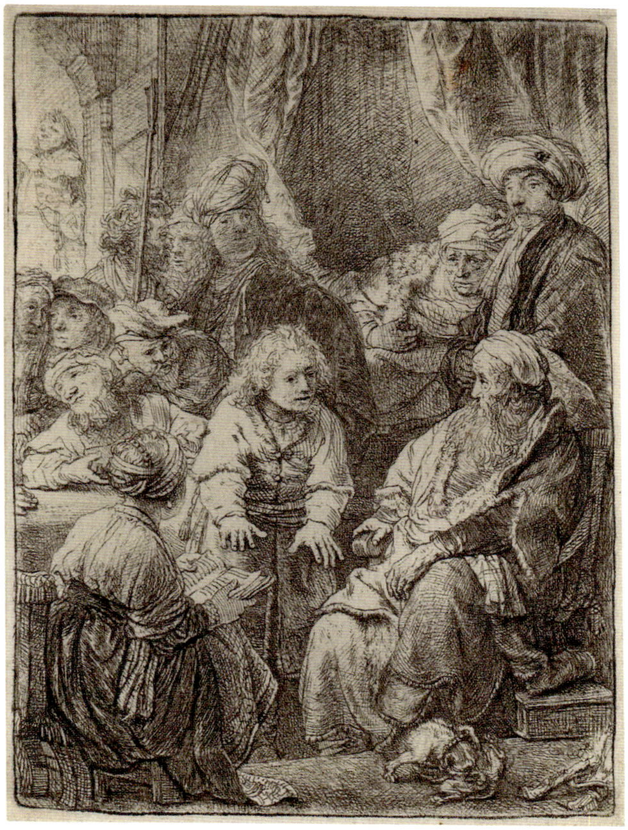

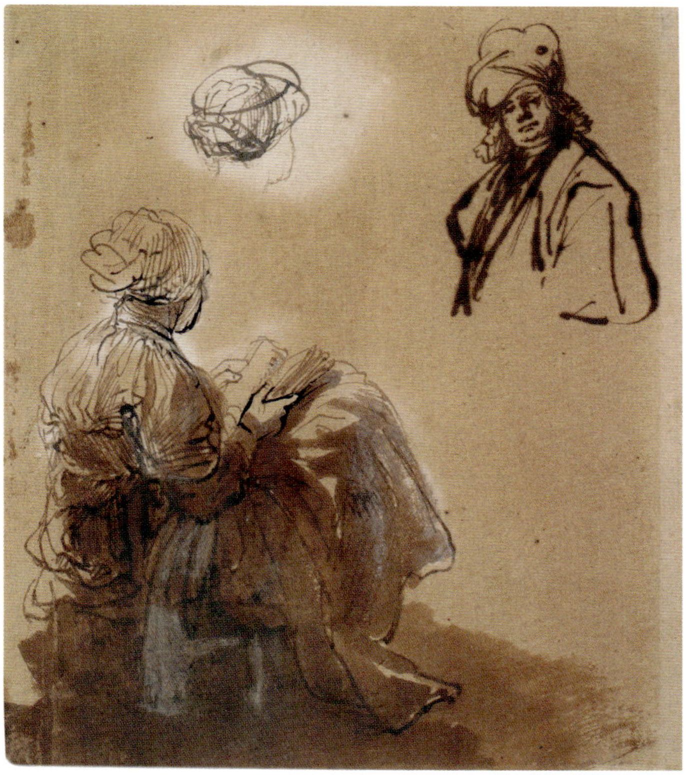

115

116 **Rembrandt Harmensz. van Rijn** (1606–1669)
Abraham and Isaac, 1645

117 **Rembrandt Harmensz. van Rijn** (1606–1669)
Three Oriental Figures, 1641

116
Etching, drypoint, and burin, 15.7 x 13 cm
1st state (of 2)
Inscribed on plate at bottom left:
Rembrandt. / 1645
Inv. 2007.260
Kunstmuseum Basel, Kupferstichkabinett,
Donation Eberhard W. Kornfeld, Bern

Lit.
B 34 (1/1)
NH 224 (1/2)
Swan 2013, 107, fig. 51
Verdi 2014, 157–59
Dresden 2019, 158, fig. 40

117
Etching and drypoint, 14.5 x 11.4 cm
2nd state (of 2)
Inscribed on plate at top right:
Rembrandt f 1641 [in mirror writing]
Inv. 2019.162
Kunstmuseum Basel, Kupferstichkabinett,
Donation Eberhard W. Kornfeld, Bern

Lit.
B 118 (2/2)
NH 190 (2/2)
White 1999, 51–52
Ackley 2003, 20
Boston 2003, no. 67
Basel 2005, no. 93
Swan 2013, no. 36
Silver 2018, 17–18

The etching from 1645 depicts the conversation between Abraham and Isaac (Genesis 22:4–8), moments before the father prepares to sacrifice his son. As they head to the sacrificial site, the boy, carrying the firewood on his shoulder, looks bewildered that they are not taking a sacrificial animal with them; Abraham assures him that God will provide. Which is precisely what happens: at the last moment, an angel intervenes in the gruesome proceedings—the sacrifice of Isaac—and a ram miraculously appears that is killed in his place.

Rembrandt diverged from the biblical text to concentrate on the psychological intensity of the rarely depicted and intimate moment. The protagonists have already arrived at the predetermined location—in the foreground on the left the altar-shaped sacrificial site can be made out, the pot of live coals they brought with them is already on the ground, Isaac has put down the bundle of firewood—and they have turned to face each other. Insistently, the task ahead notwithstanding, the father lectures to his son, solemnly holding one hand to his heart and pointing to the sky with the other, his trust in God undiminished. Isaac listens unsuspectingly to his father's words while behind his back, dark areas of shading augur the rising smoke of the sacrifice. Both figures are dressed in heavy, richly ornate fantasy robes full of exotic details; Abraham's Orientalizing traits include the belted undergarment worn beneath a fur-lined coat, the sword suspended from his waist with its ornate pommel, and a turban.

The *Three Oriental Figures* from four years earlier are characterized by similar traits: three exotically dressed figures have gathered next to the covered doorway of a house, shown at an angle, as in Rembrandt's etching *Abraham Entertaining the Angels* (cat. 118). They are engaged in lively conversation with another figure who is leaning out of the upper, open section of a Dutch door. Here, too, Rembrandt devoted considerable attention to the detailed rendering of clothing: wide, fur-trimmed coats with ermine-like shoulder adornments, richly patterned undergarments with sashes, and extravagant head coverings, among them a turban with a jeweled medallion and a flamboyant fur hat, create an exotic impression of faraway lands. As his drawings show (see cat. 19, 20), Rembrandt certainly encountered visitors from the East in Amsterdam (see cat. 21), yet the *Three Oriental Figures* and the drawing of *Abraham and Isaac* barely reference such studies from life. In their deliberate exoticism, the robes are closer to fantasy items inspired by traditional patterns and costume books. Rembrandt was aiming for a harmonious overall impression rather than an authentic reproduction of real clothing styles, combining established motifs with his own inventions.[1] Since the narrative character of the etching seems to evoke a specific scene, *Three Oriental Figures* has been tentatively linked to a number of biblical stories, without an entirely conclusive result. The most widespread interpretation, however, is the dispute between Jacob and Laban (Genesis 30:25–34). GD

1 For the relationship to reality of Rembrandt's Oriental costumes see Bahre 2006, 134, and De Winkel 2006, 255–70.

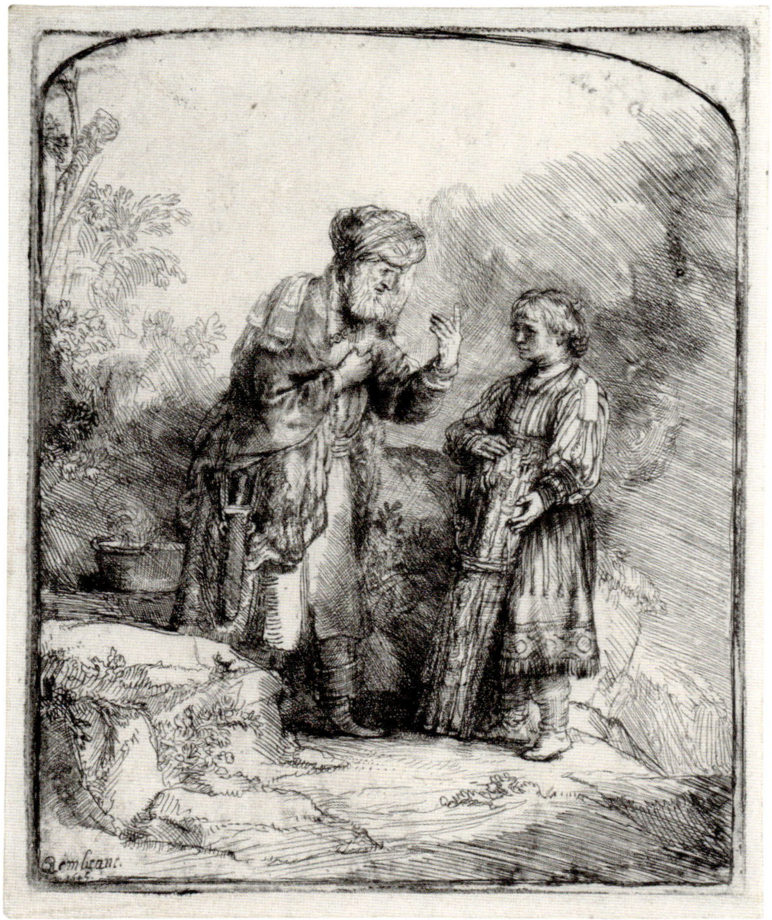

116

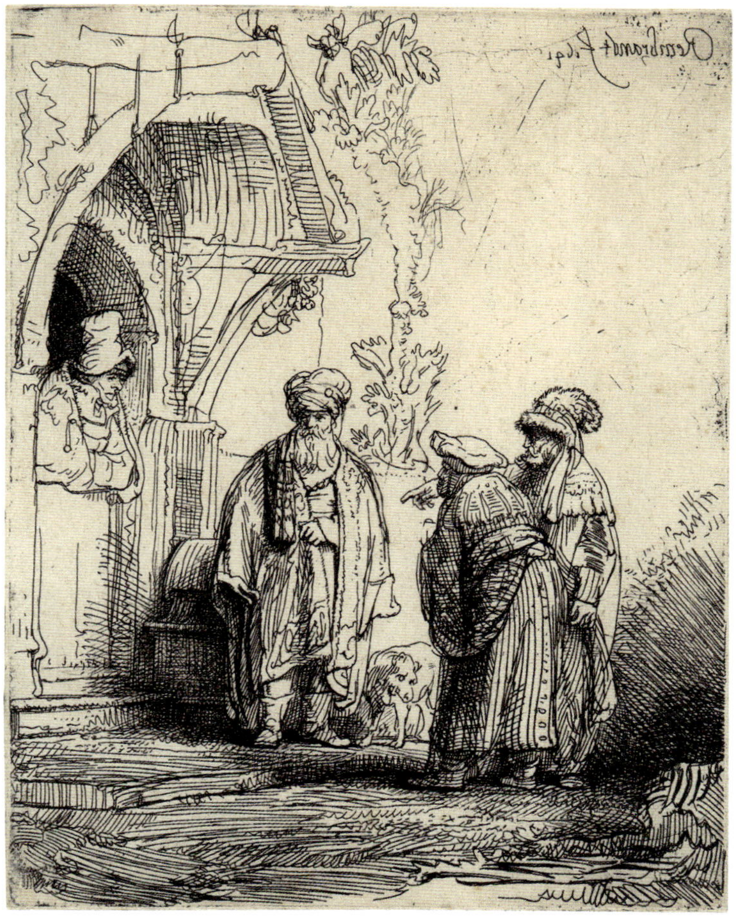

117

118 **Rembrandt Harmensz. van Rijn** (1606–1669)

Abraham Entertaining the Angels, 1656

Etching and drypoint, 15.9 x 13.1 cm
Inscribed on plate at bottom left:
Rembrandt. f. 1656
Inv. 2007.259
Kunstmuseum Basel, Kupferstichkabinett,
Donation Eberhard W. Kornfeld, Bern

Lit.
B 29 (1/1)
NH 295 (1/1)
Slatkes 1983b, 25–27, fig. 11
White 1999, 105–07
Boston 2003, 214–18, no. 142
Vienna 2004, no. 112
Basel 2005, no. 92
Manuth 2006, 56
Forberg 2015, 312–13
Denver 2018, no. 102
Los Angeles 2018, 18
Silver 2018, 8–12

In 1655–56 Rembrandt revisited the story of Abraham in two etchings that were possibly conceived as a pair (see cat. 116). One depicts God appearing to Abraham (Genesis 18:1–15), showing up unexpectedly with two attendants outside Abraham's tent. When Abraham recognizes who it is, he invites the three strangers to stay, has a calf slaughtered, and hosts them under a tree. Here, God announces to the aged patriarch that his wife Sarah was going to give birth to a son. Due to her infertility Abraham had previously fathered a son, Ismael, with the maidservant Hagar. Sarah, listening in on the prophecy, laughs out loud in disbelief and is rebuked by God. But she does indeed fall pregnant with Isaac and after his birth, Hagar and Ismael are banished.

Rembrandt relocates the incident to the entrance of a house, cut off by the left edge of the image, where Sarah is concealed behind a half-opened door. The three guests have settled down in front of it, while Abraham, who stands in a pose of humility a little lower down on the right, offers refreshments and completes the semicircle of the group. The figure of a boy, seen from behind as he shoots an arrow, points to the continuation of the story: it is Ismael who, after the banishment, proves to be a skilled archer. Departing from the pictorial tradition that Rembrandt had still observed in a painting of the same theme dated 1646 (private collection), only the two attendants are identified as angels, whereas God the Father—in defiance of the Calvinist prohibition on representing God in human form—appears as an aged patriarch with a long beard and exotic head covering, brought to the fore by lighting and relative scale. The composition of a group of men seated on a carpet around a serving platter has clear similarities to the Mughal miniature *Four Mullahs*, or rather to Rembrandt's copy of it (fig. p. 69); the physiognomy of God the Father, the jug on the right, and the lack of any real depth to the landscape in the background are also prefigured there.

In order to create an ambience that was as harmonious as possible, Rembrandt did not, as in previous instances, introduce unspecific Oriental motifs, but instead turned to contemporary Mughal miniatures that he obviously considered particularly authentic, having obtained at least some of them firsthand. Whether he actually owned the *Four Mullahs* and the other miniatures that he copied is not clear (see the essay by Gary Schwartz, pp. 56–73, and cat. 92, 96–97). Rembrandt did not slavishly follow his Eastern model; instead he used it as a starting point for his interpretations with a deeply psychological component, in which a diverse set of influences converge. Thus, for example, he left out the tree, which would have established the exact biblical setting, and replaced it with the entrance of a house that had already appeared in the same position in his 1637 etching *The Dismissal of Hagar,* but which also figures in several other works (cat. 116). The physiognomy of the two angels—which might archetypically be regarded as "Persian" or "Asian"—were added freely. The archer could even have been borrowed from Hendrick Goltzius's engraving after Raphael's fresco of the *Triumph of Galatea* in the Villa Farnesina in Rome, which would extend the frame of references further still. GD

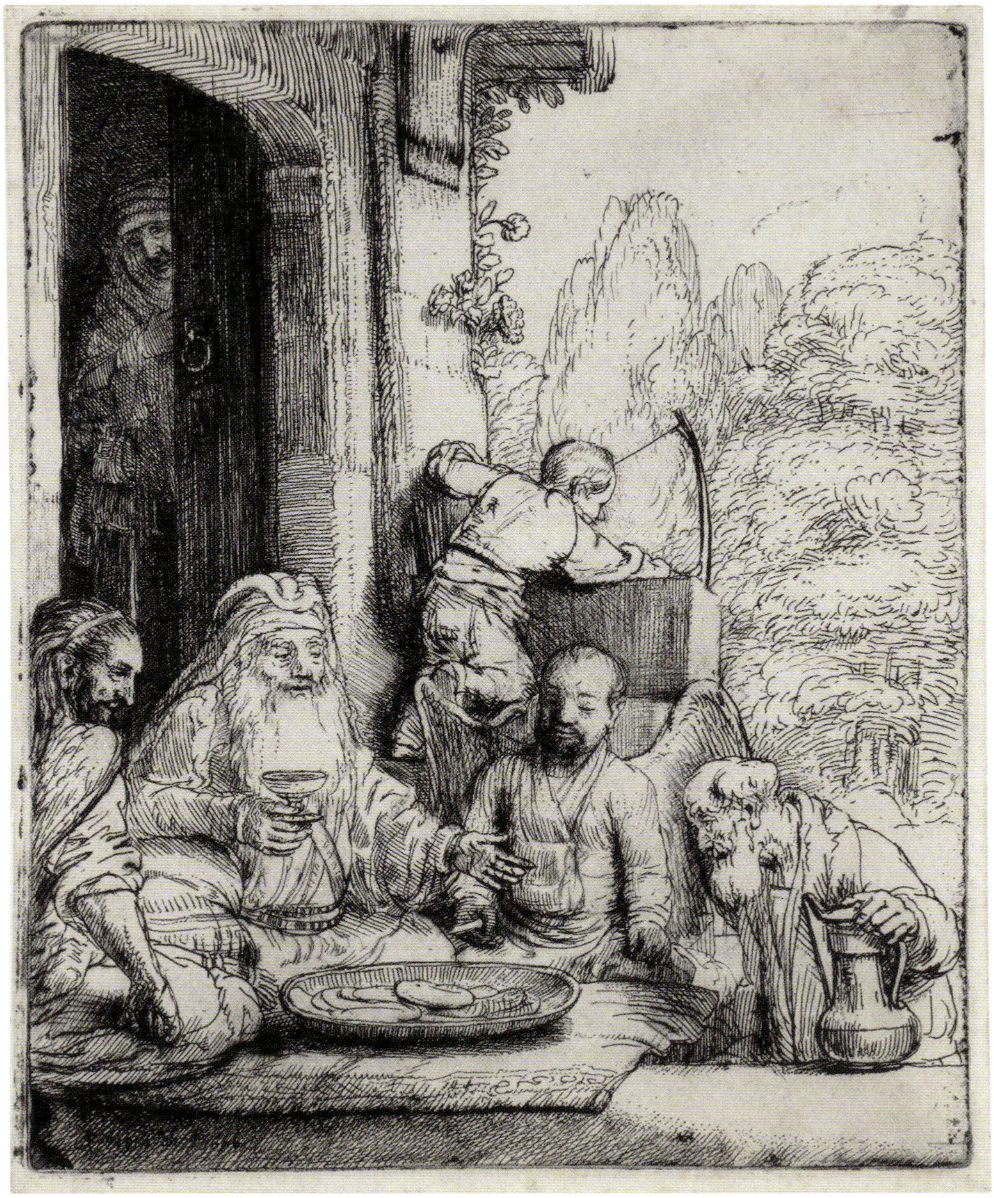

118

119 **Ferdinand Bol** (1616–1680)

Portrait of an Oriental, ca. 1665

Oil on canvas, mounted on wood, 131.5 x 101.5 cm
Inv. M1972.51
Milwaukee Art Museum, Gift of Dr. and Mrs. Roland Cron

Lit.
Blankert 1982, no. 74, fig. 82
Sumowski 1983–94, vol. 1, 284, no. 117
Milwaukee 1992, no. 2

1 Gottwald 2017.

When Ferdinand Bol moved to Amsterdam from his hometown of Dordrecht around 1636 and began working in Rembrandt's workshop, the latter had just abandoned the pictorial theme of *tronies* in Oriental costume after a good ten years of constant experimentation (cat. 99–101, 103, 106). In his efforts to adopt Rembrandt's painting style, Bol would have studied some of Rembrandt's *tronies* that remained in his studio, as well as those by other workshop employees and students who were inspired by them or had copied them.

After leaving the studio and becoming an independent painter, Bol, like his colleague Govert Flinck (cat. 3), created a series of *tronies*, among them several with Oriental and other exotic costumes, which were both indebted to Rembrandt's genre scenes and developed them further.[1] Bol took up this subject matter in the final years of Rembrandt's life—at least three decades after the latter had abandoned it, and at a time when such paintings had long since fallen out of fashion—as this *tronie* shows.

Set against an undefined spatial background, the half-length figure of a standing man is portrayed in the typical garb of an "Oriental." Over an undergarment with a sash that leaves his chest exposed, he wears a coat of asymmetrical cut that has slipped open slightly, the hem of which is trimmed with pearls and precious stones on the left. Leaning rather awkwardly against what seems to be a rounded pillar, the figure rests his right hand on a table, while holding an ornate sword with a gilded chain in his left, its hilt in the auricular style matching the seam of his cloak. The aged face, with its gray moustache and pearl earring, is bathed in luminous light, as is the neck area; the light also touches the extravagant and painstakingly wrapped turban, which is decorated with a fantastical aigrette with bird-of-paradise feathers (see cat. 2).

How much Bol's late *tronie* may owe to earlier works by Rembrandt such as *Man in Oriental Clothing* (cat. 101) or *Self-Portrait with Raised Sabre* (cat. 107), when it comes to the detailed and imaginative description of the dress and the use of light, there can be no doubt that it lifts the genre to a new level. Certainly Bol could not match Rembrandt's penetrating psychological profundity. Nevertheless his portrait—clearly that of a noble or ruler—evokes a touching moment of internal tension and struggle for self-control, due to the peculiar contrast between the disarray of the sitter's clothing, on the one hand, and his resolute expression as well as his proud display of stately insignia on the other. In fact, Bol transforms the tronie into a genre scene or single-figure history painting by scaling the figure in the painting much larger than usual, turning the traditional bust into a three-quarter-length figure. Furthermore, he charges the pictorial space with intriguing ambiguity. Thus the *Portrait of an Oriental* is an impressive testimony to the enduring fascination with the theme of the Orient as a blank page for artistic imagination, a fascination that originated in Rembrandt's circle under his influence. GD

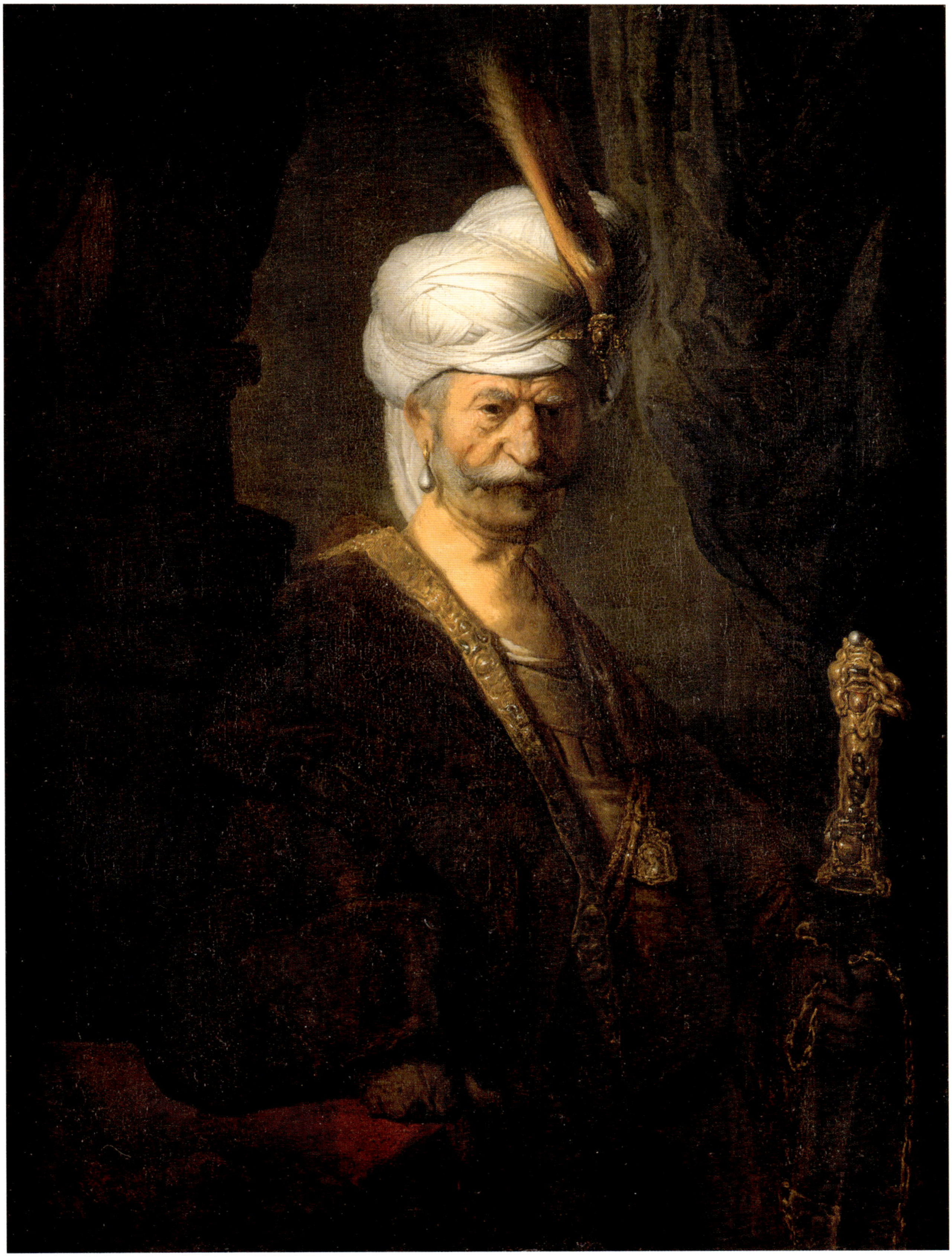

Selected Bibliography

Ackley 2003
Clifford S. Ackley, "Rembrandt as Actor and Dramatist: Gesture and Body Language in the Biblical Etchings," in Boston 2003, 17–28.

Alkmaar 1997
Sandra de Vries, *De zestiende- en zeventiende-eeuwse schilderijen van het Stedelijk Museum Alkmaar: Collectie-catalogus,* Alkmaar 1997.

Alkmaar 2016
Caesar van Everdingen (1616/1617–1678): Painting Beauty, exh. cat. Stedelijk Museum Alkmaar, 2016.

Amsterdam 1972
Nederlandse schilders en tekenaars in de Oost, 17de–20ste eeuw, exh. cat. Rijksmuseum, Amsterdam 1972.

Amsterdam 1975–79
Albert Blankert, *Amsterdams Historisch Museum: Schilderijen daterend van voor 1800; Voorlopige catalogus,* Amsterdam 1975–79.

Amsterdam 1991a
Pieter Lastman, the Man Who Taught Rembrandt, exh. cat. Museum Het Rembrandthuis, Amsterdam 1991.

Amsterdam 1991b
Rembrandt: The Master and His Workshop, exh. cat. Rijksmuseum, Amsterdam 1991.

Amsterdam 1992
De wereld binnen handbereik: Nederlandse kunst- en rariteitenverzamelingen, 1585–1735, 2 vols., exh. cat. Amsterdams Historisch Museum, 1992.

Amsterdam 1993
Dawn of the Golden Age: Northern Netherlandish Art, 1580–1620, exh. cat. Rijksmuseum, Amsterdam 1993.

Amsterdam 1998
Pictures from the Tropics: Paintings by Western Artists during the Dutch Colonial Period in Indonesia, exh. cat. Tropenmuseum, Amsterdam 1998.

Amsterdam 1999a
Rembrandt's Treasures, exh. cat. Museum Het Rembrandthuis, Amsterdam 1999.

Amsterdam 1999b
Still-Life Paintings from the Netherlands 1550–1720, exh. cat. Rijksmuseum, Amsterdam 1999.

Amsterdam 2000
Rembrandt the Printmaker, exh. cat. Rijksmuseum, Amsterdam 2000.

Amsterdam 2002a
Kopstukken: Amsterdammers geportretteerd 1600–1800, exh. cat. Amsterdams Historisch Museum 2002.

Amsterdam 2002b
The Dutch Encounter with Asia, 1600–1950, exh. cat. Rijksmuseum, Amsterdam 2002.

Amsterdam 2007a
Het aanzien van Amsterdam: Panorama's, plattegronden en profielen uit de Gouden Eeuw, exh. cat. Stadsarchief Amsterdam, 2007.

Amsterdam 2007b
Jonathan Bikker et al., *Dutch Paintings of the Seventeenth Century in the Rijksmuseum Amsterdam*, vol. 1: *Artists Born between 1570 and 1600,* Amsterdam 2007.

Amsterdam 2008a
125 jaar openbare kunstbezit met steun van de Vereniging Rembrandt, exh. cat. Van Gogh Museum, Amsterdam 2008.

Amsterdam 2008b
Norbert E. Middelkoop, Gusta Reichwein, and Judith van Gent, *De oude meesters van de stad Amsterdam: Schilderijen tot 1800,* Amsterdams Historisch Museum, Bussum 2008.

Amsterdam 2011a
Gedrukt tot Amsterdam: Amsterdamse prentmakers en -uitgevers in de Gouden Eeuw, exh. cat. Museum Het Rembrandthuis, Amsterdam 2011.

Amsterdam 2011b
Jan van Campen and Ebeltje Hartkamp-Jonxis, *Asian Splendour: Company Art in the Rijksmuseum,* Zutphen 2011.

Amsterdam 2012
Michiel van Musscher (1645–1705): The Wealth of the Golden Age, exh. cat. Museum van Loon, Amsterdam 2012.

Amsterdam 2014
Portrait Gallery of the Golden Age, exh. cat. Hermitage, Amsterdam 2014.

Amsterdam 2015
Asia in Amsterdam: The Culture of Luxury in the Golden Age, exh. cat. Rijksmuseum, Amsterdam 2015.

Amsterdam 2017
Ferdinand Bol and Govert Flinck: Rembrandt's Master Pupils, exh. cat. Museum Het Rembrandthuis and Amsterdam Museum, Amsterdam 2017.

Amsterdam 2018
1600–1700: Dutch Golden Age, ed. Gregor J. M. Weber, Rijksmuseum, Amsterdam 2018.

Amsterdam 2019
Rembrandt X Rijksmuseum, exh. cat. Rijksmuseum, Amsterdam 2019.

Amsterdam 2020
Black in Rembrandt's Time, exh. cat. Museum Het Rembrandthuis, Amsterdam 2020.

Aqajani Isfahani/Javani 2007
Hossein Aqajani Isfahani and Asghar Javani, *Safavid Wall Painting in Isfahan: Chehel Sutun Palace,* Tehran 2007.

Auboyer 1955
Jeannine Auboyer, "Un maître hollandais du XVIIe siècle s'inspirant des miniatures mogholes," in *Arts Asiatiques,* 2 (1955), 251–73.

B
Adam von Bartsch, *Le Peintre-Graveur*, 21 vols., Vienna 1803–1821, and *Catalogue raisonnée de toutes les estampes qui forment l'œuvre de Rembrandt, et ceux de ses principaux imitateurs,* Vienna 1797 (printing states added by Christopher White and Karel G. Boon, *Rembrandt's Etchings: An Illustrated Critical Catalogue,* 2 vols., Amsterdam 1969 = H, vol. 18).

Baer 2003
Ronni Baer, "Rembrandt's Oil Sketches," in Boston 2003, 29–44.

Bahre 2006
Kristin Bahre, "Orientalisierende Motive im Werk Rembrandts," in Berlin 2006, 129–43.

Bamberg 1988
Kaufleute als Kolonialherren: Die Handelswelt der Niederländer vom Kap der Guten Hoffnung bis Nagasaki 1600–1800, exh. cat. 37, Deutscher Historikertag in Bamberg, 1988.

Bandmann 1962
Günter Bandmann, "Das Exotische in der europäischen Kunst," in *Der Mensch und die Künste: Festschrift für Heinrich Lützeler zum 60. Geburtstag,* ed. Günter Bandmann et al., Düsseldorf 1962, 337–54.

Basel 1995
Mit Turban und Fahne: Aelbert Cuyps Basler Familienbildnis wiederentdeckt, exh. cat. Kunstmuseum Basel, 1995.

Basel 2000
Die Sammlung Max Geldner im Kunstmuseum Basel: Vermächtnis und Ankäufe der Stiftung, exh. cat. Kunstmuseum Basel, 2000.

Basel 2005
Rembrandt: Die Radierungen aus der Sammlung Eberhard W. Kornfeld, ed. Karin Althaus, exh. cat. Kunstmuseum Basel, Kupferstichkabinett, Basel 2005.

Basel 2011
Kunstmuseum Basel: The Masterpieces; Paintings, Sculptures, Photographs, Installations, and Videos, ed. Bernhard Mendes Bürgi and Nina Zimmer, Ostfildern 2011.

Basel 2017
¡Hola Prado! Two Collections in Dialogue, exh. cat. Kunstmuseum Basel, 2017.

Baskins 2012
Cristelle Baskins, "Lost in Translation: Portraits of Sitti Maani Gioerida della Valle in Baroque Rome," in *Early Modern Women* 7 (2012), 241–60.

Batchelor 2006
Robert Batchelor, "On the Movement of Porcelains: Rethinking the Birth of Consumer Society as Interactions of Exchange Networks, 1600–1750," in *Consuming Cultures, Global Perspectives: Historical Trajectories, Transnational Exchanges,* ed. John Brewer and Frank Trentmann, New York 2006, 95–121.

Bauch 1966
Kurt Bauch, *Rembrandt: Gemälde,* Berlin 1966.

Beekman 1996
Eric Montague Beekman, *Troubled Pleasures: Dutch Colonial Literature from the East Indies 1600–1950,* Oxford 1996.

Benesch 1954–57
Otto Benesch, *The Drawings of Rembrandt: A Critical and Chronological Catalogue,* 6 vols., London 1954–57.

Benesch 1973
Otto Benesch, *The Drawings of Rembrandt,* ed. Eva Benesch, 6 vols., London 1973.

Berlin 1989
Europa und der Orient, 800–1900, exh. cat. Festival der Weltkulturen Horizonte '89, Martin-Gropius-Bau, Berlin 1989.

Berlin 2006
Rembrandt: Genie auf der Suche, exh. cat. Gemäldegalerie, Staatliche Museen zu Berlin, 2006.

Birmingham 2004
Bartholomeus Breenbergh (1598–1657): Joseph Distributing Corn in Egypt, exh. cat. Barber Institute of Fine Arts, Birmingham 2004.

Birmingham 2017
The Barber Institute of Fine Arts, ed. Richard Verdi, London 2017.

Blankert 1982
Albert Blankert, *Ferdinand Bol (1616–1680), Rembrandt's Pupil,* Doornspijk 1982.

Bleichmar/Mancall 2011
Collecting across Cultures: Material Exchanges in the Early Modern Atlantic World, ed. Daniela Bleichmar and Peter C. Mancall, Philadelphia 2011.

Bonebakker 1998
Odilia Bonebakker, "Denomination and Iconography: The Baptism of the Eunuch in Netherlandish Art, 1520–1750," PhD diss., Kingston 1998.

Bonn 1995
Im Lichte des Halbmonds: Das Abendland und der türkische Orient, exh. cat. Bundeskunsthalle, Bonn 1995.

Bonn 2016
Der Rhein: Eine europäische Flussbiografie, exh. cat. Kunst- und Ausstellungshalle der Bundesrepublik Deutschland, Bonn 2016.

Boston 2003
Rembrandt's Journey: Painter, Draftsman, Etcher, exh. cat. Museum of Fine Arts, Boston 2003.

Bredius/Gerson 1969
Abraham Bredius, *Rembrandt: The Complete Edition of the Paintings,* revised by Horst Gerson, London 1969.

Bremmer/Hoftijzer 1998
Rolf H. Bremmer Jr. and Paul Hoftijzer, eds., "Johannes de Laet (1581–1649): A Leiden Polymath," in *Lias: Sources and Documents Relating to the Early Modern History of Ideas* 25,2 (1998), 135–230.

Brinkmann 2010
Bodo Brinkmann, "Ankäufe," in *Jahresbericht 2009 der Öffentlichen Kunstsammlung Basel, Kunstmuseum und Museum für Gegenwartskunst* (2010), 18–19.

Brook 2008
B. P. J. [Bernardus Petrus Jozef] Brook, *Vermeer's Hat: The Seventeenth Century and the Dawn of the Global World,* New York 2008.

Broos 1980
B. P. J. [Bernardus Petrus Jozef] Broos, "Rembrandts Indische miniaturen," in *Spiegel Historiael* 15 (April 1980), 210–18.

Broos 2009
Ben Broos, "Gerrit van Loo, voogd van Saskia, zwager van Rembrandt," in *Oud Holland* 122,1 (2009), 43–63.

Brussels 2015
The Sultan's World: The Ottoman Orient in Renaissance Art, exh. cat. BOZAR—Centre for Fine Arts, Brussels 2015.

Bruyn 1994
Josua Bruyn, "Een gehistorieerde familiegroep van Ferdinand Bol: Twee fragmenten in Dordrecht en Lyon," in *Oud Holland* 108,4 (1994), 208–14.

Bruyn 1997
Josua Bruyn, "François Venant: Enige aanvullingen," in *Oud Holland* 110,3 (1997), 163–76.

Budapest 2011
Ildikó Ember, *Old Masters' Gallery Catalogues*, vol. 2: *Dutch and Flemish Still Lifes 1600–1800,* Szépművészeti Múzeum, Leiden and Budapest 2011.

Budapest 2014
Rembrandt and the Dutch Golden Age, exh. cat. Szépmüveszéti Múzeum, Budapest 2014.

Burger-Wegener 1976
Catja Burger-Wegener, *Johannes Lingelbach 1622–1674,* PhD diss., Freie Universität Berlin, 1976.

Burnet 2018
Régis Burnet, "Rembrandt and the Iconography of David and Jonathan," in *Die Bibel in der Kunst / Bible in the Arts* 2 (2018), 1–14, https://www.academic-bible.com/fileadmin/user_upload/Bibelkunst/BiKu_2018_02_Burnet_Rembrandt.pdf (accessed May 6, 2020).

Chambéry 2001
Le Portrait dans les collections des Musées Rhône-Alpes: Le portrait du 16e au 18e siècle, exh. cat. Musée savoisien, Chambéry 2001.

Chapman 1990
H. Perry Chapman, *Rembrandt's Self-Portraits: A Study in Seventeenth-Century Identity,* Princeton 1990.

Cologne 1998
Arent de Gelder (1645–1727): Rembrandts Meisterschüler und Nachfolger, exh. cat. Wallraf-Richartz-Museum, Cologne 1998.

Cologne 2006
Vom Adel der Malerei: Holland um 1700, exh. cat. Wallraf-Richartz-Museum & Fondation Corboud, Cologne 2006.

Cologne 2019
Inside Rembrandt 1606–1669, exh. cat. Wallraf-Richartz-Museum & Fondation Corboud, Cologne 2019.

Courtright 1996
Nicola Courtright, "Origins and Meanings of Rembrandt's Late Drawing Style," in *The Art Bulletin* 78 (1996), 485–510.

CRP
A Corpus of Rembrandt Paintings: Stichting Foundation Rembrandt Research Project, ed. Josua Bruyn and Ernst van de Wetering, 6 vols., The Hague (vols. 1–4), Dordrecht (vols. 5, 6), 1982–2015.

DaCosta Kaufmann/North 2014
Mediating Netherlandish Art and Material Culture in Asia, ed. Thomas DaCosta Kaufmann and Michael North, Amsterdam 2014.

Daniel 2000
Norman Daniel, *Islam and the West: The Making of an Image,* Oxford 2000.

Dash 1999
Mike Dash, *Tulipomania: The Story of the World's Most Coveted Flower and Extraordinary Passions It Aroused,* London 1999.

De Groot 2009
Erlend de Groot, "The Dutch Embassy to Isfahan (Persia) in 1651–52 Led by Johannes Cunaeus: A New Interpretation of Weenix's Monumental History Painting," in Bulletin van het Rijksmuseum 57,4 (2009), 312–25.

De Hond 1994
Jan de Hond, "Cornelis de Bruijn (1652–1726/27): A Dutch Painter in the East," in *Eastward Bound: Dutch Ventures and Adventures in the Middle East,* ed. Geert Jan van Gelder and Ed de Moor, Amsterdam and Atlanta 1994, 51–81.

De Hond 2008
Jan de Hond, *Verlangen naar het Oosten: Oriëntalisme in de Nederlandse cultuur, ca. 1800–1920,* Leiden 2008.

De Hond et al. 2020
Jan de Hond, Amélie Couvrat Desvergnes, Leila Sauvage, Paolo d'Imporzano, and Forough Sajadi, "An Iranian Youth in an Album from Zwolle," in *The Rijksmuseum Bulletin* 68 (2020), 204–31.

De Silva/Beumer 1988
Rajpal Kumar de Silva and Willemina G. M. Beumer, Illustrations and Views of Dutch Ceylon 1602–1796: A Comprehensive Work of Pictorial Reference with Selected Eye-Witness Accounts, London 1988.

De Silva/Beumer 1988
Rajpal Kumar de Silva and Willemina G. M. Beumer, *Illustrations and Views of Dutch Ceylon 1602–1796: A Comprehensive Work of Pictorial Reference with Selected Eye-Witness Accounts,* London 1988.

De Winkel 1999
Marieke de Winkel, "Costume in Rembrandt's Self Portraits," in London 1999, 58–74.

De Winkel 2006
Marieke de Winkel, *Fashion and Fancy: Dress and Meaning in Rembrandt's Paintings,* Amsterdam 2006.

De Witt 2008
David de Witt, *The Bader Collection: Dutch and Flemish Paintings,* Kingston, ON, 2008.

De Witt 2017
David de Witt, "Govert Flinck Learns to Paint like Rembrandt," in Amsterdam 2017, 18–39.

De Witt 2020
David de Witt, "The Black Presence in the Art of Rembrandt and his Circle," in Amsterdam 2020, 88–119.

De Witt/Van Sloten 2017
David de Witt and Leonore van Sloten, "Ferdinand Bol: Rembrandt's Disciple," in Amsterdam 2017, 41–53.

De Zwart 2016
Pim de Zwart, *Globalization and the Colonial Origins of the Great Divergence: Intercontinental Trade and Living Standards in the Dutch East India Company's Commercial Empire, c. 1600–1800,* Leiden and Boston 2016.

Dekker 2002
Elly Dekker, The Globe between Fact and Fiction," in *News Online: Internationale Coronelli Gesellschaft für Globenkunde,* 2002, http://www.coronelli.org/publikationen/news/2002/news2002_e.html#Fic (accessed April 7, 2020).

Del Bontà 1999
Robert J. del Bontà, "Reinventing Nature: Mughal Composite Animal Painting," in *Flora and Fauna in Mughal Art,* ed. Som Prakash Verma, Mumbai 1999, 69–82.

Deluga 2008
Waldemar Deluga, "The Oriental Portraits of Aegidius Sadeler," in *Print Quarterly* 25,4 (December 2008), 424–26.

Denver 2018
Rembrandt. Painter as Printmaker, exh. cat. Art Museum, Denver 2018.

Dickey 2004
Stephanie S. Dickey, *Rembrandt: Portraits in Print,* Amsterdam and Philadelphia 2004.

Dickey 2017
Ferdinand Bol and Govert Flinck: New Research, ed. Stephanie S. Dickey, Zwolle 2017.

Dordrecht 2012
Portret in portret in de Nederlandse kunst 1550–2012, exh. cat. Dordrechts Museum 2012.

Dresden 2004
Tulpomanie: Die Tulpe in der Kunst des 16. und 17. Jahrhunderts, exh. cat. Kunstgewerbemuseum, Staatliche Kunstsammlungen Dresden, 2004.

Dresden 2019
Rembrandt's Mark, exh. cat. Kupferstich-Kabinett, Staatliche Kunstsammlungen Dresden, 2019.

Dublin 2008
Elaine Wright, *Muraqqaʿ: Imperial Mughal Albums from the Chester Beatty Library, Dublin,* Alexandria, VA, and London 2008.

Duda 1984
Dorothea Duda, "Das Millionenzimmer im Schloss Schönbrunn," in *Texte. Noten. Bilder. Neuerwerbungen, Restaurierungen, Konservierungen 1977–1983,* exh. cat. Österreichische Nationalbibliothek, Vienna 1984, 112–39.

Duda 1997
Dorothea Duda, "Die Kaiserin und der Großmogul. Untersuchungen zu den Miniaturen des Millionenzimmers im Schloss Schönbrunn," in *Malerei auf Papier und Pergament in den Prunkräumen des Schlosses Schönbrunn,* ed. Karin K. Troschke, Vienna 1997, 33–55.

Dudok van Heel 1978
S. A. C. Dudok van Heel, "Mr. Joannes Wtenbogaert (1608–1680): Een Man uit Remonstrants Milieu en Rembrandt van Rijn," in *Jaarboek Amstelodamum* 70 (1978), 146–69.

Dupré 2010
Sven Dupré, "Trading Luxury Glass, Picturing Collections and Consuming Objects of Knowledge in Early Seventeenth-Century Antwerp," in *Intellectual History Review* 20,1 (2010), 53–78.

Düsseldorf 2002
Jochen Becker, *Die niederländischen Gemälde der Sammlung Moritz Julius Binder im Museum Kunst-Palast Düsseldorf,* Hamburg 2002.

Duyvené de Wit-Klinkhamer 1966
Theresia Margaretha Duyvené de Wit-Klinkhamer, "Een vermaarde zilveren beker," in *Nederlands Kunsthistorisch Jaarboek* 17 (1966), 79–103.

Ekkart 2017
Rudi Ekkart, "Govaert Flinck and Ferdinand Bol: The Portraits," in Amsterdam 2017, 142–63.

Filipczak 2007–08
Zirka Z. Filipczak, "Rembrandt and the Body Language of Mughal Miniature," in *Nederlands Kunsthistorisch Jaarboek* 58 (2007–08), 162–87.

Floor 1979
Willem M. Floor, "Dutch Painters in Iran during the First Half of the 17th Century," in *Persica: Jaarboek voor het Genootschap Nederland-Iran* 8 (1979), 145–61.

Fock 2006
C. Willemijn Fock, "Das Interieur in der niederländischen Republik 1670–1750: (K)ein Platz für Gemälde?," in Cologne 2006, 63–86.

Forberg 2014
Corinna Forberg, "Imported Chronology: The Use of Indian Images of Kings and Gods in European Paintings and Book Art (1650–1740)," in *The Medieval History Journal* 17,1 (2014), 107–44.

Forberg 2015
Corinna Forberg, *Die Rezeption indischer Miniaturen in der europäischen Kunst des 17. und 18. Jahrhunderts,* Petersberg 2015.

Forberg 2016
Corinna Forberg, "What Does the Emperor of India Look Like? European Representations of Indian Rulers (1650–1740)," in *The Indian Ocean in the Making of Early Modern India,* ed. Pius Malekandathil, New Delhi 2016, 213–48.

Forberg 2017
Corinna Forberg, "Copying the World's Emperor: Dinglinger's Great Moghul and the French Model of Absolute Power," in *The Transformative Power of the Copy: A Transcultural and Interdisciplinary Approach,* ed. Corinna Forberg and Philipp Stockhammer, Heidelberg 2017, 375–402.

Forberg/Lunsingh Scheurleer 2018
Corinna Forberg and Pauline Lunsingh Scheurleer, "How to Succeed in Marketing Something Repulsive: A Recently Discovered Drawing of a Yogi by Willem Schellinks (1623–1678)," in *Zeitschrift für Kunstgeschichte* 81,3 (2018), 356–73.

Fraenger 1967
Wilhelm Fraenger, "Rembrandt—Synagoge und Orient," in *Castrum Peregrini* 67 (1967), 5–31.

Franke 2014
Heike Franke, "Emperors of *Ṣūrat* and *Maʿnī*: Jahangir and Shah Jahan as Temporal and Spiritual Rulers," in *Muqarnas Online* 31,1 (October 2014), 123–49.

Franken 2002
Martinus Antonius Maria Franken, *Dienaar van Oranje: Andries Schimmelpenninck van der Oije 1705–1776; Een politieke en bestuurlijke levensbeschrijving van een Gelderse luitenant-stadhouder,* Zutphen 2002.

Frankfurt am Main 2003
Rembrandt Rembrandt, exh. cat. Städelsches Kunstinstitut and Städtische Galerie, Frankfurt am Main, 2003.

Gaastra/Bruijn 1993
Femme S. Gaastra and Jaap R. Bruijn, "The Dutch East India Company's Shipping, 1602–1795, in a Comparative Perspective," in *Ships, Sailors and Spices: East India Companies and Their Shipping in the 16th, 17th and 18th Centuries,* ed. Jaap R. Bruijn and Femme S. Gaastra, Amsterdam 1993, 177-208.

Ganz 2006
Ulrike Dorothea Ganz, *Neugier und Sammelbild: Rezeptionsästhetische Studien zu gemalten Sammlungen in der niederländischen Malerei, ca. 1550-1650,* Weimar 2006.

Gifford 2008
E. Melanie Gifford, "Lievens' Technique: Wonders in Smeared Paint, Varnishes, and Oils," in *Jan Lievens: A Dutch Master Rediscovered,* exh. cat. National Gallery of Art, Washington, DC, 2008, 40–53.

Glynn 2018
Catherine Glynn, "Mughal Masterworks in Rembrandt's Hand," in *Rembrandt and the Inspiration of India,* exh. cat. The J. Paul Getty Museum, Los Angeles 2018, 29–41.

Goetz 1937
Hermann Goetz, "Rembrandt en het oosten," in *Maandblad voor beeldende Kunsten* 14 (1937), 113-17.

Goetz 1938
Hermann Goetz, "Persians and Persian Costumes in Dutch Painting of the Seventeenth Century," in *Art Bulletin* 20,3 (1938), 280-90.

Golahny 2003
Amy Golahny, *Rembrandt's Reading: The Artist's Bookshelf of Ancient Poetry and History,* Amsterdam 2003.

Gommans 2015
Jos Gommans, "Merchants Among Kings: Dutch Diplomatic Encounters in Asia," in Amsterdam 2015, 32–39.

Gommans 2018
Jos Gommans, *The Unseen World: The Netherlands and India from 1550,* Nijmegen 2018.

Gommans/De Hond 2015
Jos Gommans and Jan de Hond, "Willem Schellinks en India: Tussen werkelijkheid en illusie," in *Onbegrensd perspectief: Cultuurhistorische verkenningen,* ed. Petty Bange and Jac Geurts, Amersfoort 2015, 69–96.

Goss/Clark 1990
John Goss and Peter Clark, *Blaeu: Der große Atlas; Die Welt im 17. Jahrhundert,* Vienna 1990.

Gosselink 2015
Martine Gosselink, "The Dutch East India Company in Asia," in Amsterdam 2015, 21–31.

Göttler 2013
Christine Göttler, "The Place of the 'Exotic' in Early Seventeenth-Century Antwerp," in *Looking East: Rubens's Encounter with Asia,* exh. cat. The J. Paul Getty Museum, Los Angeles 2013, 88-107.

Göttler 2016
Christine Göttler, "'Indian Daggers with Idols' in the Early Modern Constcamer: Collecting, Picturing and Imagining 'Exotic' Weaponry in the Netherlands and Beyond," in *Netherlands Yearbook for History of Art* 66: *Netherlandish Art in Its Global Context, ,* ed. Thijs Weststeijn, Eric Jorink, and Frits Scholten, Leiden and Boston 2016, 80-111.

Gottwald 2017
Franziska Gottwald, "In Focus: Tronies in the Work of Govert Flinck and Ferdinand Bol," in Amsterdam 2017, 54–57.

Greenwich 2006
Jan van der Heyden (1637-1712), exh. cat. Bruce Museum, Greenwich, CT, 2006.

Grenoble 1994
Marcel Destot, *Peintures des écoles du Nord: La collection du Musée de Grenoble,* Paris 1994.

Grisebach 1974
Lucius Grisebach, *Willem Kalf 1619-1693,* Berlin 1974.

Gutbrod 1996
Helga Gutbrod, *Lievens und Rembrandt: Studien zum Verhältnis ihrer Kunst,* Frankfurt am Main 1996.

H
F. W. H. Hollstein, *Dutch and Flemish Etchings, Engravings and Woodcuts,* 64 vols., Amsterdam, 1954–2010.

Haak 2001
Christina Haak, *Das barocke Bildnis in Norddeutschland: Erscheinungsform und Typologie im Spannungsfeld internationaler Strömungen,* Frankfurt am Main 2001.

Haarlem 1969
H. P. [Henricus Petrus] Baard, *Halsmuseum Haarlem,* Haarlem 1969.

Haarlem 2006
Painting in Haarlem 1500-1850: The Collection of the Frans Hals Museum, ed. Neeltje Köhler, Ghent 2006.

Hahn/Weiss 2013
Hans Peter Hahn and Hadas Weiss, "Introduction: Biographies, Travels and Itineraries of Things," in *Mobility, Meaning and the Transformations of Things: Shifting Contexts of Material Culture through Time and Space,* ed. Hahn and Weiss, Oxford 2013, 1-14.

Haitsma Mulier 1997
E. O. G. [Eco Oste Gaspard] Haitsma Mulier, "The Image of Amsterdam in Seventeenth-Century Descriptions," in *Rome—Amsterdam: Two Growing Cities in Seventeenth-Century Europe,* ed. Peter van Kessel and Elisja Schulte in collaboration with Laurie Nussdorfer, Amsterdam 1997, 13-23.

Hamburg 2010
Segeln, was das Zeug hält: Niederländische Gemälde des Goldenen Zeitalters, exh. cat. Hamburger Kunsthalle, 2010.

Haveman 2015
Mariette Haveman, "De VOC-mentaliteit," in *Kunstschrift* 59,5 (2015), 12–13.

Henkel 1938
M. D. [Max Dittmar] Henkel, "Teyler, Johan," in *Allgemeines Lexikon der Bildenden Künstler von der Antike bis zur Gegenwart,* established by Ulrich Thieme and Felix Becker, ed. Hans Vollmer, vol. 32, Leipzig 1938, 573–74.

Hirschfelder 2008
Dagmar Hirschfelder, *Tronie und Porträt in der niederländischen Malerei des 17. Jahrhunderts,* Berlin 2008.

Hochstrasser 2007
Julie Berger Hochstrasser, *Still Life and Trade in the Dutch Golden Age,* New Haven 2007.

Horn 1989
Hendrik J. Horn, *Jan Cornelisz Vermeyen: Painter of Charles V and His Conquest of Tunis,* 2 vols., Doornspijk 1989.

Hundertmarck 2010
Hein F. Hundertmarck, "Das achte Weltwunder: Das ehemalige Rathaus am Dam, heute der königliche Palast in Amsterdam," in *Hausbau in Holland: Baugeschichte und Stadtentwicklung,* ed. Arbeitskreis für Hausforschung, Marburg 2010, 113–30.

Huys Janssen 2002
Paul Huys Janssen, *Caesar van Everdingen 1616/17-1678: Monograph and Catalogue Raisonné,* Doornspijk 2002.

Ingrams 1974
Rosalind A. Ingrams, "Rubens and Persia," in *The Burlington Magazine* 116 (1974), 190-97.

Israel 2007
Jonathan I. Israel, "The Republic of the United Netherlands until about 1750: Demography and Economic Activity," in *The History of the Jews in the Netherlands,* ed. Johan C. H. Blom, Rena G. Fuks-Mansfeld, and Ivo Schöffer, Liverpool 2007, 85–115.

Istanbul 2000
The Sultan's Portrait: Picturing the House of Osman, exh. cat. Topkapı-Palastmuseum, Istanbul 2000.

Jorink 2010
Eric Jorink, *Reading the Book of Nature in the Dutch Golden Age,* 1575–1715, Leiden 2010.

Kansas City 1993
Master European Drawings from Polish Collections, exh. cat. The Nelson-Atkins Museum of Art, Kansas City, MO, 1993.

Kappel 1995
Jutta Kappel, "Die Türkennot des Kaisers: Zu einigen Aspekten der Darstellung des Türkenkrieges (1593–1606) in der Hofkunst Rudolfs II.," in Bonn 1995, 125–33.

Karau 2002
Susanne Henriette Karau, *Leben und Werk des Leidener Malers Jacob Toorenvliet (1640-1719)*, PhD diss., Freie Universität Berlin 2002 [microfiche].

Karlsruhe 2015
Facing the World: Self-Portraits from Rembrandt to Ai Weiwei, exh. cat. Staatliche Kunsthalle Karlsruhe, 2015.

Karlsruhe 2019
Kaiser und Sultan: Nachbarn in Europas Mitte 1600–1700, exh. cat. Badisches Landesmuseum, Karlsruhe 2019.

Kassel 1996
Nautilus: Zeitreise im Perlboot, exh. cat. Staatliche Museen Kassel, 1996.

Kassel 2001
The Mystery of the Young Rembrandt, exh. cat. Gemäldegalerie Alte Meister, Staatliche Museen Kassel 2001.

Kassel 2009
Philips Wouwerman (1619-1668), exh. cat. Gemäldegalerie Alte Meister, Staatliche Museen Kassel 2009.

Kettering 1988
Alison McNeil Kettering, *Drawings from the Ter Borch Studio Estate,* 2 vols., The Hague 1988.

Koch 2004
Ebba Koch, "The 'Moghuleries' of the Millionenzimmer, Schönbrunn Palace, Vienna," in *Arts of Mughal India: Studies in Honour of Robert Skelton,* ed. Rosemary Grill, Susan Stronge, and Andrew Topsfield, London 2004, 152–66.

Koeman 1970
Cornelis Koeman, *Joan Blaeu and His Grand Atlas: Introduction to the Facsimile Edition of Le Grand Atlas 1663,* Amsterdam 1970.

Kolfin 2010
Elmer Kolfin, "Rembrandt's Africans," in *The Image of the Black in Western Art*, ed. David Bindman, Henry Louis Gates Jr., and Karen C. C. Dalton, vol. 3: *From the "Age of Discovery" to the Age of Abolition*, part 1: *Artists of the Renaissance and the Baroque,* Cambridge, MA, 2010, 271–307.

Kolfin 2011
Elmer Kolfin, "Omphalos Mundi: The Pictorial Tradition of the Theme of Amsterdam and the Four Continents, circa 1600–1665," in *Aemulatio: Imitation, Emulation and Invention in Netherlandish Art from 1500 to 1800; Essays in Honor of Eric Jan Sluijter,* ed. Anton W. A. Boschloo and Jacquelyn N. Coutré, Zwolle 2011, 382-92.

Kolfin 2020
Elmer Kolfin, "Black in the Art of Rembrandt's Time," in Amsterdam 2020, 12–37.

Köster 2017
Constanze Köster, *Jürgen Ovens (1623-1678): Maler in Schleswig-Holstein und Amsterdam,* Petersberg 2017.

Kratzsch 2007
Deex Autaer von Philip Angel: Eine niederländische Handschrift aus dem 17. Jahrhundert über die zehn Avatāras des Visnu, ed. Siegfried Kratzsch, Halle 2007.

Krempel 2000
León Krempel, *Studien zu den datierten Gemälden des Nicolaes Maes (1634-1693),* Petersberg 2000.

Kuipers 2014
Jan J. B. Kuipers, *De VOC: Een multinational onder zeil, 1602-1799,* Zutphen 2014.

Kuyper 1994
Wouter Kuyper, *The Triumphant Entry of Renaissance Architecture into the Netherlands,* Alphen aan den Rijn 1994.

Larsen 2017
Patrick Larsen, "The Relationship between Govert Flinck and Jürgen Ovens," in Dickey 2017, 180–203.

Lawrence 1991
Cynthia Lawrence, *Gerrit Adriaensz. Berckheyde (1638-1698): Haarlem Cityscape Painter,* Doornspijk 1991.

Leeflang 2014
Huigen Leeflang, "The Sign of Claes Jansz Visscher and His Progeny: The History and Significance of a Brand Name," in *The Rijksmuseum Bulletin* 62 (2014), 241–68.

Leeuwarden n.d.
"Paintings in the inventory of Lambert Jacobsz. in Leeuwarden, including the portrait of Maria van Eyck, wife of Hendrick Uylenburgh (2 October 1637)," in *Inventarisatieboeken* [1637–1640], Leeuwarden, Historisch Centrum, cited in http://remdoc.huygens.knaw.nl/#/document/remdoc/e4441 (accessed April 17, 2020).

Leiden 2019
Young Rembrandt, exh. cat. Museum De Lakenhal, Leiden 2019.

Lemaire 2000
Geneviève Lemaire, *Orientalismus: Das Bild des Morgenlandes in der Malerei,* Cologne 2000.

Leningrad 1990
Colin T. Eisler, *Paintings in the Hermitage,* New York 1990.

Leonhard 2007
Karin Leonhard, "Shell Collecting: On 17th-Century Conchology; Curiosity Cabinets and Still Life Painting," in *Early Modern Zoology: The Construction of Animals in Science, Literature and the Visual Arts,* ed. Karl A. E. Enenkel and Paul J. Smith, vol. 1, Leiden 2007, 177–214.

Lightbown 1969
Ronald W. Lightbown, "Oriental Art and the Orient in Late Renaissance and Baroque Italy," in *Journal of the Warburg and Courtauld Institutes* 32 (1969), 228–79.

Lloyd 2019
Stephan Lloyd, "The Derby Collection: Recent Research into a Painting from Rembrandt's Workshop," in *Stanley Estates Magazine,* August 2019, 7.

Loewenstein 1958
Jean de Loewenstein, "À propos d'un tableau de W. Schellinks s'inspirant des miniatures mogholes," in *Arts Asiatiques* 5 (1958), 293–98.

London 1988
Art in the Making: Rembrandt, exh. cat. The National Gallery, London 1988.

London 1990
Porcelain for Palaces: The Fashion for Japan in Europe, 1650–1750, exh. cat. The British Museum, London 1990.

London 1991
Neil MacLaren and Christopher Brown, *National Gallery Catalogues: The Dutch School 1600–1900,* London 1991.

London 1992
Martin Royalton-Kisch, *Drawings by Rembrandt and His Circle in the British Museum,* London 1992.

London 1999
Rembrandt by Himself, exh. cat. The National Gallery, London 1999.

London 2002
Inspired by Italy: Dutch Landscape Painting 1600–1700, exh. cat. Dulwich Picture Gallery, London 2002.

London 2004
Encounters: The Meeting of Asia and Europe 1500–1800, exh. cat. Victoria and Albert Museum, London 2004.

London 2006
Uylenburgh & Son: Art and Commerce from Rembrandt to De Lairesse, 1625–1675, exh. cat. Dulwich Picture Gallery, London 2006.

London 2014
Late Rembrandt, exh. cat. The National Gallery, London 2014.

London 2019
Inspired by the East: How the Islamic World Influenced Western Art, exh. cat. The British Museum, London 2019.

Lootsma 2017
Hilbert Lootsma, "From Stars to Satellites: The Reputation of Govert Flinck and Ferdinand Bol from Their Time to Ours," in Dickey 2017, 218–35.

Los Angeles 1997
Burton B. Fredericksen et al., *Masterpieces of the J. Paul Getty Museum: Paintings,* Los Angeles 1997.

Los Angeles 2018
Rembrandt and the Inspiration of India, exh. cat. The J. Paul Getty Museum, Los Angeles 2018.

Loughman 2008
John Loughman, "New Light on Some Portraits by Aelbert Cuyp," in *The Burlington Magazine* 150 (2008), 584–91.

Loughman/Montias 2000
John Loughman and John Michael Montias, *Public and Private Spaces: Works of Art in Seventeenth-Century Dutch Houses,* Zwolle 2000.

Lunsingh Scheurleer 1980
Pauline Lunsingh Scheurleer, "Mogol-miniaturen door Rembrandt nagetekend," in *De kroniek van het Rembrandthuis* 32,1 (1980), 10–40.

Lunsingh Scheurleer 1991
Pauline Lunsingh Scheurleer, "De Moghul-miniaturen van Rembrandt," in *Waarom Sanskrit? Honderdvijfentwintig jaar Sanskrit in Nederland,* ed. Hanneke van den Muyzenberg and Thomas de Bruijn, Leiden 1991, 95–115.

Lunsingh Scheurleer 1996
Pauline Lunsingh Scheurleer, "Het Witsenalbum: Zeventiende-eeuwse Indiase portretten op bestelling," in *Bulletin van het Rijksmuseum* 44 (1996), 167–254.

Lunsingh Scheurleer 2016
Pauline Lunsingh Scheurleer, "The Indian Miniatures in the Canter Visscher Album," in *Bulletin van het Rijksmuseum* 64,3 (2016), 194–245.

Lyon 1992
Flandre et Hollande au Siècle d'Or: Chefs-d'œuvre des Musées de Rhône-Alpes, exh. cat. Musée des Beaux-Arts, Lyon 1992.

Madrid 2009
Teresa Posada Kubissa, *Pintura holandesa en el Museo Nacional del Prado, catálogo razonado,* Madrid 2009.

Manuth 2006
Volker Manuth, "Mit Verlaub, bist du Mennonit, Papist, Arminianer oder Geuse? Kunst und Konfession bei Rembrandt," in Berlin 2006, 51–63.

Manuth/De Winkel/Van Leeuwen 2019
Volker Manuth, Marieke de Winkel and Rudie van Leeuwen, *Rembrandt: The Complete Paintings,* Cologne 2019.

Marr 2006
Alexander Marr, "Introduction," in *Curiosity and Wonder from the Renaissance to the Enlightenment,* ed. Robert John Weston Evans and Alexander Marr, Aldershot 2006, 1–20.

McNamara 2015
Simon McNamara, *Rembrandt's Passion Series,* Newcastle upon Tyne 2015.

Messling 2015
Guido Messling, *Hans de Jode: View of the Tip of the Seraglio with Topkapı Palace,* Point of View 14, Vienna 2015.

Mette 1995
Hanns-Ulrich Mette, *Der Nautiluspokal: Wie Kunst und Natur miteinander spielen,* Munich 1995.
Milwaukee 1992
Rembrandt's Students II: Ferdinand Bol, exh. cat. Art Museum, Milwaukee 1992.
Mostert/Van Campen 2015
Tristan Mostert and Jan van Campen, *Silk Thread: China and the Netherlands from 1600,* Amsterdam and Nijmegen 2015.
Munich 1983
Bayerische Staatsgemälde-sammlungen, Alte Pinakothek München: Erläuterungen zu den ausgestellten Gemälden, Munich 1983.
Münster 1994
Im Lichte Rembrandts: Das Alte Testament im Goldenen Zeitalter der niederländischen Kunst, exh. cat. Westfälisches Landesmuseum für Kunst und Kulturgeschichte, Münster 1994.
Münster/Osnabrück 1998
1648: War and Peace in Europe, exh. cat. Westfälisches Landesmuseum für Kunst und Kulturgeschichte, Münster, and Kulturgeschichtliches Museum und Kunsthalle Dominikanerkirche, Osnabrück 1998.
New York n.d.
Anonymous, *The Good Samaritan,* https://www.thekremercollection.com/pieter-lastman/ (accessed April 10, 2020).
Newark 2001
Art and Home: Dutch Interiors in the Age of Rembrandt, exh. cat. Newark Museum, 2001.
NH
The New Hollstein: Dutch and Flemish Etchings, Engravings and Woodcuts; Rembrandt, 7 vols., Ouderkerk aan den IJssel 2014.
Niayesh 2016
Ladan Niayesh, "The Fabric of Silk Power in the Sherley Portraits," in *Early Modern Diplomacy, Theatre and Soft Power: The Making of Peace*, ed. Nathalie Rivère de Carles, London 2016, 205–20.
Nieuwenhuizen 2006
Peter Nieuwenhuizen, "Sieraden van vier eeuwen oud: Het Const-thoonend luweel en het Haerlems Juweel; Tussen rederijkerij en renaissance," in *Schoon Schip* 13,1 (2006), 4–11.
Nijmegen 2002
Gelderse gezichten: Drie eeuwen portretkunst in Gelderland, exh. cat. Museum Het Valkhof, Nijmegen 2002.
Outram 2006
Dorinda Outram, *Panorama of the Enlightenment,* London 2006.
Oxford 1975
Dutch Pictures in Oxford: An Exhibition of Paintings from the Collections of the Ashmolean and the Colleges, exh. cat. Ashmolean Museum, Oxford 1975.
Oxford 1999
Christopher White, *Dutch, Flemish, and German Paintings before 1900 (Excluding the Daisy Linda Ward Collection),* Ashmolean Museum, Oxford 1999.
Paris 1967
La Vie en Hollande au XVIIe siècle, exh. cat. Musée des Arts Décoratifs, Paris 1967.
Paris 1971
Le Siècle de Rembrandt: Tableaux hollandais des collections publiques françaises, exh. cat. Musée du Petit Palais, Paris 1971.
Paris 1998
Tableaux flamands et hollandais du Musée Fabre de Montpellier, exh. cat. Institut Néerlandais, Paris 1998.
Paris 2011
Rembrandt and the Face of Jesus, exh. cat. Musée du Louvre, Paris 2011.
Paris 2016
Rembrandt intime, exh. cat. Musée Jacquemart-André, Paris 2016.
Paris 2017
Chefs-d'œuvre de la collection Leiden: Le siècle de Rembrandt / Masterpieces of The Leiden Collection: The Age of Rembrandt, exh. cat. Museé du Louvre, Paris 2017.
Pastoor 1991
Gabriël M. C. Pastoor, "Bijbelse historiestukken in particulier bezit," in *Het Oude Testament in de Schilderkunst van de Gouden Eeuw,* exh. cat. Joods Historisch Museum, Amsterdam 1991, 122–33.
Perdahcı 2016
Nurcan Perdahcı, "Lotto Type Ushak Carpets in Dutch Golden Age Painting," in *International Journal of Arts and Commerce* 5,1 (2016), 67-76, https://www.ijac.org.uk/images/frontImages/gallery/Vol._5_No._1/8._67-76.pdf (accessed March 25, 2019).
Perlove/Silver 2009
Shelley Perlove and Larry Silver, *Rembrandt's Faith: Church and Temple in the Dutch Golden Age,* University Park, PA, 2009.
Peters 2019
Monique A. F. Peters, "Allesbehalve een kleine man uit de Jordaan: Abraham Francen, een zeventiende-eeuwse Amsterdamse apotheker, arts en papierkunstverzamelaar," in *Maandblad Amstelodamum* 106,3 (2019), 113–36.
Pettegree/Der Weduwen 2019
Andrew Pettegree and Arthur der Weduwen, *The Bookshop of the World: Making and Trading Books in the Dutch Golden Age,* New Haven 2019.
Ponte 2020
Mark Ponte, "Black in Amsterdam Around 1650," in Amsterdam 2020, 44–57.
Rauschenbach 2013
Sina Rauschenbach, "Elzevirian Republics, Wise Merchants, and New Perspectives on Spain and Portugal in the Seventeenth-Century Dutch Republic," in *De zeventiende eeuw: Cultuur in de Nederlanden in interdisciplinair perspectief* 29,1 (2013), 81–100.
Rijks 2015
Marlise Rijks, "Defenders of the Image: Painted Collectors' Cabinets and the Display of Display in Counter-Reformation Antwerp," in *Netherlands Yearbook for History of Art* 65: *Arts of Display,* Leiden and Boston 2015, 54-83.
Rittersma 2010
Luxury in the Low Countries: Miscellaneous Reflections on Netherlandish Material Culture, 1500 to the Present, ed. Rengenier C. Rittersma, Brussels 2010.

Robinson 1996
William W. Robinson, *The Early Works of Nicolaes Maes, 1653 to 1661,* Ann Arbor 1996.
Roelofs 2015
Pieter Roelofs, "Painting Asia: Oriental Luxury Goods and Exotic Curiosities in Dutch paintings," in Amsterdam 2015, 229–44.
Roeper/Wildeman 1996
Vibeke D. Roeper and G. J. Diederick Wildeman, *Reizen op papier: Journalen en reisverslagen van Nederlandse ontdekkingsreizigers, kooplieden en avonturiers,* Zutphen 1996.
Roethlisberger 1981
Marcel Roethlisberger, *Bartholomeus Breenbergh: The Paintings,* Berlin 1981.
Roodenburg 2004
Herman Roodenburg, *The Eloquence of the Body: Perspectives on Gesture in the Dutch Republic,* Zwolle 2004.
Rosand 1969
David Rosand, "Rubens's Munich Lion Hunt: Its Sources and Significance," in *The Art Bulletin* 51 (1969), 29–40.
Rotterdam 1989
Topkapı en Turkomanie: Turks-Nederlandse ontmoetingen sinds 1600, exh. cat. Museum voor Volkenkunde, Rotterdam, and Museum het Princessehof, Leeuwarden, 1989.
Rotterdam 2006
Gemaltes Licht: Die Stilleben von Willem Kalf, 1619-1693, exh. cat. Museum Boijmans Van Beuningen, Rotterdam 2006.
Rotterdam 2014
Van velerlei pluimage: Zeventiende-eeuwse aquarellen van Andries Beeckman, exh. cat. Kunsthal Rotterdam 2014.
Roy 1972
Rainer Roy, *Studien zu Gerbrand van den Eeckhout,* PhD diss., Universität Wien, Vienna 1972.
Said 1978
Edward W. Said, *Orientalism,* London et al. 1978.
St. Gallen 2005
Rembrandt, exh. cat. Kunstverein Kunstmuseum St. Gallen, 2005.
Salzburg 1993
Wen verführst Du, Thamar? Ikonographische Studien zu Gemälden der Residenzgalerie Salzburg, exh. cat. Residenzgalerie, Salzburg 1993.
Salzburg 2001
Gabriele Groschner, Thomas Habersatter, and Erika Mayr-Oehring, *Meisterwerke: Residenzgalerie Salzburg,* Salzburg 2001.
Scarce 2013
Jennifer M. Scarce, "Savafid Dress and Europe," in Zurich 2013, 58–77.
Schaeps/van Ommen/Vrolijk 2005
Oostersche weelde: De Oriënt in westerse kunst en cultuur, met een keuze uit de verzamelingen van de Leidse Universiteitsbibliotheek, ed. Jef Schaeps, Kasper van Ommen, and Arnoud Vrolijk, Leiden 2005.
Schama 1988
Simon Schama, *The Embarassment of Riches: An Interpretation of Dutch Culture in the Golden* Age, London 1988.
Schatborn 1999
Peter Schatborn, "Tekeningen van Arent de Gelder," in *Arent de Gelder (1645-1727): Rembrandts laatste leerling,* exh. cat. Dordrechts Museum 1999, 111-21.
Schatborn 2017
Peter Schatborn, "Rembrandt van Rijn, Three Orientals Conversing, Amsterdam, c. 1645," in *Drawings by Rembrandt and His School in the Rijksmuseum,* ed. Jane Turner, online collection catalog, Amsterdam 2017, https://www.rijksmuseum.nl/en/collection/RP-T-1930-47/catalogue-entry (accessed March 20, 2020).
Schatborn/Hinterding 2019
Peter Schatborn and Erik Hinterding, *Rembrandt: The Complete Drawings and Etchings,* Cologne 2019.
Scheller 1969
Robert W. Scheller, "Rembrandt en de encyclopedische kunstkamer," in *Oud Holland* 84 (1969), 81-147.
Schiebinger/Swan 2005
Colonial Botany: Science, Commerce, and Politics in the Early Modern World, ed. Londa Schiebinger and Claudia Swan, Philadelphia 2005.
Schimmelpenninck van der Oye 1871
"Een Reisjournaal uit de zeventiende eeuw naar het Heilige Land: Medegedeeld door den Heer A. Baron Schimmelpenninck van der Oye," in *Kroniek van het Historisch Genootschap gevestigd te Utrecht* 26 (1871), 537–88.
Schmidt 2011
Benjamin Schmidt, "Collecting Global Icons: The Case of the Exotic Parasol," in Bleichmar/Mancall 2011, 31–57.
Schmidt 2015
Benjamin Schmidt, *Inventing Exoticism: Geography, Globalism, and Europe's Early Modern World,* Philadelphia 2015.
Schmitt 2008
Seeleute und Leben an Bord im Ersten Kolonialzeitalter, Indienfahrer, vol. 2., ed. Eberhard Schmitt, Wiesbaden 2008.
Schnackenburg 2001
Bernhard Schnackenburg, "Young Rembrandt's 'Rough Manner': A Painting Style and Its Sources," in Kassel 2001, 92-121.
Schnackenburg 2016
Bernhard Schnackenburg, *Jan Lievens: Friend and Rival of the Young Rembrandt, with a Catalogue Raisonné of His Early Leiden Works,* Petersberg 2016.
Schneider 2004
Ute Schneider, *Die Macht der Karten: Eine Geschichte der Kartographie vom Mittelalter bis heute,* Darmstadt 2004.
Schönduve 1988
Loeki Schönduve, "Antonio en Francisco Lopes Suasso: Joodse baronnen in Holland," in *Holland: Regionaal-historisch tijdschrift* 20 (1988), 49–59.
Schrader 2018
Stephanie Schrader, "Rembrandt and the Mughal Line: Artistic Inspiration in the Global City of Amsterdam," in Los Angeles 2018, 5–27.

Schumacher 2006
Birgit Schumacher, *Philips Wouwerman (1619–1668): The Horse Painter of the Golden Age,* 2 vols., Doornspijk 2006.
Schwartz 1983
Gary Schwartz, *Pieter Lastman, Jephthah's Daughter / Jan Lievens: The Four Elements, Christ Chained to the Column: Nystad in Their 121st Year, 1862–1983,* The Hague 1983.
Schwartz 1985a
Gary Schwartz, *Rembrandt, His Life, His Paintings: A New Biography with All Accessible Paintings Illustrated in Colour,* New York 1985.
Schwartz 1985b
Gary Schwartz, "Rembrandt's David and Mephiboseth: A Forgotten Subject from Vondel," in *Tribute to Lotte Brand Philip, Art Historian and Detective,* ed. William W. Clark, New York 1985, 166–74.
Schwartz 1987
Gary Schwartz, *Rembrandt: Sämtliche Gemälde in Farbe,* Stuttgart and Zurich 1987. Published in English as *Rembrandt, His Life, His Paintings: A New Biography with All Accessible Paintings Illustrated in Colour* (see Schwartz 1985a).
Schwartz 1994
The Complete Etchings of Rembrandt, ed. Gary Schwartz, New York 1994.
Schwartz 2006
Gary Schwartz, *The Rembrandt Book,* Brussels 2006.
Schwartz 2009
Gary Schwartz, "Safavid Favour and Company Scorn: The Fortunes of Dutch Painters to the Shah," in *Iran and the Netherlands: Interwoven Through the Ages,* ed. Martine Gosseling and Dirk J. Tang, Gronsveld and Rotterdam 2009, 133–53.
Schwartz 2013
Gary Schwartz, "Between Court and Company: Dutch Artists in Persia," in Zurich 2013, 152–69.
Schwartz 2014
Gary Schwartz, "Terms of Reception: Europeans and Persians and Each Other's Art," in DaCosta Kaufmann/North 2014, 25–64.
Schwartz 2019
Gary Schwartz, "Another Third Poem on Rembrandt Jews," www.garyschwartzarthistorian.nl/375-another-third-poem-on-rembrandt-jews/ (accessed August 22, 2020).
Schwartz 2020
Gary Schwartz, *A Rembrandt Invention: A New Baptism of the Eunuch,* Leiden 2020.
Schwarz 1990
Hans-Günther Schwarz, *Orient—Okzident: Der orientalische Teppich in der westlichen Literatur, Ästhetik und Kunst,* Munich 1990.
Schwarz 2003
Hans-Günther Schwarz, *Der Orient und die Ästhetik der Moderne,* Munich 2003.
Schwerin 2013
Schimmern aus der Tiefe: Muscheln, Perlen, Nautilus, exh. cat. Staatliches Museum Schwerin, 2013.
Segal 1987
Sam Segal, "Exotische bollen als statussymbolen," in *Kunstschrift: Openbaar Kunstbezit* 3 (1987), 88–97.
Seifert 2009
Christian Tico Seifert, "Leonardo und Jan Wierix: Bemerkungen zu Rembrandts 'Hochzeit Simsons,'" in *Jahrbuch der Berliner Museen* 51 (2009), 131–36.
Seifert 2011
Christian Tico Seifert, *Pieter Lastman: Studien zu Leben und Werk, mit einem kritischen Verzeichnis der Werke mit Themen aus der antiken Mythologie und Historie,* Petersberg 2011.
Seifert 2014
Christian Tico Seifert, "Pieter Lastman's 'The Good Samaritan' Rediscovered," in *The Burlington Magazine* 156 (2014), no. 1331, 99–101.
Silver 2018
Larry Silver, *Rembrandt and the Divine,* Leuven 2018.
Skeeles Schloss 1982
Christine Skeeles Schloss, *Travel, Trade, and Temptation: The Dutch Italianate Harbor Scene, 1640–1680,* Ann Arbor 1982.
Slatkes 1983a
Leonard J. Slatkes, "A 'Self-Portrait' Reidentified, an Oeuvre Reconstructed: Johannes van Swinderen (1594–1636)," in *Essays in Northern European Art: Presented to Egbert Haverkamp-Begemann on His Sixtieth Birthday,* ed. Anne-Marie S. Logan, Doornspijk 1983, 245–48.
Slatkes 1983b
Leonard J. Slatkes, *Rembrandt and Persia,* New York 1983.
Sluijter 2015
Eric Jan Sluijter, *Rembrandt's Rivals: History Painting in Amsterdam 1630–1650,* Amsterdam 2015.
Smith/Findlen 2002
Merchants and Marvels: Commerce, Science and Art in Early Modern Europe, ed. Pamela H. Smith and Paula Findlen, New York 2002.
Speelman 1908
Journaal der reis van den gezant der O. I. Compagnie Joan Cunaeus naar Perzië in 1651–1652 door Cornelis Speelman, ed. Albertus Hotz, Amsterdam 1908, https://resolver.kb.nl/resolve?urn=MMSFKB02:000036491 (accessed June 12, 2020).
Spriggs 1964–66
Arthur I. Spriggs, "Oriental Porcelein in Western Painting 1450–1700," in *Transactions of the Oriental Ceramic Society* 36 (1964–66), 73–87.
Steensgaard 1975
Niels Steensgaard, *The Asian Trade Revolution: The East India Companies and the Decline of the Caravan Trade,* Chicago 1975.
Stolte 2012
Carolien Stolte, *Philip Angel's DeexAutaers: Vaiṣṇava Mythology from Manuscript to Book Market in the Context of the Dutch East India Company, c. 1600–1672,* New Delhi 2012.
Stone Perry 1980
Barbara Ann Stone Perry, *The Eastern Motif in the Works of Rembrandt,* PhD diss., Syracuse University, New York 1980 [microfilm].
Strauss/Van der Meulen 1979
Walter L. Strauss and Marjon van der Meulen, *The Rembrandt Documents,* New York 1979.
Stuttgart 1987
Exotische Welten, Europäische Phantasien, exh. cat. Institut für Auslandsbeziehungen and Württembergischer Kunstverein, Kunstgebäude am Schlossplatz, Stuttgart 1987.
Sumowski 1979–92
Werner Sumowski, *Drawings of the Rembrandt School,* ed. and trans. Walter L. Strauss, 10 vols., New York 1979–92.

Sumowski 1983–94
Werner Sumowski, *Gemälde der Rembrandt-Schüler,* 6 vols., Landau 1983–94.

Surh 2017
Dominique Surh, "Portrait of Rembrandt in Oriental Dress," in *The Leiden Collection Catalogue,* ed. Arthur K. Wheelock Jr., New York 2017, https://www.theleidencollection.com/archives/artwork/IJ_100_isaac_de_jouderville_portrait_of_rembrandt_in_oriental_dress_2017.pdf (accessed February 25, 2020).

Swan 2013
Claudia Swan, "Lost in Translation: Exoticism in Early Modern Holland," in Zurich 2013, 100–17.

Swillens 1946
P. T. A. [Petrus Theodorus Arnoldus] Swillens, "Jacob van Hasselt," in *Oud Holland* 61,1 (1946), 133–41.

The Hague 1993
Ben Broos, *Liefde, list en lijden,* coll. cat. Koninklijk Kabinet van Schilderijen Mauritshuis, The Hague 1993.

The Hague 2001
Het Nederlandse interieur in beeld 1600–1900, exh. cat. Gemeentemuseum Den Haag, The Hague 2001.

The Hague 2002
A Choice Collection: Seventeenth-Century Dutch Paintings from the Frits Lugt Collection, exh. cat. Mauritshuis, The Hague 2002.

Thornton 1979
Peter Thornton, *Seventeenth-Century Interior Decoration in England, France and Holland,* second edition, New Haven 1979.

Troschke 1997
Karin K. Troschke, "Eine barocke Collage: Die Restaurierung der Mogulminiaturen aus dem 'Millionenzimmer' des Schlosses Schönbrunn," in *Malerei auf Papier und Pergament in den Prunkräumen des Schlosses Schönbrunn,* ed. Troschke, Vienna 1997, 18–32.

Tümpel 1986
Christian Tümpel, *Rembrandt: Mythos und Methode,* Königstein im Taunus 1986.

Tümpel 1994
Christian Tümpel, "Die alttestamentliche Historienmalerei im Zeitalter Rembrandts," in Münster 1994, 8–23.

Tuynman 2006
Pierre Tuynman, "Manuscript Caption to the 1639 Portrait of Joannes Wtenbogaert, Receiver of Inland Revenue in the Service of the States of Holland in Amsterdam and District, Appendix III," in *Rembrandt 2006: New Rembrandt Documents,* ed. Michiel Roscam Abbing, Leiden 2006, 155–68.

Utrecht 1999
Liesbeth M. Helmus, *De verzamelingen van het Centraal Museum Utrecht: Schilderkunst tot 1850,* 2 vols., Utrecht 1999.

Utrecht 2006
Jos de Meyere, *Utrechtse schilderkunst in de Gouden Eeuw: Honderd schilderijen uit de collectie van het Centraal Museum te Utrecht,* Utrecht 2006.

Valentiner 1924
Wilhelm R. Valentiner, *Nicolaes Maes,* Berlin and Leipzig 1924.

Van Campen/Eliens 2014
Chinese and Japanese Porcelain for the Dutch Golden Age, ed. Jan van Campen and Titus M. Eliens, Zwolle 2014.

Van de Velde 2014
Hildegard van de Velde, "De papegaai in de beeldende kunst van de 16e en de 17e eeuw," in *Papegaai: 'T cierlijk schoon van haare veeren,* exh. cat. Museum Nicolaas Rockox, Antwerp 2014, 49–83.

Van de Wetering 1983
Ernst van de Wetering, "Isaac Jouderville, a Pupil of Rembrandt," in *The Impact of a Genius: Rembrandt, His Pupils and Followers in the Seventeenth Century; Paintings from Museums and Private Collections,* exh. cat. Groninger Museum 1983, 59–69.

Van de Wetering 2009
Ernst van de Wetering, *Rembrandt: The Painter at Work,* Amsterdam 2009.

Van de Wetering 2016
Ernst van de Wetering, *Rembrandt: The Painter Thinking,* Amsterdam 2016.

Van der Grind 2016
Åse van der Grind, "Rembrandts ets Het scheepje van Fortuin voor Der zee-vaer lof van Elias Herckmans," in *De Kroniek van het Rembrandthuis* 2016, 40–49.

Van der Molen 2017
Tom van der Molen, "Painted Theatre: Flinck, Rembrandt, and Other Artists Paint Vondel's Joseph Trilogy," in Dickey 2017, 83–97.

Van der Veen 2008
Jaap van der Veen, "De identificatie van de zogenoemde wiskundige les door Michiel van Musscher," in *Amstelodamum: Maandblad voor de kennis van Amsterdam* 95,3–4 (2008), 46–48.

Van der Veen 2015
Jap van der Veen, "East India Shops in Amsterdam," in Amsterdam 2015, 134–41.

Van Gelder 1937
Jan Gerrit van Gelder, "François Venant, schilder," in *Oud Holland* 54,3 (1937), 137–39.

Van Gelder 2004
Roelof van Gelder, *Das ostindische Abenteuer: Deutsche in Diensten der Vereinigten Ostindischen Kompanie der Niederlande (VOC) 1600–1800*, ed. Albrecht Sauer, Hamburg 2004.

Van Gent 2011
Judith van Gent, *Bartholomeus van der Helst (ca. 1613–1670)*, Zwolle 2011.

Van Gent 2013
Rob van Gent, "Een geïllustreerde koranvertaling uit 1696, Bijzondere Collecties, Universiteitsbibliotheek Utrecht, https://bc.library.uu.nl/een-ge%C3%AFllustreerde-koranvertaling-uit-1696.html (accessed July 3, 2020).

Van Leeuwen 2018
Rudie van Leeuwen, *Beeltenissen van bestuurders en burgers als bijbelfiguren: Het bijbelse portrait historié in de Noordelijke en Zuidelijke Nederlanden van de zestiende en zeventiende eeuw,* PhD diss., Radboud Universiteit, Nijmegen, 2018, https://hdl.handle.net/2066/199526 (accessed May 12, 2020).

Van Nierop 2018
Henk van Nierop, *The Life of Romeyn de Hooghe, 1645–1708: Prints, Pamphlets, and Politics in the Dutch Golden Age,* Amsterdam 2018.

Van Straten 2005
Roelof van Straten, *Young Rembrandt: The Leiden Years, 1606–1632,* Leiden 2005.

Van Wagenberg-Ter Hoeven 2018
Anke A. van Wagenberg-Ter Hoeven, *Jan Baptist Weenix, The Paintings: A Story of Versatility, Success and Bankruptcy in Seventeenth-Century Holland,* Zwolle 2018.

Verdi 2014
Richard Verdi, *Rembrandt's Themes: Life into Art,* New Haven 2014.

Verma 1994
Som Prakash Verma, *Mughal Painters and Their Work,* Oxford and New Delhi 1994.

Vermeulen 1975–78
Urbain Vermeulen, "L'Ambassade persan de Musa Beg aux Provinces-Unies (1625–1628)," in *Persica: Jaarboek voor het Genootschap Nederland-Iran* 7 (1975–78), 145–54.

Vermeulen 1979
Urbain Vermeulen, "La Mission de Jan L. van Hasselt comme agent du Shah de Perse aux Provinces Unies (1629–1631)," in *Persica: Jaarboek voor het Genootschap Nederland-Iran* 8 (1979), 133–44.

Vienna 1923
Die indischen Miniaturen im Schlosse Schönbrunn, ed. Josef Strzygowski, Vienna 1923.

Vienna 2004
Rembrandt, exh. cat. Albertina, Vienna 2004.

Von Bockelberg 1941
Otto Heinrich von Bockelberg, "Das Morgenländische in der Anbetung der Könige: Ein Beitrag zu ihrer Ikonographie," in *Deutschland—Italien: Beiträge zu den Kulturbeziehungen zwischen Norden und Süden; Festschrift für Wilhelm Waetzoldt zu seinem 60. Geburtstage 21. Februar 1940,* ed. Kunstgeschichtliches Institut der Martin Luther-Universität, Halle-Wittenberg, Berlin 1941, 91–134.

Von Moltke 1938–39
Joachim Wolfgang von Moltke, "Salomon de Bray," in *Marburger Jahrbuch für Kunstwissenschaft* 11–12 (1938–39), 309–523.

Von Moltke 1965
Joachim Wolfgang von Moltke, *Govaert Flinck 1615–1660,* Amsterdam 1965.

Wagenaar 2016
Lodewijk Wagenaar, *Kaneel en olifanten: Sri Lanka en Nederland sinds 1600,* Amsterdam and Nijmegen 2016.

Wagner 1971
Helga Wagner, *Jan van der Heyden (1637–1712),* Amsterdam 1971.

Warsaw 2004
Jolanta Talbierska, *Rembrandt: Prints and Drawings from the Collection of the Print Room of the Warsaw University Library,* Warsaw 2004.

Warsaw 2019
Jolanta Talbierska, *Old Master Drawings from the 15th Century to the 1820s: Netherlandish, Flemish and Dutch Schools,* University of Warsaw, University of Warsaw Library, Warsaw 2019.

Wasau 1989
Delights for the Senses: Dutch and Flemish Still-Life Paintings from Budapest, exh. cat. Leigh Yawkey Woodson Art Gallery, Wasau, WI, 1989.

Washington 2009
Jan Lievens: A Dutch Master Rediscovered, exh. cat. National Gallery of Art, Washington, DC, 2009.

Wawrik 1982
Franz Wawrik, *Berühmte Atlanten: Kartographische Kunst aus fünf Jahrhunderten,* Dortmund 1982.

Weststeijn 2016
Thijs Weststeijn, "Introduction: Global Art History and the Netherlands," in *Netherlands Yearbook for History of Art* 66*: Netherlandish Art in Its Global Context,* ed. Thijs Weststeijn, Eric Jorink, and Frits Scholten, Leiden and Boston 2016, 6–27.

Weststeijn 2017
Thijs Weststeijn, *Een wereldse kunst,* Utrecht 2017.

Wheelock 2009
Arthur K. Wheelock Jr., "Jan Lievens: Bringing New Light to an Old Master," in Washington 2009, 1–27.

Wheelock 2014
Arthur K. Wheelock Jr., "Rembrandt van Rijn and Workshop (Probably Govaert Flinck): *Man in Oriental Costume*, c. 1635," in *Dutch Paintings 17th Century,* National Gallery of Art, Washington, DC, Online Editions, https://purl.org/nga/collection/artobject/572 (accessed March 1, 2020).

White 1999
Christopher White, *Rembrandt as an Etcher: A Study of the Artist at Work,* second edition, New Haven 1999.

Wilczek 1993
Amsterdam 1585–1672: Morgenröte des bürgerlichen Kapitalismus, ed. Bernd Wilczek in collaboration with Jos van Waterschoot, Bühl-Moos 1993.

Winterthur 2006
Die Kunst des Betrachtens: Holländische und andere Gemälde Alter Meister der Stiftung Jakob Briner, ed. Peter Wegmann, Winterthur 2006.

Woollett 2009
Anne T. Woollett, *Rembrandt in Southern California,* Los Angeles 2009.

Wuestman 1995
Gerdien Wuestman, "The Mezzotint in Holland: 'Easily Learned, Neat and Convenient,'" in *Simiolus* 23 (1995), 63–89.

Wuestman/Webb 2006
Gerdien Wuestman and Dianne Webb, "Withered Nell or Rembrandt's Aunt? Prints of *Tronies* and Their Titles," in *Simiolus* 32,1 (2006), 58–77.

Ydema 1991
Onno Ydema, *Carpets and Their Datings in Netherlandish Paintings 1540–1700,* Zutphen 1991.

Zell 2002
Michael Zell, *Reframing Rembrandt: Jews and the Christian Image in Seventeenth-Century Amsterdam,* Berkeley 2002.

Zurich 2005
Foundation E. G. Bührle Collection, Zurich, vol. 1, ed. Lukas Gloor and Marco Goldin, Conegliano 2005.

Zurich 2013
The Fascination of Persia: The Persian-European Dialogue in Seventeenth-Century Art & Contemporary Art of Teheran, exh. cat. Museum Rietberg, Zurich 2013.

Authors

Bodo Brinkmann, curator of Old Masters, Kunstmuseum Basel, since 2008; studied art history, German, archeology, and philosophy in Kiel and at the Freie Universität Berlin; 1990–92 assistant, Art History Department, Freie Universität; 1991 visiting assistant professor, University of California, Berkeley; 1992–2008 curator, Städel Museum, Frankfurt am Main; publications on (pre-)Romantic landscape painting and on late medieval book illustration and panel painting, including *Zu Heinrich von Kleists "Empfindungen vor Friedrichs Seelandschaft"* (1981), *Neues vom Meister der Lübecker Bibel* (1987–88), *Die flämische Buchmalerei am Ende des Burgunderreichs: Der Meister des Dresdener Gebetbuchs und die Miniaturisten seiner Zeit* (2 volumes, 1997), commentary volume for the facsimile edition of *Der Codex Rotundus: Dombibliothek Hildesheim Hs 728* (2012), *Deutsche Gemälde im Städel 1300–1500* and *Deutsche Gemälde im Städel 1500–1550* (2002 and 2005, both with Stephan Kemperdick); exhibition curator, including *Witches' Lust and the Fall of Man: The Strange Fantasies of Hans Baldung Grien* (2007), *Konrad Witz* (2011), *Caspar Wolf and the Aesthetic Conquest of Nature* (2014), *Archaeology of Salvation* (2016), and *A Passion for Paintings* (2019).

Jan de Hond, curator, Department of History, Rijksmuseum, Amsterdam, with an emphasis on the cultural history of the seventeenth to nineteenth centuries, art and science in the early modern era, and the relations of the Netherlands to the non-Western world; dissertation on Orientalism in Dutch culture; currently engaged at the Rijksmuseum in provenance research on objects from the former colonies; publications: *Verlangen naar het oosten: Oriëntalisme in de Nederlandse cultuur, ca. 1800–1920* (2008); "A Mamluk Basin for a Sicilian Queen" (*The Rijksmuseum Bulletin*, 2011, with Luitgard Mols); *Pieter Saenredam in Den Bosch* (2013, with Paul Huys Janssen); "Willem Schellinks en India: Tussen werkelijkheid en illusie," in *Onbegrensd perspectief: Cultuurhistorische verkenningen*, ed. P. Bange and J. Geurts (2015), 69–96 (with Jos Gommans); *A Narrow Bridge: Japan and the Netherlands from 1600* (2016, with Menno Fitski); "The Sword and the Album: Material Memories and an Eighteenth-Century Poetic Account on the Execution of Johan van Oldenbarnevelt," in *The Rijksmuseum Bulletin* 66,3 (2018), 204–34 (with Lieke van Deinsen).

Gabriel Dette, assistant curator of Old Masters, Kunstmuseum Basel, since 2017; studied art history, philosophy, and law in Mainz and Dijon; 2006–10 curatorial assistant and assistant curator of Old Masters, Städel Museum, Frankfurt am Main; 2011 assistant (temporary replacement), Art History Department, Goethe-Universität Frankfurt am Main; 2011–16 academic assistant, Department of Art History, Technische Universität Darmstadt; involved as assistant curator, curator, and catalog author in numerous exhibitions, including *Cranach the Elder* (2007–08), *Caravaggio in Holland: Music and Genre in the Paintings of Caravaggio and the Utrecht Caravaggists* (2009), *Botticelli* (2009), *The Golden Age of Dutch and Flemish Painting from the Städel Museum* (2010), *¡Hola Prado!: Two Collections in Dialogue* (2017), *Bilderlust* (2019).

Corinna Forberg, art historian; studied European art history, Humboldt-Universität zu Berlin, and Indian art history, Freie Universität Berlin; dissertation: *Die Rezeption indischer Miniaturen in der europäischen Kunst des 17. und 18. Jahrhunderts* (2015); research on transcultural processes in European and Indian art; 2013–15 Cluster of Excellence "Asia and Europe in a Global Context," Heidelberg, on the nature of copying and copying as a medium of intercultural exchange; professor of Iranian studies, Göttingen, since 2019; research on the staging of the Sun King with Louis XIV and the Mughal emperor Shah Jahan; recent publications: *The Transformative Power of the Copy: A Transcultural and Interdisciplinary Approach* (2017, edited with Philipp Stockhammer), "How to Succeed in Marketing Something Repulsive: A Recently Discovered Drawing of a Yogi by Willem Schellinks (1623–1678)" (*Zeitschrift für Kunstgeschichte*, 2018, with Pauline Lunsingh Scheurleer).

Susanne Henriette Karau, translator in the fields of art, culture, design, film, photography and architecture since 1991; studied art history and Dutch philology, Freie Universität Berlin and the University of Amsterdam; 2002 PhD, Freie Universität Berlin, dissertation: *Leben und Werk des Leidener Malers Jacob Toorenvliet (1640–1719)*; additional publication: "Brüderliche Bande: Jacob Toorenvliet malt das Familienporträt seines Bruders Dirck," in *Wallraf-Richartz-Jahrbuch* 67 (2006), 279–85.

Michael Philipp, chief curator, Museum Barberini, Potsdam, since 2016; studied modern history, social and economic history, and literature in Hamburg; 1995–2005 worked as an editor in Amsterdam and Berlin; 2007–16 curator, Bucerius Kunst Forum, Hamburg; publications on Stefan George and his circle, on art history and contemporary history, including *Persönlich habe ich mir nichts vorzuwerfen: Politische Rücktritte in Deutschland von 1950 bis heute* (2007); exhibitions curated in Hamburg include *Terror and Desire: The Temptation of St. Anthony from Hieronymus Bosch to Max Ernst* (2008), *Descent into the World: The Art of Mannerism in Europe* (2008), *Rubens, van Dyck, Jordaens: Baroque from Antwerp* (2010), *Dionysus: Intoxication and Ecstasy* (2013); exhibitions curated in Potsdam include *Behind the Mask: Artists in the GDR* (2017, with Valerie Hortolani), *Are Communists Allowed to Dream? The Gallery of the Palace of the Republic* (2017), and *Van Gogh: Still Lifes* (2019).

Gary Schwartz, art historian; 1971–91 publisher of art-history books; 1995 established the email blog Form Follows Dysfunction, which went online as garyschwartzarthistorian.nl in 2002 and is still active today; 1998 founded the International Council of Curators of Dutch and Flemish Art (CODART), which he directed until 2005; 1986–87 Getty Scholar, Getty Center for the History of Art and Humanities, Los Angeles; 1989 Regents Lecturer, University of California, Los Angeles; 1990 Leventritt Lecturer, Harvard University, Cambridge, MA; 2009–10 fellow, Netherlands Institute for Advanced Study in the Humanities and Social Sciences, Wassenaar; curator of various exhibitions, including *Emotions: Pain and Pleasure in Dutch Painting of the Golden Age* (Haarlem, 2014), currently preparing the exhibition *Rembrandt Seen through Jewish Eyes* (Moscow, 2022); author of numerous publications on Rembrandt including *Rembrandt: All the Etchings Reproduced in True Size* (1977), *Rembrandt, His Life, His Paintings: A New Biography* (1985), *The Rembrandt Book* (2006); other publications: *Pieter Saenredam: The Painter and His Time* (1990, with Marten Jan Bok), *Jheronimus Bosch: The Road to Heaven and Hell* (2016), *Vermeer in Detail* (2017).

Erik Spaans, journalist and art historian, with a focus on Dutch painting of the seventeenth century; publications include numerous articles on art, history, books, and film in newspapers and magazines, including *NRC Handelsblad*, *Het Financieele Dagblad*, *De Volkskrant*, *De Tijd*, *De Groene Amsterdammer*, *Museumtijdschrift*, *Dossier de l'Art*, *Oud Holland*, and *The Burlington Magazine*; author of the introductory essay in the catalog of the collection of seventeenth-century art in the Rijksmuseum, Amsterdam; books: *Paysages de France 1646: De Loire vallei getekend door Rembrandts tijdgenoten* (2006) and *Rijksmuseum Guide* (2013).

Jolanta Talbierska, senior curator and keeper of the Print Room of the University Library Warsaw; doctorate and habilitation in art history; grants from the Foundation for Polish Science, the Lanckoroński Foundation, and the Rector of the University of Warsaw; 1996–2018 study and research visits in the United States and numerous European countries; areas of research: history of European drawing and printmaking, book illustration, terminology and methodology of works on paper; teaching: University of Warsaw and the Academy of Fine Arts, Warsaw; numerous publications on various subjects in Polish, including the etchings and drawings of Stefano della Bella (2001, 2003, 2005) and Rembrandt (2004, 2006, 2008, 2009) as well as on seventeenth-century Polish prints (2011).

Roelof van Gelder, historian; studied history, University of Amsterdam; research on Dutch culture and colonial history; 1978–2009 culture editor, *NRC Handelsblad*; worked on exhibitions and television series on historical subjects; numerous publications including *Het Oost-Indisch avontuur: Duitsers in dienst van de VOC (1600–1800)* (1997, German translation 2004); *Sporen van de Compagnie: De VOC in Nederland* (1988); *Naporra's omweg: Het leven van een VOC-matroos (1731–1793)* (2003); *Zeepost: Nooit bezorgde brieven uit de 17e en 18e eeuw* (2008); *Naar het aards paradijs: Het rusteloze leven van Jacob Roggeveen, ontdekker van Paaseiland (1659–1729*) (2012); *Dichter in de jungle: John Gabriel Stedman 1744–1797* (2018).

Arnoud Vrolijk, curator of Oriental manuscripts and rare books, University Library, Leiden, since 2006; 1998 doctorate, University of Leiden, dissertation on Arabic poetry and prose of the fifteenth century in Cairo; 2001–07 president, Middle East Libraries Committee; numerous publications in Arabic studies and Oriental studies in the Netherlands, including *Turcksche boucken: The Oriental Collection of Levinus Warner, Dutch Diplomat in Seventeenth-Century Istanbul* (2012, with Jan Schmidt and Karin Scheper), *Arabic Studies in the Netherlands: A Short History in Portraits, 1580–1950* (2014, with Richard van Leeuwen), *Western Arabia in the Leiden Collections: Traces of a Colourful Past* (2016, with Luitgard Mols), *The* Thousand and One Nights *and Orientalism in the Dutch Republic, 1700–1800: Antoine Galland, Ghisbert Cuper and Gilbert de Flines* (2019, with Richard van Leeuwen).

Image Credits

Städtische Sammlung Aachen (Suermondt-Ludwig-Museum, photo: Anne Gold, Aachen): p. 35, fig. 11
Stedelijk Museum Alkmaar Collection: cat. 25
Allard Pierson, University of Amsterdam: cat. 40–41, 43.1–2, 47–48, 84, 91.1–2
Amsterdam Museum: cat. 16, 34
Collection Nationaal Museum van Wereldculturen, Amsterdam: cat. 86
Rijksmuseum, Amsterdam: p. 15, fig. 2; p. 18, fig. 3; p. 21, figs. 7–8; p. 26, fig. 1; p. 31, figs. 5–6; p. 36, fig. 15; p. 43, fig. 4; p. 49, figs. 11–12; p. 51, fig. 15; p. 63, fig. 11; p. 77, figs. 2–3; p. 79, figs. 4–5; p. 80, fig. 8; p. 83, fig. 12; p. 186; p. 282; cat. 1, 2, 17–18, 20–21, 23, 26, 32, 37, 45, 85.1–4, 88–90, 98, 101, 107, 109
Stadsarchief Amsterdam: cat. 24
Museum aan de Stroom, Antwerp (Collectie Stad Antwerpen, MAS, photo: Michel Wuyts): p. 80, fig. 9
Museum Plantin-Moretus, Antwerp (Printroom collection, UNESCO, World Heritage): p. 91, fig. 7
© Kunstmuseum Basel: p. 214; cat. 8, 35–36, 60–61, 67, 70–71, 80–82, 104–05, 110–11, 113, 116–18
bpk, Berlin: p. 21, fig. 9 (Bayerische Staatsgemäldesammlungen); p. 65, fig. 13 (Musée du Louvre, Dist. RMN—Grand Palais, Michel Urtado); p. 65, fig. 16 (Museumslandschaft Hessen Kassel); p. 58, fig. 2 (Museum für Islamische Kunst, SMB, Jürgen Liepe); p. 58, fig. 1 (RMN—Grand Palais, Benoît Touchard); p. 18, fig. 6 (RMN—Grand Palais [Musée du Louvre], Jean-Gilles Berizzi); p. 32, fig. 8 (RMN—Grand Palais, Thierry Le Mage); p. 45, fig. 5 (RMN—Grand Palais, Thierry Ollivier); p. 32, fig. 9 (Staatliche Kunstsammlungen Dresden, Hans-Peter Klut); p. 32, fig. 10 (Staatliche Schlösser, Gärten und Kunstsammlungen Mecklenburg-Vorpommern, Elke Walford); p. 63, fig. 9 (Stiftung Preussische Schlösser und Gärten Berlin-Brandenburg, Roland Handrick); p. 43, fig. 2; p. 61, fig. 8; p. 69, fig. 18 (The Trustees of the British Museum); cat. 65 (Bayerische Staatsgemäldesammlungen); cat. 73 (Staatliche Kunstsammlungen Dresden, Elke Estel, Hans-Peter Klut)
Bridgeman Images, Berlin: p. 51, fig. 16; p. 58, fig. 3 (© Christie's Images); cat. 58
Staatsbibliothek zu Berlin: p. 26, fig. 3
© The Henry Barber Trust, The Barber Institute of Fine Arts, University of Birmingham: cat. 66
© Herzog Anton Ulrich-Museum, Braunschweig, Kunstmuseum des Landes Niedersachsen: cat. 11, 78
Staats- und Universitätsbibliothek Bremen: p. 43, fig. 1
© Szépművészeti Múzeum / Museum of Fine Arts, Budapest, 2020: cat. 7, 53
Statens Museum for Kunst, Copenhagen: cat. 51
The Orientalist Museum, Doha (© National Collection of Qatar): p. 45, fig. 6
Chester Beatty Library, Dublin (© The Trustees of the Chester Beatty Library, Dublin): cat. 96
Dordrechts Museum: cat. 6
Kunstpalast Düsseldorf (© Kunstpalast, Horst Kolberg, Arthothek): cat. 39
Scala, Florence (photo: Opera Metropolitana Siena): p. 65, fig. 14
Historisches Museum Frankfurt (photo: Horst Ziegenfusz): p. 35, fig. 12
Museum of Fine Arts, Ghent (www.lukasweb.be—Art in Flanders, Photo: Hugo Maertens): p. 26, fig. 2
Musée de Grenoble (Ville de Grenoble/Musée de Grenoble, J. L. Lacroix): cat. 15
© Frans Hals Museum, Haarlem: cat. 46
Leiden University Libraries: p. 88, figs. 1–4; p. 91, figs. 5–6; p. 93, figs. 8–10; p. 97, figs. 12–14; p. 98, figs. 14–16; cat. 5, 42, 44
The British Museum, London (© The Trustees of the British Museum): cat. 108, 112, 114
© The National Gallery, London: cat. 12, 77
National Maritime Museum, Greenwich, London: p. 83, figs. 10–11
Royal Collection Trust, London (© Her Majesty Queen Elizabeth II 2020): p. 31, fig. 7
© Victoria and Albert Museum, London: cat. 94
© The J. Paul Getty Museum, Los Angeles: cat. 68
The J. Paul Getty Museum, Los Angeles (The Getty's Open Content Program): p. 36, fig. 14
Musée des Beaux-Arts, Lyon (© MBA Lyon, Photo Alain Basset): cat. 59
Museo Nacional del Prado, Madrid (© Photographic Archive. Museo Nacional del Prado, Madrid): cat. 31
© Museo Nacional Thyssen-Bornemisza, Madrid: cat. 52
Milwaukee Art Museum (© John Nienhuis, Dedra Walls): cat. 119
Musée Fabre de Montpellier (© Musée Fabre de Montpellier Méditerranée Métropole, photo: Frédéric Jaulmes): cat. 27
Bayerische Staatsbibliothek München, Munich: p. 26, fig. 4; p. 46, figs. 9–10
The Metropolitan Museum of Art, New York: p. 63, fig. 10
New York Public Library, New York: p. 77, fig. 1
© Ashmolean Museum, University of Oxford: cat. 9
Bodleian Libraries, University of Oxford: p. 46, fig. 8; cat. 93
Bibliothèque Nationale de France, Paris: cat. 87
© Fondation Custodia, Paris: cat. 57, 79
Fondation Custodia, Paris (Collection Frits Lugt): p. 18, fig. 5
Musée des Beaux-Arts de la Ville de Paris (Paris Musées/Petit Palais): p. 63, fig. 12
Musée Cognacq-Jay, Paris (Paris Musées): p. 58, fig. 4
Bibliotheek Norbertijnenabdij Postel: p. 260
Staatliche Bibliothek Regensburg: p. 43, fig. 3; p. 51, fig. 13
Museum Boijmans Van Beuningen, Rotterdam (Studio Tromp): p. 46, fig. 7
© Residenzgalerie Salzburg: cat. 63
Artothek, Spardorf (© Städel Museum): p. 15, fig. 1; p. 18, fig. 4
The State Hermitage Museum, St. Petersburg (© photo: Vladimir Terebenin, Konstantin Sinyavsky, The State Hermitage Museum): cat. 13, 28, 74, 75
Nationalmuseum, Stockholm (photo: Hans Thorwid, Nationalmuseum 2009): p. 61, fig. 7
Tel Aviv Museum of Art (photo: Elad Sarig, Tel Aviv Museum of Art): cat. 72
Koninklijke Bibliotheek, The Hague: cat. 92
Mauritshuis, The Hague: p. 35, fig. 13; cat. 76
RKD—Netherlands Institute for Art History, The Hague: cat. 102
© Centraal Museum Utrecht: cat. 4
Albertina, Viennna: cat. 97, 103
Austrian National Library, Vienna: p. 79, fig. 6; p. 80, fig. 7
Gemäldegalerie der Akademie der bildenden Künste, Vienna: cat. 64
Kunsthistorisches Museum Wien, KHM-Museumsverband, Vienna: cat. 83
Schönbrunn Palace, Vienna (© Schloss Schönbrunn Kultur- und Betriebsges.m.b.H., Digitalisat: Salon Iris): p. 69, fig. 17; cat. 95.1–2
Stichting Duivenvoorde, Voorschoten, Stichting der Heerlijkheden Oosterland, Sirjansland en Oosterstein: cat. 14
University of Warsaw Library: cat. 19
National Gallery of Art, Washington, DC: cat. 10, 100
National Museum of Wales (© Amgueddfa Genedlaethol Cymru): p. 36, fig. 16
National Trust, Wiltshire (© National Trust, Andrew Patterson): cat. 69
York Museums Trust: cat. 33
Collection Emil Bührle, Zurich (SIK-ISEA, Zurich): cat. 3, 50 (J.-P. Kuhn); cat. 54 (Lutz Hartmann)
Collection of Prince and Princess Sadruddin Aga Khan: p. 51, figs. 14, 17
The Kremer Collection: cat. 38, 55, 99
The Right Hon. The Earl of Derby, 2020: cat. 106
Private collections: cat. 29–30, 49, 56 (photo: Doro Keman, Velsen), 62, 92, 115

It has not proven possible to locate or contact copyright holders in all instances. Naturally, legitimate claims will be satisfied in the framework of the usual arrangements.

Colophon

This catalog is published in conjunction with the exhibition
Rembrandt's Orient: West Meets East in Dutch Art of the Seventeenth Century

Kunstmuseum Basel
October 31, 2020, to February 14, 2021

Museum Barberini, Potsdam
March 13 to June 27, 2021

Editors:
Bodo Brinkmann and Gabriel Dette, Kunstmuseum Basel
Ortrud Westheider and Michael Philipp, Museum Barberini

Exhibition:
Gary Schwartz

Catalog:
Bodo Brinkmann, Gabriel Dette, Michael Philipp, Gary Schwartz

Catalog Editing:
Michael Philipp, Sophie Reinhardt

Picture Editing:
Sophie Reinhardt, Julia Nagel

Kunstmuseum Basel

Executive Board
Director: Josef Helfenstein
Head of Art & Research, Deputy Director: Anita Haldemann
Head of Art Care: Werner Müller
Head of Finance & Operations Matthias Schwarz
Head of Marketing & Development: Mirjam Baitsch

Curator, Old Masters: Bodo Brinkmann
Assistant Curator, Old Masters: Gabriel Dette
Head of Exhibitions & Collections: Charlotte Gutzwiller
Registrar: Monika Mascus
Exhibition Manager: Matthias Fellmann
Conservation:
Paintings: Sophie Eichner, Annette Fritsch, Esther Rapoport, Werner Müller
Paper: Kristin Bucher, Chantal Schwenderer, Annegret Seger, Caroline Wyss Illgen, Lina Wyss
Exhibition Installation: Claude Bosch, Felix Böttiger, Urs Cavelti, Dominique Gfeller, Philipp Gueniat, Stefano Schaller
Scientific Photographer: Jonas Hänggi
Head of Communication, Media: Karen N. Gerig
Marketing: Vera Reinhard, Christian Selz
Website, Social Media: Dominik Asche
Curator of Programs: Daniel Kurjakovic
Art Education and Outreach: Hanna Horst, Christine Müller Stalder

Museum Barberini, Potsdam

Director: Ortrud Westheider
Personal Assistant to the Director: Theresa Büning
Director Finance and Administration: Claudia Thurow
Personal Assistant to the Director Finance and Administration: Nadine Müller
Chief Curator: Michael Philipp
Curator: Daniel Zamani
Publications: Sophie Reinhardt
Research Associate: Julia Nagel
Research Associate (Provenance Research): Linda Hacka
Registrar: Anne Barz
Press and Communications: Achim Klapp, Marte Kräher, Esther Knuth
Digitalization and Information Security: Remigiusz Plath
IT Administrator: Sebastian Semmler
Educational Service: Dorothee Entrup, Andrea Schmidt
Events: Marie-Christin Hupp, Julia Teller, Ines Wenzel-Hirschfeld
Guest Management: Jutta Bockhacker, Frauke Herlyn, Vanessa Souli
Accounting and Ticketing: Yvonne Benesch
Office Manager: Sandra Spudy
Head of Building Services: Carsten Loeper
Building Services: Frank Altmann, Dennis Kokert

In collaboration with:

Conservation: Felicitas Klein, Berlin, Friederike Beseler, Berlin
Exhibition Design:
Gunther Maria Kolck, Hamburg
BrücknerAping, Büro für Gestaltung, Bremen
Museum Shop:
Museum Barberini. Der Shop, Jörg Klambt

Catalog

Editorial Direction, Prestel: Markus Eisen
Graphic Design and Typesetting: BrücknerAping, Büro für Gestaltung, Bremen
Copyediting: Tas Skorupa, Berlin
Project Management: Annette Krüger, Hamburg
Translation of German texts (unless stated otherwise): Lance Anderson (chapter introductions), Catherine Bindman (foreword; catalog entries, chapters 1, 2, 4), Simon Cowper/Melanie Newton (catalog entries, chapter 5), Nicola Morris/Lucy Powell (catalog entries, chapter 7), Bronwen Saunders (catalog entries, chapters 3, 6)

Production Management, Prestel: Cilly Klotz
Separations: Reproline Genceller, Munich
Printing and Binding: Printer Trento, Trento
Typeface: Neue Haas Grotesk
Paper: Garda Matt Ultra, 150 g/m²

MIX
Paper from responsible sources
FSC® C015829

Penguin Random House Verlagsgruppe FSC® N001967

Printed in Italy

Library of Congress Control Number: 2020946430

A CIP catalog record for this book is available from the British Library.

ISBN 978-3-7913-5962-5 (German trade edition)
ISBN 978-3-7913-9056-7 (German museum edition, Kunstmuseum Basel)
ISBN 978-3-7913-9008-6 (German museum edition, Museum Barberini, Potsdam)

ISBN 978-3-7913-5963-2 (English trade edition)
ISBN 978-3-7913-9057-4 (English museum edition, Kunstmuseum Basel)
ISBN 978-3-7913-9009-3 (English museum edition, Museum Barberini, Potsdam)

www.prestel.de
www.prestel.com